THE SOCIAL SCIENCES

AND THEIR INTERRELATIONS

EDITED BY

WILLIAM FIELDING OGBURN
Professor of Sociology, Columbia University

AND

ALEXANDER GOLDENWEISER
Recently of Columbia University and the New School for Social Research

HOUGHTON MIFFLIN COMPANY
BOSTON · NEW YORK · CHICAGO · DALLAS · SAN FRANCISCO
The Riverside Press Cambridge

H
83
O5

/1661

PREFACE

THE increasing specialization in the social sciences has been accompanied by greater ignorance as well as by greater knowledge. This handicap has been especially felt because the rapidity of social change in recent years has made it difficult for branches of knowledge in the social sciences to remain within the bounds prescribed under earlier situations. Furthermore, with the rise of the modern emphasis on social research, it has been found that many problems lie in several different fields and that their solution demands methods from the various social sciences. The increasing specialization also is part of the great accumulation process in social knowledge. This accumulation process is so great that it has become exceedingly difficult for any one individual to become well oriented in the general field of the social sciences. For all these reasons it is thought that this volume of chapters on the interrelations of the various social sciences, contributed by different specialists, will serve a useful purpose.

The effort has been to make the volume realistic. The contributors were requested to deal with conditions, problems, and methods as they exist to-day. They were also asked to make their papers concrete and factual, with only a limited amount of earlier historical material and very little speculation as to the status of the sciences in the far distant future. The purpose has not been to present a volume which as a history or a prediction will be a guide for all time, but rather to develop a work that will be useful for the state of society and the social sciences as existing in the first part of the twentieth century.

Not all the contributors have dealt with their subjects in the manner and procedure suggested. There is considerable variability in treatment. Perhaps the nature of the subject-matter in many instances did not encourage uniformity. And then, of course, each writer must be allowed to see his subject in the mold in which he is accustomed to view it. This variability of treatment indeed has its advantages, particularly for the reader who is interested in a special social science, for he will profit by seeing how several authorities view it. This checking by different writers quite properly allows for more individual freedom.

The editors are assured of the great need of such a treatment of the social sciences, and it is their hope that the present volume will meet this need and will accordingly be of use.

CONTENTS

CONTENTS

CLASSIFIED CONTENTS

CLASSIFIED CONTENTS

SOCIOLOGY

THE SOCIAL SCIENCES

THE SOCIAL SCIENCES
AND THEIR INTERRELATIONS

.:.

CHAPTER I

THE FIELD OF THE SOCIAL SCIENCES

By THE EDITORS

THE DECLINE OF SYNTHESIS

IN these days of specialization, synthesis becomes increasingly difficult. Aristotle may have encompassed the entire knowledge of his day, natural, social, and philosophical. His authority held for centuries. Modern instances are rare. While Herbert Spencer, perhaps, deserved the cognomen of a modern Aristotle, it has often been remarked that each part of his synthesis was accepted as authoritative by all but the specialists in that particular branch of learning. Auguste Comte was equally comprehensive but even less accurate. Wilhelm Wundt may have come nearest to the ideal of a universal mind. Reared in the techniques of the exact and natural sciences, he subsequently extended his range so as to include, in his *Völkerpsychologie* and *Logik*, the entire domain of the social and philosophical disciplines. Among historically minded scientists Duhem, Mach, and Höffding approached but did not equal his standards, their command of the vast store of data and concepts being rather extensive than intensive. Two other men among moderns, while operating upon different backgrounds and from vastly disparate points of view, went as far in encyclopedic range of knowledge as is still humanly possible: Elisée Réclus in his *Universal Geography* and *L'Homme et la Terre*, and Merz in his *History of European Thought in the Nineteenth Century*.

The increasing difficulty of synthesis is, of course, due to the enormous accumulation of factual material as well as to diversification in method. The result is a store of knowledge so stupendous in quantity and so varied in range that human ability does not suffice to acquire a thorough mastery of more than a limited field.

The adjustment to this fund of culture on the part of scholars generally and of researchers particularly took the form of selection and specialization. Indeed, the parts selected for detailed mastery are themselves so large that one is precluded by limits of time and ability from extending one's own range. In the field of modern mathematics alone, for example, one specialist knows less about the subject of another specialist than, in former days, a physicist knew about chemistry. Even in so recent a branch of biology as genetics one geneticist finds it difficult to keep abreast with the writings of another geneticist. It may be noted in passing that in both subjects, mathematics and genetics, specialization was precipitated and sustained by a highly technical terminology.[1]

It will thus be understood how so broad a field as that of the social sciences had to become differentiated from the even broader field of the natural sciences, and how this was inevitably followed by a still further splitting-off of one social science after another.

THE EMERGENCE OF THE SOCIAL SCIENCES

In the days of Aristotle, Plato, and Pythagoras, philosophy still embraced the exact, natural, and social sciences. At the beginning of the nineteenth century the exact and natural sciences — mathematics, astronomy, physics, chemistry, geology, biology — had already left their philosophical matrix and were rapidly developing their own methods and techniques, while preserving a tendency to return to philosophy for an occasional theoretical and speculative rehauling. But the social sciences — history, ethics, law, economics, psychology, religion, esthetics, anthropology (such as it was) — were still rocking in the metaphysical cradle of Mother Philosophy. One by one the babes emerged and learned to stand on their own feet and to talk their own language, even though their gait and vocabu-

---

[1] The relevance of these reflections should not be construed as signifying a final pessimism with reference to possible synthesis and versatility even in the field of the exact and natural sciences. Departmental specialization in each field does, to be sure, lead to the creation of relatively water-tight compartments. An expert in the microscopic study of stained nerve tissues may be a tyro in functional neurology and know little about ductless glands. An excellent psychological tester may be a novice or less in hypnotism and know next to nothing about psychoanalysis. Nevertheless, scientific activity in marginal fields continues, and has in recent years received a new impetus. The great reformers of modern physical science, men like Röntgen, George Darwin, and Bohr, were equally at home in physics and chemistry. The same is true of Michelson and Millikan. Jacques Loeb was as good a physico-chemist as he was a biologist. Even shifting from one technique to another or commanding more than one simultaneously, is rare although not impossible. Max Verworn, the famous physiologist, became in his later years an excellent archeologist. Our own Roscoe Pound is both a botanist and a historical and theoretical jurist, just as Lester F. Ward was not only a sociologist but a paleontological botanist also.

lary continued for a long time to bear the traces of their maternal heritage. Sociology, already baptized by Auguste Comte, was definitely emancipated by Herbert Spencer. A similar service was performed for history by J. Ranke and Th. Mommsen; for ethics, by Wundt, Höffding, and Westermarck; for law, by J. Kohler and Steinmetz; for psychology, by Fechner, Weber, and Wundt; for religion, by Wundt, Höffding, and the Durkheim school; for esthetics, by Fischer, Th. Lipps, and Max Dessoir; for anthropology, by Waitz, Gerland, Ratzel, Bastian, E. B. Tylor, and Franz Boas.

The former unity of the social sciences which lay in their common philosophical matrix was now destroyed. However, they remained subject to common influences on account of the fact that they were all sciences of man and of the mind — *Geisteswissenschaften.*

Henceforth, man as an organism and as a psychic being became the connecting link between the natural sciences, the marginal science — psychology, and the social sciences.

THE INFLUENCE OF BIOLOGY, ANTHROPOLOGY, AND PSYCHOLOGY UPON THE SOCIAL SCIENCES

Biological facts and speculations reached over into the social field through two channels: the analogy between a biological organism and the organism of society, and the extension of evolutionary ideology from the biological to the social sphere. Fortunately for the social sciences, the "organismic theories" of society and the state were usually so far-fetched as to exert but a passing influence on social thought. The specter of Hobbe's *Leviathan* haunted us but for a moment; Spencer's elaborate "analogies" were soon discarded as dialectic fireworks; while Lilienfeld's mercilessly pedantic tomes were criticized so little only because they were read even less.

The effect of evolutionary biology struck deeper and lasted longer. The somewhat confused notions of development and progress already present in the social sciences now received a fresh impetus. Fired by the glowing panorama of social evolution thrown upon the canvas of culture history by Spencer's none too discriminating brush, aided by the fatal flexibility of the "comparative method," social scientists — the "classical evolutionists" — were filled with an unprecedented enthusiasm for system building. Thus arose the evolutionary religion of a Tylor, Frazer, Jevons; the evolutionary social and political theory of a Morgan, Kowalevski, Müller-Lyer; the evolutionary art — if not esthetics — of a Haddon, Balfour,

Hirn; the evolutionary ethics of a Wundt, Sutherland, Westermarck, Hobhouse; the evolutionary economics of a Letourneau, Bücher, Hahn. As all these writers used almost exclusively primitive data, the biological doctrine thus grafted upon social science assumed in this new domain an anthropological guise.

There was, however, one curiously significant exception to this wholesale surrender of the social sciences to evolution. History, a science inconveniently crowded with chronologized sequences of fact, remained aloof. No truly evolutionary history was ever written. Lamprecht's attempt in this direction resulted in a sort of esthetic interpretation of history; while Kurt Breysig's ambitious scheme was carried out only with reference to the peoples of prehistory. When Breysig was confronted with history, he turned his attention to other matters.[1]

We need not dwell here on the gradual demolition of the evolutionary stronghold by a new anthropology, better equipped with facts and methods, and a more discriminating psychology. This chapter of the history of thought is now common knowledge; it has, moreover, been further illumined from different angles in the essays that follow.

It took years, however, before the new anthropological orientation was incorporated in the general body of social theory. Anthropological monographs seemed forbidding, and no syntheses or popularizations were forthcoming for some time. Thus arose the anomalous situation of a rapidly advancing anthropological science coexisting with the general use of obsolete facts and theories in monographs and textbooks in the other social sciences. Even today evolutionary anthropology often functions as a family skeleton in the busy household of social theory. By and large, however, the maturer anthropological thought has been incorporated in the wider field of social study and is having a quickening effect on orientation and perspective.

The influence of psychology on the social sciences has been equally significant and fruitful. It also came in two main currents. It must be remembered that the social sciences are all, in a sense, psychological, that the facts they deal with belong to the psycho-

[1] The havoc that can be wrought in social thought by the naïve or uncritical utilization of a half-baked anthropology is well illustrated in Myres's historical study, *The Influence of Anthropology on the Course of Political Theory*. Another somewhat extreme example of how anthropological learning need not in itself save one from intellectual incompetence will be found in Margold's *Sex Freedom and Social Control*.

logical level, that the processes of intercommunication without which there could be no society and no social science, are intercommunications between minds. It is for this reason that social science and social theory were always prolific in their use of psychological terms and concepts; but until recently they used these concepts and terms none too discriminately — one is tempted to say, none too seriously.

An early wave of psychological influence came with the psychology of instincts, beginning with McDougall's famous *Introduction to Social Psychology* and reaching a climax in Trotter's *Instincts of the Herd in Peace and War*. Appraised in retrospect, instinct psychology will be seen as a blind trail in social science, which accounts for the somewhat violent recent reaction against it in such works as Josey's, Kantor's, and Bernard's.

Another wave that had its inception over a generation ago in the influence of Wundt's voluntarism and the concepts of apperception and "creative synthesis," was checked for a time, but was quickened to new life with the emergence of behaviorism, psychoanalysis, and "individual" psychology (in the sense of William Stern). We are still in the beginning of this phase, during which a complete rehauling of the entire field of social science may be anticipated.

THE SOCIAL SCIENCES IN THE UNITED STATES

Notwithstanding their amenability to common influences, the social sciences in the United States have in recent years shown a marked tendency toward parting company with one another. This applies especially to our academic institutions. The department of history, for example, or even of Spanish-American colonial history in the seventeenth century, is singled out as a sphere of activity and acquisition, and the historian may remark with justification or even pride that he is not an economist or a psychologist. Scientific societies emphasize their intellectual particularism. The political science associations meet apart from the political economy societies, and social workers from the sociologists. There are such specialized scientific societies as an Association for Labor Legislation and a National Community Center Association!

These university departments and scientific societies develop loyalties as well as jealousies. At times they almost assume the features of esoteric cults. Each particular group is trying to herd in a part of human knowledge and build a fence around it. Most scholars do not object to the spread of their knowledge, but they look askance at trespassing students from other fields.

Thus, departmentalizing and specialization, while to a degree inevitable and conducive to highest achievement, are seen to have their attendant evils. Research, discovery, and invention, which are greatly encouraged by specialization, are also sufferers if the process of isolation goes too far.

It is true that new knowledge in a particular field often develops from previous knowledge in the same field. Thus, differential calculus grew out of earlier discoveries in mathematics, in particular, out of analytical geometry. The Constitution of the United States was largely built upon the foundation of the colonial state governments. The theories of Karl Marx rested upon those of Ricardo.

Growth as an integral organic process is illustrated by the foregoing examples.

But there is another side to the picture. Growing elements in culture do not exist in isolation. They are not a closed system. Interrelations are numerous and inevitable. Culture comprises complexes and adhesions. A change in one element of a complex affects all the other elements. The growth of education, for example, cannot be seen in proper perspective without considering the contemporaneous inventions and discoveries embodied in our industrial system. Art is influenced by religion, religion by science, and medicine by both religion and science. Such influences, while natural and inevitable, are not always properly timed: there are lags.

Culture is also profoundly affected by conscious importations from without of factors and elements that had not formed part of it until imported. In fact, the most rapid and progressive changes do not occur in isolated communities through inventions from within, but in communities in contact with others, where borrowing and diffusion are frequent. Often borrowed elements undergo change in the process of assimilation, leading to new ideas and discoveries. Thus there seems to be a sort of cross fertilization. Roman culture was influenced by Greek culture, the Greeks borrowed freely from the Cretans, while Crete owed much to Egypt. And in each instance borrowing also meant assimilation and transformation.

What is true of culture in general applies to science and, as shown in the preceding pages, to social science. Specialization means refinement of method, thorough command of data, and detailed analysis; but intercommunication brings perspective, germination of new ideas, synthesis.

THE PURPOSE OF THE VOLUME

In bringing together between the covers of a book a score or more essays emanating from many minds and covering a vast field of research, the earnest wish of the editors was to present an integral picture of the present interrelations of the social sciences, with particular reference to the United States, as well as to lay bare the potentialities for future developments.

There are interrelations and interrelations. They may be too many or too few, useful or disastrous. Thus, biology has benefited the social sciences by introducing the concept of natural growth and by defining the scope and limits of man's organic traits; but, as shown above, it has also hurt them by flooding the field of social theory with the dogmatic notion of a rigidly ordered development. The "iron laws" of history assumed the form of barred cells for creative and critical thinkers. Psychology furnished the social sciences with the very canvas to embroider their conceptual designs upon, but it also injected into them the poisonous virus of a hazy ideology of instincts; and even to-day, when the advances in experimental and pathological psychology are proving of inestimable worth to social theory, the uncritical use of psychoanalysis is threatening the sanity of the sociologist and even of the tough-minded historian, while the bodily transfer of behavioristic ideas from psychology to social theory is responsible for much intellectual barrenness of the "institutional sociologists." Sociology brought brilliance and mellowness to history by teaching it that "facts are scarcest raw material" unless shot through with ideas and illumined by valuational overtones, while history imparted to sociology a wholesome respect for temporal sequences and an appreciation of the oneness and uniqueness of historic events.

The social sciences, moreover, are not merely theoretical disciplines but also tools to be employed in the solution of the concrete practical problems of an existing and developing society. As tools they must constantly coöperate, with an all but complete disregard of academic and classificatory distinctions. The problems of living society do not range themselves so as to fit the artificial isolation forced upon the social sciences by differences of specific subject and method. These problems are what they are. If they are to be solved, whatever knowledge we possess about society must be called into service, wherever needed.

The problem of poverty, for example, is related to biology because of a possible heredity factor. It also falls in the domain of psychology, for many cases of destitution are neurotic — a problem for the psychiatrist. Economics contributes to the solution, for the distribution of wealth, wages, and the business cycles are all factors in poverty. Sociology is related to the problem through population, migration, birth control, housing, city planning, old age pensions, public health measures, etc. From still other angles poverty enters the fields of political science, ethics, and education. Immigration, as a social problem, falls within the provinces of sociology, economics, anthropology, political science, jurisprudence, and education. Race problems are dependent upon information from biology, anthropology, history, economics, sociology, and statistics. A study of nationality means coöperation on the part of history, psychology, sociology, political science, economics, and anthropology. In dealing with crime one must use statistics, sociology, law, psychology, political science, and economics. Taxation is the concern of political science and economics, as well as of other sciences.

If one makes a list of research problems, even very specialized ones, and examines it with reference to the various social sciences to be consulted, one is often surprised to find how much they are interrelated in their pragmatic aspects. This is so to-day and will become increasingly so in the future, as changes in society, brought about by an efficient handling of social problems, become more frequent and thoroughgoing.

Attention, finally, must be drawn to the increasing importance of statistical methods in the social sciences. Exact measurement and numerical representation of results have, of course, been characteristic of modern science since its inception. These features are, in fact, responsible for making science what it is. Mathematical procedure, first introduced into astronomy and physics, was then applied to chemistry and still later to biology, in particular its latest and rapidly developing offshoot, genetics. The full value of the mathematical method in biology was, however, not realized until with the introduction of the calculus of probabilities a marvelously efficient technique was developed for dealing with variable phenomena. First applied to social data by Quetelet, then developed on its biological and theoretical sides by Galton and Pearon, this technique is now widely used in experimental psychology, including so-called psychological testing, in economics, and certain aspects of sociology, and even political science. The extent to which social thought and theory will pass from the sphere of opinion, conjecture, and contemplative analysis to that of fact, knowledge, and control, will depend on their permeation by these scientific methods of measurement and statistics. Even though social problems must in the last instance be solved in social terms, many problems never appear at all until the data have been subjected to statistical manipulation.

There will always be room in the social sciences, however, for the purely analytical, interpretative, and valuational approaches, for these sciences deal with man, a subjective and capricious creature, and with historic facts, which in their very nature evade complete schematization. Both man and history, moreover, are relatively impervious to the concept of law and but partly subject to control.

The reflections in the last section can be summarized in the following three propositions: The "scientific" future of the social sciences depends upon their amenability to statistical methods. The theoretical unit of these sciences is not so much man the animal nor man the psychic being as *man in society;* and if sociology is defined as *the study of the principles underlying man's social relations,* then it follows that the natural meeting-ground of the social sciences and the sphere par excellence of their interrelations are in their common *sociological level.* The social problems, finally, of a living society are no respecters of academic or methodological distinctions; however far, therefore, the social sciences may depart from each other in their conceptual specialization, they must ever be prepared for the call to pragmatic reunification and coöperation.

The following essays are offered to the student and the interested lay reader in the earnest hope that they may contribute, if but a little, to the clarification and furtherance of the social sciences, which, unless all signs deceive us, will constitute the contribution of the twentieth century to human thought and power. Civilization, nurtured and strengthened by the natural and the exact sciences, must henceforth look for its preservation and enhancement to the sciences of society.

CHAPTER II
ANTHROPOLOGY AND ECONOMICS

By N. S. B. GRAS

No Separate Study of Economic Anthropology

Economics and anthropology have grown up largely independen
of one another. Few, if any, scholars have devoted special atten
tion to the general problems of them both. Parts of economics an
history, and also of sociology and psychology, have been closel
integrated so that a somewhat special field of economic history, an
another of social psychology, have resulted. There is no such unio
of economics and anthropology. In fact, for the synthesis c
anthropological and economic studies there is not even a name. W
may speak of anthropological economics, meaning by that term
study of the ideas that primitive peoples held about economic mat
ters. Such ideas would doubtless be found to be vague, unformu
lated, and greatly confused with other matters. Such a subject i
quite undeveloped, and the interests involved, though of grea
significance, are but little noted. We may with more justificatio
speak of economic anthropology, or the study of the ways in whicl
primitive peoples obtained a living, which would, of course, be th
prologue to economic history. Although economic anthropology
is much studied in one aspect or another by anthropologists
economists, and others, there are apparently few, perhaps no
scholars, who make this subject their specialty or who comprehen
all its aspects. It is with economic anthropology that the rest o
this article deals.

Classification of Anthropologists

We may roughly classify anthropologists according to their atti
tude to economic anthropology somewhat as follows: (1) Ther
are the physical anthropologists and also some social anthropolo
gists, especially those absorbed in religion and psychology, wh
neglect the economic activity of primitive peoples. (2) Some socia
anthropologists, such as E. B. Tylor and Clark Wissler, includ
economic (or technological) anthropology in their treatment o

primitive civilization, but simply on a par with religion, the family, language, folklore, art, and the like. Many of the field-workers contributing descriptive articles to learned journals belong to this group. (3) Then there are the social anthropologists who make economic activity the foundation of social anthropology. Frazer does this occasionally, Nieboer does it with great emphasis, Thurnwald within limits, and Goldenweiser in general theory. The ideal of such a group might be stated thus: The economic changes of primitive peoples should first be discovered and then generalized, perhaps in the form of stages. Then, after non-economic developments have been learned, there should be a correlation between the economic and the non-economic. Some scholars in treating of social anthropology profess their general adherence to economic determinism and then commit the scarlet sin of jumbling up the cultures of the hunter and the agriculturist, the planting and the pasturing nomad. It does not require much familiarity with the problem, however, to discover how hard it is to make such a correlation. Indeed, an impartial survey of the difficulties of the situation either makes one feel humble, or, if humility be not the virtue, makes one doubt this particular philosophy of history.

GROUPS OF SCHOLARS IN THE ECONOMIC FIELD

Those who labor in the various economic fields may be conveniently classified along rather different lines. (1) There are many economists ("theorists") who either do not touch economic anthropology at all or do so very lightly. One group of these economists considers a very limited field of human experience (chiefly since the industrial revolution), largely because the members are absorbed in the *logical* aspects of their subject. Examples of this group are Ricardo, Mill, Seager, and Fetter. A second group, such as Marshall, Nicholson, Cannan, and Taussig, makes use of economic history, but little or no use of economic anthropology. (2) There are some economists, however, who, for sundry reasons, do interest themselves in the economic activity of prehistoric and primitive peoples. Brentano, Schwiedland, and Seligman are noteworthy instances of contemporary economists of distinction who have devoted not a little attention to the subject in question. Sometimes the purpose of such scholars is to provide a brief beginning for the more recent phenomena with which they deal at length; sometimes it is to show the influence of economic forces. One of

their main reasons for going into the distant past is their desire t
provide a contrast with present conditions. And lastly, there is th
need of finding illustrations of economic conditions not elsewhere t
be discovered. There is strong suspicion at times that they creat
the illustrations out of an imaginary past to elucidate an artifici:
present. In their treatment of economic anthropological dat:
economists prefer a very simple and summary generalization, show
ing that they are interested in the remoter past not for its own sak
but for the purposes of the present. In recent years the economist
who are most interesting to their fellows do not deal with primitiv
economic conditions at all, but (a) bring new data from contem
porary psychology and sociology, (b) apply statistical methods (
studying economic phenomena, or (c) use their powers of economi
analysis in handling the problems of current business and goveri
ment. A swing of the scholastic pendulum may again turn man
economists to the past for perspective as well as for illustratior
of the deep and abiding drives in the human make-up. (3) Th
last group consists of scholars in the economic field who go bac
to primitive conditions for the sake of completeness. They see
to uncover the whole gamut of economic evolution. The historic:
economists, such as Roscher and Schmoller, belong to this grou|
They may have thought of revamping economic theory as the:
ultimate goal, but much of their real work lay in the discovery (
economic progress. The genetic economists, such as Karl Büche:
seek the facts of the past simply that they may discover brief fo1
mulæ for expressing the steps of development, notably in the for»
of stages. Economic historians do not dip into the anthropologic:
bucket as historians, but at times they feel the need of providin
themselves with a beginning for the institutions in which they a1
interested. An illustration is found in the problem of the origi
of property. It seems easier for the economic historian, generall
interested in a particular country, to enter the prehistoric pa:
through the avenue of archeology rather than through the mo1
remote field of anthropology.

QUESTION OF AN "ECONOMY" AMONG PRIMITIVE PEOPLES

One of the most sweeping judgments about economic anthropo
ogy is that in the earliest part of man's existence there really was r
"economy" at all. Karl Bücher denied that the very primitiv
peoples had any economic organization, or made any plans in pr‹

lucing the things they needed, or developed any regular habits in their work. Accordingly he spoke of a pre-economic search for food. To be sure, if we push our inquiry back to the missing links of the human chain, we may conceivably find some such condition. But the description applies to no peoples of whom we have adequate information, although, of course, it comes nearest to being true of the most primitive hunters, fishers, and collectors. Among the somewhat more advanced peoples, Thurnwald and Malinowski have found not a little organization. The Trobriand Islanders, as Malinowski has shown (1922), have a very remarkable exchange system called the *kula*. This is a regular interchange of ornaments, those for the neck being sent in one direction and those for the arms in the opposite direction. Complicated human relationships are attached to this system, most significantly a genuine barter system in various and sundry commodities.

QUESTION OF THE DIVISION OF LABOR

Adam Smith (1776) helped to set the modern fashion of distinguishing the barbarous from the civilized state when he ascribed to the former little division of labor and to the latter a great deal. Now this is somewhat the same distinction as has just been considered under the head of "economy." That the division of labor has vastly increased is indisputable and tremendously significant. To a certain extent, however, we are left with the idea that there was no division of labor among primitive peoples; that each did all, and all did each. That there was a jack-of-all-trade capacity in the savage is not to be gainsaid; but that there was no division of labor, and no organization, religious, political, or domestic, to bring a division about, is a vastly different matter. And it is an error to lump all early peoples together in this respect: in truth, as they have progressed even in the early halting steps of change, they have increased the extent of their division of labor. About all this we obviously have need of information based on specific inquiry.

EXCHANGE OF GOODS

The division of labor was greatly facilitated by exchange, under whatever form it took. The historical economist, B. Hildebrand (1864), posited three stages — barter economy, money economy, and credit economy. Only the first two are of moment here. From recent evidence we are led to consider a stage in between barter and money economy. When we learn that the natives of the Caroline Islands use stones too large to be handled as a measure of value in exchanging goods for goods, and others use yams and coconuts for the same purpose, we are eager for more information on the subject. Following the formulation of Franz Oppenheimer, we might find on further study that the development of exchange was really somewhat as follows: pure barter, barter money economy, commodity money economy, and credit-money economy. In the second stage money would be used as a measure of value only; in the third, as both a measure of value and a means of exchange. The fourth stage, like the third, is money economy, except that the money has no intrinsic value, only such worth, indeed, as is based on the credit of a government, a bank, or an individual. This whole matter of the use of money has been precipitated by economists, and there are plenty of indications that anthropologists now have the issues more or less clearly in mind. On the other hand, it has been naturally objected by one economist, Seligman,[1] that this series of stages does not show which is the cause and which the effect. Although Lamprecht regarded money as an efficient cause, there are now probably few persons who really think that they are dealing in this connection with anything but results.

ORIGIN OF PROPERTY IN LAND

The question of the origin of property in land has long puzzled students of early conditions. Economic and legal historians have been much divided on the subject. Kemble (1849), Von Maurer (1854), Maine (1861 and 1871), and, we may add, Laveleye (1874) thought that property in land was first vested in the village group. Denman Ross (1883) and Coulanges (1889) challenged this view. A distinction which now has some vogue is that at the beginning, or near the beginning, of settled village economy, land was held not in common ownership but in co-ownership. The arable and meadow land was owned, so much by each family; and although there might have been rotation of holdings, there was no redistribution of the amount until quite late in history. There is no unanimity among economists on this subject. Schmoller and Schwiedland seem to hold somewhat to the old views, while Hildebrand [2] leans the other way. Anthropologists have had neither the legal nor the economic interest that would direct their attention very strongly to this sub-

[1] *Principles*, p. 68.   [2] *Recht und Sitte*, pp. 165–89.

ject. And indeed the dawn of the ownership of land comes quite late in the development of early peoples. Malinowski, with an eye to the economic, has pointed out how complicated rights to land really are among the Trobriand Islanders. Indeed, his work gives promise of the kind of contribution that anthropologists, not steeped in the controversy involved, might make to the subject. If ownership of land is ultimately proven to have been generally communal at the beginning, then there is perhaps an argument for its socialization or sequestration.

DIMINISHING RETURNS, INCREASE IN PRODUCTION, PROGRESS

The getting of raw products for food, shelter, and tools has been a problem of mankind from the first up to the present. For the individual at one particular time it is largely a matter of persistent and traditional effort; but for the group over a long period it is a matter of changing age-long habits so as to avoid the impending shortage of supplies. When a hunting people become more and more numerous and occupy more and more completely the area at their disposal, they find that the wild animals become fewer and fewer. They must domesticate some of the animals, or undertake agriculture, or make some other adjustment. But whatever stage they enter, they find sooner or later that greater efforts bring relatively poorer results. Accordingly, the herder must become an agriculturist and the agriculturist must improve his methods. At first a system of natural husbandry prevailed, one in which the cultivator cared naught for soil fertility, abandoning the land he had impaired till nature had again given it producing power. When this procedure threatened to leave him without sufficient good land, he adopted a system of fallowing, wherein he rested part of his land periodically and ploughed the resting part to eliminate weeds and other parasites. Later, but beyond the scope of our present interest, the cultivator might adopt a system of legume rotation, then field-grass husbandry, and finally a scientific rotation of crops. Many scholars have emphasized an increasing population as a factor in economic progress, but undoubtedly it should be regarded not only as a *cause* of advance, especially where diminishing returns set in (under the old methods), but also as a *result* of the newly discovered system. It is chiefly to economic historians, and to such historical economists as Rocher and Schmoller, that we owe our interest in changes in production and our knowledge about them.

How much more information anthropologists might provide, however, if they had more in mind the problem of balancing food supply and population! The student is commonly disappointed when he goes to anthropological treatises, general or particular, for information on this vital question.

General Economic Stages (Bücher)

Undoubtedly the theme most usually considered by both economists and anthropologists is the *general* evolution of economic endeavor. More specifically, they ask themselves through what general economic stages man has passed. The answer of Karl Bücher to this question has been most widely considered, perhaps most commonly accepted. According to Bücher's view of economic development (1893), man has passed through three stages — independent domestic economy, town economy, and national economy. Some have praised these stages because they take into account both production and consumption. They do this, in truth, but they do it badly. It is not very useful to sum up all economic progress occurring before town economy under one heading, independent domestic economy. Moreover, it is not accurate to do so. Several scholars have shown that in primitive times there was a good deal of trade. The works of W. E. Roth, Grierson, and Malinowski should be read in this connection. And since the criticism of Eduard Meyer, Von Below, and others, some of the historical examples of independent domestic economy can no longer be defended. The large slave households in ancient Greece, Italy, and North Africa, are instances in point. Of course, caution must be observed in going to the other extreme; but it would seem to be nearer the truth to say that man has been familiar with the exchange of goods in one form or another from the earliest times of which we have knowledge. At any rate, there is no shadow of foundation for independent domestic economy as an economic stage. Bücher's formulation of a closed town economy has been often attacked, and with success. His conception of national economy as an actual organization of production has also been challenged, but it is generally accepted.

Hunting, Herding, Agriculture: Hahn's Objections

The stages which have received time-honored consideration by both economists and anthropologists are the product of neither, for they go back to the ancient period, to men of shrewd observation though of little training along special lines. These stages are hunting (direct appropriation, natural existence), pasturing, and agriculture. In the first century A.D. Varro quoted Dicæarchus of the fourth century B.C. as an authority for these famous three stages. Economists and anthropologists, as well as investigators in other fields, have widely accepted them. Early in the nineteenth century, however, there arose a tiny stream of objection which has since become a river and has, to say the least, destroyed the banks of the old structure. Humboldt concluded that the aborigines of South America had not passed through the stage of pasturing. In 1874 Gerland asserted that plant culture preceded animal culture. H. Ling Roth in 1886 held that agriculture did not necessarily follow pastoral pursuits. In a Russian journal of 1890, Petri stated that the Japanese and Polynesians had never been nomads at all. In 1891 Eduard Hahn began his life's work of setting straight the question of the development of primitive production. Much impressed with American evidence, he maintained that after hunting came not pasturing but hoe culture, then the domestication of animals, and finally plough culture (or true agriculture). Hahn thought the hunter incapable of becoming a herdsman. The hunter might tame animals for sport, but he did not have the foresight to see the economic advantages of animal culture. On the other hand, he maintained, hoe culture was an easy step from the hunting stage. While man had hunted animals, woman had grubbed for roots and collected wild plants. Woman could easily go a step farther and cultivate the plants which she had formerly just gathered. Further progress depended on the domestication of animals as beasts of burden, especially for the dragging of the plough and the wagon, instruments emphasized by Hahn; it also depended on man's taking over much or most of the field work. For over two decades Hahn wrote articles and books, massing facts and arguments.[1] He has had many followers in Germany and elsewhere. Indeed, only a few scholars — for example, the economic historian Kowalevski (1896), and the sociologist De Greef (1904) — have not been influenced by Hahn's work, at least to some extent. Some, not accepting Hahn's arguments, have thrown over the whole series of stages, or have fallen back on types, dodging the difficult question of development. As anthropologists have poured in facts from America, Australia,

[1] For a list of his works, cf. *Festschrift Eduard Hahn zum LX. Geburtstag*, pp. vii–xi.

the South Sea Islands, and elsewhere, it has been necessary for economists and others to abandon or modify their old-time theories.

REPLY TO HAHN

In answer to Hahn and his school, however, the following points may be made.   (1) Although we seem to lack evidence of any hunting people undertaking herding, nevertheless there are instances (for example, Hereros and Lapps) of pastoral nomads who depend solely on their new activity of herding and their old one of hunting. Such people practice no plant culture.   It might be argued that they have degenerated from a stage of soil cultivation; but this is improbable because of the lack of evidence of the survival of the general culture which would probably have accompanied the higher stage.   (2) If hunters could domesticate animals for social, recreational, or hunting purposes, why not also for economic reasons? Why should we credit women with the capacity for developing soil cultivation out of the search for wild plants, and disallow to man a parallel capacity?   (3) There are historic instances (in Asia, Wales, Algiers) of herders (pastoral nomads) settling down to agriculture. Putting this fact together with the argument under number (1), we arrive at the age-long series of hunting, herding, and agriculture. (4) It may be true that many prominent herders have used sheep and goats more than cattle and horses, but only a slight adjustment of emphasis would enable them to breed cattle (and horses) for use in dragging both wagon and plough.   Besides, it is not to be forgotten that sheep and goats are as real factors in agriculture as are the larger animals.   (5) Hoe culture and pasturing may be parallel developments or alternates.   Hahn thought hoe culture came first. The two may have grown up side by side in some districts; or in other parts of the world, where natural conditions favored one at the expense of the other, either may have arisen to supplant hunting as the dominant occupation.   They would, of course, in any case precede true agriculture, which is taken to be the integrated combination of both plant and animal cultivation.

A NEW SERIES OF STAGES SUGGESTED

What we need is a series of stages which will be both accurate and useful.   Such stages should apply to all peoples who have had a more or less unrestricted opportunity to expand their powers.   A few peoples have been so limited in their isolated, often insular, positions that their development could in no way be taken as typical. We must allow for exceptions. Our stages must be significant for production and must be related to distribution and consumption, though the correlation, from the very nature of the case, may not be exact. Our stages must likewise be significant for both anthropology and economics; they must be useful in the association of economic and general cultural data. With these desirable qualities in mind, the present writer has worked out the following stages of general economic development: collectional economy (hunting, fishing, grubbing, and so forth), cultural nomadic economy (pasturing or planting or *both*), settled village economy (developing a true agriculture), town economy, and metropolitan economy. The chief interest in these stages at this point is that they attempt a synthesis of the old generalizations and the new discoveries of anthropological material in various outlying parts of the world.

ECONOMIC DETERMINISM

Both anthropologists and economists have been interested in economic anthropological facts partly because of their desire to explain the non-economic by the economic. Although Adam Smith lived long before Karl Marx, the formulator of the economic interpretation of history, nevertheless he sought to show that military strength has depended upon the economic stage which a people had reached. And, with less success, he maintained that the cost of justice has increased as man has progressed from one economic stage to another. In all this he followed the traditional sequence — hunters, shepherds, and husbandmen. Some modern economists [1] have accepted the economic substructure as the foundation of modern culture. The economist, Richard Hildebrand,[2] made an interesting and valuable attempt at the economic interpretation of various primitive institutions. Among social anthropologists (and sociologists working in the field of anthropology) we find many examples of scholars using the economic interpretation, for instance, Hobhouse, Wheeler, and Ginsberg,[3] also Grosse in his work on the beginnings of art and the development of the family, and Nieboer in his study of the growth of slavery. On the other hand, many

---

[1] For example, K. J. Fuchs, *Volkswirtschaftslehre*.
[2] *Recht und Sitte auf den verschiedenen wirtschaftlichen Kulturstufen*.
[3] *The Material Culture and Social Institutions of the Simpler Peoples.*

anthropologists (and psychologists and sociologists in the field of anthropology) have been interested in economic phenomena either very slightly or just as one of the phases of primitive existence. Durkheim, Wundt, and Freud attach little cultural importance to early production. The ethnologist, Hahn, ascribes the domestication of animals to religious purposes. Giddings [1] makes fun of an economic interpretation of history. He accepts the discarded stages of hunting, pasturing, and agriculture as accurate enough, but denies their value. Of course, the answer to this is that economic stages in themselves are not intended as an interpretation. They merely provide, in this connection, the background of generalized economic facts for the correlation of economic and general cultural data.

Some Distinctions in Economic Interpretation

At the very beginning of this subject of the economic interpretation of primitive culture, a very simple but often forgotten or neglected distinction should be made, namely, the difference between motive and force, conscious plan and unconscious pressure. The stoutest champion of economic determinism would now hesitate to project into the dawn of human society any extensive generalization, theorizing, or conscious balancing of alternative economic systems. The rationalization of Spencer and Tylor seems to be dead as an accepted explanation, though possessing some life as an actual practice. A second distinction of capital importance should be made, one of concern to both anthropologists and economists, namely, the difference between technological and economic interpretations of general culture. Marx has been thought to have had the technological interpretation in mind, whereas more probably he just took his chief illustrations from it. Marett would apparently make invention (technology) the basis of economic progress, and with much justification. But after all, fish-hooks and canoes, spears and tree traps, fire drills and bronze adzes, while constituting the technological foundation of economic activity, are in reality the tools and not the life of economic activity. The habits, organization, and relationship, man to man, man to woman, and group to group, in early days as now, constituted an essential part of economic doings. The ideas, magical and religious, often are fundamentally the expressions of a deeper economic association. Sex

[1] *Studies in the Theory of Human Society*, p. 40.

bonds and community of economic interest, as Thurnwald has pointed out,[1] may coincide so as to produce a social institution of great significance. If we are to take an economic, in contradistinction to a merely technological, view, the venerable series of stages — stone, bronze, and iron — recedes into the background. We may make some use of them in archeology, but we must reject them for economic anthropology, not simply because they do not hold, as they stand, but because they are only relatively significant.

ECONOMIC INTERPRETATION OF PATRIARCHY AND MATRIARCHY

The explanation of patriarchy and matriarchy along economic lines constitutes one of the most outstanding illustrations of economic interpretation in the whole field of economic anthropology. In 1893 Brentano[2] maintained that matriarchy prevailed in the hunting stage but was supplanted by patriarchy when hunting gave way to herding. Brilliant in many fields, Brentano has been wrong in several. It now seems that patriarchy came first, and, as we have noted, pasturing did not always follow hunting. Although not beyond question, it is now accepted by some anthropologists (Grosse and Thurnwald) and economists (Schmoller, guardedly, and Schwiedland) that matriarchy followed patriarchy when and where women developed plant culture, thereby assuring the group of a more continuous supply of food. But as readers of Westermarck know, it is very difficult to generalize successfully about the human family. Accordingly we may deem ourselves justified in declining to come to a decision.

SUGGESTIONS FOR RESEARCH IN ECONOMIC ANTHROPOLOGY

Some day scholars may train themselves in anthropology, economic theory, economic history, and social psychology for grappling with the issues and the problems of economic anthropology. Past studies suggest that such persons might well have the following in mind:

(1) We need more field work, actual inquiry into economic conditions, before the simpler peoples of the world have been influenced by advanced culture — in short, before they have disappeared.

(2) Such inquiries should be economic rather than technological. Pictures and specimens are not now so valuable as information

---

[1] Bānaro Society, *Memoirs of the Am. Anth. Assoc.*, III, p. 373.
[2] *Zeitschrift für Sozial- und Wirtschaftsgeschichte*, I, p. 141.

about intangible economic relationships of man to man, and man to nature.

(3) The field investigators should have in mind wealth in all its aspects, how produced, distributed, and consumed.

(4) They should seek data showing correlations with other social and natural phenomena.

(5) We need more information about the density of population and its relation to changes in production.

(6) Along with economic should go environmental studies so as to provide data that will enable us to distinguish the normal from the abnormal.

(7) Field-workers and stay-at-home generalizers should possess an intellectual and emotional detachment from the preconceptions, perhaps even the preoccupations, of the past generations of scholars.

(8) Anthropologists and economists, though working at their own special problems, might collaborate profitably to themselves. The anthropologists could provide those in the economic field with facts in return for ideas and the fundamental issues involved in getting a living.

SELECTED REFERENCES

Boas, F. "Ethnology of the Kwakiutl." *Thirty-Fifth Annual Report of the Bureau of American Ethnology*, 1913–14.
The Mind of Primitive Man. 1911.
Brentano, L. "Die Volkswirtschaft und ihre konkreten Grundbedingungen." *Zeitschrift für Sozial- und Wirtschaftsgeschichte*, I, 1893, pp. 77–148.
Bücher, Karl. *Industrial Evolution*. 1893, 1897, 1901.
Frazer, J. G. *Totemism and Exogamy, A Treatise on Certain Early Forms of Superstition and Society*, IV. 1910.
Fuchs, K. J. *Volkswirtschaftslehre*. 1901.
Goldenweiser, A. A. *Early Civilization; An Introduction to Anthropology.* 1922.
Gras, N. S. B. *An Introduction to Economic History*. 1922.
Grierson, P. J. H. *The Silent Trade, A Contribution to the Early History of Human Intercourse*. 1913.
Grosse, Ernst. *Die Formen der Familie und die Formen der Wirtschaft*. 1896.
The Beginnings of Art. 1897.
Hahn, Eduard. *Das Alter der wirtschaftlichen Kultur der Menschheit*. 1905.
Die Haustiere und ihre Beziehungen zur Wirtschaft des Menschen. 1898.
Festschrift Eduard Hahn zum LX. Geburtstag. 1917.
Hildebrand, Bruno. "Natural-Geld- und Creditwirtschaft." *Jahrbücher für Nationalökonomie und Statistik*, II, 1864, pp. 1–24.
Hildebrand, Richard. *Recht und Sitte auf den verschiedenen wirtschaftlichen Kulturstufen*. 1898.
Hobhouse, L. T., Wheeler, G. C., and Ginsberg, M. *The Material Culture and Social Institutions of the Simpler Peoples*. 1915.

Koppers, P. W. "Die ethnologische Wirtschaftsforschung, eine historisch-kritsche Studie." *Anthropos*, x–xi, 1915–16, pp. 611–51, 971–1070. (An invaluable review of the literature.)

Lucretius. *De Rerum Natura*, book v.

Malinowski, B. *Argonauts of the Western Pacific.* 1922.
"The Primitive Economics of the Trobriand Islanders." *Economic Journal*, xxxi, 1921, pp. 1–16.

Nieboer, H. J. *Slavery as an Industrial System.* 1900, 1910.

Nowacki, A. J. *Jagd oder Ackerbau? Ein Beitrag zur Urgeschichte des Menschen.* 1885.

Roscher, Wilhelm. *Nationalökonomik des Ackerbaues.* 1859, 1888.

Roth, H. Ling. *On the Origin of Agriculture.* 1886.

Schmoller, G. *Grundriss der Allgemeinen Volkswirtschaftslehre*, part I. 1901.

Schwiedland, Eugene. *Volkswirtschaftslehre.* 1922.

Seligman, E. R. A. *Principles of Economics.* 1905, 1923.

Thurnwald, Richard. "Bānaro Society: Social Organization and Kinship System of a Tribe in the Interior of New Guinea." *Memoirs of the American Anthropological Association*, III, 1916, pp. 253–391.

Westermarck, E. A. *The History of Human Marriage.* 3d ed. 1921.

Wissler, Clark. *Man and Culture.* 1923.
The American Indian. 1917, 1922.

CHAPTER III
ANTHROPOLOGY AND ETHICS
By JOHN DEWEY
COLUMBIA UNIVERSITY

PROBLEMS

THE relationship of anthropological material to ethics presents a double problem. On the one hand, there is the question of the influence of more primitive practices and ideas upon subsequent development of practice. Tradition and transmission operate perhaps nowhere else as powerfully as they do in morals. This matter, however, belongs to the history of culture, and is too vast a subject to fall under present consideration. One of its phases, however, comes within the theoretical field which is our immediate concern. Many writers tend to exaggerate the differences which mark off the more primitive cultures from those with which we are familiar to-day. Accordingly, when similarities are found they are disposed of as "survivals" of early ideas and customs. As a matter of fact, there is hardly a phase of primitive culture which does not recur in some field or aspect of life to-day. For the most part, tradition does not operate and "survivals" do not occur except where the older beliefs and attitudes correspond to some need and condition which still exist. To put it briefly, the reign of animistic ideas, of the magic and ceremonialism which are sometimes considered to be exclusively or at least peculiarly primitive, is due to modes of feeling, thought, and action which mark permanent traits of human nature psychologically viewed. The important phenomenon is not survival, but the rise of scientific, technological, and other interests and methods which have gradually and steadily narrowed the extent and reduced the power of what is primitive in a psychological sense.

INFLUENCE ON THEORIES

The other and narrower question concerns the influence of knowledge of anthropological and ethnological material upon the formulation of ethical theories and doctrines. What does such material have to teach those who now theorize upon moral problems? What use has already been made by ethical theorists of this material? Since anthropology is distinctly a recent science, this question is still a relatively new one, and it is not surprising that there is still a great lack of consensus in results.   Indeed, the larger phases of the problem and its conflicting solutions were anticipated long before any such rich store of data was at hand as now exists.   The Greeks came into contact with a variety of peoples, and their ever avid curiosity was aroused by the variety and contrariety of practices and beliefs with which they made acquaintance.   They were led to formulate the question whether there was a natural and sure basis of morals, or whether morals were wholly a matter of "convention," that is, of local customs, enactments, and agreements; or, as we might say to-day, whether there was some absolute and unchanging element or whether morals were wholly relativistic.   Both answers were given; and, as to-day, the upholders of the natural or intrinsic view pointed to the fact, or alleged fact, that amid all the diversity there were certain factors common to all peoples.   And, somewhat like theorists of the present time, they were divided in their explanation of this universal element, some attributing it to the presence of the same reason in all men — in modern language, a faculty of conscience or intuition — while others took a more objective ground and held that certain virtues and rules of obligation were necessarily involved in the constitution of any kind of community or social life.

Another example of the use by moral theorists of unorganized anthropological data is found in the lively controversy of the seventeenth and later centuries between the empirical and the a priori schools of philosophy.   Thus, we find John Locke (1632–1704), in his polemic against innate ideas, asserting that "he who will look abroad into the several tribes of men ... will be able to satisfy himself that there is scarce any principle of morality to be named ... which is not somewhere slighted and condemned by the general fashion of whole bodies of men," and citing from reports of missionaries and travelers in support of this proposition.   Similar material of a popular rather than a scientific kind supplied the stock argument of relativistic and empirical theories of morals for a long period afterwards.

KROPOTKIN

The rise of the theory of evolution in the later nineteenth century operated, however, in such a way as to stimulate a more scientific treatment of primitive morals and to promote a systematic, rather than a merely controversial, use of the growing mass of anthropological data. Prince Kropotkin's writings are typical of one phase of the evolutionary school. In his *Mutual Aid* he endeavored to show that reciprocal assistance is a fundamental factor in the evolution of the higher forms of animal life. By emphasizing this factor he found the sub-human basis of morals not in an antagonistic struggle of organisms and species against one another, but in the instincts of sociality developed through coöperation. In his *Ethics, Origin and Development*, he carried this principle further in accounting for the main concepts of human ethics. Primitive man, living in close contact with animals, keen observer of their habits, and attributing to them superior wisdom, was struck with the unified group action exhibited by animals. The first vague generalization made regarding nature was that a living being and its clan or tribe were inseparable. Thus, the instinct of sociability inherited from lower animals was made into a conscious idea and sentiment. Sociality and mutual aid were such general and habitual facts that men were not able to imagine life under any other aspect. The conditions of their own existence were such as to absorb the "I" in the clan or tribe. The self-assertion of "personality" came much later. In the constant, ever-present identification of the unit with the whole, lies the origin of all ethics. Out of it developed the idea of the equality of all members of the tribal whole, which is the root idea of justice, equity.

Kropotkin then endeavors to prove that early peoples had not merely certain lines of conduct which were honored (and their opposites shamed and ridiculed), but also certain modes which were obligatory in principle, and which in fact were rarely violated in practice. He finds, on the basis of the Aleuts of North Alaska, that there were three main categories of obligatory tribal regulation. One concerned the usages established for securing the means of livelihood for each individual and for the tribe as a whole. Then there were the rules relating to the status of members within the tribe; such as rules for marriage, for the treatment of the young and of the old, for education, and the regulations for preventing and remedying acute personal collisions. Finally, there are the rules relating to sacred matters. Kropotkin's general conclusion is that there is no tribe which has not its definite and complicated moral code. His specific conclusion is that there is a definite notion of equity or fairness and means of restoring equality when it has been infringed upon, and also that there is universal regard for life and condemnation of murder within the tribe — that is, of fratricide. The chief limitation of morals in this period is the restriction in most respects to those within the group, though some regulations pertain to intertribal relations.

Subsequent development is not altogether of the nature of advance. The absence of adequate inter-tribal regulations led to war, and war strengthened the power of the military leaders, which had an unfavorable effect upon equality and justice. The same effect was produced by the growth of wealth and the division into rich and poor, with increase of industrial skill. Moreover, the elders who were in possession of the tribal traditions in which regulations were contained, tended to form themselves into a distinct and secret class which was the germ of ecclesiastic power. In time this class united its power and authority with that of the rulers established on a military basis. The actual evolution of morals can be studied only in connection with such changes in social life as they specifically take place — that is, within definite social groups. However, there remains the one outstanding fact that notions of good and evil were evolved on the basis of what was thought good and bad for the whole group, not just for separate individuals. It is to be regretted that Prince Kropotkin did not live to undertake such a study himself, as his method of studying moral practices and ideas in definite connection with the life of particular groups is undoubtedly sounder than that of writers who use anthropological data and adopt a purely comparative method, selecting in a miscellaneous group common ideas from different peoples without adequate control by the study of the total situation of each people as an organized whole.

WESTERMARCK

The massive work of Westermarck on *The Origin and Development of the Moral Ideas* presents a larger body of anthropological data in connection with morals than can be found elsewhere, but its value is unfortunately somewhat vitiated by the uncritical adoption of an uncontrolled comparative method. His starting-point is also one-sidedly psychological. He finds that the basic moral factor in evolution springs not from the social relations out of which sentiments and ideas grow, but from the sentiments of praise and blame. These sentiments are akin to gratitude and anger or resentment, but are differentiated from the latter by not being purely personal. They have a disinterestedness and impartiality and quasi-objectivity lacking in the latter, for they are *sympathetic*. That is, they are felt on behalf of others, and of one's self as commanding the sympathetic support of others. Custom is recognized as the great factor in determining the objects and contents toward which sympathetic approval and resentment are directed. Westermarck, however, reasons in a circle in holding that custom is the factor which makes gratitude and resentment impartial and disinterested, while still holding that custom is a moral principle only because its maintenance arouses approval and its breach, resentment. The circle is significant because it follows necessarily from his excessively psychological and subjective starting-point. Westermarck, however, undoubtedly supplements in a desirable way the objective sociological methods of writers like Prince Kropotkin and the French school of Durkheim and Lévy-Bruhl by his introduction of emotional favor and resentment. However, it cannot be said that Westermarck derives his starting-point from an unbiased consideration of anthropological material. He sets out, rather, from contemporary philosophical ethical theory which since the time of Hume has been divided, at least as far as English thought is concerned, into moral theorists who make emotion primary and those who give that position to reason. Kropotkin also was influenced by contemporary issues, as his desire to find equity or equality a primary idea is connected with his bias in favor of economic communism.

WUNDT

Wundt makes considerable use of anthropological data in his *Ethics*, but he is even more influenced by the traditions of philosophic ethics. He is especially concerned in showing the importance of reflection, of a somewhat abstract kind, in the development of moral conceptions, and thus to make out that only the *materials* out of which moral conceptions were later formed by scientific and philosophic reflection were found in primitive race-consciousness — not the ideas themselves. He emphasizes the fact that the objects of primitive approbation and blame — which, like Westermarck, he takes to be primary in at least the genetic order — were mainly sensible and outward, while later ideas are reflective and inward. In spite of this fact he holds that man has always had a moral endowment, the germs of later developments being found in early practices and ideas. The actual evolution has been determined by two forces — religious conceptions and social customs and legal norms.

Wundt's bias toward "intellectualism" appears in his notion that the metaphysical element predominates in religions, namely, some kind of theory regarding the universe and human relation to it. So considered, the ideal objects which are involved in religion, especially the ideas of the gods, have served a double moral purpose: they have supplied exemplars and patterns of conduct, and through their connection with a system of rewards and punishments, they have operated as the guardians and executors of moral laws. In custom, also, there is a marked intellectual factor, since human customs involve dependence upon tradition and transmitted material; which means that they demand consciousness of the past and an outlook upon the future. A custom is thus a norm of *voluntary* action. It is intermediate between morality, properly speaking, and law — akin to morals in having at disposal a subjective disposition in the individual to conform, and akin to law in using objective means of compulsion. Gradually the two strains diverged, and only after this divergence can we clearly discriminate morals from law. In detail Wundt considers, in their bearings upon moral development, customs relating to food, habitation, clothing, work, service of others by labor, play, courtesy, rules of intercourse, greeting, etc., and the definite social forms of family, tribal, and civic life. In spite of all change of detail, these *relations* remain constant and thus supply a factor of genuine moral continuity to the variety of customs which history exhibits. Moreover, there are two constants upon the psychological side, namely, reverence and affections. The first finds expression originally on the religious and supernatural side, the latter, on the human side. But they gradually became interconnected. The outcome is that we can mark out three stages of ethical evolution. In the first, the social impulses are confined within a narrow area, and the things which are regarded as virtues are chiefly external qualities that are of obvious advantage. In the second stage, the social feelings, under the influence of religious ideas and feelings which interact with them, come to explicit recognition, and virtues are connected with internal dispositions of a socially directed character, while, however, social objects are limited to local or national groups. In the third stage, the influence of philosophy and religion makes the objects universal, as wide as humanity, and disposition undergoes a corresponding change.

HOBHOUSE

The subtitle of Hobhouse's *Morals in Evolution* is *A Study in Comparative Ethics*, and in his attempt to trace the development of morality he necessarily draws largely upon anthropological material. Hobhouse regards the idea of *good* as the central and unifying theme of morals, so that the evolution of morals is an evolution of the content assigned to this idea and of the means by which the assigned content is realized. Hobhouse raises more explicitly than other writers the question of the exact relation between sociological and moral development, and concludes that while they are intimately connected, no social development is moral save as it *expresses*, and not merely influences, the idea of good, either in its content or in the area of its application. Thus, most primitive peoples exhibit customs of equal treatment and mutual regard, but since among most peoples these customs existed as a mere fact rather than as a conscious idea, they were submerged by the rise of differences between rich and poor. The Hebrews, on the contrary, grasped the institutions as an idea, and hence were enabled to maintain them against the sociological forces which brought about a division into rich and poor. According to Hobhouse, the factors which have determined ethical evolution have been, first, the form of social organization, and, secondly, the forms of scientific and philosophic thought, including under these headings popular beliefs such as are found in myth and magic. On the social side, morals are correlated respectively with primitive family life, organized clan life, the city-state, the empire, the territorial national state. The intellectual correlation affords an opportunity for a consideration of early animism and magic. In general, the force behind custom, according to Hobhouse, is at first mainly non-ethical, namely, the belief in magic and fear of revengeful spirits. Hence guilt, involving liability to these influences, is removed by non-moral means, such as incantations, purifications, and a technique of appeasements. This stage is paralleled on the social side by the fact that wrongs are first thought of as occasions of vengeance on the part of the injured man's kin, and "justice" arises not for a moral purpose but for the sake of averting, or buying off, a feud which is harmful. But when society gradually became interested in maintaining social peace, it developed an idea of right and wrong, and not simply of harm and liability to vengeance; in a similar way there developed in religion the ideas of spirits who have an interest in protecting the helpless, the guest, the suppliant, and in punishing a murderer simply because he is a murderer. Hobhouse concludes that there are four stages of moral development, or at least one pre-moral, and three ethical. In the first, customary rules obtain, but they have no character of moral laws. Secondly, specific moral obligations are recognized but without being founded on any general moral principle. In the third stage, generalized ideals and standards are formed, but without knowledge of their basis or function. In the fourth, reflection extends to discovering the needs of human life that are served by morals, and the function of serving these needs which forms of conduct, personal and institutional, exercise, so that there is a reflective criterion for judging modes of behavior and institutions which profess to be ethical.

CONCLUSIONS

Our hasty sketch makes clear that there is still far from being a consensus of opinion regarding the significance for moral theory of anthropological data, or even as to the method by which these data should be utilized. Upon the whole, preëxisting differences in moral theories are read over into the data and employed to interpret them. However, certain converging tendencies may be made out.

First, part of the diversity is due to a desire, which cannot be realized in any case, to differentiate sharply between moral conceptions and practices, on the one side, and manners and economic, domestic, religious, legal, and political relations on the other. In early peoples these traits are so fused that attempts to mark out what is distinctively moral become arbitrary, the writer having to use some criterion which appeals to him at the present time as peculiarly ethical in character. Certain phases of conduct have in the course of time become associated with distinctive, even explicit moral ideas. But this holds for popular practices and beliefs of the present time much less than theoretical moralists suppose. In other words, present as well as early morals are largely a complex blend, and the ideas taken for granted and expounded by theorists have had but little effect on popular consciousness, except when associated with religion and law — which again illustrates a feature of primitive morals. In short, the great demand on the part of moral theory is first an objective study of the types of conduct prevailing in early societies, without any attempt at artificial divisions into morals, religion, law, and manners, and secondly, a history of the transmission and modification of these habits of life, within groups and in their contacts with one another. This is an immense task and will be accomplished but slowly.

Secondly, the emotional factor in conduct is found to be universal and intense. For the very reason, however, that it is a constant, expressing inborn psychological traits, it cannot be appealed to in explanation of differences nor of historical changes. They must be sought for rather in change of institutions and in intellectual changes — theological, philosophical, scientific.

Thirdly, while at various times the effect of modes of industry and commerce upon conduct has been very great, there is no justification for an a priori assumption of economic determinism. As a rule, its importance in early groups is relatively slight, once the demand for necessities has been met. The rise and wane of economic forces in influence is a topic for specific historic study and analysis, the same as that of any other factor. The institution of slavery, for example, has had an undoubted importance for ethics, and the origin of slavery is chiefly economic, since prior to settled agrarian life a slave was more of a liability than an asset. But military conquest, sentiments of honor and superiority, and sexual motives have also played a part in originating human slavery, and the institution once established is persisted in on other than economic grounds, after, indeed, it has become demonstrably an uneconomic device. In general, a purely economic explanation of any primitive social institution, as marriage or myths, is to be regarded with suspicion.

Fourthly, neither side in the controversy as to whether the direction of ethical development has been away from or toward greater individuality, is unambiguously borne out by the facts. The romantic notion of the eighteenth century that the savage is a type of free and independent man, is obviously contradicted by facts. On the other hand, extreme, or at least ambiguous, statements have been made about the enslavement of early men to custom. They were enslaved from *our* standpoint; but they took the customs for granted as part of the necessary conditions of life (just as we, for example, do not feel the necessity of breathing air as a restriction on freedom), and hence probably had less sense of impeded freedom than modern men. For we, with a multiplication of personal wants and aspirations, are much more sensitively aware of constraints. It can also still be said of us that there are many customs which are so much part and parcel of our lives that we are not aware of them, or at least not aware of them as hindrances, while to our descendants they may appear to have been intolerably oppressive. Thus, present economic conditions may appear in the future to have been even more constraining in the case of the well-to-do than among the poor where restriction of freedom is now alone alleged.

No Single Development

The entire question of ethical evolution or progress is often put ambiguously. There is no doubt of the failure to establish uniform and universal stages of moral development. It may also be doubted whether the attempt to discriminate a single continuous line of moral development can be successful when understood in a philosophical sense rather than as literal historic sequences. On the one hand, there are certain basic needs and relations which remain fairly constant. On the other hand, the conditions under which the needs are expressed and satisfied and the relations of man to man are sustained, undergo immense modifications. That there has been, for example, progress in scientific method and knowledge, there can be no doubt; there has been advance in economic invention and control; there has been progress in the complexity and delicacy of legal and political institutions. But these very advances have so complicated conduct, have introduced so many new problems and afforded so many new ways of going wrong, that they cannot be identified with progress in actual morality. These changes have raised the plane upon which conduct operates; they have elevated the quality of ideals and standards; but by this very fact they have multiplied the opportunities for transgressions and shortcomings. Hence the meaning of moral evolution and progress needs to be carefully defined by discrimination between two distinct matters — change of the level upon which all conduct, good and bad alike, goes on, and actual right and wrong in conduct judged by conditions prevailing at the time.

If we speak of the former as a moral evolution we must recognize that it has not been for the most part brought about by distinctively moral causes, but rather by intellectual changes, the operation of new political and economic conditions, and so forth, which have so modified habits of life as to bring about an extension of the scope of previous moral concepts and a refinement of their content. Certain forms of industry and commerce, for example, effect a great widening of the area of human intercourse, and multiply contacts among people previously separated. In consequence, previous moral ideas as to obligations and rights have to be generalized, and the attempt at generalization modifies somewhat the nature of the ideas. A like effect is brought about by scientific changes. Thus, the older association of moral practices with certain religious ideas has been broken into more than once by the rise of philosophical and scientific criticism, and in consequence the content of moral ideas has been enlarged and altered so as to be capable of statement independently of particular religious beliefs. If we use morals in a narrow sense, it probably must be denied that there has been a distinctively moral development; if we use the term in the wider sense, it becomes merged in the general theme of the changes of human culture.

Relativity and Stability

It follows that great relativity in the actual content of morals at different times and places is consistent with a considerable degree of stability and even of uniformity in certain generic ethical relationships and ideals. Changes have arisen, as just indicated, chiefly from sources not usually termed moral in themselves — science, politics, industry, and art. Within the content of morals proper there are at least two forces making for stability. One is the psychological uniformity of human nature with respect to basic *needs*. However much men differ in other respects, they remain alike in requiring food, protection, sex-mates, recognition of some sort, companions, and need for constructive and manipulative activities, and so forth. The uniformity of these needs is at the basis of the exaggerated statements often made about the unchangeability of human nature; it is sufficient to ensure the constant recurrence, under change of form, of certain moral patterns. In the second place, there are certain conditions which must be met in order that any form of human association may be maintained, whether it be simple or complex, low or high in the scale of cultures. Some degree of peace, order, and internal harmony must be secured if men are to live together at all.

In consequence of these two factors of comparative invariance, the extreme statements sometimes made about the relativity of morals cannot be maintained. Yet we do not have to resort to non-empirical considerations to explain the degree of uniformity that is found. There is no society without its modes of shared approval and disapproval, and hence none without an idea of the opposed characters of good and bad. Variations in content are great, but they spring from technological and other methods at command by which needs are satisfied, and from detailed differences in social structure. There is no community which does not regard that which contributes to its social needs and perpetuity as good. There is none which does not strongly condemn conduct which prevents satisfaction of common needs and which renders social relations unstable. Thus, there is universal condemnation of murder, if murder be defined as the taking of the life of a brother, or of a social member within the group. The exceptions that exist are not dissimilar to those which now exist in respect to taking of life by public officials, or in self-defense, or in war. They are simply not thought of as murder. Even the statements which are made about lack of regard for property have to be critically scanned. We have first to know whether and in what respects private property is a contemporary institution, how far thrift is subordinate to generosity, the relative status of the persons involved, and so forth. Till very recently, those who have insisted upon uniformity have usually done so because they thought it was evidence of a common transcendental basis for morals, while those believing in an empirical and a naturalistic basis have felt obliged to seek for and emphasize divergencies. As fast as this motive disappears, we may expect consensus of opinion to grow up concerning uniformity and divergence of morals at different periods, especially if the loose comparative method gives way to a study of the correlations within particular cultures.

SELECTED REFERENCES

Bastian, Adolph. *Der Mensch in der Geschichte.*
Dewey, J., and Tufts, J. H. *Ethics*, part I. 1908.
Dickinson, Z. C. *Economic Motives.* 1922.
Frazer, J. G. *The Golden Bough.* 3d ed. 1911–25.
Goldenweiser, A. A. *Early Civilization.* 1922.
Harrison, J. E. *Prolegomena to the Study of Greek Religion.* 1908.
Hobhouse, L. T. *Morals in Evolution.* 3d ed. 1915.

Jastrow, Morris. *Aspects of Religions and Practice in Babylonia and Assyria.*
1911.
Kohler, Josef. A series of articles upon "Recht" in various primitive peoples,
in the *Zeitschrift für vergleichende Rechtswissenschaft,* XI, XIV, XV.
Kropotkin, P. *Mutual Aid.* 1919.
      Ethics, Origin and Development. 1924 *trans.*
Letourneau, Charles. *L'Évolution de la Morale.* 1894.
Maine, Sir Henry. *Early Law and Custom.* 1891 ed.
Maspero, Sir Gaston. *Dawn of Civilization.* 1896.
Petrie, Sir Wm. Flinders. *Religion and Conscience in Ancient Egypt.* 1898.
Post, A. H. *Afrikanische Jurisprudenz.* 1887.
Rée, Paul. *Die Entstehung des Gewissens.* 1885.
Schmidt, L. V. *Die Ethik der alten Griechen.* 1882.
Smith, W. Robertson. *Lectures on the Early History of the Semites.* 1894.
Spencer, Herbert. *Principles of Ethics,* part II. Induction.
      Principles of Sociology. 1923 ed.
Steinmetz, Sebald. *Ethnologische Studien zur ersten Entwickelung der Strafe.*
1894.
Veblen, Thorstein. *Instinct of Workmanship.* 1914.
Westermarck, E. A. *The Origin and Development of Moral Ideas.* 3 vols. 1908.
Wundt, W. *Philosophische Studien,* vol. IV. 1888.

CHAPTER IV

ANTHROPOLOGY AND HISTORY

By A. T. OLMSTEAD

UNIVERSITY OF ILLINOIS

HISTORY AND ITS FIELD

HISTORY may be known and read of all men, but its definition and its content are still matters of earnest discussion. The earliest historians, Babylonian, Egyptian, and Assyrian scribes, were content to chronicle the great deeds of their royal masters or to compile brief summaries and lists. The unknown historian, so modern in his objectivity, whose work underlies Second Samuel, broke loose from this tradition and prepared for later generations a true picture of his own, but his interest was still confined almost entirely to wars, the court, and the personalities of the leading men.

A far broader view was taken by Herodotus, "Father of History," and this breadth of treatment reaches its culmination in the famous "anthropological" book on Scythia. Thucydides represents the reaction which again narrowed the historian's interests to wars and politics. Since the days of these two historians, writers of history have followed the one or the other, at times identifying history with political narrative, at other times introducing a certain amount of social content. Modern "scientific" history tended toward the more narrowly political view, though always with notable exceptions. Since the beginning of the twentieth century there has been an ever-increasing tendency toward "socialized" history, which may now be said to hold the field.

History by etymology is simply "inquiry." This sufficiently indicates the historian's desire to study the facts as scientifically as may be, but it does not delimit the field of history, nor does it indicate that "art" which has been regularly assumed to be equally necessary with its "science." A rough rule-of-thumb definition might run something like this: "History is the investigation and presentation of such known facts of the human past as are important."

Certain explanations and qualifications of this definition are needed. Historical facts are not merely those which are presented in written documents, books, manuscripts, inscriptions, tablets, papyri, or the like. They equally include material remains, buildings, paintings, objects of daily life, even to the sherds of pottery. Nor should it be forgotten that there are certain immaterial facts, such as institutions, customs, and points of view, which are of the utmost significance.

But the historian must have facts. Since the vast majority of once existing historical facts have perished without trace, he must reconstruct his history only on the basis of those which have survived. Often he may predicate the general from the typical, though never without the consciousness of possible error; or he may bridge his gaps with hypotheses. These hypotheses, however careful their utilization of the extant evidence, are scientific guesses and nothing more. So cautious has been the historian that he has been perhaps unduly skeptical of theories of the past, but it has been a healthy skepticism.

Out of the still unmanageably large number of facts preserved, the historian must choose those which are important or typical. This choice depends in part on the historian, in part on the needs of his particular age. Thus, history must be reinterpreted for each generation. What, for instance, may be mere back-stairs gossip for one generation of historians may for another generation prove to contain important indications of political divisions, which in turn may enable us to understand economic and social conditions of the most fundamental character.

Finally, historical investigation is practically worthless unless it is presented in such a manner as will cause these investigations to be known. It is noteworthy that this art, ordered into exile by the first practitioners of "scientific" history, is being revived by the present generation.

ANTHROPOLOGY AND ITS FIELD

Anthropology received its name in the "scientific" period. Its literal meaning, "science of man," accordingly represents more truly its particular field. Strictly interpreted, anthropology could include the whole of the field cultivated not merely by the historian, but by the sociologist, political scientist, economist, psychologist, geographer, or even anatomist. Such broad claims have indeed been made by reputable anthropologists, but in their own practice the field covered has been much less extensive.

Hitherto, the chief interest of the anthropologist has been in primitive peoples, whether primitive in date or in present-day practice. Certainly no portion of the human field needed immediate cultivation more urgently. Remains of earliest man were being destroyed as gravel pits were worked, his implements were being scattered abroad. The leveling process of modern education in Europe and America was wiping out old customs and sayings, survivals of primitive modes of thought. Peoples in remote corners of the earth's surface, who had existed with little change for thousands of years, were being discovered and "civilized" with such rapidity that only the fast dying elder generation retained a full consciousness of older custom and of its meaning.

This work, in so far as it relates to primitive men or primitive thought to-day, is obviously nearing its completion. There are still valuable gleanings to be made, but it may be suspected that little knowledge of a revolutionary nature will be discovered. Primitive man is becoming increasingly aware of the airplane and of alcohol, he is blessed by the missionary and the movie, he prides himself on his European garments and attempts to clothe his thoughts in European fashion. That much of the old will survive — that the Europeanization is in many respects of the most superficial character — indicates a whole series of most interesting problems for the future historian. The anthropologist is in a less happy state, for the old is going and is increasingly more difficult to secure; when secured, it is probable that, in general, it will merely add more footnote references to support the general conclusions.

With this rapid drying-up of the sources of new information, the anthropologist is once more turning to the production of these general conclusions. The earlier anthropology was, as might have been suspected, largely under the influence of the then new concept of evolution. With the fragmentary knowledge then possible, it attempted to present a scheme of things which should have universal validity. It was equally obvious that the then dominant school of historians could have little sympathy for anthropological methods or conclusions. With all their insistence on the "scientific" character of history, especially in investigation of the sources, historians clung, as always, close to solid ground. They had long realized that history is not logical, in the sense in which logic is taught in the schools, though it does have a sort of logic of its own which may be dimly perceived through the study of the entire world history. Historians considered their most insidious enemy the "philosopher of history" who undertook to rewrite history in the terms of the fashionable philosophy of his day. Early anthropology was not a little under the influence of the Spencerian philosophy, and it was only natural that this type of anthropology should be considered by the historian as but a more matured form of the "philosophy of history." In the same manner may be explained the historian's suspicion of the earlier sociology, again so largely the product of the philosophers.

There is no longer excuse for such suspicion of anthropology. Evolution is no longer given undue importance. Diffusion is recognized as the dominant force in the great majority of cases of cultural similarities, until we come to an extreme school which virtually denies all independent evolution. A priori thinking has disappeared; the present-day anthropologist has the closest touch with reality.

The Historian and the Anthropologist

In the anthropology of the present, more than in any other of the social or near social sciences, the historian recognizes the same attitude toward the facts and the same methods of investigation that he is accustomed to in his own studies. In both the anthropologist and the historian there is a strong feeling of the danger of too simple generalizations. Both have ceased to believe in a single evolution through which each people has passed or must pass, and they recognize that human development is infinitely complex, that no two races or peoples have evolved in precisely the same manner. The problem has become far more complex, but for that very reason the search for essential human nature under its myriad manifestations has become the more fascinating.

Meanwhile, the relations between anthropologists and historians have become increasingly closer. There has never existed the actual antagonism which at certain times affected the relations between the students of history and of certain other of the social sciences. Rather, the historian and the anthropologist of the past ignored one another. *Rapprochement* can now be safely made on the basis of present conditions, and without any danger from former relations of a less pleasant character.

ANTHROPOLOGY AND AMERICAN HISTORY

That this approach is actually taking place is easily evident. It is least clear in the field of conventional American history. In spite of all the excellent work done by our national Bureau of Ethnology and by our various museums, there is little evidence of the utilization of the mass of material thus furnished in the account given by the average American historian. Pre-Columbian history is virtually non-existent, so far as the histories of America are concerned. No papers on this highly interesting subject grace a meeting of the American Historical Association or the pages of the *American Historical Review*. The word "Indian" would indeed appear often in the index of a typical history of the United States, but one would find on checking these references that none of them told of Indian origins, customs, or cultures, while the Indian point of view is never so much as hinted. With a few notable exceptions, the state historical societies refuse to consider Indian history as within their proper territory. For some of the most important states of the union, information as to the Indian past is virtually non-obtainable, while year by year the Indian sites are being obliterated by the plough.

In the conventional field of American history, there is to be noted a decided progress in developing a more social view of the subject. Purely political history makes little appeal, and fuller realization of such elements in American history as the frontier, sectionalism, agriculture, and immigration, is bringing the student to problems toward whose solution much aid might be given by the anthropologists. It must be confessed, however, that the student of American history is as yet unaware of the assistance to be gained from the anthropologist.

ANTHROPOLOGY AND EUROPEAN HISTORY

Much the same situation is still to be found in English history. A quarter of a century ago, the present writer heard a famous English historian, with a characteristic wave of the hand, begin a course in English history: "We will not waste our time with the men who made flint arrows or with the Roman legions; we will take our start with the true beginning of English history, with the Angles and Saxons and Jutes." Little more would be said to-day. English history is still written as if Hengist and Horsa meant a clean sweep of all that went before. Students of British pre-history, of

Roman Britain, and of the later England still work in separate compartments, with the consequent losses. British history has likewise suffered from a somewhat marked tendency toward political narrative, though fortunately a strong minority has held faith in social history.

Modern European history has suffered in much the same manner. In the study of the highly mixed populations and cultures of Europe, it is considered more than enough if a map showing the distribution of the "races" according to their languages is included. Modern history has also suffered from the attempt to prove one "race" superior to another, but it may be doubted whether the attempt to prove all great men Nordics has done more damage than the counter-accusations as to the "blond beast." Medieval history is in somewhat better case. This is especially true in eastern Europe where the obvious complexities of the problems, the lack of a conventionalized history, and the shorter interval of time that has elapsed since written records became available, all have forced a larger use of the prehistoric material.

ANTHROPOLOGY AND ANCIENT HISTORY

It is, however, in the field of ancient history that a real *rapprochement* is taking place with anthropology. The reasons for this fortunate condition may be found in the history of these studies. To the very end of the nineteenth century, that is, in the period when "scientific" history was so largely dry as dust, Greece and Rome were not recognized as integral parts of the field cultivated by the historical profession. The first assistant professor of ancient history in an American university was not appointed until 1902, and it was not until 1909 that the American Historical Association recognized ancient history as worthy of a separate section meeting. Until then, and to no small degree since, the teaching of ancient history was one of the tasks of the professor of Greek or Latin. His interest was primarily in the classical literature, and the narrative, purely political history, was given relatively little attention. In fact, it would not be far from the truth to say that the transfer of ancient history to the department of history gave a necessary political backbone which had hitherto been sadly lacking.

From the days of the Renaissance there existed the keenest interest in classical life and literature. Since classical texts were to be minutely interpreted, illustrations of each custom must be found, and search was accordingly made in many a work which would never have been read for its own literary value. Material objects which would illustrate the classical life were even more eagerly welcomed. Manuals of "classical antiquities" were produced in great numbers, and the foundations of archeology were laid. Interest extended to the classic lands themselves. Temples were drawn and measured, minor objects were collected, until at last the day came when excavations could be begun. Step by step with the collection of archeological material went the collecting of data on the modern population, their customs, their folk lore, and much was likewise found here to illustrate the classics.

Excavation soon showed that the excavator could not stop with purely classical strata. The post-classical period was indeed despised, and much has doubtless been lost because it was dubbed "merely Byzantine." Later excavators have at least carefully mapped and planned what they have destroyed, and have collected the smaller objects.

The attitude of the classical excavator toward the strata which underlay the classical was entirely different. Problems of origins have always troubled the student of Greek and Roman history. The classical example of "scientific" historical method is Niebuhr's destruction of the legendary history of Rome. After his epoch-making book it was impossible not to recognize that the earlier recorded history of the classical world was legendary. Grote, indeed, left the blank unfilled in his *History of Greece*, but this was a counsel of despair and soon the legendary history was being turned into myths according to the accepted methods of the day. Increasing sanity showed the mythical explanation to be equally unsatisfactory, and a serious attempt was now made to extract some sort of true history from the legendary mass. Mommsen's once famous chapter on the races of Italy is absurd enough in the light of to-day, but it was at least recognition of a blank to be filled.

Excavation soon began to suggest possible answers to the question of Greek and Roman origins, and thus the classical student was launched on the study of local pre-history. His strata did not stop with the period just before the dawn of written history, but continued into the neolithic. All the material discovered must be properly published, and in securing the necessary parallels the classical investigator was led more and more afield. To-day the classical archeologist moves back and forth between pre-history and history, scarcely conscious of the boundary, and to the great scandal of certain conservatives who assert that Pindar and Pericles are being ignored for pots and pans.

When the anthropologist was ready to begin work there had been accumulated a vast store of classical material, easily accessible, well organized, and dealing with subjects known to every educated man. It was only natural that the anthropologist should utilize this material for his own study. It is highly significant that the author of one of the epoch-making books in anthropology, the *Golden Bough*, should have found his inspiration in a classic tale, and that he should be equally famous, though among a different group of scholars, as the editor of the best-known Baedeker of ancient Greece. How far this connection has gone will be realized when we read another most significant book, *Anthropology and the Classics.*

ANTHROPOLOGY AND THE ANCIENT ORIENT

Almost exactly parallel was the development of the ancient history of the Near East. Since the Bible was the Book, it was studied with even more minute care and with yet more minute illustration of every passage. Biblical Antiquities took their place on the shelf beside the Classical Antiquities, and drew much from their companions. Religious history was and remains the chief study of the Biblical scholar, and emphasis on the political history and its influence has become even more necessary here than in the case of the Greek and the Roman.

The Bible was in every man's hand, and the earliest anthropologists found much that they might use. If to-day we smile at the very thought of Samson as a sun god, inhabiting a heavenly Beth Shemesh, "House of the Sun," when the highly terrestrial Beth Shemesh has actually been excavated, it remains none the less true that the Samson story has legendary elements, and that the customs there mentioned find their explanation, as do those of many another early Bible story, according to the rules of anthropology. Here again, as in the case of the classics, the connection between Biblical study and anthropology has been close. It is, indeed, difficult to decide whether such a man as W. Robertson Smith was more eminent as an anthropologist or as a Biblical scholar. A whole series of later studies bears witness to the persistence of the anthropological method in such investigations.

With the exception of the Biblical data and a few passages in the classical writers (since proved for the most part incorrect), the whole ancient Orient was virtually unknown a little more than a century ago. The resurrection of the Orient was thus effected step by step with the progress of scientific history. During the greater part of this time the historian would have nothing to do with this virgin field. His hesitation was not entirely unjustified, for difficult and strange languages and scripts, still but half deciphered, demanded a philological training few could endure. This very fact saved it from the political historian. To this day political narrative history of the Orient in the ordinary manner is quite impossible, at least if the attention of the general reader is to be held. Interest may center on a few kings who happen to be mentioned in the Bible, a few mighty personalities emerge from the misty past; but what the general reader wishes to know is how the people lived, what they thought, how they worshiped, above all, what light is thrown on the most minute point in the sacred scriptures.

This the Orientalist can give his readers. Not only has he a list of records of every conceivable variety, and numbered by the tens of thousands, but he has other thousands of objects to illustrate the daily life, and with the finger prints of the maker or user sometimes still upon them. The beholder's imagination is stirred and he realizes the essential humanity of these age-old Orientals.

The study of Egyptian antiquities has progressed to such a degree that we can answer instantly questions of daily life which are still disputed in the case of Greece and Rome, and for which we would search in vain the histories of later peoples. Babylonian archeology still suffers from the general feeling of Assyriologists that "tablets are the thing," but this evil is in process of being remedied. Palestine has recently found excavators of zeal. The early influence of the Egyptologist is lessening, and a true Palestinian archeology is in process of development.

Nowhere is the dividing line between history and pre-history more nearly invisible than in the ancient Orient. As the Orientalist pushes back in history, the inscriptions become ever fewer and briefer, the individualities more misty. More and more the historian is forced to rely on purely material sources for his knowledge of the civilization. When the earliest pictograph is passed and he enters true pre-history he is scarcely conscious of the change, for the same general culture can still be traced back through its various levels.

The Historian and Pre-History

Conventional pre-history was developed in Western Europe. Textbooks of pre-history still devote all or nearly all of their attention to Europe. But meanwhile so many discoveries have been made in the field of Near-Eastern pre-history that the time is ripe for a re-orientation of pre-history which shall place the Near East in its central position. The well-known Hale lectures of Professor Breasted point the way; a new pre-history should follow the indicated route.

With the growth of interest in Oriental pre-history has gone the application of the anthropological method. The Bible forms, after all, but a small literature; it must be illustrated from the outside. Robertson Smith's most important discoveries, whether considered as anthropological or as Biblical, were not made primarily on the basis of the Biblical data, but by invoking the evidence of the vast Arabic literature to explain isolated references in the sacred books. With the opening of the treasure stores in cuneiform and in hieroglyphic characters, these likewise were laid under contribution by Robertson Smith's successors. Such a book as Barton's *Semitic Origins* owes as much to anthropology as to Babylonian history, while Jastrow's monumental *Religion Babyloniens und Assyriens* was possible only to one who had studied more primitive religions.

If the general historian has been slow to recognize ancient history, he is still unaware of the significance of pre-history. Certain indications show that his attitude will change. For many years high-school texts in ancient history have devoted three or four perfunctory pages to the old and new stone ages and they have been generally omitted by the teacher. A new development came in 1916 when Breasted's *Ancient Times* for the first time gave high-school students an adequate treatment of pre-history. The success of the work has been amazing, and students by the tens of thousands have been leaving high school with the feeling that pre-history is an essential part of history. Each year their influence on the general public becomes more marked.

Much the same service was performed for the general public in 1921 by Wells's *Outline of History*. Indeed, it is not improbable that when the history of historiography in the twentieth century comes to be written, this introduction of pre-history as a part of history to the general reading public may be the most significant influence attributed to that much-debated work. The year 1923 saw a final capitulation on the part of the professional historians. To the rather dryly political *Cambridge Modern History* had been prefixed a much more socialized *Medieval History*, and to this was now prefixed in turn an *Ancient History*. The first two chapters of the first volume are easily the most significant in the whole work, for these chapters by J. L. Myres present the best review of pre-history in existence. Later volumes have given equal attention to the later phases of pre-history. When the series is complete, it will afford an interesting cross-section of the anthropological interests of the various groups of historians. It begins with a pre-history which only yesterday was confined to anthropology: it ends with a present-day history which shows no signs of knowing that anthropologists exist.

RELATIONSHIP OF THE ANTHROPOLOGIST AND THE HISTORIAN

Meanwhile the anthropologists have become increasingly conscious of their relation to the historians. They discuss the relations between the two studies, with full recognition of the elements in common and of the difficulty in drawing a dividing line. We even have an anthropologist such as Lowie deliberately declaring that his book is not sociology but history.

History may be a science; it certainly does its work in a scientific manner, and its practitioners care little whether the term "science" is applied or not. However that may be, its purpose is essentially descriptive. It may narrow its interest to a single man, a single period, a single nation, or it may study the development of an institution through the ages or even attempt to picture the most essential factors of the whole human past.

It has broadened its field enormously, both in time and in space. It is taking over what has been called pre-history, and there is no reason why it should not take over the history of primitive peoples, in so far as this can be determined from written records of foreign visitors or from a study of their material or immaterial culture. There is reason to assume that this field will be increasingly occupied as it comes to be recognized that only thus can there be secured a proper background for that expansion of Europe which has been so characteristic a feature of modern times. It has already made firm its grasp on the Orient, whether in the better-known Near East, in India, China, or Japan, and in time it will include Central

Asia, just coming into the historian's view, and in all probability destined to knit together the hitherto isolated civilizations of the older Orient.

THE ANTHROPOLOGIST AND THE LAWS OF HISTORY

But when all is said, history remains essentially descriptive. All its technical processes have been evolved to that end. Yet to-day there is a growing feeling among historians that more attention should be devoted to ultimate relations. Historians now write and talk about "processes" or even "laws" of history.

Now it is of course conceivable that a certain number of historians might be specialized to deal with these "laws." But in so doing they would cease to be historians in any real sense. It is furthermore questionable whether this specialization is necessary or advisable. There is another science which deals with much and might deal with all of this field of "law in history." Its practitioners will in the future spend less of their time describing primitive peoples, as these peoples cease to be primitive. This will free them more and more for the study of "laws."

The historian is too busy already to devote more time to general principles. But he has very definite ideas as to what facts must be made the basis for general conclusions and as to the manner in which these facts must be used. He finds the anthropologist to have essentially these same presuppositions, and in so far as the anthropologist has come to general results, these results seem natural and quite uncontaminated by any "philosophy of history." In all probability, therefore, the historian will continue his humble but fascinating task of describing the particular, and will leave the evolving of general laws to his friend the anthropologist.

SELECTED REFERENCES

Alvord, C. W. "The Science of History," *Popular Science Monthly*, 1914, p. 490 *et seq.*

Barnes, H. E. *The New History and the Social Studies*, chap. IV. 1925.

Barton, G. A. *Sketch of Semitic Origins.* 1902.

Bernheim, E. *Lehrbuch der historischen Methode*, 2d ed. 1894.

Boas, Franz. *Anthropology in North America.* 1915.
　　　　　Anthropology. (*Columbia University Lectures on Science, Philosophy, and Art.*) 1908.

Breasted, J. H. *Ancient Times.* 1916.

Brinton, D. G. *Anthropology.* 1882.

Bury, J. B., Cook, S. A., and Adcock, F. E. *The Cambridge Ancient History.* 1922.

Cheyney, E. P. "Law in History," *American Historical Review*, xxix, 1924, p. 231 *et seq.*

Fling, F. M. *The Writing of History.* 1920.

Frazer, J. G. *The Golden Bough*, 3d ed. 1911–15.

Goldenweiser, A. A. "History, Psychology, and Culture," *Journal of Philosophy*, xv, 1918, p. 561 *et seq.*, p. 589 *et seq.*
  Early Civilization. 1922.

Gooch, G. P. *History and Historians in the Nineteenth Century.* 1913.

Haddon, A. C. *History of Anthropology.* 1910.

Johnson, Allen. *The Historian and Historical Evidence.* 1926.

Kroeber, A. L. *Anthropology.* 1923.

Lamprecht, K. *What is History*, trans. by E. A. Andrews. 1905.

Langlois, C. V., and Seignobos, C. *Introduction to the Study of History*, trans. by G. G. Berry. 1898.

Lowie, R. H. *Culture and Ethnology.* 1917.
  Primitive Society. 1920.

McDougall, W. *Anthropology and History.* 1920.

Marett, R. R. *Anthropology.* 1912.
  (ed.) *Anthropology and the Classics.* 1908.

Rivers, W. H. R., and others. *Reports on the Present Condition and Future Needs of the Science of Anthropology.* 1913.

Robinson, J. H. *The New History.* 1912.

Smith, W. Robertson. *Lectures upon the Religion of the Semites*, 2d ed. 1901.

Swain, J. W. "What is History," *Journal of Philosophy*, xx, 1923, p. 281 *et seq.*, p. 312 *et seq.*, p. 337 *et seq.*

Teggart, F. J. "Anthropology and History," *Journal of Philosophy*, xvi, 1919, p. 691 *et seq.*
  Prolegomena to History. 1916.
  Theory of History. 1925.

Vincent, J. M. *Historical Research.* 1911.

Wells, H. G. *Outline of History.* 1921.

CHAPTER V

ANTHROPOLOGY AND LAW

By ROBERT H. LOWIE

UNIVERSITY OF CALIFORNIA[1]

THE connection of anthropology with law is less obvious than its relations with other branches of knowledge; it is nevertheless a very real one, though restricted to special phases of both subjects. The line of contact is naturally along the study of institutions: the jurist who rises above the immediate practical exigencies of his profession is bound to survey the legal systems obtaining in alien countries and must consistently proceed to an inspection of simpler conditions; while the historian of culture cannot arbitrarily rule out of consideration the juridical conceptions found in complex civilizations.

Among the jurists who have in some measure grappled with the problems of primitive law only a few names can be mentioned here. Maine in his *Ancient Law* was perhaps the first to conceptualize the important distinction between government based on local contiguity and political coherence based on the tie of blood-kinship — an idea that through Lewis H. Morgan's *Ancient Society* powerfully affected sociological and anthropological theories of the state. Maitland, with extraordinary acumen, perceived the fragile character of unilinear evolutionary schemes at a time when practically all professional anthropologists were committed to them, and he warned anthropologists against postulating a fixed sequence of maternal and paternal descent. Vinogradoff's more ambitious attempt at the coördination of primitive and advanced law in *Outlines of Historical Jurisprudence* (Vol. I) is less satisfactory to the anthropologist because of his floundering between the modern historical and the antiquated evolutionary position in anthropological theory. His work is perhaps mainly instructive as evidence of the need for a complete résumé of juridical data rather than for particular flashes of insight.

In this connection J. Kohler merits a distinctive place of honor. From 1882 until the time of his death a few years ago he was co-editor of the *Zeitschrift für vergleichende Rechtswissenschaft*, and as such exerted a considerable influence on both jurists and anthropologists. With indefatigable zeal he perused and abstracted from ethnographical monographs the data significant for a student of comparative law, while at the same time establishing in his journal a rallying-place for those having kindred interests. Thus, anthropologists like Professor Max Schmidt and Dr. Richard Thurnwald are found among the collaborators of the later volumes in this impressive series. Above all, Kohler was interested not so much in the accumulation of unrelated fact as in the construction of a consistent philosophy of law. His article on "Rechtsgeschichte und Weltentwickelung"[1] outlines his conception of jurisprudence as merely a special department of a larger whole, culture, and expresses his firm conviction that only the cultural context of legal institutions can render them intelligible. His specifically anthropological views, to be sure, will not be widely accepted nowadays: he was a loyal follower of Bachofen and Morgan, and his temperament craved a unification of sociological fact by an assumption of eternal laws of evolution that runs counter to the tenets of our historical schools. Nevertheless, Kohler, like Morgan, and unlike Frazer, towers head and shoulders above most writers of whatever school because his espousal of unilinear evolutionism was coupled with a penetrating analysis of kinship terminologies — the acid test of competence in a student of comparative sociology. Thus, his article "Zur Urgeschichte der Ehe"[2] merits study even at the present day, and justly attracted the attention of non-German ethnologists, such as W. H. R. Rivers and A. M. Hocart.

It is the work of men like Maine, Maitland, and Kohler that suggests what to an anthropologist is naturally the most important thing in the relationship of anthropology and law, to wit, how his own discipline may benefit from a neighboring branch of learning. The jurisprudence of advanced civilizations, refined by centuries of acute intellects, is marked by a clarification of basic concepts such as the student of anthropology may well envy. There are obvious pitfalls to be avoided. Primitive customary law does not present the rigid formalism of codified law. It would assuredly be the acme of artificiality to pigeon-hole the rules of inheritance in a North American aboriginal community according to the standards of English jurisprudence. But the comparative fluidity of primitive conditions is fully recognized at the present time, and little danger

[1] *Zeitschr. f. vgl. R.*, **v**, pp. 321–34. [2] *Zeitschr. f. vgl. R.*, **xii**, pp. 187--353.

threatens from that source. The real menace lies not in ascribing a fictitious rigidity to primitive man but in following the bent, so strong in all of us, of preserving in our own discussions of primitive man an eo-logical (*sit venia verbo!*) disregard for clear thinking. It does not require an extensive knowledge of the literature or an extravagantly critical intellect to discover that when many anthropological writers use such terms as "classificatory system," "animism," or even "Neolithic," they have only the remotest idea of what range of phenomena they are attempting to designate. Epistemology may be the best and most universal prophylactic against such loose thinking, but for the anthropologist jurisprudence lies closer at hand and is a hardly less efficient corrective.

Let us now briefly summarize the results of anthropological investigations in their bearing on four main problems of legal theory — family law, property, associations, and the state.

FAMILY LAW

It may be regarded as a firmly established fact that in the earliest period which we can reconstruct by comparative researches mankind did not live in the promiscuous hordes envisaged by earlier theorists but in mainly monogamous family groups. This is the condition almost uniformly discovered among the unequivocally simplest tribes, such as the Pygmies of the Andaman Islands. Where sex communism has been reported, it invariably resolves itself on closer analysis into a set of special usages in no wise contravening the existence of the individual family, that is, a group composed of parents and children united by economic and sentimental bonds. The matter of doubtful paternity, to which great importance was once attached, is legally of no consequence: as Malinowski and others have shown, the "father" is generally the husband of the woman he has protected during the period of pregnancy. In fact, the definition of paternity may be quite conventional, as in Toda polyandry, where the husband who performs a certain rite *ipso facto* becomes father of the children born until a fellow-husband goes through the same ceremony.

In view of Sir Paul Vinogradoff's strangely vacillating position in the book cited, it cannot be too strongly emphasized that the matriarchate probably never existed and certainly did not exist in more than a very few of the instances commonly cited as proof. What we find is the totally different condition of matrilineal descent — the reckoning — of children as of kin with their mother. Even where women own the houses, as in Pueblo Indian tribes, they may be of subordinate importance in domestic and public life, and among the Iroquois the political rights granted to women never culminate in female chieftainship. In recent years Father Wilhelm Schmidt has argued that women rose to ascendancy by inventing horticulture, but while that achievement is plausibly credited to them the argument is unconvincing unless we accept an undemonstrable economic determinism.

As for maternal descent, the rejection of unilinear evolution has also led to the repudiation of the theory that maternal descent uniformly preceded patrilineal reckoning. The comparison of the rudest peoples suggests that the primeval family unit was "bilateral," that is, without undue accentuation of either the father's or the mother's side. Such factors as permanent residence of a young married couple with the wife's or the husband's kin would, however, inevitably lead to a weighting of the maternal or the paternal relatives, respectively. For example, the "matrilocal" rule would involve the co-residence of children with their mothers' brothers, who accordingly would become closer than the paternal uncles. Such a situation might develop into a full-fledged "avunculate," by which the nephew rather than the son would be considered the legal heir and successor to office. Similarly, such conditions would naturally align relatives so as to produce a nascent maternal clan (sib), while the reverse form of "patrilocal" residence would correspondingly unite individuals into a nascent paternal clan. The same results might be accomplished by other means, such as joint economic activity of mother, daughters, and granddaughters in digging roots or hoeing a plot of ground; or of father, sons, and grandsons in corresponding enterprises.

From this conception it follows that the maternal and the paternal clan are not to be conceived as evolving out of each other but as each independently arising from the bilateral family organization, according to which side happens to become stressed in consequence of specific circumstances. That an alteration of the rule of descent from maternal to paternal, or vice versa, may sometimes have occurred, may be admitted.

It is necessary to note that a "unilateral" clan organization never more than partly supersedes the bilateral family; it is something super-added that by its very existence must modify the family but cannot destroy it. As in all cases where two institutions coexist, divided loyalty may lead to conflict. How the paternal sentiment of the family type asserts itself even in a well-knit matrilineal community, has been graphically described by Dr. B. Malinowski.[1]

Family law naturally leads to a consideration of property.

PROPERTY

Is there anything in the way of property among primitive tribes? The pronouncements of many writers suggest primitive and primeval communism. These pronouncements may be definitely rejected as no longer accurately representing our present state of knowledge. With respect to certain forms of property there is often what virtually comes to communism, notably in connection with the procuring of food. But even in these extreme cases there is often a distinction between an ethical and a legal claim to the supplies in question, only the former being strictly accepted by the community. At most, it must be said that such communism as occurs is merely a partial encroachment on individual ownership rights. These rights, in some form or other, are generally recognized. As exceptions we might regard the property law of definitely autocratic or aristocratic societies (for example, in Polynesia), where a person of superior rank may *ipso facto* dispossess an inferior of any of his possessions. But this is evidently a condition at the opposite pole from communism.

One of the most interesting developments in recent years has been the accumulating proof that even among hunting tribes collective ownership of land is far from universal. Professor F. G. Speck has demonstrated that among the North East Algonkians individual families held tracts for economic use, trespass being rare and "summarily punishable." In Queensland the right of gathering roots or seeds in certain spots is restricted to families. Among the Vedda of Ceylon there is a definite transfer of ownership, and a man would not hunt even on his brother's land without permission. These facts certainly do not eliminate the occurrence of communal utilization of the soil in other regions, but they prove the difficulty of basing on such practices a generalization even for the rudest stage of economic activity.

The separate ownership of fruit-trees and of the land on which they stand in Oceania and elsewhere shows the sophistication of

[1] *Crime and Custom in Savage Society*, p. 100 *et seq.*

which primitive law is capable. Another special point of interest is the rarity of alienation: in most instances the land is never conceived as belonging to the category of purchasable goods.

If further proof for individual property rights were required, it would be found in the widespread recognition of incorporeal property rights. Even where chattels may be appropriated with the utmost freedom, as among the Andamanese, a song composer's copyright is never invaded. The same applies to the magical formulæ of the Papuan Kai and the Siberian Koryak. In some American instances the notion of individual ownership — based on a supposed supernatural blessing — is so firmly rooted that even the closest relatives acquire the relevant privileges only by a special transfer procedure.

In such cases, then, there is no simple inheritance. In other examples of the same category — and this applies to property generally — the rules of inheritance are nicely regulated. Some of a Nootka (Vancouver Island) Indian's possessions, tangible or intangible, could not possibly be kept from his heir because of the rule of primogeniture. This form of inheritance cannot be considered general; frequently the eldest-born is rather the trustee of an estate jointly held by a group of brothers. This condition is, in turn, akin to collateralism, one brother inheriting from the next older one. This was the rule of succession in Mexico and to some extent in New Zealand. Ultimogeniture (junior-right) holds sway among certain peoples, such as the Kirgiz and certain Eskimo tribes.

The rules of primitive inheritance law are exceedingly diverse and connected with numerous other institutions. Where there is a definite clan system, inheritance tends to conform to the rule of descent, so that matrilineal tribes often transmit property from the maternal uncle to the sister's son. But there are important qualifications to this correlation. Thus, in Melanesia, matrilineal land inheritance may be coupled with patrilineal succession to office, and it is a quite open question as to how far this disparity may be derived from the fusion of two antithetical idea-systems.

ASSOCIATIONS

Facts long previously recorded by naïve observers were first brought together with an appreciation of their theoretical significance when Heinrich Schurtz published his book on *Altersklassen*

und Männerbünde (1902). He demonstrated that comparative sociologists had neglected a very important phase of primitive life. The
illiterate peoples of the world were not merely grouped in families
and clans — by real or putative blood-ties — but also on the basis
of sex, age, matrimonial status, of common sympathies and purposes. Hence there have sprung men's tribal societies, age-classes,
units of bachelors and elders, feasting-clubs, trade guilds, and
religious fraternities or sororities.

Schurtz overemphasized the extent to which organizations of this
type, which are conveniently classed together as "associations," are
traceable to sex antagonism and to sexual peculiarities. It is not
true, as he contended, that women's societies are invariably pale
reflections of their masculine counterparts, and we now know that
in fairly many instances men and women may be fellow-members.
But he was right in recognizing that age is a potent factor in uniting
individuals, even though the union of coëvals may be informal or may
represent a mere subdivision of some larger whole, not the primary
basis of grouping according to his scheme. The assertion that all
associations are psychologically derived from the age-class, in other
words, is no longer defensible in the light of our present information.
That, *historically*, certain special forms of association belong together, as Schurtz believed, can hardly be doubted, but precisely
where the limits should be drawn between independent origin and
diffusion remains a moot-question. Few would doubt that the
initiation rites of Australia and New Guinea have a common source,
and many are haunted by the strange resemblances that connect
the adolescence ceremonials of West Africa and of Oceania, nay,
even of South America. Yet the latter case is naturally less convincing, and when we come to compare the age-classes of East
Africa, Melanesia, and the Upper Missouri, the similarities are of so
vague a character as to render historical connection extremely improbable.

One of the interesting features in the theory of associations is the
side-light it throws on political development.

THE STATE

Historically the anthropological problem of the state arose
through Maine's and Morgan's doctrine that a chasm divided the
governmental plan of primitive and of civilized society, the former
resting exclusively on the blood-tie, the latter on local contiguity.

It therefore remained to show the development of the latter out of the former. This was very imperfectly done by the earlier theorists. Schurtz's supplementary type of unit, to wit, the associational form, in some measure supplied the deficiency. For one kind of association, the men's tribal organization, does unite all the males of a settlement, *irrespective of the blood-tie*, and thus indirectly achieves the territorial integration of a given group.

A closer inspection of the data shows that this explanation, though excellent so far as it goes, is only a partial one since the men's tribal society is not a world-wide phenomenon, while some sort of local unification seems invariably to exist. This latter fact appears in the universal feeling of neighborliness over and above kinship ties, and in the universal recognition of certain offenses as not merely personal wrongs but public crimes. Contrary to Maine and Morgan, a primitive community is never wholly rent asunder into kin groups mutually as independent of one another as so many distinct states. The problem thus requires re-definition: it is evidently a question not of the creation but of the strengthening of the local bond, which in attenuated form must be held omnipresent.

This intensification of local affiliations may be partly effected, as we have seen, in the tribal associations. But whether these associations exist or not, it can be brought about by any imperious assertion of sovereignty. The autocracy of an African ruler and, temporarily at least, the powers vested in a special constabulary force during a Plains Indian buffalo hunt subject all the individuals within the group to a supreme law and thereby achieve the consolidation characteristic of statehood.

SELECTED REFERENCES

Barton, R. F. *Ifugao Law.* (*Univ. Cal. Pub. Amer. Archæol. and Ethnol.,* **xv,** pp. 1–127.) 1919.
Goldenweiser, A. A. *Early Civilization.* 1922.
Kohler, J. "Zur Urgeschichte der Ehe." *Zeitschrift für vergl. Rechtsw.* **xii,** 1897.
Lowie, R. H. *Primitive Society.* 1920.
Maine, H. S. *Ancient Law.* 1861.
Malinowski, B. *Crime and Custom in Savage Society.* 1925.
Morgan, L. H. *Ancient Society.* 1877.
Rivers, W. H. R. *Social Organization.* 1924.
Schurtz, H. *Altersklassen und Männerbünde.* 1902.
Thurnwald, R. *Die Gemeinde der Bánaro.* 1921.
Vinogradoff, P. *Outlines of Historical Jurisprudence,* **i.** 1920.

CHAPTER VI
ANTHROPOLOGY AND POLITICAL SCIENCE

By J. L. MYRES

UNIVERSITY OF OXFORD

ALL science has always two distinct objects, at all events as its ultimate aim: to ascertain and to formulate the truth about that aspect of existence with which it is dealing, and to extend, in reliance on knowledge so gained, our own freedom from the control and the obstacles presented in the course of events to the realization of our aims in life. The first of these, the advancement of knowledge, is the function of what we call "pure science"; the second, of those "applied sciences" by which our own age has so profoundly altered man's place in nature, and is (if there is any justification for writing this chapter at all) as directly concerned to review and revise, as better knowledge may permit, our behavior among our fellow-men.

Now it is a common experience, in the conquest of the unknown, as in other sorts of war, that advance is by rushes, along a ragged front. Reinforcements and new weapons of offense, as they become available, make good the shortcomings of an earlier phase and establish a fresh liaison on either flank of a rectified battle-line. But there is overlap, unavoidably, of objectives, and manœuvres, and personnel; and it may take time and thought to redistribute units in a revised order-of-battle.

More especially, in the human sciences, where for so long the practical needs of daily life have been urgent and solutions of current problems have been sought either directly from oracular authority or by inference from documentary precedents interpreted according to traditional and often symbolic analogies, most of the ground was already occupied by various forms of what we may describe generally as "political science," long before modern anthropology came into being through an extension of the concepts of uniformity and natural laws from physical and physiological events to human behavior above the animal plane. And not unnaturally, although occasional comparisons were made between savage and civilized behavior, as long ago as the pre-Socratic phase of Greek thought, the methods and conclusions of anthropology were regarded as in some sense special to the study of primitive peoples — meaning by this all savages and barbarians outside the pale of the great Oriental, Græco-Roman, and modern European cultures — and as alien, consequently, to the academic study of political forms habitual to those cultures.

RETROSPECT

Not that anthropology and political science pursued wholly unconnected courses, at all events from the revival of learning onwards. To the geographical hypotheses of the dependence of institutions on climates and food-quests, which are characteristic of Bodin, Grimstone, and Heylin, succeed the specifically West-African and Central American examples with the help of which Hobbes not only illustrated but evidently elaborated his *Leviathan;* the "Indian in the backwoods of America," who is the type of pre-social man for Locke; the Huron and Iroquois whom Montesquieu borrows presumably from Sagarde and Lafitau; the "Carib on the banks of the Orinoco" in the writings of Rousseau; the Polynesian of Chamisso and Forster; the Semitic and Aryan exponents of the patriarchal theory of Maine, MacLennan, and Fustel de Coulanges; and the Nair, Tibetan, and Redskin exemplifications of the "mother-right" of Bachofen and Lewis Morgan.[1]   At every stage political philosophy has drawn not merely picturesque illustrations but some of its boldest generalizations from analogies and also from contrasts between what seemed to be the simpler observances of remote and unsophisticated folk, and the more complex life and institutions of European societies.   That the presumed simplicity lay rather in the sketchiness of the traveler's tale than in primeval innocence among savages could hardly have been suspected until European observers trained for the purpose had lived among such people long enough and intimately enough to win their confidence and to discuss with them the principles on which their social order rested.   Born ethnologists, moreover, like Sagarde, Lafitau, and Dobrizhofer, have been rare, even in the modern world; and until quite recently it has been more often through some accident of geographical exploration or missionary enterprise than through

---

[1] For details see Th. Achelis, *Moderne Völkerkunde, deren Entwicklung und Aufgaben*, and J. L. Myres, "The Influence of Anthropology on Political Science," *Pro. Brit. Ass. Adv. Sci.*, reprinted with additions in *Univ. Calif. Publ. in History*, IV, p. i.

organized research into native manners or beliefs as such, that the lucky contact has been made.

LIMITED OUTLOOK OF POLITICAL SCIENCE

That ethnology has had the prospect of contributing as much new material to political science as some of its exponents have believed, results indeed less from the novelty or superior validity of ethnological conclusions than from the circumstance that until quite recently political science had for the most part derived its data from a limited range of experience — namely, from the societies of modern Europe, the ancient Mediterranean, and certain regions of the Nearer East — and similarly has had those data interpreted by men who had been brought up in one or other of those very societies and who were seldom at all fully emancipated from the social and political presumptions of their public and private life. As the second limitation applies also to ethnologists, it is not easy to estimate its effects upon other schools. Nor is it possible to point to profound changes in the principles or in the practice of political philosophers that can be ascribed to their ethnological studies; more especially as those evolutionary notions which have so largely determined the method of modern ethnology, as well as the moment of its emergence as a separate science, can be shown to have influenced the course of political inquiry directly and with far greater effect than have the contributions of ethnologists. Neither Spencer nor Buckle, for example, were themselves primarily interested in ethnological research, and their use of ethnological illustrations in support of their theories proves little more than the practice of their predecessors from Bodin to Maine. And, on the other hand, the well-marked differences in the method and in the results of political science as practiced in the principal European countries, suggest that even its ablest exponents are not only better acquainted with the political institutions which are most easily accessible, but are far more profoundly impressed by the significance of these institutions than by any common stock of examples such as ethnology might have been expected to provide. Political science, indeed, as it has been practiced hitherto, almost without exception, has interested the ethnologist rather as a confession-book of regional or national ideas and foibles than as an abstract presentation of man's place in society. Like an Oxford satirist, he sees the professors of it in each country.

"To experience turn a stolid ear: we do things differently here!"

ALTERNATIVE STANDPOINTS: SPECULATION OR RESEARCH

But while the direct influence of ethnological research on political science has been slight and indeterminate, in the method and standpoint of ethnology applied to political manifestations we see most diagrammatically the contrast between the two alternative modes of attacking such questions, under one or other of which every such examination of them must fall. Either the inquirer starts from psychological analysis of his own experiences and impulses as an individual, and from some act of faith as to the metaphysical substructure and logical meaning of his own individuality and personal experience — in which case all historical or geographical data (using those terms in the largest sense to express main departments of our knowledge of events, in their order of time or order of space respectively) become subsidiary illustrations, from a relatively illexplored context, of those states of mind of which alone he conceives that he has unqualified knowledge. Or else, accepting, by an act of faith in no way more audacious than the former, the existence of other individuals with personalities no less real than his own, and which include him in their several surveys exactly in the same sense as he includes them in his, he proceeds to investigate interactions of their behavior with his own, geographically distributed in space, historically distributed in time, and scientifically distributed in the sense that both these kinds of distribution may be apprehended by himself as related by way of cause and effect. Whether scientific observation of these interactions of the behavior of individual personalities — that is to say, of human beings in human experiences — is described as ethnology, sociology, or political science, would seem to be a matter of historical terminology; what is essential, and common to all such modes of description and procedure, is that knowledge becomes wider and more precise, and eventually more applicable to practical occasions, by observation, definition, comparison, classification, and eventual establishment inductively of uniformities of behavior, which can be tested and proved, in the logical sense, by crucial instances. Quite broadly and popularly speaking, the distinction might perhaps be maintained that in political science, which has by far the longest history of the three modes of describing this branch of knowledge, the eventual applicability of theoretical results to practical occasions is more steadily in view, political science passing insensibly first into a science and then into an art of politics; while as between the other two, sociology shares with political science — if only as in some sense a revolt or reaction from it — the claim to be of practical application, while ethnology, in so far as it has dealt with institutions or political customs, has so far concentrated its attention on extinct or obsolescent communities as to share with other branches of historical science the reproach — if it be one — of having no practical applications at all except the thankless service of mitigating the sufferings of peoples for whom the world has no more use.

There is, however, between the sociological and the ethnological outlook this more significant contrast, that while sociology specializes, as its name shows, on the social organization and institutions of a people and has been inclined to treat them in abstraction from its beliefs, its technology, and even from its economic régime, ethnology considers the social aspect of a people's activities as one aspect only of an indissoluble complex of aspirations, efforts, and achievements, our classification of which, under the headings "political," "economic," "industrial," "artistic," "religious," and the like, is an artificial dissection for purposes of analysis only; so that the same observance not infrequently reappears under several of our headings, according as our attention has been directed to its significance in the religious, artistic, or political life or habitual activities of the people we study.

The Political Animal and its Environment

Up to this point it has been possible to simplify discussion by substituting for the term "anthropology," which stands in the title of this chapter, the more special term "ethnology," which is commonly accepted as describing that aspect or department of the whole "science of man" which deals with the behavior, structure, and characteristics of human groups and with the relations between such a group as a whole and individuals composing it, considered simply as its components. Discussion could be and (in a sense) had to be thus simplified, because political science likewise deals with individuals composing societies as components simply, and leaves to other sciences, ethics and psychology, all questions of those individuals' personalities or inward make-ups; just as it leaves to anatomy or to the physical department of anthropology all questions of biological structure and function.

But it is one of the discoveries which is at last beginning to be made, even by professional exponents of political science — though hardly even now by the practitioners of the political art — that to speak of man as a "political animal" without further qualification as to the kind of man composing this or that breed of such political animals is as perilous as the economists have now discovered to be that venerable fiction, the "economic man." Very little is known yet about any correlations there may be between physical and mental characters in man; but it would be a very slovenly and incompetent ethnologist who would describe the manners and customs of a human group without mention of the physical build and racial affinities of the population, and also of the geographical make-up of its homeland, the whole complex, that is, of non-human factors, among which that population lives and against which that human group maintains that ceaseless struggle for maintenance, if not for mastery, which we call "life." These non-human factors fall necessarily within the survey of ethnology, for the sufficient reason that they frequently impose a geographical control so austere as to preclude the survival within the region which their coexistence defines of any breed of man not specially adapted by modifications of build and physique to endure it; and even where the maintenance of more than one human breed is physically possible, the limits within which any kind of exploitation is conceivable are usually so strict as to give appreciable, if not overwhelming, advantage to the more specially adapted; and even to that breed on condition of a conformity to local circumstances so rigid as to restrict human enterprise to a few mean and trivial achievements.

Reaching out thus, on the one hand into geographical environment, on the other into human anatomy and physiology, for marginal data and still more for a background and a perspective in which to judge of their significance in the life-history of a people, ethnology falls into place as that department of anthropology within which overlap with political science occurs; and its special contribution to the treatment of political problems is precisely in this wider synthesis, when it is a question of constructive interpretation. Self-centered as Greek thought was in many of its political speculations, it realized surely enough that equality, for example, was practicable only as between equals; and that while "fire burns here and in Persia," not only did climate and situation and natural fertility contribute to the "form of the State" and modify its functions, but there was also such a thing as "temperament," and that a vital factor in temperament was what we call "breed"; so that a

Scythian or an Ethiopian had no more place or prospect in a Greek city-state than a Greek would have among the Celts or Indians.

INSTINCT AND TRADITION IN MAN

Within what limits, and under what conditions, either physical breeds or geographical controls succeed or fail, when it is a question of changing the reactions which make up the customary behavior of a community, is consequently the central problem of constructive or theoretical ethnology. That this behavior is in very large measure traditional, in the strict sense, is certain; it is being imposed, that is, by the generation that trains, on the generation that is in training. Each infant in that generation comes into being unequipped with any such traditional behavior: if it comes "trailing clouds of glory," they are not of this world. It has, moreover, singularly little in the way of instinctive outfit: few if any of the higher animals are so defenseless and impotent at the start. Few, however — and perhaps for that very reason — are so impressionable and apt to learn: education (so nurses will tell you) begins, for good or evil, within hours, rather than days, after birth. It does not affect the issue that the circumstance that such first aid in education is mostly offered ignorantly or absurdly supplies one of the reasons why most people are as encumbered with inhibitions as they are. We call it the "burden of the flesh," and occasionally we see one who bears it well, literally "taking life easily," inasmuch as he enjoys a personal freedom beyond the reach of most of us. Whether, even so, these exceptional persons owe more to congenial upbringing, or to being in the literal sense free-born, is a question unanswered as yet, by psychologist and educator alike.

This digression to the borderland between physical anthropology and the psychology of the individual is less irrelevant than it perhaps appears; for the problem which it has attempted to formulate is a social and political problem also. Once grant that the adult citizen is what he is, as a component of the state to which he belongs, in consequence of either his breed or his upbringing or both, and the implications become clear, both of the wider avenue of approach contemplated by the ethnologist, to whom all categories of customary behavior are alike significant as aspects of the group-life, and of the minute study devoted in the first systematic treatise on political science, the *Politics* of Aristotle, to the political status of the child — and, we may add, of its mother — and to the pro-

vision not merely for training in civics but for liberal education of
the citizen-to-be on wide humanistic lines and sound psychological
principles.   For, equality being unattainable except among equals,
the approach to equality is by way of assimilation to a type of individual competent to assume the twofold rôle of ruling over free men,
and being ruled, in turn, though free, by other men enjoying the
same freedom.

FREEDOM AND PROGRESS

With the emergence, at this point in the discussion, of the conception of freedom, and of an individual competent to enjoy freedom in a group of free men banded together for the maintenance of
freedom, we discover a profound contrast between the data of current ethnology and those with which political science is commonly
supposed to deal.   Both alike deal with the behavior of man in
society; but we begin to see why ethnology takes so much account
of the non-human geographic controls and also of the human inhibitions on the spontaneity of individual temperaments; and also
why political science has so greatly neglected them and has concentrated its attention on the problems presented by that very spontaneity and by the conception of progress which is its social and
political counterpart.   For, as it has been justly claimed that the
borderline between ethnology and history lies at the point where
you may first truly speak of the occurrence of a "great man" and
trace from a certain date his interference with a course of events
which was as devoid of chronology, till he came, as a geological period or the life-history of a natural species, so ethnology, dealing with
the structures and functions of human groups conceived as self-
renewing and self-maintaining organizations merely or primarily —
for in this respect what the Germans call "natural" peoples
(*Naturvölker*) and the earlier political philosophy discounted as
people "in the state of nature," seem as devoid of conscious objective in their lives as is a cabbage or an oyster — makes abstraction of individual abnormalities of behavior, which are indeed uncommon here and which appear to be dealt with as summarily, when
they occur, as they are carefully precluded by that ubiquitous
system of ritual and tabu which governs life in uncivilized society.
Political science, on the contrary, itself began, as we now see to have
been inevitable, within the first type of political structure which
contemplated freedom (which in its original Greek and Roman

dress meant simply "grown-up-ness": *eleutheria: libertas*) as a legitimate and desirable end of the state, and has never ceased to take
account of that freedom as an indispensable ingredient in any social
order.   Even those systems of political philosophy which maintained a "divine right" of an absolute ruler to do as he pleased —
which at all events guaranteed freedom to him, at the cost of all
else — are contradictory of the savage ideal of kingship tied and
bound by precautionary rites and prohibitions, and politically
nugatory, just because of his divine right and majesty of deleteri-
ous initiative.   All others assume at all events an ideal of freedom
for all persons naturally free, however violent the constraints which
they may find it necessary to impose upon some people's actual
freedom in order to realize that ideal.   And they do so because,
whether Christian or Hellenic in their psychology and morality,
they are alike Kantian in their estimate of the individual personality as an "end."   Have not the most ruthless tyrannies claimed,
as their sanction, that they were "saving souls"?

Ethnological and Political Aspects of Actual Societies

There is, of course, overlap at many points.   Few societies have
risen to be sufficiently superior to their regional circumstances as to
be in a position to exploit the resources of their neighbors, without
yielding to the temptation to do so; but where the more intimate
details of aggression are available, tribal or national quarrels appear
to originate with predatory individuals, and not infrequently with
involuntary trespass of hunters or herdsmen exercising lawful occupations along an undelimited frontier.   But hostilities, like any
other emergency or upsetting of the normal,[1] are the opportunity
of the seer and the originator.   Then tabu is broken, lest it wreck
what it should conserve; precedent is over-ridden, for the situation
is seen to be unprecedented; political history begins, because (in
Greek phrase once more) the *ethnos* has become a *polis* of *politai*:[2]
a "population" has been transformed into a "state."

At the other end of the series, too, it is increasingly evident that
only rarely, if ever, is that transformation quite completed; that,
as Plato realized in Greek city-states, most political troubles arose

---

[1] It is instructive that the Greek word for "war," if we may judge from its
cognate verb, meant primarily a "mix-up" (*polemos; pelemizein*).

[2] In the Homeric poems, *polis* never means a community but always a fortress; and
the *politai* are not corporators, but a garrison.   For the transition from Homeric to
classical Greek usage see Gilbert Murray, *The Rise of the Greek Epic.*

from the survival of elements from obsolete tribal or clan-like allegiances, competing with the loyalty of individual to state, and perverting it; and that neither mere size nor mere wealth, nor emancipation from the more material "controls" of economic or regional environment, nor even security for the freedom of corporators approximately equal in their opportunities for enjoyment of it, guarantees a community against the persistence or the reëstablishment of elements within it which are literally out-law elements, maintaining themselves in as predatory and self-determined a "state of nature" as any wildling in Amazonian jungle. And between those extreme instances and the normal enjoyment of freeman's estate in any society there are many grades of inhibition by customary or traditional prejudice, scruple, superstition, of the kind that is the fascination and the despair of the collector of folklore. These manifestations are as abnormal now, as individual freedom was, in the state of nature revealed among natural societies; but in proportion as their existence and significance are realized, the scope of ethnology necessarily widens among the substructures of political science: just as the scope of physical anthropology widens when it is realized that it does make some difference (to however incalculable a degree or in however unforeseen directions) to a man's capacity to become a good citizen, whether he is of this or that build or complexion, conformable (or not) to the dominant breed, in the great state itself, or in some social or industrial compartment in it.

PROSELYTE OR GENIUS?

Whether such services, rendered by ethnological study of the more complex modern societies to the political science which deals specifically with their intensive corporate life, are or may be requited by applying the more refined criticism of social manifestations, which political science devises, to the descriptive material brought home by the field ethnologist from the simpler and more natural societies, is a question mainly for the future. Recent speculations as to the missionary activities of an ubiquitous archaic civilization, for example, assume a degree of emancipation on the part of the creators of so potent an agency, which is without parallel until the revival of learning in modern Europe, and they claim to recognize a new kind of spoor or trail where such emancipated agents have trod. In such matters normal ethnology looks partly, indeed, to the psychologist for clear notions of the processes by which the stimulus of ideas is diffused among men and the normal "burden of the flesh" is cast aside in crises of revolutionary exaltation, but partly also to the political philosopher and his pedestrian colleague, the biographical historian, for guidance in detecting genius at work upon our common humanity.

SELECTED REFERENCES

Bachofen, J. J. *Das Mutter-recht.* 1861.

Bodin, Jean. *Of the Lawes and Customes of a Common Wealth.* **1577.** English ed., 1605.

Buckle, H. T. *History of Civilization in England.* 1857–61.

Chamisso, Adelbert von. *Werke.* Vol. i. 1864.

De Montmorency, J. E. G. *The Natural History of Law.* (Pamphlet, Oxford, about 1925.)

Fustel de Coulanges. *The Ancient City.* 1894.

Grimstone, Edward. *The Estates, Empires, and Principalities of the World.* 1615.

Heylin, Peter. *Microcosmus: a little description of the Great World.* 1636 ed.

Hobbes, Thomas. *Leviathan.* 1907 ed.

Lafitau, Joseph. *The Manners of the American Savages, compared with the Manners of the First Ages.* 1724.

Locke, John. *Two Treatises on Government.* 1690.

MacLennan, J. F. *Studies in Ancient History.* **1876.**

Maine, Sir Henry. *Ancient Law.* 1861.

Montesquieu. *L'Esprit de Lois.* 1748. (Nugent's translation, 1914.)

Morgan, Lewis H. *In the Proceedings of the American Academy of Arts and Sciences*, vii, 1865–68.
Ancient Society. 1871.

Myres, J. L. *The Political Ideas of the Greeks* (Bennett Lectures). 1927.

Post, A. H. *Einleitung in das Studium der Ethnologischen Jurisprudenz.* 1886.
Comparative Jurisprudence.
Afrikanische Jurisprudenz. **1887.**

Ratzel, F. *Anthropogeographie.* 1899.

Rousseau, J. J. *Discours sur l'Origine et les Fondements de l'Inégalité parmi les Hommes.* 1922 ed.
Du Contrat Social. 1762.

Spencer, H. *Man vs the State.* 1884.
Social Statics. 1892.

Sagarde, Gabriel. *Grand Voyage au Pays des Hurons.* 1632.

Teggart, F. J. *Processes of History.* 1918.

Tylor, E. B. *Researches into the Early History of Mankind and the Development of Civilization.* 1878.
Primitive Culture. 1889.

Vinogradoff, P. *Introduction to Historical Jurisprudence.* **Vol. i.** 1923.

CHAPTER VII
ANTHROPOLOGY AND PSYCHOLOGY
By ALEXANDER GOLDENWEISER

LATE OF THE NEW SCHOOL FOR SOCIAL RESEARCH, NEW YORK

INTRODUCTION

ANTHROPOLOGY, the science of man, and psychology, the science of mind, must obviously be related in more than one way. Among other theoretical and practical contacts of these two disciplines special significance attaches to the relations characteristic of all sciences belonging theoretically to different, yet proximate levels; of the physico-chemical sciences in relation to biology, of the biological sciences in relation to psychology, and of psychology in relation to the sciences of society, including anthropology.

The attempts to solve the problems arising out of the relations of such groups of sciences have led to two significantly different tendencies. One set of thinkers are inclined to interpret the phenomena of one level in terms of data belonging to the next level. Thus we have biologists like the late Jacques Loeb who think in terms of physico-chemistry and mechanism, psychologists like Münsterberg who reduce psychology to biology or neurology, and sociologists like Allport who approach social facts with psychological tools. The other set of thinkers prefer to restrict their interpretations to unit concepts belonging to the same theoretical level as the data to be interpreted. Here belong scientists like Driesch and E. B. Wilson in biology, psychologists like Joseph Jastrow and the psychoanalysts, and social scientists like Durkheim, institutional sociologists like Kantor, and the cultural autonomists among anthropologists.

There is, however, a third position which combines the two approaches. Like most compromise positions, it is unpopular in both camps and has so far made but little headway. It is granted that nothing can happen in the biological level which would contradict the tenets of physico-chemistry, or in the psychological level, which would conflict with the principles of biology, or in the sociological level, which would go counter to the concepts of psychology. Yet, while granting this much, it may well be maintained that each level comprises phenomena *sui generis*. Now, whenever one level is interpreted in terms of another, the very features which make the first level unique unto itself, invariably and inevitably disappear. Therefore, if the autonomy of the levels is to be preserved — and there seems to be little inclination to discard categories of thought so well grounded in experience — attempts will continue to interpret each level in terms of unit concepts belonging to the same level.

In dealing with phenomena of the last two levels, the psychological and the sociological, a further complication is encountered in the fact that an altogether special significance attaches to the psychic or bio-psychic or socio-psychic unit on which society is built up — man. Nor is it a question of theoretical status, for man is no more significant theoretically than is an atom or a cell or a social unit like the family; or of existential status, for all of these units exist, experientially or at least conceptually. The special significance of man rests in his valuational halo. When with all due modesty born of scientific insight, we have laid aside the infantile vanities of primitiveness and have learned to see man's place in nature in its true perspective, there remains a residual anthropocentrism which will not be gainsaid or argued away. A warmth, an intimacy, an interest attaches to all that concerns man, and the universe has no say in the matter.

In view of these considerations it seems worth while to devote the rest of this essay to an examination of the psychological assumptions, avowed or implied, underlying some of the principal trends in anthropological thought and procedure. To do this at all adequately would require vastly more space than is here allowed, and even a superficial treatment will necessitate leaving aside many other aspects of the relations of anthropology and psychology, to which omission we are cheerfully committed.

PSYCHOLOGICAL POSTULATES OF BASTIAN'S ETHNOLOGICAL SYSTEM

The work of Adolph Bastian belongs to the nursery of anthropological thought. Temperamentally this restless traveler and ardent lover of mankind was a philosopher and mystic, which did not prevent him from extricating out of the bewildering maze of facts he had observed, a number of basically sound concepts. These were his *Elementargedanken*, *Völkergedanken*, and *Geographiche Pro-*

vinzen. Bastian perceived that mankind was everywhere and always very much the same, and he taught that this sameness expressed itself in similar "ideas" or tendencies which were ubiquitous. These *Elementargedanken*, "elemental ideas," however, never found expression except in the form of *Völkergedanken*, "folk ideas." The elemental ideas were abstractions, tendencies, or potentialities which were realized as folk ideas. The folk ideas, on the other hand, were concrete as well as definitely circumscribed in their provenience, for they were formed within certain geographical areas, and under the influence of specific historic determinants including inter-area contacts.

Writing when he did, Bastian showed great perspicacity in grasping the essentials of culture in its relations to man, geography and history. Under the guise of an obsolete terminology we recognize familiar concepts: the elemental ideas stand for the original nature of man, the folk ideas for cultural patterns (Teggart's idea-systems), the geographical provinces for culture areas.

Clarity, to be sure, was not one of Bastian's virtues. His elemental ideas remained exasperatingly vague and were in time elevated by his interpreters to the status of mystical entities. It is, however, clear that Bastian thought well of *homo sapiens* and that to him original nature comprised much more in absorptive power and creativeness than do the denuded psyches of Watson's infants or those of the poor-witted morons postulated by the diffusionists. The folk ideas also remained hazy. We hear nothing of the mechanisms which engendered them nor much about their ways of behaving. But they were *folk* ideas, that is, attitudes, concepts, and procedures grounded in the psyche of man but given definite form by social determinants and specific for different times and places. The geographical provinces in which folk ideas grew were not worked out by Bastian with any degree of precision, but again he must be given credit for perceiving that culture patterns arise with a definite local reference and that geographical factors as well as historical ones, of local or extraneous origin, coöperate in their making. Here Bastian tended to dogmatism; he vastly exaggerated the specific rôle of physical environment and thought of historic contacts in terms both too precise and too narrow, his idea being that such contacts were predetermined by geographical position (a concept recently revived by Teggart in his *The Processes of History*).

The essential sanity of Bastian's psychological, geographical, and historical perspective is also reflected in his attitude toward the problem of diffusion versus independent development, a problem the scope of which was barely adumbrated in Bastian's day. He recognized the universality of *both* processes and their basic significance for the growth of culture, leaving, as usual, the working-out of particular instances to other students.

PSYCHOLOGICAL POSTULATES OF EVOLUTIONISM

The classical evolutionists, as a group, were speculators but not theoreticians, and they fell into their methods rather than deliberately selected them. Even Spencer, in the face of the external coherence of his system and its apparent logical rigor, neglected to offer any theoretical justification of some of the salient features of his theory of cultural development. He claimed, for example, that culture evolved as an integral unit, and then proceeded to demonstrate the evolution not of culture, but of ceremonial institutions, industrial, military institutions, and so on. Nor did it occur to him that it was theoretically indispensable either to prove that these evolving aspects of culture were definitely correlated, in which case his original concept of an evolving culture might have been saved; or to claim at best that what evolved were the separate aspects of culture, and then to inquire how these evolving series were interrelated and how culture as a whole behaved. The use of the comparative method, again, was common to all evolutionists, but one would search their writings in vain for a single serious attempt to justify this procedure.

It can, I think, be shown that the psychological assumptions implied in evolutionism were throughout either erroneous or inadequate and that the theory of cultural evolution in its classical form, even if it were found valid from other standpoints — to make an assumption contrary to fact — could be condemned on this ground alone.

To make this clear let us examine the basic concepts of evolutionism: the psychic unity of man, the three tenets — uniformity of cultural developments, their gradual and progressive character — the comparative method and the use of survivals, and the rationalism and individualism of the evolutionist's interpretation of culture origins.

As to the psychic unity of man, the evolutionists, following in the

tracks of preëvolutionists like Waitz and Bastian, were certainly
on the right path.   Man is one, meaning by this not only physio-
psycho-logical unity but also availability for culture.   Fortunately
we need not go here into the question of the potential equality of
the races, for is it not a commonplace of anthropology that the most
striking cultural differences are found among peoples of one race, in
America, between the Eskimo and Maya or the Californians and
the Peruvians, in Africa, between the Kaffirs of the South, the
Baganda or Bahima of the East, and the Ewe or Yoruba of the
West, in Asia, between the migratory herders of the steppes and
tundras and the Chinese?   In this matter of psychic unity the more
critical theorists of the post-evolutionary period often exhibited
less acumen than did the evolutionists, as when Lévy-Bruhl attempted to draw a sharp line between the pre-logical mystical
mentality of the savage and the rational objectivity of the modern,
an attitude which contrasts unfavorably with Spencer's assertion that the savage is rational but misguided by deficient knowledge.

The evolutionists have not fared so well with their three major
tenets.   The tenet of uniformity has, of course, been shown to be at
variance with the facts of history; but it is also built on a false
psychology.   There may be such a thing as a limitation of possibilities in developments which keeps the figure of actual cultural
variants below the abstractly possible one, but this limitation is
never so stringent as not to leave room for a kaleidoscopic variety
of cultural growths the components of which must be sought in the
versatility of the human mind plus the play of historic accident.
If, this notwithstanding, there were to be uniformity, it could only
be explained by some quasi-organic drive which would keep the
traffic of historic events ever and ever along the same highway.
Avowedly or by implication, the evolutionists did postulate just
such a drive or urge to account for the uniformity of evolutionary
processes and stages.   But, if so, it is an urge without a locus.
Surely it is not in individuals.   Where then is it?

So also with the gradual changes, perceptible or even imperceptible.   In the light of history, they must at best be supplemented by
frequently occurring spurts, precipitations, cataclysmic changes.
In technology, art, philosophy, science, as well as in the domain of
social, political, and economic phenomena, the record of events can
only be read one way.   In this case psychology strikes deeper at the

evolutionary concept — gradual change — than does history if superficially analyzed. Changes could come gradually if there were no resistance to the pressure of the factors or forces which prompt change. In the absence of resistance cultural causes would achieve their effects smoothly and without friction or delay. This, however, is never the case. The inertia of the individual psyche is ever reluctant to yield to pressure, for every change means breaking a habit, and habits notoriously stick. This individual inertia is enhanced by the much more ponderous inertia of institutionalism which, at its points of operation, is also psychological. The result is that every change in culture is preceded by a period of delay during which there is an accumulation of those factors which prompt the impending change. When by dint of cumulative pressure (or, psychologically, summation of stimuli) the resistance is overcome, the change comes — with a spurt. Nor is this a purely temporal phenomenon, a mere delay in time. If that were so, the change when finally achieved might after all be slight, even "imperceptible." But what actually happens, as just indicated, is that during the delay, while pressure works upon resistance, the factors prompting the change *accumulate;* so, when the change comes, it is quite a jump. We know from the study of the learning process that it is not gradual but jerky. So also it is with culture, for culture, from one angle, is learning. And the psychology also is the same: the delay comes from inertia due to preëxisting habits, only that in the case of culture the inertia of the individual is greatly reinforced by institutional inertia which lengthens the delay and adds to the explosive character of the change when it does come.[1]

The weakest of the three evolutionary tenets is certainly the last: progressivism. The concept that culture (of a tribe, nation, or even the world as a whole) progresses, greatly overrates the organic integration of a culture, an integration which is basically a phenomenon of psychic assimilation and interpenetration of cultural features. But even when applied to the separate aspects of culture, as is done by the less extreme evolutionists, the concept of progress, especially when conceived as necessary, breaks down through the implied disregard of the psychology of values. For progress is a valuational concept, it is *change in the direction of improvement.* But what is

---

[1] There are also some positive reasons why cultural changes are often more nearly like DeVries' mutations than like the microscopic changes of the Darwinians, but it would carry us too far to go into this here.

improvement? Where is the standard? Who is the arbiter? If the concept of progressive change is to be preserved at all, it must become particularistic and critical, cognizance being taken of the valuational perspective.[1]

Passing to the methods of the evolutionists, it must be noted that the often criticized weakness of the "comparative method" which consists in tearing beliefs and customs from their historical settings and using them *in vacuo*, as it were, is at bottom a psychological error. For the historical setting consists of the psychological threads which tie to one another the different elements of a culture. To untie or disregard these threads is to denude the cultural element, to deprive it of the flesh and blood of reality. Similarly, when the evolutionist makes retrospective interpretations of "survivals," he places undue stress on the "fitness" of a cultural element with reference to a definite culture pattern — the importance of the mother's brother, for example, in matriarchal society — and minimizes the multiplicity of settings in which such a feature may appear with a greater or lesser degree of fitness.

One of the strangest features of evolutionary philosophy was its rampant individualism. While Spencer and Tylor, Sir John Lubbock (later Lord Avebury), Frazer, and Hartland were penning their first contributions to evolutionary sociology, the air was full of folk-psychological speculations, much was said about the group mind, about suggestion, imitation, and crowd-psychology. But the pristine individual in the evolutionist's cradle remained in a state of isolation truly splendid, and culture was made to emerge from his solitary mind like a Zeus from the head of Pallas Athena. The family, clan, religious society, tribe, simply did not exist as contributory factors to culture origins. The individual mind was represented as facing external conditions, nature; and to these it reacted, innocent of all guidance or restraint on the part of social norm or cultural pattern. This hypothetical mind, moreover, seems to have contained ideas and intellectual processes, but no emotions, conations, urges, desires, or fantasies. It is not surprising, therefore, that the speculative constructs of the evolutionist were as plausible and self-consistent as they were artificial and unreal. For consistency and plausibility are not of the stuff that history is made of; instead, it

[1] To use the term "progress" so as to cover *all* cultural change, as is done by Oppenheimer (see his essay, p. 223) is, in my opinion, going too far in the abrogation of this time-honored concept which, if properly used, may still do good service in social theory.

is wont to grab the strange and peculiar and mold these into the commonplace.[1]

Psychological Postulates of Wundt's Folk-Psychology

The charge of being largely unconscious of one's methods and assumptions to which the classical evolutionists laid themselves open, cannot be made against Wilhelm Wundt who brought to his folk-psychological speculations a mind deeply steeped in theoretical wisdom and methodological criticism. Whatever faults Wundt's thought may possess, superficiality and naïveté are not among them, and a carefully elaborated theoretical point of view runs like a scarlet thread through his entire system. Wundt was first and foremost a psychologist and he took pains to deduce his folk-psychology and his historical philosophy from the principles on which his psychology was built. In the center of these stood his synthetic view of mental processes which was superimposed upon the analytical view of the associationist school to which the evolutionists belonged. Hence the concept of *apperception*, which became the operative unit of the synthetic view just as perception and idea were of the analytical view. In the apperceptive process the mind (or part of it) faces a new perception or experience not as a mass of "ideas" but as a mass of organized or integrated "ideas." This gives the preexisting mental state an advantage, as it were, over the newcomer from the outside world. The latter is not merely absorbed and incorporated but also transformed or re-created: a *creative synthesis* takes place. A new mental product arises which is not merely a sum or juxtaposition of the old and the new but an interpenetration of the two, a process in which the old plays the predominant part. It gives the color to the new whole and is the creative agent in the synthesis.

Thus the preëxisting mental mass is far from a passive participant in the process: it is an active agency. An element of conation or will is involved. Therein lies the root of Wundt's *voluntarism* and the basis of his anti-intellectualism (another thrust at the

[1] It will be readily conceded that the picture here drawn of man in the evolutionist's Garden of Eden, is extreme. It fits only the left wing evolutionists such as Spencer and Frazer. One emotion, in particular, was often conceded to primitive man by the evolutionists, including Spencer: fear. This was made the most of in connection with religious origins. It must also be remembered that when writing of primitive man in a general way, the evolutionists often referred to other psychic qualities besides ideas. The point here emphasized is that they made such sparse use of this insight in building their theories.

evolutionists!). On this foundation Wundt builds his concept of *psychic causality* in which the effect is never equal to the cause — after the pattern of physical causality — but is always *greater* than the cause, to use this inadequate term. The effect is the cause transformed.[1]

When so much is said, a foundation is laid for a folk-psychology. For whence does an individual derive his apperceptive mass? From his experience? Yes! But this experience, even though it refer to the external world of nature, is shot through with social factors. For it is either acquired in the company of others or it is an experience *of* that company, or — if the individual experiences in solitude — the group, these "others," are already stamped into his soul, they have become an integral part of his apperceiving self and make it what it is.

Wundt made the most of this insight. He realized that the others, the group, were, with reference to the individual, the carriers of habit, of tradition. They set the pattern and held the individual to it. And patterns, historically transmitted, are culture. Culture then, taught Wundt, was a group product, a creation of the *folk*. As a culture-maker, the individual was part of the folk, the group, and only for purposes of analysis could he be separated from it, and then only with difficulty. This was particularly true, he thought, of *language, myth,* and *custom*. But by the time Wundt had elaborated this triplet (in a ten-volume work) it came to embrace language, art, myth, religion, ceremonialism, social and political organization and law. A fairly complete list, this, of the contents of culture, it will be seen, with the single and singular omission of its material aspect (in so far as this extends beyond the domain of art).

This omission of the physical basis of culture from so comprehensive a system is most significant as well as curious. It explains why Wundt's stupendous contribution must appear to the environmentalists and economic interpreters of history as so much elaborate talk about nothing (shadows, phantoms, epiphenomena!) just as their own stiff and soulless universe impressed Wundt as would the play *Hamlet* with the Prince left out. This is the price Wundt paid for being too much of a psychologist. It is as if he had become so greatly absorbed in what the mind did with experience that he

---

[1] The question of the advisability of using the term "cause" for two radically different concepts need not be gone into here.

turned his back upon the external sources of experience. In the mind, to be sure, he found the whole of culture, even material culture, but not its materials. And it is the materials which hold man in their grip, dominate economic life and industry, and tie culture to the physical environment, to plant and animal nature, to the earth, to climate.[1]

Having spotted culture Wundt proceeds to apply to this wider field his concept of creative synthesis. The apperceptive functions of individuals are then folk-conditioned. They are creative and take the form of what Wundt calls *Wandlung der Motive* and *Heterogenie der Zwecke*. Motives and purposes are in a state of constant flux, mutation, transformation. Social units assume new functions or functions give rise to new social forms. Words and phrases acquire meanings not even adumbrated in the original use. Religious customs become prototypes of moral rules or of play techniques, while moral precepts acquire religious sanctions. Objective relationships become symbols while symbols are materialized in art or objectified in social form. Objects of use come to function as adornment while things of art are put to use. Virtues turn vices and vices virtues. In the psychic domain in which culture dwells there is a constant up and down, a shifting and moving, interpenetration of meanings, transvaluation of values.

This contribution of Wundt's to the dynamics of cultural life went over the heads of the evolutionists, the diffusionists shut their doors (material all to material!) against it, the critical anthropologists were too busy disposing of their predecessors or plotting maps to do it justice. It is to be hoped that the superior discernment embodied in Wundt's concept will not be wasted on social thinkers during this period of mutation of motives and purposes in the entire field of the sciences of society.

It was almost inevitable that Wundt, having grasped the complexity of the individual psyche, the mobility of the cultural process, and the significance of values and valuations in all that concerns man, should have taken the view of history which his writings reveal. He often paid his respects to the rôle of historic accident and turned his back resolutely against the concept of law in history,

---

[1] When Wundt in the third volume of his *Logik* expatiates at length upon the theories and methods of Marx and his followers, he still finds it unnecessary to explain how and why it is that his own theoretical edifice starts in the top story, as it were, and remains there. A somewhat chastening discovery this, that even so cautious and sophisticated a spirit as Wundt's could be so blinded by subjectivism!

against, therefore, all forms of historic determinism and dogmatic stage building, including strict evolutionism.[1] Instead he elaborated a set of *principles* for history as a theoretical discipline or *trends* in history as fact. These concepts were calculated to save the student of the history of events and cultures from the discouraging fate of being confronted with an utter chaos.

But for the purposes of this essay, we have followed Wundt far enough.

PSYCHOLOGICAL POSTULATES OF DIFFUSIONISM

Whatever may be true of evolutionism, the principle of contrasting pulsations or of the pendulum certainly asserts itself in history. When an idea, a doctrine, a tendency, an institution, becomes established and popular, it tends to become dogmatic, monopolistic, exaggerated. It overreaches itself. And presently, out of the iniquities of its exaggerations, its opposite is born.

So it was with evolutionism. Its well-nigh cynical disregard of factual evidence, its methodological enormities, went too far. . . . And then diffusionism arose. Ratzel gave the new approach its first impetus. He became interested in tracing historical connections between cultural similarities. By predilection and training, a student of the concrete and material, he applied himself to such problems as the distribution of the African bow and arrow or of plate armor. With the theory and methodology of diffusion he did not make much headway, but other students picked up his work where he left it, and before long it became clear that the theory of diffusion could be used as a weapon in the fight against uncritical evolutionism. If objects, customs, ideas could be imported from without — and it was easy to show that that was so — and incorporated in a tribal culture, what became of the evolutionist's organic urge, his cultural growth from within, his stage building? At every point he was now confronted with the question: what is the historical home of this or that custom or thing? If it does not belong where you find it, your first task is to trace it to its source, and surely you can no longer deal with it as if it were a natural and inevitable outgrowth of your local culture.

The air was thick with concrete studies of diffused things and

---

[1] That, withal, Wundt himself should have emerged pretty much of an evolutionist, is another sad illustration of the only too common disparity between profession and performance even when both lie in the intellectual domain. But if he was thus misguided, the responsibility did not rest with a vicious psychology.

ideas, the fight of independent development versus diffusion was well under way, when a young German student, F. Graebner, a historian by training, entered the arena. He became the first full-fledged diffusionist, and the theory of diffusion, as he conceived it, was built out of the negatives of evolutionism. Psychic unity? Yes! But you cannot do anything with it. It collapses when confronted with cultural diversities; how, then, can it explain similarities? Man's inventive capacity? Yes! But it is not all it was cracked up to be. By and large, inventions are hard, man is lazy, and if you claim that a tricky thing has been invented twice, you have to prove it. Independent invention, moreover, is mostly an assumption. Can you spot it? Diffusion can be demonstrated. Every day brings new evidence of its actuality. Uniformity in cultural developments? Any one who has read history can see that there is nothing in it. The task of the ethnologist is that of the historian; if he is to conduct research he must apply himself to tracing cultural connections instead of reclining in his arm chair and dreaming about man's genius, similar ideas springing up in twins and triplets, and cultures everywhere passing through beautifully symmetrical stages.

In his anti-evolutionary enthusiasm Graebner neglected to set his own house in order, and diffusionism when fully developed in his *Methode der Ethnologie* becomes as dogmatic and uncritical as evolutionism itself. Many of its errors, moreover, are also traceable to wrong psychological assumptions, avowed or implied.

It is, of course, true that man's inventiveness can be exaggerated. On the other hand, evidence is not lacking that man's mind is ever actively at work. Apart from the lessons to be derived from the study of children, diffusion itself supplies confirmatory evidence. For if man were as incapable as the diffusionist would make him, diffusion itself would be impossible. It takes mind, adaptability, inventiveness, to adopt objects and ideas, to assimilate them or their uses, to transform them. Moreover, the diffusionist never tires insisting — when arguing against parallelism — that the world is full of different things. But these *different* things — and they are indeed many — had to be invented. In arguing against the independent invention of similarities, from the angle of the mental power involved, the diffusionist leans heavily upon the independent invention of differences. But the minds that could originate these differences thereby qualified for the origination of similarities, unless some other grounds can be adduced to show why this was not likely to occur.

Realizing the crucial importance for the theory of diffusion of the appraisal of cultural similarities Graebner establishes his two *criteria:* one qualitative, the other quantitative. The first refers to formal similarities, the second to their number. In his estimate of our ability to pass judgment in such matters Graebner disregards the evidence of psychology, the laboratory kind as well as that of the street. Even when comparing material objects we tend to be influenced by training, interest, point of view. Here, however, the measuring rod can be of assistance in eliminating, or, at least, minimizing subjectivism. In the social and mental domain there is no such mechanical corrective. Here our judgments are notoriously vacillating, or, what is worse, categorical but subject to grave error. Who is there who would dare to claim objectivity or detailed accuracy for his estimate of the degree and significance of the similarity between two forms of art, religion, morality, or thought? To this Graebner might reply, truthfully enough, that his system is largely built up on the basis of material culture. But this defense could be readily turned into an indictment.

If, then, estimates of similarity are at best vague and often subjective, no effort should be spared to supplement the evidence derived from inspection of objects or traits of culture by other factors, such as geographical location and the probability (or evidence) of historical contact. If that much is admitted, the next link in Graebner's argumentative chain is shattered, namely, his concept of *interpretation at a distance*, the point being that judgments of similarity and the conclusions therefrom must hold, whatever the geographical distance between the cultural objects or traits compared.

In his view of culture in its relation to its constituent traits as well as to time, Graebner commits equally grave psychological errors. His method of characterizing a culture consists in an enumeration or a catalogue of its component features, material (mostly that!), social, and spiritual. This has been rightly designated as a mechanical procedure, in a derogatory sense, for no cognizance is here taken of the inter-trait relations, in the form of associations, symbolizations, interpenetrations, which resolve a culture into trait complexes and combine these into a more or less integrated whole. Curiously enough, Graebner also holds that in intertribal contacts cultures act as units or nearly so: if one trait is diffused, others follow, necessarily so — a view more consistent with the ideas about culture of Graebner's more psychologically-minded critics than with his own. Being unaware of what holds cultural features together (psychological slip no. 1) when they constitute a local culture complex, Graebner, nevertheless, becomes convinced, justifiably enough, that they do stick together, and then holds that they continue to do so under conditions of transfer, when as a matter of fact, they break up (psychological slip no. 2). If Graebner realized that what holds them together are the psychic bonds in the minds of the human carriers of a local culture, he would have no difficulty in understanding why it is that they tend to break up and act as independent units or small clusters of units when the local bonds are severed and the human carriers left behind.

Similarly, when Graebner treats cultural features as if they were immutable, it is his psychological blind spot which prevents him from seeing things in their true perspective. Here, also, the fact that Graebner is primarily a specimen ethnologist, provides a partial justification. Objects of material culture are, relatively speaking, immutable, particularly if they remain buried underground. We say "relatively," for the use of an object may change with time, and with the use, its cultural orientation. As to the traits of social and mental culture, do they not come and go and change with years and generations and periods? Need one add that a little spiritual communion with Leipzig, where Wundt was still teaching his enlightened doctrine of valuational mutations in culture while Graebner was formulating his own system, would have saved the diffusionist much futile theorizing?

PSYCHOLOGICAL POSTULATES OF THE AMERICAN SCHOOL OF ETHNOLOGY

The work of American anthropologists during the last fifteen or twenty years has often been characterized as critical, historical, and psychological. In the few pages that follow an attempt will be made to justify this reputation, especially with reference to the psychological perspectives of our work.[1]

---

[1] For the sake of fairness to other students I want to add — what indeed is obvious — that American anthropologists do not have a monopoly of the theoretical and methodological virtues presently to be discussed. If space permitted, much work done by our European colleagues would deserve analysis in this connection. Among descriptive monographs with theoretical leanings, to mention only a few, we have Rivers' contributions on the Torres Straits islanders and the Todas, Seligman's on the Melanesians and the Veddahs, Martin's on the Malays, Spieth's on the African Ewe, Pechuel-Loesche's on other West Africans, Ehrenreich's, Von den Steinen's

With few exceptions dogmatic environmentalism has found little favor in America. While the importance of physical environment as a limiting and directing factor in cultural development is conceded, cultural form or pattern — and what is culture if not that? — is held to be but weakly correlated with environment and in no sense determined by it. Psychologically, Wissler's point (in his older work) is of special interest. He draws attention to the fact that environment, without determining a particular adjustment, does call for *some* adjustment, some cultural solution of the environmental problem. After this has been accomplished, and while the environment remains the same, the solution reached tends to persist, often in the face of better possible and even known solutions.

The concepts of independent development and diffusion, granting the ubiquitousness of both processes, are accepted as heuristic principles to be tested in particular instances. This, of course, implies the unconditional rejection of the sweeping generalizations and methodological vagaries both of evolutionism and of diffusionism.[1] Both concepts, moreover, independent origination "from within" and diffusion, have been enriched by a number of subsidiary concepts.

The concept of *convergence*, first introduced into theoretical ethnology by Ehrenreich, has been mainly elaborated in America, so far on a limited scale. It is being pointed out that, while cultural parallelisms in chronologically extended series are at best rare, convergent developments are common, thus bringing about similarities where there were differences or less marked similarities. Some convergences, in technique, form (in objects), or art, are objective, others are psychological, functional. If Wundt's principle of motivational and purposive mutation is accepted, it becomes easy to see how such convergences will come about.

In connection with diffusion, the psychological setting of the process is constantly being emphasized. To state that an object, custom, idea, has traveled from one place to another, is to give but a

and Max Schmidt's on a large number of South American tribes, Malinowski's admirable *Argonauts of the Western Pacific*, and so on to a considerable length. The same men and others such as Thurnwald, Vierkandt, Haberlandt, Montelius, Hocart, Marett, have contributed on the highest level to anthropological theory and methodology, rejecting one-sided evolutionism and diffusionism and doing full justice to the critical, historical, and psychological standpoints.

[1] This point deserves emphasis in view of the recent tendency, in certain quarters, to class American ethnologists with the classical evolutionists.

skeleton of the problem. The situation bristles with psychological issues: where did it start? Yes! but also: why? how did it travel? what happened to it on the way? when it arrived, how was it received? did it remain a foreign curiosity? was it assimilated, elaborated, transformed beyond recognition? One and all psychological issues.

The concept of *culture areas* is of interest both with reference to diffusion and from a wider historico-psychological standpoint. A culture area is Bastian's geographical province raised from a state of vagueness and abstraction to one of concreteness and relative precision. A culture area is characterized by a catalogue of traits or features, material, artistic, religious, ceremonial, social (so far like a Graebnerian culture), but also by the way such features are associated, interrelated, colored by one another (an outlook quite beyond Graebner's horizon). Such culture *complexes* show remarkable tenacity and chronological persistence. The further concept of a *culture center*, arising from the attempt to find the locus of greatest incandescence of the culture of an area with a concomitant attenuation toward the periphery, has proved less serviceable. While attractive, it is also dangerous and seems difficult of application. The facts may be too complex for so simple a formulation.

The concept of *marginal areas*, on the other hand, has been fully vindicated and opens up interesting theoretical problems with a distinct psychological reference. A marginal area is culturally an area of transition (geographically intermediary) between one culture area and another. Now, it has been pointed out that objectively a marginal area will comprise some cultural features belonging to two or more culture areas and, in this sense, be indeed marginal or transitional and less distinguishable as a separate entity. But psychologically a marginal area *is* a culture area as good as any other, with its own associations and interpenetrations of traits.

Another concept which gained precision during the study of culture areas (although it had been elaborated and applied outside of this context) was that of culture *patterns*. It was easy to observe how new cultural creations within a culture area, a tribal cluster or a single tribe, were rapidly drawn into the preëxisting scheme or configuration of traits or processes and assimilated. The rôle of the pattern concept in cultural studies, useful though it has proved in the past, has not been fully explored and is likely to prove even more quickening in the future.[1]

The study of culture areas, of tribal clusters and of individual tribes in the greatest detail and from all possible angles — a mode of procedure generally adopted by American ethnologists — is of interest also from another angle. The historical record of cultural anthropology is most fragmentary and inevitably it will remain so for all time. Whenever the anthropologist wants to turn historian, therefore, in the sense of a recorder and an interpreter of chronologically consecutive events, he must learn to rely in part on speculative reconstruction as the only means available for filling in the gaps in the record. The evolutionist and his brother in sin, the diffusionist, have done this on a sweeping scale and with dire results, largely on account of their daring but fateful disregard of the actuality of cultural life and of observable historical processes. The historian is often hard pressed because his records, even though available, are remote and difficult of critical scrutiny. The anthropologist is much worse off: only too frequently his records are not there or are fragmentary in the extreme. Where shall he look for his perspective, for an opportunity to steep himself in cultural reality comparable in kind to this lost past record? This he finds in the study of contemporaneous primitive cultures in their natural historico-geographical setting. In this work he is building on the assumption, a psychological one, that the life of culture — whatever its content — remains essentially the same at all times. By identifying himself with this life, as thoroughly and sympathetically as may be, he becomes a culture expert. He has gained a perspective which will come him in good stead when historical gaps are to be filled in.

CONCLUSION

Enough has been said, perhaps, to show how intimately the theories of cultural anthropology are interrelated with psychological insight — or the absence of it. The life of culture belongs to the psychological level. It is in the minds of men in society. If the

---

[1] An obvious homology to the culture pattern concept must be seen in Koffka's and Köhler's psychological theory of *Gestalt*. Similar categories are encountered in the study of organisms and of crystals. All these concepts are again related to the concepts of form and system in the plastic arts, music, and the abstract disciplines such as mathematics and logic. Unless we are badly misguided, a concept of the general type of *pattern* or *Gestalt* may yet come to mark an epochal advance in our conceptual explorations.

nature of this level is misunderstood, an impetus is given to vicious methodology and one-sided or artificial theory. The historian, the anthropologist, are students of life. Life is psychology. Abuse your psychology, and it will corrupt your history, your anthropology.[1]

SELECTED REFERENCES

In addition to the titles listed below consult the copious bibliographies in my "Cultural Anthropology," *History and Prospects of the Social Sciences*, pp. 210–55.

Bastian, Adolph.   *Der Völkergedanke.*   1887.
     Ethnische Elementargedanken.   1895.
     Völkerkunde.   1892.
Boas, Franz.   *The Mind of Primitive Man.*   1911.
Goldenweiser, Alexander.   "The Principle of Limited Possibilities in the Development of Culture."   *Journal of American Folk-Lore*, vol. xxvi, 1913, pp. 259–90.
     "History, Psychology and Culture."   *Journal of Philosophy*, vol. xv, 1918, nos. 21 and 22.
     Early Civilization.   1922.
     "Four Phases of Anthropological Thought."   *Publications of the American Sociological Society.* 1924.
     "Diffusionism and the American School of Historical Ethnology."   *American Journal of Sociology.*   1925.
     "Psychology and Culture."   *Publications of the American Sociological Society.*   1925.

[1] As noted in the Introduction, many aspects of the relations of anthropology and psychology have been left aside here, for lack of space. Of these, three deserve mention (by title) as of special interest.

The first is the contribution of psychoanalysis. This system of thought has so far been notable for its abuse and misinterpretation of anthropological data chiefly on account of the psychoanalyst's refusal to adopt the historical point of view. Malinowski's recent work on the basis of his Melanesian material brings welcome evidence to the fact that a more fruitful reciprocal relationship may be looked forward to in the future.

The second is the contribution of folk-psychology to the modern psychology of the individual. Wundt never tired of insisting that individual psychology can learn much from a critical utilization of folk-psychological data. It is indeed apparent that the behavior of the individual psyche under primitive conditions which can never be reproduced in modern society, must inevitably reveal many of its qualities and limitations which would otherwise remain unexplored. The functionings of the mechanisms of projection and symbolization, for example, can best be studied on the basis of such material.

The third is the contribution of technical modern psychology to anthropology. Whatever we learn about the individual may sooner or later prove useful in any science of culture. The recent explorations of the unconscious, of the mechanisms of the emotions (of which we still know so little), of the peculiarities or abnormal manifestations of psychic life, are already serving as guides and safe-guards in both sociology and anthropology. We have as yet no detailed studies of psychic abnormalities among primitives, a field from which much further insight may be expected.

Goldenweiser, Alexander. "Anthropological Theories of Political Origins," in *Political Theories: Recent Times.*

"Cultural Anthropology," in *History and Prospects of the Social Sciences.* 1924.

Hocart, A. C. "Ethnology and Psychology." *Folk-Lore,* vol. LXXV, 1915, pp. 115–38.

Kroeber, A. L. *Anthropology.* 1923.

"The Possibility of a Social Psychology." *American Journal of Sociology,* vol. xxiii, 1918, pp. 633–51.

Lowie, Robert H. *Culture and Ethnology.* 1917.

Primitive Society. 1920.

Primitive Religion. 1924.

"Psychology and Sociology." *American Journal of Sociology,* vol. xxi, 1915, pp. 217–29.

"Plains Indian Age Societies." *Anthropological Papers, American Museum of Natural History,* vol. xi, 1916, pp. 877–1031.

Malinowski, Bronislaw. "The Psychology of Sex and the Foundations of Kinship in Primitive Society." *Psyche,* vol. iv, 1923–24, pp. 98–128.

"Psychoanalysis and Anthropology." *Psyche,* vol. iv, 1923–24, pp. 292–332.

Marett, R. R. *Psychology and Folk-Lore.* 1920.

Radin, Paul. "A Sketch of the Peyote Cult of the Winnebago: A Study in Borrowing." *Journal of Religious Psychology,* vol. vi, 1914, pp. 1–22.

"Influence of the Whites on Winnebago Culture." *Proceedings, State Historical Society of Wisconsin,* 1913, pp. 137–45.

Rivers, W. H. R. Presidential Address, Anthropological Section, British Association for the Advancement of Science, *Proceedings.* 1911.

"The Loss of Useful Arts." *Westermarck Anniversary Volume.* 1912.

"Survivals in Sociology." *Sociological Review,* vol. vi, 1913, pp. 293–305.

"The Contact of Peoples." *Essays and Studies Presented to William Ridgeway,* 1913, pp. 474–93.

Psychology and Politics. 1923.

"Sociology and Psychology." *Sociological Review,* vol. ix, 1916, pp. 1–13.

Sapir, Edward. "Time Perspective in Aboriginal American Culture." *Memoir 90, Geological Survey of Canada.* 1916.

"Culture, Genuine and Spurious." *American Journal of Sociology,* vol. xxix, 1925, pp. 401–30.

"Culture in New Countries." *The Dalhousie Review,* 1923, pp. 358–68.

Spencer, Herbert. *First Principles.* 1886.

Principles of Sociology. 1893.

Wissler, Clark. *The American Indian.* 1921.

Man and Culture. 1923.

The Relation of Nature to Man in Aboriginal America. 1926.

"The Influence of the Horse on the Development of Plains Culture." *American Anthropologist,* vol. xvi, 1914, pp. 1–25.

Wissler, Clark.   "Psychological and Historical Interpretations for Culture."
         Science, vol. XLIII, 1916, pp. 193–201.
            "Aboriginal Maize Culture as a Typical Culture-Complex."
         American Journal of Sociology, vol. XXI, 1916, pp. 656–62.
Wundt, Wilhelm.   *Völkerpsychologie.*   1916.
         Elements of Folk-Psychology.   1912.
            "Ziele und Wege der Völkerpsychologie."   *Philosophische
            Studien*, vol. IV.

CHAPTER VIII

ANTHROPOLOGY AND RELIGION

By R. R. MARETT
UNIVERSITY OF OXFORD

OF the principles of method involved in the study of the rudimentary forms of religion, some are, as it were, generic, while others are specific in the sense that they relate more or less exclusively to the particular subject. Here it will suffice to deal briefly with the former, so that the latter may receive the more attention. For, whereas there can be little doubt about the strategy to be employed, the tactics are relatively uncertain, with the result that a certain confusion and waste of effort at present attend the efforts of the fighting line.

RELIGION AS A FORM OF CULTURE

Regarded generically, then, the study of rudimentary religion is a branch of cultural anthropology. To class it thus as a kind of anthropology means, in the first place, that it forms part of a science of human origins — one that, adopting the genetic or evolutionary outlook, seeks in the earlier in time, as on the whole simpler, a clue to the nature of the later, as on the whole more complex. It may be noted in passing that considerations of origin can never in themselves determine actual, and still less ideal, validity, because as the development proceeds the intrinsic quality alters. Thus, it is not for the anthropologist to pronounce judgment on questions of religious truth. His function is confined to showing how men, professing this or that religion, have actually fared at the various stages of the historical process that he traces out. Thereupon the philosopher or the theologian must, as best he can, decide how far the biologically useful can serve in this case or in any case as a measure of the true.

In the second place, if cultural anthropology is to have charge of the subject, this means that religion will be considered simply as a part of human culture. To cultivate is to tend something carefully and by so doing to make it grow. Culture, then, comprises the various ways in which man has tended his own nature so as to make it grow. Thus, from the standpoint of cultural anthropology, religion is but a means employed by man to further his own self-education. Viewed from this, the human end, religion is no influx from a transcendental region, but is something that man has made in the course of making himself. Now for the purposes of the theologian such a limitation of outlook may have serious drawbacks. For those, however, who work at the level of science, there are compensating advantages in considering religion strictly as a mode and product of human self-development. First, such a working hypothesis confines research to a definite field, namely, to history regarded as the history of human endeavor. Secondly, it imposes a definite set of methods, namely, those that are common to the empirical sciences. Other methods involving a priori thinking may be found suitable on the plane of the ideal. But on the plane of the actual, to which anthropology as a branch of natural science is restricted, empirical methods suffice to yield truth in the only form attainable under the conditions.

RELIGION AS COMMON TO ALL MANKIND

It remains to add about the study of religion in its generic character as a branch of anthropology that, if it looks only to the human aspect of religion, at least it tries to see it whole. Anthropology insists on considering human history as all of a piece. It recognizes no chosen peoples, but seeks a just perspective such as will not exaggerate minor differences, but will allow the common and essential features to stand out. Thus, although in practice it concerns itself chiefly with the beginnings of culture, and, as regards religion in particular, with its rudimentary forms, even so it is committed in advance to the search for a conception of religion that is capable of a world-wide application. Human culture being many-sided, it is found convenient to group the facts relating to its history under a number of main heads or categories, each and all of which must apply to mankind in general. Whether it be religion, or morality, or law, or fine art, or marriage that is in question, the anthropologist will not tolerate a working definition of it that shuts out any part of observable humanity from the claim to possess it in some fashion. Let a pre-religious, or pre-moral, or pre-matrimonial stage in human history be postulated by all means, if the theorist requires it as his logical *terminus a quo*. But such a theorist would be well advised to put it well back into the Pliocene — in short, back to some point at which the positive evidence concerning man breaks off altogether. So far as the human record extends, should likewise extend the leading categories of cultural anthropology, if justice is to be done to the continuity of man's traceable efforts to cultivate his natural powers.

THE NEED FOR A WORKING DEFINITION OF HUMAN RELIGION

At this point it becomes possible to pass on to the more difficult question: In what specific way is the student of rudimentary religion to set about his task? For it appears that he must proceed in the light of a definition of his subject that will apply to man in general. What Tylor calls a "minimum definition" of religion is needed — the barest characterization that will serve to keep the worker within the four corners of his field of research. Let it be remembered that the definition in question is wanted for historical, not for analytical, purposes. Its function is to delimit, not a system, but a tendency; the thing signified being, not fixed, but in process. For the historical student religion is but the greatest common measure of an untold number of religions, all of them changing, whether for better or for worse, and all of them in some sense competing. Now for the anthropologist the tendencies, or processes of connected change, which he tries to mark off and understand are essentially human activities — types of behavior in which the whole man as a feeling, thinking, and willing being finds various expression. Assuming, then, religion to be a human activity of a fundamental kind, he must, in order to grasp its specific nature, employ a double criterion: first, he must be able to distinguish it wherever it occurs by its outer traits; secondly, having so distinguished it, he must be able likewise to discern its inner motives. Roughly, these complementary modes of apprehension relate severally to the sociological and the psychological aspects of the subject. It is, however, highly desirable that the same definition should as far as possible indicate both the outward and the inward views of religion which it is the ultimate object of the anthropologist to combine. Or, since the external manifestations must be observed before the internal springs can be interpreted, a definition capable of directing sociological observation should at least allow of expansion, so that, whenever the time comes for it, psychological interpretation may be guided by means of an added clause.

Here it will be necessary, for reasons of space, to dispense with a criticism of current theories, and, proceeding constructively, to suggest a working definition of religion, such as it is hoped will be found to conform with the methodological principles just laid down.

RELIGION AS CULT

Let the anthropologist, then, try whether the following definition will not prove sufficient for all the purposes of sociological observation and description: *religion is the cult of the sacred*.   Viewed thus externally, namely, as a kind of behavior, religion is a specific kind of activity, here termed cult, which is concerned with a specific object, here termed the sacred.   As for cult, the word, though etymologically akin to culture, and having the same implication of a caring for, has the advantage of belonging to the peculiar' terminology of religion.   Thus it means a caring for that, whatever it is, with which religion is especially concerned.   Further, the word would seem always to stand for a type of religious behavior that is customary: so that without undue pressing it may be taken to stand primarily for the traditional conduct of a group.   Even if the facts of history point to the existence of forms of religious observance that are in a way private to the individual, nevertheless these forms must meet with public approval; observances which do not, however similar as regards their other features, had better not be classed under the head of cult or religion, but should be relegated to a distinct category, such as magic.   It may be added, without intrenching on psychological ground, that cult is normally marked off from most other kinds of social activity by a scrupulous care for the niceties of routine, so that it almost in itself amounts to the ceremonial habit.

THE EXPERIENCE OF THE SACRED

Next, as regards the sacred, this word too belongs to the vocabulary of religion; so that in using it we are not troubled by associations relating to irrelevant topics.   Etymologically, sacred would seem to mean separate.   Conformably with this root-meaning, the sacred may be made to stand for a type of experience which most men judge to be widely separated from ordinary experience, and tend thereupon to assign to separate objective orders, or as it were, worlds.   Thus, the cult of the sacred is a caring for the things of this other world.   The clue to the sacredness of a particular thing is to be sought, not in its objective characters as ordinary experience recognizes them, but simply in its temporary or permanent inclusion within the world of cult — the world of a distinctive experience obtained by means of a no less distinctive form of behavior. Cult and its object, the behavior and the resulting experience, though logically distinguishable as means and end, almost merge into each other when observed concretely. For, of all human activities, religion would seem to be most autotelic, the value being immanent in the very effort to realize it.

THE QUEST FOR AN INFINITE GOOD

So much, then, for an exterior definition of religion that may help the anthropologist to pigeon-hole, before trying to explain, the historical evidence specifically relating to the subject. It remains to be seen whether this definition can be enlarged so as also to include a brief but sufficient indication of the inner meaning of the historical process, and hence of the line which psychological explanation may profitably take. Let the expanded form of the definition run as follows: *religion is the cult of the sacred as symbolic of an infinite good.*

Now if the psychologist is to credit a world-wide and age-long human activity with a constant motive, it can only be by construing intelligence in a broad way and allowing that a historical tendency may involve the intelligent adaptation of a means to an end, whether means and end are or are not selected with an explicit awareness of their meaning and purpose. Thus, the conception of an infinite good may seem alien to any but the highest thought, if indeed any human thought be deemed capable of entertaining it worthily. Infinite, however, is but a negative term, and means unlimited; and it is not unreasonable that the psychologist should regard human desire as such as insatiable, or in other words, as involving the never-ending pursuit of a good such as is to be enjoyed without shortcoming or hindrance whatsoever. Nor, because the psychologist for his own purposes conceives the pursuit as never-ending, does this mean that man in his religious capacity is bound likewise to believe that the goal can never be reached. On the contrary, the reality in the sense of the ultimate possibility of a complete and an abiding satisfaction would appear to have been the motivating faith of every form of religion that the world has known. For the rest, the way in which man supplies his notion of an infinite good with such content as it needs to excite emotion and direct effort, will depend largely on the level of culture that has been reached. The good he aspires to is always the best he has hitherto known together with a *plus;* and the heart of his meaning is in the *plus.* Thus, it is wrong to say that the savage imagines the supreme good as food: as well might it be said that the Christian figures it as music. At most, as is only natural, good hunting largely colors his notion of good living and forms the point of departure of his larger hope.

Religious Symbolism

This, then, is why religion is essentially symbolic in the expression of its meaning. It seeks the *all,* but can never succeed in representing *all* except by *some,* realizing the while that *some* falls short of being *all.* Every symbol that man can use must have a particular being of its own, but this particular being is ignored in favor of the universal being of which it serves as a sign. Unfortunately, it is hard in practice completely and consistently to ignore the private nature of the thing chosen as a vehicle of suggestion. Hence literalism in religion has always been the enemy: that way lies idolatry. But, on the other hand, to regard the savage as pure idolater, pure fetishist, or what not, is to miss the point of his use of material objects to signify an immaterial power or grace which the objects are held for the time being to contain, yet in such a way as at any moment to pass it on by a kind of contagion to all sorts of other objects. It may not be so obvious, but it is nevertheless equally true, that the oral rites to which the civilized man is prone are but the vehicles of a meaning that is independent of their form, the idolater of words alone attributing efficacy to the form as such. Meanwhile, the psychology of symbolism is at present little understood, and it is an open question how far some symbols are naturally more suggestive than others as vehicles of the more refined emotions; while, again, ethnological research can do much to explain how certain symbols have traveled from one people to another, often changing much of their implication by the way. Enough, however, has perhaps been said to provide the study of rudimentary religion with a general orientation. The exterior definition marks off an ample field of historical research; and within this field the development of religion as a universal human activity can be traced throughout its complex movement by attending to its essential marks, a means, namely, symbolic prefiguration, and an end, namely, limitless good felt to be beyond all seeming and hence beyond literal expression in terms of the things of sense.

SELECTED REFERENCES

The subject of primitive religion is so vast that the following list of sources is by no means exhaustive.

Theory

Ames, E. S.   *The Psychology of Religious Experience.*   1910.
Crawley, E.   *The Mystic Rose.*   1902.
    The Tree of Life.   1905.
Durkheim, E.   *Les Formes Élémentaires de la Vie Religieuse.*   1912.
Frazer, J. G.   *The Golden Bough.*   3d ed.   1911–25.
    Totemism and Exogamy.   1910.
    Psyche's Task.   1913.
    The Belief in Immortality.   3 vols. issued.   1913–25.
Gennep, A. van.   *Les Rites de Passage.*   1909.
Hartland, E. S.   *The Legend of Perseus.*   1894–96.
    Ritual and Belief.   1914.
Hastings, J.   *Dictionary of Religion and Ethics.*   1908–21.
Hobhouse, L. T.   *Morals in Evolution.*   3d ed.   1915.
Hubert, H. F., et Mauss, M.   "Essai sur la Nature et la Fonction du Sacrifice." *L'Année Sociologique.*   1899.
    "Théorie générale de la Magie." *Ibid.*   1904.
    Mélanges d'Histoire des Religions.   1909.
Jevons, F. B.   *Introduction to the Early History of Religion.*   1896.
    Introduction to the Study of Comparative Religion.   1908.
King, I.   *The Development of Religion.*   1910.
Lang, A.   *Custom and Myth.*   1884.
    Myth, Ritual, and Religion.   1899.
    The Making of Religion.   2d ed.   1900.
Lowie, R. H.   *Primitive Religion.*   1924.
Marett, R. R.   *The Threshold of Religion.*   2d ed.   1912.
    Psychology and Folklore.   1920.
Preuss, K. T.   *Ursprung der Religion und Kunst.*   1904.
Schmidt, W.   *Der Ursprung der Gottesidee.*   1912.
Smith, W. Robertson.   *Lectures on the Early History of the Semites.*   1894.
Soderblom, N.   *Das Werden des Gottesglaubens.*   1916.
Trumbull, H. C.   *The Blood Covenant.*   1893.
    The Threshold Covenant.   1896.
Tylor, E. B.   *Primitive Culture.*   4th ed.   1903.
Webster, H.   *Primitive Secret Societies.*   1908.
    Rest Days.   1916.

Illustrative material

Europe
Farnell. L. R.   *Cults of the Greek States.*   1896–1909.
Fowler, W. Warde.   *The Religious Experience of the Roman People.*   1911.
Rose, H. J.   *Primitive Culture in Greece.*   1925.
    Primitive Culture in Italy.   1926.

Asia
Groot, J. J. M. de   *The Religious System of China.*   1892.

Rivers, W. H. R.   *The Todas.*   1896.

Skeat, W. W.   *Malay Magic.*   1900.

Wilken, G. A.   *Het Animismus bij de Volken van den Indischen Archipel.*
1884–86.

Africa

Callaway, H.   *The Religious System of the Amazulu.*   1884.

Gennep, A. van.   *Tabou et Totémisme à Madagascar.*   1904.

Junod, H. A.   The Life of a South African Tribe.   1912.

Rattray, R. S.   *Ashanti.*   1923.

Roscoe, J.   *The Baganda.*   1911.

Smith, E. W., and Dale, A. M.   *The Ila-speaking Peoples of Northern
Rhodesia.*   1920.

Oceania

Cambridge Anthropological Expedition to Torres Strait, v, vi.   1904–08.

Codrington, R.   *The Melanesians.*   1891.

Howitt, A. W.   *Native Tribes of Southeast Australia.*   1904.

Rivers, W. H. R.   *History of Melanesian Society.*   1914.

Spencer, B., and Gillen, F. J.   *Native Tribes of Central Australia.*   1887.
Northern Tribes of Central Australia.   1904.

Spencer, B.   *Native Tribes of the Northern Territory of Australia.*   1914.

Strehlow, C.   *Die Aranda-und-Loritjastämme.*   1907–10.

America

Thurn, Sir E. im.   *Among the Indians of Guiana.*   1883.

Jesup North Pacific Expedition.   1902.

Karsten, R.   *Civilization of the South American Indians.*   1926.

Smithsonian Institution, Bureau of Ethnology Reports.

CHAPTER IX [1]

ANTHROPOLOGY AND SOCIOLOGY

By EDWARD SAPIR

UNIVERSITY OF CHICAGO

PRIMITIVE SOCIETY: THE EVOLUTIONARY BIAS

JUST as unlettered and primitive peoples have an economic basis of life that, however simple in its operation, is strictly comparable to the economic machinery that so largely orders the life of a modern civilized society; and just as they have attained to a definite system of religious beliefs and practices, to traditionally conserved modes of artistic expression, to the adequate communication of thought and feeling in terms of linguistic symbols, so also they appear everywhere as rather clearly articulated into various types of social grouping. No human assemblage living a life in common has ever been discovered that does not possess some form of social organization. Nowhere do we find a horde in which the relations between its individuals is completely anarchic.

The sexual promiscuity, for instance, that was such a favorite topic of discussion in the speculative writings of the earlier anthropologists seems to be confined to their books. Among no primitive people that has been adequately studied and that conforms to its own traditional patterns of conduct is there to be found such a thing as an unregulated sexual commerce. The "license" that has been so often reported is either condemned by the group itself as a transgression, as is the case on our own level, or is no license at all, but, as among the Todas of India and a great many Australian tribes that are organized into marriage classes, is an institutionally fixed mode of behavior that flows naturally from the division of the group into smaller units between only certain ones of which are marital relations allowed. Hence "group marriage," a none too frequent phenomenon at best, is nowhere an index of social anarchy. On the contrary, it is but a specialized example of the fixity of certain traditional modes of social classification and is psychologically not at all akin to the promiscuity of theory or of the underground life of civilized societies.

If it be objected that intermarrying sub-groups do, as a matter of fact, argue a certain social anarchy because they disregard the natural distinctiveness of the individual, we need but point out that there are many other intercrossing modes of social classification, the net result of which is to carve out for the biological individual a social individuality while securing him a varied social participation. Not all the members of the same marriage class, for instance, need have the same totemic affiliations; nor need their kinship relations, real or supposed, toward the other members of the tribe be quite the same; nor need they, whether as hunters or as votaries in ancestral cults, have the same territorial associations; nor need their social ranking, based perhaps on age and on generally recognized ability, be at all the same; the mere difference of sex, moreover, has important social consequences, such as economic specialization, general inferiority of social status of the women, and female exclusion from certain ceremonial activities. The details vary, naturally, from tribe to tribe and from one geographical province to another.

All this is merely to indicate that a large and an important share of anthropological study must concern itself with primitive types of social organization.[1] There is such a thing as primitive sociology, and the sociologist who desires a proper perspective for the understanding of social relations in our own life cannot well afford to ignore the primitive data. This is well understood by most sociologists, but what is not always so clearly understood is that we have not the right to consider primitive society as simply a bundle of suggestions for an inferred social pre-history of our own culture. Under the powerful ægis of the biological doctrine of evolution the earlier, classical anthropologists tacitly assumed that such characteristic features of primitive life as totemism or matrilineal kinship

[1] It is not the purpose of this article to give a systematic survey of the different kinds of primitive social units. A very convenient summary is given by Dr. A. Goldenweiser in his chapters on Society in *Early Civilization*. He points out that these units depend on locality; blood relationship (family, in its narrow sense; group of blood relations, as roughly defined by classificatory systems of kinship terms; clan, or matrilineal sib; gens, or patrilineal sib; hereditary moiety; maternal family, as defined by actual descent from a female progenitor; marriage class); age; generation; sex; and function (groups defined by industries; religious, military, and medical societies; units defined by hereditary privilege or wealth).

There are, of course, many other kinds of association that are not so easy to classify. In practice a good many overlappings occur. Thus, a clan or gens may at the same time be a territorial unit or it may exercise a predominant influence in a village in which other clans or gentes are represented; a religious society may at the same time be an age group or a sex group; a particular maternal family, as among the Iroquois, may be the social unit which has the privilege of giving the clan to which it belongs its chief; and so on.

groups or group marriage might be assigned definite places in the gradual evolution of the society that we know to-day.

There is no direct historical evidence, for instance, that the early Teutonic tribes which give us the conventionally assumed starting point for Anglo-Saxon civilization had ever passed through a stage of group marriage, nor is the evidence for a totemistic period in the least convincing, nor can we honestly say that we are driven to infer an older organization into matrilineal clans for these peoples. Yet so convinced were some of the most brilliant of the earlier anthropologists that just such social phenomena could be inferred on comparative evidence for the cruder peoples as a whole, and so clear was it to them that a parallel evolutionary sequence of social usages might be assumed for all mankind, that they did not hesitate to ascribe to the prehistoric period of Anglo-Saxon culture customs and social classifications that were familiar to them from aboriginal Australia or Africa or North America. They were in the habit of looking for "survivals" of primitive conditions in the more advanced levels, and they were rarely unsuccessful in finding them.

CRITIQUE OF CLASSICAL EVOLUTION

The more critical schools of anthropology that followed spent a great deal of time and effort in either weakening or demolishing the ingenious speculative sequences that their predecessors had constructed. It gradually appeared that the doctrine of social stages could not be made to fit the facts laboriously gathered by anthropological research. One of the favorite dogmas of the evolutionary anthropologists was the great antiquity of the sib (clan) or corporate kinship group. The earliest form of this type of organization was believed to be based on a matrilineal mode of reckoning descent. Now while it is true that a large number of fairly primitive tribes are organized into matrilineal sibs, such as many of the tribes of Australia, it proved to be equally true that other tribes no whit their superior in general cultural advance counted clan (gens) descent in the paternal line.

Thus, if we consider the distribution of sib institutions in aboriginal North America, it is not in the least obvious that the buffalo-hunting Omaha of the American Plains, organized into patrilineal sibs (gentes), were culturally superior to, or represented a more evolved type of social organization than, say, the Haida or Tlingit or Tsimshian of the west coast of British Columbia and southern

Alaska, who possessed an exceedingly complex system of caste and privilege, had developed a very original and intricate art that was far beyond the modest advances made by any of the tribes of the Plains, and lived as fishermen in definitely localized villages, yet whose sibs (clans) were of the matrilineal type. Other American evidence could easily be adduced to prove that on the whole the matrilineally organized tribes represented a later period of cultural development than the patrilineal ones, whatever might be the facts in aboriginal Australia or Melanesia or other quarters of the primitive world. It was remarkable, for instance, that the confederated Iroquois tribes and the town-dwelling Creeks of the Gulf region and many of the Pueblos (for example, Zuñi and Hopi) of the Southwest, all three agricultural and all three obviously less primitive in mode of life and in social polity than our Omaha hunters, were classical examples of societies based on the matrilineal clan. Criticism could go farther and show that the most primitive North American tribes, like the Eskimo, the Athabaskan tribes of the Mackenzie Valley and the interior of Alaska, and the acorn-eating peoples of California, were not organized into sibs at all, whether of the matrilineal or the patrilineal type.

Countless other examples might be enumerated, all tending to show that it was vain to set up unilinear schemes of social evolution, that supposedly typical forms of archaic society had probably never developed in certain parts of the globe at all, and that in any event the sequence of forms need not everywhere have been in the same sense. The older schematic evolution thus relapsed into the proverbial chaos of history. It became ever clearer that the culture of man was an exceedingly plastic process and that he had developed markedly distinct types of social organization in different parts of the world as well as interestingly convergent forms that could not, however, be explained by any formula of evolutionary theory.

At first blush critical anthropology seems to have demolished the usefulness of its own data for a broader sociology. If anthropology could not give the sociologist a clear perspective into social origins and the remoter social developments that were consummated before the dawn of history, of what serious consequence was its subject-matter for a general theory of society? Of what particular importance was it to study such social oddities, charming or picturesque though they might be, as the clan totemism or the clan exogamy of

Australian blacks or American redskins? It is true that anthropology can no longer claim to give us a simple scaffolding for the building of the social history of man, but it does not follow that its data are a rubbish heap of oddments. It may be and probably is true that anthropology has more to tell us than ever before of the nature of man's social behavior; but we must first learn not to expect its teachings to satisfy any such arbitrary demands as were first made of it.

The primary error of the classical school of anthropology was (and of much anthropological theory still is) to look upon primitive man as a sort of prodromal type of cultured humanity. Thus, there was an irresistible tendency to see his significance not in terms of unfolding culture, with endless possibilities for intricate development along specialized lines, not in terms of place and of environing circumstance, but always in terms of inferred and necessarily distorted time. The present anthropological outlook is broader and far less formalized. What the sociologist may hope to get from the materials of social anthropology is not predigested history, or rather the pseudo-history that called itself social evolution, but insight into the essential patterns and mechanisms of social behavior. This means, among other things, that we are to be at least as much interested in the many points of accord between primitive and sophisticated types of social organization as in their sensational differences.

The Family as Primary Social Unit

We can perhaps best illustrate the changing point of view by a brief reference to the family. The earlier anthropologists were greatly impressed by the importance and the stability of the family in modern life. On the principle that everything that is true of civilized society must have evolved from something very different or even opposed in primitive society, the theory was formulated that the family as we understand it to-day was late to arrive in the history of man, that the most primitive peoples of to-day have but a weak sense of the reality of the family, and that the precursor of this social institution was the more inclusive sib (clan). Thus the family appeared as a gradually evolved and somewhat idealized substitute of, or transfer from, a more cumbersome and tyrannically bound group of kinsfolk.

A more careful study of the facts seems to indicate that the family is a well-nigh universal social unit, that it is the nuclear type of social organization *par excellence*. So far from a study of clans, gentes, and other types of enlarged kinship group giving us the clue to the genesis of the family, the exact opposite is true. The family, with its maternal and paternal ties and its carefully elaborated kinship relations and kinship terminology, is the one social pattern into which man has ever been born. It is the pattern that is most likely to serve as nucleus for, or as model of, other social units. We can, then, understand the development of sib and kindred institutions as proliferations of the universal family image. The terminology of clan affiliation or non-affiliation is simply an extension of the terminology of specific familial and extra-familial relationships. The modern family represents the persistence of an old social pattern, not the emergence of a new one. Clan and gentile organizations blossomed here and there on a stem that is still living. What is distinctive of practically all primitive societies is not the clan or gens or moiety as such, but the tremendous emphasis on the principle of kinship. One of the indirect consequences of this emphasis may be the gradual overshadowing, for a certain period, of the family by one or more of its derivatives.

DIFFUSION AND INFERRED HISTORY

Such an example as this illustrates the value of anthropological data for the fixing of formal perspectives in social phenomena. Meanwhile, if anthropology no longer indulges in the grand panorama of generalized pre-history, it has by no means given up all attempts at reconstructing the history of primitive societies. On the contrary, there is more inferential history being built out of the descriptive data of primitive life than ever before; but it is not a pan-human history, finely contemptuous of geography and local circumstance. Social institutions are no longer being studied by ethnologists as generalized phenomena in an ideal scheme, with the specific local details set down as incidental avatars of the spirit. The present tendency among students of primitive society is to work out the details of any given institution or social practice for a selected spot, then to study its geographical distribution or, if it is a composite of various elements, the distribution of each of these elements, and gradually to work out by inferences of one kind and another a bit of strictly localized social history. The greatest importance is attached to the discovery of continuities in these distributions, which are felt to be most intelligibly explained by the gradual diffusion of a given social feature from one starting point.

To-day we are not satisfied, for instance, to note the existence of maternal clans among the Haida, of Queen Charlotte Islands, and to compare them, say, with the maternal clans of the Zuñi and Hopi in the Southwest. Nothing can be done with these isolated facts. Should it appear that the clans of the two areas are strikingly similar in the details of their structure and functioning and that the areas are connected by a continuous series of intermediate tribes possessing maternal clans, there would be good reason to believe that the Haida and Zuñi-Hopi organizations are derivatives of a single historical process. But this is not the case. The clan organizations are very different and the clan areas are separated by a vast territory occupied by clanless tribes. The American ethnologist concludes that the general similarity in the social structures of the separated areas is not due to a common history but to a formal convergence; he has no notion that the antecedents of clan development were necessarily the same in the two cases. On the other hand, the Haida clan system is strikingly similar in structure, type of localization, totemic associations, privileges, and functions to the clan systems of a large number of neighboring tribes (Tlingit, Nass River, Tsimshian, Bella Bella, Kitamat), so that one is irresistibly led to believe that the social system arose only once in this area and that it was gradually assimilated by peoples to whom it was originally foreign.

Analogous cases of the diffusion of social features over large and continuous but strictly limited areas can be cited without end (for example, Australian maternal clans; Australian marriage classes; men's clubs in Melanesia; age societies in the North American Plains; caste institutions in India), and in nearly all of these cases one may legitimately infer that their spread is owing chiefly to the imitation of a pattern that was restricted in the first place to a very small area.

The Reality of Parallel Social Developments

The recent tendency has been to emphasize diffusion and historical inferences from the facts of diffusion at the expense of convergences in social structure, certain extremists even going so far as to deny the possibility of the latter. It is important for students of the structural variations and the history of society to realize the important part that the borrowing of social patterns has played at all times and on all levels of culture; but the reality and the significance of formal parallelisms should never be lost sight of. At present anthropologists are timid about the intensive, non-historical study of typical social forms. The "evolutionary" fallacies are still fresh in their minds, and the danger of falling into any one of a variety of facile "psychological" modes of interpretation is too obvious. But anthropology cannot long continue to ignore such stupendous facts as the independent development of sibs in different parts of the world, the widespread tendency toward the rise of religious or ceremonial societies, the rise of occupational castes, the attachment of differentiating symbols to social units, and a host of others. Such classes of social phenomena are too persistent to be without deep significance. It is fair to surmise that in the long run it is from their consideration that the sociologist will have the most to learn.

Few anthropologists have probed deeply into these problems. Hasty correlations between various types of social phenomena have been made in plenty, such as Rivers's brilliant and unconvincing attempt to derive systems of kinship terminology from supposedly fundamental forms of social organization; but the true unraveling of the basic and largely unconscious concepts or images that underlie social forms has hardly been begun. Hence the anthropologist is in the curious position of dealing with impressive masses of material and with a great number of striking homologies, not necessarily due to historical contact, that he is quite certain have far-reaching significance, but the nature of whose significance he is not prepared to state. Interpretative anthropology is under a cloud, but the data of primitive society need interpretation none the less. The historical explanations now in vogue, often exceedingly dubious at best, are little more than a clearing of the ground toward a social interpretation; they are not the interpretation itself. We can only glance at a few of those formal convergences or underlying tendencies in primitive social organization which we believe to be of common interest to anthropology, to sociology, and to a social psychology of form which has hardly been more than adumbrated.

THE KINSHIP "IMAGE"

It has frequently been noted that the kinship principle tends to take precedence in primitive life over other principles of social classification. A good example of this is afforded by the West Coast tribes of Canada. Here the integrity of the local group, the village, with a recognized head chief, is pretty solidly established. Nevertheless we are constantly hearing in the legends of a particular family or clan, if feeling itself aggrieved for one reason or another, moving off with its house boards and canoes either to found a new village or to join its kinsmen in an old one. There is also direct historical evidence to show that the clan or family constitution of the villages was being reassorted from time to time because of the great inner coherence and the relative mobility of the kinship groups. Among the Nagas of Assam the villages as such had little of the spirit of community and mutual helpfulness, but were split up into potentially hostile clans which lived apart from one another and were constantly on guard against attack from fellow villagers. Here the feeling of kinship solidarity, stimulated, it is true, by ceremonial ideas with regard to feuds and head-hunting, actually turned the village into a congeries of beleaguered camps. The significance of such facts is that they show with dramatic clarity how a potent social pattern may fly in the face of reason, of mutual advantage, and even of economic necessity.

The application to modern conditions is obvious enough. The ideology which prevents a Haida clan from subordinating its petty pride to the general good of the village is precisely the same as that which to-day prevents a nation from allowing a transnational economic unit, say the silk industry, from functioning smoothly. In each case a social group-pattern — or formal "image," in psychological terms (clan; nation) — so dominates feeling that services which would naturally flow in the grooves of quite other intercrossing or more inclusive group-patterns (mutual defense in the village; effective production and distribution of a class of goods by those actively engaged in handling it) must suffer appreciable damage.

FUNCTION AND FORM IN SOCIOLOGY

This brings us to the question of the functional nature of social groups. Our modern tendency is to see most associations of human beings in terms of function. Thus, it is obvious that boards of trade, labor unions, scientific societies, municipalities, political parties, and thousands of other types of social organization are most easily explained as resulting from the efforts of like-minded or similarly interested individuals to compass certain ends. As we go back to the types of organization which we know to be more deeply rooted in our historic past, such as the family, the nationality, and the political state, we find that their function is far less obvious. It is either all but absent from consciousness, as in the case of the family, or inextricably intertwined with sentiments and loyalties that are not explicable by the mere function, real or supposed, of the social unit. The state might be defined in purely territorial and functional terms, but political history is little more than an elaborate proof that the state as we have actually known it refuses either to "stay put" or to "stick to business." However, it is evident that the modern state has tended more and more in the direction of a clearer functional definition, by way both of restriction and of extension. The dynastic and religious entanglements, for instance, which were at one time considered inseparable from the notion of a state, have loosened or disappeared. Even the family, the most archaic and perhaps the most stubborn of all social units, is beginning to have its cohesiveness and its compulsions questioned by the intercrossing of functional units that lie outside of itself.

When we compare primitive society with our own, we are at once impressed by the lesser importance of function as a determinant of organization. Functional groupings there are, of course, but they are subsidiary, as a rule, to kinship, territorial, and status groups. There is a very definite tendency for communal activities of all sorts to socialize on the lines suggested by these groups. Thus, among the West Coast Indians, membership in the ceremonial or secret societies, while theoretically dependent upon the acquirement of power from the initiating guardian spirits, is in reality largely a matter of privilege inhering in certain lines of descent. The Kwakiutl Cannibal Society, for instance, is not a spontaneous association of such men and women as possess unusual psychic suggestibility, but is composed of individuals who have family traditions entitling them to dance the Cannibal dance and to perform the rituals of the Society. Among the Pueblo Indians there is a marked tendency for the priesthood of important religious fraternities to be recruited from particular clans. Among the Plains tribes the policing of the camp during the annual buffalo hunt was entrusted not to a group expressly constituted for the purpose but to a series of graded age societies, each serving in turn, as among the Arapaho, to the sibs, as among the Omaha, or to some other set of social units that had other grounds for existence.

We must be careful not to exaggerate the importance of facts such as these, for undoubtedly there is much intercrossing in primitive society of the various types of social organization; yet it remains true that, by and large, function tends to wait on alien principles, particularly kinship. In course of time, as numbers grow and pursuits become more specialized, the functional groups intercross more freely with what may be called the natural status groups. Finally, with the growing complexity of the mechanism of life the concept of the purpose of a given group forces itself upon the social consciousness, and if this purpose is felt to be compelling enough, the group that it unifies may reduce to a secondary position social units built on other principles. Thus, the clan tends to atrophy with the growth of political institutions, precisely as to-day state autonomy is beginning to weaken in the face of transnational functions.

Yet it is more than doubtful if the gradual unfolding of social patterning tends indefinitely to be controlled by function. The pragmatic temper of present-day thinking makes such an assumption seem natural. Both anthropology and history seem to show, however, that any kind of social grouping, once established, tends to persist, and that it has a life only partly conditioned by its function, which may be changed from age to age and from place to place. Certainly anthropology has few more impressive hints for sociological theory than the functional equivalence of different types of social units.

Among the Indians of the Plains, whether organized into sibs or merely into territorial bands, the decoration of articles of clothing, so far as it does not involve a symbolic reference to a vision, in which case it becomes a matter of intimate personal concern, is neither vested in particular women nor differentiated according to sib or territorial units. The vast majority of decorative motives are at the free disposal of all the women of the tribe. There is evidence that in certain of the Plains tribes the women had developed industrial guilds or sororities for the learning of moccasin techniques and similar items, but if these sex-functional groups specialized in any way in the use of particular designs, it would only emphasize the point that the decoration of clothing had nothing to do with the basic organization of the tribe. The facts read quite differently for such West Coast tribes as the Haida and Tsimshian. Here, owing to the fact that the clans had mythological crests and to the further fact that these crests were often represented on articles of clothing in highly conventionalized form, artistic expression was necessarily intertwined with social organization. The representation of a conventionalized beaver or killer-whale on a hat or dancing apron thus actually becomes a clan privilege. It helps to define or objectify the clan by so much.

Another example of an identical or similar function applied to different social units is afforded by the ceremonial playing of lacrosse among several eastern tribes of the North American aborigines. Both the Iroquois and the Yuchi, of the Southeastern area were organized into clans (matrilineal sibs), but while the Iroquois pitted their two phratries, or clan aggregations, against each other among the Yuchi the game was not a clan or phratric function at all but was played by the two great status groups, "Chiefs" and "Warriors," membership in which depended on patrilineal, not matrilineal, descent.

The Transfer of Social Patterns

Such instances are not exceptions or oddities. They may be multiplied indefinitely. Any student who has worked through a considerable body of material of this kind is left with a very lively sense of the reality of types of organization to which no absolutely constant functions can be assigned. Moreover, the suspicion arises that many social units that now seem to be very clearly defined by their function may have had their origin in patterns which the lapse of time has reinterpreted beyond recognition. A very interesting problem arises—that of the possible transfer of a psychological attitude or mode of procedure which is proper to one type of social unit to another type of unit in which the attitude or procedure is not so clearly relevant. Undoubtedly such transfers have often taken place both on primitive and on sophisticated levels.

A striking example of the transfer of a "pattern of feeling" to a social function to which it is glaringly inapplicable is the following again quoted from the West Coast Indians: The psychic peculiarity that leads certain men and women to become shamans ("medicine-men" and "medicine-women") is so individual that shamanism shows nearly everywhere a marked tendency to resist grooving in the social patterns of the tribe. Personal ability or susceptibility counts far more than conventional status. Nevertheless, so powerful is the concept of rank and of the family inheritance of privilege of every conceivable type among the West Coast people that certain tribes of this area, such as the Tlingit and Nootka, have actually made of shamanistic power an inheritable privilege. In actual practice, of course, theory has to yield to compromise. Among the Nootka, for instance, certain shamanistic offices are supposed to be performed by those who have an inherited right to them. Actually, however, these offices necessitate the possession of supernatural power that the incumbent may not happen to possess. He is therefore driven to the device of deputing the exercise of his office to a real shaman whom he pays for his services but who does not acquire the titular right to the office in question. The psychology of this procedure is of course very similar to the more sophisticated procedure of rubber-stamping documents in the name of a king who is profoundly ignorant of their contents.

A very instructive example of pattern transfer on a high level of culture is the complex organization of the Roman Catholic Church. Here we have a bureaucratic system that neither expresses the personal psychology of snobbery and place-hunting nor can be seriously explained as due to the exigencies of the religious spirit which the organization serves. There is, of course, reason to believe that this organization is to a large extent a carry-over of the complex structure of Roman civil administration. That the Jews and the evangelical Protestant sects have a far looser type of church organization does not prove that they are, as individuals, more immediately swayed by the demands of religion. All that one has a right to conclude is that in their case religion has socialized itself on a less tightly knit pattern, a pattern that was more nearly congruent with other habits of their social life.

Nor can there be a serious doubt that some of our current attitudes toward social units are better suited to earlier types of organization than to the social units as they actually function to-day. A dispassionate analysis of the contemporary state and a full realization of the extent to which its well-being depends upon international understandings would probably show that the average individual views it with a more profound emotion than the facts warrant. To the state, in other words, are carried over feelings that seem far more appropriate for more nearly autonomous social bodies, such as the tribe or the self-supporting nationality. It is not unreasonable to maintain that a too passionate state loyalty may hinder the comfort of its object in precisely the same way that an overzealous mother, wrapped up in the family image, may hinder the social functioning of her beloved son. It is difficult to view social and political problems of practical importance with a cool eye. One of the most subtle and enlightening of the fruits of anthropological research is an understanding of the very considerable degree to which the concepts of social pattern, function, and associated mental attitude are independently variable. In this thought lies the germ of a social philosophy of values and transfers that joins hands in a very suggestive way with such psychoanalytic concepts as the "image" and the transfer of emotion.

RHYTHMIC CONFIGURATIONS IN SOCIETY

Modern psychology is destined to aid us in our understanding of social phenomena by its emphasis on the projection of formal or rhythmic configurations of the psyche and on the concrete symbolization of values and social relations. We can do no more than suggest here that both of these kinds of mental functioning are plentifully illustrated in primitive society, and that for this reason anthropology can do much to give their consideration an adequate place in sociological theory. They are just as truly operative in our more sophisticated culture, but they seem here to be prevented from a clear-cut expression along the lines of social organization by the interference of more conscious, rational processes and by the leveling and destructive influence of a growing consciousness of purpose

The projection in social behavior of an innate sense of form is an intuitive process and is merely a special phase of that mental functioning that finds its clearest voice in mathematics and its most nearly pure æsthetic embodiment in plastic and musical design. Now it has often been observed how neatly and symmetrically many primitive societies arrange their social units and with how perfect, not to say pedantic, a parallelism functions are distributed among these units. An Iroquois or Pueblo or Haida or Australian clan is closely patterned on the other clans, but its distinctive content of behavior is never identical with that of any of these. Then, too, we find significantly often a tendency to exteriorize the feeling for social design in space or time. The Omaha clans or Blackfoot bands, for instance, took up definite positions in the camp circle; the septs of a Nootka or Kwakiutl tribe were ranked in a certain order and seated according to definite rule in ceremonial gatherings; each of the Hopi clans was referred to one of the four cardinal points; the Arapaho age societies were graded in a temporal series and took their turn from year to year in policing the camp; among some of the Western Bantu tribes of Africa the year was divided into segments correlated with territorial groupings. The significance of such social phenomena as these, which could easily be multiplied, is probably far greater than has generally been assumed. It is not claimed that the tendency to rhythmic expression is their only determinant, but it is certainly a powerful underlying factor in the development of all social parallelisms and symmetries.

SYMBOLICAL ASSOCIATIONS

The importance of symbolical associations with social groupings is well known. Party slogans, national flags, and lodge emblems and regalia to-day can give only a diluted idea of what power is possessed by the social symbol in primitive life. The best-known example of the socialization of symbols among primitive people is of course that complicated, indefinitely varied, and enormously distributed class of phenomena that is conveniently termed totemism. The central importance of totemism lies not so much in a mystic identification of the individual or group with an animal, a plant, or other classes of objects held in religious regard (such identifications are by no means uncommon in primitive cultures, but are not necessary to, or even typical of, totemism) as in the clustering of all kinds of values that pertain to a social unit around a concrete symbol. This symbol becomes surcharged with emotional significance not because of what it merely is or is thought to be in rational terms, but because of all the vital experiences, inherited and personal, that it stands for. Totemism is, on the plane of primitive sociology, very much the same kind of psychological phenomenon as the identification in the mind of the devout Christian of the cross with a significant system of religious practices, beliefs, and emotions.

When a Haida Indian is a member of a clan that possesses, say, the Killer-whale crest, it is very difficult for him to function in any social way without being involved in an explicit or implicit reference to the Killer-whale crest or some other crest or crests with which it is associated. He cannot be born, come of age, be married, give feasts, be invited to a feast, take or give a name, decorate his belongings, or die as a mere individual, but always as one who shares in the traditions and usages that go with the Killer-whale or associated crests. Hence the social symbol is not in any sense a mere tag; it is a traditional index of the fullness of life and of the dignity of the human spirit which transcends the death of the individual. The symbol is operative in a great many types of social behavior, totemism being merely one of its most articulate group expressions. The symbol as unconscious evaluator of individual experience has been much discussed in recent years. It needs no labored argument to suggest how much light anthropology may throw on the social psychology of the symbol.

SELECTED REFERENCES

Boas, F. *The Mind of Primitive Man.* 1911.
"The Social Organization and Secret Societies of the Kwakiutl Indians." Report, U.S. National Museum, 1895, pp. 315–733.

Codrington, R. H. *The Melanesians: Studies in their Anthropology and Folk-Lore.* 1891.

Cunow, H. *Die Verwandtschafts-Organisationen der Australneger.* 1894.
Zur Urgeschichte der Ehe und der Familie. 1912.

Dorsey, J. O. "Omaha Sociology." Bureau of American Ethnology, 3d Annual Report, 1884, pp. 211–37.

Frazer, J. G. *Totemism and Exogamy.* 1911.

Gifford, E. W. "Clans and Moieties in Southern California." *University of California Publications in American Archæology and Ethnology*, XIV, 1918, pp. 155–219.

Goldenweiser, A. A. *Early Civilization, an Introduction to Anthropology.* (Particularly chaps. XII and XIII.) 1922.
"Totemism, an Analytical Study." *Journal of American Folk-Lore*, XXXIII, 1910, pp. 179–293.

Graebner, F. *Methode der Ethnologie.* 1911.

Hartland, E. S. "Matrilineal Kinship and the Question of its Priority." *Memoirs of the American Anthropological Association*, IV, 1917, pp. 1–90.

Junod, H. A. *The Life of a South African Tribe.* 1912.

Kroeber, A. L. "Zuñi Kin and Clan." *American Museum of Natural History, Anthropological Papers*, XVIII, 1917, pp. 39–205.
Anthropology. 1923.

Lowie, R. H. "Plains Indian Age-Societies: Historical and Comparative Summary." *American Museum of Natural History, Anthropological Papers*, XI, pp. 877–984.
Primitive Society. 1920.

Malinowski, B. *The Family among the Australian Aborigines.* 1913.

Morgan, L. H. "Systems of Consanguinity and Affinity of the Human Family." *Smithsonian Contributions to Knowledge*, XVII, 1871.
Ancient Society. 1877.
League of the Ho-de-no-sau-nee or Iroquois. 1904.

Radin, P. "The Social Organization of the Winnebago Indians, an Interpretation." *Geological Survey of Canada, Museum Bulletin*, no. 10, 1915.

Rivers, W. H. R. *The Todas.* 1906.
The History of Melanesian Society. 1914.
Kinship and Social Organization. 1914.

Sapir, E. "Time Perspective in Aboriginal American Culture, a Study in Method." *Geological Survey of Canada, Memoirs*, no. 90, 1916.

Schurtz, H.   *Altersklassen und Männerbünde.*   1902.

Spencer, B., and Gillen, F. J.   *The Native Tribes of Central Australia.*   1899.

Swanton, J. R.   "Contributions to the Ethnology of the Haida."   *Memoirs of the American Museum of Natural History,* VIII, 1905.

"The Social Organization of American Indians."   *American Anthropologist,* N.S., 1905, pp. 663–73.

Thomas, William I.   *Source Book for Social Origins.*   1909.

Tylor, E. B.   *Primitive Culture.*   1889.

"On a Method of Investigating the Development of Institutions; applied to Laws of Marriage and Descent."   *Journal of the Anthropological Institute of Great Britain and Ireland,* XVIII, 1889, pp. 245–72.

Webster, H.   *Primitive Secret Societies.*   1908.

Wissler, C.   "The Social Life of the Blackfoot Indians."   *American Museum of Natural History, Anthropological Papers,* VII, 1911, pp. 1–64.

Man and Culture.   1923.

Westermarck, E. A.   *The History of Human Marriage.*   3d ed.   1903.

CHAPTER X

ANTHROPOLOGY AND STATISTICS

By FRANZ BOAS

COLUMBIA UNIVERSITY

ANTHROPOLOGY deals with the bodily form, the physiological and psychological functions, and the behavior of groups of men. It differs from many aspects of anatomy, physiology, and psychology in so far as these sciences are interested primarily in the typical behavior of the individual, whereas the group is the center of interest for the anthropologist. The anatomical form of the adult individual is fairly stable and may be described as a constant. The forms of a number of individuals composing a group are not identical, and, therefore, the anatomical problem of anthropology deals in every case with a variable.

The physiological reactions of the individual vary from time to time, and hence they are variables. When a group of individuals is studied, the variability is increased because the individuals differ in their functioning among themselves. This is equally true of mental functioning.

It follows from these remarks that in the study of any anthropological problem dealing with anatomical form, physiological or psychological function, one is dealing with variable phenomena — more variable in the study of function than in the study of form.

When, however, the development of form and function during the period of growth and decline is studied, a new variable element enters into consideration. The rapidity of change is not equal in all individuals. Thus, the variability of time is added to the variability of form and function.

Phenomena of this type can be handled only by statistical methods, and the task of the statistician in studying anthropology is the disentangling of the conditions which bring about variation.

In the study of the adult anatomical form, the statistical problem depends upon the character of the group that is to be studied. It has been observed that the types of distribution in various social groups differ considerably. It is not often that the opportunity presents itself for studying a sufficient number of individuals belonging to one group to determine with accuracy the distribution of forms. In many cases it is necessary to confine one's self to a small sample, partly for the reason that the financial resources or the number of observers at the disposal of the investigator are not adequate for obtaining a large series, and partly because the group studied is small. When, for instance, the investigator is confronted with the problem of determining the anatomical characteristics of the people of Tierra del Fuego, he has, at best, a few hundred individuals at his disposal. In other cases the total number of individuals may be even smaller. In the study of skeletal material he is confined to the few finds that represent the characteristics of a certain group. This is preëminently the case in all prehistoric investigations relating to very early times, because only very few specimens have been preserved.

In all cases where the detailed distribution cannot be investigated, it is necessary to substitute a few derived constants for the distribution of the series and, according to the generally applied statistical methods, the average and standard deviation must be used. It must be understood that under these conditions both terms have no biological significance but serve merely to identify a series. A detailed analysis based on statistical methods is impossible in cases of this kind.

In those series which are sufficiently extended to give us a better insight into the actual distribution of forms, a more searching analysis may be possible. The anatomical forms of social groups are determined partly by heredity, partly by environmental influences in the widest sense of the term, and partly by more or less artificial selection. The definition of the group may be made on a geographical, a biological, or a social basis. When the individual development in time during childhood and senility is included, the element of age may be relevant. If is, therefore, necessary in a statistical treatment to differentiate clearly between these factors. Since the elements of descent, of location, and of environmental influences are not readily separated, it seldom happens that the distribution of forms gives a clew with regard to the conditions determining the character of the variability. When, for instance, a population is investigated in which social factors determine certain aspects of bodily form, the social constitution of the unit investigated will be reflected in the distribution. When we are dealing with a closely inbred series, like certain branches of the European nobility, a small village community, or an isolated tribe, the general distribution will not show the characteristics of the various family lines which will differ fundamentally from populations that are drawn from distinctive areas that are not inbred. The statistical investigator, therefore, must be concerned not only with the series as a whole, but must try to analyze the series from these various angles.

On account of the multiplicity of the conditions reflected in the variable forms, the distributions generally have a form approximating the exponential curve. Deviations, however, are frequent. To give an example: Our knowledge of stature in Italy is based largely upon measurements of enlisted soldiers. According to law, soldiers less than 154 cms. in stature are excluded. There are also lowest limits for chest circumference and for a number of other features. It therefore follows that short individuals, but taller than 154 cms., are liable to be excluded from military service. This is clearly expressed by the great asymmetry of distribution of stature in Italy. This asymmetry is the greater, the greater the number of short statures. It is determined entirely by social selection and does not reflect the characteristics of the Italian population as determined by heredity and environment.

There are also cases in which the population of a definite district is known to be drawn from different types which happen to have settled in the same area. An example of this kind is the population of Paris, which consists partly of the relatively long-headed, lightly pigmented North French, and partly of the short-headed, more darkly pigmented Central French. Ordinarily, the descent of each individual is unknown, and it is, therefore, one of the tasks of the statistical investigator to determine from the observed distribution the composition of a mixed population of this kind.

Analogous phenomena may occur in regions in which the heterogeneous descent of the population is not known, and the investigator may be tempted to classify his material according to resemblances to types known to him. This is probably one of the most fruitful sources of error, because the assignment of an individual to one type or another depends entirely upon the subjective feeling for the importance of certain selected types. If it is said, for instance, that the Navajo of the southwestern United States are in part of Pueblo type and in part of Ute type, or of others, it must be assumed that these types are clearly in the mind of the observer and can be segregated from the total group. From a statistical point of view, it would obviously be necessary to prove the greater variability of the assumedly mixed type as compared to the component types, and it is not often that a sufficient increase of variability can be proved.

The method here employed is analogous to the method of the pathologist or physician to whom extremes of a variable type are of particular practical importance and who, for this reason, speaks of extreme constitutional types and considers the intermediate group as a mixed type. While from the point of view of practical medicine this method is undoubtedly valuable, it is entirely misleading from a statistical point of view, because it creates as types those forms which are merely extreme variants.

Our considerations indicate that true normal distributions may be expected in a very few instances only. This is much more the case when the developmental conditions are taken into consideration. The rate of growth and development is hardly ever proportionate to time, but is a complex function of the time element. In prenatal life growth is exceedingly rapid. The rapidity decreases until adolescence. Then it increases again. In adult life size becomes almost stable, but undergoes retrogressive changes of greater or less rapidity when senility sets in. Since all the phenomena of growth are dependent on the three fundamental factors of heredity, environmental influences, and time, it is a difficult although an important task to separate these three elements. When a child ten years old is considerably taller than the average of his class, it may be due to the fact that he belongs to a tall racial group, or that he is growing up under conditions which favor large size, or it may be that his development is unusually accelerated; and the problem of the segregation of these elements will be the principal task of the investigator. Because of the complex character of the relation between time and the rate of development, accelerated and retarded individuals cannot be distributed in a symmetrical way and a skew distribution must be expected as soon as the element of time plays an important part in a series.

It follows from all these considerations that the analysis of curves showing the distribution of forms cannot be made according to a standardized method. In each case it is necessary to consider the morphological problem involved, to formulate the problem, to determine the constants to be investigated, and to arrange the statistical investigation accordingly.

In the investigations of heredity much stress has been laid upon the similarity of fraternities or of parents and children as expressed by the coefficient of correlation. It must be borne in mind that the coefficient of correlation depends, to a great extent, upon the composition of a series. In a population in which all the family lines are identical, there will be no fraternal and no parental correlation, because a child of a certain form may belong to any one family line. On the other hand, in a population in which the family lines are very different, the assignment of a child to a certain type of family will be easy. In other words, in the latter case the coefficient of a fraternal correlation will be high. It does not matter in these cases whether there is selective mating or not. In a heterogeneous population in which the family lines are distinct, the high fraternal correlation will persist. From a biological point of view the only problem of importance is the relation between fraternal variability and the variability of family lines. It is quite conceivable that there may be two populations with the same distribution of individual forms, which, however, with regard to the distribution in family lines and the distribution of family lines, are entirely distinct. Similar considerations have to be made with regard to the interrelation of bodily organs in which, also, the coefficient of correlation may fail entirely to reveal the biological problem involved.

In other cases the coefficient of correlation may be a valuable means of detecting hereditary characteristics of a population. If, for instance, there is an intermingling of a short- and broad-headed population with a long- and narrow-headed population, the coefficient for the interrelation between the length and width of head may be completely reversed. Ordinarily, within the same type, a long head will be at the same time, comparatively speaking, broad; a short head will be, comparatively speaking, narrow. In the particular case here mentioned the reverse will be the case, the long head belonging to the narrow-headed type will be narrow, and the short head belonging to the broad-headed type will be wide, so that the normal value of the correlation between length and width will be materially disturbed. Wherever such disturbances occur, either unduly intensifying or unduly reducing the coefficient of correlation, heterogeneity of the series may be suspected.

One of the problems with which the anthropologist is concerned is the distinction of racial types. These types are so distributed that there is a gradual transition from the type of one region to that of another region. This is largely due to migrations and to inter-marriages, but it may also be brought about by environmental influences. The problem in these cases is that of finding a satisfactory basis of classification of form. When we are dealing with types as distinct as the North Europeans or the Central African negroes, no difficulty presents itself because the racial characteristics are well defined in each case and the differences will be greater than the range of variability. When, on the other hand, two neighboring areas are compared, there is such a degree of overlapping that it is impossible to assign each individual definitely to a certain group. The question here arises whether each individual, according to its bodily form, may be definitely assigned to one biological type or another. It is important to bear in mind that individuals that are apparently morphologically identical may represent quite different hereditary strains. Thus, for instance, if Bohemians and Sicilians of a certain definite type are selected, which can be done on account of the overlapping of the ranges of variation in each type, it is found that the children of the selected Bohemians approach the general Bohemian type, while the children of the selected Sicilians approach the general Sicilian type. In order to solve the problem of classification of types in a satisfactory way, it would be necessary to establish a standard of racial difference. Obviously this cannot be the difference between the average types, because with the same amount of difference of average type and a small degree of variability, the difference will be much more decided than in the case of the same difference of averages and a high degree of variability, which brings about a considerable overlapping of forms. The problem can be solved only by substitution of the concept of similarity for that of difference, but a satisfactory method of differentiation of type has, so far, not been found.

The remarks concerning anatomical form are equally applicable to the study of physiological and psychological function, with the difference, however, that the new element of individual variability must be taken into consideration. It will be necessary in all cases of anthropological interpretation of these phenomena to supplement the study of group distribution with a detailed study of individual variability as determined by the varying conditions of the organism.

Even in comparatively simple phenomena like the rate of the heart beat or of breathing, the influence of all the conditions upon the individual must be taken into account. For this reason many of the investigations regarding vital capacity, if determined by physiological constants or dynamometric measures, cannot be interpreted truly as characteristic of groups. Since the group distribution and the individual variability are independent of each other, the segregation of the two elements is not difficult.

Attempts have also been made to apply statistical methods to ethnographical phenomena. The success of these attempts is more than doubtful. E. B. Tylor tried to show statistically that there are definite relations between a number of characteristic forms of behavior in the family group. Czekanowsky tried to apply the methods of correlations to a number of ethnic phenomena, and these attempts have recently been repeated in other fields. The fundamental difficulty of this method is our lack of knowledge of historical connection. In order to make a statistical method a success it is essential that the phenomena counted must be independent of one another. If a number of them go back to the same historical sources they cannot be considered as separate units. If this method is rigidly applied, the number of available cases is so small that valid results can hardly be expected. It is only when an inner psychological or sociological relation can be established that methods of this kind, which, I think, do not need elaborate statistical treatment, can be utilized with any hope of success.

SELECTED REFERENCES

Questions relating to the application of statistics to anthropology are treated in *Biometrika*, edited by Karl Pearson. Investigations by him and by his associates are also published in *Biometric Laboratory Publications, Drapers' Company Research Memoirs;* in the Memoir Series of the Eugenic Laboratory Publications, and the *Annals of Eugenics.*

Czekanowski, Jan. "Verwandschaftsbeziehungen der Zentral-afrikanischen Pygmäen." *Korrespondenzblatt der deutschen Gesellschaft für Anthropologie, Ethnologie und Urgeschichte,* vol. 41, 1910, p. 107.
    "Objective Kriterien in der Ethnologie." *Ibid.,* vol. 42, p. 71.
Davenport, C. B. *Statistical Methods with Special Reference to Biological Variation.*
Martin, Rudolf. *Lehrbuch der Anthropologie.* Chapter on Statistical Methods, pp. 62–103. 1914.
Pearson, Karl. *Tables for Statisticians and Biometricians, 1914–24.*
Tschuprow, A. A. *Grundbegriffe und Grundprobleme der Korrelationstheorie.* 1925.
Westergaard, H. "Some Remarks on the Services of Statistics in Anthropological Investigations." *Medd. Danmarks Antr.,* vol. II, p. 153.

CHAPTER XI

ECONOMICS AND ETHICS

By J. A. HOBSON

LONDON

ECONOMICS AS A NATIONAL ECONOMY

ECONOMICS, like most important branches of knowledge, was an art before it was a science. Or rather it was a group of arts or policies referring to various aspects of the business side of life, chiefly related to the public interest as represented by the state. Hence the term "political economy" was primarily concerned with the regulation of trade, finance, taxation, and ways of promoting agriculture and industry, regarded from the standpoint of national security and progress. Economics, thus conceived as a branch of statecraft, necessarily carried such ethical implications as inhere in the art of politics. The "ought" is certainly not excluded from the conception and use of economics as a line of conduct directed to secure the public good by the regulation of the productive activities of the people. A definitely "national economy" must still be regarded in this light as a department of statecraft and, as an art of political control, must be endowed with an ethical content.

THE NON-MORAL ECONOMIC MAN

General economists, however, especially in England, France, and America, have striven to establish an economic science upon foundations of objective fact and law that assume certain human motives and activities as operative forces, without inquiring into their desirability from the standpoint of moral valuations. It is curious that the great treatise of Adam Smith should have been made the instrument for this sharp cleavage between the early classical economics and ethics. For Smith was a moral philosopher, and his *Wealth of Nations* was conceived by him as part of a wider exposition of a philosophy to which his *Theory of Moral Sentiments* was another contribution. As Lange and other commentators have pointed out, the pure egoism by which men were supposed to be motivated in their economic conduct, as landowners, employers, workers, and so forth, was of the nature of those "fictions" which all the sciences have employed provisionally in their discovery of "laws." Smith did not believe that in his business life man was moved entirely by considerations of self-interest, but he held that selfish interest was so potent a force that other motives might conceivably be disregarded in working out the laws of a science of wealth. It seems, however, that this fiction of Smith's became an all-sufficient working hypothesis to many of his followers. Hence, the "economic man" around whom so much controversy has waged. Close students of Ricardo and the makers of the classical school are able to adduce much evidence to rebut the charge of soulless materialism brought by Carlyle, Ruskin, and other critics against them. But this evidence does not really dispose of the charge. It only indicates a certain human inconsistency in the economists which led them to qualifications and modifications strictly irrelevant to their treatment. In other words, the scientific character of the classical economics is actually attained by a false simplification of the motives that enter into every department of economic conduct. Men were treated in this economic world "as if" they were automatons, accurately driven by greed and laziness, and so disposed to get as much and give as little as they could, regardless of other feelings and sentiments, customs and traditions. Unfortunately, Smith also gave a sort of quasi-moral sanction to this view, in his theory that by each man's intelligently following the line of his own self-interest in disposing of his productive resources, the greatest wealth of the community would be attained. This "simple system of natural liberty" was presented as a law of social harmony that gave a sort of moral justification to selfish economic conduct. Here individualism, rationalism, utilitarianism were built into the foundations of the economic science, and the consequences of this unfortunate procedure have never been satisfactorily eliminated from the authoritative science.

Failure to Confront the Moral Issues

J. S. Mill strove to humanize his study by appending to his exposition of the working of the existing economic system some speculative aspirations for a new coöperative order, in which the general body of the workers should enjoy a larger share of the products of industry and a voice in controlling the conditions of labor. He was alive to the inequitable character of the labor-bargain and the wrongs of unearned increment from the private ownership of land

and other monopolized or scarce resources.   But the main structure of his laws and principles rested upon the Smithian-Ricardian foundations and was chiefly confined to the explanation of the play of supply and demand for factors of production and their products under the guidance of the single desire for material gain, without any attempt to assess the processes by any standard of human values.

The study was almost wholly concentrated upon problems of production, the activities of agriculture, mining, manufacture, transportation, commerce, professional, official, and personal services; consumption was never made an object of serious consideration, or treated from any other standpoint than that of its bearing on further production.   The general problem of the distribution of the product between the several factors of production was never confronted, and was, indeed, incapable of confrontation as long as the laws of rent, of wages, and of interest and profit were kept separate, land reckoned in acres, labor in man-days, and capital in hundreds of pounds.

ETHICAL DEFENSE OF THE CLASSICAL ECONOMICS

But when the mid-Victorian economists were denounced by humanitarians for inculcating selfishness and materialism, a pig-philosophy, they found powerful defenders among the moralists of the age.   For the puritan morality, which inspired the new business classes in their struggle for industrial and commercial success, fitted in well with the ethics which taught that if every man applied his personal powers for his own benefit and that of his family, utilizing the opportunity which Providence, or circumstances, placed in his path, he would necessarily be contributing to the welfare of society at large.   Industry, thrift, sobriety, forethought, honesty, the staples of a sound useful personal character, were the sufficient requisites for a solid and progressive industrial society.   This moral individualism withstood all efforts of socialism to question the natural harmony which should transmute personal selfseeking into common gain, or to stress the organic nature of society as a determinant of the utility of individual effort in production.   The moral inadequacy of the individualistic harmony was, however, keenly felt by many who were not prepared to espouse socialism, especially in the form Marx and his school gave to it.   Capitalism as the robbery of laborers, manual laborers as the sole creators of wealth, the class-war as a necessity of economic evolution, were rejected by most thinkers, on ethical as well as on intellectual grounds.

The New Ethical Compromise

The central principle of the critics of capitalism, to wit, that production should be for social service and not for private profit, has always won the acceptance of moralists. But they have differed as to how far social service, as the end to which productive energy was directed, must, ought, or could, be the main *conscious* motive of the individual participants in industry. The general compromise they have reached is one that aims at making the apparatus of industry work as humanly and equitably as possible under the conditions of production and the distribution of the product, trusting that this will induce in all classes of producers some consciousness of the social utility of the whole process, although the main immediate incentive may still continue to be personal gain. Most fair-minded moralists would confess that this compromise of social reform is not a counsel of perfection. The ethical ideal would be one of a communism based on the principle, "from each according to his powers; to each according to his needs." But this is not attainable "*propter duritiem cordis.*" Much work is disagreeable and will not be done save under the pressure of need or greed; some work of skill, initiative, enterprise, or management, though not in itself disagreeable, is the natural or acquired monopoly of a few who insist upon taking its scarcity value as a personal reward, not content to perform a social service for their soul's good. There must, therefore — so runs the moral compromise — be private property, wide divergence of income, and inequality of social-economic classes. Human nature is at present, and perhaps forever will be, so constituted that without these inequalities and their incidental hardships and injustice, a reasonably productive economic system will not work. Our moralists usually round off this compromise by representing wealth, thus acquired or inherited, as a "social trust" to be administered by the owner, not for his own enjoyment, but for the public good. Incidentally the perfection of his own personality demands this philanthropic mission in order that he may not be corrupted by luxury or waste. And is it not only property but industrial power and leadership as well that are to be the subjects of this voluntary exercise of social virtue? Ruskin's ideal of Landlords and Captains of Industry, administering their estates and businesses for the good of their dependents and employees, is beginning in England to bear fruit in a large variety of forms of Whitly Councils, co-partnerships, insurance and welfare schemes, and other concessions from the older, grasping, domineering capitalism, with a view to securing the harmonious coöperation of the factors of production. Plans for bringing into this coöperation the public interest, in the person of the consumer, appeal to an increasing number of reformers as a sufficient policy of social service, removing or abating the economic and moral struggle between capital and labor, producers and consumers, and making for a more equitable apportionment of wealth.

The Conception of a Moral Trust

The distinctive character of this movement is that it relies upon the individual good will of the participants for establishing pacific and equitable arrangements. Collective consultation and agreement are, indeed, recognized as effective methods for putting industry upon a sound and just footing. But its success manifestly depends chiefly upon a spirit of generosity and voluntary concession on the part of the owning and controlling classes in their dealings with their employees and the consuming public. Its appeal to the owner is that he shall regard his property as a moral trust, to the employer that he shall regard the welfare of his employees as a chief consideration in the conduct of his business, subject only to the wider public interest his business is designed to serve. For himself he shall reserve in the shape of profits, or wage of management, what he deems to be a fair compensation for his work.

That the hardships of competitive capitalism can be softened by this sense of responsibility and social service in owners of property and controllers of industry is unquestionable. But the moralization of the economic system as a whole by such private voluntary conduct is more doubtful. The justification of property, by consideration of the public service to which its owner may devote it, serves, perhaps unconsciously, to divert scrutiny from its origin and mode of acquisition. Here and there a rich man may put his wealth to a good use. But is there any guarantee that the capacity for acquiring wealth in the operators of our economic system is linked with a capacity for judging what are the best public uses to which it may be devoted? May not the two capacities be inherently contradictory? Again, so far as the better relations of employer and employee are concerned, or the relations of producer to consumer, it is difficult to find any agreed standard for the equities which take loose shape in such expressions as "a fair wage," "a reasonable profit," or "a just price." Moreover, excepting so far as this more generous and human attitude is "good business," its adoption must remain confined to firms that by their financial strength, control of markets, or special economies of production, are removed from the full strain of competition. Under free competition it is not feasible for a few competitors to practice generosity to their employees or to the purchasers of their product. Close combination alone makes this feasible, and the moralization of the members of a combine is something of an ethical miracle. For though intelligent self-interest will go a certain way toward humanizing industry, it will not go far enough.

The State's Part in the Moral Compromise

Having some recognition of the truth that a social problem cannot be solved adequately by individual action, economists and business men sometimes realize that organized society, the state, must lend its help and its control in order to establish a general minimum rule of subsistence and decency for the whole body of the industrial population, leaving the play of business competition and coöperation to operate only above the level of this common rule. Modern ethics also usually recognizes that the state has other functions of a quasi-economic order to perform, in rendering available, on equal terms for all, such services as health, education, and some forms of recreation, which private enterprise cannot profitably undertake. But economists in general still adhere to the early conception of the state's restricted rights of interference in the business sphere. They look with jealousy and suspicion at all proposals of national ownership and operation, even of the railroads, power resources, and monetary system of the nation, as illegitimate encroachments upon private enterprise. They refuse to regard the state as the moral guardian of the nation, responsible for safeguarding its inhabitants against exploitation of monopolists. Although the state, by its protective and other services, quite manifestly ranks as an important contributor to the efficiency of economic production, the tax-revenue needed for the performance of these services is commonly regarded as a confiscation, instead of as an income earned and belonging by right to the state.

The Deeper Rift Between Economics and Ethics

There remains a deeper rift between economics and ethics in the persistent refusal of economists to submit to any standard of human equity or welfare the processes of bargaining, or price-fixing, that play the central rôle in business operations. I have already touched this point in speaking of the absence of any criterion for "fair wage," "just prices," or "reasonable profit." This defect is inherent in an economic science which, according to Dr. Pigou, "is a positive science of what is and tends to be, and not a normative science of what ought to be." So long as economists confine themselves to a purely descriptive analysis of actual economic structure and processes, this refusal of all ethical considerations is proper enough. But when they take an evolutionary view of the economic system, and concern themselves with the wills and desires of the participants in changing methods of production, discussing new relations between capital and labor, or between producer and consumer, or the functions of the state in industry, it is impossible to keep out "normative science." Adjustments in those processes of bargaining that apportion work and wealth are quite manifestly affected by the equities and human considerations which they contain, and which affect not only the physical efficiency but the good will and effective coöperation of the participants of production. An economic psychology which could devise sound methods of coördinating wills of employers and employed in some common sense of the social utility of the work they were doing would evidently be assisting in the process of economic evolution which economic science professes to study.

Ethical Interpretations of Wealth and Value

The chief barrier, however, between economics and ethics, has been the different conceptions of wealth and value taken by the two respectively. So long as wealth is envisaged in quantities of goods and services, objectively regarded, and its value in purely monetary terms, it has no human, no ethical significance. Of a given stock of goods, expressed in terms of money, you can make no estimate whatever regarding the utilities of human satisfactions it represents, even accepting a purely hedonistic calculus. For the subjective or human value, attaching to any given goods or property, may vary indefinitely with the nature and distribution of the human efforts engaged in producing them, and with the mode of their use or consumption. Economic science definitely approached this problem when the concept of producers' and consumers' surplus was introduced into the cost and utility analysis of value. But though Giessen in his *Gesetze des menschlichen Verkehrs* published the outlines of a calculus of comparative utilities and disutilities, little progress has been made along these lines. Stanley Jevons, the first British economist to realize that "political economy must be founded upon a full and accurate investigation of the condition of utility: and as we understand this element, we must necessarily examine the character and the desires of man," nevertheless failed to apply his accepted principle in any consistent way to the wants and desires of man as affected by the processes of production. For as he elsewhere asserts, "the whole theory of economy depends upon a correct theory of consumption." In this contention he has been followed by most of our neo-classical economists, who, taking consumption as the economic goal, treat the wants and desires of man exclusively from the standpoint of consumptive utility or satisfaction, ignoring the need of a corresponding recognition of human needs and desires conveyed in workmanship. Even Dr. Pigou in his recent elaborate study of *Wealth and Welfare* relates the two elements entirely through the distribution and utilization of income, giving no attention to how the processes by which the goods that form the income are produced, affect human satisfaction. Yet all economists will readily assent to the proposition that a given quantity of concrete wealth may represent a larger or a smaller amount of burdensome, painful, or injurious toil, according to the conditions of the work, the hours of labor, the sex or age of the persons employed, and so on. If, then, we were to follow Jevons in teaching his science as "a pleasure and pain economy," it would seem self-evident that what we have to do in evaluating any economic system is to set the net satisfactions arising from the two processes of production and consumption against the net dissatisfactions.

THE STANDARD OF A "GOOD LIFE"

But such an analysis of wealth and economic processes, in terms of a current hedonistic calculus, would not bring economics into intelligible relations with ethics, which requires that some standard of a good life shall be applied in the assessment of those subjective economic values. For such a purpose it would be necessary to evaluate the economic life of man according to some standards of production and consumption that were in themselves desirable as contributing to the highest current conceptions of a good personality. But this implies supplementing the study of "what is" by a study of "what ought to be." Economists, especially from J. S. Mill onwards, though formally disclaiming any such intentions, are constantly led into side criticisms which contain ethical valuations. It is impossible, for instance, to endeavor to relate economic to non-economic welfare, as Pigou does, without making the connection. Still less can we study the economic functions of the state or the economic activities included under philanthropy without realizing that ethical standards of the intrinsically valuable play an important part in the actual direction and operation of an economic system. A science or an art of economics is bound to recognize these activities and the ethics they carry as germane to its sphere of study, and cannot dismiss them as belonging to a sphere of non-economic welfare.

Those who hold that an economic system is in large measure what man wills to make it, have in effect committed themselves to the position that the arts of industry and consumption are parts of the general art of human conduct, and that while involving specialistic studies of a highly technical order, the economic values they claim to yield must be brought into adjustment to the general conception of a good life. So regarded, the economic problem presented to any community will take this shape: Given a population with certain natural resources at its disposal, certain inherited aptitudes and knowledge, needs and tastes, certain institutions, customs, and traditions, how shall they best apply their personal productive powers, and how best apportion the product so as to support "the largest number of healthy and happy human beings." This, of course, assumes that there is an accepted standard of health and happiness, and "an optimum" of population for any country conformative to that standard. But these assumptions underlie all reasonable social policy or statecraft.

SELECTED REFERENCES

Bonar, James. *Philosophy and Political Economy.* 1909 ed.
Burns, C. Delisle. *The Philosophy of Labor.* 1925.
Cannan, Edwin. *Wealth.* 1920.
Cole, G. D. H. *Social Theory.* 1920.
Hammond, J. L., and B. *The Rise of Modern Industry.* 1926.
Haney, Lewis H. *History of Economic Thought.* 1923.

Hobson, J. A. *Work and Wealth*. 1914.
Hobhouse, L. T. *Social Development*. 1924.
　　　　　　　The Elements of Social Justice. 1922.
Hobhouse, L. T., and others. *Property: Its Duties and Rights*. 1915.
Jevons, W. Stanley. *The Principles of Economics*. 1905.
Marriott, J. A. R. *Economics and Ethics*. 1925.
Pigou, A. C. *The Economics of Welfare*. 1920.
Robson, W. A. *The Relation of Wealth to Welfare*. 1925.
Ruskin, John. *Munera Pulveris*. 1872.
Smart, William. *Second Thoughts of an Economist*. In *Proceedings of the Royal Philosophical Society of Glasgow*, vol. 44. 1913.
Tawney, R. H. *The Acquisitive Society*. 1921.
Urwick, E. J. *Luxury and Waste of Life*. 1908.
Veblen, Thorstein. *The Place of Science in Modern Civilization*. 1919.

CHAPTER XII

ECONOMICS AND LAW [1]

By ROBERT L. HALE

COLUMBIA UNIVERSITY

THE SCIENCE OF LAW VERSUS THE LEARNING OF LAWYERS

IF a science of the law be taken to mean an understanding of the effect of actual or possible legal arrangements on the various interests promoted or retarded thereby, it must be evident that some understanding of economics is essential to a science of the law; for many legal arrangements have economic results. It does not follow that an understanding of the economic effects of all legal arrangements requires the professional training of the lawyer; nor does it follow that the lawyer's professional training will help in such an understanding. The lawyer's learning is not the science of the law. The lawyer must understand how to ascertain the existing law, and how to predict the development of it through judicial decisions; he must acquire the technique of presenting to courts the kind of argument likely to prevail; and he must learn to advise his clients how to adapt their behavior to the law as it exists or as it is likely to be developed or modified by judical decision. While he is likely to understand the effect of legal arrangements on the economic interests of his own clients, he is not necessarily concerned with the effect on the interests of more remote groups or persons.

SOME LEGAL POLICIES DETERMINED BY LAYMEN

There are some legal arrangements of important economic significance with the policy of which the lawyer as such is not concerned at all. Such arrangements include patent laws, tariffs, taxation, public expenditures, currency laws, and the administration of public

[1] The subject-matter of this paper is handled along other lines by John R. Commons, in a paper, "Law and Economics," in the *Yale Law Journal*, Feb., 1925, xxxiv, p. 371, and in his somewhat formidable book, *Legal Foundations of Capitalism* (1924). Since this article was written, an extremely suggestive article has appeared by K. N. Llewellyn entitled, "Effect of Legal Institutions upon Economics," in the *American Economic Review*, Dec., 1925, xv, p. 665, and an excellent book by John Maurice Clark, *Social Control of Business* (1926). Not a good deal has been written in the general field, but very many books and articles dealing with detailed problems common to law and to economics have appeared. Some of them are referred to in the course of this article.

lands. The lawyer has to take cognizance of the existence of such laws, and has to concern himself with detailed questions of their application and construction. But the economic policy governing their enactment or non-enactment is determined by the legislature, not the courts; and the lawyer's professional training gives him no special qualification for predicting the behavior of legislatures, and requires no special understanding of what would be good legislative policy.

SOME ECONOMIC POLICIES DETERMINED BY COURTS

There are other legal arrangements, however, for the policy of which the courts are more responsible; in regard to these arrangements it might be professionally advantageous to a lawyer, who has to address himself to the courts, to be trained in the economic problems involved. Typical of such problems is that of determining where the risk should lie in industrial or commercial undertakings. Such a problem of economic policy really underlies much of the development of the law concerning forged signatures and endorsements and negotiability of bills and notes,[1] implied warranties,[2] and the passing of title in sales, liability of a principal for the acts of his agents and of a master for those of his servants,[3] liability without fault and the adjustment of the conflicting interests of the stockholders and creditors of an insolvent corporation. Many of the cases on these subjects contain no reference to the underlying economic policy, but proceed instead on grounds of unreal logical analogies. There is a tendency in the direction of realism,[4] however, and this tendency will doubtless be strengthened by the type of teaching making its way into the more modern law schools.

In the administration of the anti-trust laws, the courts have to determine what sort of combinations in restraint of trade are reasonable and what are not, and this determination obviously raises fundamental economic questions as to the limits of desirable competition.[5] When the policy of competition is abandoned in favor of regulation of rates and prices, the judicial determination of the

[1] Cf. Brannan, J. D., *Negotiable Instruments Law*, 4th ed., by Z. E. Chafee (1926), p. 572.

[2] See Llewellyn, *op. cit.*, p. 667, footnote 8.

[3] See Smith, Young B., "Frolic and Detour," *Columbia Law Review*, XXIII, 1923, pp. 444 and 716.

[4] Moore, Underhill, "The Right of the Remitter of a Bill or Note," *Columbia Law Review*, XX, 1920, p. 749.

[5] See cases in Herman Oliphant, *Cases on Trade Regulation* (1923).

constitutionality of any particular rate reduction leads the courts logically into an appraisal of the economic justification of the various advantages derived by individuals from the ownership of income-yielding property. The courts have for the most part evaded the issue by purporting to hold that reductions in income are valid only when they do not incidentally reduce the value of the property; but as there could not possibly be a reduction of income without an incidental reduction of value, and as the courts have permitted frequent reductions of income, they have clearly not held in fact what they have purported to hold. Their decisions in rate cases are chiefly mere jugglings with figures, and their behavior with respect to any particular rate reduction that may be brought before them is a quite unpredictable matter of judicial whim.[1] Should a consciousness of its illogical and self-contradictory character ever clear away the fog of judicial opinions on valuation, a study of the economic functions of ownership might prove a professional asset for lawyers who argue rate cases.[2]

In the development of the common law concerning strikes and boycotts, much depends on the economic opinions of the judges as to the justification of the object for which economic pressure is applied by the unions.[3] The better law schools are teaching this subject in a realistic way, and the teaching may ultimately bear fruit in a more enlightened attitude on the part of the courts.

Nearly every statute which applies to economic life — whether it be rate regulation or labor legislation or something different — can be said to take away somebody's liberty in some respect or to deprive somebody of property; many such statutes also bring about a *net*

[1] The doctrine of "valuation" in rate cases, its adoption and history at the hands of the Supreme Court, and its fallacy, are perhaps best treated in two articles by Gerard C. Henderson, in the *Harvard Law Review*, May and June, 1920. "Railway Valuation and the Courts," *Harvard Law Review*, XXXIII, pp. 902 and 1031. Cf. also the present writer's "The 'Physical Value' Fallacy in Rate Cases," *Yale Law Journal*, XXX, May, 1921, p. 710, and "Rate Regulation and the Revision of the Property Concept," *Columbia Law Review*, XXII, 1922, p. 209, and J. C. Bonbright's "Progress and Poverty in Current Literature on Valuation," *Quarterly Journal of Economics*, XL, Feb., 1926, p. 295.

[2] For constructive proposals for handling the problem of public utility valuation, cf. J. M. Clark, *Social Control of Business*, chaps. 22 and 23; John Bauer, *Effective Regulation of Public Utilities* (1925), and Justice Brandeis, concurring, in State *ex rel.* Southwestern Bell Telephone Co. *v.* Public Service Commission, 262 U.S. 276, 1923. For another point of view of the economic merits, cf. Harry Gunnison Brown, "Railroad Valuation and Rate Regulation," *Journal of Political Economy*, XXXIII, 1925, p. 505, reprinted in part in Smith and Dowling, *Cases on Public Utilities*, pp. 1011–13. Cf. also the answer by Bauer and rejoinder by Brown in *Journal of Political Economy*, XXXIV, Aug., 1926, p. 479.

[3] Cf. *Cases on Labor Law*, by Francis B. Sayre (1922).

enlargement of liberty,[1] or promote the safety or health of the community. The Fifth and Fourteenth Amendments of the Federal Constitution prohibit the national and state legislatures (respectively) from depriving persons of life, liberty, or property without due process of law. If the United States Supreme Court feels that the considerations in favor of the statute outweigh in importance the deprivation of liberty or property involved, the deprivation will be held to be *with* due process of law and the statute upheld; otherwise it will be held to be a deprivation without due process and the statute annulled.[2] The striking of the balance can be done intelligently only if there is a realistic understanding of the economic effects of the legislation.

THE FUNCTIONS OF PROPERTY

Many of the decisions which invalidate legislation on the ground that it interferes unduly with property rights are decisions which reveal judicial ignorance of the significance of property. Property is a complex of rights and duties, the central one of which is a curtailment of liberty whereby legal duties are imposed on the non-owners of any specific piece of property to desist from trespassing thereon.[3] Every one is under a duty not to trespass, but trespassing means committing one set of acts when the word is applied to one man, and a different set when applied to another. Whether the act of entering a given house without asking consent is or is not trespass depends upon whether the act is performed by the owner or by another. With verbal equality the law curtails the liberty of every one to commit trespass; but it is not the same act that is forbidden under that name for each person. The prohibition of trespass has no content without the legal arrangements for defining what shall constitute trespass for each person. These arrange-

[1] Cf. the present writer's "Labor Legislation as an Enlargement of Individual Liberty" in the *American Labor Legislation Review*, June, 1925, xv, p. 155.

[2] This statement is believed to be substantially accurate. Not all judges put it this way, and lip service is often given to the doctrine that a statute will not be held unconstitutional unless its unconstitutionality is so clear that reasonable men cannot doubt it. Moreover, the opinions rendered in these cases frequently make only indirect reference to the Court's view of the policy of the statute, and have a specious appearance of proceeding, without regard to the Court's views, from premise to inevitable conclusion.

[3] The word "trespass" is used here for convenience in the loose, non-technical meaning of any illegal act of meddling with another's property, whether the property be realty or personalty.

ments are the rules governing the acquisition of titles to property.[1]

* PROPERTY VERSUS LEGAL EQUALITY

It is often asserted that the policy back of the institution of property (hence the policy against any but the most imperatively necessary statutory modifications thereof) is the policy of equality before the law.[2] If this means that all have the same legal rights and duties it is clearly untrue in anything but name, as we have just seen, for the duty not to trespass is a duty the content of which is different for each person. And to say that these different duties of each person are equal is meaningless, unless it be specified in what respect they are equal. Certainly they are not equal in economic significance. They are at most equal in the sense that any one who can show the existence of a right will get the same sort of legal protection as will any one else who can show the existence of the same sort of right in himself. But in that sense of the word, they would remain just as equal after any proposed statutory modification of property as they were before. In fact, it would be difficult to conceive a legal system of which that sort of equality could not be predicated. Even in feudal times any one who could show that he had the rights of a lord could get just as favorable treatment as any one else who could show he had the same rights.

Frequently, however, it is maintained that the unequal property rights are the outcome of the equal application of equal rules governing the acquisition of titles. Any one may acquire property by producing it or by voluntary contractual transfer, it is said; to put statutory restrictions on the terms which persons may incorporate in their contracts would be to disturb this equality of the opportunity to acquire property with all its incidents; it would be to revert from contract to status as the basis of our legal relationships.[3] But the opportunity to acquire property by production is not equal unless all are equally at liberty to produce it; and he who owns no raw materials or apparatus is guilty of trespass if he produces without the consent of some one who does own them. And there never

[1] The unreality of the theory of Natural Liberty in the context of property rights was pointed out by Thorstein Veblen (1904), in *The Theory of Business Enterprise*, chap. VIII.
[2] Cf. for instance, "The Menace of New Privilege," by George W. Alger, in the *Atlantic Monthly*, CXXVII, Feb., 1921, p. 146.
[3] This view is set forth by the late Professor John Chipman Gray in the Preface to the second edition of his *Restraints on the Alienation of Property* (1895).

was a time when all had approximately equal property rights in the means of production. As for the opportunity to acquire property by contract, here again there is no equality, since the man who starts with valuable property rights has a greater opportunity to acquire more than does he who starts without much property. There never was a time when all started with the same. This is particularly true when we are speaking of the persons with unequal rights who are now living; for even if we assumed that the founders of our present rich families acquired their wealth in equal competition with others, it would still be true that the living heirs had wealth-getting opportunities of greater economic value than those of the persons who started poor. And the living heirs are not identical with their dead ancestors, or with the dead non-ancestral benefactors who left them property by will. It is the law of inheritance and of wills that has attached to the facts of family relationship and of testamentary devise a legal and an economic significance; and has conferred upon the beneficiaries the status of owners of property which they themselves neither produced nor acquired by contractual transfer. This important fact is overlooked in the theory that all the present owners and non-owners started with equal legal opportunities, and that the existing inequalities in rights are the outcome of their own activities. The rôle played by the dead and by the law's unequal conferring upon the living of the rights of the dead, quite alters the complexion of the case.[1]

Equality before the law, then, is not consistent with unequal property rights. And equal property rights would be almost an impossibility. Yet if the choice were clearly revealed to be one between legal equality on the one hand and the maintenance of some sort of property rights on the other, there are few who would hesitate to sacrifice legal equality. But the social and economic policy which requires the continuance of a large degree of the inequality inherent in our property system does not preclude all modifications of that inequality. In fact, it may require many.

PROPERTY AND INTERESTS IN THE EXCLUSIVE USE OF THINGS

Some years ago Professor L. T. Hobhouse made a distinction between property-for-use and property-for-power.[2] When the

[1] For a clear and concise demonstration of the impossibility of equality of opportunity, see pp. 529–30 of "The Economics of Unionism," by Alvin H. Hansen, in the *Journal of Political Economy*, xxx, Aug., 1922, p. 518.

[2] "The Historical Evolution of Property, in Fact and in Idea," contributed to *Property: Its Duties and Rights*, new ed. (1915).

wner of things uses those things himself, the legal arrangement
which restricts the liberty of the non-owners promotes an interest
of a very different sort from that promoted when the owner does not
himself use the things owned. In the former cases the interest promoted by the arrangement usually outweighs the interest that is
affected adversely.[1]

PROPERTY AS A COERCIVE ELEMENT IN THE DISTRIBUTION OF WEALTH

When it comes to property-for-power, on the other hand, the
situation is less simple. The owner of modern industrial property
has rights whose function is not to promote his interest in the personal use of the thing owned. He desires no personal exclusive use.
The primary interest promoted is the owner's bargaining power.
Because he can determine whether the law shall render the use of
his property by others lawful or unlawful, he is in a position to impose terms for rendering that use lawful. The terms imposed on
the workers include their surrender of all share of the title to the
goods produced with the help of their labor in return for specified
money wages. After production, the owner of the plant thus becomes the owner of the products and is then in a position to impose
terms on those who would like to consume them. In return for his
making their consuming of his products lawful, they must surrender
title to a certain amount of cash, or transfer certain rights against
banks (by drawing checks to the owner). Armed with the cash or the
credit, the owner is in a position to impose terms on other owners of
other products, and to obtain finally legal permission to consume
the actual things that constitute what economists call his real income. At every point in this process, it will be noted, his bargaining power is in some degree offset by counter pressure. First, his
laborers are under no legal duty (apart from contract) to work for
him, while he *is* under a legal duty to desist from violently coercing
them to work. While the *law* will coerce them (with violence if
necessary) from eating food which they do not own, and from taking
money which they do not own, and from producing goods with the
help of apparatus which they do not own (in each case unless they
can secure the consent of the appropriate owner); and while the
result of all this coercion amounts to an indirect coercion to work in

[1] For the shift of emphasis from "rights" to "interests," cf. Roscoe Pound, *The
Spirit of the Common Law*, pp. 91–92 (1921).

some one's employ; still, the circumstances may be such as to give the workers considerable bargaining power as against the employer depending upon how tightly woven is the network of property duties which surround them, on how scarce a variety of labor each one of them possesses in his own person, and on how much opportunity they have to unite their individual powers to withhold their labor. This power to withdraw their labor gives them a certain coercive power against the owner, and lessens his power to impose terms on *them*. Then, again, the customers' power to withhold their cash or credit limits the owner's power to charge prices for the products. Finally, the owner must reckon with the power of those who own the goods which he buys for his ultimate consumption. The result is a network of coercive pressures and counter-pressures of varying strength, each pressure consisting in the last analysis either of the power to lock or to unlock the bars which the law erects against the non-owners of each piece of property, or else of the power to withhold or not to withhold labor. These pressures are what enable each person to obtain such share as he can of the goods produced by the industrial system.[2]

DISTRIBUTION OF WEALTH AND THE ECONOMISTS

The resulting incomes have been classified by economists into various categories — wages, interest, rent, competitive profits, monopoly profits. Much has been written on the distribution of wealth and on whether it conforms to costs, or to productivity, and on whether it is justified or should be reformed. Some of the discussion is question-begging, since the concept of specific productivity amounts in last analysis to the loss of production that would follow should the person who controls any factor in production withdraw that factor, and his power to withdraw it is the very essence of his bargaining power, which is the very thing in question. The bargaining power under existing legal arrangements cannot be justified by showing that it results in incomes proportionate to bargaining power. Similarly, the concept of cost is frequently (but not always) taken to mean either what the person who controls any factor of production can compel an entrepreneur to pay

[1] Compare a suggestive article "The Labor Shortage," by Henry P. Fairchild, in the *Survey*, July 17, 1920.

[2] The writer has treated this matter in more detail in an article "Coercion and Distribution in a Supposedly Non-coercive State," in the *Political Science Quarterly*, XXXVIII, Sept., 1923, p. 470.

for its use, or what the person who controls it could obtain by using it himself in the production of wealth — the result in either case depending upon existing bargaining power. There are some rewards that must be paid, however, irrespective of the bargaining system, if certain productive activities are to be expected. To what extent the existing distribution of bargaining power suffices, to what extent it more than suffices, to what extent it fails to suffice to provide the minimum incentives for the maximum production is a legitimate and not a question-begging problem. When economic discussion addresses itself to the relation between prices and costs in this sense, it is in point; and much of it does address itself to this point, not only in general works on distribution, but in the treatment of the more specific problems of the shifting and incidence of taxation. Moreover, when cost is taken to mean actual sacrifice of *anything other than present bargaining power*, a discussion of the relation of distribution to costs may be in point. But the ambiguous word "cost" should be avoided or so carefully defined as to exclude the question-begging meaning above referred to.[1]

SCIENCE AND THE NORMS OF DISTRIBUTION

Of course, the most that any legal or economic science can tell us with regard to distribution is whether any particular legal arrangements (existing or imagined) tend to make distribution conform to incentives, or to sacrifices, or to needs, or to some other norms. It cannot tell us at what norms we should aim. The choice of ends is a matter of desire or aspiration, not of fact.[2] Much of the contro-

---

[1] The writings of the leading economists on distribution are too well known to require enumeration here. For a more detailed analysis of some of the concepts of cost and incentive, the reader is referred to my "Economic Theory and the Statesman," contributed to *The Trend of Economics*, edited by R. G. Tugwell (1924). A clear exposition of the theory that interest on capital performs the function of an incentive to the production of the apparatus for further production is to be found in F. W. Taussig's *Principles of Economics* and in T. N. Carver's *Distribution of Wealth*. The passage in the latter is reprinted in one of Professor Carver's later works, *Principles of National Economy* (1921). A contrary view of the function of interest is to be found in *Profit and Wages* by G. A. Kleene (1916), elaborated into some very interesting ramifications by the same writer in an article, "Productive Apparatus and the Capitalist," in the *Journal of Political Economy*, xxxi, Feb., 1923, p. 1. Cf. on the same subject an article by A. B. Wolfe, in the *Quarterly Journal of Economics*, xxxv, Nov., 1920, p. 1. The leading work on the shifting of taxes is E. R. A. Seligman's *Shifting and Incidence of Taxation*. J. M. Clark's *Economics of Overhead Costs* (1923), is an illuminating analysis of some of the cost problems that are particularly in point.

[2] For an excellent discussion of the ethics of distribution, see Frank Chapman Sharp's "The Problem of a Fair Wage," in the *International Journal of Ethics*, xxx, 1920, p. 372.

versy over specific distributive legal arrangements, however, turns upon means rather than ends, and to this extent the controversy is in the field of economic and legal science. As some of these questions are involved in decisions affecting the validity of statutory modifications of property rights, a part of the field of economic and legal science might come properly within the range of the learning of lawyers. But lawyers are given no training in this science, because the courts usually assume that the economic consequences are justifiable simply because they are consequences of property rights which are supposed to be a fruit of legal equality; whereas in fact the property rights are part of a legal arrangement whereby the law curtails the liberty of different individuals in different degrees, and the justifiability of the particular arrangements depends on the justifiability of the economic results rather than the reverse. The courts therefore take a distorted view of the justification for particular statutory modifications of the institution. It is as if one judged the wisdom of applying the brakes with no reference whatever to the speed of the car or to the circumstances of traffic which affect the desirability of that speed.

Modifications of Property and International Conflicts of Interest

When legislation modifies the economic results of property, whether consciously or incidentally, conflicts of interest emerge. If a tax is levied on the owners of natural resources, and if the tax reduces their income so that it furnishes less of an incentive than formerly to productive activity, the output of their products will decrease and the price rise. The conflict is between the consumers and the beneficiaries of the public treasury. If, on the other hand, the tax takes away only the surplus above what was functioning as an incentive, the owners (having the same supply to market as before) will be unable to shift the tax to the consumers, and the conflict is between the owners and the beneficiaries of the public treasury. In either case, after the tax is collected there is a further conflict of interest as to the disposition of the proceeds — some having more to gain if the state spends the revenue on roads, some if it spends it on schools or public health. As a tax is a legal arrangement, the tracing out of the various conflicting interests is a matter both of legal and of economic science. If all parties to the conflict are residents of the same state, however, the question is as a rule left to the legislature for determination and becomes no part of the learning of lawyers. It might conceivably be attacked in the courts as a deprivation of property, but such cases are much rarer with regard to taxation than with regard to other kinds of modification of income distribution.

Suppose, however, it is a foreign country that imposes the tax, and that some of the interests affected are the interests of citizens of this country. If the foreign country is weak, the conflict of interests is likely to awaken the activities of diplomats, and these diplomats are likely to appeal to something that sounds like a legal principle. When Mexico attempts to levy a high tax on natural resources, the American State Department appeals to the supposed principle that property may not be confiscated by taxation [1]; the Mexican government appeals to the principle of national sovereignty. Neither principle works satisfactorily. We have already examined the soundness of the first. The second would permit a government whose legislature represents but a part of the interests in conflict to resolve the conflict without regard to the foreign interests. Even that is apt to have better results than dictation by a strong foreign government, with the accompanying seeds of war. The solution of the problem is far less simple than that of the conflict of purely domestic interests described in the preceding paragraph, where all the interests have some sort of representation in the legislature whose authority settles the conflict. In the international field, however, legal science can at least demonstrate the speciousness of the pseudo-legal principles appealed to by the diplomats. This speciousness applies not merely to the principle that owners must not be deprived of the economic benefits of their property. It applies also to the principle of the "open door," so often evoked when the foreign country is not modifying property but is devising the rules whereby titles shall vest in foreigners. The "open door" rests on the doctrine of "equality of opportunity," the inapplicability of which to any modern system of property has already been pointed out.

These jurisdictional questions of legal science may at any time enter the field of the lawyers' learning should a world court be given power to mark out the limits of national sovereignty. Should that time arise, the lawyer might be prepared for it who is familiar with the underlying economic background of the cases which now reach

[1] Cf. note of Ambassador Fletcher, reported in the *New York Times*, June 30, 1918.

our Supreme Court under the Commerce Clause. Individual states in our country may take some action in the way of taxation, conservation of natural resources and regulation of the local activities of interstate railroads or other corporations, which have an indirect effect on the inhabitants of other states; other actions they may not take. To what extent the limitations on state action worked out by the Supreme Court conform to any realistic understanding of the economic facts, is a question of legal and economic science on which the present writer is not qualified to speak.

CONCLUSION

While the economic questions which courts and lawyers must even now handle are of surpassing importance to the community, they do not yet constitute a sufficient proportion of the work of the average practitioner to induce the professional law schools to devote much time to their study. Hence the bar and bench are quite complacent over the superficial treatment accorded them. Should ability to handle these questions intelligently ever come to be regarded as a professional asset, the development of a true science of the economic aspects of the law might follow. And the growth of such a science among lawyers might lessen the influence of crude economic ideas over the formation of other legal arrangements — such as taxes and tariffs and the diplomatic coercion of weaker nations — which are not the professional concern of the lawyer. For if the learning of the leaders of the bar included training in legal and economic science, it would be less likely than it is now for the ignorant utterances of politicians and bankers and diplomats to pass as enlightened economic statesmanship; and the leaders of the bar might less frequently than at present set an example of ignorance to the laymen.

SELECTED REFERENCES

Clark, J. M.   *Social Control of Business.*   1926.
Commons, J. R.   *Legal Foundations of Capitalism.*   1924.
     "Law and Economics."   *Yale Law Journal,* xxxiv, Feb., 1925, p. 371.
Ely, R. T.   *Property and Contract in Their Relation to the Distribution of Wealth.*   1914.
Hobhouse, L. T., and others.   *Property: Its Duties and Rights.*   1915.
Llewellyn, K. N.   "Effect of Legal Institutions upon Economics."   *American Economic Review,* xv, Dec., 1925, p. 665.
Mill, J. S.   *Principles of Political Economy.*   1848–1923.
Veblen, T.   *The Theory of Business Enterprise,* chap. 8.   1904.

CHAPTER XIII

ECONOMICS AND POLITICAL SCIENCE

By CLYDE L. KING

UNIVERSITY OF PENNSYLVANIA

POLITICAL SCIENCE is the science of government. Economics is the science of making a living.

There can be no making a living save under the protection of government. And there can be no government unless men can make a living. Futile one without the other. The line where one begins and the other ends is shadowy and is never at the same place from day to day.

UNITY IN SERVICE

What, then, is the relation of political science to economics? They are as closely intermeshed as law and order and the making of a living; or as security to life and security to property.

What is the end and the aim of life? Is it the pursuit of happiness? The pursuit of happiness leads through the highways and byways of community peace and of industrial security: one is political science; the other is economics. Is it the greatest good to the greatest number? This ideal fruits only in the light of democracy in government and democracy in economic opportunity: the one is the classical concern of the political scientist; the other, of the economist. Is it the gaining of life immortal in Elysian havens? The surest road to this goal lies not through the quagmires of persecution of the flesh, but through the straight and narrow path of peaceful endeavor. There can be no peace without government and no worthy endeavor without food, clothing, and shelter. Or is the sole end of life the propagation of the species? Both the numbers and the quality of human beings depend upon the service of governments and surplus wealth. Like ants and grass, microbes and elephants, men multiply mightily only under favoring conditions.

The purpose of life is as complex as life itself. And life is a unit of which political science and economics are but theoretical parts set aside for the convenience of study, but with each as dependent upon the other as the lungs and the stomach are upon the heart.

The heart of life is what we live for, and even that varies from year to year with each of us, and from age to age with all of us. Two, but only two, agencies through which life fulfils its purpose are government and industry, and both of these agencies are servants to the great purpose.

The economist worthy of the name is a political scientist, and the political scientist is an economist. And such is also the case with the sociologist and the anthropologist, and all the other "ologists."

HISTORICAL DEVELOPMENT

It may fairly be said that specialized scientific treatises on government preceded specialized and scientific treatises on economics. The why and wherefore of government intrigued first the minds of the social scientists. Aristotle's *Politics*, Plato's *Republic*, Machiavelli's *The Prince*, and Locke's *Treatise on Civil Government* had all found concise expression in the great charters of Anglo-Saxon liberties, and, enriched by Rousseau's *Social Contract*, in the Declaration of Independence and the Bills of Rights of American constitutions before the classical economists had bequeathed their heritage to the aspiring minds of the nineteenth century.

And then came the vogue of the "Political Economists." In the "political" part of those treatises was the creative mind of the modern political scientist, and in the "economy" part, the creative mind of the modern economist. The sciences then parted for a while, to their mutual loss. And now each group again acknowledges heartily their mutual relationship.

Both sciences are being re-created in the light of the outstanding services of all the social scientists of the past century. In this rebirth the economists took the lead, particularly in the recognition of the complexity of human motives now embraced in that inclusive term "psychology." But the political scientist to-day is venturing, too, into the same fields that keep all social scientists kin.

SOME ILLUSTRATIONS

The income and the expenditures of government are the pocket nerves of political science. In summary form they make up the budget, and the budget will usually be classed as economics. However, the budget is nothing more, on the expenditure side, than services put into dollars; and the services of government constitute the main study of political scientists.

A study of the function of government leads to a study of rate regulation and price economics; of monopolies and their regulation; through the Interstate Commerce Commission, to transportation; and through the Federal Trade Commission, to commerce. The function of government leads the inquiring student into every social and economic activity. Without a study of economics one cannot judge adequately of the functions of government; and without knowledge of the functions of government there can be no adequate inquiry into economic factors in modern industrial life.

The tariff is more a problem of international relations than of economics. A tariff scheme when adopted has economic effects upon the industries it protects and also upon those for which protection is denied. But nevertheless no industrial question is fraught with greater international consequences than national tariffs. The tariff may be more an arm of the military department than a help to consumers within a nation. Moreover, national life as embodied in the word "nationalism," will find its first definite fruition in tariff walls, and the forces of international economics work to break down these tariff walls.

We are committed in this country to a policy of fair price through competition, and yet governmental agencies are set up to raise standards of competition and, by raising standards, sometimes to prevent real competition. Such are the boards for licensing pharmacists. Such boards occasionally have a greater desire to limit the number of approved pharmacists and thus raise their income rather than to raise the standard of the work done by pharmacists. Lawyers express their desire for better income through staunch licensing boards, as do doctors, engineers, architects, dentists, and undertakers. Professions have learned through governmental agencies to raise their standards of living by raising the standards of the profession through law.

Once again: The quantitative theory of money has long been held to be a bailiwick of economists only. Recent European experiences show that it has consequences of governmental and international import far beyond its economic consequences.

Further illustrations are hardly necessary, for they would but emphasize and multiply the truth, to wit, that political science and economics are dependent upon each other for their complete understanding, for each is but a part of a single and greater whole — human life.

SELECTED REFERENCES

Beard, C. A. *Readings in American Government and Politics.* Pp. xxiii, 624. 1911.

Brooks, R. C. *Political Parties and Electoral Problems.* Pp. 638. 1923.

Bryce, Sir James. *The American Commonwealth.* Pp. 963. 1914.

Burdick, C. K. *The Law of the American Constitution.* Pp. xviii, 687. 1923.

Bye, R. T. *Principles of Economics.* Pp. vi, 507. 1924.

Clay, H. C. *Economics for the General Reader.* Pp. xviii, 456. 1920.

Coker, F. W. *Readings in Political Philosophy.* Pp. xv, 573. 1914.

Dunning, W. A., Merriam, C. E., and Barnes, H. E. *A History of Political Theories.* Pp. xii, 597. 1924.

Ellis, William. *A Treatise on Government, Translated from the Greek of Aristotle.* Pp. 284. 1888.

Evans, L. B. *Leading Cases on American Constitutional Law.* Pp. xliii. 1925.

Fetter, F. A. *The Principles of Economics.* Pp. xv, 610. 1907.

Ford, H. J. *Representative Government.* Pp. vii, 318. 1924.

Gettell, R. G. *History of Political Thought.* Pp. xi, 511. 1924.

Jowett, Benjamin. *Republic of Plato.* Pp. xi, 329. 1901.

Locke, John. *Two Treatises on Civil Government.* Pp. 320. 1887.

Matthews, J. M. *American State Government.* Pp. xv, 660. 1924.

Merriam, C. E. *Political Theories.* Pp. xv, 364. 1913.

    The American Party System. Pp. x, 439. 1923.

Munro, W. B. *Municipal Government and Administration.* Vol. i, *Government*, pp. xii, 459; vol. ii, *Administration*, pp. vi, 517. 1923.

Patten, S. N. *The New Basis of Civilization.* Pp. vii, 220. 1907.

    Theory of Prosperity. Pp. ix, 237. 1902.

Rousseau, J. J. *Social Contract.* Pp. 238. 1893.

Taussig, F. W. *Principles of Economics.* Pp. xxiii, 545. 1924.

Tugwell, R. G., Ed. *The Trend of Economics.* Pp. xi, 556. 1924.

Young, J. T. *The New American Government and its Work.* Pp. xvi, 743. 1923.

CHAPTER XIV
ECONOMICS AND PSYCHOLOGY

By Z. CLARK DICKINSON

UNIVERSITY OF MICHIGAN

THE constituency of persons who are in any way concerned or curious about relations between psychology and economics includes several wings, with diverse purposes. Some, of philosophic and literary predilections, cultivate only the larger aspects of our subject, in the grand manner; they propound and answer questions like "Who killed the Economic Man?" Others, with more of the natural-science-research bent, pay scant attention to such (to them) meaningless and futile dialectics; they keep their feet on the ground of small, inductive investigations in industrial or commercial problems. Some members of both of these factions, however, may be interested in an overhauling of their common background; in reformulating their views on the general scientific status of both economic and psychological assumptions, laws, and procedure; on the distinctive features of each science; and particularly on the special nature of the area where they meet and overlap. Occasional attention to these larger working conditions will perhaps help to avoid unnecessary jurisdictional disputes.

SUMMARY

A statement at this point of the main propositions which I shall emphasize may be helpful in tying together succeeding details, though it is not convenient to develop them exactly in the same order: Economics and psychology have always been, to some extent, interdependent, because their respective studies lead them into a common ground of principles of human behavior and of human desires and satisfactions; but the assertions occasionally made, over the past forty or fifty years, that economists were neglecting their duty by failing to keep up with the styles in psychology, were in many respects inaccurate and misleading, so that although they are "well-known" they are not altogether "facts." Some have erred in underrating the part which historical "accidents" and traditions, added to the cold, essential relations among phenomena, have played in determining the methodology, assumptions, and problems of these as well as other sciences; others have made the opposite error. In general they have overstated the extent to which economics, at any time up to the present, has been built on psychological theories; and they have overstated also the extent to which the new psychology has demolished the old. Many of the "well-known facts" concerning the falsity of associationist-hedonism are not true.

Although our sciences have developed up to this point more independently than is apparent on the surface, because each cultivated only small scattering portions of its ideal field, the border between them is now beginning to be cultivated with improved tools, as both basic sciences transform their older limited abstractions into more complex and realistic propositions, by means of inductive studies which are increasingly of the quantitative type. This approach toward common concepts and methods favors a greater use by each science of materials produced in the other field; at the same time, differences in relative complexity of phenomena are likely to multiply specialized sciences in between historical economics and physiological psychology.

THE FAMILY TREES; THEIR SUPPOSED MALFORMATIONS

Suppose we begin by noticing a few ways in which both historical movements and eternal qualities of their subject-matters have tended to determine the relations between economics and psychology. It is commonly stated that the two infants (early nineteenth century) were rocked in the same cradle by utilitarians like Bentham and the Mills, with the result that both were deformed by the paregoric of psychological hedonism. Another preliminary often used is: Since economics obviously studies a sort of human behavior (namely, "business" and "government"), therefore it must always be but a branch of the master science of human behavior, which is — psychology or sociology. These plausible propositions may easily be over-developed into the opposite errors mentioned above; we must qualify them considerably even for purposes of our hasty survey.

The first assertion exaggerates the extent to which these sciences were *created* by eighteenth and nineteenth century philosophers, and hence the probability that they had similar defects of foundation. Actually, Adam Smith and the other "moral philosophers" who expounded both political economy and psychology for a hundred years after him, found the characteristics of each science considerably determined by discussions which reach back into ancient times — discussions which, on the whole, arose from distinct practical and theoretical interests. Aristotle, for example, wrote a treatise "On the Soul" which clearly foreshadows modern psychology, embracing as it does laws of association of ideas and observations on the relations of pleasures and pains to action; also reflecting, as it does, the natural-science and ethical interests of the time. But the prototypes of Smith's *Wealth of Nations* are found more largely in practical and political contexts — in Greek works on household management and the revenues of Athens, in medieval discussions of money and prices, in early modern Italian bookkeeping and business practice, and in the maxims of financial advisers to kings. To some extent the older moral philosophers considered the study of commerce unworthy of them; and certainly the development of a pecuniary measuring-technique gave impetus toward quantitative science in the economic field long before statistical units were found for psychology.

The other half-truth mentioned above, that ideal economics is a branch of ideal psychology, has been grasped by methodologists for at least several generations; but practically, down almost to the present time, both sciences have been so far from their ultimate goals that their methods and problems have been about as far apart as the study of accounting or corporation finance now is from researches on mental tests; even farther apart, perhaps, for the latter branches all make much use of quantitative technique. For some years, however, each science has been gradually separating from its antique relics of private and public administrative arts and speculations on metaphysical, ethical, and esthetic problems, the core of positive scientific capital which seems to be characteristically its own. "Pure" psychology thus cultivates the elementary facts and principles of human behavior and consciousness, while various students promote intercourse with adjoining fields of the biological and social sciences (and arts), to the end that psychology may ideally become a complete account of "the mind." Economic science, on the other hand, continues to add small increments to its old heritage of systematic knowledge concerning a special field of inter-action between man and the rest of nature, namely, the production and use of wealth. Partly, no doubt, for historical reasons, we continue to schematize these latter phenomena by means of our Laws of Supply and Demand, or of Value. Economists of all periods, to be sure, have been humane enough to notice other types of causation within their subject-matter; practically all of them have dealt in "welfare economics" as well as in "price economics." Adam Smith, for example, gave some attention to the military and cultural aspects of tariff policies, and also to the effects of minutely subdivided labor on the character of the workman. Nevertheless, it is their methods of reasoning on the effects of all manner of factors, such as tariff duties, mass production, monetary and credit techniques, on wages and other *values*, that has most clearly distinguished the work of economists from that done in other human-behavior studies, like business administration, psychology, political science, or ethical or esthetic philosophy.

Controversies over Psychological Postulates of Economics

Development of connective tissue between these two bodies has produced numerous growing pains in the way of controversy. Some of the tissues it is instructive to notice.

An early discussion of the human-nature border of economics was that of John Stuart Mill (about 1830), who remarked that for purposes of abstract economic theorizing the following postulates were assumed: (*a*) "The familiar psychological law that a greater gain is preferred to a smaller one," and three master motives which oppose this desire for gain, namely: (*b*) aversion to labor, (*c*) desire for present, as compared with future, satisfactions, and (*d*) the powerful impulses which lead to propagation of offspring.[1] These and other postulates, referring to the "economic man" or the "economic nature of man" (as the German writers would express it), have been stated and revised from time to time. The concept "perfect competition," for instance, implies something near omniscience on the part of all competitors; for, although small children are almost infallible in preferring a larger to a smaller piece of cake, they are less aware of what course is dictated by self-interest in more complex transactions. About 1871 a new and fertile set of postulates was brought into economic science by Jevons and others — the ideas associated with the Law of Demand and Diminishing Utility, which have been so useful in clarifying the reciprocal relations between the quantities of various commodities available and their prices.

[1] *Essays on Some Unsettled Questions of Political Economy*, Essay v.

Many of the classical economists were inclined toward the philosophy which sought to place ethics on rational and democratic grounds rather than theistic or intuitive, and they tended to assume that all propositions relating to human motives could be summed up in the psychological-hedonism formula: "Nature has placed mankind under two sovereign masters, pleasure and pain."

But there were always parties of opposition. Some of the leading blocs were made up of ethical-religious writers like Carlyle; some of historical economists like Knies; some of materialists like Veblen. They were always a motley crew as to positive doctrines, but they reassured one another that somehow "orthodox economics" was and is built on psychological quicksand. The idealistic attackers assert that economists have "libeled" human nature by representing the average man as a selfish, lazy creature and by ignoring his more god-like attributes. Mill and all his successors have answered the more sweeping versions of this attack by showing that economic theory properly purports to be only an abstract, simplified view of economic life, not a complete and realistic account. Wages, for example, are actually determined in part by custom and by ignorance of the real state of the labor market as well as by many other deviations from omniscient self-interest; but Mill contended that any one who had mastered the abstract theory would be better able to make the allowances necessary for such complexities and finally to understand the concrete situation than persons who have despised abstract theory and are unable to see the wood for the trees.[1]

Analogies are supplied by the laws of every other science (gravitation, for example) which cannot be applied to concrete problems without allowance for "disturbing factors," especially in the earlier stages of their formulation. Thus, in psychology, the hypothetical laws of instinct, of "reflex arcs," of variations in "intelligence," of habit-formation, are most valuable instruments when properly

[1] Mill, *op. cit.* Of course many economists, and still more politicians and business-men "economists," have disregarded this distinction and have tried to apply the abstractions directly to practical affairs. Mill wrote to Thornton in 1867, saying that the latter's book would " be very serviceable in carrying on what may be called the emancipation of political economy — its liberation from the kind of doctrines of the old school (now taken up by well-to-do people) which treat what they call commercial laws, demand and supply for instance, as if they were laws of inanimate matter, not amenable to the will of the human beings from whose feelings, interests, and principles of action they proceed." (*Letters of John Stuart Mill*, II, p. 90.)

It is true that Mill's expression quoted above ("The familiar psychological law . . .") may be interpreted as a claim to realistic psychological assumptions.

used; but since they cannot yet be fully exemplified or proved in most concrete cases, critics are usually able to persuade themselves that these laws have no validity.

And economists, like other scientists, attempt gradually to bring their hypotheses close to reality, so that their human factors will come more and more to resemble living men, and their assumptions in the law of rent approach nearer to the characteristics familiar to the real estate broker.[1] A great step in this direction was made by means of the "marginal" analysis applied to value, when it was seen that clear and usable laws of wages and interest could be drawn up without using the assumption that men are equally lazy or impatient to consume their capital.[2] The exceptional people referred to by the historical economists are thus in a measure provided for by our rubric "producer's surplus" — the idea that some producers would continue to supply their services even if the price were lower; but the "marginal" part of the supply is forthcoming, making the total supply sufficient to satisfy the demand only if the price is higher.

This defense of abstraction, then, answers pretty well the common charge that the older economics was falsely based on the supposition that men are "rational." The other common assertion, that the older sciences of psychology and economics were vitiated by false conceptions of the motivating powers of pleasures, pains, desires, and such-like entities, will presently be seen to be less formidable than is often supposed, as we notice the trend of modern psychology.

CHARACTERISTICS OF PRESENT-DAY PSYCHOLOGY AND ECONOMICS

The above-mentioned efforts of psychologists and economists to refine and supplement their older, cruder generalizations, have increased both demand and supply in borderline material. Consider first the present state of fundamental psychology. There are still abysmal differences among various sects — structuralists, animists, behaviorists, psychoanalysts, and other types of psychiatrists. McDougall, Watson, and Titchener, for example, come nowhere near

---

[1] A good example of the use of degrees of abstraction to realism is to be found in F. M. Taylor's development of the theory of rent (*Principles of Economics*, chap. 38, 8th ed.). The method, of course, in this case owes much to von Thünen.

[2] See Carver, T. N., "The Place of Abstinence in the Theory of Interest," *Quarterly Journal of Economics*, VIII, 1893, pp. 40–61; "The Theory of Wages Adjusted to Recent Theories of Value," *ibid.*, 1894, pp. 377–402.

agreeing as to which one, mind or body, is the cart, and which the horse; or what sort of harness binds them together. Consequently economists are still able to choose their psychological and metaphysical authorities to suit their own predilections. Yet there seems to be increasing coöperation among all camps toward research work that in effect tests further and further the hypothesis that both body and mind are subject to unchanging (and infinitely complex) natural laws, and that there is some definite linkage between them so that their phenomena may be studied in either the subjective or the objective aspect (that is, by introspection of one's own consciousness, or by observation of behavior), somewhat as you may study your electric system either in terms of its illumination in your parlor or in terms of its meter in your cellar. Not many sensible scientists suppose that the mysteries of mind will ever be fully explored by human investigators, or those of the body or of electricity either. It is not necessary that a student should *believe* the mechanistic hypothesis with all his heart and soul in order to be an effective psychologist or other sort of scientist, but so far as he is interested in scientific laws at all, he is interested to see how far the determinist hypothesis can be pushed,[1] not in denying on metaphysical grounds that further explanation and prediction will ever be possible.

How has this drift in fundamental psychological theory affected our social-psychological disputes over instinct versus pleasure-pain, fixity or plasticity of human nature? It provides further means for arbitration. Thus, the probability grows that we have numerous generic "innate tendencies" toward certain types of behavior, which, from the physiological or objective point of view, are congenital and hereditary characters (connections in the nervous system, hormones, or what not), whose operations (when the appropriate stimuli are supplied by the environment) give rise, in human

---

[1] As evidence for the conclusion that mental states are linked consistently to certain bodily conditions (either one you like as "cause"), we have now not merely such physiology of the sense-organs as was used by the association-psychologists, but also the remarkable similarities recently discovered between laws of "association of ideas," revealed partly by introspection, and laws of motor habit-formation, revealed by objective, statistical studies of behavior of both human and lower animals. There is also the psycho-analytic demonstration that personalities can hardly be accounted for wholly in terms of conscious states; they seem to require the assumption of "subconscious" factors, which laboratory psychologists suspect to be mainly habits whose consciousness has become dormant or non-existent.

R. S. Woodworth's *Dynamic Psychology* is a good brief statement on relations among the various psychological sects.

beings at least, to characteristic states of consciousness. The clearest cases, of course, are the reflexes and instincts, narrowly so-called, which are ready to function at birth, like sucking and crying; with their probable correlates of sensation, emotion, and feeling. Because there are so few of these reactions, which clearly owe *nothing* to experience, some students hastily propose to throw overboard the idea of instinct altogether.[1] But most of the "innate tendencies" which are of special interest to social scientists are probably described rather as flowing from congenital structures which determine in some degree the facility with which the individual may *acquire habits* of a given sort; which determine his aptitude, in short, for athletics, music, science, or politics. There are still sharp disputes among psychologists, to be sure, as to how important congenital differences of this sort are as compared with differences of opportunities for development after birth; but the analogies supplied by gross bodily characteristics, like height, which vary among individuals in close conformity with the probability curve; the series of cases from clear congenital feeble-mindedness to apparent congenital genius; and the other evidence which has accrued from biometric and mental test researches, have convinced most competent psychologists that considerable innate differences in most or all mental capacities are of the highest degree of probability. The more debatable questions are those of intercorrelations; which gifts or deficits (if any) tend to be high or low together?[2]

In this rather general disposition to believe that men are born unequal as to mental as well as to physical traits, modern psychologists differ rather sharply from their predecessors, the associationists, who were inclined to be dogmatic in their assumption that our native endowment of mental equipment is about the same from one individual to another — the appearance to the contrary being due to the omnipotence of experience in molding character. This particular "explosion" of the older psychology of "hedonism" does not greatly affect the older parts of economic theory, however, so far as I can see; though it does affect vitally the social-reform issues on which economists have always been free in expressing judgment. It is interesting to note that modern economists who talk much

[1] See, for example, *American Journal of Sociology*, May, 1924.
[2] A convenient, comprehensive, and able treatment is found in Cyril Burt's presidential address on "Individual Differences" to the psychology section of the British Association, Liverpool meeting, 1923.

of social psychology and the importance of the supposedly plastic social "institutions" for the ideal economic theory, are really so unhistoric as to repeat the general denunciations of utilitarian psychology which McDougall has popularized. Their instincts might be expected to enable them to recognize more readily their psychological kin in the old associationists, who also considered institutions plastic.

These qualitative trends in fundamental psychology seem to facilitate coöperation between psychologists and economists, for they require no very violent breaks from the traditions of either one. A more important unifying factor, between these two as well as among all sciences, is the increasing use of the universal language of statistical concepts. Statistical technique, in the form of accounting and public records, was developed first, I believe, in relation to economic and political data, because of its practical utility in these fields and the early emergence of manageable measuring units. Adam Smith's political economy, therefore, was in some degree a quantitative science of human behavior, for many of his observations rested finally on some kind of governmental or private bookkeeping. Experimental psychology reached the quantitative stage fifty years or more ago; and now it is a commonplace that in both sciences inductive attempts to establish empirical quantitative relationships (or "laws") are receiving rather more attention than the dialectic development of abstract theory. For this reason the above-discussed disputes as to whether the "psychological assumptions" implied in economic generalizations are sound, are attracting relatively less notice than was the case a generation ago.

An important aspect of this quantitative and empirical trend in both sciences is the growing emphasis on "objectivity" of method. The important sense of this term, I think, is that propositions or data are generally of the highest scientific value when they may be verified by any competent observer, and hence are not to be suspected of depending on any individual's bias or untransmissible skill.[1] Such objectivity is usually associated with some sort of measurement and repeating of observations, if it is no more exact

[1] J. B. S. Haldane points out that at present social and psychological sciences are less serviceable practically, for many purposes, than empirical skill such as politicians, preachers, actors, and business managers acquire. But such skills are less readily and accurately transmissible from one person to another than are objective scientific formulæ: and so their relative serviceability for practical control may in time become reversed, as has been the case in many manufacturing industries. (*New Republic*, Dec. 3, 1924.)

than taking a vote among several authorities as to which is the prettier girl or picture. Such a canvass as this illustration assumes does not necessarily give much objectivity, since the authorities consulted may all have imbibed their views from a common, and perhaps an unreliable, source. Data on consciousness, as to clearness of attention and so on, may thus be collected from numerous subjects, and their common features will be relatively free from personal idiosyncrasy, *provided* that the subjects are not told too much of what they should expect to see, and that negative as well as positive instances are faithfully reported. In these respects the work of structuralists like Titchener is characterized by a large measure of objectivity (which at bottom is only due regard for general logical principles), while the output of the psychoanalysts, who also collect numerous introspections, is as yet much less so.

CHARACTERISTICS OF RESEARCH IN BORDERLINE FIELDS

From these tendencies which affect our two sciences as wholes, let us turn to a brief inquiry as to how their respective natures affect, and are affected by, researches in their common frontier. At the outset we may say that most of the concrete psycho-economic papers thus far presented, which actually attempt to utilize techniques and important principles drawn from both sciences, are of the *deductive* and *abstract* type (the present essay may be regarded, perhaps, as an example). They attempt to show how a few broad concepts from one side may be used by or attacked from the other. Thus, we have numerous papers on the significance of the psychological concepts of instinct, of "interest," of insanity, for economics. (See bibliography at the end of this paper.) Oddly enough, few if any writers have yet attempted to discuss the significance of economics-materials for psychology.

Inductive, quantitative studies, on the other hand, in the borderland which is part of the *ideal* domains of both economics and psychology, have shown but little interaction of the larger characteristic methods and principles of both sciences. To illustrate: We have researches by economists on mass-reactions to partially controlled stimuli like prices, profits, wages, and taxes, all of which are continually enlarging our total knowledge of the regularities in human behavior and are, therefore, actually contributing raw materials for the psychology of the future. On the other side we have psychologists "applying" their techniques to problems of advertising, selling, and personnel administration, with practically no reference to distinctively economic *science* — for labor turnover or advertising data, investigated by logical statistical procedure, can scarcely be called parts of economics until somebody has shown how they make useful additions to the general body of that science. (Similarly, a bank clerk is often not much of a financial scientist, though he has complete mastery over the causation in one part of the field.) We realize, of course, that in the end these psychology-in-business researches are sure to furnish new and vital contributions toward the ideal economics which would explain all phenomena within the world of bargain-and-sale; but in general, those students who are able to understand the experimental technique involved have not been sufficiently interested in relating the work to economic science to study the latter seriously.[1]

Better integration is found, I fancy, between physiology and psychology in studies of fatigue and efficiency. From this fascinating firing-line of research are coming also, it is true, some very promising approaches toward interpenetration of psychology and economics, or at least a quantity of high-grade ore for refiners who are fairly competent in both basic sciences.[2]

Although it is convenient to classify psycho-economic researches into the two main categories of commercial and industrial or personnel problems, in accordance with the main sources of raw materials, it will soon be recognized that a great range of important classes of topics are susceptible of inductive investigation. Practically any division of economics involves a "human factor," whose mental reactions may be most comprehensively studied by

---

[1] Cf., however, A. W. Kornhauser's paper, "Intelligence Test Ratings of Occupational Groups," *American Economic Review*, xv, March, 1925, Supplement, pp. 110–22, and an earlier paper by R. M. Woodbury, "General Intelligence and Wages," *Quarterly Journal of Economics*, xxxi, 1917, pp. 690–704, for excellent beginnings, from the psychological and economic sides respectively, toward connecting mental-test research with economic doctrine.

[2] Cf. the paper on "The Interconnection between Economics and Industrial Psychology," given by Eric Farmer (who is an investigator for the British Government's Industrial Fatigue Research Board) before the joint meeting of the Economics and Psychology sections of the British Association, Liverpool, 1924 (abstract in *Journal of the National Institute of Industrial Psychology*, ii, April, 1924, pp. 78–83); various papers by Elton Mayo (investigator in the University of Pennsylvania's Department of Industrial Research), for example, "Revery and Industrial Fatigue," *Journal of Personnel Research*, Dec., 1924, pp. 273–81; and *Economics of Fatigue and Unrest*, by P. Sargant Florence (a Cambridge economist who has investigated fatigue by means of factory statistics). The reports of the New York State Ventilation Commission supply excellent examples of interpenetration of experimental psychology and physiology.

some reference to psychological science. In dealing with the motivation and the welfare of consumers we have a range of problems, including causation of wants, diminishing utility, the valuation and marketing processes, the basic laws of demand by commodities, the psychical mechanisms in business cycles, comparisons between desires to purchase and satisfactions realized when purchases have been carried out, and so on. Again, looking at our human subjects successively as workers, savers, risk-takers, citizens, we must eventually work out, as nearly quantitatively as possible, the influences which affect invention and technical progress, and a host of other relations; and we must even come back some time to great riddles like those with which psycho-economic speculation in a manner started: I mean the part of economic factors in determining social evolution, and the prospects of manipulating that evolution toward a more satisfactory social-economic situation for all people. In most of these cases the ground has been scratched, often greatly to the credit of the pioneers, but as compared with older fields of scientific work, they remain virgin soil.

Will it be long before the texts of both basic sciences will show riper fruits of this interaction than the generalities on instincts and hedonism? Doubtless we should not make too much of Watson's references to industrial studies in his treatment of the organism at work, nor his appeal to life insurance statistics for evidence against the supposed human acquisitive instinct;[1] but if you consider how much the present texts of psychology owe to past experimental work in the laboratories of educational processes — tests given to school children, and so on — you may not doubt that not merely the theory of individual differences in mental traits, but most other departments of our sciences, will gradually take cognizance of inductive work both in the laboratories and in the shops of industry.

SELECTED REFERENCES

The following references are intended to represent most of the various shades of opinion on our topic:

Anderson, B. M., Jr. *Social Value.* 1911.
Bagehot, Walter. *Economic Studies.* 1880.
Bentham, Jeremy. *Introduction to the Principles of Morals and Legislation.* 1789.

[1] Watson, J. B., *Psychology from the Standpoint of a Behaviorist,* chap. X and p. 255.

Boehm-Bawerk, E. v. *Positive Theorie des Kapitales*, dritte Auflage, zweiter Halbband. 1912.

Bonar, James. *Philosophy and Political Economy, in some of their Historical Relations.* 1893.

Boucke, O. Fred. *A Critique of Economics.* 1922.

Bücher, Karl. *Arbeit und Rhythmus.* 1897.
   Evolution of Industry. 1893.

Bye, R. T. "Some Recent Developments of Economic Theory," esp. Sec. 3, in *The Trend of Economics*. 1924.

Clark, J. Maurice. "Economics and Modern Psychology," *Journal of Political Economy*, XXVI, 1918, pp. 1–30, 136–66.

Copeland, M. A. "Professor Knight on Psychology." *Quarterly Journal of Economics*, XL, Nov., 1925, pp. 134–51.

Davenport, H. J. "Scope, Method and Psychology in Economics." *Journal of Philosophy, Psychology, and Scientific Method*, XIV, 1917, pp. 617–26.
   Value and Distribution. 1908.

Dibblee, George B. *Psychological Theory of Value.* 1924.

Dickinson, Z. C. *Economic Motives.* 1922.
   "Quantitative Methods in Psychological Economics." *American Economic Review*, Supplement, XIV, 1924, pp. 117–26.

Farmer, Eric. "The Interconnection between Economics and Industrial Psychology." *Journal of the National Institute of Industrial Psychology*, II, April, 1924, pp. 78–83.

Jevons, W. S. *Theory of Political Economy.* 1871.

Kitson, H. D. "Economic Implications in the Psychological Doctrines of Interest." *Journal of Political Economy*, XXVIII, April, 1920, pp. 332–38.

Knight, F. H. "Economic Psychology and the Value Problem," *Quarterly Journal of Economy*, May, 1925; "Fact and Metaphysics in Economic Psychology," *American Economic Review*, XV, June, 1925, pp. 247–66; also his contribution, "The Limitations of Scientific Method in Economics," in *The Trend of Economics*; and other articles.

Kornhauser, Arthur W. "Intelligence Test Ratings of Occupational Groups." *American Economic Review*, Supplement, XV, March, 1925, pp. 110–22; "The Motives-in-Industry Problem." *The Annals*, Nov., 1923.

McDougall, W. *An Introduction to Social Psychology.* 1908.

Mill, James. *Analysis of the Phenomena of the Human Mind*, new ed., edited by J. S. Mill, with notes by A. Bain and others. (A landmark in associationist-hedonist psychology.) 1869.

Mill, J. S. *Essays on Some Unsettled Questions of Political Economy.* 1844.
   System of Logic, esp. book VI. 1844.

Mitchell, Wesley C. "The Rationality of Economic Activity," *Journal of Political Economy*, XVIII, pp. 97–113; 197–216; "Human Behavior in Economics: A Survey of Recent Literature," *Quarterly Journal of Economics*, XXIX, 1914, pp. 1–47; "The Rôle of Money in Economic Theory," *American Economic Review*, Supplement, VI, 1916, pp. 140–61.

Ogburn, W. F. "The Psychological Basis for the Economic Interpretation of History." *American Economic Review*, Supplement, March, 1918, pp. 291–305.

Parker, Carleton H. *The Casual Laborer and other Essays.* 1915–18.

Robertson, D. H. "Economic Psychology." *Economic Journal*, XXXIII, June, 1923, pp. 178–84.

Snow, A. J. "Psychology in Economic Theory," *Journal of Political Economy*, XXXII, Aug., 1924, pp. 487–96.

Stuart, H. W. "Hedonistic Interpretation of Subjective Value." *Journal of Political Economy*, IV, Dec., 1895, pp. 64–84.

Taussig, F. W. *Inventors and Money-Makers.* 1915.

Tugwell, R. G. "Human Nature in Economic Theory." *Journal of Political Economy*, XXX, June, 1922, pp. 317–45, and his other writings, including his "Experimental Economics," in *The Trend of Economics*, edited by him, 1924.

Veblen, Thorstein. "The Preconceptions of Economic Science." *Quarterly Journal of Economics*, XIII, Jan. and July, 1899, pp. 121–50; 396–426; XIV, Feb., 1900, pp. 240–69; "Why is Economics Not an Evolutionary Science?" *Quarterly Journal of Economics*, XII, July, 1898, pp. 373–97, and other writings.

Viner, J. "The Utility Concept and its Critics," *Journal of Political Economy*, Aug., Dec., 1925, pp. 369–87; 638–59.

Wagner, Adolph. *Grundlegung der Politischen Oekonomie*, esp. book I. Part I. 1st ed. 1879.

Wicksteed, P. H. *The Common Sense of Political Economy, including a Study of the Human Basis of Economic Law.* 1910.

Wolfe, A. B. "Functional Economics" (esp. Sec. 4), in *The Trend of Economics.* 1924.

Woodbury, R. M. "General Intelligence and Wages." *Quarterly Journal of Economics*, XXXI, 1917, pp. 690–704.

CHAPTER XV
ECONOMICS AND STATISTICS[1]
By WARREN M. PERSONS
HARVARD UNIVERSITY

THE contributions of statistics to the science of economics depend, first, upon the scope, nature, and continuity of the available quantitative data relating to the production, stocks, exchange, distribution, and consumption of wealth, and, second, upon the development of appropriate statistical methods for handling the particular numerical data — such as time series — and the particular problems — such as the measurement of the influence of each one of a group of factors — with which economics is concerned.

What are, precisely, "the particular numerical data with which economics is concerned"? Numerical data expressed in units of value — prices of commodities and securities, wages, rents, interest rates — are obviously to be classified as economic statistics. Data expressed in physical units — yards, pounds, ton-miles, bushels per acre, kilowatt-hours, British thermal units, horsepower — when they are utilized in problems relating to the wealth-getting or wealth-consuming activities of men, are also to be classified as economic statistics. That is to say, if the argument is economic to which the numerical data of other fields are addressed, the data are economic statistics.

The term "economic statistics" may be defined broadly, therefore, to include all the numerical data of mass-phenomena which have an economic application. But there are certain data, expressed in units of price or quantity, which are *primarily*, or even exclusively, applicable to economic problems and economic theory. In the following survey the writer has particularly in mind the narrower rather than the broader field of statistical data.

THE GROWTH OF STATISTICAL DATA

To investigators and students of economic theory the volume and quality of the statistical data at their disposal to-day seems

---

[1] The author is indebted to his colleagues, Professors Crum, Young, and Taussig, for counsel and suggestions in the preparation of this article.

inadequate and unsatisfactory. But the data are inadequate and unsatisfactory only with respect to the economists' demands and vision. Comparing the data now available with those available previous to 1919 one finds that there has been a pronounced addition during the last six years to the body of "thorough realistic statistics." In fact the accumulation of new statistical series has been greater in the United States during the six-year period just elapsed than in any similar period of the past — and a like statement is probably true of Canada, Great Britain, and certain other countries. The recent increase in statistical material has resulted largely, of course, from the stimulus of the war-time necessity for information. But for the twenty-five years preceding the outbreak of the war the collection and publication of data had been increasing at an accelerated pace.

Even though the body of economic statistics has greatly expanded during the last thirty-five or forty years, the investigator finds that the *lacunæ* are still numerous, especially of data for less than annual periods. Thus, extensive monthly data relative to the physical production of important minerals and manufactured commodities, freight traffic, new building construction, retail and wholesale distribution, and banking conditions are available for only one country, the United States, and for a comparatively short period of time, since 1919.[1] The only data available in monthly form for most countries are: statistics of wholesale prices of commodities; index numbers of wholesale prices, retail prices, and cost of living; the production of a few leading commodities, such as coal, petroleum, iron and steel; exchange rates; unemployment; and statements of the condition of central banks. The price data are fairly complete back to 1913 or earlier, but figures for physical production, for the most part, are scattered.[2] Fairly extensive figures are available for the annual production in the United States of manufactured articles since 1899, and minerals and crops since 1879,[3] and less extensive figures are available for certain other countries and shorter periods

---

[1] Such data may be found currently in the monthly *Survey of Current Business* of the United States Department of Commerce, the monthly *Federal Reserve Bulletin*, and various private journals and statistical services. Annual summaries may be found in the *Statistical Abstract* and *Economic Yearbook* of the Department of Commerce. The Harvard Economic Service publishes a *Monthly Statistical Survey* and an annual *Statistical Record*.

[2] See the *Bulletin Mensuel* of the International Institute of Statistics, The Hague.

[3] See E. E. Day, "An Index of the Physical Volume of Production," *Review of Economic Statistics*, Sept., 1920–Jan., 1921.

of time.[1] Index numbers of prices are available for the United States in monthly or quarterly form back to the Civil War, and for Great Britain in quarterly form back to 1779, but those indexes have only recently been computed.[2]

Many of the records, which constitute the material for statistical research, have resulted by accident rather than by design. For instance, our figures for the personal distribution of incomes are a by-product of tax administration; bank clearings are a consequence of the process of check collection; and figures for building permits have resulted from the regulation of urban construction. It is only in comparatively recent years that such statistical by-products have been supplemented by special collections of data definitely planned to answer specific social or economic questions.[3] And it is a still more recent development for various organizations, such as journals, trade associations, and governmental agencies, to collect and publish current data, such as bank debits and figures for stocks and production of goods, expressly for the purpose of estimating economic tendencies.[4]

THE DEVELOPMENT OF STATISTICAL METHODS

The material with which the economist *as statistician* is concerned consists of quantitative data relating to the multitude of facts and events of the complex world of affairs in which we are immersed. In technical language, the material is numerical, refers to mass-phenomena, and is connected with the wealth-producing and wealth-consuming activities of mankind. The scientist, working in this field, has two objects: first, of *describing* specific mass-phenomena as simply and completely as possible by means of tables, charts, averages, index numbers, mathematical functions, and other statistical devices; and second, of *judging* his results with the object of making statistical inferences. In this description and judgment he may be obliged to adapt his statistical methods to the economic material with which he is concerned, or even to originate appro-

[1] See, for instance, J. W. F. Rowe, "The Physical Volume of Production for the United Kingdom," *Special Memorandum* of the London and Cambridge Economic Service, Oct., 1924.

[2] See J. L. Snider, "Wholesale Prices in the United States, 1866–91," *Review of Economic Statistics*, April, 1924, and N. J. Silberling, "British Prices and Business Cycles, 1779–1850," *Review of Economic Statistics*, Supplement 2, Oct., 1923.

[3] See, for instance, W. I. King, *Employment Hours and Earnings in Prosperity and Depression*.

[4] Cf. *The Problem of Business Forecasting*, p. 4.

priate methods.   But it is possible for the economic statistician to utilize a large portion of the statistical technique developed in connection with the general theory of probability and applied to data in other fields than economics.

INVERSE PROBABILITY

The fundamental problem of practical statistics, in economics or in any other field, is the problem of "inverse probabilities."[1] This is the problem of estimating the accuracy of a sample, of judging the significance of a difference between two averages, or of arriving at the constitution of an unknown "universe" on the basis of incomplete numerical data.   A solution of the mathematical problem by Bayes was communicated to the Royal Society of Great Britain in 1763.[2]   Laplace published a similar solution in 1774, and gave the expression for the *normal* curve of the distribution of errors in 1783.[3]   Forty years later Gauss, starting with the normal law of distribution of errors, derived the method of least squares.   This method was promptly adopted in the physical sciences for arriving at the "best " value of a measurement from repeated observations affected by "accidental" errors,[4] and the Gaussian method remains to-day the standard process for reducing physical observations. The calculus of probabilities was applied to birth-rates, mortality, testimonies, and court judgments before the time of Laplace.   In his *Philosophical Essay on Probabilities* Laplace speaks of applying "to the political and moral sciences the method founded upon ob-

---

[1] Cf. Pearson, Karl, "The Fundamental Problem of Practical Statistics," *Biometrika*, Oct., 1920, p. 1.

[2] *Philosophical Transactions*, LIII, 1763, pp. 376–98.   Bernouilli's theorem (of which Bayes's theorem is the inverse) was published in 1713.   This theorem assumes that the a priori probability of an event's occurrence is *p* and proves that (under certain conditions) the most probable *proportion* of its occurrences to the total number of occasions is *p*.   Professor J. M. Keynes, following Bernouilli, looks upon probability as the measure of the strength of our expectation of a future event and, therefore, subjective.   (*Treatise on Probability*, pp. 4, 282.)   Professor J. L. Coolidge, following most mathematical treatises, defines probability as " a statistical, that is to say, an experimental science, and the mathematical problem is to establish rules which yield correct and valuable results."   (*An Introduction to Mathematical Probability*, p. vi.)   Whether one considers Bayes's or Bernouilli's theorem the "central theorem of statistical probability" (Keynes, *op. cit.*, p. 337) may depend upon whether he adopts the subjective or objective definition.

[3] Cf. Pearson, Karl, *Biometrika*, Oct., 1920, pp. 1, 25.   Professor Pearson says: "Laplace anticipates Gauss by some 40 years. . . . Many years ago I called the Laplace-Gaussian curve the *normal* curve, which name, while it avoids an international question of priority, has the disadvantage of leading people to believe that all other distributions of frequency are in one sense or another 'abnormal.'   That belief is, of course, not justifiable."

[4] Cf. Coolidge, J. L., *op. cit.*, chap. VII.

servations and upon calculus, the method which has served us so well in the natural sciences." He gives illustrations of various applications of the calculus of probabilities to the "moral sciences," but not to economics.[1] Its significance for and applications to economic statistics have been of comparatively slow growth.

In 1837 Poisson extended Bernouilli's theorem by dispensing with the assumption of equal a priori probabilities at every trial and thus arrived at a somewhat different curve of distribution from that of Laplace and Gauss.[2] Poisson gave the title "law of great numbers" to the principle underlying the regularity of distribution of observed facts, as expressed in his theorem. Adolphe Quetelet was much impressed by the work of Laplace and Poisson and became greatly interested in the application of the law of great numbers to the field of social statistics. His imagination was struck by the regularity which he found in the distribution of human statures, birth-rates, deaths from suicide, crimes, and other social phenomena. Quetelet was the popularizer of the theory of probability as applied to social statistics and the leading influence in broadening the collection of data. Sir Francis Galton and Wilhelm Lexis, however, contributed more than Quetelet to the founding of modern statistical method; and Karl Pearson and F. Y. Edgeworth were preëminent in its development.

Between 1875 and 1879 Wilhelm Lexis published a series of papers in which he made an approach to the problem of probability by observing the dispersion of actual birth-rates for different populations and times round their mean value. From this objective approach he concluded that all actual distributions of birth-rates did not correspond to the assumption of a *general* subjective probability and could not be accurately described by the normal curve. He assumed, as a result of this conclusion, that any general probability was made up of sets of special probabilities, and that the a priori probabilities would vary from set to set. These assumptions lead to a distribution which might have (a) normal dispersion (equal to that of the Bernouilli distribution), (b) subnormal dispersion, or (c) supernormal dispersion.[3] The contribution of Lexis

[1] Laplace, *Philosophical Essay on Probabilities* (English translation by F. W. Truscott and F. L. Emory), chap. XI. This essay was printed as an introduction to the *Théorie Analytique des Probabilités* in 1814.

[2] Cf. Rietz, H. L., editor, *Handbook of Mathematical Statistics*, chap. VI, "Bernouilli, Poisson, and Lexis Distributions."

[3] *Handbook of Mathematical Statistics*, pp. 85–87; Arne Fisher, *The Mathematical*

and his followers was mainly to relieve the theory of probability of its rigid assumptions and to make the theory more realistic by approaching it from the statistical side. The methods of Lexis were developed and applied by himself and his followers — Von Bortkiewicz, Tschuprow, Czuber, Westergaard — chiefly in connection with vital statistics (birth-, death-, and marriage-rates), but the same methods are applicable to certain economic statistics, such as unemployment ratios by states. The statistical problems, in these cases, are, of course, those of sampling and judging the significance of the dispersion of series on the assumption of non-normal (Lexian) distribution of the items.[1]

In 1885 an economist, Professor F. Y. Edgeworth, read a notable paper at the Jubilee of the Royal Statistical Society on Methods of Statistics in which the application of the theory of probability, developed by Laplace and Lexis, to the field of economics was explained and illustrated.[2] In his discussion the author made the very significant statement that "the Law of Error is equally applicable to the elimination of chance, whether it is, or is not, fulfilled by the observations whose means we are comparing." This principle is clearly an extension of the Laplace-Gaussian concepts, and is of prime importance for the application of the law of error to economic statistics.

Professor Edgeworth demonstrated his extension of the law of error in 1905.[3] "*The law of great numbers,*" he says, "states that if numerous observations, each obeying (almost) any particular law of frequency, are taken at random, their sum (or more generally linear function, or approximation thereto) will approximately obey the normal law of error."[4] This theorem provides the justification for applying the theory of probability to the problems of sampling and computation of means from economic data differing markedly from the normal type.

Theory of Probabilities, 1915, chap. x; Keynes, *Probability*, chap. xxxii, and Lexis's works there cited.

[1] C. V. L. Charlier, Swedish astronomer and mathematician, and Arne Fisher, Danish-American actuary, are recent non-German writers who have developed and applied the Lexian theory.

[2] *Jubilee Volume of the Statistical Society*, p. 182.

[3] Edgeworth, F. Y., "Law of Error," *Cambridge Philosophical Transactions*, 1905, and "Generalized Law of Error," *Journal of the Royal Statistical Society*, LXXI, 1906.

[4] Edgeworth, F. Y., "On the Probable Errors of Frequency Constants," *Journal of the Royal Statistical Society*, LXXI, June, 1908, p. 389. The article quoted is one of a series on the subject published in vol. 71 of the *Journal*, pp. 381, 499, and 651, and vol. 72, p. 81.

CORRELATION

The measurement of correlation between two or more series of corresponding items is the second problem, the solution of which is of the greatest importance to economic statistics. Indeed the problem of correlation, that is, of interdependent variations, is one aspect of the general problem of probability — the other aspect, which we have just considered, is connected with independent variations. To Sir Francis Galton is due the credit for discovering the correlation calculus. In his *Natural Inheritance*, published in 1889, Galton started from the relationship between parent and offspring and passed to the idea of a coefficient measuring the correlation between pairs of individual measurements.[1] In the early nineties Karl Pearson, F. Y. Edgeworth, W. F. R. Weldon, and others, starting with Galton's idea, developed the "coefficient of correlation" (r) for linear regression, found the probable error or r, and extended the theory to *multiple* and *partial* correlation, or correlation between several variables.[2] Karl Pearson has devised and recommended the "correlation ratio" for measuring correlation between two variables with non-linear regression, but the general problem of correlation, either for two or more variables, has not been solved.

The Galton-Pearson coefficient of correlation was developed in connection with biological studies and applied to parts of measurements of organs in the same or related individuals. Of a different type from biological measurements is the major portion of the data with which economics deals. Economic data consist largely of aggregates, averages, or relative numbers defined for selected time units, and these items, being *ordered* in time, have a characteristic conformation. The problem of the measurement of correlation in time-series of statistics thus demands special methods.[3] This prob-

---

[1] Cf. Pearson, Karl, "Notes on the History of Correlation," *Biometrika*, Oct., 1920, especially pp. 25, 28, 40. "Galton," he says, "created the subject of correlation; there is nothing in the memoirs of Gauss or Bravais that really antedates his discoveries" (p. 40).

[2] See especially Karl Pearson, "Regression, Heredity and Panmixia," *Philosophical Transactions of the Royal Society*, Series A, CLXXXVII, 1896, p. 253; F. Y. Edgeworth, "On Correlated Averages," *Philosophical Magazine*, 5th Series, XXXIV, 1892, p. 190; W. F. R. Weldon, announced coefficients of correlation, or "Galton's functions," as he called them, as early as 1890 ("Notes on the History of Correlation," by Karl Pearson, *Biometrika*, Oct., 1920, p. 41).

Coefficients of partial correlation measure the linear correlation between any pair of several variables *when the remaining variables are kept constant*.

[3] Cf. *Handbook of Mathematical Statistics*, chap. x on "Correlation of Time Series," by W. M. Persons.

lem has received attention only during the last five or ten years, mainly from writers in the United States.[1]

PERIODIC VARIATION

The problem of the correlation of time-series of economic statistics leads directly to the investigation of the various types of fluctuations — seasonal, cyclical, secular, or irregular — which time-series exhibit.[2] Are such fluctuations periodic or irregular? Is it possible to isolate different types of fluctuations? Provided that there are periodic fluctuations in one series, are there similar fluctuations in related series? These are problems to which the technique of Harmonic Analysis has been applied in the last ten years.[3] Economic series are rarely long enough, and the fluctuations (if they exist) are not sufficiently regular to enable harmonic analysis to yield positive results. It would seem that the periodogram offers the best *general* method for studying periodicities, but it cannot be said, at the time of the present writing, that such analysis has been fruitful. Periodicities in economic series have been neither demonstrated nor disproved by the application of the periodogram method.

The problem of seasonal variation in economic series is in an important respect — the known yearly period — less complicated than the general problem of periodicity. Methods have been devised for determining the regularity of movements from month to month and computing indexes of seasonal variation, upon the assumption that the seasonal variation is uniform for the period in question. Methods have also been devised for computing indexes upon the

[1] The "variate difference correlation method" was offered as a solution of this problem in 1914 (see articles by "student," Dr. O. Anderson, and B. M. Cave, and Karl Pearson, in *Biometrika* for April and November, 1914). But the method was based upon assumptions which could not be retained for series of economic statistics. (W. M. Persons, "On the Variate Difference Correlation Method and Curve-fitting," *Quarterly Publication of the American Statistical Association*, Dec., 1921, pp. 949–52, and Karl Pearson and E. M. Elderton, "On the Variate Difference Correlation Method," *Biometrika*, March, 1923.) The studies of seasonal and cyclical fluctuations during the last five years by various writers in *Review of Economic Statistics* and in the *Journal of the American Statistical Association* bear directly upon the problem of the correlation of time-series.

[2] Persons, W. M., "Indices of General Business Conditions," *Review of Economic Statistics*, Jan., and April, 1919.

[3] Moore, Henry L., *Economic Cycles*, and *Generating Economic Cycles*; Beveridge, W. H., "Wheat Prices and Rainfall in Western Europe," *Journal of the Royal Statistical Society*, May, 1922, p. 412; and Crum, W. L., "Cycles of Rates on Commercial Paper," *Review of Economic Statistics*, Jan., 1923, p. 17, and "Periodogram Analysis," chap. xi of the *Handbook of Mathematical Analysis*.

ssumption of a gradually changing seasonal variation.[1] But it annot be said that methods for investigating seasonal or other ypes of periodic fluctuations have become standardized.

INDEX NUMBERS

There is no branch of economic statistics that shows the advance f statistical method during the last twenty-five or thirty years nore clearly than index numbers of prices. In 1869 Professor N. G. Pierson, the distinguished Dutch economist, expressed the pinion that "all attempts to calculate and represent average novements of prices, either by index numbers or otherwise, ught to be abandoned."[2] This extreme view was probably ot held by the majority of Professor Pierson's contemporaries, ut nevertheless it indicates the skepticism of the time toward ndex numbers of prices. To-day no economist would take such position.

Previous to the middle of the last century, studies of the theory nd application of index numbers were exceedingly meager and scattered. W. S. Jevons, who in 1863–65 advocated the use of the simple geometric mean and worked out annual index numbers for English prices back to 1782, may be considered the "father of index numbers."[3] He kindled interest in the subject, but it was not until the eighteen-eighties that other studies of the theory appeared — by the Italian economist, Messedaglia, in 1880, by Edgeworth n 1887–89, and by Westergaard in 1890. At about the same time Sauerbeck and Soetbeer began publishing their well-known indexes for England and Germany. The general study and use of index numbers, however, did not really develop until after 1900 with the work of Edgeworth, Walsh, Fisher, Bowley, Pigou, Flux, Mitchell, Young, Knibbs, and others. Irving Fisher, a leading authority on the subject of index numbers, says that "although we may push back the date of their invention a century and three quarters, their current use did not begin till 1869 at the earliest, and not in a general way till after 1900. In fact, it may be said that their use is only seriously beginning to-day."[4]

[1] Crum, W. L., "Progressive Variation in Seasonality," *Journal of the American Statistical Association*, March, 1925, p. 48.

[2] "Further Considerations on Index Numbers," *Economic Journal*, March 3, 1896.

[3] Fisher, Irving, "Landmarks in the History of Index Numbers," in *The Making of Index Numbers*, p. 459, Appendix IV.

[4] Fisher, Irving, *op. cit.*, p. 460.

The foregoing survey shows that the important developments of statistical methods — of probability, sampling, and curve fitting; simple and partial correlation; periodicities and periodogram analysis; and index numbers — have occurred since the eighteen-eighties and that the applications to economic statistics have mostly taken place since the opening of the present century. During the last twenty-five years there has been a remarkable growth of the technique of statistics, but the development of methods strictly adapted to handling two of the most important, if not the most important, problems of economic statistics — the general problems of correlation and periodicity of time-series — is in its infancy.

STATISTICAL ANALYSIS IN ECONOMIC THEORY

Economists of the present day, for the most part, are not interested in dogmatic generalizations concerning the appropriate logical method to be used in economics. They do not dispute concerning quantitative versus qualitative analysis in the development of economic science, for they do not question the legitimacy of applying quantitative analysis to concrete economic problems or to general economic theory.[1] But they are interested in the concepts and assumptions used in statistical arguments, the advantages and limitations of statistical induction, and the probable fruitfulness of statistical analysis.[2] The economists of thirty-five or forty years ago who discussed the logical methods of their science do not give us many examples of the fruitfulness of statistical analysis, but they do give us valuable notions of the nature of economic laws and the logical position in economics of statistical induction.

John Stuart Mill, the leading economist of his time, called his method "the Concrete Deductive Method." The concluding book of Mill's *System of Logic*, published in 1843, is "On the Logic of the Moral Sciences." In this book Mill says: "The Social Science, therefore, ... is a deductive science ... after the model of the more complex physical sciences. It infers the law of each effect from the laws of causation on which that effect depends; not, however, from the law merely of one cause, as in the geometrical method; but by considering all the causes which conjunctly in-

[1] Cf. Mitchell, Wesley C., "Quantitative Analysis in Economic Theory," *American Economic Review*, March, 1925.

[2] See, for instance, chapters by various authors in *The Trend of Economics*, ed. by R. G. Tugwell.

luence the effect, and compounding their laws with one another. ts method, in short, is the Concrete Deductive Method." The mperfections of the a priori method are great, he continues, espe-ially when applied to society with its numerous conflicting endencies. But there is an appropriate remedy: "This remedy onsists in the process . . . of Verification. . . . The ground of con-idence in any concrete deductive science is not the a priori reason-ng itself, but the accordance between its results and those of ob-ervation a posteriori. Either of these processes, apart from the ther, diminishes in value as the subject increases in complication."

Sometimes there is an actual inversion of the two processes, Mill ays, so that "instead of deducing our conclusions by reasoning, and erifying them by observation, we in some cases begin by obtaining hem provisionally from specific experience, and afterwards connect hem with the principles of human nature by a priori reasonings, vhich reasonings are thus a real Verification."[1]

W. S. Jevons expressed what can probably be called the present-lay view of the position and possibilities of statistics in economics. Vriting in 1871 he said:[2] "The deductive science of Economy must e verified and rendered useful by the purely inductive science of tatistics. Theory must be invested with the reality and life of act." As an illustration of a statistical treatise "which treats ertain questions of Political Economy in a highly scientific and nathematical spirit," Jevons cites a work on *Railway Economy* by)ionysius Lardner, issued in 1850, and says: "The relation of the ate of fares to the gross receipts and net profits of a railway com-any is beautifully demonstrated, in pp. 286–293, by means of a iagram. It is proved that the maximum profit occurs at the point vhen the curve of gross receipts becomes parallel to the curve of xpenses of conveyance."[3] The work of Jevons himself offers illus-rations of the application of statistics to economics, especially in he field of index numbers of prices.[4]

This brief survey of the attitude of certain leading economists of n earlier generation toward the application of statistics to eco-omic science may be concluded by quoting from J. N. Keynes's cope and Method of Political Economy and Marshall's *Principles*

---

[1] Mill, J. S., *A System of Logic*, 8th ed., book VI, chap. IX, §1.
[2] Jevons, W. S., *The Theory of Political Economy*, pp. 26, 28.
[3] *Ibid.*, pp. 17, 18.
[4] See his essay on "A Serious Fall in the Price of Gold Ascertained," *Investigations* Currency and Finance.

of Economics, both published in 1890. The functions of statistics in economic theory, according to Keynes, are the following:[1]

First: "To suggest empirical laws, which may or may not be capable of subsequent deductive explanation." An illustration of an empirical law is the cyclical movement of business, first disclosed by repeated occurrence of financial crises and the fluctuations of commodity prices and other statistical indexes of business conditions. Another illustration is the seasonal movements of money rates. Theories of the origin and nature of cyclical and seasonal fluctuations did not precede, but followed, the collection of statistical data. Thus, Professor F. W. Taussig observed from a chart showing the silver currency in circulation in the United States each month, 1878–91, "a very distinct increase in the outgo or circulation of silver in the latter half of each year. That increase shows itself regularly," he observed, "even in years like 1885, when the general movement was toward a reduction in the volume outstanding." He then explained the observed autumnal expansion as a phase of the "crop moving" demands. The steadiness of this particular phenomenon indicated the additional conclusion, "that the outgo of silver money into circulation has by no means proceeded with that regularity which the legislature expected and intended, but has been very greatly affected by circumstances beyond legislative control."[2]

Second: "To supplement deductive reasoning by checking its results, and submitting them to the test of experience." This is the same idea as that more recently expressed by Professor Henry L. Moore in the phrase, "the statistical complement of pure economics."[3] Professor Moore's work offers some of the best illustrations of this type of analysis. For instance, he has made statistical test of the correlation between wages and cost of subsistence, between wages and the specific product of labor, between the increase of capital and the increase of wages, and between the general status of the laborer and the concentration of industry. The result of these tests is that the efficiency theory of wages "tends to be realized in actual practice."[4] Professor Moore has also made statistical tests of the

---

[1] *Scope and Method of Political Economy*, chap. x, "On Political Economy and Statistics," p. 325.
[2] Taussig, F. W., *The Silver Situation in the United States*, 2d ed., pp. 14–15.
[3] Cf. Professor Moore's article on "The Statistical Complement of Pure Economics," *Quarterly Journal of Economics*, Nov., 1908, pp. 1–33.
[4] Moore, H. L., *Laws of Wages*, p. 188.

aws of supply and demand.[1] Numerous other illustrations, with
ess mathematical flavor, might be cited as statistical tests of eco-
aomic theory. Thus, Professors John H. Williams, Jacob Viner,
and Frank D. Graham have tested various phases of the theory of
nternational trade.[2] It is evident, of course, that statistical tests
nay be thoroughgoing or partial. The course of many economic
arguments often turns upon the possibility of establishing specific
acts, of making specific comparisons, or, to use a phrase suggested
by Professor Taussig, "of verification in spots." Economic litera-
ure contains many such partial applications of statistics to eco-
aomic theory.

Professor Alfred Marshall's *Principles of Economics* was pub-
ished just a few months before Keynes's book on *Scope and Method
of Political Economy*. Marshall's view of the future of statistical
analysis in economic theory was suggested in his *Principles* in 1890.
But it was not until seventeen years later that he made an explicit
forecast of the development of such analysis. In an address before
the Royal Economic Society in 1907, he said: "Disputes as to
method have nearly ceased. . . . *Qualitative* analysis has done the
greater part of its work — that is to say, there is a general agreement as to the characters and directions of the changes which
various economic forces tend to produce. . . . Much less progress
has indeed been made towards the *quantitative* determination of the

[1] Moore, H. L., "Elasticity of Demand and Flexibility of Prices," *Journal of the
American Statistical Society*, March, 1922, and "A Moving Equilibrium of Demand
and Supply," *Quarterly Journal of Economics*, May, 1925.

[2] Williams, John H., *Argentine International Trade Under Inconvertible Paper
Money, 1880–1900* (Harvard Economic Studies, 1920). The author says: "The
purpose of the inquiry has been to test the theory of international trade under conditions of inconvertible paper money. . . . Accepting the data as on the whole adequate for our purpose, what they indicate is a partly general correspondence with
theoretical reasoning. . . . Two points brought out in the inquiry deserve special
emphasis, as indicating possible modifications, or at least the need of a more careful
restatement, of theory. . . . Too little attention has been given to the depressing
effects of the rising (gold) premium upon imports. . . . The presence of depreciated
paper money by no means renders necessary any dislocation of exchange" (pp. 256–
58).

Viner, Jacob, *Canada's Balance of International Indebtedness, 1900–13* (Harvard
Economic Studies, 1924). The author states his main purpose as that of making an
"inductive verification of the general theory of the mechanism of international
trade."

Graham, Frank D., "International Trade under Depreciated Paper. The United
States, 1862–70," *Quarterly Journal of Economics*, Feb., 1922, pp. 200–73. The
author says: "The purpose of the study was to subject to an inductive test the
theory of international trade under depreciated paper advanced by Professor Taussig in the issue of this Journal for May, 1917. . . . On the whole the theory receives
substantial verification" (pp. 220, 273).

relative strength of different economic forces. That higher an
more difficult task must wait upon the slow growth of thoroug
realistic statistics." [1]

Vilfredo Pareto, writing in the same year as Marshall, made th
forecast that "the progress of political economy in the future wil
depend in great part upon the investigation of empirical laws
derived from statistics, which will then be compared with know
theoretical laws, or will suggest derivation from them of new laws."
This concept of the possible origin and result of statistical investiga
tion was in accord with that expressed by J. M. Keynes, seventeer
years previous, which we have quoted on an earlier page.

Professor Henry L. Moore, who has made more notable contri
butions [3] to the development of "a statistical complement of pur
economics" than any other American writer, conceives of eco
nomic theory as a distinctly valuable "first approximation t
reality" and of "an inductive statistical complement of the pur
science without whose development the a priori instrument mus
lack effectiveness." [4] The actual results of Moore's statistical worl
in part verify pure theory,[5] in part suggest revisions of statement,
and in part suggest new laws.[7]

The bearing upon economic theory of the statistical investiga
tions of other writers has also been partly to verify, partly to call fo
emendation, and partly to suggest restatement. Thus, the result
of Professor Williams's studies of the "Balance of Internationa
Payments of the United States" [8] were to verify the existence of th
a priori invisible elements in international trade. The results o
Professor Mitchell's studies of the business cycle were, in his words
to show that "none of the theories of business cycles summarized i
Chapter I seems to be demonstrably wrong, but neither does any

[1] Marshall, Alfred, "The Social Possibilities of Economic Chivalry," *Economi.
Journal*, March, 1907, pp. 7, 8.

[2] *Giornale degli Economisti*, Maggio, 1907, p. 366, quoted by Henry L. Moore
in the *Quarterly Journal of Economics*, Nov., 1908. Pareto's forecast was undoubtedly suggested to him by his empirical "law of the distribution of incomes."

[3] Moore, Henry L., *Laws of Wages; Economic Cycles: Their Law and Cause; Forecasting the Yield and the Price of Cotton; Generating Economic Cycles*.

[4] *Quarterly Journal of Economics*, Nov., 1908, p. 2.

[5] *Laws of Wages*, p. 188. The efficiency theory of wages tends to be realized in
actual practice.

[6] *Economic Cycles*, chap. IV. The demand curve for an instant of time, *ceteris
paribus*, is replaced by one based on yield and price statistics over a period of years.

[7] *Generating Economic Cycles*, chap. II. The crop cycle is the cause of the economic
cycle.

[8] *Review of Economic Statistics*, July, 1919, July, 1922, Oct., 1923, and Supplements, April, 1920, and June, 1921.

one seem to be wholly adequate." [1] Professor Fisher states the origin and results of his inductive study of price indexes as follows: "The present book had its origin in the desire to put these deductive conclusions [of the Appendix to Chapter X of the *Purchasing Power of Money*] to an inductive test by means of calculations from actual historical data. But before I had gone far in such testing of my original conclusions, I found, to my great surprise, that the results of actual calculation constantly suggested further deduction until, in the end, I had completely revised both my conclusions and my theoretical foundations. Not that I needed to discard as untrue many of the conclusions reached in the *Purchasing Power of Money;* for the only definite error which I have found among my former conclusions has to do with the so-called 'circular test' which I originally, with other writers, accepted as sound, but which, in this book, I reject as theoretically unsound." [2]

In view of these results — and the results of other writers as well — it appears that future statistical investigations may lead to verification, revision, or, possibly, entire restatement of some economic laws. Dispute as to which one of the three results will be most apt to follow such investigations would seem futile.

Statistical investigations of the future, then, may be expected to make substantial contributions to economic theory, by both verification and emendation. But there are some economic questions to which statistical studies have not given an answer, and it is impossible to say that such studies will ever furnish an answer. Thus, the inductive verification of Fisher's equation of exchange, in Fisher's words, "is not completely to establish the quantity theory of money, for the equation does not reveal which factors are causes and which effects." [3] The equation of exchange "is only a statement of the problem of price levels," [4] and it is difficult to see how statistics can ever finally settle the question as to whether the sequence runs from prices to money and credit, or from money and credit to prices. To give a second illustration, statistics may never give us an answer to the question: Does the periodical glutting of the market and the occurrence of business depression arise from

[1] Mitchell, Wesley C., *Business Cycles*, p. 579.
[2] Fisher, Irving, *The Making of Index Numbers*, p. xii.
[3] Fisher, Irving, *Purchasing Power of Money*, p. 298.
[4] Laughlin, J. Laurence, "Money and Prices," discussion at the Twenty-Third Annual Meeting of the American Economic Association, *Bulletin of the American Economic Association*, April, 1911, p. 67.

mal-distribution of wealth and over-saving — Hobson's theory — or the time-using capitalistic process and the inability of producers accurately to forecast consumption — Aftalion's theory? A third economic question to which statistics has not given an answer, and may never be able to give one, is the net effect of tariff or free trade on the prosperity of a country.

The reasons that statistical investigations do not give us the basis for answering certain economic questions, such as those just cited, are not the same in all cases. Thus, in the first case cited, even though there were perfect correlation between the fluctuation of prices and the concurrent flow of purchasing power, these variables might be joint effects. In the second illustration, both mal-distribution of wealth and the time-using capitalistic process presumably result in the same objective phenomena: first, over-production of capital goods, and second, over-production of consumption-goods. The distribution of wealth and the capitalistic process are interdependent; it would appear impossible to alter one without changing the other (for instance, by socializing industry) so that if either be altered, the reason for a consequent change in production would be in doubt. Moreover, the concepts of "mal-distribution," "capitalistic process," and "over-capitalization" are so broad that statistical measures of them are difficult or impossible to secure. In the third illustration, tariff versus free trade, the differences between countries are too great and the instances too few to enable us to come to a conclusion from statistical evidence concerning the direct or inverse correlation between prosperity and free trade. If we had the records of many countries, say one hundred, over a period of years, perhaps the method of partial correlation would give dependable results.

The statistical investigations cited in the preceding pages prove, if proof be needed, that the devices of economic statistics — tables, charts, averages, index numbers, measures of dispersion and probable error, frequency curves, and coefficients of correlation — are not arguments. They merely furnish the basis for statistical inference. There is nothing novel in the argument of the statistician. Nor is there anything persuasive in the technique of probability, unless that technique is based upon assumptions which can be retained in practice.

Statistical investigations of the future, as in the past, may be expected to start with either current economic theory or some empirical observation as a "first approximation" and proceed to verification or emendation of economic law. Statistical description and statistical inference, then, may be expected to make economic theories more realistic, and in general to give us more certain and useful answers to economic questions; but some questions, such as the quantity theory of money, and free trade versus protection, are not likely to be answered by statistical investigations.

SELECTED REFERENCES

Edgeworth, F. Y., "On the Application of the Calculus of Probabilities to Statistics." *Bulletin de l'Institut International de Statistique*, xviii, 1909.

"Methods of Statistics." *Jubilee Volume of the Statistical Society*, 1885, p. 182.

Keynes, J. M. *A Treatise on Probability.* 1921.

Keynes, J. N. *Scope and Method of Political Economy*, chap. x, "On Political Economy and Statistics." 1891.

Laplace. *Philosophical Essay on Probabilities*, English trans. by F. W. Truscott and F. L. Emory, chap. xi. This essay was printed as an introduction to the *Théorie Analytique des Probabilités* in 1814.

Mill, J. S. *A System of Logic*, 8th ed., book vi, chap. ix. 1844.

Mitchell, Wesley C. "Quantitative Analysis in Economic Theory." *American Economic Review*, March, 1925.

Moore, Henry L. "The Statistical Complement of Pure Economics." *Quarterly Journal of Economics*, Nov., 1908.

Pearson, Karl. "The Fundamental Problem of Practical Statistics." *Biometrika*, Oct., 1920.

CHAPTER XVI

HISTORY AND ECONOMICS

By EDWIN R. A. SELIGMAN

COLUMBIA UNIVERSITY

THE relations between history and economics can be envisaged from a double point of view — the influence of history upon economics, and the influence of economics upon history.

THE INFLUENCE OF HISTORY UPON ECONOMICS

Taking up first the influence of history upon economics, it need scarcely be pointed out that the science of economics as it was developed primarily by the classical school was essentially unhistorical. It was unhistorical in a double sense: in the first place, it concerned itself with ascertaining the laws which govern the production and distribution of wealth as it existed at that time primarily in England. In the second place the mere fact that it dealt with such an analysis left no room for an attempt to elucidate either the connection between the facts of a former time or the laws of the development of the phenomena. The founders of the classical school were indeed aware of the limitations of their subject, and accomplished admirable work in undertaking the explanation of the facts of their immediate economic environment. Some of their successors, however, made an over-hasty use of their ideas, erecting into so-called laws what were at best simply maxims of expediency, and attempting to apply to entirely different conditions the conclusions which they had drawn from the facts of British life. The consequence was the elaboration of a system of thought which proved to be continually more unsatisfactory because of its inelastic character and its growing aloofness from the facts of a changing economic environment.

The first reaction against the classical school came from the historical school of economists, the chief votaries of which were found in Germany, although important representatives existed also in England and elsewhere. As a result of their labors three consequences ensued in the relation between history and economics.

THE STUDY OF ECONOMIC HISTORY

The first was the impetus given to the study of economic history. It was pointed out that while the science dealt primarily with an analysis of the existing facts of industrial society, the facts themselves were influenced by, and were an outgrowth of, the essentially different facts of former economic conditions. As soon, however, as this was realized, the way was opened for a study of these former economic facts; that is, of economic history. The real contributions, however, to economic history, have been made not by historians but by economists. This is true with some rare exceptions even at present, and is entirely explicable. For the historian in general can with difficulty be expert in all the multiform phases of human interest which constitute either the present or the past of human society. Just as the history of architectural development can best be unraveled by the student who is versed in the laws of architecture, so the far more intricate and baffling explanation of past economic life can best be undertaken by the scholar who understands the science of economics and who is accustomed to disassociate the economic phenomena from the other complicated facts of life. The real discoveries of note in economic history have therefore been made almost entirely by economists or by historians who have been trained in the science of economics. On the other hand, the historical economist must not only be skilled in the science of economics: he must be an economic historian, that is, trained in history. In other words, he must have the professional equipment of an historian; he must know his historical material and be familiar with the technique of interpretation. Above all, he must have that historical sense and power of imagination without which no good history can be written. In this way it may be said that economics has become penetrated by history.

THE HISTORICAL LAWS OF ECONOMIC LIFE

There is a second way in which history has influenced economics. As soon as it was recognized that economic facts are what they are because they constitute an outgrowth of what has previously existed, the demand arose for an explanation of the reasons by which the former facts were transmuted into the present facts. In other words, an effort was now made to explain what might be called the historical laws of economics or the economic laws of history. So far as the economists were concerned, there were scholars who even declared that the real function of economics was primarily to elucidate these historical laws of economic life. We find even in Roscher, Knies, and Hildebrand some rash generalizations to this effect. Two at least of these three scholars, however, devoted a large part of their careers to essentially different efforts, which can only in insignificant respects be distinguished from those of the classical school. For most of their subsequent work had to do with clarifying the laws which explained the interrelation of existing facts. Their earlier work, however, was not lost and modern economics has become sufficiently tolerant to include within its purview the endeavor to explain the becoming as well as the being. Indeed, the modern economist finds in not a few instances that his effort to explain the relations between existing facts is considerably facilitated by a knowledge of the way in which the actual phenomena have grown out of those of the past. History thus fructified economics by teaching it to realize that there is an essential validity in the historical laws of economics.

THE HISTORY OF ECONOMIC THEORY

Finally, history has influenced economics in a third way. As soon as it was seen that the economic life of the past, so essentially different from that of the present, had also had its problems, and that the scholars and statesmen of bygone ages were no less concerned in meeting their difficulties than are those of to-day in meeting our own, the entire attitude toward the history of economics, that is, the history of economic doctrine, was changed. In fact it may be said that the history of economics has in this sense been an outgrowth of economic history. The older view was to the effect that the history of economic thought was of very slight utility. If economics is the science of analyzing the true relations of wealth as we see it, the attempts at explanation by the scholars or statesmen of a former age are necessarily erroneous or even puerile. As one writer has put it, the more perfect such a science becomes, the shorter is its history. To thinkers of this type of opinion the study of the history of economics is useless or, if useful at all, only in the sense of studying the perennial conflict between error and truth. As soon, however, as the conception of relativity of theory replaces that of absolutism, the situation is altered. While the explanation of past economic interrelations as given by their contemporaries may be entirely incompetent to solve any problem of our present, it may none the less have achieved some measure of success in illuminating the particular facts with which they had to deal. From this point of view we should not be justified in refusing to those thinkers the name of economists or in denying that the explanations which they advanced were economic explanations, more or less well calculated to elucidate their difficulties. In this way the history of economics becomes an essentially fruitful study in helping us not only to arrive at a better explanation of past facts but also to appreciate the progressive unfolding of the human intellect in its endeavor to interpret the filiation of ideas.

In these three ways, therefore, through the study of economic history, through the elaboration of historical laws of economic life, and through the study of the history of economic theory, economics may be said to have been influenced and interpenetrated by history.

The Influence of Economics upon History

More important, however, has been the influence of economics on history, in that it has completely transformed the modern attitude toward the explanation of historical life.

For a long time historians were content with immediate and surface interpretations of the past. Attention was directed primarily to the actions and the lives of the leading personalities, and more especially of the political rulers. Explanations of national and international occurrences were found in the personalities — their likes and their dislikes, their friendships and their enmities; and when these did not suffice, a further explanation was sought in diplomatic entanglements, in racial or in religious rivalries. The history of the past thus became in large measure a history of great men.

Already at an early period, however, some thinkers, like Aristotle and Thucydides, had called attention to certain factors which underlay this development and thus emphasized what has in modern times come to be known as institutional history. For a long time, however, even after modern historical investigation had reached the stage of institutional research, attention was still centered upon the political aspects of the problem. Familiar to all is Freeman's statement that history is past politics. In the interval, there came progress along two separate lines, even though chiefly in a sporadic as well as a sketchy manner. On the one hand, the influence of climatic and geographical conditions upon political life had been stressed by a number of writers, some of them even dating back to classic antiquity. More important was the emphasis put by other thinkers upon the development of social institutions and the connection between social and political development. The resulting generalizations, however, were vague in the extreme, and of but little help in elucidating the real connection. It was reserved for Karl Marx to popularize the new conception of the influence of economic considerations and thus to found the theory which has become known as the economic interpretation or the materialistic interpretation of history.

THE DOCTRINE OF KARL MARX

In one sense, indeed, Karl Marx was not the originator of the theory. We find that not a few of his predecessors, whom he was in the habit of deriding as sentimental socialists, put emphasis on economic interpretation. This is especially true of the French socialists. But what Marx accomplished was to place his own interpretation upon this general theory of the interdependence of economics and history, and to make it the foundation of his organic structure of scientific socialism, of which the doctrine of class conflict was the coping stone. Economics thus to him becomes the explanation not only of sociology, but of anthropology, of law, of politics, of ethics, and in fact of all the various manifestations of human society.

The original Marxian philosophy was based upon the intimate connection between social relations and the productive forces of society. In changing the mode of production mankind necessarily changes all its social relations. "The handmill creates a society with the feudal law; the steam mill, a society of the industrial capitalist." Or, as he puts it in another place: "It is always the immediate relations of the owners of the conditions of production to the immediate producers in which we find the innermost secret, the hidden basis, of the entire social structure, and thus also of the political form. The method of production in material existence conditions social, political, and mental evolution in general."

NON-SOCIALIST INTERPRETATIONS

The theory of the economic interpretation of history may be said to have engendered a complete revolution. So far as the economists are concerned, it led to an interesting development. Although modern socialism is essentially a practical movement, and even though the most recent manifestations of socialism, as under the soviet régime in Russia, have very largely divorced themselves from Marxian theory, not a few thinkers of the last quarter of the nineteenth century enrolled themselves under the banners of so-called scientific socialism, which is simply another name for Marxism. The socialist thinkers who had become interested in the economic interpretation of history because of its socialistic implications and conclusions naturally identified economic interpretation with socialism. The great mass of economists, however, who were interested in history but whose investigations and analyses of economic phenomena brought them to conclusions inconsistent with socialism, while accepting the theory of the economic interpretation of history in the sense of the general influence of economic upon social conditions nevertheless opposed the peculiar variant which alone interested Marx. All kinds of non-socialistic economic interpretations have been advanced during the past half-century. There is really nothing in common between the economic interpretation of history and the doctrine of socialism except the accidental fact that the originator of both theories happened to be the same man. Socialism is a theory of what ought to be; historical materialism is the theory of what has been. The one is teleological, the other is descriptive; the one is a speculative ideal, the other is a canon of interpretation. Just as the Marxian economics must not be confused with economics in general, so the Marxian interpretation of history is by no means synonymous with the economic interpretation of history.

THE LACK OF MATERIALISM

In its general signification, however, the economic interpretation of history has been assailed from two sides: for some, the doctrine is too materialistic; for others, the doctrine is not materialistic enough.

The critics of Marx on the last count base their objection on the concessions that he and Engels made toward the end of their careers. These critics emphasize anew the materialistic doctrines which were applied by some of the eighteenth-century French philosophers to intellectual life in general. But they reënforce their doctrines by an appeal to the modern mechanical explanations of biology, as represented especially in the work of Jacques Loeb. If all living organisms are in virtue of that doctrine to be explained fundamentally in chemical, physical, and mechanical terms, social life surely cannot escape the same basic explanation. According to all such thinkers, not only is *homo faber* antecedent to, and the explanation of, *homo sapiens;* not only is civilization itself the outgrowth of the chance invention of the first tool: but every succeeding step taken by human beings in mental, social, or moral progress is to be explained in the same way by the influence of similar successive inventions. According to such thinkers, while Karl Marx was indeed the first great sociologist, he made too many concessions to his opponents. The law of history must be a unitary law like the law of life: if there is such a thing as unity in multiplicity, it is the unity and not the multiplicity that must be stressed. Just as the mechanical forces are the unifying and all-sufficient explanation of life in general, so the conditions of production are the unifying and all-sufficient explanation of the life of man in society, that is, of civilization.

The Excess of Materialism

The chief criticism of Marx has, however, come from the other side, namely, from those who believe that Marx has gone too far. Such thinkers object to the economic interpretation of history for two reasons: first, that it is essentially materialistic and fatalistic; and second, that it neglects the ethical and spiritual forces in history.

The fatalistic objection is that the doctrine is opposed to the theory of free will. Ever since the time of Huxley, however, this criticism has lost its force. Every man indeed has will power and may decide to act or to refrain from acting, thus showing that he is in this sense a free agent. But whether he decides in the one way or the other, there are certain causes operating within the organism which are responsible for the decision. The function of science is to ascertain what these causes are. Man like other beings is what he is because of his environment, past and present — that is, the environment of his ancestors as well as of his own. His congenital and acquired characteristics are such that under certain conditions he will always elect a certain course of action. The negation of the influence of social environment in fact excludes the very conception of law in the moral disciplines. It is therefore an obviously incorrect statement to assert that the theory of economic interpretation is incompatible with the doctrine of free will. If by determinism we mean moral fatalism, determinism is not involved at all. Given a certain set of conditions, the great mass of the community will decide to act in a certain way. If the conditions change, the common ideas will change with them. But the conditions, so far as they are social in character, are created by men and may be altered by men, so that in last resort there is nothing fatalistic about progress. Men are the product of history, but history is made by men.

Economics and Ethics

So far as the other phase of the subject is concerned, the discussion of the last few decades has brought the majority of thinkers to the conclusion that the economic interpretation of history is not materialistic in the sense that it neglects spiritual factors in history. It is now generally recognized that even individual ethics are the outgrowth of social forces. Whatever truth there may be in the intuitive or transcendental theory of ethics as a part of the cosmic scheme, all individual morality is the outcome and reflex of social considerations. As the etymology of the common terms "good" and "dear" clearly shows, the material always precedes the ethical: in the same way the economic conditions of society continually modify the ethical conceptions. Compare, for instance, the ancient and the modern ethical theory on such questions as those of slavery, of feudal rights, and of dueling.

The economic interpretation of history does not seek to deny or to minimize the importance of ethical and spiritual forces. It is, however, only on the border line and during the transition from the old social necessity to the new social convenience that the ethical reformer makes his influence felt. The economic conception of history does not really neglect the spiritual forces; it seeks only to point out the terms on which the spiritual life has hitherto been able to find its fullest fruition.

Since the theory of economic interpretation of history was first advanced, considerable work has been done in elucidating the march of history. To choose only a few examples, there is now a substantial unanimity of opinion that the origin of political organization itself is to be sought in economic considerations. The state was an outgrowth of the preceding clan organization of society, as a consequence of the effort to protect private property. The rise, the growth, and the disappearance of slavery, again, are now recognized to be the inevitable consequences of the connection between the growth of population and the amount of available free land. The migration of nations or the so-called irruption of the barbarians into Europe is everywhere conceded to be due primarily to the search for a more abundant food supply. To come to somewhat later events, we now know that the struggle between Rome and Carthage turned primarily upon the control of Sicily as the granary of the empire; and that the decay of the Roman Empire is intimately associated with the gradual exhaustion of the arable land.

Again, the researches of the economic historians have emphasized the facts that the growth of the absolute monarchy and of nationalism in the sixteenth and seventeenth centuries was the reflex of economic conditions; that the discovery of the new world was due to the effort to ascertain a shorter route to the spice islands; that the English and the French revolutions in the seventeenth and eighteenth centuries were almost entirely ascribable to economic reasons. More recent studies have elucidated the economic causes of the growth of American individualism and of the changes in constitutional interpretation. Finally, not a little excellent work has been done in emphasizing the economic connotations of the Crusades, of the colonization of America, of the Reformation, of even such seemingly unrelated developments as that of cathedral building in the Middle Ages and of the manifestations of modern art and music.

METHODS OF INTERPRETING HISTORY

In one sense, indeed, there are as many methods of interpreting history as there are classes of human activity. There is not only an economic interpretation of history, but an ethical, an esthetic, a political, a jural, a linguistic, a religious, and a scientific interpretation of history. But it is now widely recognized that in the presence of the niggardliness of nature the primary explanation of social life must continue to be that of the adjustment of material resources to human desires. This adjustment may be modified by intellectual and spiritual forces, but in last resort it still remains an adjustment of life to the wherewithal of life.

In this sense history has been broadened and deepened. While there still remains an ample field for the military or esthetic or scientific or religious historian, history in the sense of the unfolding of the vital forces of civilization has been interpenetrated by economics. Even if he does not subscribe to the doctrine of economic interpretation as the fundamental explanation of history, the modern historian cannot afford to neglect the economic phases of progress. Thus, while economics owes much to history, history owes still more to economics.

SELECTED REFERENCES

Adler, Max. *Causalität und Teleologie im Kampfe um die Wissenschaft.* 1904.
   Marxistische Probleme. Beiträge zur Theorie der materialistischen Geschichtsauffassung und der Dialektik. 1913.
Barnes, H. E. *The New History and the Social Studies.* 1925.
   (ed.) *The History and Prospects of the Social Sciences.* 1925.
Barth, P. *Die Philosophie der Geschichte als Sozialwissenschaft.* 1897.
Beard, C. A. *An Economic Interpretation of the Constitution of the United States.* 1913.
   The Economic Basis of Politics. 1922.
Below, G. V. *Probleme der Wirthschaftsgeschichte.* 1924.
Bernstein, E. *Zur Theorie und Geschichte des Sozialismus.* 1904.
Berr, H. *La Synthèse en Histoire.* 1911.
Biermann, W. E. *Die Weltanschauung des Marxismus.*
Borcharat, Julian. *Der historische Materialismus.* 1922.
Brandenburg, E. *Die materialistische Geschichtsauffassung.* 1920.
Braunthal, Alford. *Marx als Geschichtsphilosoph.* 1920.
Breitfeld, A. *Die geschichtsphilosophischen, historischen und politischen Anschauungen von Marx und Engels.* 1922.
Bucharin. *Theorie des Historischen Materialismus.* 1920.
Croce, B. *History: Its Theory and Practice.* 1921.
Cunow, H. *Die Marxsche Geschichts-Gesellschafts-und Staatsauffassung.* 2 vols. 1920.
Delbrück, H. *Die Marxistische Geschichtsauffassung in Preussische Jahrbücher.*
   Die Marxsche Geschichtsphilosophie. 1920.
Engels, F. *Der Ursprung der Familie, des Privateigenthums und des Staats.* 1884.
   The Development of Socialism from Utopia to Science. 1898.
Földes, B. *Die Hauptströmungen der sozialistischen Gedankenwelt.* 1923.
Giddings, F. H. *Studies in the Theory of Human Society.* 1922.
Greulich, H. *Uber die materialistische Geschichtsauffassung.* 1897.
Hammacher, E. *Das philosophisch-ökonomische System des Marxismus.* 1909.
Helander, S. *Marx und Hegel.* 1922.
Hobhouse, L. T. *Social Development: Its Nature and Conditions.* 1924.
Jacobson, G. *Die materialistische Geschichtsauffassung im Lichte der neueren soziologischen Forschungen.* 1921.
Koester, Otto. *Zur Kritik des historischen Materialismus.*
Kraus, Emil. *Die geschichtlichen Grundlagen des Sozialismus.* 1921.
Lacombe, P. *De l'Histoire considéré comme Science.* 1894.
Labriola, A. *Essais sur la Conception matérialiste de l'Histoire.* 1897.
Lafargue, P. *Idéalisme et Matérialisme.* 1895.
Lamprecht, K. *Alte und neue Richtungen in der Geschichtswissenschaft.* 1896.
Loria, A. *The Economic Foundations of Society.* 1899.
Mankes-Zernicke, Anne. *Over Historisch-materialistische en Social-democratische Ethick.* 1918.

Marx, K. *Die Heilige Familie und Kritik der Kritischen Kritik.* 1845.
　　　　　Misère de la Philosophie. 1847.
　　　　　Zur Kritik der politischen Oekonomie. 1859.
Masaryk, T. G. *Die philosophischen und soziologischen Grundlagen des Marxismus.* 1899.
Meyer, E. *Zur Theorie und Methodik der Geschichte.* 1902.
Robinson, J. H. *The New History.* 1912.
Salvadori, G. *La Scienza Economica e la teoria dell' Evoluzione.* 1901.
Scalia, Carmelo. *Il Materialismo Storico e il Socialismo.* 1920.
Schmoller, G. *Ueber einige Grundfragen der Sozialpolitik und der Volkswirthschaftslehre.* 1898.
Seignobos, C. *La methode historique appliquée aux sciences sociales.* 1901.
Seligman, E. R. A. *The Economic Interpretation of History.* 1902.
Simmel, G. *Die Probleme der Geschichtsphilosophie.* 1892.
Schlesinger, A. M. *New Viewpoints in American History.* 1922.
Shotwell, J. T. *Introduction to the History of History.* 1922.
Sombart, W. *Sozialismus und soziale Bewegung.* 8th ed. 1919.
Stammler, R. *Wirthschaft und Recht nach der materialischen Geschichts auffassung.* 1896.
Teggart, F. J. *The Processes of History.* 1918.
Thomas, F. *The Environmental Basis of Society.* 1925.
Todd, A. J. *Theories of Social Progress.* 1918.
Troeltsch, Ernst. *Der Historismus und seine Probleme.* 1922.
Tugan-Baranowski. *Theoretische Grundlagen des Marxismus.* 1905.
Veblen, T. *The Place of Science in Modern Civilization.* 1909.
Weisengrün, P. *Der Marxismus und das Wesen der sozialen Frage.* 1900.
Weber, Max. *Gesammelte Aufsätze zur Wissenschaft.* 1922.
Wallace, W. K. *The Trend of History.* 1922.
Williams, Maurice. *The Social Interpretation of History.* 1921.
Woltmann, L. *Der historische Materialismus.* 1900.

CHAPTER XVII

HISTORY AND POLITICAL SCIENCE

By ARTHUR N. HOLCOMBE

HARVARD UNIVERSITY

THOUGH there is universal agreement among political thinkers and writers that the data of politics are the acts of men, there is no similar agreement concerning the source from which the materials of a science of politics should be derived.

THE HUMANISTIC POINT OF VIEW

The view which is doubtless most widely held at present was well expressed by the late Viscount Bryce in his presidential address before the American Political Science Association on "The Relations of Political Science to History and to Practice." "The laws of political science," he said, "are the tendencies of human nature and are embodied in the institutions men have created. These tendencies are so far uniform and permanent that we can lay down general propositions about human nature and can form these propositions into a connected system of knowledge." To these preliminary observations there will probably be general assent on the part of political thinkers and writers. But Bryce proceeded further. "The materials of political science," he declared, "are the acts of men as recorded in history." This was a point which he wished particularly to emphasize. "In other words," he continued, "they are such parts of history as relate to the structure and government of communities. Political science takes all the facts that history gives us on this subject and rearranges them under proper heads, describing institutions and setting forth those habits of men and tendencies of human nature which correspond to what in the sphere of inanimate nature we call natural laws. Thus, your science may be defined as the data of political history reclassified and explained as the result of certain general principles. . . . They [the historical facts] are so disposed and arranged as to enable us more easily to comprehend what we call the laws that govern human nature in political communities, so that we can see these laws as a whole in their permanent action and can apply what we have learned from history to the phenomena of to-day and to-morrow."

This is a view of the relationship between history and political science which puts a high value on the study of history. "If once we grant that historic truth is attainable," one of the most enthusiastic historians of this way of thinking, Sir John R. Seeley, has argued, "then there can be no further dispute about its supreme importance. It deals with facts of the largest and most momentous kind, with the causes of the decay and growth of empires, with war and peace, with the sufferings or happiness of millions." But history deals not only with the sufferings and happiness of the millions who are dead and gone. If it is worth anything, Seeley insisted, it should enable us also to anticipate the lessons of time, and thereby diminish the sufferings and enlarge the happiness of the living in the present and the future. "We shall all no doubt be wise after the event; we study history that we may be wise before the event." It was with such considerations as these in mind that Seeley merged the study of history with political science. "Destiny," he said, "will be the result of the working of those laws which it is the object of political science to discover." And again: "I tell you that when you study English history, you study not the past of England only, but also her future." This is the view which Seeley summed up so neatly in his oft-quoted couplet:

> History without political science has no fruit;
> Political science without history has no root.

It converts the study of history from a pleasant literary pastime into an exacting scientific pursuit, comparable to the labors of the natural scientists in their laboratories. It encourages the attempt not only to sift, arrange, and dispose in the most agreeable manner the facts which history records, but also to ascertain what help can be rendered to citizens and statesmen by placing the facts of history and the conclusions of political science at their service.

The Theological Point of View

Another view attaches comparatively little importance to the facts of history as material for a science of politics. After the fall of Napoleon the Third and the collapse of the Second French Empire, Henry the Fifth, head of the house of Bourbon and legitimate heir to the throne of France, could have worn the crown if he had been willing to accept the tri-color and thereby attest his recognition of the principle of popular sovereignty. But he would rule by divine right or not at all, and the scepter eluded his grasp. It has been said that the Bourbons learned nothing and forgot nothing. Certainly they had not learned much from history. In general, believers in the divine right of kings could not be expected to learn much from history. Their political science was founded upon a special revelation in which the facts of history played a minor part. Learned theologians like Bossuet might write universal histories in which the record of events served to point a moral or adorn a faith; but in the opinion of the faithful the authority of rulers and the processes of government enjoyed a higher sanction than any that could be derived from the philosophy of history. The theological school of political thought may appeal to history to show the folly of unauthorized political ideas, but its members need no other materials for their political science than are afforded by the materials of their theology.

This view was once almost universally accepted in the Western World. People then used to say that at the bottom of their politics they always found theology. Although this can no longer be said with equal truth, the theological point of view persists and will continue to do so. Practical statesmen, who have learned their trade in the school of experience (which is a good school, though the tuition is high), must deal as best they may with those who, lacking experience themselves, will not learn from history, which is the record of the experience of others. Bismarck was a practical statesman who had learned much both from personal experience and from the study of history. Throughout his political career he had constantly to deal with those whose theology rendered them comparatively indifferent to the course of events. In January, 1871, when in the palace at Versailles, the King of Prussia was about to be proclaimed head of the newly founded German Empire, a furious controversy raged over the title which the triumphant monarch should assume. Those who believed in the divine right of the House of Hohenzollern — and they were many and powerful — insisted that William should be proclaimed Emperor of Germany. William agreed with them. But those who had studied their histories to better purpose and were aware of the rising political consciousness of the German people argued that the proper title would be Emperor of the Germans. This was the view of Bismarck. The contending theories of popular sovereignty and divine right were profoundly involved in the war of words. No settlement could be reached. And so, when the time came to hail the new wearer of the imperial crown, the awkward dilemma was evaded by raising a cheer for the German Emperor. The dubious title stuck to the Hohenzollern rulers as long as they retained their power. Churchmen, however, as well as statesmen, have learned much from history in recent years, and the theological school of political thought cannot be as indifferent to the logic of events as in former times.

THE RATIONALISTIC POINT OF VIEW

It is not only the theologians whose political science has been largely derived from other than historical sources. Their arch-opponents, the rationalists, have been almost equally indifferent to the study of history.

The point of view of the rationalistic school is well illustrated by the opinion of Hobbes, a great figure among the early English rationalists. He despised not only the political philosophies which were founded upon the authority of the traditional theology, but also those which were laboriously extracted from the annals of the past. If he had read as many books as others, he boasted, he would have been as ignorant as they. In his celebrated political treatise, *Leviathan; or the Matter, Form, and Power of a Commonwealth*, he set forth a complete theory of the state, in which the authority of the most arbitrary rulers is derived from the consent of the governed through a social compact. According to this theory the social compact is the very essence of the justification of governmental power; yet Hobbes was utterly indifferent as to whether or not history afforded any examples of such a compact. Whether the social compact were fact or fiction, the sanction of sovereignty was equally rational, Hobbes insisted, because it was grounded "upon the known natural inclinations of mankind and upon the articles of the law of nature." But upon examination the "known natural inclinations of mankind" proved to be neither more nor less than Hobbes's personal sentiments concerning human nature, and the articles of the law of nature became identical with the rules of conduct which seemed to him reasonable for mankind as he viewed it. Since he held human nature in low esteem, it is not surprising that he identified the law of nature largely with the principle of self-preservation. Political thinkers and writers who held a better opinion of mankind were bound to reject Hobbes's political theory. As Locke pointed out, good rulers had no need of such a justification, and tyrants could not be helped by it.

THE REVOLUTIONISTS

The political theory of the American revolution was mainly rationalistic, but it followed Locke rather than Hobbes. Jefferson was too shrewd a politician to neglect any weapon that could help his cause, and in penning the official justification of the declaration of independence he was careful to appeal not only to "the laws of nature" but also to those "of nature's God." But the materials of his political philosophy were derived neither from theological authority nor from recorded history. They were "self-evident" truths. In other words, they were truths which did not depend for their validity upon confirmation by historians or ecclesiastics. It was enough that they satisfied the consciences of the "good people" of the United Colonies.

It is significant that revolutionary leaders are so often distinguished for their youth. Jefferson himself was only thirty-three when he wrote the immortal Declaration. Youth is naturally rationalistic. It takes time to gain experience through personal participation in affairs, and it takes time to learn the lessons of the experience of others through the study of history. But the rational faculties appear to attain their full development in early manhood, and in default of a stock of personal observations or historical learning they must operate on the most acceptable materials that are available. Such materials must be largely derived from speculative philosophy. It is not surprising that in periods of revolutionary change, when youth has the best opportunity to come quickly to the front, "glittering generalities," as the sophisticated elder statesmen like to call them, obtain their strongest hold on the minds of the leaders of men. In the second American Revolution, if the formation of the more perfect Union under the Constitution of 1787 may be so described, young men were still to the front. Madison, the most influential member of the Convention, was in the middle thirties, and Hamilton, the most brilliant, though not the most influential, of them all, was even younger. Madison, however, was a prodigious student of history, and Hamilton had already had such experience in politics as rarely comes to men of twice his age. In general, the framers of the Constitution were more empirical in their political thinking than the earlier revolutionary leaders, and their omission of a declaration of rights from the original draft seemed to many contemporary critics a deliberate repudiation of the rationalistic political theory which had been consecrated by the Revolution.

There was a similar course of political thought in revolutionary France. Rousseau, the political thinker and writer whose influence was in the ascendant at the height of the Revolution, affected to fortify his political doctrines by apposite citations from the experience of the Greeks and Romans, but his convictions gained their force from his stupendous faith in the rights of man. He was, indeed, as thoroughly rationalistic as Hobbes, and, having a very different opinion of human nature, was as fairly entitled to put his trust in the masses of the people as Hobbes was to put his in princes. It cannot be said that one was any less logical than the other, though, starting from radically different premises, they properly arrived at radically different conclusions. As the Revolution developed and the Mirabeaus and Lafayettes gave way to the Dantons and Robespierres, youth and rationalistic politics more and more dominated the scene. Danton was only thirty-five when Robespierre sent him to the guillotine. Robespierre himself was thirty-six, and Saint-Just, the most congenial of his confederates upon the Committee of Public Safety, was only twenty-six when the disillusioned remnants of the Convention revolted against their despotic sway and ended the "reign of reason" by a restoration of common sense. The creative faculties of the rationalistic type of mind seemed less potent than the critical and the destructive faculties, and the statesmen who so successfully overthrew the old régime proved incapable of establishing the new. Eventually the fruits of the Revolution were harvested by men whose ability to profit by the teachings of experience more than made up for their previous inattention to the lessons of history.

Though the revolutionary rationalistic political theory suffered severely from its neglect of the facts of history, it was able to shake the credit of its theological rival and to secure for its principal dogmas unprecedented popular support. So successful were the political movements which were executed in their name that they continue to the present day to cast their spell upon the minds of multitudes. In the political philosophy of Hobbes and Rousseau, of Locke and Tom Paine, the social compact and the natural rights of man may be no more than magnificent fictions; but in the history

of modern democracy they are facts as substantial as the fundamental laws of the Third French Republic or the Constitution of
the United States.

The Utilitarians

Another division of the rationalistic school of political thought
consists of philosophers like Bentham who, having rejected the fiction of a social compact as unhistorical, proceeded to theorize on
politics without any historical basis at all.   The doctrine of natural
rights they brushed aside as a plain contradiction in terms.   Seeking some definite principle from which a science of politics could be
deduced, they found it in the supposed fact that all men seek
pleasure and avoid pain.   In that respect they thought men could
be measured and compared.   It seemed, therefore, possible to construct a veritable science of politics from materials which would
render the political scientist as independent of the imperfect and
unreliable annals of the past as the chemist or the astronomer.

The Benthamites or utilitarians made one great contribution to
the methodology of political science.   They insisted upon the importance of statistics for an understanding of affairs of state, and
thereby contributed to the adoption of quantitative rather than
merely qualitative methods of political reasoning.   Instead of dis-
coursing pleasantly upon the rights of man and the national honor,
they directed attention to birth- and death-rates and the distribution of wealth.   Refusing to admit that political authority could be
justified once for all time by any such process of reasoning as might
have persuaded rational men in a hypothetical state of nature to
give up their hypothetical natural rights for the blessings of civil
society, they set out to discover whether existing governments
could be justified by their works from day to day.   They loved to
dwell upon such prosaic matters as interest rates and rates of wages,
price-levels, stocks of commodities on hand, imports and exports,
and the volume of production.   This was much less romantic than
sounding the praises of the golden age when "wild in woods the
noble savage ran" with liberty, equality, and fraternity for all.
But it was much more helpful to statesmen.

The utilitarians, however, were guilty of at least one grave error.
Pleasure and pain are indeed facts about human nature, but, as
Graham Wallas has convincingly demonstrated, they are not the
only facts that are important to politicians.   Men have rational

opinions concerning the ways and means of pursuing pleasure and avoiding pain, and they also have natural impulses and instincts which under the complex conditions of life in the modern world often seem to work directly against the happiness of their possessors and to increase pain instead of diminishing it. Religious, racial, and class prejudices, to mention only one set of irrational, or at least non-rational, factors in modern politics, play an important part in the actual course of events — how important it is impossible accurately to measure. The utilitarians were not wholly blind to the influence of these factors upon the fortunes of men, but they seemed incapable of making due allowance for the non-rational modes of thought and conduct in the development of their own political philosophy. It is unwise to assume, as the utilitarians were too prone to do, that men always act from self-interest, and that, therefore, when we see what a man does, we can know with certainty what he thinks his interest to be. It seems the incurable defect of the rationalistic school of political thought that it overestimates the reasonableness of mankind. High-minded rationalistic thinkers like the younger Mill might dedicate their lives to dispassionate study of the problems of their time; but the Palmerstons and Disraelis and Gladstones who chiefly gained the suffrages of their fellow men were forced to do much of which the Mills strongly disapproved in order to maintain their sway.

Contemporary Schools of Political Thought

The history of political thought in recent times has been largely a history of efforts to liberate the mind not only from the domination of the traditional theology in political affairs, but also from that of the rationalistic thinkers. The authority of religion and abstract reason alike has been challenged, and the right of appeal to the verdict of experience has been ever more firmly maintained. Among the political thinkers of modern times who have insisted upon the submission of theories of the state and of government to the test of experience, the foremost was Montesquieu. Historians have claimed him as the founder of the historical school of political science because he filled his pages with references to the records of the past and endeavored to support his conclusions upon the experience of the ages. But his use of historical materials was often faulty, and though he gave new dignity to the study of history, he did not succeed in raising it to the level of a science. Anthropogeographers have claimed him as the founder of the anthropogeographical school because he emphasized the political effects of topography, food supply, soil, and climate. But his inferences from the facts of natural environment, though always interesting and often astonishingly shrewd, were also often astonishingly superficial and unsound. Most of the contemporary schools of political thought, indeed, may be traced back more or less directly to Montesquieu, but he cannot be definitely assigned to a place in any of them. His was the honor of being the first great empiricist of modern times, and the empirical school of political thought, which he may properly be credited with founding, led the attack upon the established dogmas of the theological and rationalistic schools.

THE EMPIRICAL SCHOOL

The greatest service of the empirical school of political thought was to insist upon the importance of observing with a critical eye the political practices of contemporary peoples. Montesquieu, who did this with rare discernment, made solid contributions to the theory of government. But he also committed serious blunders; and those who trod in his footsteps could not fail to recognize the necessity of checking their observations upon contemporary politics by more careful study of the history of the past as well as more systematic analysis of the non-political factors in the history that was in the making. The empiricists exercised an influence which it is easy to underestimate upon the reconstruction of Europe at the close of the revolutionary age, but in the scientific world their authority presently gave way to the more specialized schools which sprang up on all sides. The metaphysicians, the historians, and the anthropogeographers, the biologists, the sociologists, and the psychologists, all have made substantial advances in the study of politics, but all must acknowledge their indebtedness to the empiricists for their preliminary work in the development of modern political ideas. The metaphysical, the historical, and the anthropogeographical schools of political thought, the ethnographical, the sociological, and the psychological schools, each has made its own contribution to the contemporary stock of ideas, but all testify to the soundness of the methodology which the empirical school introduced, and seek to check their conclusions by scientific study of the political behavior of men. They differ more or less from one another, however, in the importance they attach to the study of history as the source of material for a science of politics.

The Metaphysical School

The metaphysical school of political thought inherited from the rationalists their disposition to give to the study of politics a systematic and philosophical character, and from the empiricists its members learned the importance of submitting their political philosophy to the test of experience. Thus they became interested in history as a source of materials for their theorizing, and political philosophy tended to become a systematic philosophy of history. This tendency culminated in Hegel, whose metaphysical theory of the state was the climax of his entire philosophical system. His conception of the state as the synthesis of the conflicting ideas of liberty and authority gave a new impetus to political philosophy, but Hegel was more than a political philosopher. He seems fairly entitled to recognition as a political scientist, though his contribution to political science is less valuable in itself than through its influence upon the work of others. Political science must begin with the classification of states, and Hegel proposed to classify them in accordance with the various ideas of liberty exhibited by their peoples and with the various modes of reconciling the particular idea of liberty with the general idea of authority. His attempt to construct a series of classes, beginning with the oriental despotism and proceeding through the higher types of state exemplified by the ancient Greek commonwealth and the Roman empire to its final perfection in the Teutonic monarchy, cannot be regarded as successful. But Hegel did succeed in emphasizing the importance of historical materials for the development of a science of politics and in encouraging a new faith in the reign of law in history and in the progressive evolution of mankind. Hegel's successors in the metaphysical school have wisely retracted some of his errors, but they have added little to the substance of his achievement.

The Historical School

The historical school of political thought in the strict sense of the term dates from the close of the French Revolution. The *Code Napoléon*, which was the final achievement of the revolutionary rationalism, remains a great monument to human reason. But when Savigny persuaded the German jurists to defer the codification of the Germanic law until its spirit should be better understood, the spell of the rationalistic school was definitely broken and the way was cleared for the adoption of new methods of political

thought.   At first the historical method was most profitably employed in the study of jurisprudence and political economy. Though the Germans eventually yielded to the rationalistic arguments in favor of codification, sagacious jurists like Gierke continued to demonstrate the value of historical studies for the improvement of the law.   Likewise the historical economists from Roscher to Schmoller showed the importance of a knowledge of economic history in the analysis of contemporary economic problems and in the development of sound economic policies.   The historical method scored its most spectacular triumph when Marx and the "scientific" socialists applied the economic interpretation of history to the theory of the state and of government.   The doctrines of the class struggle and the inevitable ultimate victory of the proletariat may be the result of a disproportionate attention to one particular kind of historical facts, but they inspired masses of men with a new interest in the study of history and a better appreciation of its practical significance.   Meanwhile other groups of historians were directing attention more particularly to the influence of geographical and racial factors in history, and the anthropogeographical and ethnographical schools of political thought were introduced upon the scene.

The Anthropogeographical School

The anthropogeographical school of political thought, like the historical school proper, is often traced back to Montesquieu. His chance remark, after describing the relation which he believed he had discovered between the English system of government and the enjoyment of the blessings of liberty, that "this beautiful system was first invented in the woods," suggested the thought that if life in the woods leads to the development of characteristic political institutions such as the English system of representative government, other geographic factors must also have their characteristic consequences, and the influence of geography upon the history of institutions and of political ideas in general must be an important subject of scientific study.   Buckle was one of the ablest historians who wrote with this thought in mind, and the point of view exemplified by his *History of Civilization* would have exerted a greater influence upon the development of political science had it not been overshadowed by the impressive discoveries of Darwin in the field of biology which were announced to the world at that time.   It remained for the learned German geographer, Friedrich Ratzel, to demonstrate the importance of an anthropogeographical interpretation of history and to develop a field of study which at the hands of a growing number of accomplished writers is becoming increasingly serviceable to political science.

Ratzel was greatly influenced by Hegel, as is clearly shown by the quotation which Wells has made so widely known through the introduction to his *Outline of History*. "A philosophy of the history of the human race, worthy of the name," Ratzel wrote, "must begin with the heavens and descend to the earth, must be charged with the conviction that all existence is one — a single conception sustained from beginning to end upon one identical law." This was a view of the philosophy of history which might easily lead to an exaggerated estimate of the importance in human affairs of the particular class of phenomena in which its holder might happen to be interested. Some of the anthropogeographers, indeed, have fallen into this error, and, like certain advocates of economic and racial interpretations of history, have produced grossly one-sided explanations of the course of events. Ratzel himself, however, and the ablest of his successors, notably Miss Semple, Brunhes, and Vallaux, largely avoided this mistake. From the geographical and climatic standpoint, Southern California bears an extraordinary resemblance to the Holy Land, but the anthropogeographers have considerately refrained from predicting for its inhabitants a history similar to that of the people of Israel. With the proper qualifications the materials furnished by human geography are among the most promising that are becoming available for an acceptable interpretation of history and for the development of a true science of politics.

THE ETHNOGRAPHICAL SCHOOL

The ethnographical school of political thought is related less directly than the anthropogeographical to the historical and empirical schools. The mechanistic conceptions of the state and of government, for which the Newtonian physics prepared the minds of Montesquieu and the other empiricists, were radically different from the organismic conceptions that were fostered by the Hegelian metaphysics and the Darwinian biology. The latter conceptions emphasize the opinion that constitutions are not made but grow, and hence the adoption by students of politics of the point of view nd the scientific methods of the evolutionary biologists stimulated more eager search for historical materials than was the practice when political thinking was influenced to a greater extent by the supposed analogies between physics and politics. Yet even before the advent of the Darwinian biology there were students of politics to whom Montesquieu's remark about the Germanic origin of the English system of representative government suggested the thought that the kind of people who invented such a beautiful system in the depths of the woods must have possessed a peculiar genius for politics. This, transmitted to their descendants, would endow all the Germanic people with an extraordinary political capacity. Thus, one division of the historical school, under the leadership of such writers as Freeman and Gobineau, helped to build up the Anglo-Saxon and Teutonic myths which did so much in the later nineteenth century to lend an appearance of scientific validity to vulgar racial prejudices. The Darwinian biology tended to confirm many of these prejudices, and in the hands of writers like Houston Stewart Chamberlain prepared the way for the perfected Nordic myth which still serves to justify in many quarters the domination of alien races by imperialistic world-powers. A better result of the new view of history which the evolutionary biology promoted was the impetus which it gave to the sociological approach to political science.

THE SOCIOLOGICAL SCHOOL

When Comte first declared that the time had come to transform the philosophy of history into a veritable science, the materials for a serviceable sociology were sadly lacking. The poverty of his actual contribution to political science, despite the fundamental soundness of his method, is sufficiently attested by the fate of his proposals for the conduct of public affairs by the priesthood of humanity. There could be no hope of a dictatorship of the sociologists until through the study of history they had developed a science of politics which would actually be superior to the empirical art of the practical politicians. It was not enough for Comte to say, "Let there be a new science." It was necessary to provide the materials for it. The Spencerian sociology gave the sociologists a fresh start and rendered a valuable service by infusing the modern philosophy of history with the spirit of the evolutionary biology; but Spencer's conclusions outstripped his data and it presently became clear that the sociologists were only on the threshold of their new science. Durkheim may not have been wiser than many others, but he was certainly more candid when he declared that the time had not come for formulating the principles of sociology. His theory of political evolution from the primitive kinship state through the territorial state to the commonwealth of the future based upon functional association, is suggestive of the constructive work which may be done by sociology in the great career which still lies before it, but for the present the sociologists must remain immersed in the comparative study of history and in the statistical analysis of contemporary society. Their greatest contribution to the advancement of political science has been their insistence upon a sound methodology. More than any other modern school, they have emphasized the importance of deriving the materials for a science of politics from the study of history.

The Psychological School

The latest of the schools of political thought is the psychological school, and of all the successors of the empirical school it is the least disposed to seek the materials of political science in the records of the past. Agreeing with the others that the data of politics are the acts of men, it insists upon the advantages of studying the evidence at first hand rather than through the imperfect and uncertain records of past performances which constitute the stuff of history. The advantages of constructing a science of politics from materials gained by observing directly the political behavior of living men, are indeed very great. The political scientist who adopts this method is not dependent upon the accuracy and impartiality of historical writers whose observations he cannot easily verify and whose inferences he cannot submit to the test of experiment under controlled conditions. The social psychologists, to be sure, are apparently no more capable than the historians of employing the experimental method for the testing of their political hypotheses; but at least they have rendered excellent service to political science by warning the student of politics against the tendency to exaggerate the intellectuality of mankind, which the rationalistic tradition so strongly encourages. They have accumulated an impressive mass of material for the use of the political scientist, but they have yet to demonstrate, if indeed they really wish to do so, that he can afford to neglect the data which may be obtained from the study of history.

SCIENTIFIC INTERPRETATIONS OF HISTORY

There has been a truly remarkable growth in the authority of history since the time when the rationalists were proclaiming the natural equality of mankind and Herder said that it was not permitted to speak the dishonorable words, "races of men." With the possible exception of the social psychologists, most students of politics are doubtless now content to repeat after Gobineau that "the tribunal of history has been the only one that is competent for a rational judgment on the character of mankind." But what is the judgment of history on the character of mankind? And to what extent is it now possible for the students of politics to derive from history adequate materials for a genuine political science?

THEIR INADEQUACY

The answers to these questions are far from satisfactory. The study of history reveals the influence of three main factors upon the development of human institutions, racial inheritance, geographical and climatic environment, and economic and social environment. But what is the relative importance of each? The students of history are in hopeless disagreement. The ethnographical interpretation of history lays great stress upon the first; the anthropogeographical, upon the second; the economic and social interpretations, upon the third. Mr. Lothrop Stoddard, having read Gobineau and Houston Stewart Chamberlain and Madison Grant, finds in alleged "racial realities" the key to the history of Europe. Mr. Ellsworth Huntington, having read Buckle and Sir H. J. Mackinder, finds the key in "climatic energy." Mr. Morris Hillquit, having read Marx and Engels, finds it in the "class struggle." The course of history is made to turn upon the shape of the skull and the color of the skin, or upon the mean annual temperature and precipitation, or upon the methods of raising food and fabricating clothes and shelter. The political scientist has no means of reconciling the differences between these one-sided interpretations of history, and he gets little help from their authors in the formulation of principles of politics. But when he turns from the ethnographical and physiographical and economic historians to the sociologists and psychologists he does not greatly improve his position. Sociology in its turn is dependent, as Comte rightly pointed out, upon the development of the antecedent sciences, and, to say nothing of other obstacles, the imperfection of modern social psychology seems to make a true science of sociology, as Durkheim confessed, unattainable at present.

There can be no genuinely fruitful science of any kind without agreement upon the definition of fundamental terms. The controversies of the psychologists over the meaning of such terms as instinct and intelligence do not encourage great expectations on the part of students of politics from the science of psychology in the near future. Philip Guedalla's mordant gibe about the infant science of psychology with all its data and no conclusions and of sociology with all its conclusions and no data, is perhaps as unfair to the psychologists as to the sociologists; but the fact remains that the materials for a science of politics based upon the acts of men must still be mainly derived from historical sources. The attempt to deduce such a science from the laws of human nature received a trial at the hands of the rationalists, and their failure shows the magnitude of the task which confronts the modern social psychologists. J. B. S. Haldane may be unduly pessimistic when he suggests that the psychologists will need another two or three centuries before they will be beating the practical politicians at their own game and usurping their power, but the time foreseen by the Webbs in their fascinating book, *The Constitution of the Socialist Commonwealth of Great Britain*, when the present empirical art of politics shall have become a scientific profession carried on for the most part by a dominant bureaucracy of expert economists duly trained in political psychology, seems at least as remote as the dictatorship of the sociologists envisaged by Comte.

The Province of Historical and Political Science

The most competent students of politics, having diligently searched through recorded history for the materials of their science and having also observed with care the political behavior of their contemporaries in public and private life, have taken an exceedingly modest view of the province of historical and political science. Bryce, for instance, whose qualifications for expressing an opinion were at least as good as the best, remarked that "historical study is a fine tonic for the system, but does not furnish prescriptions for every-day ailments." And he added: "Cherish no vain hopes of introducing the certitude or the authority of science into politics. If you help to create among the most enlightened part of a nation the right temper and attitude, if you strengthen their sense of civic luty, if you enforce the need there is for accurate knowledge of facts, and intelligent reasoning from the facts, you will have done as much as can be expected and more than has ever yet been accomplished." If this were all that Bryce had to say on the value of a knowledge of history to the student of politics, the hope of deriving from that source the materials for a genuine political science would be faint indeed. But Bryce did not stop there. He concluded his discussion of the relations of political science to history and to practice in a much more hopeful vein. "It is an experimental science," he declared, "for though it cannot try experiments it can study them and note the results. It is a progressive science, for every year's experience adds not only to our materials but to our comprehension of the laws that govern human society." What more is needed to justify the continued search for materials which shall enable the student of politics, if not to perfect a science which must long remain the most imperfect of all the sciences, at least to raise the standard of political thought among the peoples of modern states? It may well be that no great improvement in government can be expected in the near future through the application of scientific methods to the study of politics, but surely it is possible gradually to strengthen each man's sense of obligation to the whole community to the end that the time may come when men will create better institutions than any they now possess and will operate them in a nobler spirit.

The Need for a Political Interpretation of History

The first requirement of the political scientist who wishes to make better use of historical materials is a more serviceable interpretation of history. Metaphysical, economic, physiographic, racial, sociological, and psychological interpretations of history have made solid contributions to political science, and, as they become less imperfect, may be expected to make even more substantial contributions. Froude's dictum, that "the address of history is less to the understanding than to the higher emotions," must be rejected. But the historical materials for a science of politics are still very hard to use. It is unlikely indeed that the science of politics can be greatly improved without important previous improvements in the underlying sciences. Yet the political scientist cannot pause while all other scientists remain at work. He cannot make an end of his labors until the others bring theirs to an end. For his own immediate purposes his greatest need is a political interpretatio of history.

The ultimate inadequacy of every political interpretation of his tory has been demonstrated by Barth in his valuable treatise, *Th Philosophy of History as Sociology*. But while no interpretation o history that is merely political can take the place of the more funda mental interpretations, a sound political interpretation is indispensa ble for the more scientific utilization of the materials which histor affords for the study of politics. Most political interpretations o history have been based upon a classification of forms of govern ment. This has been a grave defect, since the external form of gov ernment is but a superficial expression of the true nature of th state. Political science must begin with the classification of states and no satisfactory classification of states is possible that does no look beyond the forms of government to the political processes, and behind the processes to the systems of ideas which give the processe their character. Teggart was on the right track when he said tha "the distinguishing feature of any group will be, not its language implements, institutions, but its particular idea-system, of whicl these other manifestations of activity are varying expressions." And again he properly reminds us that "if we are to consider the content of life in addition to the exterior forms of human associ ation, the study before us must concern itself with the factors and processes through which the idea-systems of different groups have come to be as we find them to-day."

THE IMPORTANCE OF HISTORICAL JURISPRUDENCE

A sound political interpretation of history must be based upon an analysis of the purposes of the members of states, the purposes of their rulers, and above all, of their peoples. Are the rulers pursuing mainly private purposes, or are they held to a course of conduct which insures mindfulness of purposes which are truly public? And if they are pursuing public as well as private purposes, what is the nature of those purposes? Are they mainly concerned to provide merely for the common defense, or are they trying also to insure domestic tranquillity and to promote the general welfare in what ever ways they can? Above all, what are the prevailing ideas of liberty and of justice? These are the most important elements in the idea-systems of states. Historical studies of every kind will help to open the door to a sound political interpretation of history,

ut the master-key is historical jurisprudence. Yet the political
cientist will not forget that a knowledge of the laws of a state is not
nough. It is necessary also to know to what extent they are en-
orced, and to what extent they respond to the requirements of the
eople. There must be careful discrimination between what Dean
ound has called the law in books and the law in action. Finally,
n important lesson for the political scientist is to be learned from
he sage who said that he did not care who wrote the laws of his
ountry if he could write its songs.

SELECTED REFERENCES

Babbitt, I. *Democracy and Leadership.* 1924.

Barnes, H. E. *The History and Prospects of the Social Sciences.* 1924.
    Sociology and Political Theory. 1924.
    The New History and the Social Studies. Chap. VIII. 1925.

Barth, P. *Die Philosophie der Geschichte als Soziologie.* 2d ed. 1915.

Bosanquet, B. *The Philosophical Theory of the State.* 3d ed. 1920.

Bryce, James. "The Relations of Political Science to History and Practice."
    American Political Science Review, III.

Catlin, G. E. G. *The Science and Method of Politics.* 1927.

Chamberlain, H. S. *The Foundations of the Nineteenth Century.* English
    trans., 2 vols. 1910.

Comte, A. *A General View of Positivism.* Bridge's trans., Harrison's ed.
    1908.

Dunning, W. A. *A History of Political Theories.* 3 vols. 1902–20.

Durkheim, E. *De la Division du Travail Social.* 1st ed. 1893.

Febvre, Lucien. *A Geographical Introduction to History.* 1924.

Flint, R. *A History of the Philosophy of History.* 1893.

Ford, H. J. *Representative Government.* 1924.

Freeman, E. A. *Comparative Politics.* 1873.

Froude, J. A. *The Science of History.* 1864.

Gettell, R. G. *History of Political Thought.* 1924.

Gobineau, A. de. *Essai sur l'Inégalité des Races Humaines.* 2d ed. 2 vols.
    1884.

Haldane, J. B. S. "Science and Politics." *New Republic,* Dec. 3, 1924.

Hegel, G. W. F. *Lectures on the Philosophy of History.* English trans. 1857.

Hobbes, T. *Leviathan; or the Matter, Form, and Power of a Commonwealth,
    Ecclesiastical and Civil.* 1651.

Hobhouse, L. T. *The Metaphysical Theory of the State.* 1918.
    Social Evolution and Political Theory. 1911.

Holcombe, A. N. *The Foundations of the Modern Commonwealth.* 1923.

Huntington, E. *Climate and Civilization.* 1924.

Laski, H. J. *A Grammar of Politics.* 1925.

Lippmann, W. *Public Opinion.* 1922.
    The Phantom Public. 1925.

Locke, J. *Two Treatises on Government.* 1690.

MacIver, R. M. *Community, a Sociological Study.* 1917.
    The Modern State. 1926.

McDougall, W. *Social Psychology.* 1908.
    The Group Mind. 1920.

Marvin, F. S., *Progress and History.* 1916.

Marx, K., and Engles, F. *The Communist Manifesto.* 1848.

Mencken, H. L. *Notes on Democracy.* 1926.

Merriam, C. E., and Barnes, H. E., eds. *A History of Political Theories, Recent Times.* 1924.

Pound, Roscoe. *The Spirit of the Common Law.* 1921.
                  Interpretations of Legal History. 1923.
                  Introduction to the Philosophy of Law. 1922.

Ryan, J. A., and Miller, M. F. X. *The State and the Church.* 1922.

Seeley, J. R. *The Expansion of England.* 1891.
            Introduction to Political Science. 1896.

Semple, E. C. *The Influences of Geographic Environment, on the Basis of Ratzel's System of Anthropogeography.* 1911.

Stoddard, L. *Racial Realities in Europe.* 1924.

Teggart, J. F. *The Processes of History.* 1918.
           The Theory of History. 1925.

Vaughan, C. E. *Studies in the History of Political Philosophy.* 2 vols. 1925.

Vinogradoff, P. *Introduction to Historical Jurisprudence.* 1923.

Wallas, Graham. *Human Nature in Politics.* 1908.
              The Great Society. 1914.
              Our Social Heritage. 1921.

CHAPTER XVIII
HISTORY AND PSYCHOLOGY

By WILSON D. WALLIS

UNIVERSITY OF MINNESOTA

THE historian long posed as the recorder of events; those who turned to the task of a history of history have had their revenge. The historians of history have shown us that the historian is as frequently a recorder of prepossessions as a recorder of events. The supposed objectivity of the task of the historian has always its subjective tinge. His records reflect his point of view in approaching the task; he pictures events rather than photographs them.

This variance in the point of view of historians is reflected in the schools of history. Though old schools like that of Bossuet, declaring that all history is a record of divine intervention, have gone out of vogue, they have been succeeded by others as deeply steeped in prepossession. We now have the economic historians, seeing in economic forces the determining and fundamental factors of history-making; we have the culture historians, seeing in prevailing culture forces the determinants of historical progress; we have the "great man" historians, Carlyleans of a later century, declaring that history is only a summary of biographies.

Many historians are men of action or of strong partisan conviction, and prone to interpret history in terms of the political values current in their day and country. Even when the historian is a recluse he reclines in one set of predispositions rather than in some other. Thus do men make of history an ally rather than a counselor; it becomes a means of propagating their own convictions. Progressives as well as conservatives take history into their keeping and use it as propaganda.

That history presents many examples of a stubborn set of mind which refuses to weigh the evidence or even deliberately tips the scales, should, perhaps, not be surprising; for the task of the historian is a delicate one. Langlois and Seignobos describe for the historian the technique of his work; they tell him, in part, what to seek as well as how to seek. But who will brighten his path and lighten his task by defining for the historian the goal of his efforts?

True, he resurrects and preserves the past; but the scandalous newspaper columns do as much.

INTERPRETATIONS OF HISTORY

Carlyle finds history only biography writ large. Karl Lamprecht and H. Taine find it in the genius of the people working itself out through the centuries, the personages being but actors in a drama staged by the nation and created by the national genius.

Froude, one of the greatest of the English historians, frankly declares there is no science of history, but only individual taste: history is what the historians make it, and they make it anything they like.

Max Nordau agrees that the caprice of the historian has, so far, been the determining factor in the making of history; but, he insists, the historian must not choose; he must imitate those old *chronicleurs* who made record of what happened — earthquakes, plagues, floods — and did not choose from among the materials at hand. But were not these *chronicleurs* selecting their material as much as present-day historians are selecting it? They have omitted many outstanding facts of which they were cognizant — the shifting clouds, the rain or sun, the soughing wind, the change of apparel, the conversation of men, and a million other facts which daily fell beneath their notice, or at least beneath their record. A historian who did not select would furnish poor reading; he would have no principle of treatment; his heterogeneous facts would surfeit the most protean intellectual ostrich; it would take years to write the history of a single day, and the reading of such a history would send the victim to the madhouse. The matter has been well put by Anatole France. In commenting upon the statement of M. Bordeau that "history is not and cannot be a science," France observes:

History is the written presentation of past events. But what is an event? Is it any fact whatever? No, sir. It is a noteworthy fact. Now, how is the historian to judge whether a fact is noteworthy or not? He judges according to his taste and caprice, follows his own idea, in short, proceeds after the manner of an artist. For facts do not of their own nature divide themselves into historical facts and non-historical facts. Again, a fact is something extremely complex. Does the historian represent facts in all their complexity? No, that is impossible. He represents them stripped of the greater part of their detail, consequently truncated, mutilated, different from what they were.

Sir W. W. Hunter says in the preface of one of his histories of India that he hopes the book will reach the hands of many who look upon history as a record of events rather than as a compendium of philosophy. But can any intelligible record of events be given which is not, at the same time, a compendium of philosophy? As Faure says, "What history is there that the historian does not interpret?" The worst of it is, as Voltaire points out, that in history one finds error succeeding prejudice and prejudice succeeding error, putting to flight both truth and reason.

Motive and Predisposition in History

What history should be we leave for the present to P. Lacombe and Hegel, and turn our attention to a brief consideration of what it has been.

Herodotus does not deserve the double honor of father of history and father of lies. He certainly did not invent the latter — let human nature be credited with all it deserves — and it may be doubted whether to any extent he gave way to this frailty. As a matter of fact there is no more justification for accusing Herodotus of intentionally falsifying than for accusing Ptolemy of a like crime in alleging that our planet was the fixed center of the universe about which sun, moon, and stars revolved. Herodotus's errors were as much errors of the intellect as were those of Ptolemy. He saw things as a Greek of his day. This was inevitable. Practically all his descriptions of other peoples, as, for example, when he discourses of the Egyptians or of the Scythians, show in profound manner the naïve Greek point of view.

Many motives, unconscious as well as conscious ones, enter into the historian's account. Livy's patriotism prevented him from mentioning the conquest of Rome by Porsenna, although he was familiar with that fact. According to Grote, the early English historians, from Hardyng and Monmouth to Holinshed and Milton, recorded the descent of the English kings from Brutus and Julius Cæsar. Later historians who suppressed this account as fabulous were accused, because of such suppression, of want of patriotism and were branded as criminals.

Events affecting America have been much distorted by historians. Even the adult American reluctantly admits the truth in Kipling's taunt that the Colonies did not revolt while enemies to the north and west threatened them, but only after England had defeated France and removed the French menace. Then they remembered the cause of freedom, refused to help pay for the war, and proclaimed the right to self-determination. Another Englishman who has turned his attention to the history of our Revolutionary War, or, as he calls it, the First American Civil War, reminds us that

New England was founded and colonized by men of prudence, who thought it wise to retire from any further dealings with Stuart misrule, leaving the contention to stronger purposes and sturdier minds. The migrating Puritans, having thus left better men to settle a quarrel which they themselves had contributed to inflame, have accustomed themselves to think of the English they abandoned as a people of degenerate mind. They have contracted a habit of alleging the superiority of their motives, the purity of their faith, their supreme fortitude, in comparison with the conduct and character of the men who stood by the old ship and weathered her through the breakers to calmer and deeper waters. The men who remained behind in England — Cromwell, Pym, Hampden, Milton, Falkland, and the rest — were tainted with corruption, while the refugees who quitted their native land because there were laws compelling every one to go to meeting in old England, reënacted those laws with a little alteration of detail, as salutary provisions for the maintenance of order and decency in New England.

The history textbooks used in the United States have been written with a marked bias with regard to the period of the Revolution. Of forty textbooks in use prior to the past two decades, thirty-two, used in one hundred and nineteen centers, display more or less pronounced Anglophobia; the remaining eight books, used in fifteen centers, have a fairly moderate attitude toward Great Britain. Among fifty-three books in use in 1918 thirty-three, used in one hundred and twenty-three centers, display varying degrees of Anglophobia, whereas twenty, used in sixty-eight centers, are more or less impartial. In a total of ninety-three books it is possible to count on the fingers of one hand the books that point out that in the American Revolution,

the claims of Great Britain were, at their worst, only the ordinary claims of mother countries upon their colonies at that time. It is evident, therefore, that a very high percentage of those who have passed through the schools of the United States must have learned to regard the attitude of George III and his ministers as unusual and exceptional; and a very considerable majority must have imbibed a feeling of actual hatred toward Great Britain. One is tempted to suspect that the historian of the future, coming across the lines:

'Hate by water and hate by land,
Hate of the head and hate of the hand.

· · · · · · ·

We love as one, we hate as one,
We have one foe, and one alone,
                ENGLAND!'

might easily fall into the trap of attributing them to an American author of the nineteenth century.

A prejudice against the United States, as marked and as universal as the prejudice against England which has pervaded our textbooks, has been characteristic of the textbooks used in Canada; a prejudice which has "led to a bitter and morbid treatment of many episodes in the relations between the two countries; it has magnified tenfold, for instance, the importance of the War of 1812; and it has encouraged, curiously enough, a foolish depreciation of the qualities of the American people."

Oddly enough, a formidable line of English historians have themselves exaggerated the case in behalf of the Americans quite as much as have the American historians.   The source material on which they drew was that of the party in England opposed to the Tory régime, which, like all political parties, enlarged the faults of its opponents.   Thus, the prejudice of enemy historians, instead of offering a corrective to American interpretations, only enlarged the distortion because they copied from a similar prejudice.   Apparently they did not take warning from the fate of Phrynichos, who was fined for reminding the Greeks of their defeat at Miletus.   Some similar fate may be expected by one who ventures, too insistently, to remind us of our national defeats, mistakes, or epochal impotencies.

In any case, the past is not immutably known, nor is it unchangeable.   We can alter our relation to the past and thereby alter the proportion the past bears in our vital history; it is "a series of half-dead seeds, any of which may be revived by a changed relation to it."

INFLUENCE OF PSYCHOLOGY UPON HISTORY

Guyot overstates the case when he alleges that history is merely a psychological analysis, but certainly history is as various as the psychological theories of the times in which it is written.   Psychological reconstructions are constantly being made and these are injected into the past.   When the psychologist gives us a new interpretation of his contemporaries, he gives us a new interpretation of Julius Cæsar and Napoleon Bonaparte; for if these men were not like unto ourselves, we cannot hope to understand them. To know ourselves anew is, therefore, to know them anew. Whenever the understanding, or misunderstanding, of our contemporaries undergoes a change, so likewise does our understanding of our predecessors. Every new psychological insight, therefore, is a new insight into historical personages.

The most important of the psychological interpretations which bid fair to lead to far-reaching reconstructions in history are probably the following:

Recent psychology gives new insight into motives. Those which concern history most intimately are the economic and political motives and those associated with personal ambition. Marx, Loria, and Beard describe the possibilities, or supposed possibilities, which lurk in economic motives, not to say in the play of economic determinism. Guizot, Thiers, and the long line of nationalistic historians in Germany after 1870 were influenced by political motives, as was Burke in an earlier day; and interpretation of personal ambition is the leading-string through much of the history of medieval Italy, Germany, and France.

What Factors Make History?

If the historian had nothing to do but record events in the order in which they happened, his task would then not be simple, but his aim would be clearly defined; but chronological sequence is not the purpose of history, being merely the manner in which it carries out its purpose. The events which history records must be not merely so many beads on a string, but rather so many events that are interconnected, that spring from some common underlying cause or motive. The discovery of the string which holds the events together, of the cause responsible for the happenings which the historian records, is a part of his task, and perhaps the larger part, as it is the more important. Here, where interest begins, begins also the enigma of the historian who can more easily state *when* and *where* and *which way*, than the *why* and *wherefor*. How, for example, shall he rate the factor of race? Shall he, after Gobineau, declare that race is the determiner of history, time and circumstance being merely the media through which race genius finds its inevitable expression? Did Anglo-Saxon civilization come to the fore because of the racial qualities of the carriers of that civilization, or was race but an indifferent medium? Recent analyses by psychologists reflect back upon the historical fates of the peoples whose racial qualities are rated by psychological tests as high, medium, or low.

Unfortunately, the psychologist has confused race with nationality or culture, and has palmed off as race characteristics what after all are only culture or nationality characteristics. Historians, or pseudo-historians, already have misapplied these psychological fumblings, injecting into history the initial errors of the psychologists.

What importance shall the historian attribute to the various psychological agencies which in all times and places make history? Shall he attribute European progress to qualities inherent in race? Do the factors which make for progress originate in the group, or in extraneous groups? Is Greek civilization the outcome of influences arising from within the Greeks in Greek lands, or is it due to influences pouring in from surrounding cultures? What importance shall the historian attribute to remote as compared with immediate purposes, to conscious as compared with unconscious motives? Do the times make their problems, or are they made for them?

What importance shall the historian attribute to geographical influences? Are they external influences which act independently of the mind which dwells amid them? As such they have frequently been treated, yet psychological analysis tells us that external forces are influences only when they are stimuli, consciously or unconsciously responded to by an organism. In short, until one knows environment, or feels environment, or responds to the stimuli of environment, it has little or no psychological play. Why does coal influence the aboriginal American of three centuries ago in one manner, that is to say, scarcely at all, and the present-day English-speaking American in quite another way, if not, in part at least, by reason of a different apperception of "coal"? New knowledge makes the old into a new environment.

The story of economic motivation is similar. Loria and Beard, for example, offer economic interpretations of history which could scarcely have been developed prior to a science of economics. Indeed, economic history has its beginnings in the last half of the eighteenth century, as for example, in the writings of Turgot, when economic science was beginning to get its stride. Then social and historical development was described from a new angle, the angle of economic pressure and response to economic factors.

In contrast with these interpretations are the interpretations of the culture historians who point to the influence of surrounding or antecedent cultures, a movement well under way soon after the Renaissance. The tolerance of one culture for the culture of its neighbors or for that of its predecessors influences its own development — an attitude which at basis is an attitude of mind. Indeed, it was this attitude of mind which made the revival of learning possible and gave us the new Graeco-Roman civilization which we call Western European.

Frequently we find a group that is a psychic entity, possessing unity and self-completeness which make it a supra-individual thing. The psychic qualities of the group cannot be obtained by adding up nor yet by averaging the qualities of the individuals who compose *the group*. Social psychology is a study of the behavior of groups which function as units among other unit groups. Each nation has a psychology peculiar to itself: the social psychology of the English is not that of the French, that of the Germans, nor that of the Italians.

What it is is recorded in what the nation does, and in what the constituent parts do. Social psychology may give an account of the component parts, or may describe the functioning of the nation or group as a unit rather than as a composition of coördinating parts. Most important of all the new views in psychology, possibly, is that which has developed under the guise of social psychology or allied branches. If the group has a mind, then that mind must react upon the progress of the group as well as influence greatly the behavior of the component members of the group. It is, of course, the antithesis of the "great man" theory of history, a denial of the Carlylean interpretation of causal factors. The first clear presentations of this view must be credited to H. Taine and Karl Lamprecht, with their theories that a people has a "spirit" which carries it from decade to decade, unfolding its destiny.

MENTAL PATTERNS IN RELATION TO HISTORY

That this is and will remain a fruitful field for psychological historical work is probable. Much emphasis was given this point of view in the work of German historians who exalted the German *Kultur*, a culture pattern peculiar to Germany. At the present time we have a promising revival of it with new interpretations and new implications in the school of *Gestalt Theorie* now being developed by a group of German psychologists. A corollary of this interpretation is the conception of a mental pattern applicable to a given group, a mental pattern in which the parts are interwoven and interdependent, so much so that a part cannot be understood without an understanding of the whole, for the parts are interdependent. In their totality they function as a culture unity which is as real as the individual mind. In almost any culture group the forces which hold the group together are not the sum of uncorrelated individual efforts but a complex and functionally united enterprise composed of various interdependent groups of enterprises. The mental pattern of English civilization is as real as the mental attitude of any of her statesmen, and, in the world of international statecraft, a much more important thing. Only the historian who is psychologically trained, or the psychologist who is historically trained, will be able to comprehend that mental pattern; but he who does comprehend it grasps a reality of much significance.

The things which contribute to this mental pattern are essentially of psychological-historical nature. First and foremost, perhaps, is tradition, as much a matter of psychology as of history. For tradition is selection of a portion of the past, a portion which becomes a conscious incentive for present and future action; and tradition shifts when culture emphasis shifts. At every new turn of political or cultural aims a people shifts its traditions, eliminating some elements, selecting new ones.

Custom is the partner of tradition, and a fly-wheel of society. It acts upon the individual by suggestion and by way of direct stimulus. One can no more escape the impulsions of custom than the pull of gravitation. Each culture group, often each political unit, can be distinguished by its customs. Some of these customs are of minor significance, some are of great culture importance.

Opinion, too, takes an objective aspect and may be one of the powerful stimuli in group life. Was it not public opinion which kept the Greek citizenry in line with tradition and custom, which enabled the populace to ostracize unpopular leaders and substitute men who were more to the liking of the inhabitants? Did not public opinion hold sway in Rome in many an affair of state? If the opinions of one's compatriots are a matter of concern, if they incite to action or deter, then such opinion must be rated as a historical force.

The historian cannot be blind to the rôle of ideas in group life nor to the importance of the continuity of the social psychology, the continuity of the mental life of the group. There is about it something supra-individual, as there is about language and political structure. Mind in the making is one of his problems, and no plea of its difficulty excuses failure to face it.

Nor, if he aims at thoroughness and enlightening insight, will he be able to escape the problem which the psychologist is now bringing to our attention — the problem of purpose or mechanism in historical forces. Do they move in predetermined manner to their fulfilment, or is purposive direction, deflection, modification, possible, or only illusory? Could history have been different from what it is, or to be different would it have been necessary to start out with another sort of universe and another sort of creature than this *homo sapiens?*

Psychological analysis is, of course, only one of the tools of the historian, whose tool-chest already contains a multitude of implements. That it is a tool which he must use is brought home to us by the extent to which historical reconstructions depend upon the interpretation of facts and events as well as upon their discovery. Every new psychological interpretation reflects back upon the field in which the historian works, and colors his inferences as well as his findings. He must select from amid the data at hand, and no selection can be apart from his estimate of the meaning of the facts or events which he adduces. Since history deals with man it can never dispense with interpretations of mind, either mind in the individual or mind in the mass. Indeed, it might be said that in the last analysis it is only with the manifestations of mind that history is concerned.

SELECTED REFERENCES

Adams, George B. "History and the Philosophy of History." *American Historical Review*, XIV, pp. 221–36.

Barnes, H. E. "Psychology and History." *American Journal of Psychology*, 1919.

Bourdeau, Louis. *Histoire des Historiens*. 1888.

Bradley, F. H. *The Presuppositions of Critical History*. 1874.

Bryce, James. *Modern Democracies*, II, chap. II. 1921.

Butler, Samuel. *The Fair Haven*. Chap. III. 1913.

Carrier, Lyman. *The Beginnings of Agriculture in America.* Chap. I. 1923.

Corcoran, T. *The Teaching of History. Studies,* XII, June, 1923, no. 46, pp. 249–60.

Croce, Benedetto. *History: Its Theory and Practice.* English trans. by D. Ainslie. 1921.

Crozier, John B. *Civilization and Progress.* 1909.

De Pierrefew, Jean. *Plutarch Lied.* 1924.

Fisher, S. G. "Legendary and Myth-Making Process in Histories of the American Revolution." *Proceedings of the American Philosophical Society,* LI, 1912, pp. 53–76.

Foster, W. E. *The Point of View in History.* 1906.

France, Anatole. *Penguin Island.* English trans. 1909.

Freeman, E. A. *Methods of Historical Study.* 1886.

Grant, I. F. *Everyday Life on an Old Highland Farm.* Chap. II. 1924.

Held, F. E. *Christianopolis,* pp. 232–35. 1916.

Klüver, Heinrich. "The Problem of Type in 'Cultural Science Psychology.'" *Journal of Philosophy,* XXII, April 23, 1925, pp. 225–34.
"Psychological and Sociological Types." *Psychological Review,* XXXI, 1924.

Lacombe, Paul. *De L'Histoire Considerée Comme Science.* 1894.
La Psychologie des Individus et Des Sociétés chez Taine Historien des Littératures. 1916.

Lamprecht, Karl. *What is History?* 1922.

Lowie, R. H. *Primitive Religion.* Chap. IX. 1924.

Maine, Sir Henry. *Village Communities in the East and West.* Chap. I. 1876.

Mathews, Shailer. *The Spiritual Interpretation of History.* 1917.

Mougeolle, Paul. *Les Problèmes de l'Histoire.* 1886.

Nordau, Max. *The Interpretation of History.* English trans. 1910.

Payne, Edward J. *The History of the New World Called America.* Chaps. 1, 2, 15. 1892.

Robinson, James H. *The New History.* 1913.

Spencer, Herbert. "What Knowledge is of Most Worth?" *Westminster Review,* 1859.
The Study of Sociology. 1920 ed. Chap. II.

Stockbridge, Frank P. "What Washington did for a Living and How He Succeeded in Becoming the First Millionaire in America." *Collier's National Weekly,* Feb. 21, 1925.

Teggart, Frederick J. "Anthropology and History." *Journal of Philosophy,* XVI, pp. 691–96.
"Prolegomena to History. The Relation of History to Literature, Philosophy, and Science." *University of California Publications in History,* IV, pp. 155–292. (Valuable bibliography.)
The Processes of History. 1919.

Troeltch. "Historiography," in Hastings' *Encyclopædia of Religion and Ethics.*

Voltaire. *Siècle de Louis XIV.* 1775–1922.
Essai sur Les Mœurs. 1775–1835.

Wallis, Wilson D. "Motive and Caprice in Anthropology and in History." *Journal of Philosophy, Psychology and Scientific Method,* XVII, 1920.
"The Influence of Anthropology upon History." *Scientific Monthly,* Nov., 1917.

Wallis, Wilson D. "Mental Patterns in Relation to Culture." *Journal of Abnormal Psychology and Social Psychology*, xix, 1924, pp. 179–84.

"The Independence of Social Psychology." *Ibid.*, xx, 1925.

Introduction to Sociology. Chap. xvii. 1927.

Williams, J. M. *The Foundations of Social Science.* Chap. xxi. 1920.

Wissler, Clark. *The American Indian.* 2d ed., pp. 386–88. 1922.

Woodbridge, F. J. E. *The Purpose of History.* 1916.

Biography. Interesting psychological reconstructions will be found in:

Brooks, Van Wyck. *The Ordeal of Mark Twain.* 1920.

Gardiner, A. G. *Prophets, Priests, and Kings.* 1914.

Portraits and Portents. 1926.

Guedalla, Philip. *The Second Empire.* 1923.

Fathers of the Revolution. 1926.

Harlow, Ralph. *Samuel Adams.* 1923.

Strachey, Lytton. *Life of Queen Victoria.* 1921.

Eminent Victorians. 1918.

CHAPTER XIX

HISTORY AND SOCIOLOGY

By FRANZ OPPENHEIMER

UNIVERSITY OF FRANKFORT

SOCIOLOGIST AND HISTORIAN

BETWEEN sociologists and historians there has existed since the first inception of sociological ideas, even since the time of Condorcet, a sharp difference, a state of battle, which grows out of two different sources — a psychological and a scientifico-logical.

The psychological difference is based on the fact that all the older writing of history viewed and evaluated events from the standpoint of the upper class. It was, as soon as it had grown out of the embryonic stage of writing mere annals or chronicles, of three kinds: first, court historiography, with the clearly set task of glorifying the deeds and creations of the ruler; or secondly, it was clerical philosophy of history, which explained events from the standpoint of the ruling church as the carrying out of a divine plan of salvation, and was for this reason necessarily quietistic, conservative, anti-revolutionary; or finally, it was history-writing of the third estate, which had either already gained control of its state or was at least preparing to do so, and if it had not already attained to complete victory politically, at least it already possessed sufficient economic means to want political control and to be able to force it in the not too distant future. On the other hand, the first representatives of sociological thought viewed things as socialists *from below*, and this attitude has never been entirely lost by their successors, as for example Comte, who had primarily bourgeois tendencies.

Closely connected with this psychological difference is the scientifico-logical. All older history-writing had thrust the strong *individual*, the hero, into the center of the story, had conceived him as the real motive power of the events: the court historiographic method did this as a matter of course; the clerico-ecclesiastical conception did it, with the difference, however, that it regarded rulers, lawgivers, and the like, as instruments of God; and the bourgeois writing of history, in line with its general individualism, did it by abandoning the idea of a "genius" come from God and conceiving instead "genius" as eminent personal endowment. In contrast with this, the sociological conception, for the very reason that it viewed things *from below*, represented the masses as the real bearers of historical events. This is collectivistic; the older history-writing was individualistic.

This is a difference, moreover, which does not stop at the surface of things: it leads to the deepest depths. A science of history aimed essentially at the individual cannot possibly conceive the notion of seeking the laws of history (unless it be to feel out instinctively the divine plan of salvation working itself out in it), for there can be no law of the individual. But sociology in its first representatives proceeded from the philosophy of western Europe, which was oriented in mathematics and natural science, and took its beginning in Descartes; it was therefore as a matter of course intent on conformity to law, and from its collectivistic standpoint could well hope to be able to find such lawfulness. To it, then, the science of history, such as it found in existence, naturally seemed positively unscientific. Not only did the socialist, Condorcet, think so, but also after him the real founder of sociology as a science, Auguste Comte, who immediately opened the attack. Historians were for him the thing which he scientifically most despised, "specialists" whose banal doings would have to be overcome by a new specialty, "the study of scientific generalities"; the writing of history, he said, had in aspect not lost its descriptive and narrative character to that day and was far from being a true science, since its childish over-valuation of genius would be impossible in a true science. The second progenitor of the young science, Herbert Spencer, was no more polite. He leaves to history-writing, at most, description, saying that history is to be compared to sociology as biography is to physiology. And similar expressions were used by the man who first synthetically united western European sociology with the middle European philosophy of history, Lorenz von Stein. This critical attitude extends down to the present day; only a short time ago a German sociologist, L. Von Wiese, remarked caustically to the pure historian, von Below, that "since the days of Spencer there had existed among sociologists a lively distrust as to the reliability of the material which history supplies us." [1]

No wonder that those who had been attacked so unexpectedly and so rudely, defended themselves. Even the demand to change

[1] The literary citations in our *Allgemeine Soziologie*, pp. 125–26.

their course, to see things from an entirely new angle, could not be expected to be received kindly; for always and everywhere "the capitalists of the mind defend themselves against expropriation." Now, however, to the antipathy for the socialists and the anger at the disturbers of the peace was added also resentment against the bold attackers, and the tone of the polemics betrayed the mental attitude.

Now the young branch of knowledge, in its first systems, made blunders enough, which enabled those already ensconced in science to decline to recognize it at all. They said it was "monistic in method," that it tried to handle social philosophy with the tools of natural science, that it often confused pure sociology, which explains causes, with social philosophy, which refers to values, that it undertook, for example, to derive what ought to be from what is, and that it evinced here and there often enough a lack of the necessary critical attitude toward its sources and of caution in its synthesis. Comte's attempt at a scientific universal history contained, side by side with some downright brilliant portions, a large number of easily refutable peculiarities and undeniable mistakes, and thus people held sociology — such is human nature — responsible for the sins of the sociologists, threw them both overboard, and declared the whole undertaking a priori unscientific and unviable. The sentence of condemnation on the part of the Rector of the University of Brussels, Van der Reft, is well known; even recently von Below, a good historian of the old school, has taken the same stand and has characterized sociology as an "omnium-gatherum science" and, with Alfred Dove, as a "loan shop of word-masks."

The quarrel must be fought to a conclusion. For sociology, as the *theoretical science of the social process* as such and as a whole, cannot think of renouncing its right to treat the chief and most interesting part of this process, *social progress*.[1] It cannot content itself with investigating its subject only in the cross-section, so to say, in the axis of space; in order to get closer to its goal it must be allowed to investigate it in the longitudinal section, in the axis of time, in order to be able to find from the synthesis of these two considerations the law of the whole. That was Comte's great ob-

---

[1] By "progress" we understand, leaving aside every other connotation connected with the word, solely the changes of the social process — or what amounts to the same thing, human society — taking place in the dimensions of time. For example, a clear retrogression, such as "a cultural loss," may according to our definition be a part of progress.

ject; he consigned it to all his successors, and most of them took over the inheritance with this charge. Spann is almost the only one who has shunted history out of his system, and that apparently is only for the present. (We are not speaking here of the representatives of that tendency which already seems outworn, which came from Simmel, but was finally given up by him as well, which conceives sociology as a purely formal science, analogous to logic and grammar.)

WHAT IS HISTORY?

Let us ask, then, first, what the writing of history is. Its battle with the sociological conception of history, particularly in the form of the so-called materialistic philosophy of history, has forced its representatives to a consideration of their position, task, and method, so that the problems are now stated with some accuracy and probably admit of a decision.

Wilhelm Dilthey distinguishes first of all between the natural sciences and the mental sciences. The former treat that which is forever foreign to us, which comes to us from without and is recognizable through our senses, just to what extent we do not know; the latter, however, have as their material that which is immediately accessible and familiar to us from our own observation — life and consciousness. In the case of the former, we can only connect cause and result from without; in the case of the latter, we, as a part of feeling, willing, recognizing life, see from within into the true connection of things, and can understand it by empathy.

The general field of the mental sciences is historical, social, reality. They can make concerning the mental sciences three different kinds of statement: *historical*, by expressing the real that is got by perception; *theoretical*, that is, constituent contents of this reality derived by abstraction; and *practical*, which express judgments of value and prescribe rules. We are interested here in the first class. Dilthey says that the conception of the singular, the individual, is as much a subject of science as the development of abstract uniformities.

In this discussion we have first of all to state what is most important for us, namely, that the social historical reality admits besides the historical consideration also a theoretical one that is deductive and aiming at conformity to law. But we will not content ourselves with that; we will ask whether the assuredly possible empathetic consideration of the singular and individual can be recognized as *science*? Suffice it for us here that Dilthey has been most decisively contradicted from his own camp, that of the defenders of the hitherto prevailing method of history-writing: that is, what he portrayed was not science but *art*. Writing history, then, is an art, a conception which not long since a historian of the rank of Beloch expressed in no uncertain terms.

Heinrich Rickert, the most famous logician and methodologist of Germany, will not admit that writing history is an art, and rightly; for as a matter of fact, that about a work of art which is the reproduction of individual reality is esthetically unessential. In order to save the writing of history as a science, he distinguishes, contrary to his predecessor, *materially*, between natural science and cultural science, and *formally*, between the method of natural science and the historical method. Within the scope of cultural science comes everything and every occurrence which we lift out of the sum of reality because they have for us a particular importance or significance, so that we see in them more than mere nature. And whenever we investigate such things or occurrences with regard to their separateness and individuality rather than their existence, in so far as it is determined by general laws, then we are making use of the historical method (which incidentally is just as applicable to subjects of natural science as the method of natural science is to the subjects of cultural science).

Here, again, we wish to assert that that deduction clears even more decidedly the way of sociology as a generalizing branch, that is, one proceeding according to the method of natural science, from the social, historical reality, than does Dilthey's conception. But we will not content ourselves with that either; we will inquire further whether Rickert succeeded in rescuing the writing of history as a science of the individual.

This seems doubtful. Rickert, as the eminent logician that he was, knew of course that, as Kant says, there can be no particular without the general. We can understand only what we can classify under general conceptions. And so, also, the writer of history can by no means do without such general conceptions. Even Spencer pointed out in the case of a number of historians, among them the famous Froude and Kingsley, that they, who *ex professo* deny all conformity to law in history, not only recognize it *de facto*, but also make it the basis of their discussions. Bouglé ironically and strikingly calls that involuntary sociology. And just as the historian cannot even start his work if he does not believe in a certain conformity to law in human mass activity, he likewise cannot proceed a step further if he does not have a system of general conceptions. What could the historian possibly do if he did not possess the concepts "state," "economics," "rule," "politics," "literature," "revolution," "people," "city," and so on?

In order to evade this difficulty, Rickert constructs for historical work special so-called complex concepts, which are not to be deduced by abstraction, but in some way or other probably to be made by empathy, and which are supposed to embrace the whole range of presentation. He names as an example the idea of the Renaissance. It seems doubtful whether there can be such concepts at all; whether it is not a question rather of outgrown images, approximately what Spinoza characterized as "*notiones universales*," unclarified, obscure masses of ideas, or really only words which come in where there is a lack of ideas. It seems to us that here, just as in the case of Dilthey, the vivid, artistic appreciation of a personality, an individual group, or a *Zeitgeist* is being confused with scientific activity.

It cannot possibly escape a mind of the caliber of Rickert's that, to say the least, questionable things are here being asserted; and we shall get at the core of the problems if we trace the way by which he reached these constructions. He says that the historians wish to portray the ever individual reality in its individuality; they see this as their task, and to it logic must do justice. Otherwise the work of Ranke and all the other famous historians would not be scientific!

The syllogistic *petitio principii* is obvious. That which is to be proved is used as a premise of the proof. The real question is whether the great historians were not mistaken when they considered their work scientific work.

The solution must really be that the great historians were, to be sure, great scholars, but that it is nevertheless doubtful whether what they produced may be, or indeed has to be, called science. In order to write history, one must possess scientific qualities of a high order: one must at least be a great philologist and have all the capabilities of a diplomat, numismatist, and so forth. Eduard Meyer, who has a masterly command not only of Latin and Greek, but also of all the Near Eastern languages, is certainly a great scholar, as is also Mommsen, who besides his most thorough philological training was also an eminent jurist. Furthermore, the critical handling of the assembled material calls for decided scientific ability, above all, for acumen. But that does not prove that the *product* of these scientific labors is *scientific* history.

Here we can still see that the writing of history had its origin in Humanism, which was quite essentially philology, that is, the science of language. To the rapt devotion of that generation to antiquity, every single fact that was handed down from the history of the Greeks and Romans seemed immensely valuable, and it was axiomatic that the most painstaking establishment of all those facts was a worthy goal of effort. And that may still be uncontested from the standpoint of philology; but for us philology is no longer history! To us it is, from the standpoint of history-writing, nothing but one of its auxiliary sciences, as from the standpoint of philology the writing of history is one of its auxiliary sciences.

HISTORY-WRITING AS DESCRIPTIVE DOCTRINE

What, then, has the writing of history been heretofore if it is neither art nor science? We consider it an esthetic activity. Leonard Nelson in his *Kritik der praktischen Vernunft* (*Critique of Practical Reason*) has shown that ethics is composed of two parts, the doctrine of duty, which grows out of the moral interest, and the doctrine of the ideal, which comes from the esthetic interest. The former gives categorical imperatives, the latter, categorical optatives. For its prescriptions are not hypothetical, nor yet imperative, and still they have a relation to the will. And he shows further that every higher, that is, non-sensual, positive value can only have its root here: for every moral value is only negative, produces only — for undutiful action — negative, incompensative lack of value. All the cultural values come, then, from the esthetic interest, which alone is capable of giving stress to value.

In pursuance of these thoughts, we consider history-writing a *descriptive doctrine of the ideal*. That fits in beautifully with the very common idea that history should and can be the schoolmaster of mankind — a conception which would be quite senseless if one tried, like the representatives of history-writing, to treat it as a science and yet denied all conformity of events to law, but which on the other hand has good grounds if one conceives the writing of history as a doctrine of the ideal which sets up models to be lived up to and wishes to offer to the will categorical optatives of heroic action.

And this corresponds even better with the utterances of important historians and philosophers of history. Mehlis writes, for example, that history has the best of intentions with regard to its heroes. Dilthey says, "The biographer ought to view man *sub specie æternitatis*, as he himself feels at moments when there is only a vestment and veil between himself and the divinity, and he feels himself as near to the starry heavens as to any part of earth." Even Goethe assigned to history the task of "awakening enthusiasm"; Troeltsch says of Machiavelli that he contented himself with a psychologically viewed typification of history as a guide in present action; Schleiermacher thinks "that history is the picture book of moral philosophy, and moral philosophy is the formulary of history"; and Eduard Meyer says "that all presentation of history is not only science but art, and moreover not only in the matter of outward form, as in the case of every work of literature, but also as to content in shaping the object."

And what is more — and this is where the true sociological viewpoint is expressed — history is always the doctrine of the ideal from the standpoint of a *definite group*. Every group, particularly every class (in the wider sense of the word where it means rank and caste), *reads its group ideals into history and brings them forward in the form of idealized personalities, institutions, and conditions as everlasting models and guides for present action*. Or in other words, the historian writes history "*sub specie*" of what he orthodoxly considers "*æternitatis*," which in reality, however, is nothing but his "personal equation" (Spencer): and that is his group's stock of norms which have been instilled into him by education, imitation, and tradition. To illustrate by a single example, a historian, Treitschke, famous not only for his scientific achievements, in his *Politik* (I, p. 86) boasts of the Germans, that is, of himself, that they are "free from political traditions and prejudices." There is no question of his orthodoxy, and neither can one doubt his inseverable connection with his social group, that of Prussian conservatism with a strong big-agrarian coloring.

In so far as they are all the expression of the personal equation of their teachers and writers, that is, the expression of the chance disposition of the group to which those personalities belong, all mental and cultural sciences are not the subjects of sociological investigation, as is assumed — they are *its objects*. It is the most priceless gift which the young discipline of sociology has yet brought to science and mankind, that it has caused us to recognize this hitherto almost completely neglected viewpoint of criticism. It demands to know the personal equation of every investigator in one of its fields in the same way as that is expected of the astronomer making observations; and it demands of every critic that in the case of all older works and the recent ones as well, he first of all determine what ideal of class or group the author (orthodoxly) served or serves, and what, for this reason his "*thema probandum*" was or is. This psychological test opens the way in many cases for the logical test and leads to the proton pseudos of deduction.

This new method is already being used to-day as a matter of course, consciously or unconsciously, by all the important representatives of the history of the mind: a pleasing result particularly of the materialistic criticism of history, and a new proof of the fact that even an incorrect theory, if it is only brilliant enough, can accomplish a great deal for the advancement of science.[1]

We will mention as one of the most important representatives of this critical tendency Wilhelm Hasbach, who has already handled the method with complete mastery in his classical investigations concerning the *General Philosophical Principles of the Political Economics Founded by François Quesnay and Adam Smith*. We ourselves have consciously and on principle applied it in all our research on the history of the dogmas of economics, both in the case of preceding sociologists in our *Allgemeine Soziologie*, and to history-writing in an extensive excursus on the history of the *Great-Men Theory* (p. 911 *et seq.*). A work on the state soon to appear (the second part of *Das System der Soziologie*, of which hitherto the first volume, *Allgemeine Soziologie*, and the third, *Oekonomik*, have been available, each in two half-volumes) also treats from the same critical viewpoint the doctrines of the state from canonical times to the present. That this method, applied to the writing of history, produces extremely valuable results is proved by a piece of research, as yet only in the form of a sketch, by my pupil Gottfried Salomon, Privatdozent at the University of Frankfort on the Main, on "History as Ideology" (in *Wirtschaft und Gesellschaft*, Festgabe für Franz Oppenheimer, 1924). He proves here conclusively that all history-writing is the weapon of the various clearly recognizable parties of political life; for instance, in the Middle

---

[1] Concerning the materialistic conception of history compare *Allgemeine Soziologie*, p. 911 *et seq.*

Ages, of the papal party or that of the local rulers, or perhaps of the imperial party; or in modern times, of the states, or of absolutism, or of the third or fourth estates; and that the position taken each time corresponds exactly to the interests of the orthodoxly-represented social group.

According to that, the writing of history ceases to be the *opponent* of sociology and becomes its *subject of study*. It serves as an important index of the class situation, out of which grew the individual work by virtue of the social-psychological determinism which was an insurmountable obstacle for the sociologically naïve man.

The Sociological Method

The first task of sociological history-writing is, accordingly, one of criticism. It has to put the generally accepted axioms of the historians under the microscope and test them to see if they hold good in fact, if they in fact are true. Where the axioms of the different classes, especially of the bourgoisie and the prevailing Socialism, contradict one another mutually, the task is already solved in part — the axioms are already confuted or at least shaken. But where the two schools solely devoted to science start from the same fundamental axiom, there the whole work is yet to be done. One of the firmly seated propositions of this sort is the "law of previous accumulation," from which the whole bourgeois as well as the whole Marxian doctrine proceeds as from an incontestably true principle — that doctrine by virtue of which the social classes everywhere without any interference of extra-economical force, from merely inner, merely economic forces, have developed from a state of original equality, and after the restoration of equality would have to develop again from absolutely the same forces. In other words: history has *existed*, to be sure, but has *effected* nothing; conquest, enslavement, subjection, dominance, state, and foreign policies have remained without effect on the present state of humanity. On this theory alone communism sensibly rests: if it is true, rational equality can be restored and maintained only by the elimination of those forces of economic competition between those unequally endowed.

I have time and again attacked this pseudo-law, and with, I think, successful arguments have refuted it as completely false (most recently in *System der Soziologie*, I, p. 987 *et seq.*, and III, p. 206 *et seq.*) without, however, thus far being able to get a fair debate from those attacked. In the second volume of *Das System* I have laid bare in a detailed analysis from the standpoint of intellectual history, the ramifications of the theorem and have shown that it is one tangle of dogmatic metaphysical postulates in connection with crude, even ridiculous, misunderstandings. (A short extract has appeared in the *Festschrift für Lujo Brentano*.)

After the completion of this task of criticism, which will perhaps uncover still other principles of present-day writing of history, just as widespread and just as false, the second and positive task is to *portray* history by taking the correct conception of the origin of the state and the classes as a basis. An attempt of this sort is to be found in our *Grossgrundeigentum und soziale Frage* (second edition), where we have portrayed German history, especially of the Middle Ages, purposely ignoring the law of previous accumulation in all its forms, even in that of the Malthusian law of population, and have reached new views. The book has never till this day (it appeared first in 1898) been criticized by an expert; there is only a private, very appreciative statement by Karl Lamprecht (printed in the preface to the second edition). If strength and life hold out, my co-worker, Fedor Schneider, and I will complete in the fourth volume of *Das System der Soziologie*, which we have undertaken, a delineation of the social and economic history of Europe from the tribal migrations to the present, handling this great theme without the use of the false explanations of the law of previous accumulation, that is, proceeding from the principle of the "sociological idea of the state."

THE LIMITATIONS OF METHOD

This first attempt on a large scale will have to show what sociological history-writing, which has already proved itself in the field of mental history, can do in that of political history. But here it must be said that it is not in a position to accomplish, and is neither willing nor obligated to accomplish, what some of its opponents demand of it — the setting up of mathematically exact "laws of nature" for history. That is a ridiculous demand of us which proves nothing more than that the originators of it have little notion of the conception of a law, that they confuse a limited class with the main concept. Only in mathematical physics, for example, in astronomy, are there laws of this precision; the other natural sciences have to get along with laws of much lesser range, and often enough even with mere empirical rules. One cannot demand of sociology, which has to do with even more complicated aggregates, any greater precision than, for instance, of meteorology. We have expatiated on this subject in our *Allgemeine Soziologie* to a considerable extent, namely, in connection with Cournot and Eulenburg, and will only refer to that discussion now.

In the second place, it is to be noted at the outset that sociology, conceived in its modern significance as the purely causal science of the social process, is not in a position *by itself* to illuminate history-writing completely. It needs on every hand the coöperation of social philosophy, that is to say, ethics, which is oriented in values and itself assigns values.

And thirdly, it must be said that sociological history-writing, as an inductive theoretical science, is for this very reason not in a position to do justice to the purely individual, for the reason that no single theoretical science can do this, since it reasons away from the individual. It must therefore decline to reveal the secret of the so-called supersocial personality — the great leader, scholar, saint, and so forth. Here there still remains for the real, individualizing writing of history a wide field of activity in which it will likewise have to work in common with social philosophy.

But even here, too, sociological history-writing has indispensable preparatory work to do. For it is scarcely ever disputed and nowadays is regarded as proved, that even the strongest, the most ingenious, individual is and remains deeply entangled in the standards of his group. He towers, at times very high, above his fellows, but he never stands outside their intellectual circle. Only comparative inductive generalization can ascertain, even in the case of the greatest personalities, how large the individual scope is within which they are able to emancipate themselves from their group imperatives. Until this general conformity to law is determined, every evaluation of the historical personality is purely arbitrary and not in the least binding. Only the lack of such general, sociological preparatory researches has made possible the absolutely ridiculous overvaluation of the "great men" which reached its highest point in Treitschke and degenerated in Carlyle (hero-worship) into a Messianic cult, which annuls the usual great-men theory since it recognizes in the whole course of the world's history only a very small number of geniuses.

That is about all that is to be said about the relation of history-writing and sociology to-day. The practical application is that the sociologist, in whatever part of this great field he may choose to work, should take the most sincere pains to become acquainted with his own personal equation and properly to take it into account. Only then will the so-called mental sciences begin to be sciences in the real, strict sense of the word. Only when this is done, will sociology be able to attain its highest goal of becoming the schoolmaster of man, who will never rise from the pitiful barbarism in which he is living until he has learned by unprejudiced science to master the most powerful of all elementary processes, the social process, with as much surety as he controls steam and electricity to-day. *Nothing is so practical as theory.* And never did a time need a correct social theory more than does our day — this world of the white man which threatens to go under in the collision of Western Capitalism and Eastern Bolshevism.

SELECTED REFERENCES

Barth, Paul. *Die Philosophie der Geschichte als Soziologie.* 1897. 2 Aufl.

Below, Georg von. *Soziologie als Lehrfach.*

Bernheim, Ernst. *Lehrbuch der Historischen Methode.* 1889. 5 und 6 Aufl.

Bouglé, Célestin. *Qu'est-ce que la Sociologie?* 3d ed. 1914.

Breysig, Kurt. *Der Stufen-bau und die Gesetze der Weltgeschichte.* 1905.

Buckle, H. T. *History of Civilization in England.* 1858.

Comte, Auguste. *The Positive Philosophy.* Trans. by Harriet Martineau. 1833.

Croce, B. *Theory and History of Historiography.* Trans. by D. Ainslee. 1921.

Dilthey, Wilhelm. *Einleitung in die Geisteswissenschaften.* 1883.

Eulenburg. "Naturgesetze und Soziale Gesetze." *Archiv für Sozialwissenschaften,* XXXII *et seq.*

⎯⎯ "Ueber Gesetzmässigkeiten in der Geschichte." *Archiv für Sozialwissenschaften,* XXXV.

Fueter, Eduard. *Geschichte der Neueren Historiographie.* 1911.

Giddings, F. H. *Principles of Sociology.* 1896.

Gumplowicz, Ludwig. *The Outlines of Sociology.* Trans. by F. W. Moore. 1899.

⎯⎯ *Die Soziologische Staatsidee.* 1902.

Hasbach, Wilhelm. *Die Allgemeinen Philosophischen Grundlagen der von François Quesnay und Adam Smith Begründeten Politischen Oekonomie.* 1890.

Kistiakowski, Theodor. *Gesellschaft und Einzelwesen.* 1899.

Lamprecht, Karl. *Moderne Geschichtswissenschaft.* 1905.

Mayr, Georg von. *Gesetzmässigkeit im Gesellschaftsleben.* 1877.

Pareto, V. *Traité de Sociologie Générale.* 2 vols. 1917.

Quételet, Adolphe. *Sur la Physique du Globe.* 1861.

Ratzel, Friedrich. *Anthropogeographie.* 1899.

Rickert, Heinrich. *Die Grenzen der Naturwissenschaftlichen Begriffsbildung.* 1902.

Ross, E. A. *Foundations of Sociology.* 1905.

Rothacker, Erich. *Einleitung in die Geisteswissenschaften.* 1920.

Schäffle, Albert. *Bau und Leben des Sozialen Körpers.* 1896.

Simmel, Georg. *Grundfragen der Soziologie.* 1917.

Small, A. W. *General Sociology.* 1905.

Spann, Othmar. *Kurzgefasstes System der Gesellschaftslehre.* 1914.

Spencer, Herbert. *Principles of Sociology.* 1876.

> *Study of Sociology.* 1874.

Stein, Lorenz von. *Geschichte der sozialen Bewegung in Frankreich.* 1855.

Wiese, von. "Die Soziologie als Einzelwissenschaft." Schmoller's *Jahrbuch für Gesetzgebung, Verwaltung und Volkswirtschaft im Deutschen Reich*, XLIV.

> "Zur Methodologie der Beziehungslehre." Kölner's *Vierteljahrshefte*, I, no. 1.

CHAPTER XX
HISTORY AND STATISTICS

By HAROLD U. FAULKNER

SMITH COLLEGE

PAUCITY OF STATISTICS IN EARLY HISTORY

A CENTURY ago statistics were rarely used in the writing of history; to-day the historian finds that statistical data, accurately arranged and intelligently analyzed, are quite often his most important asset in reconstructing the past and interpreting the present. This new emphasis upon the place of statistics in history implies, quite obviously, both a shift in historical methodology and a general revolution in the whole philosophy of history. Before statistics could be widely used by historians, the conception of history itself had to expand to include an infinite variety of subjects hitherto neglected, and the historian himself had to become more scientifically minded. At the same time, the wider use of statistics was predicated upon a simultaneous advance in statistical technique.

Numbers, of course, and in some cases very elementary statistics, were used by the early historians; but as long as the story of alliances, wars, dynasties, rulers, and political intrigue formed the stock in trade of writers of history, there appeared to be little call for statistics. The ancient historians had some appreciation of the importance of economic and social factors, but they did not allow that appreciation greatly to influence their narrative. The medieval chroniclers wrote of the conflicts of feudal society, but their haphazard estimates of the relative strength of competing armies could hardly be dignified by the name of statistics. The Protestant Revolt, with its overpowering interest in religion, brought in its wake much ecclesiastical history, but little interest in statistics; and the economic revolutions of the sixteenth and eighteenth centuries revived the political narrative. The struggle of the new middle class for political power led the most brilliant chroniclers of the period to expend their energies in the dreary waste of constitutional history. It was a time when abler men than Freeman agreed with the absurd statement that "history is past politics, politics is present history." Constitutional historians could have made good use of statistics, but they rarely did.

THE EMERGENCE OF THE NEW HISTORY

Fortunately, the same forces which were influential in producing the constitutional history of the eighteenth and early nineteenth centuries were also undermining its influence. The political revolutions precipitated by the rising bourgeoisie were the inevitable result of the commercial and industrial revolutions, and the tremendous alteration in the material conditions of human life which ushered in a new civilization could not help but profoundly affect the outlook of historical scholars. The rise and fall of dynasties and the story of wars and rumors of wars paled into insignificance before the epoch-making effects of the spinning-jenny and the steam-engine. Historians began to see in the wars of nations a struggle for markets and raw materials, and in the conflict of political parties the age-long friction between diverse economic interests and social groups. Pressing on the heels of the bourgeoisie were the proletariat, likewise demanding to be somebody politically; and again historians had to take into consideration the fact that other groups than the aristocracy had played a rôle in history.

This new interest in economic and social history was not a sudden phenomenon, but developed gradually throughout the nineteenth century. Economists like Malthus, searching in history for data to prove their theories, began the process of undermining the old structure. The fortress of political history was sadly shattered by Buckle's penetrating observations on the influence of geographical factors, and almost demolished by Karl Marx's brilliant diagnosis of history as a class struggle dominated by economic determinism. Economic history was now taken up in earnest, and it was but a short time before social history was drawn into its orbit. The old guard still defends antiquated history as written by Droyson, Stubbs, Burgess, and Holst; but the younger scholars and their followers are now caught by a different vision. In this shift toward a new history no aid has been more important than that rendered by statistics, and it is quite doubtful if much of significance could have been accomplished without such assistance.

The *rapprochement* of history and statistics was also influenced by the scientific revolution of the eighteenth and nineteenth centuries. The rising scientific spirit no longer sought for explanations of economic and social phenomena in the wrath of God or in the movement of heavenly bodies, but in causes which might be ascertained, if searched for patiently. A railroad wreck might still be described as "an act of God," but no scientifically minded person believed it to be. Darwin and Wallace lit the fires which were to consume the old-fashioned conception of the universe, and the modern historian, discarding teleology and demanding a more scientific reason than the divine purpose for the phenomena which he observed, found in statistics a tool which enabled him to work with a surer touch.

THE COLLECTION OF HISTORICAL STATISTICS

Before statistics could become an important part of the historian's equipment, responsible agencies must be established to collect data and a statistical technique developed. Ancient governments frequently attempted census enumeration to aid in levying taxes, classifying inhabitants, and determining military strength. Efforts toward the same end were made during the middle ages, the famous Domesday Book of William the Conqueror being perhaps the most famous example. These enumerations, however, were spasmodic and inadequate, a rich mine to the present historian but merely a suggestion of the subsequent development of governmental statistics. The gathering of statistical data with reference to commerce and trade was immensely stimulated by the mercantilist statesmen of the sixteenth and seventeenth centuries, but it was in Prussia in the eighteenth century that the modern foundations of the systematic and periodic collection of statistical data were laid.

The lead taken by Prussia was soon followed elsewhere. The United States took its first biennial census in 1790, and England its first in 1801, and as the nineteenth century progressed the innumerable bureaus and committees of the various governments with cumulative speed piled their data mountain high. In no nation has this passion for statistics been more evident than in the United States. From the surveys of Tench Coxe and Timothy Pitkin to the latest report of the Interstate Commerce Commission there has been a steady advance both in the technique and in the adequacy of the data. Fortunately, these census enumerations have been ably directed, and a history of American statistics might conceivably be written around the careers of the notable census enumerators of the first century of our national existence — J. B. DeBow, Francis A.

Walker, "the greatest all-around master of the science of statistics," Robert P. Porter, Carroll D. Wright, Henry Gannett, William R. Morrison, and S. N. D. North. But the census enumerations and the work of the Permanent Census Office (established March 6, 1902) comprise but a small part of the statistical data provided by the government. The numerous bureaus of the Departments of Agriculture, Interior, Commerce, and Labor, to say nothing of such special organizations as the Federal Trade, Interstate Commerce, and Tariff Commissions, literally deluge the public with their products. More recently, to complement the activities of the government, commercial and endowed organizations have been busy collecting data on their own initiative or endeavoring to interpret the statistics which the state and federal bureaus liberally shower upon them.

Economists, sociologists, and historians, although gasping for breath, have not been completely swamped in this deluge of statistics, chiefly because of the simultaneous progress in statistical method. The development of statistical technique from the days of Sebastian Munster and Pierre d'Avity to Adolphe Quetelet and Francis D. Walker involves not only the growth of the science of statistical mathematics but also an enlarging concept of the uses to which numbers can be applied in the measurement and interpretation of social phenomena.

THE MEETING OF HISTORY AND STATISTICS

With historians increasingly receptive to the importance of economic history, with statistical methodology advanced to a status in which practical use of numerical data can be made by the historians, and with the land flooded with statistics, the stage would seem to be cleared for a wide use of statistics in history. While the economic historian has seized upon statistics with avidity, the majority of historians have been slow to take advantage of this new tool. Innate conservatism, unwillingness to work with strange implements, and lack of interest in the type of history which lends itself to the use of statistics partly explain this attitude. The union of history and statistics in the end depends upon the appreciation by historians of the primary significance of social and economic history, and their willingness to approach their subject from this angle. The economic interpretation of history is certainly not accepted *in toto* by the majority of historians, but the importance of economic history is. When historians advance beyond the stage of intellectual acceptance and actually teach and write the new history, then statistics, as far as history is concerned, will come into their own.

Professor Robinson has described history as "all that we know about everything that man has ever done, or thought, or hoped, or felt."[1] Although this definition is too narrow, for it does not include biological and geographical history before man, it undoubtedly describes the chief field of historical interest. Fortunately for the historian, statistics likewise are chiefly concerned with man and his activities. The science of statistics arose in the tabulation and organization of mortality data and of census enumerations. Even to-day the life and activities of man are the chief subjects for statistical research — the number and distribution of people, the wages and standards of labor, the production and consumption of commodities, the cost of living, the organization and exchange of wealth. The study of man as a social and economic animal remains the chief function of statistics and is rapidly becoming that of history.

THE USE OF STATISTICS BY HISTORIANS

What have historians done with statistics? To the out-and-out economic historian statistics have been the *sine qua non* of his work. Therold Rogers, H. de B. Gibbons, W. J. Ashley, William Cunningham, Gilbert Slater, Sidney and Beatrice Webb in England, D. R. Dewey, N. S. B. Gras, John R. Commons, and others in America have based much of their work on statistics. Some of the most interesting examples of the use of statistics, however, have been made by historians not primarily interested in economic development. Albert H. Lybyer, for instance, by an examination of prices of oriental wares exploded the long-held theory that the conquest of the Eastern trade-routes by the Turks precipitated the Commercial Revolution.[2] Charles A. Beard, by an examination of the economic interests involved in the struggle for the constitution and by calling to his service the most obvious and elementary use of statistics, has completely revolutionized the earlier conception regarding the origins of that document.[3] George Louis Beer in like manner has

---

[1] *History of Western Europe*, p. 1.

[2] "The Influence of the Ottoman Turks upon the Results of Oriental Trade." *Annual Report of the American Historical Association*, 1914, pp. 127–33.

[3] Beard, C. A. *An Economic Interpretation of the Constitution of the United States.*

shattered certain of the older views as to the effects of British mercantilism upon the American colonies.[1] Frederick J. Turner's studies of the correlation of glacial drifts and literacy show the unexpected but fruitful fields open to the historian who would call statistics to his aid. This type of correlation is vastly different from the enumerations of the early chroniclers.

To the historian who asserts that it is his business to deal with "men and the deeds of men" and that the use of statistics is not his "proper method" and cannot become his "principal tool," it must be conceded that men are units which differ from one another in complex variations.[2] Furthermore, it should be conceded at once that statistics have a varying value when applied to historical events. Statistics may have the greatest value in interpreting the French Revolution, the Continental System, or the fall of Napoleon, and yet be of little use in explaining Napoleon's character or his decisions. In like manner the historian, just as the economist, may easily be led astray by inadequate statistics, faulty methods, and erroneous conclusions, and his customary lack of training in statistical technique makes it the more necessary for him to be on his guard.

At best statistics provide but one of many tools with which the historian must equip himself. But whether he pursues his task by means of the geographical, the psychological, the anthropological, the economic, or the political approach, or, forsooth, attempts the almost superhuman task of combining them all, he still finds himself resting heavily upon statistical data, compared and correlated. If he is a teacher of history he finds it advisable to resort to pictograms, historiograms, and graphs of various sorts. The attempt to picture history by the plotted line on statistical graphs has become so universal that it has even won its way into the pedagogy of secondary education, and statisticians have apportioned a special field for historical statistics.

Statistics have on the one hand made the task of the historian easier and on the other, more difficult. A new tool has been provided which should enable him to make more accurate deductions, but at the same time it has made his task harder. Where statistical data can be brought to bear on a subject, generalizations without

---

[1] Beer, G. L. *Origins of the British Colonial Policy 1578–1660; British Colonial Policy 1754–1765; The Old Colonial Policy.*

[2] Hull, C. H. "The Service of Statistics to History." *Publications of the American Statistical Association*, XIV, pp. 30–39.

their use are no longer in order.   At the same time statistics have widened the scope of historical research.   But most important of all, statistics have lent valiant aid in stimulating the development of economic and social history, a tendency which has given to that ancient study a new purpose and a new youth.

SELECTED REFERENCES

Adams, G. B.   "History and the Philosophy of History."   *American Historical Review*, xiv, pp. 223–36.

Barnes, H. E.   "History, its Rise and Development."   *Encyclopedia Americana*, 1922 ed.
The New History and the Social Studies.   1925.

Bailey, W. B.   *Modern Social Conditions*, chap. i.   1906.

Bowley, A. L.   *The Nature and Purpose of the Measurement of Social Phenomena.*   1915.

Chaddock, R. E.   *Principles and Methods of Statistics.*   Part i.   1925.

Hankins, F. H.   *Adolphe Quetelet as Statistician.*   1908.

Hull, C. H.   "The Service of Statistics to History."   *Publications of the American Statistical Association*, xiv, pp. 30–39.

King, W. I.   *The Elements of Statistical Method.*   Chap. xv.   1913.

Koren, John, ed.   *The History of Statistics.*   1918.

Mayo-Smith, R.   *Statistics and Economics.*   1899.

Meitzen, August.   *History, Theory, and Technique of Statistics.*   Trans. by Roland P. Falkner.   1891.

Persons, W. M.   "Some Fundamental Concepts of Statistics."   *Journal of the American Statistical Association*, xix, pp. 1–8.

Robinson, J. H.   *The New History.*   1912.

Schmeckebier, L. F.   *The Statistical Work of the National Government.*   1925.

Seligman, E. R. A.   *The Economic Interpretation of History.*   1905.

Shotwell, J. T.   *Introduction to the History of History.*   Chap. xxvii.   1923.

CHAPTER XXI

POLITICAL SCIENCE AND PHILOSOPHY

By GEORGE H. SABINE

OHIO STATE UNIVERSITY

A DESCRIPTION of the present state of political philosophy is difficult because the subject is now in a great measure unformed. The
interest in it among students both of philosophy and of politics is
indeed great — certainly greater than it was only a few years ago.
But it is clear that we are in a period of transition when a variety
of tendencies are affecting political thought and moving, presumably, toward a new crystallization in a pattern differing fundamentally from the political philosophy of a generation ago. For
the present, however, it is impossible to say what this pattern will
be. The purpose of this paper, accordingly, is not to state a political philosophy even in outline, or to give an exposition of current
political theories. All that can be done is to suggest the direction in
which thought about the nature of political institutions has moved
and appears to be moving, and to indicate certain tendencies which
seem destined to have an important effect upon the future of political philosophy.

THE CLASSICAL POLITICAL PHILOSOPHY

It will make for clearness if we begin by indicating the point of
departure — what might be called the classical political philosophy
— from which recent political theory takes its rise. Owing to certain historical conditions that were fundamental to the development of modern political institutions, the classical political theory
revolved mainly about two conceptions, the state and the individual. For the state is admittedly the most significant, as it is incom-
parably the most powerful, of modern social institutions. And in
the course of its development it achieved a unique control over its
subjects which enabled it either to crush or to subordinate the multitude of medieval corporations and associations, already rendered
moribund by the evolution of modern economic and social conditions. Thus the individual was left actually in a condition of relative isolation; and because the need for establishing the state's

preëminence over other corporate bodies was urgent, political thinkers were prone to exaggerate the degree of that isolation. Thus it happened that these two entities, the individual on the one side and the sovereign state on the other, were the two points from which all the problems of political philosophy were envisaged.

Accordingly political philosophy became at once a theory of sovereignty and a theory of rights, with the inevitable problem of showing some sort of logical relation between the two. The political problem might be approached from two directions. Starting with the assumed rights of the individual, it was a question how the state could rightly exercise the coercive power which was admitted to be necessary even to sustain those rights. Or, assuming the sovereign power of the state, it was a question of drawing the limits within which the individual could rightly claim exemption from universal regulation by the state. In either case, however, the majority of political theorists (neglecting the extremists on either side) agreed that both principles must be maintained: neither the rights of the individual nor the coercive power of the state could be surrendered. Without pausing to specify by reference to particular authors, let us note briefly the general characteristics of political theories developed from this point of view.

In the first place, they show the prevailing rationalism which has tended, until recently at least, to characterize all modern philosophy. This means, on its negative side, that a relatively low estimate was placed upon the worth of custom and tradition, which were conceived mainly as repressive, irrational, and burdensome. From these the enlightened individual must liberate himself, as far as possible, if he is to attain a rational type of life. It followed almost necessarily that institutions, both social and political, were regarded with suspicion — often justified, no doubt, by the facts — and their scope of action was jealously limited. The general tendency was to extend the individual's sphere of private control and activity as far as political expedience would permit. The reasonable action of the individual, moreover, tended to be identified with enlightened self-interest. Relieve the mind of its burden of traditional and customary prejudice, and the individual will readily perceive for himself the nature of his needs; free him from repression by institutions created and directed by the interests of privileged classes, and he will find by his native good sense the best means to satisfy those needs. And with such minimum of regulation as is indispensable, the pooled self-interest of all individuals will achieve the general well-being of the group.

In the light of this sort of rationalist individualism, juristic thought set up a definite goal as the end at which law ought to aim. This end is to secure to the individual an unimpeded exercise of his own free will, within the sphere which the state may safely leave to individual initiative. Not only is the state so to limit its action as to leave the individual free, but its legitimate field of activity is to prevent invasions of this freedom by other individuals. The end is in general the greatest amount of freedom possible, the coercive action of the state being properly confined to cases where an undue expansion of individual liberty would threaten liberty itself. The type of the state's activity is accordingly found in the administration of the criminal law and the law of property and contract. So far as possible the supplying of all sorts of services is to be left to individual initiative, controlled by the ideal of leaving the freedom of contract as untrammeled as may be. That some types of contract were "contrary to public policy" was not indeed lost sight of, but the tendency was to confine such limitations as narrowly as possible. The ideal is that the state shall keep the lists open for the widest possible exercise of free choice on the part of the individual.

On the side of ethics this type of political philosophy assumes the fundamental value of individual initiative or of free, spontaneous individuality. It is assumed almost without argument that the social interest or well-being is merely the well-being of all the individuals concerned, since the community is, as Bentham says, only a "fictitious body."[1] In effect, therefore, the state's defense of rights was limited to cases where a rather tangible self-interest was felt to exist, and the desirability of leaving each individual to judge of his own interests was in general unquestioned. This bias was of course favorable to the extension of democratic political institutions, and the theorists of Bentham's time were content to assume, pursuant to their belief in the efficiency of enlightened self-interest, that such institutions would inevitably further the ends of individual liberty and spontaneity. To John Stuart Mill this was far from obvious; in fact, the fear that a democratic majority might itself prove tyrannical and oppressive formed an important note in his essay *On Liberty*. This essay is the classical defense in

[1] *Principle of Morals and Legislation*, chap. I, § IV.

nineteenth century ethical literature of the profound social value of individual freedom. Still later, when it was apparent that English legislation was turning more and more toward certain limitations of the freedom of contract, the older individualism was given its last militant statement in Herbert Spencer's *The Man versus the State*.

In brief outline this represents the main features of what may be called the classical political philosophy. It runs in terms of the concepts of sovereignty and individual rights; it is rationalist and individualist; it lacks the conception of social interest; it conceives liberty largely as unimpeded freedom of contract; it exalts the value of individual initiative and enterprise. From this type of theory, more recent political thought has diverged. Indeed there is no aspect of the older theory which has not been subject to far-reaching modification. We must, therefore, indicate the nature of these changes in order to see the direction in which political philosophy has been moving.

Positive Liberty and Social Function

British philosophy in general suffered an almost revolutionary change during the seventies and eighties with the rise of Neo-Hegelian Idealism and the almost complete disappearance of the traditional English Empiricism. Even a little earlier a change took place in public opinion which began to make itself effective in politics. Professor Dicey, in his *Law and Opinion in England*, estimates that the ideals of Bentham's philosophy dominated English legislation until 1865 or 1870; at about this time a change is discernible in the direction of what Dicey calls "collectivism." A new political philosophy to conform to this change first appears in the ethical idealism of T. H. Green.

It is not too much to say that Green exerted a decisive influence upon liberal political thought by insisting that freedom of contract, and in fact the whole policy of defending for the individual a circle of indetermination and free choice, is a means and not an end. How far it may be desirable to leave men to their own devices, or to put upon them the task of working out their own salvation without organized social aid, depends upon circumstances. It will evidently not be the same, for example, in all conditions of economic organization or for all classes. Green apparently had mainly in mind the English agricultural worker and the Irish tenant farmer, but his argument has an obvious and even a broader application to industrial workers, and it was given added point by the great and growing mass of legislation intended to regulate conditions of labor in industry.

The essence of freedom, according to Green, consists in the possibility which the individual possesses of doing and being something worth doing or being, and the purpose of liberal legislation is to create, so far as this can be done by law, the conditions of such a positive achievement. A formal liberty to contract, under circumstances which make the terms of the agreement virtually involuntary, is freedom only in name. Similarly, from Green's point of view, the coercive power exercised by the law is not its sole or even its most significant feature. It aims rather at the positive development of human good and uses repression as a means to this end. It aims by means of organized political coercion to offset actual but unorganized coercion — in other words, to "hinder the hindrances" to a good life. The constructive effect of Green's philosophy is, therefore, to substitute a positive for a negative idea of freedom; political liberalism is to be measured by the degree in which it preserves the conditions of a humanly valuable life. In practice, this has worked out to the conception of what has been called the "national minimum" — a fixed point, whether of education, or economic competence, or sanitation, below which it shall be considered bad public policy to allow any large portion of the population to fall. Among later writers who adopt a generally idealist point of view, Professor L. T. Hobhouse has best developed this aspect of Green's thought.

In yet another respect English idealism furthered an important change in the principles of political philosophy. Idealism was influenced in part by the theory of the state in German philosophy, especially in the philosophy of Fichte and Hegel, but still more by a revived interest in the Greek conception of the state and by certain elements of Rousseau's political philosophy which are traceable very largely to that author's admiration for his own native city state, Geneva. In principle, the change proposed by the Idealists, especially by F. H. Bradley and Bernard Bosanquet, consisted in substituting Plato's view that the state rests on functions for the traditional view that it rests on rights. The whole ethical significance of the individual consists in the fact that he has a social work to perform, that he has what Bradley calls a "station" and its attendant duties. Any claim that he may make to rights or liberties depends for its validity upon the fact that his duties require a certain liberty of action as the condition of their performance. The "general will" of the state, therefore — to use the phrase that Bosanquet adopts from Rousseau — is the sole foundation both of individual rights and of right in general; whatever ethical value the individual has arises from his being an agent of the general will. Even his "freedom " comes by the subordination of his private will to the general will.

The idealist political philosophy is thus a thorough-going rejection of the older individualism. It stands for the fact, which no thinker would now deny, that society in one way or another is a factor in every act that the individual performs and in every claim to freedom that he can make. Indeed, in the form given it by Bradley and Bosanquet, it has some of the characteristics of a reaction. It quite unnecessarily exaggerates the part that conformity plays in the individual's social nature and neglects the fact, so excellently urged by Mill, that individual spontaneity, and therefore non-conformity, is itself a social function of the first importance. For theoretical purposes, however, its most serious defect is that it tends both to idealize the state and to identify the state with society at large. It tends to assume, therefore, that society, like the state, is a single, centrally organized system in which all lesser social groupings are assigned a definite and subordinate place. It accordingly fails to take account of at least two fundamentally important classes of facts about modern political conditions, to wit, the great diversity and looseness of social groupings within the modern state and the extension of many social groupings beyond the state. In other words, though it stresses functions rather than rights, it still continues to conceive its problem in terms of the traditional entities, namely, the state and the individual.

In a modified form, moreover, English idealism carries on the rationalist tradition in political philosophy. It wholly abandoned, to be sure, the old notion that enlightened self-interest was the guiding motive of conduct and a sufficient inducement to socially and politically desirable conduct. In the place of enlightened self-interest it put the general will of the state itself, which it conceived as the standard both of what was socially desirable and of the individual's ultimate self-interest. But like self-interest for the older political philosophy, the general will is supposed to present a rational standard of conduct. The system of moral, legal, and political institutions is the embodiment of a reasonable mode of life such as the individual would choose if he were able fully to subordinate his errant impulses to rational control. For the idealist, therefore, as for the individualist, reason is the guide of the social and political life, but the idealist gives an Hegelian interpretation of reason. Reason for him is objective, embodied in the historically evolved social system, rather than the standard of subjective judgment.

POLITICAL IRRATIONALISM

In respect to this implicit rationalism of political thought, however, whether in the older form of individualism or in the later social form, the philosophy of the last quarter of a century has shown perhaps its most violent reaction and its most radical change of front. This phase of political philosophy is indeed quite in line with certain aspects of philosophy generally. From Schopenhauer through Nietzsche to Bergson, there has run a stream of irrationalism in philosophy which could scarcely be paralleled in any other period of thought since the Renaissance. In political thought, moreover, the tendency appears to have gained strength from other than philosophical sources. So far as the conception of individual conduct is concerned, the combined effect of biological and psychological studies of instinct has been very great. The overwhelming evidence of the importance of instinctive factors in human conduct has been interpreted to the disparagement of intelligence and its power to direct action. The irrationalist implications of modern psychology have no doubt been exaggerated, though indeed the old psychology of enlightened self-interest is hopelessly dead. Graham Wallas's *Human Nature in Politics* is the classical criticism of rationalism in political conduct. On the other hand, the idealist interpretation of social institutions as the embodiment of reason has been the subject of an equal reaction. Even the Hegelian theory of social development itself had been partly responsible for Marx's economic interpretation of the different types of social and political structure. The theory of class struggle as means of ameliorating social conditions, the substitution of direct action of minorities for political action, and the acceptance of proletarian domination as the end of the class struggle, represent social and political irrationalism at their farthest stretch. All these have been represented by theoretical defenders as normal developments of Bergson's philosophy of creative evolution.

This clash between the implicit rationalism of the older political philosophy, including idealism, and the avowed irrationalism of certain later political theories has largely been the occasion for the important social philosophy developed in this country by Professor Dewey. The theory of instrumentalism is directed equally against rationalism and irrationalism. All the values which have traditionally been considered metaphysically, or from the point of view of their place in ultimate reality, Professor Dewey would reinterpret as having an instrumental use in political, moral, and social situations. Indeed, the special function of philosophy is to rationalize the various possibilities that present themselves when social and moral interests are in conflict, and thus to find the means for their adjustment and regulation. Against irrationalism, however, Professor Dewey is equally concerned to urge that this readjusting and regulating function, which is the specific task of intelligence, is really effective. The supposed antithesis between impulse or instinct and reason is quite false, which can readily be seen when the proper psychological function of reason is understood.

Professor Dewey's philosophy, therefore, has developed from a theory of the rôle of thought in the life of the individual, and from this central point he has worked out to a theory of the social functions of thought. His thesis is that thinking is a phase of human conduct which has to do with the adjustment and reorganization of impulse and habit when for any reason they meet with some obstacle which impedes their normal unreflective modes of operation. So long as we are doing only those things which habit and impulse are fully equipped to do, reflective thinking simply does not occur. If, however, the smooth road of habitual conduct proves to be blocked, and the impulse is thwarted in mid career, there results a "tension" or feeling of need which requires thought or reflection for its solution. Its mode of operation consists in a dramatic rehearsal of the possible and rival lines of action and the assessment or valuation of each in terms of its relevance to the existing situation. It issues normally in a choice, which is simply the finding in imagination of something that can supply the stimulus to overt action, so that active conduct proceeds upon its way again. Its significance, however, consists in the fact that the new overt action represents a readjustment or reorganization of habit and impulse in the light of their failure to meet and cope with the obstacle in question. In this sense the function of thought is instrumental.

It will be perceived that this theory, though it confines the significance of reason to a purely human function, nevertheless assigns a definite and an important rôle to ideas, and therefore to social, moral, and political ideals. Such ideals are not the remote ends in which action is to cease, but rather the significance, the meaning of the action as it goes on; they are the means by which present activity is released. Ideals, therefore, are a part of every social situation which presents a variety of possible solutions and where there are alternative policies which require valuation. They are the plans or patterns by which the problem conceivably might be solved and form, therefore, an aspect of every political situation. They in no way suggest political Utopias or impossible flights of political imagination, but rather the growing-edges by which political policies and political institutions are shaped into more adequate instruments for realizing individual and social purposes. The primary purpose of philosophy, in common with the social sciences, as Professor Dewey conceives it, is to bring intelligence to bear upon social and political problems, to introduce a measure of human control into the solution of them, just as the physical sciences have made possible to a large extent the control of the physical environment.

If we look back now at the classical political theory from which we started, we can see that its chief characteristics have been fundamentally changed. The ideal of *laissez-faire* has disappeared both in theory and in practice; the state has been loaded with the obligation to preserve the positive conditions of at least a minimum human achievement; the individual has been subordinated to a society which is itself conceived as some sort of organic whole; and the conception of rights as a basis for the theory of the state has tended to be supplanted by the conception of function or service. Potentially more far-reaching than any of these changes, however, is the tendency to regard the individual in his social behavior, and society in its structure and development, as a congeries of forces, irrational in their nature and but little amenable to intelligent control. As we have seen, the need of correcting this potential irrationalism while recognizing the importance of instinctive and impulsive factors in conduct, has formed one of the most serious problems in recent philosophy. In general, however, the political philosophy so far referred to had followed the traditional modern form; that is, it had run in terms of the two entities, the state and the individual, and their relations. The tendency to depart radically from this tradition, and accordingly to question the unique significance of the state among social institutions and perhaps even among political institutions, has been an important aspect of recent political theory.

THE STATE AND ASSOCIATIONS

This tendency apparently arose in the first place from a reawakened sense of the reality of that other great social entity, which from the first has stood beside the state in Christian societies, the Church. A Roman Catholic thinker, like Lord Acton, felt the deficiencies of a purely individualist liberalism at a time when the ancient question of church and state was supposed to have lost its importance for political theory. Thus he says in his essay on "The Protestant Theory of Persecution":[1] "Religious liberty is not the negative right of being without any particular religion, just as self-government is not anarchy. It is the right of religious communities to the practice of their own duties, the enjoyment of their own constitution, and the protection of the law, which equally secures to all the possession of their own independence." At a much later date the idea contained in this sentence was elaborated by John Neville Figgis in his *Churches in the Modern State*, which seeks to show that a society such as a church, as the organ of its members' religious life, must claim a measure of self-direction proportional to the significance of its task.

A far more effective claim in behalf of communities or corporate bodies, however, has come from certain students of the law, not only in England and Germany, but especially in France. In England the argument was best stated in Frederic W. Maitland's now famous introduction to his *Political Theories of the Middle Age*. Maitland's general conclusion, based upon Otto von Gierke's study[2] of the conception of corporations in Teutonic law, is that a corporate body, in so far as it has its own corporate purpose and activities, is not the creature of the state but a real personality. Indeed, the state itself is merely one species of the genus corporation, and the power claimed for and exercised by the state must be justified by

---

[1] *The History of Freedom and Other Essays*, p. 151 *et seq.*
[2] *Das deutsche Genossenschaftsrecht*, 4 vols.

the importance of the purposes and modes of activity for which it stands, and consequently by arguments which, *mutatis mutandis*, will apply also to other species of corporation. What gives the argument weight for present-day political theory is not its historical soundness, or its general agreement with a certain view of the Church, but rather the fact that it accords with a highly important phase of the evolution of modern industrial societies, to wit, the great development of associations, most of them designed to further some special interest of their members, many of them exceedingly powerful, and nearly all of them in no particular way dependent on the state except in the negative sense of not being positively illegal. It is, therefore, a grotesque over-simplification to confine political theory to the relation merely of the state and the individual. It is perfectly true, as Acton says, that liberty is less a matter of individual freedom than a possibility of unimpeded functioning for communities other than the state.

The work of the French jurist, Duguit, has greatly strengthened the tendency to recognize the political significance of such communities or corporate bodies, especially those having an industrial importance such as labor organizations. His views are based upon the theory of the division of social labor of the sociologist Durkheim,[1] a conception which, as we have seen, was revived from Plato by the English idealists also. Behind law and the state is the solidarity of society itself, which requires the continuous rendering of certain services for satisfying human needs. In accordance with this conception of functions, Duguit considers the type of the state's activity to be the providing of public services. Indeed, the state is at bottom a collection of agencies to organize and manage public interests, such, for example, as education, transportation, or public health. Between services of this sort rendered by agencies of government and those rendered by private persons or corporations, there is no very obvious social difference; the main need is that the service shall be continuously rendered, with due regard for the interests of all concerned, including the social interest embodied in the service itself. Any agency that renders such a service is, therefore, virtually public in its significance and may reasonably claim the self-regulating authority that is needed for its healthful continuance. The extensive literature on guild socialism is a witness to the large part that this idea plays in present day economic

[1] *De la Division du Travail Social.*

and political thought.   Among English writers Professor H. J. Laski has made the most serious effort to bring these ideas to bear on political theory.

What effect these ideas may ultimately have upon political organization and consequently upon our ideas of political institutions is as yet far from clear.   In an allied field, that of jurisprudence, they have already had a more positive effect in producing a new conception of the ends to be served by law.   As we have seen, Duguit holds that the end of law is to keep the avenues open for that interchange of services upon which the life of society rests.   A somewhat similar view has been cogently set forth in this country by Professor Roscoe Pound.   According to Professor Pound's theory the end of law is to safeguard interests and to satisfy claims and demands with the least friction and waste.   Especially in a modern industrial society, with its manifold associations for the furtherance of special interests, the claims and demands of groups and individuals overlap and conflict in the most bewildering fashion, and the realization of any of them depends upon their organization and regulation.   It is the end of the law so to order them as to make as many as possible of them effective.   "Looked at functionally, the law is an attempt to reconcile, to harmonize, to compromise these overlapping or conflicting interests, either through securing them directly and immediately, or through securing certain individual interests or delimitations or compromises of individual interests, so as to give effect to the greatest number of interests or to the interests that weigh most in our civilization, with the least sacrifice of other interests." [1]   Jurisprudence is, therefore, a sort of human or social engineering; its procedure needs to be frankly instrumental.   Professor Pound quotes with approval the saying of William James that the guiding principle for ethics is "to satisfy at all times as many demands as we can," and the affinity of his thought to the philosophy of Professor Dewey is obvious.

The Drift of Political Philosophy

In conclusion, we may sum up by enumerating the changes which seem likely to affect in an important way a future restatement of political philosophy.   The outline of a theory is as yet scarcely discernible, and the negative consequences of the many-sided dis-

[1] "A Theory of Social Interests." *Proceedings of the American Sociological Society*, xv, p. 44.

cussion now going on are far clearer than the positive or constructive implications. We have for the present a drift rather than a result.

In the first place, it seems clear that the conception of individual rights and their protection will have to be relegated to a place of secondary importance, and the first place assigned to the conception of interests, individual, corporate, and social, and their protection and regulation. The notion of a claim or an interest is really simpler and more general, since a right is merely a claim which has obtained social or legal recognition and protection. It is, moreover, far less subject to the serious ambiguities which in the past have continually beset the term "right" when used in political theories. At the same time the notion of an interest has the advantage of being positive, whereas rights, at least as actually interpreted, were often negative and formal. Most important of all, perhaps, is the fact that it is easy to recognize social interests which cannot be identified with the rights of any assignable individuals and which still imperatively require protection. The idea that the state exists to protect rights was really the correlate of a certain political and social theory, the theory that a group could be identified with the aggregate of its members and that the protection of the rights of all individuals would be equivalent to a protection of all the interests involved. Under the conditions of any highly industrialized society, however, there are bound to be numbers of social interests which do not admit of so simple an analysis. The conception of social interest is quite as clear as the conception of an individual right, and the means for its protection need be no harder to apply.

It apparently follows that for ethical philosophy the use of the conception of personality must largely disappear, or at least the conception must be greatly modified. In effect, a person for ethical and political philosophy was a subject of rights, and this was largely a negative conception; it meant for the most part non-interference. Kant's saying, that the sum and substance of morality consists in treating persons as ends and not as means, which is the most incisive formula for stating the fundamental value of persons, is perhaps not devoid of meaning as suggesting a certain ethical attitude, but it is hopelessly vague as a rule for dealing with any concrete situation. What is needed is an analysis of the interests and activities of which the individual's life is made up. For even his individual well-being depends upon the release of normal modes of activity; self-development or self-expression in the large means practically nothing.   And, moreover, his interests and activities are points at which he comes in contact with institutions and with groups.   Indeed, it may be said that both persons and groups are merely forms of organization; the materials organized are in both cases activities and interests.   A conception of the ends to be attained by legislation or public policy must be formed in terms of the claims, demands, activities, and interests affected, whether these are viewed as belonging to individuals, or as the special concern of an association, or as embodied in an institution.

In this connection it is perhaps worth pointing out that this view in no way implies the loss of individual personality or its absorption, in any bad sense, in groups.   There is nothing which ought to obscure the significance of John Stuart Mill's fine defense of the social value of non-conformity.   That group life can be and often is repressive is a fact and not a theory; on the other hand, the notion that conformity is identical with social value, is a theory and not a fact.   Certainly there is no easy way to reconcile, either in theory or in practice, the conflicts that arise between organization and unimpeded action.   But it is clear that to keep open the field of experimentation through individual initiative is itself a real social interest, just as it is clear on the other side that the claim to a free field of action can be justified only on the ground that the exemption from interference has more than individual significance.

If the general end to be aimed at is taken to be the regulating and safeguarding of interests, with a view to satisfying as many demands as possible with the least friction and waste, due regard being given not only to the number of interests but also to their importance, it seems clear that for the foreseeable future, at least, the state will have to be conceived as the ultimate social organ for their evaluation.   In the last resort, of course, this function of evaluation can never be fully organized; what we vaguely call public opinion with regard to questions of moral and political right and individual and social expedience is nothing more than the inchoate sense of the relative worth of the interests concerned, so far as these interests are understood.   But to be effective, evaluation requires its organs, and there does not appear to be any agency better fitted than the state to become the guardian of what may be called the total social interest, or the greatest balance of interests realizable under given conditions.   This conception of a greatest balance of interests, indefinite though it is, cannot be dispensed with at least as a regulative ideal of political philosophy.

It apparently follows that political theory must change its point of attack. The problem is not exclusively, or perhaps even mainly, the relation of individuals to the state, but rather the relation of the state to social groups other than itself. For interests organize themselves almost spontaneously in associations for their own preservation. In many cases to assume such associations to be purely private and voluntary may be little better than a fiction; their actual power has to be reckoned with, and both their purposes and their power to realize them are corporate rather than individual. It would accordingly be a main function of the state to regulate and coördinate the activities of these embodiments of special interests; for without regulation their pulling and hauling becomes intolerably wasteful and vexatious. The regulation of organized interests, however, by no means implies their mere subordination to the state or their absorption into a political system as this has commonly been understood. Nothing is more obvious than the excessive complexity of the exchanges of service upon which a modern society depends for its existence. Anything like their effective regulation would appear to depend, therefore, upon a virtual decentralization of the state itself, so far as the actual rendering of services is concerned, and the use of the corporate body itself for purposes of self-regulation in putting policies into effect. The analogy of the holding corporation has been suggested as the type of organization required, or the notion of a federalization of function rather than of territorial units. Such a change of organization would imply a significant modification, though not the abandonment, of the conception of delegated authority. The state would apparently have to confine itself to fixing the limits of jurisdiction and adjudicating conflicts. At the very least it would amount to a considerable departure from the closely centralized state upon which the theory of state sovereignty was traditionally formed.

Finally, there would have to be a corresponding change in the relation conceived to exist between the state and law. The elements of a federalized state would have to be conceded some degree of law-making or ordinance-making authority to carry on their own proper functions. The decentralization of the state would mean largely a decentralizing of law-making authority, and a purely formal description of the relation of the legal sovereign to the law would be less applicable to the concrete fact. In the end this would probably mean a reversal of the theory that the sovereign is the maker of law, which was the normal expression of a period characterized typically by centralized legislation, in favor of the view that the sovereign is really the creature of law. Such a change would be in line with the tendency of all civilized states to define the competence of officials and to make them legally responsible, and also in line with what apparently must follow the strengthening of international law to a point where governments themselves are held legally responsible for what would now be deemed sovereign acts. What would remain of legal sovereignty would be mainly the fact that any body of law is relatively at least a unified system, together with the fact that there existed a legal apparatus for resolving conflicts of authority.

SELECTED REFERENCES

Barker, Ernest. *Political Thought in England from Herbert Spencer to the Present Day.* 1915.
    "The Discredited State." *Political Quarterly,* v, p. 101.

Barnes, H. E. *Sociology and Political Theory.* 1924.

Bentley, A. F. *The Process of Government.* 1908.

Bosanquet, Bernard. *The Philosophical Theory of the State.* 1899.

Bradley, F. H. *Ethical Studies.* 1876.

Burns, C. D. *Political Ideals, their Nature and Development.* 1915.

Coker, F. W. "The Technique of the Pluralistic State." *American Political Science Review,* xv, 1921, p. 186.

Dewey, John. *Democracy and Education.* 1916.
    Reconstruction in Philosophy. 1920.
    Human Nature and Conduct. 1922.

Duguit, L. *Les Transformations du Droit Public.* Trans. as *Law in the Modern State,* by F. and H. Laski. 1919.

Dunning, W. A. *A History of Political Theories, Rousseau to Spencer.* 1920.

Figgis, J. N. *Churches in the Modern State.* 1913.

Follett, M. P. *The New State.* 1918.
    Creative Experience. 1924.

Gettell, R. G. *History of Political Thought.* 1924.

Greene, T. H. *Principles of Political Obligation,* Works, II. 1879–80.
    Liberal Legislation and Freedom of Contract, Works, III. 1881.

Hobhouse, L. T. *Liberalism.* 1911.
    The Metaphysical Theory of the State. 1918.
    The Elements of Social Justice. 1922.

Krabbe, H. *The Modern Idea of the State.* Translation and Introduction by George H. Sabine and Walter J. Shepard. 1922.

Laski, H. J. *The Problem of Sovereignty.* 1917.
    Authority in the Modern State. 1919.
    The Foundations of Sovereignty. 1921.

MacIver, R. M. *Community; a Sociological Study.* **1917.**
    The Modern State. 1926.

Maitland, F. W. *Political Theories of the Middle Age.* Translated from von Gierke's *Genossenschaftsrecht.* Introduction. 1900.
    Moral Personality and Legal Personality. Collected Papers, III. 1911.

Merriam, C. E. *History of the Theory of Sovereignty since Rousseau.* 1900.
    American Political Ideas: Studies in the Development of American Political Thought. 1865–1917, 1920.

Merriam, C. E., and others. *A History of Political Theories, Recent Times: Essays on Contemporary Developments in Political Theory.* 1924.

Mill, J. S. *On Liberty.* 1859.
    Considerations on Representative Government. 1860.

Pound, Roscoe. "A Theory of Social Interests." *Proceedings of the American Sociological Society,* XV, 1920, p. 16.
    The Spirit of the Common Law. 1921.
    Introduction to the Philosophy of Law. 1922.
    Interpretations of Legal History. 1923.

Sabine, G. H. "Pluralism, a Point of View." *American Political Science Review,* XVII, 1923, p. 34.
    "The Concept of the State as Power," *Philosophical Review,* XXIX, 1920, p. 301.

Spencer, Herbert. *Social Statics.* 1851.
    Man versus the State. 1884.
    The Principles of Ethics. Part IV (Justice). 1891.

Wallas, Graham. *Human Nature in Politics.* 1908.
    The Great Society. 1914.
    Our Social Heritage. 1921.

Wilde, Norman. *The Ethical Basis of the State.* 1924.

CHAPTER XXII

POLITICAL SCIENCE AND PSYCHOLOGY

By FLOYD H. ALLPORT

SYRACUSE UNIVERSITY

I

THE FIELD OF POLITICAL PSYCHOLOGY

THE observation that with increasing knowledge the demarcation between the various sciences tends to disappear is illustrated through the recent development of political psychology. This science deals with data which are commonly called political; but it deals with them from the viewpoint of a science of individual human nature. Such an integration of disciplines in a common field is the more impressive since it combines a "social" with a "natural" science, thus challenging the familiar distinction between these two types of discipline.

A glance at recent developments within these two fields will help us to understand the origin and possibilities of the new science of political psychology. Upon the side of political science there has come about a reaction from the description of political structures, departments, and constitutional rights and powers. An attempt has been made to probe the dynamics of political control, seeking causation, not in the *modus operandi* of government, but in the motivation of individual leaders or representatives of economic and other interests. The rôle of the average citizen in the political democracy has been subjected to damaging scrutiny. Fully as striking changes have occurred in the science of psychology. The emphasis in America has shifted from man as possessed of a stream of consciousness, containing inner perceptions, ideas, and feelings, to man as an organism adjusting his behavior by learning, thinking, and emotional reaction to the necessities of his environment, or so shaping his environment as to provide for himself and posterity new tools for the better satisfaction of needs. So long as the intro- spective psychology dominated, there was little chance of calling attention to the interrelations between human beings. The view- point was solipsistic, each individual looking within himself rather than toward the activities by which he stimulated, or responded to, others. Stimulus-response psychology, however, in spite of admitted limitations, has led us to consider the behavior of human beings as stimuli to other individuals, or as responses to such stimuli. The result has been the rise of an objective science of *social psychology*. The behavior viewpoint has thus made possible a verifiable approach to political data. There is no check upon the inner experiences (thoughts and feelings) either of leaders or of the masses; but there can be made a verifiable estimate of their behavior, whether in the form of writing, speaking, nodding, forming organizations, or casting ballots.

In these mergings of the activities of psychologists and political scientists it must not be thought that the gain is entirely upon the side of the latter. Fields of human behavior are here explored which could never be known to the laboratory psychologist working only with the responses of the isolated individual. Even in the laboratory situation, the cultural patterns of habit, such as those of political behavior, are often a factor in the subject's response, whose influence the psychologist cannot estimate apart from a knowledge of the political culture of the group. The so-called "pure" psychologist can tell us *how* people think, learn, and experience feelings, in the sense of the mechanisms and processes involved in those acts, but he cannot tell us *what* people at large think (that is, common verbal stereotypes), what they feel (common, or public sentiment), or what common habits (cultural responses, customs) they have acquired. The approach to the latter phenomena, through the combined viewpoint of psychology and the social sciences, will, as Professor Judd has shown, enrich our knowledge of human nature itself.[1]

Psychological research in the political field, as in the social sciences generally, may be classified under two heads. The first may be called the "common segment" aspect, and the second, the "face-to-face" situation. These heads represent not precise divisions of subject-matter, but different phases of orientation to the common data. They are points of view which aid in theoretical analysis and bring to light strategic points of attack either for scientific investigation or for practical control.

THE COMMON SEGMENT VIEW

In this approach we isolate and determine the distribution of a

[1] Judd, C. H. *The Psychology of Social Institutions.*

characteristic common to a large number of individuals in the designated political group. The feature selected might be near the biological level, such, for example, as the incidence of a disease, or the distribution of intelligence levels in a community or a country. Or it might be upon a sociological level, such as a classification according to vocational status, education, or income. Again, from a psychological viewpoint, we might select the incidence of certain political attitudes in the group concerned. How many people, for example, are inclined toward high tariff, prohibition, racial intolerance or militarism? What is the distribution of individuals who are members of, and loyal to, the Republican Party, the American Federation of Labor, or the Methodist Church? The determination of public opinion is a major problem of the "common segment" method. Group traditions, mores, and laws may likewise be viewed as widely distributed habits or "segments" characteristic of many individuals.[1]

THE FACE-TO-FACE SITUATION

The second approach to political behavior may best be defined through its contrast with the first. Human beings may be regarded not as bundles of segments which we may select at will for purposes of classification and control, but as integrated wholes in which each segment plays its part, in interaction with all the others, toward the vital economy of the entire organism. No one segment dominates completely in the biological and psychological organization of the individual. If one obeys the will of party leaders, it is only because, in some way, loyalty to this particular party has a value with reference to one's needs, interests, and point of view. Because of the uniqueness of an integrated personality the common segment view cannot be employed to exhibit it. The behavior here concerned can be shown only in the face-to-face contacts of individuals. Political relationships as seen from this approach are not groupings of common interests and attitudes, but reactions of individuals, considered as personalities, to one another. The chief

[1] The common segment notion is merely a somewhat broader statement for Professor Giddings' concepts of "likemindedness" and "pluralistic behavior." It conforms closely with the approach which he has developed in his book, *The Scientific Study of Human Society*. Professor J. R. Kantor has also employed this idea in his theory of "cultural reactions." Cf. his article, "What are the Data and Problems of Social Psychology," *Journal of Philosophy*, xx, 1923, p. 449, *et seq.* The common segment view covers most of the phenomena included by sociologists under the term "derivative" or "secondary group."

problems illuminated are personal ascendancy and leadership, social movements as expressions of personality, committee work, discussion, and the emergence from such deliberations of new laws and institutional patterns aimed at the resolution of conflicts.

II

PROBLEMS FORMULATED MAINLY UPON FACE-TO-FACE RELATIONSHIPS

A situation is rarely found which represents either a wholly common-segmental relationship or a wholly face-to-face situation. Both forms are combined within the same individuals, and are distinguished not so much in the behavior presented as in our view toward that behavior. A good illustration is to be found in the rise of Fascism in Italy. We have, on the one side, the peculiar traits of Mussolini's personality: his drive for power, his shifting political philosophy, his apparent shrinking from the examination of his inward nature, losing himself instead in the control of the outer environment, his virtual identification of himself with the state and the conception of a rejuvenated Italy. On the other side, we must consider the previously established institutions of central and local government of Italy, the nationalistic traditions, and the hero-worshiping tendencies of the Italian people. The two points of view are thus supplementary. For purposes of research and discussion, however, it is convenient to separate them. We shall discuss in this section certain phases of problems as viewed in terms of personalities and their face-to-face behavior and adjustments.

No satisfactory technique has yet been devised for the study of personality. The obvious approach would seem to be to divide the individual into certain traits and capacities and to attempt the construction of a test-scale for measuring each of these characteristics. Traits are here conceived to be basic and early-developed systems of habit. This procedure, however, has been fraught with so many obstacles that except for the measurement of scholastic intelligence and a few simple capacities, little progress has been made. We have still no adequate means of appraising an individual's degree of emotionality, ascendance, perseverance, objective- or subjective-mindedness, vocational aptitude, level of ethical conduct, character, and similar important traits. The difficulty has been due partly to superficial analysis and definition, partly to the unavoidable artificiality of the test situation in the attempt to evoke the basic responses of personality, and partly to the absence of available objective criteria against which to check the validity of the estimates given. As for the organic and physiological factors and their possible correlation with political behavior, though suggestive results have been obtained, we are even farther from practicable methods than in the study of behavior traits themselves.

The basic difficulty is perhaps not the lack of a measuring technique, but of definition. Is there really such a thing as a trait of personality? A certain form of behavior may be shown in one situation but contradicted in another. This fact shows the necessity of discovering more fundamental modes of response, not obvious on the surface, but underlying large sections of the individual's behavior, and explaining what seem superficially to be inconsistencies. We find, for example, such an apparent contradiction in the career of Theodore Roosevelt. How did it happen that a man bred in such an aristocratic tradition, and the advocate of power and the strenuous life, should appear as the champion of the common people in a new party organized against economic power and oppression? The contradiction seems to be resolved when we select as a basic trait, not Roosevelt's political philosophy, which may be largely a rationalization, but his life-long drive of struggling against obstacles. Originating in childhood in his fight against physical handicaps, this trait seems to have extended in later life to the conquest of wild animals, enemies in war, obstruction in Congress, graft in politics, and monopolistic control by the trusts.

The search for the fundamental trait shows the importance of a genetic study, following the individual's life back into the years of childhood. Systematic questionnaire studies may here be combined with a modified psychoanalytic approach. A challenge is thus given to the entire trait approach, considered as a measurement of characteristics seen in a cross-section of the life stream. If we had all the traits isolated and their degrees measured with accuracy, we should still be very far from the goal. We need also the *longitudinal* approach, which shows the origin and development of the habit patterns and enables us to predict their future significance in the personality. Of even greater importance, perhaps, is the fact that the longitudinal study reveals how the various traits and capacities *function together*, and which ones are more basic and prevalent in the behavior pattern than others. It shows, moreover, how excellence in one trait may compensate for defect in another, how plans of life are worked out which give all the traits expression, or how the failure to find such a career leaves some of them suppressed and involved in a condition of inner tension and conflict.

Though we are still groping in the dark for a really scientific combination of methods, some light can be thrown by the techniques and interpretations now available upon the rôle of personality in public affairs. One might, for example, investigate the manner in which a leader possessing a specific pattern of personal traits comes to be selected, as it were, by the circumstances of a situation. The nomination and election of Warren G. Harding afford materials for such a study. Often the traits by which one climbs to a position of authority in the political scheme are widely different from those requisite for effective administration while in authority; and a period of failure and readjustment inevitably follows. There is frequently a discoverable relationship between dynamic elements of the leader's personality and his acts in office. The outlook of the executive upon life, and his peculiar drives, prejudices, and set of values help to determine the political and social products constructed by his administration. The civil and institutional reforms achieved by Gladstone are an illustration. The idealistic leaning of Woodrow Wilson, combined with his skill in the use of language, was a potent factor in building a structure designed to harmonize the nationalistic enmities of Europe and the world. An example upon the judicial side can be found in the personality traits of judges in the higher courts. In those cases where no clear-cut legal criterion exists for the decision, there can be found a constant though defensible and well-rationalized slant toward the social philosophy of the particular judge. Another problem capable of investigation links personality with the social psychology of prestige. It is interesting to observe which of the outstanding traits of a leader are used to create a popular "image" of the man, and to measure, if possible, the discrepancy between this social image and the true personality. There is, finally, to be considered the effects of a career upon the further development of the leader's personality. The situation reacts backward upon the individual; leadership is a process, not of one-sided control, but of give and take. The office of presidency, for example, helped Abraham Lincoln to resolve his inner conflict between humility and ambition by the expression of both these traits in his political acts.[1]

[1] The significance of the total situation in political and social life as shown through

The study of non-official as well as official leadership is important for political science. Such leadership is exerted by the outstanding individual or the spokesman of public opinion. Opinion upon any public issue can be measured by presenting each individual in a chosen sample of the population with a scale of attitudes ranging from the logically extreme view on one side of the question to the logical extreme upon the other, and asking him to check the statement which most nearly expresses his own attitude.[1] Interesting distributions of opinion are thus obtained, reflecting sometimes strong agreement (a large number of checks) upon a moderate position, and sometimes the splitting of the mass of votes upon two or more steps of the scale according to alignments of interest or subjection to different species of propaganda. We shall return later to these distributions as measures of public opinion. At present our interest centers in the possible relationship between personality and the position checked upon such an opinion scale.

We are especially concerned with the characteristics of the person who chooses a statement selected by only a very few of the group and lying perhaps at one extreme of the scale, as contrasted with the personality of an individual choosing the attitude characteristic of the large majority. By using the percentage of individuals who fall in the same step as the person chosen, we may compute for that person an index showing his *degree of typicality*. The "typical" and the "atypical" upon any question form suggestive categories for studying the connection between political attitude and trends of the personality. Of especial importance is the question whether an individual is typical or atypical only upon a given question or upon the larger part of his social and political attitudes. That is to say: Is there a tendency toward individual constancy of typicality index for different issues? If so, the man with a high average typicality index might be regarded as a "political weathervane." He would be in high demand by all politicians desiring a short-cut to the ascertainment of public opinion. The atypical individual, on the other hand, would be important as an index of social change and as a means of suggesting the traits of personality one might

mutual interaction of its factors has been forcefully developed in Mary P. Follett's recent book, *Creative Experience*.

[1] Allport, F. H., and Hartman, D. A. "The Measurement and Motivation of Atypical Opinion in a Certain Group." *American Political Science Review*, XIX, no. 4, pp. 735–60. Although this method has thus far been confined to experiments with college students, it may be possible to adapt it to larger and more diversified communities.

expect in leaders of minorities and in social movements of the crusading order. Tentative studies have already revealed in the personalities of atypicals a high level of intellectual interest, an intensity of feeling, and a firm conviction of the truth of their atypical opinions. Investigations of the intelligence and emotional factor of atypical individuals have also been started. The scientific study of the typical and the atypical individual is thus clearly possible and promises results of some significance for political science.

The difficult problem of radicalism, conservation, and reaction ism lies largely within this field. "Radical" and "reactionary" are names commonly applied to persons holding views of low typicality at respectively opposite extremes of the attitude-scale. Much theorizing has been done upon the motivation of these groups, and some suggestive interpretations have been made showing the presence of emotional factors, rationalizations, projections, over-correction for feelings of inferiority, and other defense mechanisms.[1] Although we may be fairly certain of their existence in some cases, it is difficult to weigh scientifically the importance of these explanations. We are faced at the outset with a problem of definition. Do we mean, in calling a person a radical, that he possesses a radical view on a certain political question, or that he is a *radical by nature* and will therefore express radical views on almost every question? Scientific caution would compel us to insist upon the first formulation and to refuse to speak (until further evidence) of a radical or reactionary personality, but only of a radical or reactionary opinion as defined by political standards. It is commonly assumed that individuals are characteristically radical, conservative, or reactionary. This assumption must be tested. Although psychological differences have been suggested between conservative and radical thinkers, there is also evidence that the mere degree of typicality (regardless of whether reactionary, conservative, or radical) seems the more constant and significant category. The important question then arises as to what is the psychological nature of atypicality? What are the personality traits of atypicals?[2]

[1] Cf. Wolfe, A. B., *Conservatism, Radicalism, and Scientific Method;* Allport, F. H., *Social Psychology*, pp. 268–74; and Ogburn, W. F., "Bias, Psychoanalysis, and the Subjective in Relation to Social Science." *Publications of the American Sociological Society*, XVII, 1922, pp. 62–74.

[2] Allport, F. H., and Hartman, D. A., *op. cit.*; also, "A Technique for the Measurement and Analysis of Public Opinion." *Publications of the American Sociological Society*, XXXII, 1926, pp. 241–44.

Moore, H. T. "Innate Factors in Radicalism and Conservatism." *Journal of Abnormal and Social Psychology*, XX, 1925, pp. 234–44.

Thus far we have considered mainly the estimates of factors making up personalities and the more general manner in which personalities fit into the social situation. The specific contacts between individuals are the media through which the integrated patterns of traits are evoked or given expression. In the free give-and-take of discussion the personality functions as a whole. In relation to leadership we observe, first, the more obvious complementary attitudes, such as ascendance and submission, between leader and followers.[1] Of especial, though neglected, significance, is social behavior upon a basis of equality rather than of subordination; as, for example, the deliberations and discussions in face-to-face groups. In the round-table, the arbitration conference, and the working committee, there arise peculiar and novel effects, amounting sometimes to social inventions. These conditions result from the evoking of trained habits of thinking in one individual by the stimulus of a different viewpoint formulated by another. Miss Follett has pointed out the importance of this process in the resolution of conflicts. Little can be accomplished so long as we consider conflict as a group-wise pitting against each other of two detached, segmental interests. The solution is to be found, not in the institutionalized (common segment) approach, but in considering the relation of the demands to the entire personalities from which they emanate. Through face-to-face discussion there may emerge a deeper, more personal significance of the demand, that is, what the disputant *really* wants; and upon such a basis we may proceed to a more fundamental and satisfying adjustment.[2] An important task of the political psychologist is the revealing and measurement of these effects, and the suggestion of techniques for their more effective use.

III

Problems Formulated Mainly upon the Common Segment Approach

Shifting our point of view now from whole personalities and their interactions, we shall consider those problems which can be understood only by seeing all the individuals of the political group oriented, not toward one another, but toward some situation com-

---

[1] Suggestive though somewhat fanciful interpretations of this relationship have been developed by the psychoanalytic school. Cf. Freud, S., *Mass Psychology and the Analysis of the Ego*, and Rivers, W. H. R., *Psychology and Politics*, chap. 2.

[2] Follett, M. P., *op. cit.*

mon to them all; and exhibiting thereby the distribution of some common characteristic or mode of behavior. By far the most politically important type of common segment is that of opinion on public issues. Before we can analyze public opinion, however, it is necessary to give some attention to a more fundamental and biological characteristic, the distribution of native capacity to form opinions, to learn, and to solve problems — in short, the classification of the citizens with respect to levels of intelligence.

The development of tests to measure native capacity in school children has led to the definition of intelligence in terms of mental age. Degree of intelligence is measured by rapidity of its development. When applied to adults, however, this standard and the tests based upon it become dubious. In the first place, native capacity probably becomes mature by a given age; hence, since each adult has reached what for him is the limit of growth in capacity, some criterion other than stage of development must be found for comparing his capacity with that of his fellows. This task is extremely difficult, for adults are more highly specialized in their activities than children. Following, as they do, widely different vocations, there is no common situation or measure of success, as in the case of school children, which can be employed as a test. Moreover, there is no way of measuring the rôle of maturity and experience which, though not in itself innate, nevertheless sharply distinguishes one man from another and contributes to what we call the "intelligence" of his actions.

In spite of the many pitfalls of mental measurement, at least one conclusion of political significance is assured. Whatever the type of test-scale used, the population in any large sample arranges itself according to the probability curve of normal distribution. Those of mediocre attainment in the scale comprise the large majority or mode of the curve. Increasingly inferior individuals shade off in numbers at one end, as do the superior individuals or geniuses at the other. For this reason a "government of the people," so far as these tests may be taken as criteria, will be a government of mediocre laws, policies, and statesmanship. The theory which seems to underlie American democracy is that no one man can be trusted to govern for the welfare of others. The people must govern directly by the means of majority assent; that is, there must be self-government. Between the safeguarding of public interest as the direct expression of the masses and the efficient administration of public affairs as the work of the intelligent few, lies the dilemma of the political scientist. The psychologist has done little to help him solve this problem; but he has drawn his attention sharply to one horn of the dilemma, and has taught him to become increasingly skeptical both of the political ingenuity and the quality of judgment to be expected at the hands of public opinion.[1]

Already critical of the much-used term "public opinion," political scientists are beginning to coöperate with the psychologists in the attempt to form a better definition and to devise, if possible, methods of measurement in this important field. The notion of public opinion has become entrenched not only in popular usage but in agencies of control, so that resistance is offered to an analytical approach. The labor of conducting adequate experiments is great. Only a few tentative researches upon method, mainly in connection with universities, have thus far been completed. Organizations for formulating and controlling opinion are flourishing in abundance; but the facilities for scientific study of opinion are hopelessly meager. The suggestions which we shall give here pertain chiefly, therefore, to future development.

The desired direction for the study of public opinion can best be indicated by contrasting two ways of dealing with it. The first is the traditional way, namely, that of the editor or campaign manager, the publicity director and spokesman. The other attitude is the scientific one, which shuns all popular appeal and works only through patient and tedious research. We shall call them for convenience the *publicity approach* and the *scientific approach* respectively. In the following summary of their differences the writer believes that a scientifically useful definition of public opinion will emerge.[2]

(a) The *publicity* method works through newspapers, political speeches, and various forms of visual and auditory propaganda, with the major purpose not of investigating public opinion, but either of creating it or of formulating an opinion alleged already to exist. The *scientific* method employs no organ for building up or

[1] Cf. Goddard, H. H., *Human Efficiency and Levels of Intelligence*, especially pp. 95–128; Martin, E. D., *Psychology (Lectures in Print)*, lecture 12; Brigham, C. C., *A Study of American Intelligence;* Gosnell, H. F., "Some Practical Applications of Psychology to Politics." *American Journal of Sociology*, xxviii, 1922–23, pp. 735–43; Lippmann, W., *The Phantom Public.*

[2] It should be borne in mind that the terms "publicity" and "scientific" are used in the following discussions to refer to methods, not to persons. A publicist may at times take a scientific attitude, and a scientist may occasionally employ publicity.

controlling public opinion except for experimental purposes. Its purpose is purely one of investigating the present status of opinion

(b) The publicity method deals only with statements of content which are accredited to the majority of citizens in the political unit. This is accomplished through either (1) selecting that opinion which seems likely to be accepted by the great number, or (2) creating by propaganda the acceptance of a certain stated opinion. The scientific process, on the other hand, deals not only with the majority acceptance but with the views of all minority groups as well. It does not select a statement for majority agreement, but tries to give a comprehensive and accurate picture of the entire range of opinions at a given moment.

The publicity man, in other words, asks the question, "What will the public agree upon?" And when he has decided this point to his satisfaction, he says, "This view is public opinion." The scientist, on the other hand, asks, "What is the opinion, or what are the opinions, of individuals comprising this public regarding this issue? If there is not complete agreement, in what proportion is acceptance distributed upon all possible attitudes which are relevant to the question? What are the geographical, institutional, or other differences with regard to acceptance of different proposals?" The publicist considers that without a goodly consensus or agreement there is no public opinion. For the scientist there is always public opinion (that is, opinions) so long as individuals are able to hold coherent views upon a question.

(c) The publicist uses the word "opinion" in the sense of the logical content of the stated view; that is, as the verbal presentation, or stimulus. The scientific student uses it to denote the attitudes and thought processes existing in the neuro-muscular pattern of the individuals making up the public. For him public opinion is in terms of response.

(d) As a means of *ascertaining* public opinion, the *publicity* viewpoint comprises two methods. The first is making a canvass of newspaper publicity, editorial opinion, public speeches, and political advertisement to which the people in a certain locality have been subjected — surveying, in other words, the local and representative centers for the formulation and control of opinion. The second means is the use of the straw vote or referendum ballot, usually to be answered by "yes" or "no," thus forcing the attitudes of the citizens who vote into one or the other of these categories. The *scientific* approach, on the other hand, deals not with centers of opinion formation, but with individuals; and it deals with them by a more discriminating process than the use of the customary ballot. A scale is presented to the individual on which he is asked to check his opinion, not as merely positive or negative, but upon all the logically discriminable attitudes which one might hold upon the question. It is thus possible to measure the distribution of opinion among a sample of a mass of individuals and to indicate this distribution [1] numerically or graphically.

In discussing the values for social science to be derived from a technique of measuring opinion, the first to be mentioned is the substitution of measurement for guesswork. The merit of the scientific approach is that it enables us to ascertain public opinion directly and quantitatively rather than through the general impression of an editor or a leader who considers himself in close touch with public affairs. Due respect must be paid to the keen ability to sense public opinion that is possessed by many politicians. There is also perhaps some truth in Roosevelt's dictum that he knew what the American people were thinking, not through any mystical intuition, but because he himself was a typical American citizen. The scientist, however, wishes a more objective and verifiable method of measuring his phenomena. The publicist, thinking as he does habitually in terms of eliciting and molding opinion, may argue that no public opinion really exists until it is created through being publicly expressed. Since it has been his business thus to create it, he will maintain that he is in the best position to know what the public opinion is. This claim may be allowed to stand tentatively with respect to the publicist's own definition, namely, that public opinion is a statement which is accepted by the majority. It is obviously false, however, if applied to the scientific definition, since the latter is concerned with the distribution of differences of opinion as well as with the majority agreement. The argument that newspapers are so edited as to stimulate circulation and that

[1] The construction of these scales and the types of distribution resulting from their use have already been described in connection with the measurement of atypicality.

In addition to the references there given, the following attempts at the use of attitude scales may be mentioned: Rice, S. A., "The Political Vote as a Frequency Distribution of Opinion." *Journal of the American Statistical Association*, March, 1924; Willey, M. M., and Rice, S. A., "William Jennings Bryan as a Social Force." *The Journal of Social Forces*, XI, 1924, no. 3; and the *Syracuse University Reaction Study*, prepared at the School of Citizenship and Public Affairs, Syracuse University.

editors are keen to sense the public acceptance, although true, does not cover the question. The factors involved are too complex. Newspapers may sell upon the basis of pictorial or sensational features rather than upon policies with respect to public issues.

But even from the publicist's standpoint of a consensus, we may deny that public opinion exists only when it is given expression. It is possible to have such an agreement without public expression having taken place. Suppose, for example, that in a large industry there is announced a probable lowering of the wages of all the workers. An issue would thus be created separately in the attitude of each worker, quite apart from any public agitation upon the question. If measurement could be taken at that moment, there would be found a practically unanimous agreement against such a proposal. It is true that situations of this sort are speedily taken up by agitators or "spokesmen"; and the factors of behavior in crowds enter to increase intensity of conviction and energy of action. The illustration, however, proves that there can be a strong alignment of opinion without external propaganda or control. It is such alignments that the scientific method aims to measure.

A second scientific ideal is ability to predict future events. In addition to propaganda and fortuitous happenings, there exist certain attitudinal determinants of the future opinions of individuals when they are confronted by a new situation. Propaganda cannot be implanted from a blue sky: it must work with habitual attitudes and sentiments already present. Long before prohibition became a wide legislative issue, many people were stirred by such stories as Ten Nights in a Barroom; while many had espoused individualistic philosophies with regard to governmental control over personal habits. Largely out of such raw materials the strong prohibition and anti-prohibition alignments of the present day have been built up. A technique of measurement applied to these underlying attitudes may enable us to make intelligent predictions as to the future trend of opinion.[1]

A third goal of scientific measurement is that of control over social change. The knowledge necessary for control depends upon the ability to measure changes produced by carefully controlled experimental conditions. The measurement of change thus be-

[1] It is, of course, conceded that propagandists may *use* these psychological determinants in ways which we cannot readily foresee.

comes a question of fundamental importance. It is frequently assumed that one can determine the manner in which opinion has changed over a given interval by noting the changes in the editorial policies of newspapers during that period. There is, however, no way of knowing whether the change of editorial policy follows and depends upon the change of opinion, or vice versa. Does the newspaper editor create public opinion or merely express it, or perhaps both? There is no way of answering this question until the lay of opinion is actually measured before a newspaper takes up an issue, and a corresponding measurement made under controlled conditions after newspaper publicity has been employed.[1] Such methods should be used to measure the influence not only of propaganda, but of religious revivals, educational material, face-to-face discussion, and other agencies which affect wide-spread attitudes.

The situation, however, is made still more complex by the entrance of another circular process. A number of authorities have included as a part of their definition of public opinion the fact that each individual accepts the stated opinion as the view also of his fellows. This acceptance operates psychologically as a kind of compulsion to strengthen and still further extend the acquiescence of the individuals concerned. Merely to express a view as the opinion of the majority is to produce through the impression of universality an acceptance of that view by many persons who would not otherwise conform to it.[2] Both editors and political speakers in their frequent references to the public play upon this susceptibility to the view of the supposed majority; and such appeals probably affect voting to a large extent. There occurs to the

[1] A few attempts have already been made in the measurement of opinion-change in universities. See Willey and Rice, "William Jennings Bryan as a Social Force," *loc. cit.*, also Rice, S. A., "Differential Changes of Political Preference under Campaign Stimulation." *Journal of Abnormal and Social Psychology*, XXI, 1926, pp. 297–303. Further development, however, is required both in the technique and in the resources for such investigations.

[2] To express this view in extreme form: If most of the individuals in a community could be made to believe that a certain opinion, x, is the opinion of the majority in that community, and if there is no possibility of individuals checking the truth of this assertion, then x *will be likely to become the opinion of the majority*. Public opinion may be said from this standpoint to be the opinion which the individual thinks is characteristic of the public. Attempts are being made to measure the specific extent of this influence in the Reaction Study of Student Opinion conducted at Syracuse University. A general discussion of the "impression of universality" and "attitude of conformity" are given in the writer's *Social Psychology*, chaps. 11, 12.

For an experiment to determine the effect of majority opinion upon judgments of value, see H. H. Moore's article "The Comparative Influence of Majority and Expert Opinion." *American Journal of Psychology*, XXXII, 1921, pp. 16–20.

writer but one method by which this use of "public opinion" as a tool can be exposed, and the fictitious element introduced through the impression of universality separated from those genuine alignments which would exist in the absence of such devices. That method is the measurement upon an attitude scale of the opinions held by a sufficient sample of individuals, either (a) before and after the employment of the type of publicity just described, or (b) after the use of such publicity, with the added requirement in the scale for the subject to state the source of his convictions, and the part played in them by agencies pretending to express the "will of the majority." It is probably of greater importance than is commonly recognized that actual, discrete opinion be measured as accurately as possible, and that citizens, as a protection against certain forms of publicity, be informed of the distribution of this opinion.

Not only in the problem of measuring public opinion is there opportunity for coöperation between political scientist and psychologist, but also in studying the psychological nature of opinion itself. We enter here the field of verbal habits or, as Lippmann has called them, "stereotypes." All voting, except upon vital issues and alignments, probably rests upon this relatively superficial basis. One may study the formation of such stereotypes by the introspective method combined with a kind of psychoanalytic procedure. By discovering certain ideas, images, emotional biases, and previously formed convictions associated with a political attitude, one can often determine the source from which it was acquired, and may view the part it plays in the general pattern of thought and feeling of the individual. Stereotypes have been investigated in the fields of racial aversions, patriotism, and judgments of personalities by familiar outward signs. Tentative correlations have been made between the acceptance of stereotypes and intelligence and scholarship. Attitude studies for detecting proneness to "stereotyping" have been used to measure the success of political science courses in developing a critical habit of thought, and the transfer or spread of this tendency to new questions.[1]

The relationship of social and political attitudes to propaganda is a further subject for coöperative investigation. Thus far interest has centered largely on the materials of propaganda, such, for

[1] Good general discussions of this field are to be found in Walter Lippmann's *Public Opinion* and Graham Wallas's *Human Nature in Politics*, part I, chap. 2. On the experimental side, consult Rice, S. A., "Stereotypes as a Factor in Judging Human Character." *Journal of Personnel Research*, v, 1926, no. 7.

example, as stimuli for evoking instructive and emotional reactions, or the use of "colorful" words to arouse sentiments of hatred, repugnance, anxiety, approbation, or love. But here, as in public opinion generally, the study of the stimulus alone is insufficient. We need, as in public opinion, a measure of response tendencies before and after the propaganda has been brought to bear if we would understand its true significance.[1]

The negative aspect or absence of political opinions is a point of attack equally important to the student of a working government. Inertia or indifference, the most significant factor in non-voting, is usually due to the fact that the individual has not acquired attitudes of sufficient strength upon the question at issue to impel him to vote. Few persons probably have genuine reasons for *not* voting. Their negligence should be interpreted rather as the lack of reasons or motives *for* voting. The gap between political institutions and personal human interest cannot be bridged by appeals to civic pride, or by such questionable analogies as "training for citizenship," or developing a civic morale of peace comparable to that in war time. Insight and critical attitude can be fostered by schools and universities; but the most difficult problem is the establishing of a drive for participation in public affairs. The old "instinct pedagogy" has failed in this task. But perhaps the difficulty lies not with our educational methods, but with the nature of the social order which these methods are expected to implant in the individual. So long as the political process abstracts only one relatively unimportant segment of the individual's life, holding it aloof from the rest of his personality, indifference to politics will remain.

There remains to be suggested a phase of the common segment approach which opens a new and an extensive field to the student of political behavior. The political order comprises not only similarity of stereotypes, beliefs, and opinions, but also common ways of behaving in the more stable relationships of life. All citizens react in a relatively fixed and predictable manner with reference to a policeman, a traffic signal, a tax collector, or the ex-

[1] For an indirect, introspective measurement of the effects of propaganda, cf. Meier, N. C., "Motives in Voting, a Study in Public Opinion," *American Journal of Sociology*, XXXI, 1926, pp. 199–212.

For general references on propaganda the following may be consulted: Martin, E. D., *Psychology (Lectures in Print)*, lectures 14 and 16, and *The Behavior of Crowds;* Dunlap, Knight, *Social Psychology*, chap. 8; Weeks, A. D., *The Control of the Social Mind*, and *The Psychology of Citizenship*.

change in labor or commodities which they expect for a dollar bill. Not only does each one respond in a regular and predictable manner toward such objects, but each knows that others may be depended upon to behave in the same way. Social organization, and the rise of political and economic institutions, are thus made possible. It might even be said that these common habits of response underlying ordered relationships, considered together with their appropriate stimuli, *are* the institutions of society.

Let us take, for example, the notion of law. From the psychological standpoint law is not an objective fact or system which serves as a stimulus to which the individual reacts by obedience and conformity. It exists essentially only in the attitudes of individuals who accept it. Their habits of conformity to a verbal code *constitute* the law. Individuals react not so much *to* the law, as *with* the law, in the sense in which we say a man lifts a stone "with" his hand. Law, and government based upon it, are psychological phenomena; they are imbedded in human behavior. A similar analysis might be made of all those "institutions" which have been traditionally considered as making up the "structure of society." Such structure is reducible to attitudes of individuals and variations in such attitudes, both as to content and as to degree of generality. Political psychology, therefore, implies a re-formulation in terms of individual human behavior of the hypothesis which has served as the background of much social thinking and investigation.

IV
Conclusion: The Identity of Political Science and Psychology

Psychologists and political scientists are beginning to join their efforts in analyzing the dynamic processes, rather than the configurations, of human life. In this chapter the writer has tried to state as he sees them the significant trends of this coöperative research, and to forecast some future possibilities. Political psychology rests, on the one hand, upon the study of the individual. It requires a deeper understanding and a clearer technique for the study of personality than exist at present. With progress in the study of contacts of personalities we may hope to increase our knowledge of leadership and of the face-to-face activities of individuals from which political processes emerge. In addition to this, the political psychologist must study, not individuals as wholes, but those common segments of ability or behavior characteristic of large numbers of individuals. In the field of public opinion such work is needed to measure the data and check the generalizations of the publicity agent. The factors of individualized response in so-called public opinion should be separated from the influence of social pressures. Eventually the political psychologist assails the very mold in which political action is cast. Leadership, social movements, public opinion, discussion, legislation, citizenship — all activities through which government is conducted — are phases of human behavior. But more than that: government itself is behavior. Conceived as a structure, or an institution, it is behavior of a different sort from those more obvious and spectacular processes mentioned above: it consists of deeper, more stable, and more generalized attitudes. But it is, none the less, behavior. The formulation of political structure as psychological and as lying within the individual has implications both for social theory and for experiment.

If the reader up to this point has agreed in principle, one significant conclusion remains: It will be possible for political scientists to cease considering their field as one of formal description and legalistic philosophy, and regard it as a *natural science*. And furthermore, when so regarded, political science and behavioristic psychology become one and the same thing. While it is true that not all behavior is pertinent to political action, nevertheless all political action is behavior. There will, of course, be a difference of opinion as to whether the political scientist should accept a complete merging of his field with that of the psychologist. Many believe, and perhaps justly, in the existence of political facts *per se* and in an order of reality cast in terms of social and political structures. Perhaps they are right. If so, the foregoing analysis is still serviceable as a description of the same phenomena upon a lower, or psychological, level. Some persons, however, will choose to discard the structural view as descriptively possible but as barren of promise for scientific understanding and control. These persons will see in the relation between political science and psychology not an overlapping but an identity.

SELECTED REFERENCES

General scope and methodology

Follett, M. P. *Creative Experience.* 1924.

Giddings, F. H. *Studies in the Theory of Human Society.* 1922.

Gosnell, Harold F. "Some Practical Applications of Psychology to Politics." *American Journal of Sociology,* xxviii, 1922–23, pp. 735–43.

Kallen, H. M. "Political Science as Psychology." *American Political Science Review,* xvii, 1923, pp. 181–203.

Merriam, Charles E. "The Significance of Psychology for the Study of Politics." *American Political Science Review,* xviii, 1924, pp. 469–88.

"Progress in Political Research." *American Political Science Review,* xx, 1926.

Personality, leadership, and the study of atypicals

Allport, F. H., and Hartman, D. A. "The Measurement and Motivation of Atypical Opinion in a Certain Group." *American Political Science Review,* xix, no. 4, pp. 735–60.

Michels, Robert. *Political Parties.* 1915.

Moore, H. T. "Innate Factors in Radicalism and Conservatism." *Journal of Abnormal and Social Psychology,* xx, 1925, pp. 234–44.

O'Higgins, H., and Reede, E. H. *The American Mind in Action.* 1924.

Wolfe, A. B. *Conservatism, Radicalism, and Scientific Method.* 1923.

Public opinion, propaganda, and citizenship

Lippmann, Walter. *Public Opinion.* 1922.

Martin, E. D. *Psychology* (*Lectures in Print*), lectures 12, 13, 14, 16. 1926.

Merriam, C. E., and Gosnell, H. F. *Non-Voting.* 1924.

Rice, S. A. "The Political Vote as a Frequency Distribution of Opinion." *Journal of the American Statistical Association,* March, 1924.

"The Behavior of Legislative Groups: a Method of Measurement." *Political Science Quarterly,* March, 1925.

"Differential Changes of Political Preference under Campaign Stimulation." *Journal of Abnormal and Social Psychology,* xxi, 1926, pp. 297–303.

Wallas, Graham. *Human Nature in Politics.* 1908.

Willey, M. M., and Rice, S. A. "William Jennings Bryan as a Social Force." *The Journal of Social Forces,* xi, 1924, p. 3.

The psychology of political structure

Dunlap, Knight. *Social Psychology,* chaps. 5 and 7.

Ginsberg, M. *The Psychology of Society.* 1921.

Lippmann, Walter. *The Phantom Public.* 1926.

Pillsbury, W. B. *The Psychology of Nationality and Internationalism.* 1919.

CHAPTER XXIII
POLITICAL SCIENCE AND STATISTICS
By JOHN A. FAIRLIE
UNIVERSITY OF ILLINOIS

"STATISTICS" and "politics" are words which have had, and still have, a wide variety of meanings; and any consideration of the relations between the two will depend largely on the particular sense in which each of the words is used. In etymological origin the two words are closely related. "Statistics" was derived from the Latin *status*, with the meaning of the political state, or of the Greek πολις; and the early use of the word "statistics" in the latter part of the eighteenth century has been defined as "that branch of political science dealing with the collection, classification, and discussion of facts ... bearing on the condition of a state or community." [1] In its later use, however, it has come to be restricted to numerical data, on the one hand, and on the other, to be extended to include economic and social facts not distinctly political, and, still further, to include data on subjects other than those dealing with the social relations of mankind.

At the same time, the word "politics," formerly used to cover the whole field of social relations, has come to be limited to the study of governmental institutions, and, in a special sense, to the art of party organization and the control of public elections.

I

Historically, the development of the interrelations between these fields may be traced along several lines: (1) the collection of numerical data by governmental agencies, (2) the comparative study of political institutions based on descriptive facts; and (3) the scientific analysis of numerical data relating to political systems.

Official and other records of numerical data are to be found in the oldest records of organized political communities — in Egypt, in the cuneiform tablets of the Babylonians, in China, and in the calendars of the Maya inscriptions of Central America. In Greece there were official records of population, taxes, and lands. The

[1] Murray's *New English Dictionary*.

Romans had a well-developed official census taken at intervals, as well as other numerical records. Official data relating to church lands were compiled under Pepin the Short and Charlemagne in the eighth century; and some records of this sort have been preserved in France, notably the *Polyptique de l'Abbé Irmion* (of the Abbey of Saint-Germain de Près) of the year 806 A.D.[1] The well-known Domesday Book of William the Conqueror (1086) stands out as the most important comprehensive official census, not only in England but of any country, before the nineteenth century. Other less extensive official reports were made at occasional intervals during the later Middle Ages. But no regular and systematic records were made until later.[2]

DESCRIPTIVE STATISTICS

"Statistics" in the eighteenth century sense of description and comparison of political conditions may be traced from Aristotle's studies of the constitutions of 158 states, of which the Constitution of Athens has alone survived. Similar descriptive studies were also made by Polybius.

A new series of such writers began in the sixteenth century. Machiavelli, who is said to have founded the modern scientific study of politics, made use of descriptive data in his political writings. So, too, did Jean Bodin, more extensively in his *Republic* (1577) which, besides the discussion of sovereignty and forms of government, considers public revenues and the influence of climate on government, recommends a periodical census of property, and sets forth what he calls arithmetical, geometrical, and harmonic proportions as applied to political regimen. Comprehensive accounts of political institutions and conditions were written by Sebastian Muenster,[3] by Sansonivi and Botero[4] in Italy, and by Étienne Pasquier in France, in the latter half of the sixteenth century.[5]

---

[1] Koren. *History of Statistics*, p. 226.

[2] The use of numerical data must have been closely limited by the cumbersome Latin system of notation, and little development was possible before the use of the arabic numerals introduced in Europe about the twelfth century.

[3] Professor at Heidelberg and Basle. His *Cosmographia* appeared from 1536 to 1544.

[4] Sansonivi, *Del Governo di regni et dello republiche antiche et moderno*. Botero, Ragioni di stato, 10 vols. *Relaziones Universali*. The last-named book gives estimates in figures of the areas, revenues, taxes, military strength, and commerce of the various countries.

[5] Pasquier, *Recherches de la France.,*

In his *Introduction to the Literature of Modern Europe*, Hallam notes that after the theoretical discussions of the sixteenth century, political writings in the early part of the seventh century assumed "more of an historical, or, as we might say, of a statistical character. Learning was employed in systematic analysis of ancient or modern forms of government, in dissertations explanatory of institutions, in copious and exact statements of the true, rather than in arguments upon the right or the expedient." [1]

In the eighteenth century there was greatly increased activity in this field of descriptive writing.[2] To Achenwall, professor at Göttingen, has usually been ascribed the first definite use of the word "statistics" (*statistik*) for such studies of the government and resources of political states, though similar terms had been previously employed by others.[3] Büsching began the publication of comparative official statistics in more detail about the same time.[4]

The works of these writers contained descriptions of various

---

[1] Vol. III, p. 156. Among such writings may be noted a study of *Les États, Empires et Principautés du Monde*, by Pierre D'Avity; and a numerous series of small volumes on the political constitutions of European states, issued by the bookdealers Elzevir, in Leyden, known as the *Respublicæ Elzeviranæ*. Lectures of this nature were also given by Herman Conring at Helmstedt, and afterwards published; and similar lectures were given by others in various places. Antoine Serra (1613) wrote on the causes of wealth and factors affecting the rate of exchanges, one of the first scientific studies in political economy.

[2] Gundling, *Ueber den jetzigen Zustand in Europa*.
Kemmerich, *Anleitung zur Staatswissenchaft der heutigen Welt*.
Thomas Salmon, *The Present State of All Nations*, 3 vols.
Everand Otto, *Primæ linæ notitæ Europæ rerum publicarum*.
Machten der Morgentheden van Europa.
Tegenwordige Staat der Vereen. Nederl. 21 vols.
Entnick, J., *Present State of the British Empire*.
Thaarup, *Danske Monarchies Statistik*.
Lagerhug, *Swea Rikes Staatskumschap*.
Fast, *Staats und Erdbeschrankung der Helvet. Eidgenossenchaft*.
Galanti, *Nuova Descr. geogr. e polit. della Sicilie*.
Lueder, *Kritische Geschichte der Statistik*.

[3] Achenwall's essay, *Vorbereitung zur Staatswissenschaft der Europäischen Reiche*, was written in 1748 and included in a larger work published a year later. Among other works by Achenwall may be noted his *Observations on North America*, based on data from Dr. Franklin (1749), translated in the *Pennsylvania Magazine of History and Biography*, 1903, and his *Observations on the Finances of France*.

The term "statist," for one skilled in public affairs, was used by Sidney (1584), Sir Thomas More (1590), and Shakespeare (*Hamlet*, V, II, 33–1602). The adjective form *Microscipium statisticum* was used by Helenus Polotanus (Frankfort, 1672); Philander von Ettenwald, *statista; rationes statisticæ*, by Aldenberg (1682); *bibliotheca statistica* by Thurman (1701); and *Collegium statisticum* by Schmeizel (died 1747) in lectures on the constitutions, revenues, and policy of states.

[4] *Neue Erdbeschreibung; Vorbereitung zur grundlichen und nützlichen Kenntniss der geographischan Beschaffenheit, und Staatsverfassung der europäischen Reiche.*

countries, their climate and population, their products and constitutions, but had little numerical data. Sometimes the descriptions
were printed in tabular form arranged in parallel columns, called
statistical tables.   Then, numerical data were included in such
tables, which thus formed a transition to the later use of the word
"statistics."   Important works of this kind were those of Henri
Crome, published in 1785,[1] Zimmerman's *Political Survey of Europe*,
and the compendious *Statistical Account of Scotland*, in 21 volumes,
by John Sinclair.[2]

Meanwhile there had been developments in the collection of
official numerical data and in methods of analysis. Registration
of births, marriages, and deaths was introduced in Augsburg in
1501 and afterwards in other German cities (Breslau, from 1542 to
1599, and in London, from 1550 to 1592); also, special inquiries
on various subjects were occasionally made by other official agencies.   Early in the seventeenth century, Sully, as superintendent
of finances, introduced for a time more systematic financial records
and reports in France; and in the latter part of the same century
similar methods were revived, developed, and placed on a more
permanent basis by Colbert.   In 1719, the regular collection of
official data on population and other matters was begun in Prussia;
and Frederick the Great extended the scope of the work.

Advances in the analysis of numerical data were made in England by John Graunt in his *Observations on the Bills of Mortality*,
by Sir William Petty in his *Essays in Political Arithmetic*, which
included studies of population and public finance, and by the
astronomer Halley in his study of the Breslau tables of mortality,
which laid the basis for a theory of vital statistics and life insurance.
Other important studies of numerical data were made by Charles
Davenant and Gregory King, officials in the English revenue offices.[3]

[1] *De la Grandeur et de la Population des États d'Europe*, 15 tableaux et une carte
synoptique.   Crome was professor of geography, statistics, and administration at
Dessau and Giessen, the author of numerous works, and editor of journals dealing
with administration, politics, and statistics.

[2] Zimmerman states that this science (statistics) was becoming a favorite study in
England; and an article in the *Critical Review* of the same year (vol. 68) refers to his
work as properly statistical, consisting of tables with a general comparative view of
forces, the government, the extent and population of the different countries.   Sinclair refers to the German use of the word, but states that he uses it in a broader sense
to include an inquiry into the state of a country.   The third edition of the Encyclopedia Britannica (1797) refers to statistics as a word lately introduced to express a survey of any kingdom, county, or parish.

[3] Davenant, *Of the Use of Political Arithmetic*, and *Two Discourses on the Publick
Revenue and Trade of England*.   King, *Natural and Political Observations and Conclusions on the state and condition of England*.   Extracts used by Davenant, but not
published until 1801.

In the eighteenth century, Bernouli, in his *Ars conjectandi*, formulated the general "law of large numbers"; and Süssmilch made further contributions to the analysis of vital statistics.[1]   In France Montesquieu discussed problems of population, and Messance, Moheau, and Lavoisier took up problems of estimating the number of inhabitants and agricultural resources.[2]   In England, Hume wrote an essay on population, Arthur Young wrote on *Political Arithmetic*, William Playfair developed the use of charts as a means of presenting numerical data on public finance and commerce,[3] and Malthus published his famous essay on population. Schlözer, the most influential pupil of Achenwall, wrote in 1804 his *Theorie der Statistik*.

At the beginning of the nineteenth century some further progress was made in the collection of official statistical data.   An official census of population was taken in the United States in 1790, and repeated every ten years.   The first regular census was taken in Great Britain in 1801.   Bureaus of statistics, established in France in 1801 and in Prussia in 1805, compiled and published useful reports.   Statistical bureaus were also established in several other countries, but continued only for a short time.   The prolonged war and the political reaction which followed were not conducive to further development.   During this period, also, the specialization of social studies in the universities, with the rise of political economy, public law, and geography as distinct fields, took over important branches of the field of statistics as conceived by Achenwall and his followers.   An active controversy arose between the older school and the newer group of numerical statisticians.

A new period of statistical development began about 1830. Statistical societies were organized in France (Marseilles 1827, Paris 1829), England (Manchester 1833, London 1834), and the United States (1838).   Official bureaus of statistics were revived and their activities extended, and new offices were organized, in Belgium (1830), in the British Board of Trade (1832) and Home

---

[1] *Betrachtungen über die göttliche Ordnung in den Veränderungen des menschlichen Geschlechts aus der Geburt, dem Tode, und der Fortpflanzung desselben erwiesen.*

[2] Westergaard, "Method and Scope of Statistics."   *Publications of the American Statistical Association*, xv, p. 234.   Meitzen, *History, Theory, and Technique of Statistics*, translated by R. B. Falkner.

[3] *Lineal Arithmetic.   Statistical Breviary and Atlas; A Statement of the Finances and Revenues of Great Britain.   An Inquiry into the permanent Causes of the Decline and Fall of Wealthy Nations.   A Statistical Account of the United States of America.*

Office (1834), in Russia (1834), in Austria (1840), and the German Zollverein. An International Statistical Congress was held at Brussels in 1853, followed by other meetings in other European cities at intervals of several years; and an International Statistical Institute was organized at London in 1885.[1]

In later years governmental statistical offices have been established in great numbers. A bureau was organized in Italy in 1861. A bureau of statistics was created in the United States Treasury Department in 1866, and a permanent census bureau was established in 1902. Such bureaus are now to be found in most central governments, in most of the American states, and in some cities — and with a wide range in the scope of their activities.

THE SCOPE OF STATISTICS

Along with these developments came important changes in the conception of statistics. Some writers adhered to the view that statistics dealt with the description and comparison of political states. One group restricted it more definitely to the political field of state constitutions. Others extended it to include all facts relating to the condition or status of states,[2] linking both the original and the political meanings of the Latin word *status*. Still others emphasized mainly the compilation and analysis of numerical data relating to social conditions, and some extended it to numerical data in other fields.

The analysis of numerical data was advanced by the development of the theory of probabilities by Laplace, Fourier, and Cournot,[3] and by its application to population studies and problems in political economy. John R. McCulloch, author of *A Statistical Account of the British Empire*, held that the object of the statistician is to describe the condition of a particular country at a particular period.[4] The Belgian statistician Quételet made extensive social studies based on numerical data,[5] hoping to find in the figures laws of the cosmological order and the world's history. F. Dufau

[1] Koren, *History of Statistics*.

[2] Cf. Von Mohl, *Die Geschichte und Literatur der Staatswissenschaften*, part XIX.

[3] Laplace, *Essai philosophique sur les probabilités;* Fourier, *Notions générales sur la population;* Cournot, *Exposition de la theorie des chances.*

[4] *Political Economy*, I, 59.

[5] *Mémoires sur les lois de naissance et de la mortalité à Bruxelles; Recherches sur la réproduction et la mortalité de l'homme aux différent âges; Sur l'homme et le développement de ses facultés; Lettres sur la théorie des probabilités appliqués aux sciences morales et politiques; Du système sociale et des lois qui le regnent; Sur les tables de mortalité.* Cf. Columbia University Studies, vol. 31, no. 4, *Quételet as a Statistician.*

explained his work on statistics as the theory of a study of the laws according to which social facts develop, while Moreau de Jannes defined statistics as the science of social facts expressed in numerical terms.[1]

In its program of 1838, the London Statistical Society declared that statistics did not consist merely of figures, but that "all conclusions should be drawn from well-attested data and shall admit of mathematical demonstration." [2]   About the same time J. E. Portlock, a British geologist, held that all actual things, or facts, qualities, and the like which could be collected in numbers were statistics.[3]   A writer in the *London and Westminster Review* took the position that "statistics is merely a form of knowledge — a mode of arraying and stating facts which belong to various sciences." [4]

Cournot considered that statistics covered the collection and comparison of numerous facts of every kind in order to ascertain numerical relations which denote regular causes.   In 1850 Dr. C. G. A. Knies, in a study of conflicting views of statistics, proposed that the descriptive statistics of Achenwall should be designated as the science of the state (*Staatenkunde*), and that the term statistics should be restricted to the study of numerical data such as had developed from political arithmetic.[5]   These opinions with regard to statistics as based on numerical data of all kinds have been followed by M. Block (*Statistique de la France*), Adolf Wagner, and Rümelin of Tübingen (*Zur Theorie der Statistik*), and have come to be generally accepted.[6]   By the end of the century Professor Mayo-Smith stated that "statistics consists in the observation of phenomena that can be counted or expressed in figures." [7]

---

[1] *Éléments de Statistique.*   [2] *Journal*, i.

[3] An address explanatory of the objects and advantages of statistical inquiries, Belfast, 1838.   Portlock was connected with the Ordnance Survey of Ireland.   He compiled data on the physical aspects, geology and economic resources of Ireland, and in 1837 he founded a geological and statistical office at Belfast.

[4] Vol. 29, p. 70.   Harriet Martineau (in *Society in America*, ii, p. 292) remarked: "There is a great virtue in figures, dull as they are to all but the few who love statistics for the sake of what they indicate."   In 1829 F. B. Hawkins published a book on *Elementary Medical Statistics*, which he defined as "the application of numbers to illustrate the natural history of man in health and disease."   In 1845 appeared Nelson's *Contributions to Vital Statistics.*

[5] *Die Statistik als selbständige Wissenschaft.*

[6] Maxwell in his *Theory of Heat* referred to "a statistical view of the subject" distributing molecules into groups.   An article in the *Journal of the Statistical Society* in 1881 (vol. 44) referred to statistics of pig iron, coffee, population, revenues, etc.

[7] *Statistics and Sociology.*   Cf. also, A. Russell, *Principles of Statistical Inquiry* — in re United States Census of 1840; and J. G. C. Kennedy, *Progress of Statistics* (read before the American Geographical Society, 1859).

II

The interrelations between statistics and politics at the present time may be considered with reference to (1) the governmental agencies for the collection of statistical data, and the statistical data on political and governmental organization and activities, and (2) the scientific analysis of political statistics.

Governmental Agencies

Government statistics form by far the largest volume of statistical data, and the official statistical agencies are among the most important means for the analysis of statistical data. Such official agencies are of importance to the student of political institutions in two ways. In the first place, they are the principal source for adequate and well arranged data on the organization and operation of the government; and in the second place, the organization and interrelation of such agencies furnish a problem in the administrative organization of the government. A brief account of such agencies in some of the more important governments will serve to illustrate these conditions.[1]

France had, perhaps, the earliest specialized official statistical office, and has one of the best developed systems at the present time. Bureaus of statistics have been organized in the ministries of Justice (1827), Commerce (1833), Public Works (1844), Finance (1877), Agriculture (1881), and Labor (1906). The last, although recently established, now publishes the more general statistics. There is also a Superior Council on Statistics, organized in 1885, an advisory body, composed of representatives from the various ministries, from Parliament, and from learned societies. Statistics are also compiled and published by other departments. The principal criticism of the arrangements is the need for more centralization and more specialization. Central bureaus of statistics are lacking in many departments, and a larger degree of central control over all the statistical agencies would bring about more effective coöperation. The city of Paris has a well-organized bureau of statistics, established in 1879, which issues an *Annuaire Statistique* and other useful publications.

In Germany, official statistical offices were established in the more important states during the first half of the nineteenth century; and statistical work was also organized by the Zollverein.

Koren, *History of Statistics;* Zahn, F. W., *Die Statistik in Deutschland.*

After the formation of the Empire, an imperial statistical office was set up in 1872, which has been continued with a well-organized staff of professional statisticians and assistants. The statistical offices in the several states have also continued, in active coöperation with the imperial office. Some of the more important states, such as Prussia, Bavaria, Würtemberg, and Hesse, have central statistical commissions. About fifty of the larger cities in Germany maintain municipal bureaus of statistics, that of Berlin dating from 1882; and in addition to their local reports, these bureaus coöperate in a *Statistical Year Book* of German cities, published at frequent intervals. A German Statistical Association was organized in 1911. Official statistics in Germany are classified in four main divisions: central statistics, handled by the central bureau and officials of the *Reich;* federal statistics, based on general plans formulated by the central bureau for the *Reich*, collected by the several states, and compiled and published for the *Reich* as a whole; special statistics, collected and published by the several state bureaus on their own initiative; and communal statistics, collected by the municipal bureaus, but to a large extent based on common plans.

In Great Britain the collection of official statistics is marked by a high degree of decentralization. Each department carries on its own work in its own way. The raw material is abundant and carefully collected, but the results fall short of the potential utility because of the lack of general supervision and coöperation. The most important agencies are the statistical department of the Board of Trade (1832) and the Registrar General's Office (1837); but extensive and useful reports are also published by the Treasury, Home Office, Ministry of Health, Board of Education, Board of Agriculture, Post Office, and other departments. Several of these departments publish useful statistical data on local administration and finance. Official statistics are also published by many of the local authorities, and there are also unofficial compilations of such data. But the organization of special statistical offices and the systematic analysis of statistical data seem to be less developed than in the German cities.

Although official enumerations of population and other data were made in the American colonies before the Revolution, and although the census was taken by the national government every ten years from 1790, and other numerical data, especially on finance and commerce, were published both by the national and the state governments, the first permanent statistical office to be organized in the United States was the bureau of statistics in the treasury department in 1866. Other agencies dealing largely with statistical work have since been established: for example, the bureau of labor (1884), the interstate commerce commission (1887), the comptroller of the currency, the bureau of education, and the department of agriculture. In 1902 a permanent census bureau was established, and in 1903 the creation of the department of commerce and labor brought together in one department a number of statistical agencies and provided for two new agencies. The creation of a department of labor in 1913 transferred two of these statistical agencies; and later legislation has set up a number of other separate agencies, such as the federal trade commission and the shipping board.

During the World War the number of statistical agencies was further multiplied, and a central bureau of planning and statistics was provided for coördinating a considerable part of the statistical work; but this central board went out of existence with most of the other war agencies.[1]

A report on the statistical work of the United States government in 1922 shows forty-four different offices engaged in this field. Five of the main departments each have from four to eight bureaus engaged largely in statistical work, while there are a dozen other offices of this kind outside any of the main departments. With such a multiplication of agencies there is a vast deal of duplication and overlapping as to the general fields. In several instances ten to twelve different agencies are collecting statistics of the same kind.

The most important of these statistical agencies is the bureau of the census in the department of commerce. A report issued by the United States Bureau of Efficiency recommended that the collection, tabulation, and dissemination of all non-administrative statistics should be centralized, so far as practicable, in this bureau, and that its name should be changed to the Bureau of Federal Statistics.[2]

[1] *Publications of the American Statistical Association*, no. 125, 1919, pp. 223, 275.

[2] United States Bureau of Efficiency, *A Report on the Statistical Work of the United States Government*. A later study, *The Statistical Work of the National Government*, by L. F. Schmeckebeier, issued by the Institute of Government Research, takes another view. It holds that "it is the almost unanimous verdict of men experienced

An enormous amount of statistical data is collected by these numerous agencies of the national government, covering not only all branches of the national government and some material on state and local government, but also economic and social facts on a great variety of subjects. But the data are far from being well correlated and analyzed. The *Statistical Abstract for the United States* brings together a large mass of figures; but prepared by a bureau in the department of commerce it emphasizes the statistics of commerce and is therefore less serviceable on other matters. There is no general and comprehensive plan of coöperation between the national and the state governments, as in Germany. Statistics on state and local governments are very inadequately brought together.

The statistical activities of the national government deal largely with those phases of national life which are considered of public and especially of political interest. The population census is taken primarily for apportionment; statistics of foreign trade and manufactures, wages and prices have relation to tariff laws and policies; statistics of finance, money and banking, railways and immigration, are largely by-products of administrative and government control. On the other hand much of the statistical work of the department of agriculture, the geological survey and the bureau of mines, and the census vital statistics are based on larger economic and social interests.[1]

The several states also publish a great many statistical data, and most if not all of them have a number of statistical bureaus. In 1869 Massachusetts established the first bureau of labor statistics; and such bureaus now exist in practically all of the states. In some states the collection and publication of labor and industrial statistics have been concentrated in a single department. For the most part, however, the statistical work of the states is handled by a large number of separate agencies; and there is little or no effort to combine and correlate the data on different topics even in a single state, and still less for the United States as a whole. In a number of states there is published a *Manual* or *Year Book*, includ-

in governmental statistical work that a great consolidated statistical office will result in neither economy nor greater accuracy," but that "there is undoubtedly need for an agency that would coördinate the work of the several organizations in the statistical field."

[1] Young, A. A., in the *Publications of the American Statistical Association*, XVIII. p. 873.

ing data on a considerable variety of subjects; but these data are usually put together hastily and with no coherent plan. Statistical data about local governments are especially defective. Reports of schools are better than those in other fields; and about a dozen states compile and publish statistics of local finance.

There is also a large output of statistical reports by municipal and other local authorities, but these reports are still less carefully and systematically made. Many cities of importance publish no comprehensive reports, and issue only detached departmental reports which vary widely in quality and which in some cases are not published. A few cities have established municipal bureaus of statistics which do useful work, as in Boston and Chicago.

The general result of this situation is the lack of anything like adequate statistical data on administrative and political conditions in the states and local governments in the United States. In a number of states tables of primary and election returns are published in considerable detail; but there is no official compilation of such data for the country as a whole. Also, there is no general compilation of judicial, police, and criminal statistics for the United States, or even for a single state; and in but a few places are the local reports of much value. Statistics of state and municipal finances are published by the United States census bureau; school statistics, by the bureau of education; and statistics in some other fields of governmental activity, by various bureaus in the national government; but this information is so scattered that it is difficult to know about all that is done.[1]

A large number of international organizations have been established which deal with statistics. Some, like the International Institute of Statistics, deal with methods and the coördination of statistics. Most of them are concerned with statistics in a particular field, such as the International Institute of Agriculture, the International Bureau of Commercial Statistics (Brussels), and the International Labor Office. In 1920, the Council of the League

---

[1] Cf. Robinson, L. N., *History and Organization of Criminal Statistics in the United States;* "Improvement of Criminal Statistics in the United States," *Publications of the American Statistical Association,* XVII, June, 1922, p. 157; Hill, J. A., "Coöperation between State, Municipal and Federal Bureaus in the Compilation of Criminal Statistics," *Journal of Criminal Law,* XII, Feb., 1922, p. 529; Sutherland, E. H., *Criminology,* chap. 2. Some unofficial efforts have been made to compile municipal statistics. A *Municipal Year Book,* edited by M. N. Baker, was issued in 1902; and a similar publication was issued for 1924 and 1925 by the *American City* magazine.

of Nations appointed a temporary commission to report on existing international statistical agencies, their relations to the League of Nations, the desirability of a central advisory council and the further development of international statistics.[1]

SCIENTIFIC ANALYSIS OF POLITICAL STATISTICS

In the recent development of more systematic analysis of numerical statistics in political studies, we may first note statements of general principles as to the value of numerical data and mathematical methods by philosophical writers, and later take up some important cases of the use of numerical statistics by students of political affairs, and some studies by technical statisticians in the field of politics.

The utilitarian philosophers with their basic principle of the greatest good to the greatest number, might be expected to favor the use of numerical methods in applying the principle to problems in all branches of social relations.   David Hume, in an essay to show *That Politics may be reduced to a science*, held that "so great is the force of laws, and of particular forms of government, and so little dependence have they on the humors and tempers of men, that consequences almost as general and certain may sometimes be deduced from them, as any which the mathematical sciences may afford us."

Jeremy Bentham, in his *Theory of Legislation*, discussing the assessment of pleasures and pains by the various factors that determine their value, considered that "these provide the elements of a moral calculus, and legislation may thus become a mere matter of arithmetic."   Later, in dealing with more specific problems, he favored the registration of land titles, population, births, marriages, and deaths, publication of national accounts and lists of official fees, dues, and tolls, and fixing standards of quantity and quality.[2]

Comte, in laying the basis for a scientific study of social conditions, while believing that the general law of progress is fixed in direction beyond the power of human control, held that the rate of advance is subject to modification by physical and by moral causes that may be measured, and among the latter are political combinations.[3]

---

[1] *Publications of the American Statistical Association*, XVII, p. 629.
[2] *Theory of Legislation*, chaps. 8, 52.
[3] *Système de Politique Positive.*   Dunning, *History of Political Theories, from Rousseau to Spencer*, 391.

George Cornwall Lewis, in his *Methods of Observation and Reasoning in Politics*, urged the importance of facts or statistics in this study: "The first department of Politics, therefore, serving as a foundation for all the rest, is that which concerns the registration of political facts. This department may be described generally as consisting of history and statistics; but it includes all the methods adopted for preserving in an authentic and permanent form the meaning of political facts as they occur." [1]

Buckle, in his *History of Civilization in England*, hoped to place all historical science on the basis of statistics.

W. S. Jevons regarded political economy as a mathematical science and attempted to put its main definitions in the shape of quantitative formulæ.[2] His works on currency, taxation, and finance were based on analyses of numerical data; and he is said to have pointed the way to the method of "legislation by statistics" which has become the general rule in recent decades.[3]

Professor Sheldon Amos, author of one of the earliest works on *The Science of Politics*, in noting indications that the study of politics was being placed on a platform of higher scientific exactness than ever before, wrote:

One of these indications is the large and discriminating use of statistics. The collection and due use of statistics belong to very modern times . . . all the more advanced governments . . . rival each other in the breadth, fullness, arrangement, and clearness of the numerical information they obtain on all the groups of national fact which are susceptible of being tabulated in a systematic shape. . . . The comparison between the numerical results obtained at one time and place and another, and between those presented in different countries is becoming a political method increasing in prevalence and repute. . . . When the limits of application are duly recognized, and care is taken to distinguish legal and political causes from those which are purely ethical or sociological, the study and use of statistics must be regarded as a most valuable ally, and an unmistakable proof of the scientific character of political studies.[4]

The present-day view of the relation of statistics to political science, and also to other social sciences, has been expressed by Professor Mayo-Smith: Statistics, which is defined as the science of social masses,

---

[1] Page 554. Elsewhere he refers to Germany and Achenwall as originating the branch of descriptive politics called statistics, indicating that he does not limit the word to numerical data.

[2] *On the Mathematical Theory of Political Economy*, read before the Manchester Statistical Society, 1871. Cf. Walras, *Théorie Mathématique de la Richesse Sociale.*

[3] Barker. *Political Thought from Spencer*, p. 207.

[4] *The Science of Politics*, p. 18.

is the fundamental and general social science, observing social masses directly and furnishing material to all other sciences. ... Statistics occupies a peculiar position towards all the special social sciences. It first of all studies the social masses as pure process of nature, as in the statistics of sex, births, deaths, and physical characteristics. In these respects it has many relations with natural science, especially anthropology. In the second place, statistics furnishes materials for all the special social sciences, especially political economy. In political science, it is also extremely helpful, inasmuch as administrative statistics are often used to guide state action.[1]

Professor Von Mayr, of the University of Munich, has classified statistics as one of the secondary political sciences, along with economics and sociology, as distinguished from the primary political sciences of constitutional and administrative law and politics.[2]

With this recognition of the value of numerical statistics in the scientific analysis of political problems, came more extensive use of the greater amount of numerical data collected through official bureaus. This was, however, largely in the overlapping zones where economic and social problems seemed to call for political action, such as taxation and public finance and problems of social welfare, and comparatively little in the more exclusively political field.

This situation is indicated by an examination of the *Journal of the Royal Statistical Society* of London. A list of papers read before this society during its first half century (1834–1887) is grouped in seven divisions — commercial, industrial, financial, moral and social, political, vital, and miscellaneous. The political group includes comparatively few papers on statistics of elections, legislation, and local government. The groups on financial and on moral and social statistics, covering the overlapping fields, include a much larger number of papers on such topics as banking, currency, debt, revenue and taxation, poor relief, crime, education, and judicial administration.

So, too, in Mulhall's *Dictionary of Statistics* there are only a few short tables of what may be called political statistics in the most restricted sense, on such matters as the civil service, elections, and parliament, but a larger number in the overlapping fields, on army and navy, crime, education, finance, post office, and police.[3]

[1] "On the Study of Statistics." *Political Science Quarterly*, x, 1895, p. 475, reviewing Von Mayr, *Statistik und Gesellschaftslehre*.

[2] *Begriff und Gliederung der Staatswissenschaften*.

[3] Mayo-Smith's volumes on *Statistics and Economics* and *Statistics and Sociology* include data on matters of political interest, such as population, crime, migration,

The *Publications of the American Statistical Association* also deal mainly with economic and social statistics, including some papers in overlapping fields of political interest, on such matters as urban growth, public finance, criminal statistics, and government statistical offices, but with very few on exclusively political problems.

Until the end of the nineteenth century most of those primarily concerned with distinctively political problems, as such, apparently avoided the use of standards of quantitative measurement in their work. A striking illustration is seen in the writings of the late Lord Bryce, which while based on a greatly extended field of observation, make but little use of numerical statistics; and, indeed, Lord Bryce frankly expressed his belief that political data could not be measured with precision and that on this account politics could not be considered as an exact science.

In the present century, however, a number of writers have made more extensive use of numerical statistics in the study of the most distinctively political problems. Among these may be noted works on proportional representation, by John R. Commons and John H. Humphreys; Stanwood's *History of Presidential Elections;* A. L. Lowell's analysis of party voting in legislative assemblies (in his *Government of England*) and of popular voting on constitutional and legislative measures (in his *Public Opinion and Popular Government*); and G. M. Harris's *Problems of Local Government* (1911).

This tendency has been followed in more recent studies of political parties in America by A. N. Holcombe, Stuart A. Rice, and others.[1] Mr. Rice has also published articles on the "Political Vote as a Frequency Distribution of Opinion" and "Some Applications of Statistical Method to Political Research." Professor Charles E. Merriam has an interesting chapter on "Numbers and Politics" in his *New Aspects of Politics;* and numerical data have been analyzed in the study of *Non-Voting* by Merriam and Gosnell.

In the recent *Publications of the American Statistical Association* are several studies of this kind: A paper on "A New Method of Apportionment of Representatives," by E. V. Huntington, professor of mathematics at Harvard University, and a "Report upon

money and credit, and finance, but none on the most distinctively political problems, such as elections, and legislative or administrative action. Cf. also Charles H. Pearson, *National Life and Character*, chap. 3, on "Some Dangers of Political Development," discussing large armies, large cities, and large debts.

[1] Holcombe, A. N., *The Political Parties of Today*. Rice, S. A., "Farmers and Workers in American Politics." *American Political Science Review*, xix, 1925, pp. 500, 527, 615.

the Apportionment of Representatives" by a committee of statistical experts, which dealt with a more scientific application of mathematics to this problem.[1]

There has also been a considerable development of more systematically organized research on political subjects, based largely on numerical and other measurable data. In England such work has been done mainly by official agencies, more especially by temporary royal commissions. The commission on municipal corporations which reported in 1835 is one of the earliest and most important illustrations. Later examples are the Machinery of Government Committee of 1918, the commission on London Government, 1922, and the commission on Local Government appointed in 1923.

In the United States such studies have been made by both governmental and unofficial agencies. On a small scale some work of this kind has been done by legislative and municipal reference bureaus. More important studies have been made by some of the numerous temporary commissions and permanent administrative agencies. The largest number of these have been in the field of taxation and public expenditures. A group of special importance comprises the comprehensive studies of public administration by efficiency and economy and other commissions, resulting in general plans of administrative reorganization. There have also been many surveys in the field of education, and in other particular branches of public service.

A number of bureaus of governmental research, supported by private funds, have been established for the intensive study of governmental conditions. The Institute for Governmental Research at Washington, D.C., and the New York Bureau of Municipal Research have been the most important. The investigations of these bureaus have been mainly in the field of public administration and much of the work has been done by accountants and engineers making use of numerical data.[2]

Some of the difficulties and problems in the use of numerical statistics in political studies may be noted. Much of the data on political subjects are as yet by no means complete; and some of the data are not always accurate. There is, therefore, need for more

---

[1] *Publications*, xvii, nos. 135, 136; xix, no. 145.
[2] Twenty Years of Municipal Research.

systematic work in the collection of data and more careful methods of securing reliable data. A good deal could be done by bringing together material on political and governmental action that is scattered in the various state and local public offices, on such matters as elections, public finance, legislative proceedings, and the records of judicial and administrative activities. This probably could be done most effectively through agencies of the national government; but there is much material of this sort that could be more easily made available by the aid of private funds than the observational and experimental data of the students of the physical and biological sciences.

There are also, however, many political phenomena for which anything like complete records will be practically impossible, and some that have not as yet been reduced to precise measurements. In such matters there are problems as to the formulation of inquiries and the collection and use of partial and sample returns, and the comparison of general estimates from different sources. Studies on such problems have been made by the round tables at the National Conferences on the Science of Politics on a number of topics, such as the measurement of public opinion, a technique for testing nominating methods, methods for investigating problems of legislative organization and activities, the study of judicial review of legislation, methods of appraising civil service laws and the activities of civil service commissions, a study of state supervision of local finance, proposals for rating the efficiency of city government, and problems of international organization.[1]

There is also need on the part of students of political problems for attention to methods of analysis, comparison, and presentation of statistical data. An unmanageable mass of figures may be made to demonstrate important conditions by proper selection and arrangement in convenient tables. Charts and diagrams are also effective means to indicate the relations of a large body of statistics. These devices may, however, be abused so as to give erroneous impressions, and it is important to learn how to use them so as to emphasize conditions and conclusions that are warranted by the data.

[1] *American Political Science Review*, xviii, 1924, p. 119; xix, 1925, pp. 104, 371. Cf. Thorndike, E. L., *An Introduction to the Theory of Mental and Social Measurements*, 2d ed., revised; Bowley, A. L., *Nature and Purpose of the Measurement of Social Phenomena*; Montl, Guzman I., *De la estadistica i de su importancia politica i adminsitrativa*; Allen, W. H., *Efficient Democracy*.

In comparing numerical data, there is further need for distinguishing the significance of averages, means, and curves of distribution; of considering the relative merits of percentages, per capita figures and other bases of comparison, and of understanding varying degrees of positive and negative correlation.[1]

There is, finally, need for recognizing the limitations of statistical methods, both in the quantity and quality of available data and in the extent to which numerical measurements are applicable; and for the recognition of the continued place for other methods of observation and analysis of political phenomena.

SELECTED REFERENCES

Bertillon, J.   *Cours Élémentaire de Statistique Administrative.*   **1895.**
Cyclopedia of American Government, III, 420.   (E. D. Durand.)
Holcombe, A. N.   *The Political Parties of Today.*   1924.
Koren, John, ed.   *History of Statistics.*   1918.
Lalor's *Cyclopedia of Political Science,* III, 812.   (M. Block.)
Lowell, A. L.   *Public Opinion and Popular Government.*   1913.
Lueder.   *Kritische Geschichte der Statistik.*   1817.
Mayr, George von.   *Begriff und Gliederung der Staatswissenschaften,* 3d ed.   1910.
Meitzen, August.   *History, Theory, and Technique of Statistics.*   Trans. by R. B. Falkner.   1891.
Mohl, Robert von.   *Die Geschichte und Literatur der Staatswissenschaften.* 1855–58.
Merriam, C. A.   *New Aspects of Politics.*   Chap. 4.   1925.
Merriam, C. A., and Gosnell, H. F.   *Non-Voting.*   1924.
Rice, S. A.   *Farmers and Workers in American Politics.*   1924.
Schmeckebeier, L. F.   *The Statistical Work of the National Government.*   1925.
U.S. Bureau of Efficiency.   *A Report on the Statistical Work of the U.S. Government.*   1922.

American Political Science Review.
Allport, F. H., and Hartman, D. A.   "Measurement and Motivation of Atypical Opinion in a Certain Group," XIX, Nov., 1925, p. 735.
Arneson, B. A.   "Non-Voting in a Typical Ohio Community," XIX, Nov., 1925, p. 815.
Barnhart, J. D.   "Rainfall and the Populist Party in Nebraska," XIX, Aug., 1925, p. 527.
Catlin, G. E. C.   "The Delimitation and Measurability of Political Phenomena," XXI, May, 1927, p. 255.
Roach, H. G.   "Sectionalism in Congress, 1870–1890," XIX, Aug., 1925, p. 500.
Reports of Conferences on the Science of Politics, XVIII, Feb., 1924, p. 119; XIX, Feb., 1925, p. 104.
Rice, S. A. "Some Applications of Statistical Method to Political Research," XX, May, 1926, p. 513.

[1] Cf. Bailey and Cummings, *Elements of Statistics;* Jerome, H., *Statistical Method;* Odell, C. W., *Educational Statistics;* Rietz, H. L., ed., *Handbook of Mathematical Statistics;* Forsyth, C. H., *Introduction to Mathematical Analysis of Statistics;* West, C. J., *Introduction to Mathematical Statistics.*

Quarterly Publication of the American Statistical Association.
> Gehlke, C. E. "On the Correlation between the Vote for Suffrage and the Vote on the Liquor Question," xv, 1916–17, no. 111.
> Huntington, E. V. "A New Method of Apportionment of Representatives," xvii, 1920–21, no. 136.
> Report upon the Apportionment of Representatives, xvii, 1920–21, no. 136.
> Rice, S. A. "The Political Vote as a Frequency Distribution of Opinion," xix, 1924, no. 145.
> Young, A. A. "National Statistics in War and Peace," xvi, 1918, no. 121.

CHAPTER XXIV
SOCIOLOGY AND ECONOMICS

By A. B. WOLFE

OHIO STATE UNIVERSITY

THE NATURAL AND THE INSTITUTIONAL ASPECTS OF ECONOMICS

ECONOMICS deals with relations between man and nature as well as between man and man. It thus holds a unique place among the social sciences. Economic processes, within limits fixed by nature, follow the grooves of institutionally sanctioned habit, and vary with the changing form and content of culture. Economic doctrine must to that extent be relative, and must have a certain coöperative consistency with the content of the other social sciences. Some of the processes with which it deals, however, while conditioned by cultural factors, for example "the state of the arts," are fundamentally and universally fixed in their essential technological character by the facts of physical nature.

The fact of diminishing returns, for example, is a fact of nature. So also, essentially, is the economy of large-scale production and of the use of instrumental capital. Many other economic phenomena rest upon technological considerations which would be but slightly affected no matter what changes in the social order might take place. Division of labor and the superior technological efficiency of specialization, the use of money, the phenomena of joint cost, and the existence of differential advantages due to situation, are illustrations in point. Such matters belong essentially to the field of economic technology. They are not primarily psychological or institutional, and to a degree they can be treated by the economic technologist without much reference to cultural connections.

However far aloft into the psychological and cultural realms economic theory may rise, therefore, its feet must remain firmly planted on the earth.

It is well to emphasize these facts at once, and to keep them in mind; for in considering a subject like the present one there is always a temptation to find relations where none or only tenuous ones exist.

It seems fairly evident that the specialist in the primary technological fields of economics have little specifically to gain from sociology. Such fields are public finance, money and banking, transportation, and public utilities. On the other hand, although a great part of the extant vast literature of economics can be of no service to the sociologist, except, like every other record, as raw data for the study of attitudes and intellectual history, a full knowledge of the broader aspects of economic technology, regarded from the point of view of its influence on social organization and cultural evolution, is essential to him. Not only are there these important, some say fundamental, influences on the rest of our culture,[1] but economic technology discloses certain rather refractory physical limits, as possibly psychology does behavioristic limits, to what we may reasonably expect in the way of cultural improvement. It would be less in order to mention this fact had not some sociologists, under the influence of sentiment, shown a tendency to overlook it, as for instance in certain traditional optimisms with regard to agriculture, power, and invention in relation to population growth.

Economics is more than technology, however. It is noteworthy that among the younger theorists there is a distinct tendency either to take technological principles for granted — and consequently sometimes to forget them — or to leave them to specialists. The strongest movements to-day are those toward institutional economics and toward the study of the evolution and causative sequence of economic organization and attitudes. The desideratum is a dynamic institutional interpretation of the economic phase of human cultures. Besides the purely technological phase, we may distinguish three aspects of this more modern economics. It involves (1) a study of individual behavior (motivation, attitude, action) in relation to wealth and income; (2) a study of contemporary organization and institutions which have to do directly with wealth and income, and with other institutions to the extent that they influence, or are influenced by, the economic processes; (3) a study of the economic phase of the evolution of culture. Economics is thus at once a cultural and a technological (and from a functional point of view, also a teleological) subject. The relative

---

[1] Cf. for example Thorstein Veblen's theory of the cultural implications of the machine process, *The Theory of Business Enterprise*, chaps 2, 9; *Absentee Ownership and Business Enterprise in Recent Times: the Case of America.*

dynamic and institutional phases of economics correlate with social psychology and culture history, the teleological phase correlates with ethics also, and the technological phase with the logic of nature.

THE PROBABLE FUTURE CONTENT OF SOCIOLOGY

Any attempt to define the sphere of sociology is sure to be unsatisfactory. By general concensus of opinion, the old sociology has gone into more or less voluntary bankruptcy,[1] though it is probable that more will be saved from the effects of the defunct concern than its hostile critics and many of the younger sociologists think. There can be, of course, no precise agreement as to what the new sociology, if there is to be any, will be. Some are asserting that sociology will be exclusively social psychology, others that it will be a working partnership between social psychology and culture history. There has been for some time a violent reaction against the older sociology's short-circuiting analogies and borrowings from biology. Lately comes the positive assertion that sociology must declare its independence not only from biology but from psychology and from all the sciences that deal with phenomena below the superorganic plane. From this point of view, sociology must confine itself to the superorganic plane strictly, and interpret culture in terms of culture.[2]

On the other hand, the biological sociologists are by no means ready to give up.[3] There are certainly social processes, chiefly of group conflict and selection, which, while not strictly biological, can be brought under social psychology only by greatly extending the meaning of the term. And some of these processes are of great interest to the economist.[4]

Culture can doubtless be interpreted in its own terms, but the interpretation will not be fully satisfying. Orientation *in* the superorganic, or social, plane is a matter of two dimensions — contemporary cross-section analysis, and cultural history; but com-

---

[1] Small's *Origins of Sociology* shows almost pathetic realization of this fact.

[2] This position is taken by the leading American anthropologists. Cf. Kroeber, A. L., "The Possibility of a Social Psychology," *American Journal of Sociology*, XXIII, March, 1918, pp. 633–50. Cf. also Case, C. M., *Outlines of Introductory Sociology*, pp. xviii–xxii.

[3] Cf. Bushee, F. A., *Principles of Sociology*; Keller, A. G., *Societal Evolution*; Huntington, E., *The Character of Races*.

[4] Cf. Carver, T. N., *Essays in Social Justice*, and *Principles of National Economy*, *passim*.

plete orientation with regard to a given social phenomenon involves knowledge not only of what accompanies that phenomenon in present culture and what lies back of it in history, but what lies under it in the lower, mental organic (behavioristic), and vital organic (biological) planes.[1]　Such interpretation could properly be called sociological.　And such interpretations sociology must aim to give if it retains any of its old aspiration to arrive at a unitary view of social phenomena.　The present trend of sociologists toward social psychology and culture history and, with regard to method, away from the temptation to premature generalization in favor of monography, is a healthy one, and it is so strong a trend that for a considerable time sociological research and writing will be almost wholly in these fields.

POSSIBLE CONTRIBUTIONS OF THE SOCIO-PSYCHOLOGICAL ASPECT OF SOCIOLOGY TO ECONOMICS

Because of this fact, and also because of our limited space, it is advisable in what follows to take sociology as a combination of social psychology and culture history, and to think of sociology, as Case suggests, not as a category in a rigidly logical classification of the sciences, but as a movement of thought, a movement which may be the leaven of the social sciences but which may itself be destined to disappear.[2]

For social psychology it is possible to distinguish two lines of research: (1) the external, social mechanism present in all inter-individual or group inter-stimulation and response, and (2) specific institutional influences on attitudes and habits.[3]　In both lines of research it can render signal service to economic theory, and in time not a little to the actual technique of economic organization at those points where the efficiency of organization palpably depends largely on the type of human behavior needed.

Economics needs full knowledge of the social mechanism in its socio-psychological (inter-stimulation) aspect — knowledge of cultural diffusion, of institutional pressure (social control), of the mechanism of the derivation of individual habits and attitudes,

[1] Cf. Weiss, A. P., "Behaviorism and Behavior," *Psychological Review*, XXXI, January, 1924, pp. 32–50, and March, 1924, pp. 118–49.　For the contrary emphasis see Case and Kroeber as above cited.

[2] Case, *op. cit.*, p. xxi.

[3] It is doubtful if Allport's distinction between the fields of social psychology and sociology will hold.　Cf. his *Social Psychology*, p. 10.

through a socially directed learning process, from the institutional norms established in the existing cultural complex (social adaptation). In simpler terms, it needs accurate and critical knowledge of the mechanism of custom, convention, fashion, imitation and emulation, rivalry, social facilitation, and whatever other categories further research in social psychology may settle upon. Economics should also profit from such studies as the social psychologists, in the light of their knowledge of psycho-social mechanisms, see fit to make of specific institutional influences and controls, especially those which play an important rôle in shaping economic attitudes or are themselves more profoundly and directly touched by the economic phase of culture.

The most obvious illustration lies in the theories of value and distribution. The institutional approach has of late been most prominent in value theory.[1] The classical and marginalist economists have either assumed that demand is the expression of rationally calculated want, or refused, as does Cassel,[2] to consider its origin at all. The institutional economists investigate the cultural origin and nature of demand. With them, demand is conventional, the result, in large part, of institutional pressure and prestige.[3] Such analysis is by no means the whole theory of demand, much less of value. It is rather the indispensable foundation for a true insight into economic value as the economist understands the term, of a more realistic understanding of the market process than we can hope to have from a quasi-mathematical analysis, alone, of the superficial phenomena of the pricing process.[4]

The socio-psychological theory of demand seems in a fair way to be worked out satisfactorily. Not so with distribution. The whole theory of distribution needs reworking in the light of a better knowledge of the way in which the distributive process is affected by socio-psychological, or institutional, influences — of customary

[1] Cf. Cooley, C. H., *Social Process*, part VI; Anderson, B., Jr., *Social Value*, and *The Value of Money*, chap. 1; Veblen, T., *The Theory of the Leisure Class*.

[2] *The Theory of Social Economy*.

[3] Cf., however, Cooley's very proper distinction between "human nature values" and "institutional values." (*Social Process*, chap. 24.) The pioneer in this field was of course Veblen. (*The Theory of the Leisure Class*.) His analyses, and Cooley's, are more easily comprehended than Anderson's somewhat metaphysical "absolute value."

[4] Cassel's conception of the function of the pricing process as that of distributing goods in accordance with the "importance" of wants, illuminating as it is, does not really go to the bottom of things, since it throws no light whatever on what determines the "importance." The institutional economists appeal, in effect, to social psychology for light on this latter problem.

standards and ideals as to what is "proper" or "fair" return, of the weight of tradition, of class emulation, and of institutional drags which impair the scientific value of any theory based on the assumption of a virtually frictionless free competition.   Concrete illustration, space permitting, could be given for the theory of wages, especially explanation of differences in wages.   The element of custom and tradition is not given sufficient attention.   The lower wages of women, for instance, are attributed fundamentally to biological sex factors.   The institutional factors associated culturally with sex in a man-made world are overlooked.   In the theory of interest, we have as yet no adequate systematic investigation of the social and institutional influences — such as class standards of living, rivalry, security, and non-pecuniary incentives — on saving and the supply of capital.   Similar institutional influences should receive attention in the theory of profits.   Throughout the theory of distribution social psychology can be brought to bear to test the validity of the traditionally accepted postulates, most of which may be essentially true, but some of which may be found to be unconscious rationalizations in defense of a cultural complex familiar and therefore taken as final.

In general, social psychology should put the economist in position to secure a deeper and more symmetrical understanding of motives, including non-economic incentives;[1] of the important economic rôles of habit and custom and of our institutional social inheritance at large; and of the formation, perpetuation, and modification of specific economic beliefs, sentiments, and attitudes, including the astonishing vitality of many ancient but still honorable economic fallacies.[2]   It should help to correct some erroneous preconceptions, now bolstered by the crude biological generalizations and the claptrap terminology of the race psychologists, with regard to the sources and nature of differences in economic capacity between individuals and between races; it should aid in further research into the psychological and social results of any given economic system; and it should stimulate a wider range of vision in the treatment of many specific economic problems, such as population, conservation, capital formation, industrial management, and labor relations.

[1] Cf. Douglas, P. H., "Non-Economic Incentives," in *The Trend of Economics*, edited by R. G. Tugwell.

[2] An interesting monograph could be written on the social psychology of the tariff, for instance.

Possible Contributions of Economics to the Socio-Psychological Aspects of Sociology

If economics has much to gain from social psychology, it also has something to give. The moment the social psychologist turns from the analysis of the general characteristics of the psycho-social mechanism present in every type and phase of social inter-stimulation and response, to specific institutional relations, he is in an atmosphere permeated with economic interests and influences. Without adopting an exclusively economic interpretation of culture, we must admit the permeative character of the economic interest. No institution, from the family to the church, and few social relations, escape it.

This interfusion of all culture with the economic phase of culture needs analysis from both ends — by the economist and by the specialists in the specific fields (political, educational, moral, ecclesiastical, and so forth) in which the economic influence is seen. Among the economic factors in question may be catalogued vocational interests, business enterprise, vested interests, economic dependence and intimidation, pecuniary standards of success, economic rivalry, concentration and control of capital, speculative and predatory attitudes, new-country attitudes, the influence of the machine process, detachment of the workers from ownership of real property, motives (on the part of both worker and manager) for restriction of output and inefficiency, and the cultural significance of intensified pecuniary "drives."[1]

More specific discussion of the economic factors in institutional life would involve the presentation of much that is obvious: for example, the economic changes which have brought about the transformation now taking place in the family; factors of the economic environment in the causation of those abnormal mental complexes and maladjustments which express themselves in what we call crime; the unconscious economic bias, the quasi-economic, quasi-predatory standard of cultural values which underlies the myth of Nordic superiority (superiority in what?) and the naïve materialistic (Western) standards by which we judge progress.

The Relation between Economics and the Culture-History Aspect of Sociology

In the small space remaining we can say but little on the other

[1] As depicted, for instance, in Theodore Dreiser's *The Financier.*

half of our subject, the relation between economics and the culture-history aspect of sociology. Presumably sociology will take up the analysis of cultural change or evolution at the point where anthropology and ethnology drop it,[1] if indeed they consent to drop it at any point. There will then be a possibility of correlation between dynamic economics, concerned with the economic part of the stream of culture, and sociology, which, ultimately at least, will seek to gain some unitary view of the cultural movement as a whole.

"The sciences which are in any peculiar sense modern," says Veblen, "take as an (unavowed) postulate the fact of consecutive change." [2] Economics is arriving at this point of view belatedly, and the development of a thoroughly evolutionary and dynamic economics is the difficult and laborious task which lies before us.[3] This does not mean that economics is to be a mere section of culture history or that economics texts are to be turned into treatises on *Kulturgeschichte*. It means merely that economists, not content with deductive, or even with statistical, cross-section analyses of the phenomena of the moment, will more generally than in the past bring historical criticism and knowledge of genetic development to bear upon the interpretation of contemporary economic organization and process.[4]

This movement, which is just now occasioning evidences of some irritation which may on the whole have a salutary effect, is bound to work a noteworthy change in the immediate future of economic theory. Economic history, of however broadly cultural and philosophic a scope, cannot displace economic analysis, especially for the more technological phases of economics mentioned earlier in this chapter. It will, however, help to hold contemporary economic analysis to the main track of cultural realities, afford a curtain on which to project our knowledge of present economic forces and tendencies, and help us in the future to avoid those pseudo-psychological subtleties and over-refinements which occupy so large a

[1] Cf., for example, Wallas, Graham, *Our Social Inheritance*.
[2] "The Evolution of the Scientific Point of View," in *The Place of Science in Modern Civilization*, p. 32.
[3] Cf. Veblen, T., "Why is Economics not an Evolutionary Science?" *The Place of Science in Modern Civilization*, pp. 56–81.
[4] As typical of what is here in mind the work of Veblen and of Sombart may be cited; for the latter, especially his *Der Moderne Kapitalismus*, 6th ed. Commons's *Legal Foundations of Capitalism* may also be mentioned. Cf., also, the work of Roscoe Pound in the field of jurisprudence.

place in the theory of the last generation of economists. One element of progress, at least, is that Crusoe economics, isolated islands, and the conjectural history of the thrifty savage who saved his fish and became a capitalistic entrepreneur have already faded out of reputable economic literature.

Adequate knowledge of the historical development of the money economy, of banking and credit, of business cycles, of tariff systems and the growth and persistence of mercantile attitudes — that is, knowledge of the history of particular technological phases of our present economic organization — is essential to a clear perspective on the economic technology of the present. This specialized technical history will hardly be supplied by the sociologists, although, as in the field of money, anthropology may be of some service where it is deemed desirable to go back to origins. This needed technological history will be supplied, as in the past, by the specialists in the various technical fields.

It is from a broader angle that economics can profit from the work of the culture historians — from the point of view of social economy in the broad sense, and the place and significance of economic institutions in the whole stream of culture. What the culture historian can do, not only for the economist but for any other social science specialist, is to help him get an adequate perspective. He can do this for the economist, however, only if he possesses reasonably respectable knowledge of the economic culture of the present. If he does not show that he has such knowledge, the economist will continue to be skeptical with regard to the value of his services. If the past gives a perspective on the present, the present also inevitably gives us a selective viewpoint from which to look back on history.

It is clear that the cultural point of view should have a profound influence on the writing of economic history, apart from the highly specialized histories of the technological elements in our economic life. Economic history, until recently, has been more akin to archæology and factual chronology than to an attempt to reveal the significance of economic evolution in relation to other parts of the stream of culture. This is why more did not come of the German historical school of economics. To write an adequate economic history, a broad knowledge of the main flows in the other cultural streams — political, philosophical, theological, moral — is necessary; we can hold this to be true even though we think the economic phase of culture the fundamental one, largely determinative of the course of the other streams.[1]

A similar statement would hold true of the history of economic doctrine. That there is no comprehensive history of economics which in an illuminating and scholarly way correlates the history of economic theory with the evolution of political and philosophical theories and with the general attitudes and spirit of the times, is owing in part to the modern separatism among the social sciences, and in part perhaps to the fact that the writing of such a history is a task demanding so wide a grasp that no one is yet brave enough to attempt it.

This calls to mind the skepticism which the special social scientist is wont to evince with regard to sociology. His view usually is that the sociologist, essaying to treat culture or society as a whole, is attempting an impossible task. The comparative lack of lasting achievement on the part of the older sociology gives point to this skepticism. But if we rule out of court the pretentious array of premature laws and generalizations of the old sociology, and ask only that scholars in the several social science fields lay aside their mutual suspicions and remember that they are all dealing with aspects of the stream of activities, attitudes, and institutions which we call human culture, the skepticism will have less justification.

The point to be emphasized is that just as economic institutions of a given time must be treated in close correlation with the other contemporary aspects of culture, so the stream of economic change is a sub-stream of the total cultural movement and is constantly influencing, and being influenced by, its other elements. Each cultural stream may be investigated by its own specialists, but not adequately unless they have reasonably wide and fresh knowledge of the main features of the collateral culture movements.

Whether there is place for the sociologist, as a general surveyor and interpreter of the cultural streams taken collectively; whether this task is the proper function of the historian; whether each social science will insist on making its own general survey and determining for itself where the significant cross currents flow; whether, indeed, the task is possible at all, are questions upon which we need not commit ourselves. The central fact is that a broad knowledge of culture history is essential: the particular tag it is to bear is not.

[1] Cf. Keller, A. S., *Societal Evolution*, pp. 139 *et seq.*, 234 *et seq.*

SELECTED REFERENCES

Allport, F. H.   *Social Psychology.* 1924.

Anderson, B. M., Jr.   *Social Value.* 1911.
          The Value of Money, chap. 1. 1922.

Barnes, H. E.   *Sociology and Political Theory,* pp. 14–23, 67–73. 1924.

Boucke, O. F.   *A Critique of Economics,* chap. 9. 1922.

Carver, T. N.   "The Behavioristic Man." *Quarterly Journal of Economics,* XXXIII, November, 1918, pp. 195–200.

Case, C. M.   *Outlines of Introductory Sociology,* pp. XV–XXXVI. 1924.

Clark, J. M.   "The Socializing of Theoretical Economics." *The Trend of Economics,* edited by R. G. Tugwell. 1924.

Cooley, C. H.   *Social Process,* part VI. 1918.

Douglas, P. H.   "The Reality of Non-Commercial Incentives in Economic Life." *The Trend of Economics,* edited by R. G. Tugwell. 1924.

Ellwood, C. A.   *Sociology in its Psychological Aspects,* pp. 33–35. 1912.

Giddings, F. H.   "Further Inquiries of Sociology." *Publications of the American Sociological Society,* XV, 1921, pp. 60–67.
          "The Sociological Character of Political Economy." *Publications of the American Economic Association,* series I, vol. III.

Hamilton, W. H.   "The Institutional Approach to Economic Theory." *American Economic Review,* Supplement, VIII, March, 1918, pp. 309–18; discussion, pp. 318–24.

Haney, L. H.   "The Social Point of View in Economics." *Quarterly Journal of Economics,* XXVII, Nov., 1913, pp. 115–39; XXVII, Feb., 1914, pp. 292–321.

Hayes, E. C.   *Introduction to the Study of Sociology,* chaps. 7, 8. 1918.
          "The Social Control of the Acquisition of Wealth." *Publications of the American Sociological Society,* XII, 1918, pp. 111–30. Also in *American Economic Review,* Supplement, VIII, March, 1918, pp. 194–211.

Hobhouse, L. T.   *Social Development, Its Nature and Conditions.* 1924.

Kantor, J. R.   "The Institutional Foundation of a Scientific Social Psychology." *American Journal of Sociology,* XXIX, May, 1924, pp. 674–85.

Knight, F. H.   "The Limitations of Scientific Method in Economics." *The Trend of Economics,* edited by R. G. Tugwell.

Kroeber, A. L.   "The Possibility of a Social Psychology." *American Journal of Sociology,* XXIII, March, 1918, pp. 633–50.
          "The Superorganic." *American Anthropologist,* N.S. XIX, April–June, 1917, pp. 163–213.

(Both the above are reprinted in part in C. M. Case's *Outlines of Introductory Sociology.*)

McKenzie, R. D.   "The Ecological Approach to the Study of the Human Community." *American Journal of Sociology,* XXX, Nov., 1924, pp. 287–301.

Mitchell, W. C.   "The Prospects of Economics." *The Trend of Economics,* edited by R. G. Tugwell. 1924.

Patten, S. N.   "The Reconstruction of Economic Theory." *Essays in Economic Theory,* edited by R. G. Tugwell.

Philippovich, E. von.   "The Infusion of Socio-political Ideas into the Literature of German Economics." *American Journal of Sociology,* XVIII, Sept., 1912, pp. 145–99.

Ross, E. A.   *Foundations of Sociology,* pp. 309–27. 1905.

Small, A. W.   *The Meaning of Social Science.*   1910.

　　　　　Adam Smith and Modern Sociology.   1907.

　　　　　"The Future of Sociology."   *Publications of the American Sociological Society,* xv, 1921, pp. 174–93; discussion, pp. 194–202.

　　　　　Origins of Sociology, 1924.   Published also as a series of articles in the *American Journal of Sociology,* Jan., 1923, to Nov., 1924.

Smith, T. V.   "Work as an Ethical Concept."   *Journal of Philosophy,* xxi, Sept. 25, 1924, pp. 543–54.

Taussig, F. W.   "Alfred Marshall."   *Quarterly Journal of Economics,* xxxix, Nov., 1924, pp. 1–14.

Tugwell, R. G.   "Experimental Economics."   *The Trend of Economics.*   1924.

Veblen, T.   *The Place of Science in Modern Civilization.*   1919.   The chapters on "The Place of Science," "The Evolution of the Scientific Point of View," "Why Economics is not an Evolutionary Science," and "The Nature of Capital."

　　　　　The Theory of Business Enterprise, chaps. 2, 9.   1904.

Weiss, A. P.   "The Aims of Social Evolution."   *Ohio Journal of Science,* xxiii, no. 3, 1923, pp. 115–34.

　　　　　"Behaviorism and Behavior."   *Psychological Review,* xxxi, Jan., 1924, pp. 32–50; March, 1924, pp. 118–49.

Wolfe, A. B.   *Conservatism, Radicalism, and Scientific Method,* pp. 241–51. 1923.

　　　　　"Functional Economics."   *The Trend of Economics,* edited by R. G. Tugwell.   1924.

Young, Kimball.   "The Need of Integration of Attitudes among Social Scientists."   *Scientific Monthly,* xviii, March, 1924, pp. 291–305.

CHAPTER XXV
SOCIOLOGY AND ETHICS
By PITIRIM A. SOROKIN
UNIVERSITY OF MINNESOTA

LOGICAL INTERRELATIONS OF SOCIOLOGY AND ETHICS

THE principal task of ethics in the past has been an elaboration of the prescription of *what ought to be* and *what ought not to be*. Since the ethics of the Bible and the Sacred Books of India and China, since the works of Plato and Aristotle, up to the contemporary treatises in ethics, this task has been and still is regarded as the principal task of ethics.[1] So far as sociology professes that its scientific task consists in the study of social phenomena *as they have existed, do exist, and will exist,* there is no direct connection between the two disciplines. The reason for this is that the world of *what ought to be* and *what really is, or has been, or will be* are quite different and lie in quite different planes. The judgments of *ought to be* are not aimed to find the truth, whereas the cognitive judgments of existence have the truth as their only objective. "Love thy neighbor," "kill thy enemy," and other similar expressions are neither true nor non-true. They do not pretend to state that between *A* and *B* there *exists* such a relation. They simply demand an obedience regardless of whether their *what ought to be* really exists or not. On the other hand, cognitive judgment always says what does exist or does not exist, and never *what ought to be*. Natural science and other real sciences study the reality as it is, irrespective of whether it is "good" or "bad." The phenomena

---

[1] This is recognized by all prominent ethicists, even by those who do not limit the task of ethics by this prescription of "what ought to be." Cf. Wundt, W., *Ethik,* I, pp. 8–10; Stammler, R., *Theorie der Rechtswissenschaft,* p. 23 *et seq.;* Binding, *Handbuch des Strafrechts,* pp. 1–10; Birkmeyer, *Studien zu dem Hauptgrundsatz* etc., p. 166 *et seq.;* Rickert, H., *Zwei Wege der Erkenntnistheorie,* Kantsstudien, XIV; also *Die Grenzen der naturwissenschaftlichen Begriefsbildung,* last part; Natorp, P., *Sozialpädagogik,* pp. 1–190 *et seq.;* Windelband, W., *Praeludien;* Sidgwick, H., *Methods of Ethics,* 4th ed., p. 4; Green, T. H., *Prolegomena to Ethics,* 3d ed., p. 9; Dewey, J., and Tufts, J., *Ethics,* pp. 1–3; Höffding, H., *Ethik,* Germ. tr., p. 24; Croce, B., *Philosophy of the Practical,* p. 42 *et seq.;* Eucken, R., *Ethics and Modern Thought, passim;* Boutroux, E., *Education and Ethics,* Introduction and p. 53 *et seq.;* Ladd, G. T., *What Ought I to Do, passim;* Hayes, E. C., *Sociology and Ethics,* p. 30 *et seq.* With still greater reason this may be said of almost all "pure and philosophical" ethicists like Lotze and Kohen.

of death, plague, murder, and war are recognized by many as something "bad"; and yet science studies them as carefully as any "good" phenomena.[1] In our cognitive judgments we are free from the judgments of *ought to be*. And, vice versa, our judgments of valuation (*ought to be*) are independent logically from the judgments of existence and from the existing reality itself. In spite of the existence of plague and war, one may say that they ought not to exist, or that they are evil. In spite of the non-existence of universal love, one may say that it ought to exist. The same idea is well expressed by the great French mathematician and philosopher, H. Poincaré. He says:

There is no and cannot be any scientific ethics as there is no and cannot be an unmoral science. The reason is very simple: namely, grammatical. If both premises of a syllogism are in the indicative, the conclusion will be also in the indicative. All postulates and judgments of science are and can be only in the indicative. The most sophisticated dialecticians may manipulate these principles as they like: all that they can obtain will be in the indicative also. They never can obtain judgment which would run: do this or don't do that. This is the difficulty which all ethicists always find. They try to prove scientifically a "moral principle." They must be excused because it is their business.[2]

Correspondingly, scientific law which *describes* the existing relations among phenomena, and moral law, which *prescribes* a definite form of conduct and *valuates* the phenomena as good or bad, moral or immoral, are laws quite different and do not have logically anything in common.[3] Similarly, as poetry represents a kind of social thought quite different from science, judgments of valuation represent a kind of social thought quite different from the scientific

[1] This was well understood by Saint Thomas Aquinas: "In scientiis nor quaeritur nisi cognitio veritatis. In scientiis operativis, finis is operatio." (*Summa Theologica*, Ia, q. 14, art. 16.)

[2] Poincaré, H., *Dernières Pensées*, essay: *La Moral et la Science*. Cf. for the detailed analysis of the above statements, Pareto, V., *Traité de Sociologie Générale*, chaps. i–v and *passim;* Pearson, K., *The Grammar of Science*, chap iii; Kelsen, H., *Hauptprobleme der Staatslehre*, pp. 1–94; Durkheim, E., *Règles de la Méthode Sociologique*, 2d ed., p. 51; *L'Année sociol.*, ix, p. 324; Lévy-Bruhl, L., *La Moral et la Science des Mœurs*, chap. iii and *passim;* Boutroux, *op. cit.*, chap. iii; Husserl, *Logische Untersuchungen*, i, p. 29 et seq.; Sorokin, "Are Ethics a Normative Science and Does Any Normative Science Exist?" in *Crime and Punishment*, Introduction; Sorokin, "The Category of Ought to Be and Its Application in Science," *Juridichesky Vestnik*, January, 1917; cf. also Sigwart's analysis of "Sollen" in his *Logik*.

[3] Though the judgments of valuation like "this is good" have an appearance similar to cognitive statements, nevertheless, their nature is quite different. Cf. the analysis in the indicated works of Poincaré, Pareto, Kelsen, Husserl, Pearson, Sorokin, and others.

judgments. Similarly, as there is neither scientific nor non-scientific poetry, there is neither scientific nor non-scientific ethics. Each of them, poetry, science, and ethics, has its own criteria of valuation. To try to measure them with the same criteria is no better than to measure a distance by the unit of weight, and vice versa.

If this point is clear, then it is very easy to distinguish scientific statements from ethical evaluations wherever they are given. Their mixture is logically inadmissible. Such are the logical interrelations of sociology and ethics as a discipline which prescribes *what ought to be*.

FACTUAL INTERRELATIONS OF SOCIOLOGY AND ETHICS

If we turn now to the problem as to what are the factual interrelations between the sociological and the ethical treatises and between the sociologists and the ethicists, the picture appears very different from the above logical interrelations. In the first place, the great ethicists happen to be the great social thinkers or sociologists too; and vice versa.[1] Confucius, Mencius, Plato, Aristotle, Cicero, Seneca, Dante, St. Thomas Aquinas, Machiavelli, Hobbes, Locke, B. Spinosa, Rousseau, Montesquieu, Ferguson, Malthus, A. Smith, Kant, Hegel, Fichte, S. Simon, Auguste Comte, Bentham, J. S. Mill, Spencer, to mention but a few of the leaders, have been ethicists as well as social thinkers or sociologists. In the second place, their works have been dedicated to the study of the social phenomena as they existed and at the same time to the valuation of the phenomena from the standpoint of how they *ought to be*. It is hard to find any work of these authors in which the cognitive judgments are not intermingled with those of *ought to be*. This situation continues to exist up to the present time. There are very few if any sociological works that are free from ethical valuations like, "this is desirable or undesirable," "useful or harmful," "progressive or regressive," "just or unjust," "moral or immoral," "social or anti-social." Whole divisions of sociology, such as "theory of progress," "applied sociology," and "social control," are in essence nothing but the discussions from the standpoint of what ought to be. Almost any textbook in sociology not only teaches but at the same time preaches, and preaching sometimes

[1] The same is true in regard to economists, political thinkers, and ethicists. Cf. Ayres, C. E. *The Nature of the Relationship Between Ethics and Economics*, chap. III.

occupies a much greater place than teaching.[1]   There is no need to point out the fact that the great majority of political and journalistic writings represent nothing but preaching.   On the other hand, it is equally difficult to find a treatise in ethics which does not represent a mixture of the ethical valuations with the cognitive judgments.   The traditional division of ethics into "the physics of mores" and "the metaphysics of mores" shows this clearly. There has not been a single system of ethics, not excluding even that of Kant, that has succeeded in building a "pure ethics" without consideration, analysis, study, and description of facts as they have existed or were thought of as existing.   Such has been and is the real situation.

THE PRESENT TREND IN THE RELATIONSHIP BETWEEN SOCIOLOGY AND ETHICS

Every one who has studied the recent trend in both disciplines can but notice that ethical treatises are becoming more and more saturated with the factual materials supplied by sociology, anthropology, and other social sciences.   The reasons for this are at hand. In the first place, the last few decades in sociology and other social sciences have been marked by an enormous work in the collecting and analysis of *mores*, customs, ceremonies, moral opinions, and prescriptions as they have existed among the most widely differing peoples and at different times.   Thanks to this procedure it has become impossible for even the most ardent partisan of a "pure ethics" to ignore the obtained data.   When these data were lacking, an ethicist could speculate as he pleased.   Now, under existing conditions, to continue to build "a system of pure ethics" means practically nothing but to be busy with a childish work which can scarcely bring any credit to its author or be influential in practice.

In the second place, any ethicist may postulate anything as the highest moral principle or moral value — happiness, solidarity, human welfare, "the Golden Rule," the categoric imperative, oneness, harmony or what not — but in order to show that his formula is right he must explain why his postulate is the highest principle or moral value.   To give reasons means, practically, to turn to facts

---

[1] It is curious to note that even those sociologists who, like Durkheim and Lévy-Bruhl, have tried to put out of the science of sociology all judgments of valuation, did not accomplish this.   See Deploige, S., *Le Conflit de la Moral et de la Sociologie*, pp. i–xvi.   Richard, G.   "Sociologie et Métaphisique," in *Foi et Vie*, June and July, 1911.

and to try to show that they really prove the validity of his contention. This is necessary because at the present time references to "God's will" or to a metaphysical principle of nature are not sufficient.

In the third place, the formula of the highest moral principle in all ethical systems is so broad and indefinite that it is practically meaningless. Being so, it does not and cannot give any concrete indication as to what one ought to do in a given situation. To say that "the highest goodness is happiness" is nothing but a substitution of one unknown for another. What is happiness? What forms of conduct lead to it? When? Under what conditions? The general formula does not give any answer to such concrete problems. This may also be said of all highest moral principles given by the ethicists. Therefore such formulæ are practically useless. In order to be able to indicate what ought to be done, ethics must give some concrete rules. To formulate such rules the ethicist must know customs, mores, mechanism of human behavior and its stimuli, causal relations between different factors that influence human behavior and social life, the concrete circumstances of each case, and so forth. These data are given by sociology, anthropology, psychology, biology, and by other sciences. Without a knowledge of these data an ethicist can give only purely theoretical and useless recipes or the prescriptions which instead of curing may poison, instead of improving may aggravate individual or social sickness. Hence, an increasing dependence of ethics, as an applied art, upon science. As in the growth of biology the time of the ignorant medicine-man passed by, so in the growth of the social and psychological sciences the time of the metaphysical ethicist is also passing by.

In the fourth place, I admit that any ethicist may postulate an ideal of *ought to be* if he pleases. But if he is free from facts in this respect, he is bound to know their causal relations in order to realize his ideal in the easiest and the most efficient way. Whether he chooses a communistic or a capitalistic type as an ideal of social organization, he must know the forces, means, and ways which may lead to a realization of his ideal. Otherwise there is no use of his metaphysical theorizing. The same may be said of any plan of social reconstruction — improvement of family, diminution (or even increase) of crimes, modification of religion or political constitutions. These reasons account for an increasing dependence of ethics or any social applied discipline on sociology and other sciences. Future ethics is likely to be an elaborated discipline which, like the science of medicine, will indicate the concrete ways and means of doing what ought to be done under any given situation. At the basis of these prescriptions will lie the causal relations indicated and discovered by other sciences which study the reality as it is.

ETHICAL ELEMENTS IN CONTEMPORARY SOCIOLOGY

As I have already stated, the contemporary sociology still contains in abundance ethical evaluations and similar preaching judgments. Nevertheless, during the last two decades there appeared the tendency, which seems to be growing, to abolish, or at least to reduce, these elements as much as possible. Durkheim, Lévy-Bruhl, de Roberty, Waxweiler, W. G. Sumner, F. H. Giddings, and recently V. Pareto, not to mention many other names, represent this tendency. In my opinion it must be supported. Logically, as I have endeavored to show, all this valuation lies outside of the realm of science. Psychologically, moralizing considerably hinders an objective study of the real situation and leads to partiality and one-sidedness. Factually, in the majority of the cases it remains still purely metaphysical, not being based on a really scientific scrutiny of the corresponding facts and their causal relations.[1] Under such conditions a moralizing sociologist is no better leader of the social reconstruction movement than a medicine-man of the past or a speculative ethicist. Through his speculative preaching he compromises the science of sociology, and, like a speculative reformer, he may facilitate an aggravation of social situation instead of an improvement. These reasons are sufficient to understand the urgent necessity for getting rid of moralizing and valuation within the realm of sociology as a science. If sociology and other social sciences are going to grow they must follow the natural sciences in this respect. This does not mean any underappreciation of moral values. But it does mean that everything is proper in its own place. Moreover, I am convinced that the greater the purely scientific progress of these sciences, the greater power they will have to serve our practical needs and ethical purposes. The natural sciences, being already free from ethical elements, serve

[1] See a series of appropriate remarks in Giddings, F. H.' *The Scientific Study of Human Society*, chap. III. University of North Carolina Press.

our needs more efficiently than any social and political discipline. "Discovery of causal regularities is a self-sufficient and primary task of sociology. When this is done the results may serve other needs. To mix this and ethical tasks means to do harm to both of them," rightly says Pareto.[1] "Facing the facts the physical and biological sciences have made known to us has enabled us to live more comfortably and longer than men once did. Facing the facts that the social sciences are making known to us, and will make better known, should enable us to diminish human misery and to live more wisely than the human race has lived hitherto. It will be discovered one day that the chief value of social science, far from being academic, is moral," no less rightly says Professor Giddings.[2]

SELECTED REFERENCES

See the works quoted in the text; besides these works see:

Baldwin, J. Mark. *Social and Ethical Interpretations in Mental Developments.* 1902.

Bayet, A. *L'Idée de Bien.* 1908.

Bureau, P. *La Crise Moral des Temps Nouveaux.* 1908.

Chapin, F. Stuart. "Moral Progress." *Scientific Monthly*, May, 1915, pp. 467–71.

Delvolvé, H. *Rationalisme et Tradition.* 1910.

Dewey, John. "The Evolutionary Method as Applied to Morality." *Philosophical Review*, XI, no. 2.

D'Hautefuille, Fr. "Le Charactère Normatif et le Charactère Scientifique de la Morale." *Revue de Métaphysique et de Morale*, Sept., 1911.

Draghicesco, D. *Le Problème de la Conscience.* 1901.

Durkheim, Émile. *De la Division du Travail Social.* 1893.
　　　　　　 "Les Jugements de Valeur et les Jugements de la Realité." *Revue de Métaphysique et de Morale.* July, 1911.
　　　　　　 The Elementary Forms of Religious Life. 1915.

Fauconnet, P. "La Morale et la Science des Mœurs." *Revue Philosophique*, 1904.

Fite, Warner. "Moral Valuations and Economic Laws." *Journal of Philosophy, Psychology and Scientific Method*, XIV, p. 10.

Fouillée, A. "La Moral et la Religion Humanitaires." *Revue des Deux Mondes*, March, 1912.
　　　　　　 "La Science des Mœurs remplacera-t-elle la Morale." *Ibid.*, Oct. 1, 1905.

Frazer, J. G. *Psyche's Task, A Discourse Concerning the Influence of Superstitions on the Growth of Institutions.* 2d ed. 1913.

Gaultier, J. de. *La Dépendance de la Morale et l'Indépendance des Mœurs.* 1907.

Gillet, M. S. "Les Jugements de Valeur et la Conception Positive de la Morale." *Revue des Sciences Philosophiques*, Jan. 20, 1912.

Goldenweiser, A. *Early Civilization.* 1922.

---

[1] Pareto, *op. cit.*, pp. 1599–1600.　　　　[2] Giddings, *op. cit.*, pp. 37–38.

Gusti, D. "Die soziologische Richtung in der neusten Ethik." *Viertel Jahresschrift für wissenschaftliche philosophie und Soziologie*, 32, Neue Folge VII, 1908.

Hobhouse, L. T. *Morals in Evolution.* 1915.

Hobhouse, L. T., Wheeler, G. S., and Ginsberg, M. *The Material Culture and Social Institutions of the Simpler Peoples.* 1915.

Höffding, H. "On the Relation between Sociology and Ethics." *American Journal of Sociology*, x.

Lowie, R. H. *Primitive Society.* 1920.

Mayr, Georg von. *Statistik und Gesellschaftslehre*, III. *Moralstatistik.* 1917

Naville, A. "La Moral Conditionnelle." *Revue Philosophique*, 1906.

Novgorodzeff, P. J. *Ob obshtchestvennom Ideale.* 1923.

Oettingen, Alexander von. *Die Moralstatistik in ihrer Bedeutung für Sozialethik* 1882.

Oppenheimer, Franz. *The Rationale of Punishment.* 1913.

Parodi, D. *Le Problème Moral et la Pensée Contemporaine.* 1910.

Perry, R. B. "Economic Values and Moral Values." *Quarterly Journal of Economics*, xxx.

Petrajitzky, L. *Introduction to the Theory of Law and Ethics.* 1907.

Roberty, E. de. *Constitution de l'Éthique.* 1899.
　　　　　Les Fondements de l'Éthique. 1900.

Ross, E. A. *Social Control.* 1920.

Sidgwick, H. "The Relation of Ethics to Sociology." *International Journal of Ethics*, 1899.

Simmel, G. *Einleitung in die Moralwissenschaft.* 1892–93.

Small, A. *The Significance of Sociology for Ethics.* 1902.

Sorel, G. *Reflections on Violence.* 1912.

Spencer, Herbert. *The Principles of Ethics*, I, II. 1891.
　　　　　Social Statics. 1883.

Steinmetz, S. R. *Ethnologische Studien zur ersten Entwicklung der Strafe*, I, II 1894.

Sumner, W. G. *Folkways.* 1906.

Tufts, J. H. "Ethics in the last Twenty-Five Years." *Philosophical Review* Jan., 1917.

Weber, Max. *Gesammelte Aufsätze zur Religionssoziologie*, 3 vols. 1922–23.

Westermarck, E. *The Origin and Development of Moral Ideas*, I, II. 1906–08.

CHAPTER XXVI
SOCIOLOGY AND LAW
By ROSCOE POUND
HARVARD LAW SCHOOL

THE DEVELOPMENT OF AN ISOLATED, SELF-SUFFICING SCIENCE OF LAW

IT is commonplace that in the nineteenth century the rapid increase in the volume of knowledge and multiplication of details, together with academic specialization and the exigencies of teaching programs in universities, led to the setting off of a number of separate social sciences, each defined analytically, assigned a rigidly limited field, and provided with a definite content and peculiar method. Indeed jurisprudence had been tending in this direction since the sixteenth century. From the thirteenth to the seventeenth century, jurisprudence and ethics and politics were treated along with theology as applications of its principles. But in the latter part of the sixteenth century the Protestant jurist-theologians began to emancipate the science of law from theology, and the emancipation was completed by Grotius (1625). In the seventeenth and eighteenth centuries, jurisprudence, politics, and international law were treated together under the name of the "law of nature and nations." A common philosophical foundation was set up which was taken to suffice for all three. Given this philosophical foundation (natural law), the details of jurisprudence, politics, and a science of international relations were supposed to be reached by deduction or by rational speculation. In the nineteenth century the specialization proceeded still further. Jurisprudence was set off as a separate science. All connection with politics, legislation, or ethics came to be abandoned. All suggestion of contact or cooperation with the rising science of sociology was rejected. Moreover, whereas in the past there had been but one method of jurisprudence — in the Middle Ages a theological scholastic-logical method, and in the seventeenth and eighteenth centuries a rationalist natural-law method — the nineteenth century developed and set off three distinct methods: a metaphysical method, a historical method, and an analytical method, each of which assumed to be the one method of jurisprudence, equal to doing all the work of a complete, self-sufficing science of law.

It is true that the adherents of these methods made certain concessions. The metaphysical jurist might consider that history verified what he found and demonstrated philosophically. The historical jurist might admit that the metaphysical jurist could by philosophical reasoning justify what judge or jurist had discovered as the principle behind given phenomena of legal history. Also, the historical jurist might speak of historical jurisprudence and analytical jurisprudence as complementary. But beyond general concessions of this sort, each method pursued its separate and exclusive path. Moreover, the analytical jurists so defined their field (taken to be the whole field of jurisprudence) as rigorously to exclude therefrom everything but an attempt by analysis and comparison of established legal precepts to reach a body of universal legal principles of developed law, depending on certain necessary conceptions involved in the very idea of law. Until there was an authoritative legal precept, bearing the guinea-stamp of the state, there was nothing for the jurist to consider. Economists might study the raw materials of legislation. Politics might have to do with the mechanics of lawmaking. Ethics might have to do with principles by which the lawmaker should be governed, or by which the judge should be guided in applying the law. But in the eyes of the analytical jurist, the judge was to be constrained by logic to follow one inevitable road to his decision. The science of legislation might treat of the scope and subject-matter and methods of conscious lawmaking. Such things were no business of judge or jurist. Their turn came when a legal precept had come into being, and then only. Nor was the jurist to look behind the legal precept nor outside of the defined limits of his field — "the province of jurisprudence," study of the nature of law, thought of as a body of legal precepts, study of the "necessary conceptions" of law and of the "pervading conceptions" of developed legal systems, and working out of a comparative anatomy of the two developed bodies of legal precepts, the modern Roman law and English law.

Analytical Jurisprudence

Analytical jurisprudence had its fullest development in England, where, indeed, it still flourishes. But English and Anglo-American analytical jurisprudence have their counterpart in *théorie générale du droit* and *allgemeine Rechtslehre* on the Continent. In England it began during the legislative reform movement of the last century, and its founder (John Austin, *The Province of Jurisprudence Determined*, 1832) was a disciple of Bentham. On the Continent it became important in the latter part of the nineteenth century. Before that time, however, the historical jurists in Germany had combined an analytical method with historical theory, so that English analytical jurists were able to draw largely upon the German pandectists. In any of its forms it dealt with law from the inside only and excluded from its conception of law the traditional technique of judge and jurist, which is the enduring element in legal systems, and the body of received ideals as to the end of law and as to what legal precepts and the application of legal precepts should be in view thereof, which in the long run are the controlling element in the administration of justice. It gave a critique of the law of a time drawn from the least enduring element of that law itself. It was an ordering of legal precepts. So far as it attempted criticism it was a critique of the form of the law, not a critique of its content nor of its workings. Its presuppositions were: (1) that there was a "pure fact of law," distinguished from the "sources of law" and hence from morals and all ideas of what ought to be law; (2) that law was a body of legal precepts consciously established by a definite source of political authority; (3) that a body of law might be treated as something made once for all, as it were, at one stroke; (4) that a body of developed law might be assumed to be complete, that is, to contain express or implicit precepts for every case and conceptions applicable to all situations by mere logical development; and (5) that application of legal precepts was a purely mechanical logical process. Obviously these are the presuppositions of a period of legal stability in which the task of the jurist is one of organizing and harmonizing the results of a past period of legal growth. In such a period the jurist seeks to make of the law a body of logically interdependent precepts, to be applied mechanically to cases within their express purview and developed by formal logic to meet the exigencies of new cases. In other words, he endeavors to treat all law as if it were a body of rules of property or rules of commerical law.

The Defects of an Exclusively Analytical Science of Law

Five defects of the legal science of the immediate past are chiefly attributable to exclusive employment of the analytical method.

(1) Juristic study was confined to making the law internally coherent. Internal coherence is important in order to insure certainty, and what Bentham called "cognoscibility" — that is, to make the course of the administration of justice uniform and predictable. Such things are valuable because they tend to maintain the social interest in the general security. But there are other things to be regarded. The nineteenth-century systematists pursued internal coherence as a sole end. In consequence the law often got out of touch with the course of human life which it was to govern. Much of the abstractness and artificiality of the law of the last generation was the result of this mode of scientific study of law.

(2) As a general theory of law drawn exclusively from the modern Roman law and from modern English law it led to attempts at a purely mechanical administration of justice, which have brought about, by way of reaction, something like a revival of personal government in the form of continually increasing resort to, and reliance on, administrative boards and commissions. It brought all questions to the test of principles of arrangement and "necessary" or "pervading" conceptions reached by comparative study of analytically ideal forms of the modern Roman and modern English law. These principles and conceptions were assumed to be universal and to be adequate potentially to deciding every possible case. Criticism of principles and conceptions with reference to the ends to be subserved was rejected as no part of the science of law. Hence there was a tendency to forget that the administration of justice is a practical matter. It was taken to be enough if legal precepts were logically coherent and authoritatively established.

(3) Analytical jurists aimed at thorough logical development of established precepts through rigid deduction. Hence they aimed at an impossible degree of certainty. They sought a certainty which should enable every item of judicial action to be predicted in detail with absolute assurance. As a result the logical development of received legal precepts or doctrines to their strict conclusions was taken to be the highest judicial virtue. "Strong decisions," in which an arbitrary result was reached by a rigid logical method and applied with a high hand, were approved, without perceiving that the "logic" usually consisted in excluding all things but an abstract formula as the basis of judicial reasoning. This sort of thing has brought logic into disrepute in recent juristic writing.

(4) Analytical jurisprudence had a bad influence upon lawmaking

whether legislative or in the form of judicial decision. It conceived of law as something made consciously and deliberately and denied the name of law to anything which did not proceed definitely from a determinate lawmaking or law-declaring agency of politically organized society. All ethical, social, or economic features of scientific thinking about law were rejected. Law was law because it was the declared will of the state or because the tribunals of the state had so decided. Thus arbitrary legislation and arbitrary judicial establishing of legal precepts were invited and encouraged.

(5) Definite setting off of law from ideals of law and insistence upon complete separation between law and morals blinded us for half a century or more to factors of the first importance in the actual working of the legal order. It led to an illusion of certainty where in practice there was uncertainty. It led to a saving of the face of legal theory by ingenious covering up of compromises and adjustments of conflicting or overlapping interests, and so to groping for solutions of new problems where, if courts and jurists had recognized what they were doing, they might have proceeded much more intelligently.

The Beginnings of a Reaction

In the present century jurists have become conscious that the distinctions between the several social sciences are necessitated, not by the nature of things, but simply by the requirements of division of labor. Indeed, except in the case of analytical jurists they had never wholly given up connections of jurisprudence with other social sciences. In their ethical interpretation of legal history, the nineteenth-century metaphysical jurists kept up a certain relation between jurisprudence and ethics. The political interpretation urged by the historical jurists kept up a certain connection between jurisprudence and politics. The economic realists protested against "the habit of considering separate sciences or departments of knowledge in irrational isolation" and sought to make a new connection of jurisprudence with economics. Most of all, the positivists and the rise of sociology in time made jurists conscious of the need of a broader basis for philosophy of law, for legal history, and even for doctrinal and institutional study with reference to new problems of an urban, industrial society.

Philosophy of law was the first to seek a broader range of materials outside the limits of developed law. As far back as the last quarter of the nineteenth century continental philosophers of law began to avail themselves of anthropology and ethnology. Likewise, historical jurists began to urge that the materials of legal history were not to be restricted to the classical Roman law and the medieval Germanic law. Beginning with attempts to reconstruct a law of the primitive Aryans by comparative legal history, this movement culminated in attempts at a universal legal history, as a part of the history of civilization, and endeavors to construct a historical philosophy of law on that basis. Movements of this sort were reinforced by social psychology, which led to study of juristic and judicial processes rather than exclusive attention to doctrines, institutions, and precepts. Later they were reinforced by a revival of philosophical jurisprudence, which had been dormant in the latter half of the last century, but was awakened by the demand for juristic creative activity in a new era of legal growth. Thus, in the present century there has been a growing tendency to give over exclusive methods, to break down the nineteenth-century schools, and to unite jurists, on the one hand, in a social-philosophical school of several well-marked forms, and, on the other hand, in a sociological school, depending chiefly on the position from which they come to their new alignment and on the problems with which they have to wrestle in the immediate sphere of their activities.

The Effect of the Rise of Sociology

In the past fifty years the development of jurisprudence has been affected profoundly by sociology. The older mechanical sociology affected the science of law by its insistence upon thinking about groups. Thus it had much to do with bringing us to give up the abstract individual as the central point in juristic thought. Also this insistence upon a social theory led jurists to seek to relate law more critically to other social phenomena. Later the biological sociology brought about more thorough study of primitive legal institutions and gave impetus to the unification of the social sciences by establishing connections with anthropology and ethnology. Still later the psychological sociology gave us a more adequate account of the traditional element in legal systems, turned attention to the problem of judicial and juristic method, and made us aware of the traditional art of the lawyer's craft as an element in law and a factor in legal development. The nineteenth-century schools were therefore driven to rebuild on broader foundations, and movements began which led to the social philosophical jurisprudence of to-day. As law came to be thought of as a social phenomenon, and the legal order as a specialized social control, not to be understood entirely apart from the whole, the much debated question as to the nature of law took on a new aspect. It came to be seen that a chief juristic problem was one of valuing competing claims in order to determine what interests shall be recognized and within what limits. Thus it became clear that a rigid separation of jurisprudence and ethics could not be maintained. Also the task of the law was seen as one of adjusting or harmonizing conflicting or overlapping human claims or desires, and metaphysical questions as to the scope of the law became practical questions as to the inherent limitations of legal machinery and the possibility of better things with improved machinery. The idea of efficacy of intelligent effort replaced the juristic pessimism of the historical school. To-day jurists consider the legal ordering of society functionally and debate the end of law rather than the nature of law. These radical changes in jurisprudence are chiefly owing to the movement for unification of the social sciences which marked the beginning of the present century, and the chief credit of that movement is due to sociology.

THE DEVELOPMENT OF SOCIOLOGICAL JURISPRUDENCE

While the nineteenth-century historical school and the analytical school are still well represented in jurisprudence and each numbers many adherents in law faculties, these schools are now on the defensive. The active schools are the social-philosophical jurists, and a rising school of sociological jurists. The latter school is still to some extent formative. Differences that exist or have existed among sociologists are reflected in differences of view among sociological jurists. It is not so easy to attribute a definite creed to them as it is to formulate the creeds of the several nineteenth-century schools. But the tenets of those schools began to be formulated more than one hundred years ago, whereas the first attempts to formulate a creed for sociological jurists date from the second decade of the present century. In consequence certain misconceptions of sociological jurisprudence are not uncommon. As the subject has followed the development of sociology, and so has gone somewhat rapidly through the changes that have marked the growth of that science, there are those who assume that they may lay hold of some tentative doctrine of a past stage and insist that sociological jurists must adhere thereto for all time. Thus, because the first type of sociologist regarded legal institutions and legal doctrines as products of an inexorable mechanism of social forces, excluding all possibility of effective creative activity, it is often assumed without warrant that such must be the position of the sociological jurist of to-day. Others assume that because at one time sociology went through a descriptive stage, sociological jurisprudence must therefore be a mere gathering of data as to the legal institutions of primitive peoples. Other critics assume that the ethnological and biological interpretations of legal history, which went along with the biological sociology, must inevitably be accepted by the sociological jurist forever after. These things are as much in the past in sociological jurisprudence as they are in sociology. The characteristic marks of the sociological jurists of the present are that they study law as a phase of social control and seek to understand its place in the whole scheme of the social order; that they regard the working of law rather than its abstract content; that they think of law as a social institution which may be improved by intelligent human effort and hold it the duty of jurists to discover the means of furthering and directing that effort; and that they lay stress upon the social purposes which law subserves rather than upon theories of sanction.

PRESENT RELATIONS OF SOCIOLOGY AND JURISPRUDENCE

While sociology has done much for jurisprudence, jurisprudence has been utilized less in sociology than its possibilities warrant. Legal phenomena are not the least significant of social phenomena. The social adjustments made or attempted by the legal order and the detailed history of their development, since law was first definitely set off from an undifferentiated social control by the jurists of republican Rome, have been recorded in law books and have been studied in all their possibilities of logical development by generations of specialists, and in all their possibilities of practical application by generations of judges. The mere cataloguing of the interests or claims or desires which have pressed upon the law for recognition, of those which have been recognized and secured and those to which recognition has been denied, and of the devices by which the law has sought to give effect to those which it recognized, might be as useful for sociology as it is coming to be for jurisprudence. Sociology of law may well be an important item in the program of the sociologist. But there remains much that sociology may do for jurisprudence. A chief problem of jurisprudence is to work out a method whereby to value conflicting or overlapping claims or desires and to determine which to recognize and to what extent. Thus far jurists have had to rely chiefly upon philosophy for this purpose. Social psychology is beginning to assist. Much is yet to be done, however, before we may hope to find a method adequate to the demands of a new period of growth, and our main hope must be in the further development of the social sciences. Again, a leading problem of jurisprudence to-day is individualization of the application of law. Here the most significant achievements have been in connection with social work, and these achievements need to be organized and made available for the law through the studies of sociologists. Also, we may expect much from sociology in connection with the problem of enforcement of legal precepts, which is now in the foreground in America. This problem cannot be solved with legal materials exclusively. It must be studied as part of the whole subject of social control as we seek to reshape the legal materials handed down from the rural, agricultural society of nineteenth-century America to meet the needs of the urban industrial society of to-day.

SELECTED REFERENCES

The nineteenth-century schools

Bryce, James. *Studies in History and Jurisprudence.* Essay 12. 1901.
Pollock, F. *Oxford Lectures,* pp. 1–36. 1890.
    Essays in Jurisprudence and Ethics, pp. 1–30. 1882.
Pound, R. "The Scope and Purpose of Sociological Jurisprudence." *Harvard Law Review,* xxiv, 1911, p. 591.
Vinogradoff, P. *Historical Jurisprudence,* i, pp. 103–60. 1923.

Analytical jurisprudence

Austin, J. *Jurisprudence,* 5th ed. 1861–1879.
Gray, J. C. *The Nature and Sources of the Law,* 2d ed. 1909.
Holland, T. E. *Elements of Jurisprudence,* 13th ed.
Salmond, J. W. *Jurisprudence,* 7th ed. 1891.

Social-philosophical jurisprudence
Social Utilitarian
    Ihering, R. von. *Der Zweck im Recht,* 6th ed. The first volume is translated by Husik under the title *Law as a Means to an End.* 1877–1905.
        Scherz und Ernst in der Jurisprudenz, 13th ed.

Neo-Kantian

Stammler, R.   *Wirthschaft und Recht*, 5th ed.   1896.
        Lehre von dem richtigen Rechte.
        Lehrbuch der Rechtsphilosophie, 2d ed.   1923.

Neo-Hegelian

Berolzheimer, F.   *System der Rechts- und Wirthschaftsphilosophie.*   Vol.
        2 translated as *The World's Legal Philosophies.*   1904.
Kohler, J.   "Rechtsphilosophie und Universalrechtsgeschichte," in Holt-
        zendorff, *Enzyklopädie der Rechtswissenschaft*, i, 7th ed.
        Lehrbuch der Rechtsphilosophie, 3d ed., 1st ed. translated by
        Albrecht as *Philosophy of Law.*
        Moderne Rechtsprobleme, 2d ed.

Revived natural law

Demogue, R.   *Notions Fondamentales du Droit Privé.*
Duguit, L.   *L'État, le Droit Objectif et la Loi Positive.*
        *Le Droit Social, le Droit Individuel, et la Transformation de
        l'État*, 2d ed.
        Les Transformations Générales du Droit Privé.   Trans. in *Conti-
        nental Legal History Series*, ii, chap. 3.
Geny, F.   *Méthode d'Interprétation et Sources en Droit Privé Positif*, 2d ed.

The economic interpretation

Dicey, A. V.   *Lectures on the Relation between Law and Public Opinion in
        England*, 2d ed.   1914.

Sociological jurisprudence

Brugeilles, R.   *Le Droit et la Sociologie.*
Cardozo, B. N.   *The Nature of the Judicial Process.*
        The Growth of the Law.
Cosentini, F.   *Filosofia del diritto.*   1914.
Ehrlich, E.   *Soziologie und Jurisprudenz.*
        Grundlegung der Soziologie des Rechts.   1913.
        Die juristische Logik.
Holmes, O. W.   *Collected Legal Papers*, pp. 167–202.   1920.
Kantorowicz, H. U.   *Rechtswissenschaft und Soziologie.*
Kelsen, H.   *Ueber Grenzen zwischen juristischer und soziologischer Methode.*
        1911.
Kornfeld, I.   *Soziale Machtverhältnisse.*
        Allgemeine Rechtslehre und Jurisprudenz.
Pound, R.   *The Spirit of the Common Law.*   1921.
        Introduction to the Philosophy of Law.   1922.
        Interpretations of Legal History.   1923.
        Law and Morals.   1924.
Rolin, H.   *Prolégomènes à la Science du Droit.*

On the whole subject, see R. Pound, "The Scope and Purpose of Sociological
Jurisprudence." *Harvard Law Review*, xxv, 1911–12, pp. 140, 489; P. de Tour-
toulon, *Principes Philosophiques de l'Histoire du Droit*, translated as *Philosophy
in the Development of Law*, 1908–19.

CHAPTER XXVII
SOCIOLOGY AND POLITICAL SCIENCE
By HARRY ELMER BARNES
SMITH COLLEGE

THE SOCIOLOGICAL POINT OF VIEW

WITH the rise of a more dynamic and synthetic political science, as promoted by such writers as Gierke, Maitland, Figgis, Laski, Duguit, Beard, Bentley, Pound, Merriam, and Holcombe, it was inevitable that sociology should play an ever larger part in furnishing writers of this orientation with materials to illustrate, amplify and defend their position. The reason for this is obvious. Sociology is the only social science which views and analyzes the social processes in a comprehensive fashion, attempting to discover, describe, and evaluate the operation and significance of the various geographic, biological, psychological, economic, political, and cultural factors which produce the institutions and activities of human society. Therefore, when political scientists have in recent years made an effort to relate political behavior to social behavior in general, they have been compelled, whether consciously or unconsciously, to adopt the viewpoint of sociology and to found their subject-matter upon information either derived from sociology or properly analyzed and classified in accordance with sociological concepts.

THE RELATION OF SOCIOLOGY TO POLITICAL SCIENCE

With regard to the relation of sociology to political science, there is general agreement among all sociologists of repute. Sociology is that general and basic social science which is concerned with the evolution of organized society and the political community, both of which political science assumes as existent at the outset of its studies, making little or no effort to investigate the subject of how society has evolved from the loosely organized primitive tribal situation to the very recent and highly regimentated condition which characterizes politically organized humanity. Sociology is devoted, further, to the study of the development and the functioning of all the diverse organizations for social control, of which the state is only one of the most prominent and powerful. Sociology is also very immediately and directly interested in the changes and modifications effected by these various agencies of social control, among them the state, in the structure and processes of human society. Political science, assuming at the outset the existence of the state, concentrates its attention primarily upon an analysis of the state and the mechanism of government, and it is only indirectly concerned with the broader problems of social origins, structure, functioning, and control, or with the reaction of the state upon social life and group behavior in general.

Once we get clearly in mind this matter of the nature of these two social sciences, their relation becomes obvious. Sociology must derive from political science its intimate and ever refreshed knowledge of the concrete details of political behavior, organization, and activities. Without the recourse to the data of political science, sociology, when dealing with political materials, could scarcely avoid lapsing into a priori political philosophy. On the other hand, political science can be pursued intelligently only by accepting as indispensable prolegomena the sociological discoveries and generalizations with respect to the origins and underlying foundations of society, political institutions, and law. As Professor Giddings has well stated this point: "To teach the theory of the state to men who have not learned the first principles of sociology is like teaching astronomy or thermodynamics to men who have not learned the Newtonian laws of motion."

THE NATURE OF THE STATE

The sociological views as to the nature of the state have, naturally, varied in keeping with the development of sociological thought and the particular interests or line of analysis of the individual sociologists. In the earlier stages of the rise of sociology most of the attention given to the state was that devoted to an analysis of the resemblances between the state and the individual biological organism. While the organismic school produced a vast literature, the result of their work was primarily to demonstrate the similarity of functional coördination as between the organs of the organism and the various agencies in the state. They were thus led to emphasize the necessity of having as harmonious relations as possible between the different organs of political society.

Far more important has been the work of sociologists in their effort to envisage the place and position of the state with reference to the origins and functioning of social organization at large. With a few exceptions, sociologists are universally agreed that society is the more general and basic fact, term, and organization which refers to and embraces all the diverse forms of associated life, whether that life be among animals or men. The state, on the other hand, is a highly specialized association, perhaps the most important and powerful of a number of fundamental types of organs or agencies which are utilized by society in order to make it certain that collective life shall be more safe, efficient, and dynamic. Though its roots extend far back into the early history of mankind and society, the state, as it is envisaged in modern political terminology, is a comparatively recent product of social evolution, and by its very origin, as well as by its specific nature and functions, is demonstrably a creation and creature of society as a whole. This is in reality the basic point of departure for the sociological analysis of political problems, and it constitutes one of the most prominent and distinctive contributions of sociology to the theory of the origin and nature of the state.

As it is with regard to other social institutions, so it is with the state: its nature can best be understood by an analysis of its most fundamental social functions. In general, the sociologists have refused to be satisfied with metaphysical abstractions as to the functions and purpose of the state, and have made an endeavor to get at the real nature of the political process. In so doing they have reverted to the attitude and line of analysis embodied in the writings of the more profound students in previous centuries. They have pointed out clearly that society is a complex of the most diverse types of groups each of which is given coherence and energy through the possession of common interests or sets of interests. If allowed to struggle without external supervision or control for the advancement of these divergent and frequently conflicting interests, society would quickly disintegrate into anarchy. In order to prevent this disastrous possibility, the state has evolved to furnish the necessary supervision and restraint for this conflict of interests, so that social justice and progress will result rather than exploitation and anarchy — in other words, so that social conflict may be rendered a beneficial rather than a destructive process. The conflict of interest-groups is the vital and dynamic factor in the social process; the state is the indispensable umpire or regulator of these struggles and the ultimate partial adjustments. Government is the agency through which these groups carry on the public phases of their conflicts and secure to a greater or lesser degree the objects of the multifarious group interests. By thus envisaging and describing the state as the umpire of the social process, the sociologists have established what is unquestionably the central position in the new or dynamic political science and the only rational or intelligent point of departure for a detailed study of the specific activity of the various institutions and processes in the political life and activities of man.

This conception of the state as the dominant supervisory power in the social process of group conflict has inevitably led various writers to consider the relation of the state to the other purposive groups of which society is constituted. This has brought a number of writers to an analysis, and in some cases to an acceptance, of what is generally known as political pluralism. These writers hold that the state is but one of a plural number of groups which make up society. The state exists primarily for the purpose of adjusting the relations of these groups to one another, and of each and all of them to the state. Most of these writers of the pluralistic school deny any unique nature or power in the state, repudiating entirely the adulatory Hegelian conception of the supreme and ineffable nature of the state. They would merely accord to the state the chief coördinating function in society, and recognize that thus far in social evolution the state has been intrusted with a greater amount of coercive power than any other social agency. Some members of this group, such as Gierke and his disciple Maitland, would attribute both to the state and to other constituent groups a real psychic personality. A number of related theorists, such as MacIver, Tönnies, Stein, and Baldwin, have carried this analysis still further by distinguishing between the spontaneous social groupings, which they designate as communities, and the various consciously organized or purposive groups of which the state is as yet the most powerful. MacIver, in particular, has emphasized what he looks upon as the unique importance of the community, holding that the spontaneous organizations of social life and activity must be given an ever larger share in guiding and controlling the collective life of man.

THE ORIGINS OF THE STATE

In dealing with the important problem of the origins of the state sociology has been able to bring together in scientific fashion the contributions of anthropogeography, psychology, anthropology, and institutional history, so as to clarify the whole problem of political origins to an unprecedented degree. Through taking into consideration the various natural factors which play a part in determining the concentration and movements of peoples, sociology has been able to make it clear why states originated in certain definite localities on the globe, and has helped in this way to explain not only the existence, but the characteristics and destinies of the diverse political entities which have thus far made their appearance.

From psychology the sociologists have been able to draw their information with respect to the various factors producing human sociability and collective or group life. The importance of such psychological factors as sympathy, mutual aid, gregariousness, the consciousness of kind, imitation, and group domination over the individual has been thoroughly analyzed and their significance in the genesis of human associations clearly expounded. Sociologists have further shown the close similarity between the psychic factors that produce society and those which have brought about the state. Such forces as fear, group intimidation of the individual, the assertiveness of powerful and dominating personalities, pluralistic response to given situations, imitation, and assimilation, have all played their part in making possible the genesis of a systematic and permanent assertion of political authority in society, and in creating those attitudes of obedience and respect essential to the perpetuation of any such authoritative control.

In tracing concretely the history of the state the sociologists have relied primarily upon the progress of anthropological research. At first they tended to accept the theories of Sir Henry Sumner Maine that the state originated in a patriarchal period of social organization. Bachofen and other later and better informed writers soon proved, however, that the theory of a universal and primordial patriarchal stage of society was fallacious. While we now know that the contention of this school that the earliest form of social and political organization was a matriarchate or female rule is not supported by the available facts, nevertheless these writers performed a good service in destroying the patriarchal theory. For a generation sociologists tended to accept the anthropological theories in regard to political origins which were set forth in the famous book of Lewis Henry Morgan on *Ancient Society*. He contended that human society had passed through successive periods in which the female organization of society invariably antedated the paternal organization. He worked out an orderly and universal succession of social and political types from the most primitive promiscuous group to the political society of the classical period. The more critical anthropologists of the present generation, led by Professor Boas and his students, have proved, however, that this succession of maternal and paternal society does not square with the concrete data assembled from the study of primitive peoples. There is no evidence whatever that the female organization of society is an older one than the paternal. Neither is there any evidence that maternal organization has ever been independently transformed into a paternal form of society. Further, it has been shown that in many cases there is no gentile society whatever among primitive peoples, but rather a simple family-village organization, with bilateral descent, much like the rudimentary forms of contemporary social groups. Diversity rather than unity seems to characterize the primitive, as well as the historical, forms of social and political organization.

As to the actual historical development of the state, the sociologists have pointed out how, in the first place, there is no sharp break between pre-political and political society. Even in primitive society there are various forms of group organization for diverse public purposes which cut sharply across ordinary kinship lines. The majority of sociologists have accepted the point of view which has been expounded by various writers from the time of Polybius to that of Hume and Ferguson, and, in our day, by Bagehot, Spencer, and Gumplowicz and his followers, namely, that the political state was gradually welded together as the result of long-continued warfare among primitive groups. The conquest of one group by another brought about an ever greater amount of authoritative and coercive control of the conquerors over the conquered, while in the process of successive conquests there were wrought out the various institutions and organizations within the state devoted to the exercise of this political control. In spite of the dominating part played by war in political origins, other sociologists, such as Sutherland, Kropotkin, and Novicow, have pointed out how many pacific factors, particularly sympathy and the adjustment of economic processes through law, have played a very significant part in the subsequent development of states. The thoroughly synthetic view of political origins is well represented in the writings of such men as Giddings, Hayes, Stein, and Tarde, who have given proper attention to both military and economic elements in the history of the state.

The Elements of the State

One of the most important contributions of sociology to political science has been a more realistic and vital elucidation of the essential elements in the composition and activities of the state. While the political scientists have long insisted that every state must include such elements as population, territory, and sovereign power, they have rarely made any effort to analyze these factors in such a way as to indicate their bearing upon political processes and the nature of political institutions. Sociologists have, on the contrary, made a detailed analysis of all the essential elements in the state, indicating how their characteristics and diversities operate to produce the specific institutions and problems of political life, with the great varieties of expression which these manifest.

With regard to population, the sociologists interested in demography have made detailed studies, particularly in connection with census reports, of birth- and death-rates, age classes, industrial groups, distribution of wealth, distribution of population, vitality classes, and so forth, all of which information has a direct bearing upon the specific problems of statesmanship. Along with this demographical work may be mentioned the more dynamic studies of the biological destiny of man by the social selectionists such as Pearson, Holmes, Schallmeyer, Ammon, and Vacher de Lapouge, who have devoted themselves to the problems of (1) whether the human race is improving or deteriorating physically with the progress of civilization, (2) the possibility of improving the race through artificial selection or eugenics, and (3) the bearing of differential biology and psychology upon aristocracy and democracy. Then there is the wide range of problems involved in the rate of population increase and its relation to the natural resources of any country. This field of study includes not only the increase of population through the birth-rate, but also any addition through immigration. The latter aspect of the case introduces a consideration not merely of the increase in the total volume of the population, but also the many issues involved in the mixture of various ethnic types and the resulting difficulties of assimilation. Finally, the sociologists, such as Hankins, working with anthropologists and psychologists, have shown that it is necessary to disregard to a large extent the element of race in political institutions and processes, because of the indeterminate nature of race and the great mixture of races in all contemporary civilizations.

With regard to territory, or the geographical factors in politics, the sociologists have been able to appropriate the remarkable work done by geographers in the last generation to show the various ways in which the state is compelled to reckon with such facts as topography, natural resources, soil, climate, routes of communication, cultural isolation or contacts, and strategic position. At the same time, more critical sociologists have been able to derive from the cultural historians and anthropologists a sufficiently discriminating attitude so as to avoid the absurdities of the old theory of direct geographical determinism. Although every state is, in differing degrees, affected by all the physical factors of material nature, there is no strict determinism, as widely different forms of political life appear in similar geographic environments, while highly uniform political institutions evolve under very divergent geographic conditions. Professor Giddings, in particular, has made an effort to work out a synthesis of the interaction of geographic and psychological factors as they combine to produce the various forms of the state and political theory. Perhaps the most important element in the newer sociological interpretation of the geographical aspects of politics has been to insist that geographical influences operate primarily in an indirect rather than in a direct and immediate fashion. Regional geography and dynamic politics are now in rapport.

One of the most substantial contributions of sociology to the elements of the state has been the sociological analysis of the origins and real nature of sovereignty. Philosophers and political scientists have devoted much space to a metaphysical discussion of the problem of sovereignty, but few have ever made a realistic study of just how it is possible for one group in human society to exercise coercive authority over another group, or have analyzed the limitations which concretely exist in the execution of this supposedly absolute authority. Sociologists have clearly indicated that there is no such thing as inherent and primordial political sovereignty. The power of any group to assert authority over another group has been the slowly evolving product of human folkways, customs, and institutions which have developed the attitudes of both assertion on the one hand and submission and obedience on the other. Without these socio-psychic factors no such thing as political authority could be exercised for a moment. Further, political authority is not original or independent: it is but one phase of general social control. The nature of the class which exercises sovereignty and the general psychological basis of its powers at any given time will depend chiefly upon the particular type of social organization in existence. In the earliest period political sovereignty rested to a large extent upon the alleged ability of the ruling classes to bring into play supernatural forces and powers, while to-day political sovereignty depends very largely upon the possession of economic ascendancy. In other words, it has been due almost entirely to the work of sociologists that the notion of sovereignty has been transformed from the metaphysical absolute of Burgess or the legalistic "determinate superior" of Austin into a concrete secular concept with definite social, economic, and psychological sources, uses, and limitations. The sociologists have demonstrated that sovereignty is not original, absolute, universal, or unlimited; that political power of any sort is but rarely supreme in any society; that political power is derivative rather than original, arising from social, economic, and psychic forces; that sovereignty cannot be studied as an isolated entity, but only in its social setting and in the light of the evolution of the state within society; and that sovereignty in its deeper significance is a sociological rather than a political or legal problem, however important the determination of the legal superior may be in concrete instances for juristic purposes.

Since the time of Aristotle the most penetrating students of political problems have laid stress upon the very great significance of economic conditions for the determination of the nature and variety of political institutions and problems. If the state exists primarily for the purpose of mediating between the various conflicting interests in society, it is obvious that political theory cannot well ignore what is probably the most important and persistent cause of social groupings and the chief source of conflicting human interests. This is particularly true of the period since the Industrial Revolution of the last two centuries, which has not only enhanced the importance of economic factors in society, but has also enormously increased the number and complexity of economic groups, with the resulting intensification of the difficulties of statesmen in mitigating and controlling the conflicts of the various contesting interest-groups. Professor Beard has admirably summarized the importance of the economic factor in politics: [1]

The grand conclusion, therefore, seems to be that advanced by our own James Madison in the Tenth Number of the Federalist. To express his thought in modern terms: a landed interest, a transport interest, a railway interest, a shipping interest, an engineering interest, a manufacturing interest, a public-official interest, with many lesser interests, grow up of necessity in all great societies and divide them into different classes actuated by different sentiments and views. The regulation of these various and interfering interests, whatever may be the formula for the ownership of property, constitutes the principal task of modern statesmen and involves the spirit of party in the necessary and ordinary operations of government. In other words, there is no rest for mankind, no final solution of eternal contradictions. Such is the design of the universe. The recognition of this fact is the beginning of wisdom — and of statesmanship.

Finally, such sociologists as Durkheim, Sumner, Thomas, and Ogburn, together with the cultural anthropologists and historians, insist that it is quite impossible to view these various elements in the state as isolated entities. One must look beyond these significant factors taken separately or merely juxtaposed, namely, to human culture, which is the product of these various elements working in different and varying combinations upon the human organism. The state, from this point of view, appears both as a creation of cultural factors, being continually changed and recombined within it, and as one of the most conspicuous of cultural institutions in itself.

THE PROCESS OF GOVERNMENT

In dealing with the problem of the functions of the state and the process of government the sociologists have made another contribution to realism in political theory. In the first place, the sociologists correctly insist that society is a collection of groups rather than of individuals. These groups tend to organize about certain definite interests, and seek to dominate other groups in order that they may more effectively realize their group interests. Government is the mechanism through which the dominant groups exer-

[1] Beard, C. A., *The Economic Basis of Politics*, p. 99. (Knopf.)

cise their control over the process of group conflict and legalize the exploitation of and dominion over the subordinate groups. Ultimately, in a relatively perfect state of political development, it may be hoped that government will function chiefly in the way of securing an adaptation and a reconciliation of these conflicting interests.

The process of government, then, becomes a method of so manipulating political bodies and institutions as to allow the more powerful groups to secure their aims and ambitions. The relative importance of any department of government depends primarily upon the success with which it is able to advance the interests of dominant groups or to mediate between the conflicts of various interest-groups. Normally the legislature is the chief arena in which these interest-groups contend, and the usual method of domination or adjustment is what has been called in this country "log rolling." While used in general as a term of opprobrium, it is in reality the characteristic technique of legislation.

The recognition of the actual process of government as one of advancing or adjusting group interests has led to new theories with respect to the reconstruction of representative government. It has been contended that the old territorial or geographic units have lost their vitality and rationale with the progress of modern industrialism and professionalism, and some of our most progressive sociologists and political scientists suggest that these territorial units should be replaced by a system of representation based upon the selection of lawmakers by the various vocational or professional groups in society. It is asserted that this would produce greater popular interest in party government, and secure far more capable and intelligent representatives. Others, in sympathy with the general aims of the vocational representationists, maintain that it would be quite impossible to discover any adequate method of weighing or distributing the number of representatives to be drawn from these various groups. They would solve the problem by choosing our legislators through present-day methods, but at the same time limiting legislation to general policies, while the specific application of these policies would be handed over to highly competent and specialized administrative commissions. Finally, another thoughtful group of writers suggests that instead of vocational representation the best way out of the injustices and inefficiency of the contemporary party system is to be found in a system of proportional representation.

The sociological theories as to the process of government and the nature of representation lead naturally to the sociological view of the nature of the political party. The political party is viewed by sociologists, not as a metaphysical body designed to promote the abstract good of society, but as the specific organization through which interest-groups seek to promote their special objects and ambitions. The party is an interest-group, or a combination of interest-groups, brought together in an organization which can advance in a powerful way the aspirations of any group or combination of groups. The most powerful parties are those which can unite the greatest number of interest-groups, without sacrificing at the same time the indispensable minimum of coherence and unity. In spite of the selfishness and corruption of political parties, there is little doubt that the conflict of political groups is one of the most dynamic influences in social life. The chief danger is to be found in a situation like that which has developed in the United States, namely, the disappearance of fundamental causes of group struggle as between different political parties, and a concentration of party conflict almost exclusively upon the spoils of office and the stolen fruits of political power.

Sociologists have also made important contributions to the explanation of the sources of the remarkable psychic and social power exercised by political parties. Graham Wallas, Walter Lippmann, Seba Eldridge, and others have shown how the chief appeal made by parties comes through various symbols and shibboleths which attract the emotional response of the voters. While parties are supposed to be augmented primarily through the strength of their program and intellectual appeal, it is a manifest fact that discussion and intellectual acumen have no chance whatever when pitted against powerful emotion-bearing symbols, shibboleths, and catch-words. The great statesman has no chance whatever against the political spell-binder. All of these various contemporary sociological doctrines with respect to the political party have been brought together in a remarkable synthesis by Robert Michels. He shows how modern democracy necessitates representative government, and how representative government produces the political party, which brings in its train political machinery and bosses, who soon lose their sense of responsibility and use their power for the purpose of exploiting rather than representing the mass of the citizens. Their control of elections, the press, and political offices makes it easy for them to delude, intimidate, or manipulate the populace at will. In this way the very requirements and necessities of democracy in the way of representative government are self-defeating.

THE SCOPE OF STATE ACTIVITY

With regard to the scope of state activity there are, of course, wide divergences of opinion among sociologists. On the one hand, we have writers like Spencer, Sumner, and Novicow, who favor a system approximating anarchistic *laissez-faire*, while at the opposite extreme are such writers as Lester F. Ward, Ludwig Stein, and Albert Schaeffle, who favor something highly similar to state socialism. The majority of sociologists are found aligned somewhere between these extreme positions. The most discriminating sociologists take an eclectic position and contend that there can be no valid absolute statements as to what the state should or should not do. The functions of the state inevitably bear a close relationship to the nature of the environing society. Certain social and cultural conditions would demand a large degree of state intervention, while in other groups the welfare of society would be most certainly advanced by permitting a high degree of personal liberty and independence. This view has been well expressed by Giddings, who holds that "the worst mistake that political philosophers have made has been their unqualified approval or condemnation of the rule of *laissez-faire*"; by Cooley, who contends that "we must take the relative point of view and hold that the sphere of government operations is not, and should not be, fixed, but varies with the social condition at large. Hard-and-fast theories of what the state may best be and do, whether restrictive or expansive, we may well regard with distrust"; and by Ross, who maintains that "it is idle to attempt to lay down definitely the proper functions of the state, because its scope should depend upon such variables as the trend of social relationships, the development of the social mind, the advances of technique, the talent available for government, and so forth." In general, this group of sociologists emphasizes the fact that the scope of desirable state activity will, roughly, vary directly with the complexities of the social order and the social, economic, and cultural inequalities prevailing in any group.

The State and Social Progress

The attitude of sociologists toward the relation of the state to social progress is, of course, directly dependent upon their notion concerning the proper scope of state activity. The individualists, such as Spencer, Novicow, and Sumner, believe that social evolution is a natural and spontaneous affair, which cannot be accelerated, but may actually be obstructed and confused by human intervention. On the other hand, writers sharing the views of Lester F. Ward believe firmly that man will become progressively more capable of artificially determining the future state of human society, and that the function of the state in this process must of necessity become ever more marked and indispensable. Ward and his disciples would, however, insist upon the necessity of basing statesmanship upon an ever more perfect body of social science if this aspiration is to become an assured success. The eclectics, naturally, take the view that the achievements of the state in promoting social progress will depend largely upon whether or not social conditions at any given time and in any given group require active and extensive state intervention. But even many of this last group are inclined to believe that, with the greater complexities of the Post-Industrial Revolution civilization, we are likely to need an ever greater degree of state activity.

Liberty and Rights

The sociological views on liberty and rights are closely interrelated with the sociological theory of social control and sovereignty, as well as with the theories of the scope of state activity. In the first place, sociologists quite correctly insist that after all, political liberty, which is usually what is referred to by political scientists when using the term liberty, is only one phase of the situation. As Hobhouse has pointed out, we must have a conception of liberty broad and comprehensive enough to relate to every phase of human interests and activities. It is obvious that with this conception of liberty in mind, it follows naturally that the state can deal with only one relatively narrow field of the whole problem of liberty. The amount of liberty which will exist, and likewise the nature, methods, and types of social domination, will depend primarily upon the social and cultural conditions prevailing in the group. Custom, convention, club and class etiquette, religious scruples, and public opinion will often, if not invariably, exert more influence in limiting the complete freedom of individual action than the state or other political institutions.   Even with regard to political liberty sociologists correctly emphasize the fact that liberty is not anything arbitrary that can be enjoyed or determined independently of any specific social situation.   The amount of state activity, with the resulting degree of curtailment of individual liberty, is, as we have pointed out above, very largely dependent upon general conditions in society.   The higher the level of culture and the more homogeneous the society, the greater the amount of liberty that can be enjoyed.

Likewise, with respect to political rights, the sociologists have completely destroyed the old metaphysical notion that man possesses any inalienable or primordial natural rights which date back to a period before the origins of human society.   The sociologists insist that rights are nothing more nor less than the immunities that are granted to the individual in any given society by the state. They are simply the rules of the game in the social process at any given place or time.   The nature, extent, and number of these rights will be determined solely by the social situation which creates the particular degree of state intervention and political evolution in vogue at the given moment.   In dealing with the interesting question of "natural" rights, the sociologists hold that there may be some possibility of restating this concept in valid sociological terms.   Natural rights may be viewed as those personal immunities which the evolutionary process has shown to be best adapted to securing relatively rapid social evolution and a high degree of social efficiency.   Professor Giddings has suggested that this view of natural rights would necessitate our holding that there may be natural rights of the community, as well as natural rights of the individual. ,

WAR AND INTERNATIONAL RELATIONS

With regard to war and international relations, the sociologists have made some interesting suggestions.   While a few, such as Gumplowicz, believe that war is still a necessary and desirable factor in social progress, most sociologists at the present time contend that whereas war performed a valuable function in the creation of states, it has long since become a very dangerous anachronism, and is to-day probably the chief menace to the human race. Sociologists, with their grip upon the underlying causative realities of social life, are able, however, to make it clear that we cannot hope for an end of war unless we eliminate the basic causes of war in population pressure, economic rivalry, savage patriotic psychology, and racial and national egotism.

Particularly suggestive have been the theories of De Greef and others with respect to the social basis of political boundaries. De Greef has well insisted that political boundaries, even if they are of the best, namely, those which conform to natural geographic barriers, can scarcely be expected to possess permanent validity. The real boundaries between neighboring peoples are the lines of equilibrium of social pressure. A powerful and dynamic group is always bound to intrude upon a weaker neighbor, whatever the nature or the location of the arbitrary political boundaries which separate them. If we are to limit the causes of war which inhere in imperfect boundaries, we must make some provision for the continual readjustment of political boundaries to the changing equilibration of social pressures.

The majority of sociologists view the present day national state as but the contemporary stage in the evolution of political life. They look forward to the gradual evolution of a world-state, which will ultimately be attained through the previous acceptance of loose federations and leagues of nations. But the sociologist has a word of caution against too great optimism with respect to the rapidity with which this desirable end can be achieved. Successful political unity cannot well precede cultural unity, or at least toleration for other cultures, and international sympathy.

SELECTED REFERENCES

Barnes, H. E. *Sociology and Political Theory.* 1925.
Beard, C. A. *The Economic Basis of Politics.* 1922.
Bentley, A. F. *The Process of Government: a Study of Social Pressures.* 1908.
Bristol, L. M. *Social Adaptation.* 1915.
Brunhes, Jean. *Human Geography: an Attempt at a Positive Classification, Principles and Methods.* 1920.
Carr-Saunders, A. M. *The Problem of Population.* 1922.
Catlin, G. E. G. *The Science and Method of Politics.* 1927.
Coker, F. W. *Organismic Theories of the State.* 1910.
Cole, G. D. H. *Social Theory.* 1920.
Conklin, E. G. *The Direction of Human Evolution.* 1921.
Dickinson, Z. C. *Economic Motives.* 1922.
Febvre, Lucien. *A Geographical Introduction to History.* 1925.
Giddings, F. H. *The Responsible State.* 1918.
Goddard, H. H. *Human Efficiency and Levels of Intelligence.* 1920.
Grant, Madison. *The Passing of the Great Race.* 1918.

Gumplowicz, Ludwig. *Grundriss der Soziologie.* 1885. Trans. by F. W. Moore as the *Outlines of Sociology.* 1899.

Hankins, F. H. *The Racial Basis of Civilization.* 1926.

Hobhouse, L. T. *Social Evolution and Political Theory.* 1911.

Holcombe, A. N. *The Foundation of the Modern Commonwealth.* 1923.

Holmes, S. J. *The Trend of the Race.* 1921.

Huntington, Ellsworth. *Climatic Changes, their Nature and Causes.* 1922.

Jenks, Edward. *The State and the Nation.* 1919.

Krabbe, Hugo. *The Modern Idea of the State.* 1922. (Trans. by Sabine and Shepard.)

Laski, H. J. *Studies in the Problem of Sovereignty.* 1917.
　　　　A Grammar of Politics. 1925.

Lippmann, Walter. *A Preface to Politics.* 1913.
　　　　Public Opinion. 1922.
　　　　The Phantom Public. 1926.

Loria, Achille. *The Economic Foundations of Society.* 1899. (Trans. from the 2d French ed. by L. M. Keasby.)

Lowie, R. H. *Primitive Society.* 1920.

MacIver, R. M. *Community, a Sociological Study.* 1917.

Merriam, C. E., and Barnes, H. E., eds. *A History of Political Theories: Recent Times.* 1923.

Michels, R. *Political Parties.* 1915.

Ogburn, W. F. *Social Change: with Respect to Culture and Original Nature.* 1923.

Oppenheimer, Franz. *The State.* 1914.

Pearson, Karl. *National Life from the Standpoint of Science.* 1905.

Pound, Roscoe. *Interpretations of Legal History.* 1923.

Ross, E. A. *Social Control.* 1909.

Small, A. W. *General Sociology.* 1905.

Spencer, Herbert. *Man versus the State.* 1884.

Sumner, W. G. *What Social Classes Owe to Each Other.* 1883.

Tarde, Gabriel. *Social Laws.* 1907. (Trans. by H. C. Warren.)

Tenney, A. A. *Social Democracy and Population.* 1907.

Todd, A. J. *Theories of Social Progress.* 1918.

Trotter, W. *Instincts of the Herd in Peace and War.* 1916. (New ed. 1919.)

Veblen, Thorstein B. *Theory of the Leisure Class.* 1918.

Wallas, Graham. *Human Nature in Politics.* 1908. (New ed. 1922.)

Ward, L. F. *Applied Sociology.* 1906.
　　　　Outlines of Sociology. 1898.

CHAPTER XXVIII
SOCIOLOGY AND PSYCHOLOGY
By L. L. BERNARD
UNIVERSITY OF CHICAGO

SCIENCES GROW UP ABOUT PROBLEMS

THE several sciences, like Minerva, were born full-fashioned from
the mind of Jove, or at least from that great complex of human
speculation and rationality which attempted to account for the nature and the meaning of things. If Minerva arose as Intellect out
of the troubled brain of Jupiter it must have been because the
ancient master god had a problem, and he had to bring thought to
bear upon it. That is the way sciences always come into existence.
They represent the organization of data and method around a
group of problems of sufficient importance and distinctness for the
explanatory analysis and synthesis involved to be labelled with a
characteristic name of their own. Sometimes this new field of
problems and explanatory data is split off from an old field of
problems that has become oriented in such a direction as to exclude
the new problems which it seems necessary, for reasons of human
interest or need, to consider. In other and doubtless less numerous cases, these groups of problems arise like new stars, out of a
nebulous condition of popular thought and tradition, and rapidly
take on systematic form and assemble their data from all sides and
sources for explanatory purposes. In a measure, psychology as a
science came into existence by the former method, and sociology
is in part at least the product of the latter process. Psychology
came to us from philosophy and metaphysics. Sociology also has
its connections with the older disciplines, but it arose largely out of
the folk mind. It is of dual origin.

When a science first appears as an independent field of thought it
assumes for itself a certain artificial separateness which is not completely justified by the facts. This is a protective device designed
consciously or otherwise to insure its integrity in the face of the
jealousy of the older disciplines. It is also in large measure a real
separateness due to the limitations of scope of the new science consequent upon its newness. But gradually its problems multiply

and their territory expands and the No Man's Land which at first separates the sciences begins to be invaded and to disappear. Sometimes these invading parties of thinkers and investigators are hostile, and it is necessary to establish some sort of arbitrating body to determine the territorial rights of the contending principalities of the sciences. At other times the exploring parties are wholly friendly and are willing to coöperate to the best of their ability. Sociology and psychology have reached that stage of their development where their No Man's Land is no longer an unknown wilderness, and very recently there have been some rather heated arguments as to rights of possession. To this sort of controversy the present discussion will not contribute. It is our viewpoint that since sciences, like the simpler phenomena of ideas, beliefs and theories, are organized around problems — in the last analysis, problems of adjustment — it is the business and the privilege of these several sciences to draw their data from whatever sources are available to them. Facts are as free as the air and they belong to any person or science that can use them. We cannot define a science in terms of the source of its data: the definition must be made in terms of the application of these data to problems. Sciences are, therefore, characterized by their problems and the statements of solutions which they offer, and these problems are likely, and in the course of time are compelled, to overlap. And therewith the isolation of the sciences tends to disappear.

THE INTERMEDIATE SCIENCE OF SOCIAL PSYCHOLOGY

Already a great intermediate science has begun to appear between the intellectual frontiers of psychology and sociology, which seems to some of the leaders in both of the old sciences to threaten to absorb, or at least to transform, the most fundamental content of both. This new science is social psychology, and it is not yet a generation old. It arose in part by splitting off from older disciplines, especially from ethical writings like the *Theory of Moral Sentiments* by Adam Smith. Such writings were in some measure the forerunners of the type of social psychology recently rendered so illuminating and so popular by Professor Charles H. Cooley. Its roots are also in the past disciplines, especially the metaphysical speculations about conscience and instinct which became so prominent toward the close of the eighteenth century. Professor William McDougall has formulated for us this phase of social psychology. But even more, this new science of No Man's Land between psychology and sociology sprang almost independently out of the problems of community contacts and developments in communication consequent upon the type of civilization which the industrial revolution brought us along with its cities, markets, transportation, telegraphs, telephones, and the like. Bagehot, from his busy office in Lombard Street, and Tarde, in his seat on the judicial bench, began to formulate observations regarding new collective processes and uniformities to make clearer our understanding of the new world of contacts as it has come to be. The content of these processes is primarily psychic, but their significance for adjustment lies overwhelmingly in the social plane. They are true collective phenomena concerned with group processes which rest upon uniform or similar experiences in individual minds. They are, therefore, both psychological and sociological in character. Modern sociology becomes largely social psychology, and psychology itself finds most of its stimuli sources in collective contacts or groups.

The Field of Psychology

For this reason the old schematic segregation of psychology and sociology has less significance than it once possessed. If we accept the older definition that psychology is the science of the mind, we at once confront the fact that mind is primarily the product of social pressures. If we prefer the statement that psychology is the study of the behavior of organisms mediated primarily through a nervous system, we must remember that this behavior, at least in our complex modern world, is conditioned quite as much by society as by the neurons and other aspects of the organism. Child and Herrick have recently made it sufficiently clear that behavior patterns are not matters of fixed heredity but are integrated and reintegrated, phylogenetically and ontogenetically, as the result of the metabolism and motility of the constituent protoplasms reacting upon the environment. If we desire to retain a distinct and logically segregated field for psychology we must find it in behavior processes. A recent writer declares that the unit of investigation of psychology is the neuron. But this is also largely the field of neurology. Perhaps we should paraphrase and modify this statement to say that the problem of psychology is to find out how the organism behaves through the mediation of its neural processes when the sense organs are stimulated or a memory complex functions. Some of the behavioristic psychologists will claim that this definition is too narrow in so far as it limits the field of psychology to neurally mediated behavior. They apparently would merge psychology with physiology as well as with neurology by including all behavior, however mediated, within its scope.

At whatever point we settle the limits of psychology — and we shall not be able to determine them to every one's satisfaction — our discussion clearly shows that there is no clear-cut distinction between this and neighboring sciences. We may properly say that psychology lies between the general sciences of biology and sociology and that it overlaps at numerous points with the various subdivisions of each. It studies neural mechanisms (described for it by neurology) and their behavior in a conditioning environment. This conditioning environment is not simple, for it consists on the one hand of the physiology of the organism (for example, the endocrines) which supports the neural mechanisms, and on the other hand, of the mechanisms which are themselves connected with the external environment through a vast multitude of gateways or sense organs, especially those of the exteroceptive senses, which make it possible for these mechanisms to be immediately and profoundly responsive to the external world, which in our day is primarily social. To say that psychology is concerned with individual behavior is well enough, if we can prove that there is any such thing as an individual or as individual behavior. Perhaps, after all, the reputed science of individual psychology is as much an abstraction as the individual is himself an abstraction. But on the whole they are both useful abstractions. The individual and his behavior, even if not independent and unconditioned by environment, are convenient symbols or nodal points for our thinking. And may we not say that the fiction of an individual psychology is useful in this same process of isolating symbolically the nodal points in our thinking processes or in guiding our behavior, because it provides us with symbols by means of which we can classify objects and divide up our environments into such categories as will enable us to adjust ourselves the more readily to them?

THE SPHERE OF SOCIOLOGY

Sociology, on the other hand, is concerned with the collective, as distinguished from the hypothetical individual, adjustment of organisms to the environment. Such collective adjustment, of course, involves individual adjustment also, and therefore it implies the functioning of behavioristic processes which are both psychological and physiological. It is because of this fact that it has so often been said that the data of sociology rest immediately upon those of psychology and biology. Here, again, we see well illustrated the fact that the distinction between biology and psychology and sociology is one of the degree of the differentiation of problems. The statement of the problems of each more extensive or general science assumes the solution of the problems of the science upon which it rests — an assumption which, in practice, is not always justified. Thus, the sociologist, studying group life or the planes and currents of social phenomena, does not wish, as sociologist, to trouble himself about the neural processes involved in the behavior of the individuals who constitute the groups or participate in the psycho-social planes and currents. Similarly, the psychologist would like to disregard the problem of the physiology of the neurons. But such independence of fields is not possible in practice in connection with highly dynamic sciences which are growing rapidly in content and method. It would be possible only if each antecedent science could be developed fully before the subsequent and more general science attempted to build upon it. There is no such time relationship of complete antecedence and subsequence among the sciences. All of the sciences react upon one another, especially the more general upon the more specific. They also stimulate one another. There is no preordained direction in which the sciences must move in their development. The investigator in any science may at any time find that he cannot go farther effectively without some bit of knowledge which ordinarily might be supposed to be provided by some antecedent and related science. If such data are not ready to his hand he may undertake to supply them himself by some means at his disposal. An example of this situation has recently arisen on a fairly large scale between sociology and psychology. The sociologist needed to know more about the relative importance of instinct and environmental pressures in shaping the affairs of men than either the psychologist or the biologist was prepared to tell him. Consequently, much of the recent work in these fields has been done by the sociologists themselves, and not always with the complete approval of the psychologists and biologists, who have sometimes felt that their territories were being invaded. But here, again, we should remember that no science has any copyright on facts; they belong to whoever can make use of them.

Sociology is concerned with the collective adjustment of individuals to environment. It is therefore, but not exclusively, interested in uniform or relatively uniform social processes. Variant social processes may always arise as incidental to any problem or process of adjustment, and they are most likely to occur when social change is most active. The uniformities and similarities of behavior with which sociology is largely concerned arise from the uniformities both of the inner organization of individuals and of the external environment, which is largely the antecedent social environment. The internal uniformity of individuals rests upon the organization and the integration within the protoplasms of these individuals — chiefly in their nervous systems — of behavior patterns which are in general outline much alike, although they may differ greatly in detail. Thus, we say that human nature is everywhere fundamentally much the same. This protoplasmic integration or set is partly hereditary, especially in the older tissues, having been selected through long periods of time. But it is also, particularly in the cerebral cortex, organized for each individual, according to his education or training in the largest sense. Thus, phylogenetically and ontogenetically we find arising in the protoplasms, of which the neural are the most significant for psychology and sociology, behavior patterns which predispose individuals to respond similarly to stimuli. This similarity of response and interaction of individuals upon one another, with the variations which make for change, gives us that objective fact which we call society.

THE OVERLAPPING OF THE SCIENCES

These behavior patterns integrated in the neural protoplasms constitute the subject-matter of psychology. It is the task of psychology to study these patterns in process of formation and in action. Whether psychology shall study for itself the structure of the sense organs, the physiology and anatomy of the nervous system, and the physiology of the endocrines, or leave these tasks to the physiologist and the neurologist, is at least to some extent a matter of interpretation of the scope of the subject. In practice no rigid dividing lines are drawn between physiology, neurology, and psychology. In like manner no definite separation can be made between the tasks of the psychologist, the social psychologist, and the sociologist. The psychologist cannot exclude from his attention the stimuli which call forth the responses of the protoplasmic behavior patterns. These stimuli are largely social. Neither can the sociologist neglect entirely the nature of the behavior patterns, upon which his social process uniformities and variations are so dependent. The psychologist is likely to speak of these behavior patterns as tropisms, reflexes, instincts, and habits.

Social psychology illustrates especially well this overlapping of interest. At the present time we have two well-defined and conflicting conceptions of social psychology. Those who approach the subject from the standpoint of their training in psychology insist upon confining their attention to those processes which go on within the individual, leaving the whole field of collective responses to the sociologist. Allport, perhaps the most outstanding protagonist of this viewpoint, defines social psychology as the science of the social behavior and social consciousness of the individual, and by social behavior he means the stimulations and reactions arising between the individual and his fellows. What he describes is always something occurring within the behavior of the individual. To Ellwood, as representative of those who approach social psychology from the standpoint of sociology, social psychology is the subject which deals with the psychic aspects of social groups and social life generally. It has to do especially with mental inter-stimulation and response, particularly as evidenced by such processes as suggestion, imitation, and sympathy. Ellwood is thinking primarily of the collective aspect, of the social uniformities, although he is not unmindful of the fact that they depend upon behavior patterns which are integrated within the protoplasms of the individual organism. The opposition of viewpoints is so strongly marked that social psychology may be split over the controversy and the psychologists and the sociologists may each develop their own particular brands of the science. While the existence of the controversy is evidence of a degree of separateness of viewpoints and problems between psychology and sociology, it also affords striking evidence of overlapping, in that social psychology is in itself a sort of capsheaf science designed to lie across the dividing line of the two older sciences.

The Significance of Environment for Behavior

If we may trust the recent work of Child, the uniformities and similarities of behavior patterns in the protoplasms of the individual organisms derive immediately or ultimately from the conditioning environments. The organism is an adjusting mechanism or system of mechanisms. Its forms and structure are functions of the adjustments which are necessary to enable it to survive. Adjustment is the chief category in the life process; the processes of life are those of adjustment. From this viewpoint the environment looms before our scientific vision as an extremely important factor in the development of individual behavior patterns and of types of social organization alike. We cannot expect to understand either individual or collective behavior without also having before us an analysis of the environment and its pressures as they serve as stimuli and produce responses in individuals and in groups. Responses by individuals and by collectivities of individuals are not genetically different things, for collective response varies from individual response only in the degree of the multiplication of individual responses of identical or similar characters. Multiple or identical stimuli acting upon several individuals possessing similar behavior patterns produce normally a collective response or a reasonably uniform social behavior. The general uniformity of environment is responsible for both the similarity of stimuli which results in a collective response and a social uniformity of behavior.

A Classification of the Environments

It is important, therefore, to present at this point a brief analysis of environment in its various forms in order that we may grasp the factors which tend to produce individual and collective uniformities of response or psychological and sociological behavior. The environments may be classified in outline as follows:

I. The physical environments
   1. Cosmic
   2. Physico-geographic
   3. Soil
   4. Climate
   5. Inorganic resources
   6. Natural agencies (falling water, winds, tides, etc.)
   7. Natural mechanical processes (combustion, radiation, gravity, etc.)

II. The biological or organic environments
   1. Micro-organisms

2. Insects and parasites
3. Larger plants used for food, clothing, shelter, etc.
4. Larger animals used for food, clothing, etc.
5. Harmful relationships of larger plants and animals
6. Ecological and symbiotic relationships of plants and animals acting indirectly upon man
7. Prenatal environment of animals
8. Natural biological processes (reproduction, growth, decomposition, assimilation, excretion, circulation, etc.)

III. The Social Environments
   1. Physico-social environments
      (1) Tools
      (2) Weapons
      (3) Ornaments
      (4) Machines
      (5) Transportation systems
      (6) Communication systems
      (7) Household equipment
      (8) Office equipment
      (9) Apparatus for scientific research

   2. Bio-social or organico-social environments
      (1) Medicines and perfumes of an organic character
      (2) Domesticated plants
      (3) Domestic animals
      (4) Parasitical body growths, germ cultures, etc.
      (5) Animals used for power purposes, including slaves
      (6) Animals used as pets, including parasitical persons, favorites, "fools," jesters, etc.
      (7) Regimented human groups, such as armies, working-men, students, citizens
      (8) Human prenatal environment
      (9) Parental and family, neighborhood, and group environments generally
   3. Psycho-social environments
      (1) Individuals that carry culture and communicate it as behavior to other persons.
      (2) Collective behavior, the uniformities of which are known to us as custom, tradition, convention, beliefs, folkways, mores, fads, fashions, etc.
      (3) Symbols of behavior or externally stored language content, found in books, periodicals, antiquities, archæological remains, etc.

IV. Composite or institutionalized derivative control environments

(derivative combinations of the various types of environments organized for purposes of social control)

1. General
2. Special

THE FUNCTIONING OF THE ENVIRONMENTS

All of the above environments may and do operate upon organisms, especially human organisms, as stimuli, and serve to mold their behavior patterns in the race and in the individual. Thus, all of the environments here outlined serve to condition both individual and collective responses and are, therefore, significant for both psychology and sociology. The physical and biological environments represent the conditioning influence of nature in relatively unmodified form upon the organism, and this influence is exerted both directly and indirectly. In modern societies the physical environment no longer directly conditions individual responses in the most important matters of adjustment, but rather indirectly by determining the conditions under which the individual is stimulated and responds to his fellows. The organic environment acts more directly upon man, especially through micro-organisms, insects, food, and vegetal conditions. The ecological and symbiotic relationships of the organic environment are decidedly indirect conditioning factors in that they determine human responses by creating and limiting his food and protective environments.

The physico-social and the bio-social environments are derivative in character, for they are the products of the reaction of man himself upon the two antecedent environments as described in the preceding paragraph. They are created in the process of adjustment of man to nature and to these two social environments themselves. Tools, weapons, ornaments, machines, apparatus, and equipment of all kinds constitute the physico-social environment which arises out of the physical natural environment as a result of man's transformation of his physical world in the process of living or adjustment. In a similar manner man has transformed the organic world so as the better to meet his adjustment needs. The domestication of plants and animals, the fabrication of clothing, shelter, and ornaments, the production of tools, of medicines, the use of animals as beasts of burden and as pets, have greatly enriched the human life process and have contributed no small amount to those utilities and satisfactions which we call civilization. Man himself creates these environments as a phase of his behavior in a social situation. This creative work in the transformation of natural environments into the lower grades of social environments is not always a conscious process. In its more primitive aspects man is scarcely aware of his inventions, so unobtrusively do they come. But gradually empirical invention gives way to or is supplemented by projective invention, and the process of human social adjustment becomes not only conscious but also largely, if not mainly, purposive.

The inventive process by which the physico-social and the bio-social environments are created from the underlying natural environments is both psychological and sociological. It involves the establishment of protoplasmic gradients and dominants and the integration of behavior patterns in the neural protoplasms of the individual organism on the one hand, and the coöperation of individuals in a social situation, in the construction of inventions, and in their selection for survival on the other hand. Likewise, these inventions, which constitute the socialized natural environments, in their turn react upon individuals as stimuli and produce in them those protoplasmic modifications as behavior patterns which we term habits. Since these habits appear in large numbers of individuals adjusting themselves to a fairly uniform environment, the physico-social and the bio-social enviroments are thereby responsible for the creation of new social processes or uniformities, which in turn enter into the content of a new phase of the social environment, the psycho-social.

THE PSYCHO-SOCIAL ENVIRONMENT UNITES PSYCHOLOGICAL AND SOCIOLOGICAL FACTORS

The psycho-social environment represents the union of psychological and sociological processes in objectified and, generally, in conventionalized or stabilized form. This environment, or complex of environments, consists of all of those psychic processes which can be sufficiently objectified through language, and standardized and stabilized in some collective or more or less uniform manner so as to serve as environmental controls in the integration of behavior patterns in others, that is, in those who are stimulated by these objectified psychic processes. If such processes are to be operative uniformly as social environmental stimuli, they must be stabilized and even standardized, and this takes place in varying degrees. Thus, we find in a complex modern society vast series of standardized objectified behavior processes, such as customs, traditions, conventions, beliefs, folkways, mores, fads, fashions, crazes, science, and whatever other forms the processes may assume. Less standardized and stabilized, but still objectified into the content of the psycho-social environment, are conversations, rumors, propaganda, public opinion, and the like. Even more primitive in origin in some aspects are the symbols of language and gesture and other attitudinal values and contacts. But more modern, at least in their more highly perfected forms, are the storage containers of these symbols of attitudes and meanings, which we call books, pictures, statuary, musical compositions, and the like. It is in these collections of symbols carrying highly stabilized meaning and attitudinal content stored in symbolic containers with physical form that the psychic processes reach the highest type of their objectified development. For example, the behavior content of books or pictures does not need to be carried in conscious detail in the human mind, but may be set aside in storage symbols until required. Then it can become effective both as psychological and as sociological factors in reinstating or in creating anew individual behavior patterns and collective behavior processes.

The psycho-social environment, created as the objectified and organized and stabilized collective form of the individual psychic behavior processes, is the newest and yet the most voluminous and most important of all the environments. It unites the psychological and the sociological factors of behavior in the life-adjustment process. Like the other and antecedent social environments, it is itself the product of the adjustment of man to nature and of man to the social environments. It appeared when man began to think about his adjustment problems and to invent symbols and systems of symbols for the communication and the preservation of that thought. Its beginning was in language, even in the lowest types of language, such as gesture and pantomime and emotional expression. It also sprang out of the tendency of many men to do the same or like things in similar situations, and to value and preserve these uniformities of behavior through remembrance and imitation as in the recognition and following of custom, tradition, convention, public opinion, science, and so on. Man has found a vast utility in coöperation, and he facilitates this coöperation in the performance of his tasks, both consciously and unconsciously, by valuing the abstract and intangible uniformities which he discovers in collective behavior as soon as he is able to see society in the abstract instead of merely perceiving men individually through the senses. Of course, it is not necessary for man to become aware of these uniformities of collective behavior through processes of abstraction before he is able to conform to them and to coöperate with his fellows in a social situation. The psycho-social environment had begun to evolve long before any one was aware of it. In early stages of social life men imitated the behavior of individuals, not principles or concepts. This latter type of imitation came much later and is by no means the general practice even among ourselves. Thus, the psycho-social environment came into existence functionally long before it was recognized as environment, a recognition which it is only now beginning to achieve in a way comparable to its actual importance.

THE CONTROL ENVIRONMENTS INTEGRATE INDIVIDUAL AND COLLECTIVE BEHAVIOR

The fourth type of environment is an organized and derivative environment, usually in some degree institutionalized. It is a composite of all the other environments, or at least of such of them and of such phases of them as need to be brought to bear upon any particular situation. It is spoken of as derivative because it is composed of the elements of the other environments possessing logical integrity which are operative upon any special situation or problem. Thus, we might take as examples of the general aspects of this derivative or composite institutionalized environmental complex the economic environment, or the racial, educational, or political environment. More specific phases of environments of the same type, often cutting across phases of the general derivative control environments here cited, would be such national environments as the French or Scandinavian, or a conservative, a masculine, a Southern, a Buddhist, or a revolutionary environment. Such environments are, of course, not always completely institutionalized, but in the main they are. As will be observed from the examples given, they are essentially control environments, serving to mold individuals who are subjected to them after a particular type. It is the derivative institutionalized environments which function most intimately in the formative process of personality building. The fact that many, perhaps scores or even hundreds, of these environments may operate upon an individual, either successively or simultaneously, in the course of a life-time, accounts for the many-sided characters which persons in the modern world have. It explains in part, also, why they exhibit such contradictory elements of character, and accounts in some measure for the neurotic traits which arise out of conflicts due to incompletely integrated personalities.

The derivative or composite institutionalized environments are composed primarily of elements of the psycho-social environments, but they also contain such elements of the other environments as are necessary to the performance of their control functions. The distribution of these composite elements of the contributing environments is, of course, not uniform in all of the institutionalized or derivative control environments. For example, in a national environment, such as the Scandinavian, there would be a much larger proportion of the natural physical and organic environmental factors as compared with the social environmental factors than would be found in a religious or in an ethical environment. In the latter instance the psycho-social factors would predominate overwhelmingly. Also, we might expect to find the physico-social and the bio-social environmental factors more developed in the French (derivative control) environment than in the Russian or Egyptian environment; and here, also, the elements of the psycho-social environment would be of a higher order of development.

Since the derivative control or institutionalized environments are engaged so definitely in the molding of personality in conformity to characteristic types, it is quite apparent that in these, as in the psycho-social environments, the psychological and the sociological processes come in close contact and are mutually dependent upon each other. It is in these derivative control environments that the data of social psychology, the connecting science between psychology and sociology, disclose themselves to the investigator. And it is to the further organization and perfecting of these environments as social and individual control agencies that the principles of social psychology, as well as of psychology and sociology, are mainly applied, when these principles have been generalized from the data of observation and experiment. It is these functionally organized control environments, rather than the general antecedent or constituent environmental planes, that are responsible in practice for the integration of specific behavior patterns in the protoplasms of the individual organisms. That is to say, these derivative control environments provide the stimuli which integrate and activate the neuro-psychic behavior processes of the individual. And it is the uniformity or institutionalized character of these derivative control environments that provides the similarity of responses which constitute individual behavior into the collective or social. Thus, we see that the psychological and the sociological factors meet on common ground in the functioning of these derivative control environments.

The Fundamental Principle Generalized

We may now advance to a generalization which perhaps has already become sufficiently evident. The relationships of the sciences can be understood only through the concrete comparison of their data as applied to the formulation and solution of their problems. In the case of the mental and social sciences, this comparison of problems and data is best accomplished by means of a study of the environments operating as stimuli calling forth individual and collective responses, for the subject-matter of the mental and social sciences is behavior patterns which arise in the process of making adjustments to an environmental situation. Therefore the data of the mental and social sciences appear, and their problems are disclosed, only in the adjustment situations which are the objective aspects of what we sometimes call the life processes of organisms, individual and social. This is the procedure that has been followed in this chapter, and it is believed to be justified on the ground that it discloses functional instead of merely logical relationships between the sciences under consideration. And in the long run logic, if it is sound, must be determined by functions rather than functions being determined by logic.

Summary and Elucidation

By way of summary and elucidation of the argument of this chapter so far, it may be said that the science of psychology lies between biology and sociology and overlaps both. It studies the organization and functioning of behavior patterns in the neuro-protoplasms of individual organisms, especially those of the human species. Its chief organized and logically schematized contact

ith sociology is through the newly integrated overlapping science
f social psychology.

Sociology, on the other hand, is the general science of collective
ehavior and has its immediate roots in psychology, especially
hrough social psychology; but it also has functional connections
vith all of the other sciences, especially with biology, which is
oundational to psychology. Since the social and mental sciences
riginated in the attempt to state and solve problems of the adjust-
nent of organisms — especially of human organisms — to their
nvironments as a phase of the life process, sociology is concerned
rimarily with collective or coöperative adjustment of individuals
o environment, just as psychology is interested primarily in the
roblems and technique of individual adjustment to environment.
The fact that the sociologist may become absorbed in the details of
elationships between individuals, or that the psychologist may be
vholly occupied with the technique of behavior responses, does not
nvalidate the statement that the significance and function of both
ciences are to be found in connection with adjustment to the life
rocess as a whole. While each science is oriented primarily
oward the problems here indicated, it also has a secondary orienta-
ion toward the major problem of the other science. Thus, psychol-
gy is concerned chiefly with the integration and functioning of
ehavior patterns in the protoplasms of individual organisms and
he functioning of these behavior patterns in the process of adjust-
nent to environment. Sociology, since it is concerned with collec-
ive behavior, must also have a secondary interest in this same
problem, while its primary concern is with the organization of
ollective behavior patterns in the group or social organism —
that is, in social organization and in the functioning of social organizations with relation to one another and to individuals. Psychol-
gy must also concern itself sufficiently with group organization
and collective behavior to determine the nature and source of the
stimuli which integrate and condition the behavior patterns of the
organism.

Hence sociology must interest itself in three main sets of phenomena: (1) the organization of individual behavior patterns as
factors conditioned by environmental pressures and as factors conditioning social organization and collective behavior. The actual
investigation of the phenomena may be left, in most cases at least,
to the psychologists. When active in this field of phenomena, the

sociologist recedes temporarily into the field of social psychology to formulate and organize the data of social contacts. (2) The primary interest of sociology is in the study of social organizations and collective behavior as conditioned by and as the conditions of individual behavior. (3) In order to determine this two-fold relationship between individual and collective behavior, between the integration of individual and collective behavior patterns, it is necessary for sociology to construct an analysis of the environments which condition the individual and social behavior under review. Such an analysis has been outlined schematically and discussed briefly in this chapter.

THREE MAIN CONTACTS OF SOCIOLOGY WITH PSYCHOLOGY

Consequently, sociology comes in contact with psychology through these three types of studies as follows: (1) In an analysis of the inherited and acquired (instinctive and habitual) neuro-psychic traits of individuals which are basic conditions of collective adjustment to environment and which arise out of the adjustment process, either phylogenetically or ontogenetically. These data pertain to psychology when studied as individual traits merely, but they are equally sociological data when they are considered as functioning in the collective adjustment processes. (2) The processes of social organization which are psycho-social, especially such processes as communication, suggestion, imitation, and the projected conceptual types of social organization, such as tradition, custom, convention, fad, and fashion, as discussed above under the heading of the psycho-social environments. Here also belong the psycho-social functions of the great formative institutions, such as education, law, religion, morals, and art. (3) In the institutionalized or derivative control environments (which are concretely functional as well as conceptual) consisting primarily of the objectified aspects of the psycho-social environment. These environments utilize the objectified psychic processes and the symbols and stored meaning complexes of the psycho-social environments to fashion individual behavior according to type and thus to perpetuate their own integrity.

In addition to these functional contacts with psychology, sociology is also concerned with those aspects of social organization which are more directly determined by the impact of the natural and social environments antecedent to the psycho-social. But the independent action of these environments upon social organization is relatively meager. In the main, the natural and lower social environments are effective only through neuro-psychic responses, and those modifications of the natural environments which we have called the physico-social and the bio-social are themselves the product of behavior which is primarily psychic. Thus the functional relationship between the data and the problems of psychology and sociology is close and constant. The two sets of phenomena cannot be disentangled in the concrete adjustment processes of life. They overlap fundamentally to such an extent under modern conditions of environmental pressures that we are driven to the conclusion that the independence of the sciences is more a matter of the technique of abstract logical distinction than of concrete experience and observation. Perhaps we may say that the tendency is for the sciences to merge in their concrete applications, as is evidenced by the rise of the connecting science of social psychology which now occupies so large a sector of each neighboring science.

CONTACT OF SOCIOLOGY WITH PSYCHOLOGY THROUGH DERIVATIVE SCIENCES AND DISCIPLINES

The close functional relationship between psychology and sociology might also be illustrated very effectively by means of an analysis of the data and the problems of various applied psycho-social sciences which fall between psychology and sociology in the field of applied science much as does social psychology in the field of theoretical science. Especially do education, mental and social hygiene, psychiatry, and psychoanalytic technique illustrate this dual relationship. Each of these sciences or disciplines must make extensive use of the data of physiology, neurology, psychology, social psychology, and sociology in order to project and realize its remedial and preventive adjustments of the individual personality to its environment. The same is essentially true of various other fields of interest and practice which have not yet attained the dignity of the characterization of applied sciences but which remain as more or less effectively integrated arts, such as advertising, business practice, practical politics, professional propaganda, religious revivals, and professional reform. Here also the art is effective in the degree to which the data of psychology and sociology, of biology and social psychology are brought into functional relationship and applied in an integrated manner to the problems of practice in the several fields concerned.

CONTACT THROUGH THE CONCEPT OF BEHAVIOR PATTERNS

The most concrete of all the relations between psychology and sociology is to be found in the data and in the scientific organization of the data pertaining to the integration of individual and collective behavior patterns. We have already spoken of the way in which these patterns are integrated in the neuro-protoplasm of the organism under the influence of environmental pressures. It has also been shown that collective behavior consists of similar or identical response of the several individuals of the same group behaving under the influence of the same stimuli coming from a common source or by reënforcement from one another. The psychologist has for some time had an active interest in the actual patterns of behavior which arise out of this organismic integrating process. In early times, when thinking was primarily in theological and magical terms, behavior was looked upon as the result of the personal willed act of some god or spirit, or as the impulsion of some occult power. Permanent internal behavior patterns were not conceived as necessary to the proper adjustment of the organism to its environment. The effective environment itself was looked upon as supernatural, rather than as natural or social in a human sense. Under such conditions there could be no human psychology properly speaking. Neither was there any sociology, unless, indeed, it were of supernatural beings to whom men were in the main in the relation of vassals or slaves.

But with the development of a metaphysical theory of the cosmos and of human behavior and relationships, in which relatively constant essential principles and forces or powers took the place of arbitrary external will as determinants of human action, behavior patterns began to be assumed within the individual. These were at first very general, such as reason and intuition, the various virtues and the vices, and conscience. Reason was, for Socrates, largely interchangeable with his Daimon or Ruling-spirit, and it was in fact the depersonalized essence of a spirit, in its inception. It was, however, a sort of nascent behavior pattern or behavior complex by virtue of the fact that it resided constantly within the individual and was not merely unassimilated will imposed upon him from without. Likewise the virtues and vices and conscience were but resident depersonalized and intellectualized spirits which caused men to act and think according to type or pattern. The metaphysical theory presumed a sort of elemental behavior, according to which there were as many types of behavior as there were elemental virtues and vices (depersonalized spirits) resident in human nature. It was altogether comparable in its naïveté to the contemporaneous theory that there were four types of matter — earth, water, fire, and air. It marked, however, the beginning of human psychology, because behavior was thenceforth conceived as dependent upon an inner or psychic mechanism.

But it was a metaphysical psychology which then began its existence, the stimuli being regarded as arising not from one's immediate environment and fellows, but from external, mystical entities, such as *nous* or *natural law*, which were supposed to rule the world and to influence the individual and collective behavior of men through some sort of infiltration of their essences into the individual through the processes of "reason" and intuition. This old metaphysical psychology is not even yet entirely obsolete among the mystics, and it was the leading brand of psychological thinking in Germany, in the school of Lotze, not so very long ago. The theologians still cling to it longingly, but with only a shadow of their old conviction. The sociology which corresponded to this psychology was also metaphysical. The uniformities of collective response or behavior were likewise conceived as induced by the same sort of infiltration from these universal external essences. Human or political law was but an imperfect copy of divine or natural law, which resided somewhere in the profound and mystical recesses of the universe. Public opinion, in so far as it existed in an age when there was little of spontaneous popular expression, customs, traditions, beliefs — all of the contents of the psychosocial environment as we know it — was but an emanation from this infinite fund of orderly universal principles. Men were but recipients of the universal bounty, not themselves the creators of their collective life.

The Rise of Scientific Psychology and Sociology

But gradually the metaphysical psychology has evolved into a scientific theory of behavior. Neurons and reflex arcs have been discovered, and the behavior entities of the anthropomorphic virtues and vices have given way — or are in process of giving way —

to sets and complexes, to habits and attitudes, which are known to be built up out of the raw material of the elemental behavior patterns. These elemental behavior patterns residing within the neuro-protoplasm of the organism have also been isolated and named, and we call them random impulses (corresponding to random movements), tropisms, reflexes, and instincts. Out of these the social man, living under the pressures of complex environments, constructs more complex and variable or flexible acquired behavior patterns to take care of his adjustments to his rapidly and constantly changing world. In the past these synthetic acquired patterns were themselves often confused with the more original behavior patterns, the instincts, but the further development of scientific analysis in the field of behavior is teaching us to draw more effective distinctions in this connection.

Gradually also the psychology of the stimulus has evolved from the mystical and metaphysical to the scientific. Sense organs — twenty-two types of them — were discovered and classified, and stimuli-response processes were studied qualitatively and quantitatively. Definite and concrete connections were established between environmental factors and the neuronic mechanisms and responses of the organism. As a result, metaphysical essences gave way to psycho-physical processes in accounting for the behavior of individuals just as rapidly as speculative philosophy or metaphysics retired before the advance of laboratory methods and concrete critical observation. In like manner the general infiltration concepts of metaphysical "reason" and intuition have been transformed into critical psychological concepts of attention, analysis, synthesis, judgment, and the like. They have become psychophysical processes instead of metaphysical entities.

Sociology has in the meantime undergone a like transformation from a metaphysical to a scientific method and content. As late as the eighteenth century Vico wrote a book to account for "the common nature of nations" in terms of the universal principles of natural law, thus giving evidence that sociological theory was still metaphysical. But the students of environment were at work and gradually they have amassed their data regarding environmental processes. Modern scientific sociology is based on the assumption that collective behavior is the result of relatively uniform environmental factors stimulating relatively uniform responses in similar human organisms. This collective response organizes individuals into groups; and the study of groups and of group behavior is the subject-matter of sociology.

MUTUAL DEPENDENCE OF PSYCHOLOGY AND SOCIOLOGY

Scientific sociology and scientific psychology are based upon exactly the same assumptions regarding the relation of behavior to environment. Both assume the environmental origin of the stimulus and both assume behavior patterns in the neuro-protoplasm which are the joint result of transmitted protoplasmic constitution and of environmentally induced differentiation of their mechanisms. Psychology studies the inner or organismic patterns. Sociology studies the external or collective behavior patterns, the organization and behavior of men in groups. Psychology measures psycho-physical phenomena. Sociology measures social or collective phenomena, communication, environmental pressures, and multiple response. At almost every point the two sciences supplement each other, and with an adequate understanding of their functions and methods they can be made to coöperate fully in securing that chief objective of all life, adjustment to environment — an adjustment which is for man essentially collective as well as individual.

SELECTED REFERENCES

Allport, F. H.   "The Group Fallacy in Relation to Social Science." *Journal of Abnormal Psychology and Social Psychology*, XIX, 1924, pp. 60–72.
                  Social Psychology. 1924.
Bernard, L. L.   "A Classification of Environments." *American Journal of Sociology*, XXXI, 1925, pp. 318–32.
                  Instinct: A Study in Social Psychology. 1924.
                  An Introduction to Social Psychology, chaps. I–III. 1926.
                  "Invention and Social Progress." *American Journal of Sociology*, XXIX, 1923, pp. 1–33.
                  "Recent Trends in Social Psychology." *Journal of Social Forces*, II, 1924, pp. 737–43.
                  "Significance of Environment as a Social Factor." *Publications of the American Sociological Society*, XVI, 1921, pp. 84–112.
Child, C. M.   *Physiological Foundations of Behavior.* 1924.
Duprat, G. L.   "L'Orientation actuelle de la Sociologie en France." *Revue Internationale de Sociologie*, XXX, pp. 464–81.
Ellwood, C. A.   *The Psychology of Human Society.* 1925.
                  "Relations of Sociology and Social Psychology." *Journal of Abnormal Psychology and Social Psychology*, XIX, 1924, pp. 8–12.

Ellwood, C. A. *Sociology in its Psychological Aspects.* 1912.

Gault, R. H. *Social Psychology.* 1923.

Goldenweiser, A. "Psychology and Culture." *Publications of the American Sociological Society,* XIX, 1924.

Hall, G. Stanley. "Social Phases of Psychology." *American Journal of Sociology,* XVIII, pp. 613–21.

Herrick, C. Judson. *Introduction to Neurology.* 3d edition.
    Neurological Foundations of Animal Behavior. 1924.

Kantor, J. R. "The Institutional Foundation of a Scientific Social Psychology." *Journal of Abnormal Psychology and Social Psychology,* XIX, 1924, pp. 46–56.

Kulp, Daniel H., II. "The Inter-Relations of Social Psychology and Sociology." *Journal of Social Forces,* III, 1925, p. 260.

Leuba, J. H. "Sociology and Psychology." *American Journal of Sociology,* XIX, pp. 323–42.

Lowie, R. H. "Psychology and Sociology." *American Journal of Sociology,* XXI, pp. 217–29.

Mead, G. H. "Social Psychology as Counterpart to Physiological Psychology." *Psychological Bulletin,* VI, pp. 401–11.

Ogburn, W. F. *Social Change.* 1923.

Rivers, W. H. R. "Sociology and Psychology." *Sociological Review,* IX, pp. 1–13.

Vico, G. B. *Scienza Nuova.* 2d. ed. 1853.

Watson, J. B. *Behavior; an Introduction to Comparative Psychology.* 1914.

Williams, J. M. *The Foundations of Social Science.* 1920.

CHAPTER XXIX
SOCIOLOGY AND RELIGION

By DANIEL BELL LEARY

UNIVERSITY OF BUFFALO

I
THE GENERAL PROBLEM

SOCIOLOGY and religion, taking these words in any of their various meanings, are fundamentally though intricately related; the relationships, furthermore, are of various types and orders. Historically, social conditions have often shaped religious practices and reflected social needs; and vice versa, religious demands have modified social customs and social behavior. Psychologically speaking, religion in particular and social conduct in general, are the expression of certain common and fundamental factors of original human nature, though this statement does not mean that there are specific social or religious instincts or mechanisms.

THE PROBLEM, AND METHODS OF INVESTIGATION

It is when we endeavor to separate social activity of a general nature from behavior which is specifically religious under one definition or another, and to study each under its respective designation of sociology or religion, that we begin to sense and weigh the intricacy and number of the relationships obtaining. It is, as a matter of fact, a theoretical separation that we make, not an actual one that we find. It thus becomes an inevitable question, once different individuals and groups have made their definition of either field of investigation, as to what, namely, is the relationship of the two as social studies. What has the student of sociology to offer in the way of content or method, assumptions, psychological background, interpretations, or results that the student of religion needs to use in order to round out his understanding of his chosen field of study? And, contrariwise, what has the sociologist, pure or practical, overlooked that the learnèd in religious matters, historically and objectively orientated, can offer? What, in brief, is the relation of sociology to religion, and religion to sociology? Our investigation will first consider the matter from the point of view of sociology and religion as bodies of organized social knowledge and resumés of the past; we will then consider them as methods of social control and programs for the future of society.

Let us go at it bit by bit. Sociologists, as a modern group, at any rate, are prone to assume a reasonably objective point of view; that is, they look for explanations of social phenomena in terms of, say, climate, race, conquest, natural resources, and so on, all of which, if carried to logical and psychological conclusions, point to social affairs in general as the expression of the original nature of man in his natural habitat. In all this, and speaking particularly, of course, of modern sociologists and recent sociology (not all of a piece, but with a fundamental similarity), the preponderating influences are the so-called natural and biological sciences with psychology as a mediating agent between them. On the other hand, students of religion and, in the main, writers on the study of religion (with certain notable exceptions, perhaps most of them very recent) have been less influenced by the methods and approach of these groups of sciences. They have, to a considerable extent, lingered in the realms of interpretation — linguistic explanations that assume what is pseudologically proven — and have been loath to see in the mutual and differential interaction of man and nature the true explanation of all of the phenomena of their field of interest and research. Hence religion, as a field of study, needs reinterpretation from the point of view of sober students of society and social phenomena in general, though this generalization has its exceptions. On the other hand, where religion has overemphasized self-expression and minimized the environment as a *vera causa*, sociology has, at times and in individuals, under-emphasized the human aspect of living. It is man-and-nature; not just the sum of the two, but the differential activity which is the give and take of the two things, each of which reflects the other. The researches of religion show, on examination, a certain warmth and human touch that is lacking in the more severe of the objective studies of social behavior as a whole which, in their objectivity, have lost sight of the subject.

THE NEED FOR OBJECTIVITY, REALISM, AND AN EVOLUTIONARY POINT OF VIEW

Ultimately, both undoubtedly need a re-analysis of their present indivisibles, their structural atoms, and their methodological assumptions. Where the student of religion deals, at times, with dubious transcendentals, the sociologist deals with transcendentals equally dubious but of another realm and order. Both would gain by consideration of the meaning of "as if"; both would improve by a study of each other's merits and defects. The apparently greater objectivity of general sociology is sometimes to be doubted; it may exist, but without question both religion and sociology can approach much nearer to an actual objectivity. This (to express an opinion) is possible in so far as they reproduce or equal the behavioristic study-observation attitude of the natural sciences.

Still further, though of course related to the above, is the fact that a fish out of water is to that extent the less a fish. And sociology in general, except when as a system or a survey it gives due and proportioned regard and value to religious matters. nullifies its conclusions with respect to everything else. All the more is the study of religion less satisfactory if it is just that and nothing more; religion is religion as much in relation to other things as by itself.

As a further aspect of general attitude and approach, we can say, with but little need of qualification, that the evolutionary point of view has quite thoroughly and quite generally permeated recent significant sociological studies, and while this effect is more recent in religious studies it is now quite general even there. But with regard to another general concept of modern thought, namely, relativity, the more general sociological studies have been more open to its influence than has the field of religion. While comparative studies of religious phenomena have been made, the general attitude of comparison has not, it seems to me, been as open, as objective, and as free from ulterior motives as in the general field. Comparative studies in religion often seem to be motivated by a conscious or an unconscious desire to show the superiority of home products or kindred behavior. In sociology the comparative studies seem more truly productive of what comparison implies, that is, the finding of common origins, the noting of individual differences and the tracing of their causes. In short, at the present time, the sociologist is more likely to concede that all values are human, social or individual, and that all are psychological at bottom.

BEHAVIORISM, DETERMINISM, AND THE SCIENTIFIC APPROACH

All through his work, in other words, and admitting still further possibilities, the sociologist is more desirous and more capable of taking the "as if" attitude, a relativistic point of view, and of approaching a thoroughly behavioristic, pragmatic, and concrete standpoint. The sociologist is more willing to use the technique of S—R and all that it implies than is the religious student, who, even when he consciously aims at such an objective description, still seems to imply something else behind it all. In so far as the student of religion does thus imply some hidden x behind the scene he ceases to be student and becomes propagandist. The older periods in the history of the physical sciences, with their forces, powers, entities, and what not, have quite completely disappeared; almost as completely have such things disappeared from sociology as a general study; but from certain subdivisions of the total field, notably religion, with perhaps ethics, esthetics, and legal science trailing it, they have not been eliminated. Religion is still as a study, with acknowledged exceptions, tinged with animism, indeterminism, chance, and a capricious, undefinable Will.

The above has, in the main, concerned itself with method, assumptions, content, and attitude in general; it remains here to say something of results and interpretation, though a more concrete examination of them is best deferred for a slightly different approach below. But note here, in general, that sociology is increasingly productive; if it does not bake bread it at least endeavors to do so. It does not merely exhibit its wares but aims to be sure they will satisfy the buyer. Sociology asks for a human evaluation; religion still tends, though there are signs of imminent change, to dogmatize on values and to point out benefits authoritatively; there is hesitancy in accepting the pragmatic trail. This is not so true of the sociologists, properly speaking, who have ventured into the field of religion; there we find the attitude, as in sociology in general, of trial and error, experiment, comparison and evaluation in terms of human nature. Such students of religion are not so apt to indulge in mere exhibitionism; but we leave the details of this for our second approach.

II

Relative Values in Sociology and Religion

All the above has been, clearly enough, comment on what might be called official accounts of social phenomena under the respective headings of sociology and religion — the one a general account, and the other somewhat limited and specialized. But one may ask, and quite properly, in the more practical sense of sociology as a social program, as a collection of mores, as a platform for social activities leading to what we soundingly call progress — What then? And of religion in the sense of, say, our individual and group relations to the great Unknown — What? What relations here? There are many, both as interesting and as important in a concrete sense as the somewhat more abstract considerations of the foregoing.

In other words, both of our concepts of sociology and religion have a double meaning. On the one hand, sociology is descriptive, analytical, historical, and explanatory; religion, in the same sense, is the same thing, keeping in mind the qualifications we have indicated above. On the other hand, in a more practical and a more dynamic sense, sociology is a program, a stimulus to change and progress, a pattern for new social behavior and group activity; and religion, keeping our general qualifications in mind, is much the same thing. All science, in the final issue, is art and application; especially so is social science because of its nature and its origin in human needs rather than in a spirit of pure logical research.

Sociology aims, finally, at results, creative effects, the externalization, in institution and in behavior, of a better knowledge of social stimuli and social responses than have gone before. Religion aims at the same thing but, as we shall see, the errors of the more theoretical survey are tremendously emphasized in the practical program. And it is quite apparent, from any adequately scientific point of view, that religion, in the practical program which it must follow, though it may emphasize and enliven certain paths to certain goals, cannot, because of metaphysical partiality and also because of an overemphasis of certain human desires and needs, lead in the movement toward social change — call it progress or betterment. Religion tends to make the wish father to the thought and belief, and even to the so-called proof; the true relationship must be either the reverse or of a different kind — wish and thought may join to produce reality when they come to terms with each other.

HUMAN NATURE AND VALUES

Religion deals with deferred values. No sociology that aims at being something more and something greater than a mechanical or logical system can deal merely or even primarily with deferred values. Human beings, for good or for evil, since they are what they are, learn, act, react, plan, withstand, and value in terms of what the psychologists call (under the general head of "laws of learning") readiness, exercise, and effect. Human beings do what they are ready to do, and any system of religion which advocates conduct or dogmatizes on values for which the group and its constituent members are not psychologically, physiologically, institutionally, and culturally ready, must remain merely a system in a book. As in mathematics and the physical sciences, so in social affairs, change is continuous; there is no jumping. To become *this* from being *that*, the steps in between must be taken, and religion as a practical program tends to insist on a jump for which there is no impulse or incentive since there is no psychological readiness or biological background. Sociology, as a general program, must be the John the Baptist to prepare a way.

Sociology can and should stimulate conduct for which, on grounds not properly discussed here but which are clearly the result of a sober analysis of the nature of man in relation to the nurture, physical and social, which is the arena of his activity and of which he is both producer and product, there is scientific basis. Sociology can and should base each new step on what is and what has been, as well as on what should be. Religion leans too much to the merely *should be*, and the obligations are more often than not fantastic rather than logical or psychological.

Religion fails also in using or attempting to use, at least in any proper sense, the second characteristic generalized from a study of organic behavior in general and called above the "law of exercise." As we shall see below, religion errs in being other-worldly to an exclusiveness that is stifling both to this and to the imputed other world; but here we need merely note that religion cannot well give practice and exercise in its program when that program is essentially of another world and for another time. In so far as religion counsels ethical or moral behavior, it is to that extent less religion and more sociology. And we have noted this from a near-by point of survey in Part I also. Practice, if wisely directed, adequately motivated, and satisfactorily rewarded, makes for attainment, though the old adage of practice and perfection is too sweeping. Religion cannot gain through practice since there is no field for practice in the here and now, and here and now are undeniably factors in any concrete program, however much present considerations of the future may enter into it. We are human now, whatever we may become later.

And, finally, since religion does not base itself on real readiness and cannot indulge in real practice, it cannot give to its practitioners real satisfaction. To be sure, one can always debate words; but by the word "real" in this context is meant the biological and psychological condition that is normal and that makes for vitality in the individual and the group. Religious feelings are, of course, as real as any others, but in the sense of the word real as used above they are not of the first order; they are acquired, secondary, substitutes, defenses, a system of breastworks behind which, when other things are barren, unkind, ruthless, and worthless, we retreat. To say this is not to deny the verity of religious concepts: that is another story. The present criticism is of religion as a workable way of living, a demonstrable way of thinking, and a practical program for societal growth and accomplishment.

THE NEED FOR COÖPERATIVE WORK

Yet, or so at least it would seem to the writer, a union of sociology and religion is possible in the practical, utilitarian, work-a-day world of here and now, based on the union of research and analysis of the two fields as outlined in Part I. It would seem that we can still use something of both that will become something better than either alone. Our relation to the great Unknown, as such, and in such disproportionate terms, is too vague for everyday use. On the other hand, the things that are intellectually within our grasp, that we can see, handle, become familiar with, and concretely realize, are sometimes insufficient for our emotional satisfaction. We would be great even if we are not; we would traffic, even phantastically, with the Sublime (if we can only forget that we have ourselves limned its every detail) since we tend to find such traffic stimulating and flattering.

This being so, sociology and religion must work together; fact restraining fancy and fancy enlivening fact makes for something greater than either alone. The man in the street is not an ardent, alert, discriminating, and sober student of facts. He prefers visions (apart from everyday affairs of an economic nature) to verifications, pleasant hopes to merely possible attainments, freely given but intangible rewards to hard-won conquest of self and nature. But all this, both the fact and the fancy, can be had in one package. Sociology and religion, in practice and in theory, can be mutually adjusted. Just as instinct and intelligence can come to work consistently and harmoniously in one and the same man, so a program of the widest social scope can be based on both knowledge and vision and can command both intellectual agreement and emotional interest.　Unless mores and ideals, facts and plans, the now and the future, are compatible, sociology and religion will always be rivals where they might be, to the gain of all concerned, coöperators.　But as matters stand at present, mores and ideals are compatible from neither the religious nor the sociological point of view, let alone from a common point of view.

All of which, of course, is highly general.　To develop the details of such a program is for the future, and for sociologists and religionists as a group, not for a man and his system.　The day of dogmatic individualism in the field of the social sciences is gone; sociology has become socialized, though religion has not kept pace with it. "What shall *I* do to be saved?" is, socially speaking, almost at zero value, and even religiously is of low order of merit.　The social sense would show better in such a query as: "What shall I do so that my community shall be blessèd?"　Religion, when sobered by broad social knowledge and tempered by concrete social aims, may become more and more an institution in the dynamic, progressive, and behavioristic sense of the word, and become less of a curative, solacing device.　Religion must do not dream, impel not comfort, express not sublimate, be positive not metaphysical.　But such a religion would also be a sociology.

SELECTED REFERENCES

Bernard, L. L.　*Transition to an Objective Standard of Social Control.*　1911.
Boynton, R. W.　*Unitarianism and Social Change.*　1919.
Brown, W. M.　*Communism and Christianity.*　1924.
Carpenter, Edward.　*Pagan and Christian Creeds.*　1921.
Chapin, F. Stuart.　*Education and the Mores.*　1911.
Cohen, Chapman.　*Religion and Sex.*　1919.
Connybeare, F. G.　*Myth, Magic, and Morals.*　2d ed.　1910.
Davenport, F. M.　*Primitive Traits in Religious Revivals.*　1920.
Dewey, John.　*Reconstruction in Philosophy.*　1917.
Durkheim, Émile.　*The Elementary Forms of Religious Life.*　1912.
Edwards, L. P.　*The Transformation of Early Christianity.*　1919.
Hall, G. Stanley.　*Jesus, the Christ, in the Light of Psychology.*　1923.
Henke, F. G.　*A Study in the Psychology of Ritualism.*　1910.
James, William.　*Varieties of Religious Experience.*　1916.
Joyce, G. H.　*Principles of Natural Theology.*　1923.
Kolnai, Aurel.　*Psychoanalysis and Sociology.*　1922.
Leary, Daniel B.　*Philosophy and Education.*　1921.
　　　　　"Modern World Order and the Original Nature of Man."
　　　　　International Journal of Ethics, April, 1922.

Leuba, J. H.   *Psychology of Religious Mysticism.*   1925.
        A Psychological Study of Religion.   1912.
McConnell, S. D.   *Confessions of an Old Priest.*   1922.
McGiffert, A. C.   *The Rise of Modern Religious Ideas.*   1915.
Martin, E. D.   *The Mystery of Religion.*   1924.
Perry, W. J.   *The Origin of Magic and Religion.*   1924.
Schleiter, Frederick.   *Religion and Culture.*   1919.
Schneider, H. W.   *Science and Social Progress.* (Arch. of Philosophy.)   1920.
Sellers, R. W.   *The Next Step in Religion.*   1918.
Shotwell, J. T.   *The Religious Revolution of Today.*   1913.
Small, Albion W.   *Significance of Sociology for Ethics.*   1902.
Vaihinger, Hans.   *The Philosophy of "As If."*   1924.

CHAPTER XXX
SOCIOLOGY AND STATISTICS
By WILLIAM FIELDING OGBURN

STATISTICS AND SOCIOLOGY AS SCIENCES

IT has been said that statistics is not a science but a method. Statistics is certainly a method, for it is essentially a tool that is of use to other sciences. Statistics is also a science, but it is different in kind from the other social sciences. The subject-matter of statistics is the statistical methodology. In this sense it resembles mathematics. Statistics, like mathematics, is a developed, organized body of knowledge, as any science is, but the knowledge it develops is about a method.

The relationship, then, between sociology and statistics is not so much the overlapping, or the points of contact, of two areas of knowledge similar in nature, but is rather that of the applicability of a special method to sociological material.

Definitions of the scope of sociology are likely to be unsatisfactory, for sociology is in a formative state and its outlines are neither stable nor definite. Most definitions of sociology are what the makers of the definitions think that sociology ought to become. Such definitions are not based on the status of the science as it exists, and hence are not sufficiently realistic for the purposes of this volume. On the other hand, a definition of sociology as it exists at the present time is not likely to last, since the scope of the science will change. We shall, then, speak of sociology as its subject-matter is treated in the general works on the subject and in the courses listed under the title of sociology in university catalogues. It will therefore be considered as dealing with the treatment of such general subjects as social organization, social institutions, social evolution, the relation of the group to the individual, the history of culture, the adjustments of inherited nature and culture, social aspects of biology, social psychology, social ethics, and with such specific subjects as population, race, the family, social work, poverty, crime, public health, the position of women, marriage and divorce, social aspects of religion, social legislation, social conditions of industrial life, and community work.

Measurement and Statistics

A body of knowledge ought not to be called a science until it can be measured. Certainly those sciences that are most exact have carried measurement the furthest, and the least scientific are those that make least use of measurements. The insistence upon measurement as a criterion of science may seem very exacting, for much knowledge is not expressed in terms of measurement. But knowledge that cannot be expressed in terms of measurement is often surprisingly uncertain. Unmeasured observations are like impressions; that is, they are very likely to be distortions of reality. These distortions may be only slight, however, so that the approximate knowledge may be usable for practical purposes.

But not all measurement is statistics. The experimental method, the case method, the historical method, and the descriptive method are not generally statistical, yet they may be based upon measurement. Statistics is essentially a quantitative method; it derives conclusions from numbers of cases or observations. The quantitative method is needed most when the phenomenon studied is highly variable. The results of a laboratory experiment are not greatly variable for the information desired, hence the results, if checked a few times, are sufficiently exact for usable purposes. Statistics, as a study of large numbers, is not necessary in such cases. The death-rates of a population, however, are highly variable and demand statistical treatment. Sociology, as a study of society, deals often with large numbers, and needs statistical measurement.

Even measurement of a single case may be treated statistically, particularly where very great accuracy is desired, as in astronomy. In such instances, the case is observed many times and the observations are treated statistically. So also in certain mechanical measurements where there are slight variations, the variations are studied according to the laws of large numbers when great accuracy is desired. Even where certain events occur rarely, as in history, they may in a strict sense be thought of as a sample of a theoretically much larger number. Thus, all our knowledge is fundamentally of a statistical nature; but practically we make no such use of statistics in many of the observations of science.

Statistics as an example of the quantitative method is, of course, not confined to simple tabulation as a more accurate description. The elaborate and refined technique of statistics enables one not only to make accurate observation but thereby to discover frequently much additional knowledge. The statistical technique, particularly as developed in recent years, greatly aids the study of the different causes of phenomena. This technique is the common property of statisticians and needs no exposition here. It may be appropriate, however, to note that causation is practically correlated variation. In a controlled experiment in the laboratory, the scientist measures the influence of one factor as a cause by varying it while at the same time holding all other factors constant, and then measuring the effect of the variation on this factor. Statistics may achieve the same result with essentially the same method in the social sciences where the controlled experiment is impractical. A device particularly appropriate for such control is the regression equation containing more than two variables, usually derived from multiple correlation. For with this equation the different variable factors may be held constant while any one is varied, and the effect of its variation on the result may be measured. For instance, such causes as those affecting the price of farms, as yield per acre, distance from market, value of improvements, amount of rainfall, can each be measured with exactness by an equation with all these factors in it as variables, through varying one factor and holding the others constant. The regression equation is thus similar to the laboratory experiment. There are also other statistical devices for holding factors constant.

It is not the purpose here to set forth an account of statistical technique, of which there are excellent expositions in many books. The purpose is rather to point out the essentially scientific nature of statistics as to accuracy of observation and measurement, and also as a technique in measuring causes. Furthermore, it is claimed that the method of the more exact experimental sciences is in fundamental character much the same as statistics. Of all the methods in sociology, statistics has the highest scientific value.

STATISTICS AND OTHER SOCIOLOGICAL METHODS

Statistics, despite its excellent scientific ranking as a method, has had so far only limited use in sociology. Sociology has relied in the past on various other methods. Nearly all, however, may be said to point toward statistics as an ideal. Thus, the descriptive method is more accurate the more statistical it is. The historical method as it is applied to recent events makes more use of statistics. The case method, as it ceases to have the individual case as its objective and as it is used more for summaries and generalizations, becomes statistical. The few experiments possible in the social sciences can be tested adequately only by statistics. Even the theoretical and the analytical methods are dealing more with the construction of hypotheses that must be verified by statistics. It is not by preference but because of practical limitations that these other methods are used instead of statistics. These various other methods will be considered separately for the purpose of estimating the extent to which each one uses the statistical method.

The historical method in sociology is used chiefly in the study of the development of social institutions, the analyses of social processes, and the accounts of social changes of the past. It is also used, at least as an approach, in the investigation of any particular social phenomenon. The historical method as used in sociology has several interesting aspects. Here it is not concerned so much with determining the accuracy of a single event as an end, but rather with using these events for the purpose of determining social processes. The historical method has very great importance in sociology as a check to the speculative theorizing and loose interpretations that have characterized much sociological writing in the past. This method is valuable also because social phenomena grow out of past conditions. The social process in the development of an institution is continuous, and any particular stage is determined by the past conditions of that institution as well as by the influences of contemporary institutions. Thus, an understanding of the family, the church, or the law depends upon a knowledge of their past. Educational practices grow out of and are influenced by educational practices as truly as they are affected by industry or the family. The importance of history, therefore, appears to be greater in sociology than in, say, physics or chemistry. The historical method is becoming extensively used in sociology in America as well as in Europe.

It seems unlikely that statistics will be used to a very great degree in the historical method in sociology in measuring the influence of the past, at least the far removed past, on account of the great difficulty of obtaining statistical data. But in the future the past will have been more adequately represented by statistics, and statistics will be used more. There are, however, many aspects of the past, such as laws, customs, religions, and social conditions, which do not lend themselves readily to statistical treatment. The historical method is, therefore, largely based on facts but not on statistics.

The descriptive method is very closely allied to the historical method; but there are many descriptive studies of present conditions that involve little history. In so far as the descriptive method implies existing conditions, then, the connection with statistics is closer than is the connection of the historical method, for the reason that statistics are more easily obtained for the present than for the past. Much descriptive work in sociology is not very careful or thorough, bearing some resemblance to reporting work for contemporary journals. Careless description is very much to be deplored in sociology, and the situation is ripe for the application of statistics. Indeed, the sociological survey and the statistical investigation are in frequent use as a new type of description. An account of Russia in 1917 is likely to be journalistic; but a survey of the economic and social conditions of immigrants in the United States will be largely quantitative. Not all descriptive studies lend themselves to statistical treatment, even though they may be factual; for example, studies of court procedure, comparative legislation, and the conditions of life of a primitive people. Many descriptive studies must be brief yet comprehensive in scope. Such studies involve selection and valuation, where practically statistics can help very little. These selected descriptions, whether in brief compass or a great range of material, are, of course, very likely to be untrustworthy. Most description to-day is not statistical, and some will always be non-statistical, despite the growing use of the technique of the survey, the questionnaire, the case method, and the social investigation.

A method that has become specialized and that is in frequent use is the case method. This method in the past has been employed in the field of social work, particularly in the work of relief agencies dealing with individuals in distress. It is quite technical and demands special training. In a modified form it has been extended to the study of other cases, such as delinquents, school children, orphans, cases of malnutrition, and various maladjusted individuals. This method has been further extended, so that the case, representing variously the results of different factors, has become the unit in many statistical and social investigations, particularly in studies using the questionnaire. The case method began with the purpose of dealing with the individual case as such; but it led rapidly to

generalizations.   It then becomes statistical.   At the present time
the records of case histories are not often made in classifications that
can be tabulated; but it is only a question of a short time, it is
thought, before they will be fitted to refined statistical methods.

The experimental method, as it is known in the laboratory sciences, is not applicable to sociology.   Yet there is a good deal of
experimenting done in society.   These experiments are undertaken
for the supposed social usefulness of the experiment at the time, and
hence they are not purely experimental.   For instance, the prohibition of the liquor traffic may be an experiment, but it was not
designed solely as an experiment, as are laboratory experiments.
The effects of such experiments can, of course, be tested best by the
statistical method.   It is not absolutely necessary, however, that
the results of such an experiment be quantitatively measured.   The
people may adjust themselves to an experiment such as direct legislation through the use of the initiative and referendum, either accepting it or discarding it without measuring its effects accurately.
But an adequate appraisal of a social experiment calls for facts,
certainly many of which should be treated statistically.   Some effects of experiments, it should be noted, are extremely difficult to
measure statistically; such, for instance, are the effects of prohibi-
tory legislation on the feeling for liberty; and there are practical
limits to the use of statistics in testing social experiments.

Lastly, a method frequently found in sociological treatises is often
described as the theoretical, the analytical, the subjective, or the
deductive method.   These methods may best be appraised after a
brief discussion of how science develops.   Science proceeds through
the verification of hypotheses.   But first hypotheses must be formulated.   In the early stages of a science the formulation of hypotheses is by no means a simple thing.   Such is certainly the case in
sociology.   There is first felt a demand for information.   The questions are usually too general, and they are framed without sufficient
reference to the tools and evidence to be used in answering them.   In
this stage where verification and evidence are little used, the issues
are rather complex, and hence theories rather than specific hypotheses are the concern of writers.   The theories are tested primarily
by the logic of different critics as to consistency, relevancy, and so
on, instead of being tested by facts.   These theories are synthe-
sized into social philosophies, still more difficult to test by facts.
There is in these theories and social philosophies much emphasis on

evaluation, concepts, and outlines. Some confident writers use a few illustrations and seem to consider them as factual proofs; so that what are really theories are set forth as conclusions or generalizations. In these stages the quantitative method finds little place. But as concepts become clarified and as the general questions become broken up into specific ones, there is greater use of statistics. A number of phases of sociology are at this point now; such, for instance, as the study of social institutions, the history of culture, the processes of social change, and certain modern social problems. Very probably, however, many sociological problems, such as the relations of the individual to society, progress, social psychology, public policies, and larger social programs, will continue to be treated in this earlier manner for some time to come.

The foregoing account of the relations of statistics to different sociological methods indicates that statistics is the ideal objective of the methods, but that statistics, however desirable, is at present impractical as a method within a great range of material, although its use is decidedly on the increase.

Subjective Influences and the Use of Statistics [1]

While the statistical method is by no means in general use among sociologists, the absence of the quantitative method in certain fields of sociology is a greater detriment than is popularly supposed, perhaps greater here than in other sciences. The reason for this may be stated as follows: A theory that is unproven by the facts has some reason for having come into existence. Where it is suggested by facts, how it came to be is understandable. But very frequently desire is the force that makes the theory come into being. Where facts are absent, desire may supply supposed facts, as in the unreality of day-dreams. Of course theories are not so unrealistic as day-dreams, but desire has the power of distorting observations from reality, and desire has a strong selective influence in causing particular data to be noted and other data not to be noted when the phenomena to be studied are complex. So, also, in recollecting and in forgetting, processes present in all intellectual work, desire is highly selective. In brief, where the materials dealt with are such as to be stimuli to the emotions, theories, even though suggested by facts, have a strong probability of being untrue in varying degrees. They tend then to be untrue pictures and false solutions. As the emotion of the poet and the artist (rightly) prevents their work from being realistic, so also the emotion of the social investigator tends to make an untrue picture of reality when the details of the problem affect his feelings. Historical textbooks, for instance, in dealing with wars present quite different pictures, depending upon in which of the warring nations the book was written and published.

Sociology deals with a great deal of material that has emotional associations, such as religion, race, the distribution of wealth, politics, the family, marriage, ethics, and social reform. In such cases, the absence of all the facts is very liable to produce seriously erroneous results. The materials of astronomy or geology present no such stimuli to the emotions, and in these sciences theories suggested by a few facts would thus seem less liable to be far removed from the truth. It is not only the complexity of social phenomena that makes the science of society so difficult, but also the emotional nature of the material. It is probable that the application of logic has helped very little to make these theories less unreal. Perhaps criticisms by those whose emotional associations are contrariwise has helped more.

These foregoing remarks appear to be applicable to the use of facts in general rather than to the use of statistics in particular. But the distorting influence of emotion seems to be so strong that the exacting requirements of science are not met except by great precision, such precision as is found in the quantitative method and in refined statistical analysis. Often rough and loose handling of facts is not enough. This disturbing element of feeling is particularly potent in social philosophies, in social programs, and in social problems strongly influenced by ethical considerations.

Where the Statistical Method is Used

The use of statistics in the social sciences is comparatively recent. Scant statistical data were collected a century ago. Statistical method grew out of mathematics, particularly out of studies in probability. The method was applied to various types of practical measurement and was found particularly useful in astronomy. That part of sociology in which statistics has found widest use is demography. In taking censuses, various nations have for a century or more made records of a number of attributes of population, such as age, sex, mental condition, race, and occupation. Very intensive work has been done, particularly in vital statistics; and in the field of public health the statistical method is widely used. States have collected for some time good records regarding the status of various industries, especially agriculture. Statistics are also obtainable where data have been measured in terms of money, as, for instance, prices, wealth, debts, taxation, trade, and income. Physical production is now being measured and recorded in different areas and for different industries. Statistics is also rather highly developed in the study of conditions affecting labor in industry, such as hours of labor, accidents, wages, employment and unemployment, costs of living, strikes, and productivity. Many special statistical investigations have been made of poverty and consumption. A beginning is now being made in subjecting the whole field of business to statistical analysis, and with distinct success. In the field of education, on the governmental side, administration is now quite accurately measured and analyzed, and the pedagogical process is being reduced to measurement in the treatment of grades, psychological tests, and studies of growth. The physiological measurement of men and of races of men is making slow but steady progress, accompanied by refined statistical analyses. Problems of heredity and environment and eugenics are attacked statistically. The data of political elections have been subjected to some statistical analysis. One of the most fruitful applications of statistical work is in the various special studies and investigations of modern social problems. In a survey made in 1924 of the research work being done by members of the American Sociological Society, it was found that one third was of a definitely statistical nature. These special statistical investigations cover a surprisingly wide and varied list of topics. These are some of the more important topics of sociology that are being treated statistically.

As to statistical methodology, much of it is quite generally and widely applicable, such as averages, variation, correlation, probability, curve fitting, sampling, and various other mathematical techniques. But various specialized forms are being developed, useful chiefly in studying social forms. These specialized techniques have been developed in connection with such subjects as index numbers, actuarial work, psychological tests, studies of time series, anthropometry, the questionnaire technique, the case method, varieties of record taking, vital statistics, curve fitting, sampling, and partial correlation. Statistical methodology is becoming specialized in forms of adaptation to various types of subject-matter. About one third of the articles published in the

Journal of the American Statistical Association during the past five years have been concerned primarily with the development of statistical methodology. As methodology in statistics becomes more specialized and differentiated, it becomes more closely integrated with the subject-matter.

These remarks, though they indicate the wide use of statistics, do not give an adequate conception of the rapid extension of the statistical method during the past half-century, during the past decade, or even during the past five years. This extremely rapid growth ought certainly to be considered in trying to predict the future use of statistics in sociology.

WHERE STATISTICAL METHOD IS NOT USED

From the foregoing section the reader will be impressed by the wide use of statistics in sociology, and rightly so. But it must be remembered that the great majority of writing not only does not employ the statistical technique, but is seldom if ever based on quantitative material. Only about six or seven per cent of the members of the American Sociological Society were members of the American Statistical Association in 1924. This scarcity of statistical method in sociology may be seen by observing the writings in the various broad divisions of the sociological field.

In the anthropological phases of sociology statistics is very rarely used. Where it is used most is in physical anthropology, especially in the study of races and environmental influences on man. There have been but few statistical studies of cultures, institutions, and customs of primitive man. While the historical and descriptive method is widely used and growing rapidly in anthropological sociology, the use of statistics will probably be quite limited.

Biological sociology is largely concerned with the theories of evolution as applied to society, qualities of racial stock, and the influence of biological man on culture and of culture on stock. Much of these writings are not at all statistical, but the studies of the qualities of the racial stock are frequently based on statistics, and the most notable use of statistics is in this field.

Social psychology is still largely in the theoretical stage and deals mainly with concepts, definitions, outlines, and valuations. Only in a few detailed and highly specialized studies has statistics been used. The future of statistics in social psychology will depend in part upon the success of measurement in psychology and the perfection of such tools as the psychological tests and the growth of quantitative methods in certain studies of culture.

Historical sociology is becoming distinctly factual, but the facts are rarely quantitative, except in certain phases of economic history and in the study of some more recent phases of social institutions. It seems very probable that historical sociology, which comprises a very large part of sociological writings, will be largely non-statistical.

Social theory has been and still is almost completely devoid of statistics. The majority of sociological works have been in this division of sociology. It is very probable that social theory as such will in the future occupy proportionately a smaller portion of sociological writings and will gradually become better fitted to testing by statistics. A much larger portion of social theory, however, will in the near future be tested by facts of a non-statistical nature, rather than by the statistical method proper.

Political aspects of sociology, particularly theories of the state, liberty, justice, law, and governmental functions, are little touched by the statistical method; however, a beginning has been made of the use of statistics.

It appears, then, that a very large part of sociology is not likely to be in the near future a fertile field for the use of statistics. This is particularly true of the history of earlier movements and institutions, of certain larger theories dealing with concepts and the delineation of factors, treatments of moral codes, accounts of customs, public policies, and larger social programs. Although many modern social and economic problems lend themselves to statistical treatment, a very large number do not. It is hard to see far into the future. A remarkable and an unpredicted change has occurred in the past ten years in the use and valuation of statistics.

CRITICISMS OF THE STATISTICAL METHOD IN SOCIOLOGY

There are, of course, criticisms of the use of statistics in sociology. These criticisms are usually of a rather trivial nature and are frequently made by individuals who are quite ignorant of statistical methods. Very few persons question the fundamental position of statistics in the theory of knowledge, and few doubt its high scientific validity. The criticisms usually deal with the practical aspects of its application. Those that are trivial from a far-reaching viewpoint are mentioned only because throughout this paper the aim h is been to stress the practical and the realistic conditions at the present time.

Some critics find statistics untrustworthy and misleading. There are the so-called statistical lies. This condition is, of course, just the opposite of what statistics stands for — accuracy and fact. The fault is with the inadequate use of the tool and not with the tool itself. It is true, however, that statistical fallacies can be exposed more convincingly than can the fallacies in other types of intellectual work.

The criticism that statistical works are uninteresting and unintelligible seems hardly worthy of comment, except to note that critics should differentiate between what is the discovery of knowledge and what is the spreading of knowledge that has been discovered. Statistics may sometimes be an obstacle in the second process, though of course facts are a check against the distortion in the spreading process of knowledge once discovered.

Moralists and reformers sometimes believe that statistics must always be secondary to purpose and the attainment of the purpose. In their view, statistics neglect values. To them statistics are hardly necessary as a help in defining their desires or an assistance in making their valuation. Furthermore, determination and free will-power are more important than statistics in carrying out their programs. Their feeling about statistical work is that effort put forth in painstaking statistical bits of work might better be spent in action. This attitude is the old argument, in new form, against the limitations of science and determinism. But statistical knowledge helps decidedly in the formulation of desires in social terms, and no program can be carried out by will-power alone. Any constructive program must deal with materials, tools, and processes; otherwise it is unworkable.

A more important criticism is that sociology in its present stage needs to deal with formulation of concepts, delineation of boundaries, evaluations of factors, and preliminary testing by logical criticisms. This is undoubtedly true. But if such theories be constructed with more specific reference to the probable evidence that will prove them, much less waste will occur. Furthermore, such concern with theories does not preclude the use of statistics where feasible.

Before discussing this criticism further, an important corollary to it should be mentioned. It is argued that the great prestige which statisticians give to verification operates to retard the use of initiative and originality. Statistical usage focusses upon phenomena that can be measured, and these phenomena are often selected for study not because of their intrinsic importance but simply because it is easy to get the data and simple to measure them. To these critics many statisticians seem to be "puttering around," as it were, with work that is not of much importance, and yet they receive much approval for such work. The approbation given to statistics is felt to be accompanied by an ostracism of other intellectual work that is not verification. Hence there is a tendency for these research workers to deal only with problems that can be proved with data. Statistics, therefore, becomes tyrannical, retards initiative, does not help in the question of values, deals largely with fragmentary bits of knowledge and neglects the important questions which social beings are most interested in inquiring about.

In reply to such criticisms, statisticians may state that at present, at least, statistics has hardly attained any such dominating position. Theory and ethics rather hold the leadership now, though statistics may soon reach such a position of power. The emphasis upon verification in sciences will not be exclusive of originating ideas, and their construction into hypotheses is as essential to science as the verification of these hypotheses. All that statisticians ask is that these initiatory theories be expressed in propositions that can be tested by the tools of science. Too frequently definitions and analyses and classifications have been unrealistic and artificial, so that when the practice of measurements has developed these theories have had to be abandoned or recast into workable hypotheses.

The critics are right, however, in insisting that statisticians should make no claim to a monopoly of method in sociology. If the method of sociology were exclusively restricted to statistics, the knowledge we should have would be more precise and exact, but it would be very restricted. We certainly know much more about the structure and the functioning of society with regard to such subjects of statistical study as population, production, and death-rates, where statistics is highly developed. Our knowledge may be crude and only approximate in the non-statistical fields, but in a society where we must act and live it is better than none at all. And it should not be forgotten in appraising the relation of statistics to sociology that there may be much science in sociology without statistics. Facts and records that are not subject to treatment according to the laws of large numbers may give sufficient accuracy and verification in many fields for most practical purposes.

Finally, it should be observed that science grows by accumulation. Discoveries, inventions, new knowledge, are added to the existing stock. Furthermore, these new elements are usually very small. Inventions, as additions of something new, are seen after analysis to be not nearly so large as they popularly appear to be. An invention is rather a small step in a process, though its significance may be great. Science is a process growing by small accretions. There are discoveries, big in significance; but their coming is hard to predict and they are rare. The new elements of knowledge are determined in part by the existing elements, and for this reason the addition of a desired element cannot be secured by will-power and enterprise alone. Their appearance is a part of the process, the nature depending upon existing elements. Primitive man needed and desired medical progress as much as modern man, and worked at it as arduously; but modern medical achievements are more dependent upon previously existing elements than upon desire and will-power.

Statisticians are engaged in this accumulative process of bringing together small bits of real knowledge. One may ask if this scientific process of growth by small accretions is helped by the larger speculative theories. Perhaps these theories help less than is customarily supposed. Many of them are discarded, as was the supernaturalism of primitive man. The curiosity of primitive man led him to theorize about the universe and to try to answer questions of great importance to him, but with only slight regard for fact. The result was supernaturalism, which had to be completely discarded as of no help to science. The similarity of social theories to primitive supernaturalism is only slight, for social theories are somewhat closer to facts. Still, much social theory is rather far from fact and will probably be discarded, without having been of any material assistance to the development of science. There is thus some doubt as to how much social theories help in the accumulative process of science; but certainly statisticians are engaged in adding exact knowledge to the existing stock, and thus solidly helping its growth.

SELECTED REFERENCES

Bowley, A. L. *The Measurement of Social Phenomena.* 1915.

Czuber, E. *Wahrscheinlichkeitsrechnung und ihre Anwendung auf Fehlerausgleichung, Statistik und Lebensversicherung.* 1921.

Edgeworth, F. Y. "Observations and Statistics: an Essay on the theory of errors of observations and the first principles of statistics." *Cambridge Philosophical Transactions.* 1885.

Giddings, F. H. *The Scientific Study of Human Society.* 1924.
"The Service of Statistics to Sociology." *Quarterly Publications of the American Statistical Association.* March, 1914.

Hart, Hornell. "Science and Sociology." *American Journal of Sociology,* Nov., 1921.

Julin, Armand. *Principes de Statistique Théorique et Appliquée.* 1921.

Keynes, J. M. *A Treatise on Probability.* 1921.

Koren, John, ed. *The History of Statistics: their Development and Progress in Many Countries.* 1918.

Mayo-Smith, Richmond. *Statistics and Sociology.* 1895.

Merz, J. T. "On the Statistical View of Nature." *A History of European Thought in the Nineteenth Century.* 1912.

Mills, F. C. "On Measurement in Economics." *The Trend of Economics,* R. G. Tugwell, ed. 1924.

Mitchell, W. C. "Quantitative Analysis in Economic Theory." *American Economic Review.* March, 1925.
"Statistics and Government." *Quarterly Publications of the American Statistical Association.* March, 1919.

Moore, H. L. *Laws of Wages.* 1911.

Niceforo, Alfredo. *La Méthode Statistique et ses Applications aux Sciences Naturelles, aux Sciences Sociales, et à l'Art.* 1925.

Pearl, Raymond. *Medical Biometry and Statistics.* 1923.

Pearson, Karl. *The Grammar of Science.* 1911.

Venn, John. *The Logic of Chance.* 1888.

Westergaard, Harold. "Scope and Method of Statistics." *Quarterly Publications of the American Statistical Association,* Sept., 1916.

Yule, G. V. *An Introduction to the Theory of Statistics.* 1922.

CHAPTER XXXI
THE SOCIAL SCIENCES AND BIOLOGY
By FRANK H. HANKINS
SMITH COLLEGE

Historical Background: Malthus and Spencer

THE definite emergence of biological viewpoints in the social sciences considerably antedates the development of the Darwinian theory of natural selection. There were, on the one hand, the writings of Franklin, Malthus, and others dealing with the economic and social significance of man's propagative instincts and capacities, and on the other, the writings of Kant, Fichte, and Hegel, presenting the concept of society as an organism with a consciousness, a will, and a destiny all its own. It was, however, at least in the English-speaking world, the writings of Spencer and Darwin, establishing the modern evolutionary theory, that centered the attention of many scholars on the significance of the new biology for man and society.

The new approach did not displace but tended rather to supplement and give new meaning to the older theories. Thus, the work of Darwin and Wallace was admittedly inspired by Malthus's famous *Essay*. While the Malthusian doctrine clearly implied a struggle for existence and a consequent selection, it limited its attention primarily to the rate of multiplication and the consequent implications for political, economic, and ethical theories. Even in the antecedent *Observations on the Increase of Mankind* (1751), Benjamin Franklin had reached a fairly clear perception of the struggle for existence, not only among men but throughout animate nature. But it had passed almost unnoticed. Not only was Malthus in his thinking unaware of the immense philosophical and scientific significance of his own implications, but his work did not, at the time, result in a new biological orientation. Another half-century of discussion was needed to make the broader aspects of excessive fecundity clear.

In his famous essay, "A Theory of Population Deduced from the General Law of Animal Fertility,"[1] Spencer had taken direct

[1] *Westminster Review*, 1852, elaborated as part VI of *The Principles of Biology*.

dissent from Doubleday's hypothesis,[1] that excessive feeding checks fecundity whereas limited or deficient nutriment stimulates it, and had advanced the hypothesis of an opposition between individuation or individual development and activity, and genesis or reproductive fecundity. This doctrine rested on the fundamental principle of Spencer's general theory of evolution as an equilibration of energy, which, translated into biological terms, implied a constant tendency throughout the organic world toward more perfect adaptation. Such adaptation was to be accomplished by the survival of the fittest brought about by the struggle consequent upon excessive fecundity. On the physiological plane the doctrine implied the evolution of larger and more complicated brain and nerve structures. On the social plane it implied a movement of social organization and institutions toward that state of perfection represented by an anarchistic Utopia peopled only by highly intelligent, thoroughly moral persons of feeble passions. For it was imagined by Spencer, under the seducing effects of his own generalizations, that man would move toward such an adjustment to a controlled and well-regulated nature, that life would be long and population would become stationary through an equilibrium of births and deaths. Meanwhile the increased development of man's brain would, in consequence of the inherent opposition of self-development and reproductive capacity, have brought it about that his natural unrestrained fecundity would have fallen to somewhat above two children per married couple, or only enough to maintain the equilibrium of births and deaths.

Before passing on to Darwin we may pause to note the judgment of a half-century and more on some of Spencer's views. In the identification of evolution with progress there was in Spencer a fundamental contradiction. Though he expressly stated that evolution meant only a more perfect adaptation and therefore produced deterioration of function and structure as well as elaboration,[2] his *Sociology* and *Ethics* are pervaded with the implication that human nature and social institutions will develop toward certain ideals predetermined in the mind of the philosopher. In these pretentious idealizations Spencer was wholly illogical. If the fundamental law of life is equilibration between organism and environment, then no final goal can be reached in a changing universe; and

[1] *True Law of Population.*
[2] Cf. especially the passage in *Principles of Sociology*, part II, par. 50.

the end of all change will be death, absolute and universal. Until that end is reached social forms may pass through many periods of development and devolution, in each of which progress, in the sense of movement toward certain human ideals, in some respects may be accompanied by retrogression in other respects. This means merely that under the infinite variability of circumstance there arises an infinite variety of social forms, customs, and institutions each adapted to the special conditions producing it. This also means that there is a vast difference between evolution and progress. Spencer was so thoroughly imbued with the notion that there was a mysterious tendency in man to move through certain steps to certain ideal ends that he did not succeed in avoiding the fallacies of the old philosophy of history. His view was largely responsible for the orthogenetic evolutionary school of anthropologists which held that societies travel through certain inevitable stages from savagery to civilization. The theory of evolution warrants no such rationalizations. Retrogression is as evolutionary as advancement, for evolution posits only a universal causation. What a pity that sociologists cannot grasp this idea, stop their pious moralizing, and place their work under the same logic and criteria which have made science the greatest boon man has yet discovered!

Spencer anticipated that human fecundity would decline with an increase in brain and nerve structure and increased demands on human energies for nervous growth and multiplied activities. But no such increase in nervous organization has occurred. Moreover, Professor Carr-Saunders [1] has collected a mass of evidence to show that the potential fecundity increases with advancement in civilization, owing to the increased quantity, variety, and regularity of food, and the greater protection from the elements and bacterial enemies which increased knowledge gives. That the increased wear and tear, especially the increased nervous strain of our complicated society, causes some reduction in the fecundity of the cultivated classes to-day is indicated by Professor Raymond Pearl's demonstration [2] that farmers are more active sexually than professional men. Spencer was clearly right in contending that the energies of the organism cannot be expended for growth, maintenance of bodily warmth, resistance to weather extremes, and simi-

[1] *The Population Problem*, 1922, especially chap. v.
[2] *The Biology of Population Growth*, 1925, chap. viii.

lar drains, and still be available for propagation. But he erred seriously in assuming a continuous organic evolution of man.

It is convenient here to consider also the development of the organismic analogies. Following Spencer, though to some extent independently, numerous writers exhausted human ingenuity in finding analogies between society and organisms. In this gay intellectual sport Paul Lilienfeld in Germany, Albert Schaeffle in Austria, and Alfred Fouillée, René Worms, and Jacques Novicow in France were the prize-winners, although similar comparisons are widely scattered throughout the literature of all the social sciences.[1] Spencer had never deluded himself into thinking that society was truly an organism. He was careful to point out that the likenesses were only analogies, and that there was the fundamental difference that parts of organisms are unified whereas the members of society are discrete, have central censoriums, and constitute the only feeling and acting units. He thus concluded that the only genuine analogy between society and an organism is the mutual dependence of parts in both. Society, he held, is not comparable to any particular type of organism, plant or animal; it is superorganic.[2] If such a conclusion satisfied Spencer's individualistic political philosophy, it was far from satisfactory to the French extremists, Worms and Novicow, who did not hesitate to call society an organism pure and simple and to argue that sociology would make no progress toward scientific realism until it fully accepted that concept.

We cannot here trace the ramifications of these conceptions. It seems quite impossible to think of society in its totality, whether as body politic, as an enduring economic concern, or as an evolving community, without resort to organismic terms. Moreover, fundamental problems of all the social sciences are involved in the question whether state or community be end or means. The fact of the matter would seem to be that society, or the state as the comprehensive social institution, must be viewed as an entity with a life of its own, to which, in the long run, the interests of individuals are subordinated. One of the basic conditions affecting all the social sciences is this: the individual struggle for existence is so dominated by the group struggle that in all matters vital to the

---

[1] Cf. Ward, L. F., "Contemporary Sociology." *American Journal of Sociology*, VII, 1902, p. 479 *et seq.*

[2] *Principles of Sociology*, part II, especially chap. XII.

whole group the individual becomes a means and not an end. Man is both gregarious and self-dependent, social and individual, altruistic and selfish. If he appears to be an end in times of peace, he is ruthlessly sacrificed in times of group crisis. The individual has rights, but they are, in fact, only the privilege of acting in his own interests so long as his interests and his mode of satisfying them do not conflict with the purposes of organized society. The social group grants the individual no greater extension of rights than it believes to be in its own interest, and never holds even these inviolable in times of crisis. The truly Leviathan character of the social organization is thus revealed. Indeed, on its negative side, the after-war conditions in Austria, Russia, and elsewhere evidenced the significance of the organic view of the social whole, for in the absence of those infinitely numerous, varied, and delicate adjustments which make a nation a going concern, millions of individuals starved and anarchy reigned over realms of death and desolation. Whole civilizations thus rise and fall as unitary phases of world history.

Society is, thus, much more than mere mechanical juxtaposition of individuals; it is a finely integrated and delicately balanced system of relationships which give it life, power, and sufficient permanency to play a rôle in the universal drama. Society shapes the individual's personality, gives him purpose, and sets him to work for himself in order to serve it.[1] Because of man's gregariousness and his mental powers, society becomes, as Professor Giddings says, interstimulation and response, out of which are built cooperation, concerted volition, and the multiform elements of social culture which in turn become the agents of social control and the integration of minds. Religion appears to be "a group sentiment of safety."[2] Ethical codes regulate individual behavior in the group interest. Economic organization, domestic arrangements, laws, principles of justice, the power of political agencies, are all justified and modified by the criterion of group power and welfare. One must also observe, however, that if man be thus gregarious and subject to social domination, he is also the only feeling and calculating social unit; he is individualistic to a degree. In consequence, those individuals who are shrewd and bold, especially if equipped with

[1] Cf. Follett, M. P., "Community is a Process." *Philosophy Review*, XXVIII, 1919, pp. 576–88.
[2] Ward, L. F., *Pure Sociology*, p. 185.

special knowledge or skill, may flout the racial and social interests more or less successfully. All the social sciences are thus more or less entangled in dilemmas growing out of man's dual nature. In politics this gives rise to the antinomy of liberty and authority; in economics, to that of individualism versus socialism in all their variations; in ethics, to the dualism of codes regulating in-group and out-group relations. The facts thus warrant no extreme positions; these oppositions of principle are inherent in the nature of man and society. The latter is not an organism; and yet its organic nature cannot be overlooked.[1]

DARWINISM AND SOCIAL LIFE

It was, however, the works of Darwin that reset the stage for a presentation of the rôle of biological factors in human destiny. *The Origin of Species* contained a vast illumination of the significance of that surplus fecundity which Franklin and Malthus had emphasized. This entailed a struggle for existence involving the elimination of the ill-adapted, and reproduction through the better-adapted. The universal variation among the individuals of a species was in this manner given a profound meaning for both individual and race. There was also emphasis on the importance of heredity, and on the effects of domestication and of geographical environment. Immediately numerous minds were set going on the significance of the new biological foundation for social philosophy, and this impetus was even accentuated by the discussion in *The Descent of Man* and *Selection in Relation to Sex* of man's genealogical history. The denial of the special creation of man and the advancement of a mechanistic explanation of his evolution from lower animal forms constituted an even greater revolution in dominant modes of thought than resulted from the creation of new heavens by Copernicus. The heliocentric view, disturbing as it was, nevertheless affected only slightly man's conception of himself as the special object of divine solicitude. But the natural-history view of man not only struck a vital blow to prevailing theistic philosophies but forced a reconsideration of fundamental questions of psychology, ethics, politics, and sociology, gave a fresh impetus to anatomy, physiology, anthropology, and archæology, and a new

[1] For a restatement of the organic theory with fresh arguments for its validity, cf. Arthur Dendy, *The Biological Foundations of Society*, chap. III; a more acute analysis reaching conclusions very similar to Spencer's is made by R. Austin Freeman, *Social Decay and Regeneration*, chaps. III and IV.

orientation to general biology, zoölogy, botany, geology, and palæontology. In fact, all the phenomena and institutions of social life have come to be treated under the biological evolutionary conceptions of variation about types and patterns, of continuous change, of struggle for survival and selective elimination, and of adaptation. Indeed, under the suggestive impulsion of the universal nisus of organic life in developing countless varieties to fit every nook and corner of the physical world, Henri Bergson (and before him Lester F. Ward) readapted even the theory of creation to evolutionary concepts. Thus, Darwinian evolutionism exerted a revolutionary influence on the whole of modern thought. By bringing man and all his works within the scheme of a mechanistic natural order, Darwin freed all the social sciences from the benumbing fears of religious authoritarianism and the paralyzing certainties of transcendental philosophizings.

Variation, Heredity, and Environment in Relation to Individual Differences

We need not here enter upon an outline of the primary tenets of Darwinism and their rejection, modification, and further development through the researches of Weismann, De Vries, Mendel, Wilson, Morgan, Jennings, and others. With a minimum of reference to biological technicalities we may proceed at once to a discussion of the significance of certain concepts for an understanding of man and his institutions.

There is no exception to the fact that individuals, though belonging to the same general stock, differ one from another. Moreover, the work of Galton and Pearson, following on that of Adolphe Quételet, has made it clear that the statistical distribution of the variates of a fairly homogeneous population takes a form more or less like the curve of the distribution of chances. That this general form holds for all traits seems indicated by a multitude of anthropometric, educational, and psychological researches using modern statistical methods. In the ideal case of symmetrical distribution the variations result from the random combinations of an infinitude of minute factors each of which has an equal probability of being either present or absent. That was the original assumption of the Darwinian biometricians, but in practice it is found that this idealized form rarely occurs — that it is only approximated more or less roughly. This lack of symmetry may be due (1) to the smallness of the group studied, which brings into play the variability of samples from a general population; (2) to the lack of fundamental homogeneity in the hereditary factors present in the population, as when two or more racial elements are mixed in unequal proportions; (3) to the unit of measurement itself, which may or may not be directly expressive of the underlying natural factors; or (4) to a fundamental lack of equality in the chances of some combinations as compared with others. That is, there may be a certain prepotency or dominance in the hereditability, or at least in the measurable manifestation, of certain traits as compared with their opposites. While, therefore, one may be certain that a reasonably homogeneous group will show variation about typical or modal values, the assumption of normal distribution is only a convenient hypothesis in the absence of adequate facts from which the actual form may be deduced.[1]

The primary question, then, has to do with the source of the variations in physical and mental characteristics observable among people living together in the same society. In the first place, it is so evident that both heredity and environment are important that we have on the one hand the Galton-Pearson biometric school and the "mental testers" claiming that heredity is nearly the whole cause, and environment scarcely measurable in its influence; and on the other hand, a vast number of sincere students, mostly non-biologists, educators, social workers, and democratic idealists, who find the hereditary factor negligible, and environment, experience, and training alone worthy of serious consideration. The development of modern genetics under the stimulus of Mendel, showing that inheritance is carried on by means of genes or "discrete packets of diverse chemicals"[2] arranged systematically in the chromosomes like beads on a string, each gene being unchanging and unchangeable, tended greatly to strengthen the case for heredity. It did, in fact, establish beyond peradventure of doubt that these genetic factors do set a definite limit to the possible development of the individual constitution.

But there is also no doubt, in view of the experimentation of the last few years, that the assumption that a given set of genetic factors would manifest themselves willy-nilly in a perfectly definite

---

[1] Cf. for a very clear and keen discussion of this matter, E. G. Boring, "The Logic of the Normal Law of Error in Mental Measurement." *American Journal of Psychology*, XXXI, 1920; pp. 1–33.

[2] Jennings, H. S., "Heredity and Environment." *The Scientific Monthly*, XIX, 1924, pp. 225–38.

physical form was carried altogether too far.   This assumption was derived from the grossly simple and now questionable conception of unit characters.   One may recall here some of the early work of the American geneticists, led by Professor Charles B. Davenport, in which it was assumed that not merely eye-color, hair-color, skin-color, and so on, were unit characters, but also a multitude of psychic traits including, among other vague and little understood conditions, wanderlust, feeble-mindedness, and epilepsy.   All that was a gross simplification.   It is found that at least fifty genes are coördinated in the production of so simple a trait as eye-color in Drosophila.   The genetic factors that enter into a man are, therefore, exceedingly numerous, numbering scores of thousands. Through their interaction with one another, with the egg cytoplasm and with the nourishing blood stream, the embryonic development is achieved.   There is indubitable proof that in the simple organisms this development is more or less plastic, so that different traits may be produced from the same genetic factors by different environments.[1]   And yet such alterations are more or less narrowly limited with respect to each trait; and different organisms vary greatly in their manifestation of measurable alterations in response to environmental changes.   Simple organisms are much more plastic than highly complex ones.   Moreover, and most important of all, whether there shall be any response at all and the very nature of the response to fresh environmental stimuli, are determined by the genetic factors themselves.

These factors thus show a certain plasticity of response to environmental conditions, a fact which must not be confused with the wholly unproven inheritance of acquired characters.   If this be true below the human level, it must be true to some extent of human inheritance also.   One must be extremely skeptical, however, of sweeping conclusions relating to man but drawn from laboratory experiments on plants, fruit-flies, and salamanders, or the alcoholization of guinea pigs and chickens.   All the evidence available indicates that the human hereditary constitution is remarkably stable, that, as regards the physical make-up, like produces like with little variability traceable to such variations in environmental conditions as are found among people of the same society.[2]   Nu-

[1] For a brilliant over-statement of this fact see H. S. Jennings, *Prometheus or Biology and the Advancement of Man.*
[2] Cf. for a report of numerous experiments, S. J. Holmes, *Studies in Evolution and Eugenics*, pp. 40–45.

merous researches of the biometricians show this constancy of physical resemblance of parents and children and the relatively slight effects of environmental differences. While, therefore, the new biology compels one to speak of heredity *and* environment rather than heredity *or* environment, one is led astray if he concludes that the weight of the two factors is always the same. Their relative importance in any particular instance can be determined only by the biometrical methods making use of the coefficient of correlation, or by the Mendelian method of tracing traits from one generation to another. In either case one must conclude from present evidence that for the physical traits, the hereditary factors of individual development are much weightier than the environmental variations occurring within any social group.[1]

The crucial case, however, relates to mental ability. Under the stimulus of modern democratic idealism and the almost religious attachment to the gospel of education, there is an overweening desire to set the mental traits in a class by themselves. The steady accumulation of critical data, however, from the earliest researches of Galton [2] to the latest findings of the mental testers, all consistently points to the same conclusion, namely, that the general level of intellectual power is inherited. The brain and nerve structures, the basis of all psychic powers, are inherited according to the same genetic principles as govern other physical organs. The evidence for this is not merely the general fact that humans have human brains, nor merely the specific fact that special types of brain, as white or negro, are inherited, but the still more specific fact that feeble-mindedness runs in families, as does also superior mental ability, even to certain kinds of highly specialized capacities, such as musical and artistic ability.[3] An extremely important piece of corroborating evidence is the relative constancy of the mental level.[4] And a still further corroboration of quite equal importance

[1] For popular summaries of many researches see *Eugenics Laboratory Lecture Series.*

[2] *Hereditary Genius.*

[3] One may refer here to the various studies of Galton, Thorndike, Newman and Merriam on twins; the Eugenics Record Office studies of *The Nam Family, The Hill Folk;* Professor Goddard's *The Kallikaks;* A. E. Winship's *The Jukes-Edwards;* and similar works.

[4] Cf. Baldwin, B. T., and Stecher, Lorle I., *Mental Growth Curve of Normal and Superior Children, University of Iowa Studies in Child Welfare,* II, no. 1, 1922; Hollingworth, L. S., *The Psychology of Subnormal Children;* Rosenow, C., "The Stability of the Intelligence Quotient," *Journal of Delinquency,* v, 1920, pp. 160–73; Terman, L. M., *The Intelligence of School Children,* chap. IX, and "Mental Growth of the I.Q.," *Journal of Educational Psychology,* XII, 1921, pp. 325–41.

is the high correlation among mental capacities or performances in different types of activity.[1]

If, then, mental level or brain power is fundamentally a matter of inheritance, environment — in which is included every factor of experience, education, and specific training — appears primarily responsible for the cultivation of habits, tastes, and social manners, general modes of behavior, and points of view.   But as we are considering only the differences among persons in the same society, we must note here that the underlying hereditary constitution is the primary factor in determining the ease and perfection of achievement in these matters.   At the Vineland, New Jersey, Training School the effort to teach low-grade feeble-minded children to read is no longer considered worth while.   At the other extreme very high-grade children learn to read almost of their own efforts.[2]   The well-endowed not only learn more rapidly but they continue to learn longer, and are thus able to move up the social scale to higher levels. Then, it seems highly probable that inheritance is primarily responsible for certain character traits which are often as important for success in life as mental level.   Here are such qualities as level of energy, resistance and hardihood of constitution, slowness or rapidity of movement, stolidity or affectability of temperament, aggressiveness or timidity of disposition.

We reach the conclusion, then, that there is a continuous gradation of natural ability; that differentiating grades include idiot, imbecile, moron, borderline, dull, retarded, normal, superior, gifted or talented, brilliant or potential geniuses.[3]   That there is a correlation between social status and physical quality is shown by the variation in height with occupational level and the relative frequency of congenital defects by social status.   That there is a correlation between social status and mental ability is demonstrated by the army psychologists who found a gradation of median intelligence from C− for laborers, general miners, and teamsters, through C for various types of skilled workers, and B for dentists, mechanical draftsmen, accountants, and civil engineers, to A for engineer officers.   It certainly could not be claimed that such results were exact or definitive: on the other hand, it may be insisted

[1] Cf. Hollingworth, L. S., *Special Talents and Defects;* Thorndike, E. L., "On the Organization of Intellect," *Psychological Review,* 1921.

[2] Cf. the very notable *Genetic Studies of Genius,* i, ii, by L. S. Terman, and others, Stanford University Press.

[3] Cf. Wallin, J. E. W., *The Education of Handicapped Children.*

that they correspond more or less closely with a vast quantity of additional data. No one, I suppose, would be inclined to doubt that unskilled workers are in brain power on an average inferior by inheritance to skilled workers, as are the latter to men in the professions.[1] For these different grades of natural ability the social environment, education, and training can never be equalized.[2] It is the human organism that is dynamic, not the environment. If it is the environment that selects the responses which shall have value for survival or for success in life, it is the organism that determines whether there shall be a response, and if so, what. It results that some find the means of personal salvation where many remain starved and stunted.

Such views have a pertinent bearing on the gospel of democracy. It can no longer be contended that men are equal in any respect — physical, mental or moral, civil, political, or economic. Nor does there appear to be any process of education or training whereby they can be made any more equal than they are now. It has often been pointed out that there is an antagonism between liberty and equality, because under a system of individual liberty inherent differences result in inequalities of intellectual attainment, economic resources, and political and social prestige. But it has not often been realized that an increase and a diversification of opportunities for education and training have the effect of increasing the differences among men instead of diminishing them. This is an amazing result in view of the fact that the primary tenet in the democratic philosophy has come to be a demand for an ever greater equalization of opportunity.

But it should be observed that the growth of modern democracy has been accompanied by an enormous increase in the differentiation of social life. The division of labor has intensified social integration and multiplied the complexity of social adjustments which the individual must make if he is to count among the successful. This process has made necessary a vast extension of facilities for education and training as means of expediting the formation of

---

[1] Cf. *Memoirs of the National Academy of Sciences*, xv, chap. 15, "Intelligence Rating of Occupational Groups"; also Bridges, J. W., and Coler, L. E., "The Relation of Intelligence to Social Status," *Psychological Review*, xxiv, 1917, pp. 1–31; Brimhall, D. R., "Family Resemblances Among American Men of Science," *American Nation*, a series in vols. 56 and 57.

[2] Cf. in addition to the foregoing references: Hopkins, L. T., *The Intelligence of Continuation-School Children in Massachusetts;* and Stedman, L. M., *Education of Gifted Children.*

habits and the spread of ideas essential for such individual adjustment. But these efforts have not prevented a widening of the extremes of wealth, of political power, and individual prestige. Social stratification is, no doubt, somewhat less rigid; it has many more layers, as befits a complex organization; but it exists and in its main outlines resembles the caste systems of more simple communities. Many family strains have remained at much the same social level through the revolutionary social changes of the last century. Democracy itself has come in practice to accept the fact of inherent inequality and has begun to establish schemes of manual training for those of low mentality quite different from the general education of the mass, which is still different from the highly specialized and technical training of the superior. There is in this a rough process of social selection. There is an elimination from the public schools at nearly every grade, but more marked after the sixth. The very high mortality of the dull and backward would be greatly increased if standards were elevated slightly. Even as it is the high schools belong to the classes and are seldom attained by the children of the masses. It is often argued that a college education enormously increases the chances of success; but it is truer to say that a very large proportion of those who have the ability to achieve distinction take a college education on the way. Opportunity means nothing to those who lack some of the mental or character traits to seize it; while, on the other hand, the capable find opportunity where the incapable see only hindrance.

The individualistic democracy of the eighteenth and early nineteenth centuries gradually gives way, therefore, to increasing state regulation. We may here note only one phase of this, the increasing community control of the relatively incapable. Experience seems to demonstrate the value of preserving as large a scope for individual initiative as is consistent with the similar privileges of others. Personal responsibility is the basis of the moral order. And yet the state has gradually extended its control over wider and wider classes of persons. Here are included first the criminal and definitely anti-social; then the insane, deaf-mute, and blind; and later still the epileptic and the feeble-minded. These categories are being gradually widened. Meanwhile, the increasing complexity of the social order has compelled the state to place more or less under its special protection large masses of proletarian workers by organizing for them insurance schemes against the effects of accident, unemployment, sickness, and old age. Thus, millions of individuals in European countries and increasing numbers in America are given a special social status somewhat below those who enjoy all the dignities of free citizenship.[1] Such status is roughly a recognition of biological fact. Even individual liberty rests on organic soundness and fitness; and there is no social arrangement which will prevent the inherently shrewd and clever, the energetic and persistent, from acquiring more power and personal freedom than their opposites.

Space does not permit the further elaboration of these points in relation to political democracy. Suffice it to say that the old doctrine of *vox populi vox dei* appears to be utter nonsense. The voice of the people is too often only the voice of ignorance, superstition, fear, and bewildered minds. Democracy becomes a helpless and panic-stricken mob in the absence of capable leaders. The danger of democracy is not its unwillingness to follow; it must perforce do that like a flock of sheep. The danger is threefold; first, that it may not develop a sufficient number of capable leaders; secondly, that it, like the European countries in 1914, may be deceived and led to its own slaughter by clever and ambitious men; and thirdly, that the growing complexity of culture may make too great a strain on republican institutions.

Only one point further can here be made in relating the findings of differential biology to the economic order, namely, the importance of finding out the capabilities of each individual as early as possible, adapting his training thereto, and guiding him into suitable occupational pursuits. In the present state of knowledge such a scheme dare not approach rigidity. There must be sufficient flexibility of direction to allow for the ignorance of educators and the unforeseeable latencies of individual development. A start has been made in this direction and it promises much for individual well being and for social efficiency. It points to the realization of the Platonic ideal of justice, a social organization in which every man will fit according to his capacities.

Space does not permit an adequate application of the theory of organic variation to the problem of human leadership. In the much-debated question of the origins of great men, one thing seems perfectly clear, namely, that men who achieve a genuine distinction are superior by nature. They arise from all social ranks and arrive

[1] Cf. Belloc, Hilaire, *The Servile State.*

at their elevation often by the most unexpected paths. The fecundity of the upper classes in persons of superior endowment appears to be distinctly greater than that of the lower classes.[1] In the second place, and contrary to popular superstition, God does not raise up adequate leaders in every social crisis. Nor, in the third place, is there any ground for supposing that the quantity of potential genius of a high order is uniform from period to period. On the contrary, really eminent ability is extremely rare, and, like the rare combinations in the theory of probabilities, almost certain to appear with a marked irregularity.

In answer to the question whether their number can be consciously increased, biology replies, "Yes, by selective reproduction." But on the human plane this matter is not simple. We do not want any of that fantastic type of eugenics which a decade and more ago regaled the world with the prospect of specialized breeds of musicians, artists, stevedores, and ditch-diggers. Such specialized breeding seems neither desirable nor possible. Superiority runs in families and tends to be preserved by assortative mating; the spread of eugenic propaganda may increase this tendency. There is some ground for believing that race crossing tends to increase the frequency of superior types. In any case, there can be little doubt that a complex demotic group supplies a wider diversity of talent than a racially pure one. There is a popular faith that education will greatly increase the supply of genius. But education and social opportunity do not create superior ability. If one compares England before and after popular education, or a nation in which little attention is given to popular education, such as France, with one like the United States where it is an object of deep solicitude, one may almost query whether it may not be an inhibitor rather than an accelerator in the development of first-rate talent. Moreover, there is no indication that the effects of education are inherited. This is a most fortunate provision. When one reflects on the enormous amount of bad teaching, bad environment, bad habit formation, and evil experiences of one sort and another, which affect all persons more or less, no feature of organic life appears more fortunate from the social viewpoint than the protection of inheritance against all influences which do not reach the germ cells themselves.

[1] For a very recent contribution cf. S. S. Visher, "A Study of the Type of the Place of Birth and of the Occupation of Fathers of Subjects of Sketches in *Who's Who in America*," *American Journal of Sociology*, xxx, 1925, pp. 551–57.

There thus seems little of a positive sort that a society can do to increase its fecundity in men of super-talent.

There has recently been an enormous furore over the question of racial differences, but with more heat than illumination. The study of biological variations furnishes the key to the correct viewpoint. It is observed in the study of related species, whether paramœcia, sweet corn, or guinea pigs, that there is an overlapping in the statistical distribution of traits. The same sort of overlapping is found in the stature, head form, and other traits of physical man; it is found in the distribution of the intelligence quotient of children whether taken (1) by contiguous ages, (2) by contiguous school grades, (3) by social classes as shown by the occupations of the fathers, (4) by nationality, or (5) by races. The same fact of differences of norm or type but overlapping distribution is found also in the mental scores of adult males whether taken (1) by occupation, (2) by nationality, or (3) by race.[1]

We thus have an enlightening principle. With reference to any particular trait one so-called race differs from another more or less as to type but with a greater or lesser degree of overlapping in the statistical distribution of individual members. Since all races are human, differences must be those of degree or quantity rather than those of kind or quality. There are, thus, differences in average stature, average complexion, average cephalic index, average size of brain, and average mental ability. Such a viewpoint warrants neither the violent rantings and fantastic claims of Gobineau, Stoddard, or McDougall in their well-known works, nor the obfuscating dust-throwing of certain dogmatists of racial equality. It does warrant the tentative conclusion, however, if one may take the results of recent researches as indicative, that fully one-fourth of the Negro Americans are superior in native intelligence to the average of the so-called Nordic Americans.

It warrants the conclusion also that a genuinely sound immigration policy would select immigrants, not on the basis of race or nationality, but on the basis of physical and mental fitness. It is

[1] Cf. the *Memoirs of the National Academy of Sciences*, xv; Brigham, C. C., *A Study of American Intelligence;* Ferguson, G. O., "The Psychology of the Negro," *Archives of Psychology*, no. 36, 1916; Garth, T. R., "The Results of Some Tests on Full and Mixed Blood Indians," *Journal of Applied Psychology*, v, 1921, pp. 359–72; Pressey, S. L., and Teter, G. F., "A Comparison of Colored and White Children," *Journal of Applied Psychology*, III, 1919, pp. 277–82; Young, Kimball, "Mental Differences in Certain Immigrant Groups," *University of Oregon Publishers*, no. 11, 1922; and similar studies.

frequently objected that race mixture is itself a source of deterioration, but genetic research indicates that neither outbreeding nor inbreeding are likely to be injurious to quality provided the stock is sound to begin with.[1] Superior Italians mated with superior Germans will almost certainly give rise to superior offspring. Races too diverse may be excluded for social, if not for biological, reasons. Otherwise it would seem that America might establish a system of unrestricted immigration of persons who in physique and mental level exceed the average of the native population.

THE STRUGGLE FOR EXISTENCE AND NATURAL SELECTION

It is often stated that natural selection has ceased to operate on man. Nothing could be further from the truth. Not only has natural selection not ceased to operate, but there is no conceivable social arrangement that could bring about such a condition. What is usually meant by such a statement is, perhaps, that the human species have ceased to evolve toward a higher form. According to Darwinism excessive fecundity results in a struggle for existence out of which arise new varieties through the selection for survival and reproduction of the better-adapted varieties. But it is not certain that natural selection does produce new varieties; its main function, in any case, is to preserve the adapted. One must rid himself of the notion that natural selection always favors the superior, as judged by certain human valuations. It is not necessarily progressive in its influence, though in its narrow connotation as commonly used it operates to preserve racial soundness by preserving the strong and eliminating the weak. In a broad and inclusive sense, however, every social arrangement or situation is selective in that it tends to favor the multiplication of certain types rather than their opposites. In this sense even reversed selection is a type of natural selection operating through the same methods to alter the hereditary composition of the population. From the standpoint of biology the fundamental question of civilization is how the totality of selective processes, of which there are a multitude, are affecting the inheritance of those qualities essential for leadership and social coöperation.

Natural selection operates in two ways, through differential death-rates (selective mortality or lethal selection) and through differential birth-rates (selective fecundity or reproductive selection).

[1] Cf. East, E. M., and Jones, D. F., *Inbreeding and Outbreeding.*

In both ways it produces its effects through the contribution which different types make to the composition of the next generation. There can be no doubt that both methods operate on man. Space does not permit the summation of the voluminous evidence which has been accumulating since the early work of Galton, Jacoby, Hansen, Ammon, and Lapouge on social selection, to the more precise work of Pearson, Pearl, and other biometricians and eugenicists. They have made it plain that just as families come and go, so the composition of the various social classes, nobles, aristocrats, burghers, and peasants undergo a constant flux of heritable elements.[1]

Certainly the conclusion may be drawn from the evidence of differential birth- and death-rates that the quality of the population fluctuates from generation to generation. As Darwin said, there is no inherent tendency of man to progress. This is true both organically and socially. Professor Pearson in one of his soundest investigations has shown that one half of those born in one generation descend from one eighth of those born in the preceding generation.[2] One is, therefore, warranted in picturing the average hereditary qualities of any community as varying up and down over a greater or lesser range in consequence of climatic, bacterial, and social factors. It seems clear also that western nations with their marked urbanization are more subject to the effects of differential fecundity now than a few generations ago. There is a vicious process, noted two generations ago by Ammon, Hansen, and Vacher de Lapouge,[3] whereby the city attracts the able, energetic, and ambitious from the country and in one or two generations sterilizes them. There is thus a certain folk depletion of the countryside. While this process is in its ascendant phase the highly complex and dynamic life of the cities and hence the whole culture of the community may be rapidly progressive, growing in color, complexity, and quality of achievement in many directions. It seems to occur during such a phase that city populations, having drawn to themselves an undue proportion of the best blood of the nation, are strikingly more fecund in superior men and women than the countryside. Indeed, in the latter appear areas of more or less complete

[1] For a list of pertinent references see various sections in Holmes, S. J., *Bibliography of Eugenics*.

[2] Popularized in "The Groundwork of Eugenics," *Eugenics Laboratory Lectures Series*, no. 2, 1909.

[3] See Ripley, W. L., *Races of Europe*, chap. xx.

stagnation inhabited by an obviously inferior stock. But it is not improbable that a final effect of these processes is to increase the complexity and delicacy of the social organization at the very time that the potential fecundity of the population in superior types of ability is being undermined so that civilization collapses of its own weight.

Practical policies to meet this situation are not easy to formulate. In the long run the natural processes are inexorable. Christian sympathy and altruism would preserve the unworthy at the expense of the race and of civilization. On the other hand, a ruthless destruction of the unfit is unthinkable. Some mild efforts to curb the inferior are being made through segregation in various types of institutions and colonies and by artificial sterilization. There appears no reason why some additional millions of persons might not be either similarly segregated in more or less self-sustaining colonies, or similarly sterilized. At the same time the purposeful dissemination of birth-control knowledge among the uninformed classes should have some effect in checking the too rapid multiplication of strains of less than average ability. The greatest question, however, is whether the individuals of high native ability can be induced to undertake family responsibilities on a larger scale. To this end the widely advocated projects for the endowment of motherhood seem wholly unpromising. Nor does it seem possible that society can ever make it economically advantageous for persons of relatively high social status to have larger families.[1]

Many aspects of the bearing of the struggle for existence on social life still remain to be treated. A generation ago the question whether these biological processes warranted a ruthless competition and a Nietzschean heartlessness was much discussed. The view taken here is that the struggle between groups overshadows that between members of the same group and compels a mollification of the latter. Social solidarity becomes a primary factor in group strength; and this involves such mutual aid and coöperation as will raise the integration and efficiency of the group to a maximum. There is a vast variation, however, in the form and extent of social solidarity in times of peace as compared with times of war. Both war between groups and internal competition have played important rôles; there is little ground for supposing either to have ceased.

[1] For an ingenious scheme of taxation with eugenic aims cf. Siemens, H. W., *Race Hygiene and Heredity*, chap. 10.

War has become so enormously wasteful, however, that intelligent substitutes must be found for it. Similarly, competition is often wasteful of health, vigor, skill, and knowledge, and may be checked by the perfection of education, vocational guidance, collective bargaining, regularization of employment, and an extension of social regulation. But so essential to human effort is rivalry that no society is soundly organized which violates Sumner's dictum that "he who would be well taken care of must take care of himself."[1] Spencer was right in insisting that no society can afford to purchase a temporary expansion of mutual helpfulness at the price of racial deterioration. If, then, the severity of the internal struggle is to be reduced, intelligent means of preserving racial soundness must be found.

Nature is inexorable in the long run in giving the torch of civilization to strong and capable peoples; but these have a wide range of possible political and social organization. Democracy's insistence on an equality of opportunity finds its surest justification in the fact that selection can work effectively in the preservation of the organically superior only when the start in the race of life has been equalized as much as possible. What is wanted is training so diverse and so applicable to every grade of ability and type of personality that each may be fitted with the greatest economy of effort — individual and social — into effective coördination with the social whole. This will maximize individual satisfactions and elevate social power by eliminating the wastes of individual maladjustment, that is, by perfecting the social integration. The illogical democrats are those who insist on society's undertaking all sorts of schemes for social amelioration but who scoff at the idea of eugenic legislation. All civilization is an artificial construct. The artificial is superior to the natural only so long as it takes full account of natural processes. If the law of the jungle is to give way to a peaceful and ameliorative social order, nature's regard for racial soundness must be satisfied.

SELECTED REFERENCES

A complete classified list of books and articles will be found in S. J. Holmes, *Bibliography of Eugenics*. Many references are contained in the preceding pages. A few titles of special value include the following:

Bateson, Wm. *Biological Fact and the Structure of Society*. 1912.
Castle, W. E. *Genetics and Eugenics*, 3d ed. 1924.

---

[1] *What Social Classes Owe to Each Other*, Yale University Press, chap. VI.

Conklin, E. G.   *Heredity and Environment in the Development of Man.*   1923.
  The Direction of Human Evolution.   1923.
Ellis, Havelock.   *A Study of British Genius.*   1904.
  The Task of Social Hygiene.   1912.
Eugenics Laboratory.   *Lecture Series* and *Memoirs.*   (London.)   1907–14.
Eugenics Record Office.   *Bulletins* and *Memoirs.*   (Cold Spring Harbor.)   1911, 1912.
Galton, Francis.   *Essays in Eugenics.*   1909.
  Hereditary Genius.   1869.
  Inquiries into Human Faculty.   1908.
  Natural Inheritance.   1889.
Gates, R. R.   *Heredity and Eugenics.*   1923.
Guyer, M. F.   *Being Well-Born.*   1918.
Holmes, S. J.   *The Trend of the Race.*   1922.
  Studies in Evolution and Eugenics.   1923.
Keith, Arthur.   *The Antiquity of Man.*   1925.
Machin, Arthur.   *The Ascent of Man by Means of Natural Selection.*   1925.
Morgan, T. H., and others.   *The Mechanism of Mendelian Heredity.*   Rev. ed.   1923.
Newman, H. H.   *Readings in Evolution, Genetics and Eugenics.*   1923.
Newsholme, Sir Arthur.   *Vital Statistics.*   (Pertinent chapters.)   1924.
Pearl, Raymond.   *Studies in Human Biology.*   1924.
Pearson, Karl.   *National Life from the Standpoint of Science.*   1901.
Popenoe, P., and Johnson, R. H.   *Applied Eugenics.*   1918.
Second International Congress of Eugenics.
  Vol. i.   *Eugenics, Genetics and the Family.*   1923.
  Vol. ii.   *Eugenics in Race and State.*   1923.
Thomson, J. Arthur.   *What is Man?*   1924.
  The System of Animate Nature.   1924.
  Darwinism and Human Life.   1919.
Wiggam, A. E.   *The Fruit of the Family Tree.*   1924.

CHAPTER XXXII
THE SOCIAL SCIENCES AND EDUCATION
By WILLIAM H. KILPATRICK
COLUMBIA UNIVERSITY

THE main endeavor in this chapter is to exhibit the interrelations of social science with education by presenting briefly the current treatment of certain educational problems which are outstandingly social in nature. In certain instances education leans so directly on the social sciences that little more can be attempted than a bare statement of the educational problem with the appropriate reference to the social science treatment.

I
INTRODUCTORY VIEW

Education is a matter of behavior-changes. In its efforts at the control of those changes, conscious education will go to two principal sources of help: first, to psychology to learn more about the determinants of behavior and consequently to see better *how* to change it; second, to the social sciences to see the bearing of the various possible behaviors on life and consequently to learn better when or what behavior is good, and why. Especially to be considered in the second inquiry is the social milieu in which the behavior under consideration is located. Having found which behavior is good and how behavior may be changed, conscious education then seeks to get the desired behavior embodied in the growing individual. Our first rough generalization thus is easy. We look to the study of social life to give us both the aim and the content of education.

THE SCHOOL AS A SOCIAL AGENCY

The school is the principal agency of society for the purposive control of education. A glance at its history will help us to see the changing conditions under which it works and, more particularly, the enlarging sphere of its social relationships. The story is not new, but it is necessary, perhaps, for a background. At the first, anthropology must be our guide.

Education long antedated the school. Before the school arose, the child's life in the family and in the surrounding group served to initiate him into the many established ways of meeting life's demands. The girl helping her mother learned in time the full round of the woman's duties. The boy too, either in mimic action or by actual participation, acquired the knowledges and skills needed for acting the part of a man. Our later thinking will be helped if we note that the subject-matter of this early education consisted exactly of the established current ways-of-behaving. The method of learning was imitation and participation. The teacher was the mother or the father or other elder who embodied in his life the needed behavior and who took more or less care that the young person should learn to reproduce properly the hereditary forms.

When in time the amount and more particularly the kind of current culture became such that it could not safely be left to the chance concern of the nearest older members of the group, then the school originated. Throughout its career the school has thus existed side by side with an older type of education which was more informal but at the same time more inherent in life itself. The essential duty of the school has at all times been to care for what would otherwise be lost from the social process, or would at any rate be unsatisfactorily preserved. This has meant that the school has especially cared for the more complex formulations, which as a rule are less obviously connected with the ordinary affairs of life and require more assiduous care for their learning. In connection have gone likewise such tools of learning as have been needed for the mastery and the preservation of these more complex matters.

CHANGES IN THE SCHOOL'S FUNCTION

While it is true that these two types of education, the more incidental and the more formal, have existed side by side through the centuries, the relative emphasis, particularly of late, has been greatly changed. First, as civilization has grown more complex the amount to be transmitted has been increased. The invention of writing marked a notable advance, increasing greatly the content to be transmitted and at the same time adding a distinctly new type of transmission tool. Latterly the growth of modern science has added tremendously to the burden of transmission. Until quite recently, as history goes, the literary and scientific heritage and the school that transmitted it were kept largely for the few. For a century or two this has been changing at an accelerating rate.

Owing partly to demands of practical efficiency, partly to more humanitarian considerations, and partly to increased wealth, a larger proportion of the young are now attending school, and for a more extended period. For our purposes quite as important are the changes in the educative function of home and community occasioned by the coming of modern industry. In losing its many industries to the factory, the home has lost not only relatively but actually in educative function. In certain important respects the same is true of the community. These losses in the educative function of the home and community have increased the load of the school, not merely in degree but quite as much in kind: in degree, in that there are now more things to teach; in kind, in that the school must now provide, in a sense not hitherto true, for actual life experiencing in order that certain important social habits and attitudes may still be learned. That the school must now provide "life" and no longer merely prepare for life has for the study of education far-reaching implications.

From the foregoing survey it would seem clear that the school as it looks to the future of the youth committed to its care must in a new sense and in an increasing degree consider both the details of life and the unification of these details into a satisfactory whole. True enough, many lament and not a few deny that the school must necessarily undertake this integrative function. But it seems unavoidably true that the school is and must remain the residuary legatee of all society's otherwise undischarged educative functions. This is, as we have seen, the raison d'être of the school's existence. Through a better education of the rising generation something may be done to help home and church discharge better their historic function; but meanwhile the school must take facts as it finds them and discharge the duties now facing it.

PRESENT DEMANDS ON THE SCHOOL

In the matter of new details to care for, it is hardly too much to say that each institutional subdivision of life is making ever new and greater demands upon the school. Religion, once the mistress of the school, is in many quarters raising eager eyes to the school for renewed help. Morals, the concern of all, are, as every school man knows, making more insistent demands than ever before that the schools care for them. As concerns government and politics, there is urgent demand that the schools make citizenship their special concern. Timid citizens, alarmed by the threat of impending radicalism, call upon the schools to make themselves into propagandist agencies in order to defend the constitution and otherwise to bulwark the threatened established faith. Business interests have long demanded that the schools pay more effectual attention to the spelling and composition of the pupils. In later years vocational preparation has found ever stronger advocates. And as if all this were not enough, health, leisure time, and home economy must receive new and worthy consideration. There might be a comic element in all this were the matter not in fact so serious. Civilization is changing very rapidly. New demands so arising are very acute and very great. Each line of demand on the school must at least be considered. Fortunately, in this chapter we do not have to solve the problems so raised. It suffices for present purposes to see that in very fact literally every important aspect of life turns to the modern school for help. And, as was indicated, the demand is not exhausted by the sum of the details. The unity and wholeness of life must as truly be cared for. The modern school in its care for the young, in literal fact, faces all of life, in detail and as a whole. Its task is very complex.

II

OUR PROBLEM RESTATED

All of the foregoing, however, is but the setting for our problem. The problem itself is somewhat different, including all the foregoing and more: What are the interrelations of education considered as an object of careful study with the various social sciences? If education were more assuredly a science or even if the whole study of education could ideally become a science, we might word our question: What are the interrelations of the science of education with the social sciences? But education can never become *a* science. Much of education is already scientific, some of it much more strictly so than some of the social sciences, and larger areas will yet be brought into the domain of science. But if education will conceive its task adequately it must, in the judgment of this writer, recognize the fact that one permanent aspect of its outlook must forever defy final scientific formulation. Actual education is too closely tied to the aims and values of life, and life is too truly infinite, to allow final formulation. This, however, does not lessen the dependence of the study of education upon the social sciences, rather the contrary. Since education must consider the whole of life, there can be no social science which is not called upon to render needed help.

THE UNIVERSITY STUDY OF EDUCATION IN THIS COUNTRY

The study of education has gone further in this country than in other countries, and it may be an interesting aside to ask how this state of affairs has come about. The newness of the study, too, gives added point to this aside, since both its history and its content will be novel to many.

How came our country to enter so markedly into this new study of education? First, the American mind is, as regards practical matters, distinctly adventurous. Frontier conditions, abundant nature, rapidly growing industrialism, the commingling of cultures — these factors have given the American an open-mindedness in practical if not in theoretical matters that inclines him to social experiment. He will try anything at least once, and he is in considerable degree pragmatic in his tests. Second, our country has changed so rapidly in size and wealth and character that school arrangements and machinery would not stay fixed. A larger and larger proportion of children have been attending school. Democracy has given voice to hitherto submerged opinions, and curricular changes have been demanded. The literary tradition has thus not been so strong here as elsewhere. Growing populations have demanded ever newer buildings, growing wealth has allowed ever better buildings. The how and why of school buildings and their use has forced itself into consideration in unwonted degree. Further, within a century entirely new administrative machinery has had to be contrived in order to care for the ever growing education. Inevitable school problems have been ever more insistent. Third, the rapid coming of the immigrant stocks to our shores gives us, above all peoples, the problem of amalgamating multiform cultures. Partly because of a rapidly growing population, partly because of our democratic doctrines, partly to make our democratic machinery work more effectively, partly because of vast immigrations, social theory plays a large part in American educational thinking. What other countries can do slowly by merely handing down the cultural inheritance, we have to hasten by school action. How to fit the school to these great tasks has required a new consideration of old procedures. Fourth, American education offers for evaluation a bewildering variety of experimentation.   Forty-eight states show forty-eight different state systems, while our cities, relatively autonomous, represent almost infinite subvarieties.   Every conceivable variation of administrative device has been tried, many good, most of them bad.   Meanwhile the friends of education have had to safeguard the schools against possibly the most enterprising politicians known to man.   Under such considerations public school administration has been studied here as nowhere else.   Fifth, partly for reasons named in another connection above and partly from more obscure causes, America has specialized in marked degree in the study of psychology.   This pronounced interest interacting with a prior interest in education has led to an intense study of the psychology of learning.   Success has attended the endeavor, and content and direction have alike been given to the study of education.

These several factors together with others that might be named have concurred to bring about in this country a very conscious theoretical and practical study of education.   Correlative machinery has naturally been needed, and the last quarter of a century has seen the rise here of institutions devoted to the study of education which surpass in all essential respects not only those of any other one country but even those of the whole remaining world.

III

The principal part of this chapter, as was stated at the outset, is to consist in the brief treatment of a number of basic problems in education which especially show connection with the social sciences. It seems but fair to warn the reader that only a selection of problems can here be considered and that the treatment is necessarily superficial, and moreover that both selection and treatment are such as commend themselves to this writer.   Any one else would in both respects make a different showing.

EDUCATION AS SOCIAL RENEWAL

Every one who thinks at all of such matters is clearly conscious of the biological renewal of society.   Death removes, birth adds, the group remains.   And the group that remains is thus, paradoxically enough, always the same and yet always different.   It is less often considered that while the same things are analogously true of the cultured life of the group, it is education, not mere birth, that must

add.   That is, it is to education that we must look for the maintenance through renewal of the cultural continuity.

To the student of the social sciences this fact baldly stated seems
so obvious as to be a commonplace.   But looked at further it is
seen to have fruitful implications not only for the management of
education, but possibly also for the better understanding of society.

At the heart of this maintenance of society in the cultural sense
through education, lies communication.   Originally this took place
primarily between the old and the young as the latter learned to
share in the necessary social enterprises; but communication is in
fact essentially present wherever there is coöperation in any joint
endeavor.   Many naïvely conceive of communication as the passing of an idea from one person to another on the pattern of trans-
ferring of physical objects from one person to another, but the
analogy is very misleading.   Ideas cannot be so passed, and even if
they could, communication would include more than this.   For
communication in the full sense to take place, there must be a prior
basis of like-mindedness.   Understanding and emotion in the one
person must answer in a measure to understanding and emotion in
the other, else, as we say, "misunderstanding" is likely to ensue.
Communication implies, then, first and fundamentally a common
basis of shared emotional and thought life.

It is, however, exactly this sharing of interests that makes people
into a social group. Physical proximity does not suffice. The needed
element is such a sharing of interest as manifests itself in common
purposes and joint enterprises.   And in joint enterprises communication is the factor in and through which the active uniting takes
place.   But wherever actual communication takes place between
two people, each one is in some measure modified.   Each gets somewhat of the other's idea and feeling, each relates this in turn to what
he already knows concerning the other, concerning himself, concerning the matter at hand.   Emotions arise and are correspondingly related.   Attitudes are built.   Action follows, habits result.
Such changes constitute education.   In a word, from actual communication education has taken place.   It thus comes about that
communication, serving as the essential factor in the actual common pursuit of shared interests, means at exactly one and the same
time both the essence of society and the essence of education.

How this conception will serve as a criterion for judging certain
practices of current life can here be only indicated.   In the relation-

ship involving the modern division of labor, the demands of the criterion would cut so deep as probably to be rejected at once by most persons.   But the contention is none the less urged that social relationships of any and all sorts are sound and good in the degree that education goes on continuously in and through them, and bad in the degree that education is hindered.   Under existing conditions the professions clearly have superiority to the trades in this respect.   The degree to which it is now feasible to make industrial life conform to this criterion is a question which we cannot here consider, although any deficiency therefrom must correspondingly hurt life.   It is but the converse of this position to say that living together in joint enterprises furnishes the best conditions for education.   The presence of others furnishes the needed stimulation and the needed checking of results, both requisite to provoke and discipline thought and feeling alike.   The significance of this fact for the management of education is great.

The various conceptions here developed will help the school to remain true to its function.   It is a commonplace that institutionalism is the pronounced sin of institutions.   The school thus too easily becomes merely scholastic, merely academic.   If education is clearly seen to be the essential factor in social renewal, education perforce becomes a bigger thing than merely covering the traditional school requirements.   It will thus be easier for the school to see that its aim is really one with that of the social process, namely, to further the active sharing of interests among all as truly as to help in the effectual pursuit of these interests.   When the part that communication properly plays in life is better appreciated, the procedure of the school will be less restricted to a formal preparation for examination and more given to the purposeful pursuit of activities vital to the pupils.   Thus, education if conceived as social renewal is the better able to help in the understanding and management of both school and society.

EDUCATION AS THE BUILDING OF THE SELF

Self-building is obviously correlative with social renewal as discussed above and also with the progressive understanding of the outside world.   But the use of the term may serve to call helpful attention to certain factors that might otherwise be too much overlooked.

Let it at once be said that nothing mystical or transcendental is contemplated in the present use of the word "self." Difficulties, true enough, abound; but the discussion is here intentionally limited to matters on which there is substantial agreement in scientific psychology.

That the human being is essentially active is almost a truism. Mental emptiness has justly been said to be one of the greatest of annoyers. The infant's consequent activities result in such organization of experience as continually remakes his outlook and abilities. As such organization increases, the setting up of conscious ends and the conscious choice of means become alike more definite characteristics. Although there are obscure and controversial elements involved, it seems safe to say that man differs from the brute at least in this, that he has a larger store of memories and out of them constructs a notion of the past and places remembered events relatedly in this past. At the same time, partly by a social process later to be discussed, he constructs a notion of himself as an abiding unity which has existed continuously throughout this past and by anticipation probably will exist at least for a while longer in the future. The self, then, is, by definition if one so prefers, this constructed notion of abiding unity in relation to which man sees his life as a whole. Since the factor of choice plays so large a part in man's life, we find ourselves for certain purposes extending the notion of the self just reached so far as to make the self the basis of consideration in making choices. Each choice looks to the future for its realization, but at the same time bases itself upon the experiences of the past.[1]

With the self so defined and so related to choice, it becomes at once evident that people for one cause or another choose and act sometimes with one set of factors at work in determining the outcome and at other times with another set so determining. As each such satisfactory act tends by well-known psychological laws to leave a tendency to repeat the act, it is clear that the act of choosing tends in time to build an abiding aggregate out of which like choices are more likely to occur. When the individual acts frequently, now in answer to one set of conditions and now to another markedly

[1] If any reader be afraid of the word "choice" as implying again something mysterious, it will serve all present purposes to think of choice as merely the successful outcome among contending tendencies to action when the confronting situation is complex enough to stimulate to contradictory responses. In like manner we might have defined the setting up of an end as merely a complex instance of delayed response. And in the same way the terms past and future might be defined from the parts they play in the analyses here used.

different, different choice-bases are likely to be built. A small boy off with his companions is likely to build and present a somewhat different character from the one that manifests itself in the presence of father, mother, and other adults of the group. For some purposes we may think of such a person as having different selves. A drunkard who at one time will have his drink at all costs and at another time is filled with remorse at such conduct would represent a pronounced instance. Still more extreme are the well authenticated instances of dual personalities. From this point of view a self is any aggregate within a person's make-up which tends to result in a consistent line of choices. A divided-self is one that shows two or more subordinate selves, while a unified self is one in which there are no such significant divisions. The proper growth of the self presents always new material which calls for a continual process of unification. Without arguing the question we may say that there are strong moral and practical reasons for wishing one to work always toward the unity of selfhood.

With this rather extended psychological basis we are ready to turn to the social discussion of the self. It is at once evident that physically each person is dependent upon his two parents for his initial existence, and also upon his elders, usually his parents, for his continued existence during his early state of absolute dependence. It is equally true that under modern social conditions each one remains his whole life long dependent upon others for his continued physical welfare, not to say actual existence. But this physical dependence does not exhaust one's social debt. As Baldwin and others have pointed out, the very notion that each one has of himself grew up in his social situation, so that much that each one now finds in himself he first identified in those about him, and in like manner much that he now sees in them he first met in himself. One's very self is thus in this very essential way socially constructed. But even this does not yet exhaust one's social indebtedness. When we turn to our thought forms and content, including also our whole moral outlook, and ask how much of this is dependent upon communication with others, we may without entering upon controversial grounds admit that one's mind is what it is only because of one's social environment. The self is, then, inherently and essentially social. Without the help of others we, as we know and value ourselves, had in very truth not been at all.

The self so understood and so built becomes, as the moral agent in society, the chief object of concern to the educator. Ethics and education here meet, the one defining the kind of conduct needed, the other translating this demand into actuality by superintending the building of character. What is the type of education correlatively needed? The self is admittedly built by the successive choices it effectually makes. That the building of the self may be done adequately, a social environment which shall call out and give opportunity for the practice of the necessary social conduct is essential, and this process must go on under such conditions as shall help the individual to pass intelligently upon the moral success or failure of his acts. The process is, of course, not to be understood as limited to morals as commonly but narrowly comprehended. All social relationships are involved. Before the school came into existence education proceeded in inherent connection with actual social life. Since the formalization of school work the essential social setting of the educative process has too often been forgotten, but always to the detriment of the child and the hindrance of the educative process. The contention here made is that the self is actually to be constructed of all that the school properly seeks to give; and that fact and skill, habit and attitude, knowledge and appreciation, each best comes as the child in a life situation meets the need for it. Only in this way can such traits be adequately conceived by the learner or adequately welded into the structure of his self. Proper self-building demands, then, a social environment in which the agent-learner can and must meet the progressively unfolding demands of the total life situation. Only in such a situation can educative thinking and educative choices adequately take place, or the requisite opportunity for overt behavior be found. Only when all these concur can an adequately social self be built.

One further corollary will conclude the applications here drawn from the conception of social self-building. Since the self is thus built in and from a social environment, it at once follows that every properly sensitive parent must be concerned with the conditioning environment that surrounds his child. And a part of this environment is the entire community in which the child lives. To be sure, a conscious and selective care may under favorable conditions greatly increase the relative effect of a specially secluding home and school environment. We could not if we would deny that exclusiveness of social contacts is within limits a real possibility. But under modern conditions of communication, all kinds considered, the community in which one lives reaches outwardly in ever greater inclusiveness and inwardly with ever closer penetration. No care however great can exclude the real influence of the great outside world. Each one inevitably lives in his own times and within this world. In this way the education of all hangs together. This is in fact nothing else than the all-inclusive, all-penetrative social fabric functioning in its most significant aspect, the educational, in the life of each of its constituent parts. To every one, then, who adds the dimension of time to his sense of social responsibility, a scheme of universal education becomes a necessity, and under democratic conditions this means public education.

EDUCATION AND DEMOCRACY

The value of popular education for the proper working of democracy is a modern commonplace. In this country within the past hundred years the zeal of our people for its public schools has become so great as to seem to many from abroad a religious enthusiasm. We do not have to evaluate this zeal in order to affirm that however important an educated citizenship may be for the proper working of a political democracy, the relationship between education and democracy is far from being exhausted by this one connection. Indeed, we may assert as a thesis in the presentation of this phase of the question that the more content we give to the two conceptions of education and democracy, the more inherently do they seem related. The more does each imply the other.

"A Democracy is more than a form of government; it is primarily a mode of associated living, of conjoint communicated experience."[1] If we look at the actual society about us, we find diverse conditions, some better, some worse. Probably the commonest instance of the better is where people so coöperate as to increase the sharing of interests among themselves and others, while the commonest if not the universal evil is where men so act as to hinder the sharing of interests. Whether or not these observations constitute definitions of good and evil need not here detain us, but they help us see the direction which a democratic social process will properly take. Caste and hereditary status mean lines that hinder the sharing of interests. Inequality before the courts means that some hold interests to the exclusion of others. Universal suffrage is a device for facilitating the sharing of interest in matters of governmental management.

[1] Dewey, *Democracy and Education*, p. 101.

But the initial sharing of any one interest furnishes an instance of education. In it one or both of the parties attain a wider point of view, each sees further into the other's inner life and is himself in some measure therein reconstructed. Our discussion on the essential educative character of communication is pertinent here. It is thus easy to see that when society moves in the democratic direction, education takes place. It is equally true that other things being equal such a move creates a situation which makes easier the further sharing of interests, and this in turn means more education. Democracy and education mutually imply and demand each other. Each as it increases mutually brings the other into existence. Each is essential to the other.

If the foregoing has seemed unduly general, an instance may help to clear it. In times past nothing has been commoner than for a sub-group to nurture its young so that on growing up they would hold the tenets of the sub-group as practically permanent prejudices. If we would criticize such a practice it matters little which line of criticism we take, whether that of democracy or that of education. Both paths arrive at the same goal. To treat young people in this partisan fashion is to take an unfair advantage of them. It is, as Kant said, to treat them not as ends in themselves, but merely as means to ends which their elders hold. It is to make sure that these young people shall not when grown share interests across party lines. Thus does a consistent democracy condemn such a practice. But education is equally opposed. This is no real education, but a warping — a mere training to ideas chosen in advance. It is a blind indoctrination, an enslaving, not the freeing of the individual's powers so that he may choose intelligently in the full and impartial light of the facts in the case. Education and democracy thus alike forbid any system of treatment that would give parents and elders perpetual control over the young. If any further illustration were necessary the evils of current propagandism would probably suffice. Here again do education and democracy, properly understood, stand together in their condemnation of a hurtful practice. The inherent connection of democracy and education is thus the better seen as each from its own basis is the more adequately interpreted. Each works for the other's goal.

EDUCATION AND PROGRESS

That improvement along many lines is possible if only we put

4

orth proper endeavor is a proposition that need not be argued. That much at least is true, even though many entangling controversies stand ready to entrap us if we claim more. Vast improvements along distinct lines are evident, however men may differ about the net outcome of it all. So understood and so limited, progress is another conception that holds intimate relationship with education. One has but to mention the word "research" to see one of the important connections between the two. How necessary a proper education is to effectual research and how potent proper research is for the increase of knowledge, require no discussion. "Academic freedom" is another phrase and conception bearing testimony to the connection between education and progress. Freedom of speech and press are much the same thing carried into the great outer world of affairs, where they affect the education of the people at large. Such connections between education and progress are obvious enough.

To cite a type of current controversial issues will help further to show the mutual bearings which education and progress have on each other. Many who seek to prevent a change of view along a given line, as for instance about war or marriage or the Virgin Birth, interpose a doctrine which if accepted would render futile any educative endeavor. War, we are thus told, is founded on an ineradicable instinct for fighting; it is vain to speak of abolishing war until we have changed unchangeable human nature. In like manner the Virgin Birth is vouched for by such a revelation that man's arguments against it, even if apparently sound, are in reality the fallacious work of Satan. As to the instinct for war, when we examine it carefully we seem, interestingly enough, to find the strongest support for war to be not in instinct but exactly where education itself has been the potent factor, namely, in socially inherited customs and traditions. Man's nature, while not appreciably changing from generation to generation in the new-born babe, seems to be the most plastic known substance when we consider the infinitely many and varied changes that take place within the lifetime of different individuals. Here at any rate education seems to be exactly the key to the door of change.

Are we, then, to conclude that there are no limits to what education can do? Before answering we must see to it that this apparently simple question does not conceal an ambiguity. Education as effect and accordingly as a sign of the basis and possibility of change must be distinguished from education as intentional cause of change. It was intimated above that human nature as found at birth has probably changed little if any in many thousands of years. Moreover, it varies within any "race" or nation much more than from race to race or nation to nation. From these considerations it seems fair to conclude that the wide cultural differences we see between any two groups, whether contemporary or widely separated in history, represent, whatever else may be said about them, exactly different changes that have been brought about within the lifetime of those who exhibit the contrasts. And as such changes are precisely educational in character it might be concluded that education must therefore be very powerful indeed since it can show to its credit such contrasting results. And thinking thus some might go on further to conclude that a program of educational endeavor is therefore capable of changing civilization in very marked degree. Such a line of reasoning, however, would be in part fallacious by reason of the ambiguity referred to. It is fair to conclude from the widely contrasting cultures that man has the educational plasticity necessary for learning such diverse things. This would certainly mean a very high degree of plasticity, and it might reasonably be inferred that this proved plasticity would probably suffice for learning a new culture differing in turn as widely from any hitherto known. Such an argument would be tenable, but the case for using greater educational endeavor as an agency to effect great cultural changes must be based on other considerations. The needed plasticity we may admit is available, but will the plasticity be utilized? Will educational endeavor — the schools, the pulpit, the press, the sum of organized effort — be strong enough to prevail over the inertia and the opposing educative effect of all other related social institutions? We might, for instance, set out to eliminate the practice of drinking intoxicating liquors from the rising generations. There is no known psychological condition that would prevent. In fact, quite the contrary. Such a consummation might well be psychologically feasible if the proper educative conditions were granted. But can we get these needed conditions? Many things oppose. A host of people live among us who are already strongly addicted to drink. In most of them the inclination to drink will probably resist any eliminative measures. A host of social customs makes it easy for new recruits to join the drinking group. Innumerable references in literature have their effect. A host of money-lovers will for personal gain encourage the sale of intoxicants. When such opposing conditions are taken into account, the probability of success is greatly lessened. Human educability may well suffice, but it is difficult for the educative endeavor to secure the requisite freedom of opportunity.

Shall we, then, conclude that educational endeavor is powerless to effect social changes? By no means. No such general conclusion can be drawn. Each case must be judged on its own merits. In general the greater the number of people who must agree on a new program the less likely will agreement be had. Also, the more sweeping the change that is proposed the less likely in general that the necessary agreement can be secured. But also, as everywhere else, the more strongly is endeavor put forth the greater is the probability of success. Here as everywhere else: Within limits endeavor counts. Nor have discussions of determinism and the like any more bearing here than they have on winning at football. Other things being equal, the team that tries the hardest is most likely to win. Any player who is "determined," in any way or for any cause, not to try, will if found out be put off the team, and properly so. But loyal supporters of the team know in practical measure how to marshal the determinants of players' wills, and within limits they succeed in doing so. They produce results. So is it in the larger game of life. It need not be denied that some proposed social schemes have found "nature" more favorable to them than to others. But considering the plasticity of human nature the general conclusion would seem safe that conscious education will as a rule succeed or fail according as it can or cannot secure greater "access" to this plasticity than can other contending social forces.

Among practical questions touching access to this available plasticity, the separability of young from old is significant. If the proposed change is one in which the bulk of the young can feasibly differ from the bulk of the old, the change is much easier to introduce. Education can more easily get in its work. Taste in literature is thus far more plastic to efforts at change than is spelling. The young and the old, the unfixed and the fixed, need not necessarily read the same books, but with English spelling or the calendar the case is different. It is difficult to have two sets of spelling or two calendars going side by side. The old and fixed who control affairs will not consent. Under such circumstances some customs indefensible to thought seem destined to last forever. The practical question of introducing reform through education seems, then, to be largely that of finding a way to educate the young in the new without requiring the old to change with them.

A moral question involved in the foregoing is important for education. It was once generally counted proper for the old to determine through the schools what the young should or should not think along any given line. Objection to this has already been voiced in the discussion of Education and Democracy above. Now it may be affirmed that the old are under severe moral limitations in such matters, much severer than most persons have even yet been willing to admit. The restraints are of two kinds. The first is in such matters as spelling or weights and measures where it would be easy, were we starting anew, to improve greatly on what we have. Here the old ought to restrain themselves from a mere selfish opposition to the novel if the advantage to future generations would in the long run be very considerable. The second pertains to matters more inherently controversial, such as socialism, for example. In such involved political and social problems, changing too with the times, the old ought to restrain themselves very severely from trying to "indoctrinate" the young with the present preferred opinion. They ought, moreover, to take great pains to prepare the rising generation to think with reliable independence about such matters. If this can be brought about, the power of the school to improve affairs will be greatly enhanced. In this consideration democracy, education, progress — all three unite to help one another reach the goal which all jointly hold in view.

THE STATE AND EDUCATION

Education increasingly becomes a major enterprise of the modern state. In no connection does education make more numerous or more definite calls upon social science. At the outset the theory of state support and control of education must correlate with one's theory of the state. Education is here constantly reaching out into new territory and in turn calling constantly for larger support. Taxpayers object. What is right and proper? There are many other questions. What shall be the upper limit of compulsory attendance? Shall the state provide secondary education for all of secondary school age? Irrespective of mental endowment? And if the family purse does not permit, shall the state by a subsidy make it possible for the capable and willing child to continue? And what about higher education? Shall the state provide it? For all who wish it? In medicine as well as in the customary liberal arts? If yes, shall tuition be charged? And equally to all? Is this a democratic procedure?

In all such matters how shall supporting funds be raised? From the district, the county, or from the state at large? What equalization of burden shall the state undertake? Shall the federal government help to equalize the burden of elementary and secondary education throughout the nation? If so, how? And what about control from Washington? Shall the appropriating body make the curriculum? Partly? Altogether? Not at all? Directly or indirectly? Shall doctrines objectionable to minorities, as evolution and vaccination, be required in publicly supported schools? Suppose the majority the other way, shall such doctrines be forbidden? What about religion? Shall it be taught in the public schools? If so, which and how? If no, shall the Bible be forbidden or shall it be read and prayers recited? If yes, what version of the Bible and what prayers? Shall the school make outside arrangements with the churches to teach religion? If yes, shall attendance at church school be compulsory?

These by no means exhaust the questions that arise under the head of state and education. They range, as is evident, all the way from the most highly theoretical to the most immediately practical. How shall school boards be chosen? Shall the school board be financially independent of the local political authorities? If yes, always or only in the case of an elective board? Shall the merit system of appointment be used? Shall equal pay for men and women prevail?

In some of these cases political theory is ready with an accepted answer. In every case what political science has to offer is useful if not essential to a proper consideration of the problem. Increasingly does school administration find itself turning to students of public finance and the like for immediate help and direction. As the study of education grows, its connections with related social fields become more and more articulate, and nowhere more than in matters of state support and control.

IV

In the university study of education we see probably better than anywhere else the dependence of education upon the social sciences.

Attention has already been given to the causes that have developed the advanced study of education in this country. For the sake of those not familiar with this truly remarkable development it should be stated that the university study of education as found in this country is not primarily concerned with the immediate preparation of teachers for the elementary and secondary schools, but rather with three other problems, the preparation of teachers of teachers, the preparation of school administrators, and original research into all kinds of educational problems. A glance at some of the fields of university study will help us to see the service here rendered by the social sciences.

The history of education was the first field of education to reach academic respectability. It includes much more than a mere history of schools narrowly considered. A principal aim is to help break the cake of preconceived and customary outlook so as to force the student and future practitioner to see more adequately the task that faces education. This calls for a very broad study of civilization and the part that education in its many aspects has played therein. It is no accident that the most epoch-making of our histories of education was written by a scholar who had been trained as a sociologist and who began his career as a teacher of general history. A recent interest in this field, the product largely of the Great War, is nationalism and its interrelations with curriculum making and administration. So also have retarded civilizations come in for new study. Here again civilization is studied, this time to see what it is and how to effect it, specifically how to "modernize" it and how best to weld together old and new. History, sociology, anthropology, political science, must here unite with lesser contributions from other fields to serve the history of education as it attacks its varied problems.

Because the philosophy of education is primarily concerned with those conflict points where contradictory demands are made from the outside upon education, this field shows perhaps the widest range of interrelationships with other fields of thought. Many of these fields we have already discussed. A typical problem, an actual instance, may serve to illustrate the natural setting from within which deeper problems inevitably arise.

In a city where the public school has hitherto been dominant, a slum district has extended itself till many children of recent immigrant families, low in morals and cultivation, are entering the schools hitherto patronized almost exclusively by the wealthiest and best educated families of the city. Many of the latter are much disturbed, some propose to organize private schools for their children, while others advocate a districting scheme for the public schools where the children of a designated area are to be admitted only to the school set apart for that area. What should be done under such circumstances?

The matters here involved have surprisingly many ramifications. One proposed solution, the private school, at once raises a host of questions, some of which have already been considered. Why have public schools? Are private schools democratic? Is a good citizen warranted in supporting a private school? To answer these questions intelligently we must go still deeper. What is democracy? What, if any, moral obligations are involved? And again yet deeper. What is the right relation of the individual to the group in such matters? What is meant by right? What constitutes right and wrong? Evidently ethics and sociology have to answer for education their most fundamental questions.

But we have not exhausted even the question of private schools. There is some tendency to legislate all such schools out of existence. What stand shall we take? There is a contrary demand to subsidize all schools which meet certain state requirements, practically apportion public funds to private and parochial schools. What is the right position with regard to these two demands? Clearly, as suggested earlier, we must ask about the state and the limitations, if any, upon its rights. Political science must here help us. But other matters have now become involved. What are the respective spheres of control among state, church, and home? Here the knottiest of all embittering disputes arise. Many fundamental conceptions need to be clarified. Other social fields must come to our aid.

Space does not suffice even to exhaust this one subordinate question of private schools. Experimentation and progress are yet to be discussed, with the dangers of a state monopoly in education which Herbert Spencer and J. S. Mill feared; but other things press upon us. Enough has been shown to make clear the fact that the philosophy of education has no lack of problems that connect it fundamentally with a very large area in the social sciences. If we went further and discussed, as we should in any full course, the problems of leisure time, health, vocational education, we should reënforce the judgment from many different angles. Educational sociology is a newer title to indicate especially an effort to bring the pertinent methods and content of sociology over into the field of education. Under whatever name the wider social bearings of education be studied, the results are the same for the inquiry at hand. Education is indeed correlative with life and must use the studies of all the specialists to help meet its problems.

The largest place in our university schools of education is given to the practical management of schools and school systems. Divisions of study here correspond to the different actual positions found in practical education. School administration will study especially the management of systems of schools, state, county, or city. Higher education, normal school education, secondary education, elementary education, rural education, kindergarten, vocational education, tell the tale of their special fields by their titles. A goodly number of problems arising here have already been touched upon under the head of the State and Education. Public school finance is perhaps at present the most insistent of these. Taxation, bond issues, and budget-making are accordingly fields in which specialists from the appropriate social sciences can give very concrete help to education.

Possibly the best concluding problem to illustrate the interrelations of education with the social sciences is that of the curriculum. In elementary, secondary, and higher education, all three, this problem is acute. In elementary and secondary education it is, on the theoretical side, the most insistent problem of the day. New times demand a new curriculum. Tradition has lost its sway. But the problem is very complex. To fix ideas by an illustration let us consider the proposition to make a unified course in the social sciences for the secondary school. From various considerations the division and separation of this field among history, geography, and civics, while customary, is not satisfactory. So a single unified course is proposed, a general social science course somewhat similar to the course in general science which is now winning its way in the field of science. Let it be further agreed, as is now common, that the school shall not so much teach solutions to social problems as build intelligent interest in them and intelligent knowledge about them, giving meanwhile efficient methods of attack upon them. A first effort, then, is to select the most promising problems, noting particularly that it is the *future* citizen whose education concerns us. The whole range of the social sciences is then surveyed to pick problems that will probably be most strategic to social life a half generation hence.   The amount of work entailed by one actual study along this line would astonish any one not acquainted with the investigation.   Suppose the problems selected, next must come a selection of material pertinent to their treatment, reliable and effectual for the youth — another task involving a wide survey.   The question of how to teach it all we can fortunately leave to other papers.   Enough has been said to show that broad as is social life, just so broad must be the study that would select for our youth the best for them to study in the social field.   Every social scientist is a potential contributor.   Here as everywhere else studied education, being inherently social, must get from the social sciences absolutely essential assistance with which to do its work.

Our survey must close as it began.   Education is concerned with such changes in behavior as make life better and richer.   Life must mean social life; and the study of how people live together in society must show us the direction toward better living.   The selected experiences of the race preserved for us in our customs and ideals constitute for us our institutional life and so furnish the means for individual development.   Education must, then, for its primary subject-matter study society and its processes.   In the actual educative process it must socially condition the living of the young in such way that they will have the stimulus and the opportunity to use the best that has been achieved.   Properly done this will mean increasing self-control over the life process itself.   In this a true conserving and a true progressing are united in one.   That all this may go well, education must at each point avail itself of the organized stores that the social sciences have to offer.   Their stores are its storehouse, their wealth its wealth.

SELECTED REFERENCES

Bagehot, Walter.   *Physics and Politics.*   1887.
Baldwin, J. M.   *Individual and Society.*   1911.
           Social and Ethical Interpretations.   1906.
Barker, Ernest.   *Political Thought in England: from Herbert Spencer to the Present Day.*   1915.
Betts, G. H.   *Social Principles of Education.*   1912.
Brown, W. Jethro.   *The Underlying Principles of Modern Legislation.*   1915.
Bryce, James.   *Modern Democracies.*   2 vols.   1921.
Burgess, E. W.   *Function of Socialization in Social Evolution.*   1916.
Bury, J. H.   *History of Freedom of Thought.*   1913.
           The Idea of Progress.   1920.
Carver, Thomas N.   *Principles of Political Economy.*   1919.

Chafee, Zechariah, Jr. *Freedom of Speech.* 1920.

Coe, G. A. *Social Theory of Religious Education.* 1917.

Conn, H. W. *Social Heredity and Social Evolution.* 1914.

Cooley, C. H. *Social Process.* 1918.

Croly, H. *The Promise of American Life.* 1912.

Cubberley, E. P. *Changing Conceptions in Education.* 1916.

Dewey, John. *Democracy and Education.* 1916.
     Human Nature and Conduct. 1922.
     School and Society. 1915.

Ellwood, C. A. *Introduction to Social Psychology.* 1917.

Fite, Warner. *Individualism.* 1911.

Giddings, F. H. *Elements of Sociology.* 1898.

Goldenweiser, A. A. *Early Civilization: An Introduction to Anthropology.* 1922.

Hadley, A. T. *Relations between Freedom and Responsibility in the Evolution of Democratic Government.* 1903.

Hobhouse, L. T. *Social Evolution and Political Theory.* 1911.

Jensen, Jens P. *Public Finance.* 1925.

Lavisse, Ernest, et Rambaud, Alfred. *Histoire générale du IVᵉ siècle à nos Jours.* 2ᵉ ed. 12 vols. 1893–1905.

Lippmann, Walter. *Public Opinion.* 1921.

Lowell, A. L. *Public Opinion and Popular Government.* 1914.

MacIver, R. M. *Community: A Sociological Study.* 1917.

Mill, J. S. *On Liberty.* 1913 ed.

Monroe, Paul. *Brief Course in the History of Education.* 1907.

Ogburn, W. F. *Social Change.* 1923.

Reisner, E. H. *Nationalism and Education.* 1922.

Robbins, C. L. *The School as a Social Institution.* 1918.

Seligman, E. R. A. *Essays in Taxation.* 1923.

Smith, W. R. *Introduction to Educational Sociology.* 1917.

Snedden, David. *Educational Sociology.* 1922.

Strayer, G. D. (Director). *Report of the Educational Finance Inquiry Commission.* 1924.

Todd, A. J. *Theories of Social Progress.* 1918.

Wallas, Graham. *The Great Society.* 1914.

Wells, H. G. *An Outline of History.* 1920.

Wilson, Woodrow. *The State.* 1918.

CHAPTER XXXIII

THE SOCIAL SCIENCES AND THE NATURAL SCIENCES [1]

By MORRIS R. COHEN

COLLEGE OF THE CITY OF NEW YORK

THE business of mapping out the proper domains of the various sciences was an integral part of the social philosophy of Auguste Comte, and a dominant interest of American sociology in its earlier years. The actual progress, however, of the various sciences since Comte's day shows that it is not only foolish but mischievous for the sociologist, philosopher, theologian, or moralist to lay down any law restricting the scientific work of the physicist, astronomer, chemist, or biologist. It is fortunate that Comte did not have the actual power to introduce his well-intentioned order into the business of scientific research. If he had, we should now be without our knowledge of the chemical composition of the stars and without the knowledge gained by studying chemistry and biology according to the methods of physics. Science is an exploration of the unknown; and it need not surprise us that prediction as to the outcome of few other human adventures is as hazardous as that concerning the direction which the future progress of any science will take. This reflection need not prevent us from trying to arrive at clear ideas as to the distinctive traits which characterize the social sciences. We may, however, be warned by it against the possible hindrance to the growth of science by the setting up of absolute boundaries on the basis of present incomplete knowledge. Our safest way seems to be to take account of the most influential views that have actually prevailed as to the relation between the natural and the social sciences, and to submit them to critical analysis, thus making the entire situation a little clearer.

The Aristotelian doctrine of the four causes suggests four points of comparison:

---

[1] *Editors' Note:* Professor Cohen's paper as submitted to the editors contained four sections that unfortunately could not be included in this volume because of limitations of space. These sections dealt with "The Three Kinds of Laws in the Natural Sciences," "The Meaning of Social Statistics," "Tendencies as Laws," and "The Theory of Types." These topics, however, will be treated in a forthcoming book by Professor Cohen.

I

The Subject-Matter of the Social Sciences

The distinctness of the words "social" and "natural" inevitably suggests that the subject-matters denoted by them must be mutually exclusive. Yet few persons seem willing to maintain such a sharp dichotomy between natural and social facts as to call the latter un- or non-natural. Social facts and the human beings between whom they take place are located in physical time and space. Deprive these social facts of their physical elements or dimensions and they lose their usual meaning and cease to have reference to anything existing.

These reflections suggest that we must not conceive the social and the natural sciences as mutually exclusive. Rather should we view them as dealing with parts of the same subject-matter from different points of view. The social life of human beings is within the realm of natural events; but certain distinctive characteristics of social life make it the object of a group of special studies which may be called the natural sciences of human society. In any case the empirical or historical fact before us is that many questions are clearly both in the physical and in the social realm. We may, if we like, draw a sharp line between physical and social anthropology, between physical and economic geography, and perhaps even between individual psychology as a natural science and social psychology as a social science. But the distinction is in any case a thin and shifting one. When we come to the study of linguistics or of epidemics, or to the various branches of technology, we see the breakdown of all the sharp separations so far suggested between the natural and the social sciences.

Can we avoid all difficulties by boldly declaring that:

1. ALL SOCIAL PHENOMENA ARE SIMPLY PHYSICAL?

The affirmative is maintained by those monistic materialists who now call themselves behaviorists. In line with the modern positivistic tradition they speak the language of empiricism and induction; but clearly no mere accumulation of facts can adequately prove the absence of some factor in social phenomena other than those taken into account in physics or biology. In point of fact, these monistic materialists, like A. P. Weiss,[1] base their stand entirely on the a priori argument that since social phenomena must

[1] *A Theoretic Basis of Human Behavior*, 1925.

manifest themselves in time and space, they must, like physical phenomena, be constituted by matter or electrons in motion. But the fact that social phenomena always involve physical elements fails to prove that they contain nothing else. The fact that X is a man does not disprove that he is a scientist. Our behaviorist friends do not seem to have learned that while general physical elements are necessary they are not sufficient to determine the meaning of social phenomena.

What differentiates the group of facts we call social from other physical facts? Consider the simplest possible social event, a salutation, for example, the doffing of the hat to a lady. Physics describes the mechanism of the motion, and bio-chemistry describes the energy-transformation which makes the motion possible. But the social significance of the act is not thereby indicated. Social descriptions involve categories altogether different from purely physical ones. To describe men as showing deference or as seeking food, mates, and so on, does not give us their physical coördinates. The behaviorist uses the categories of stimulus and response. But if the stimulus is purely physical and the response is equally so, how can we get anything as distinctive as the social categories? From the laws that are common to all physical phenomena you cannot deduce those that are distinctive of a given group. Something more and distinctive is needed for the description of social phenomena.

Moreover, the behaviorist himself must and does admit that there often are no determinate relations between the physical dimensions of stimuli and their social responses. The same physical stimulus, the sight of pork, for example, may be followed by the most diverse social responses on the part of Arabs and Russians. Also, all sorts of different physical stimuli, for example, a pistol shot and a light signal, may lead to the same social response, for instance, the starting of a race.

The idea that if we take social facts on a large scale we shall find their determining physical conditions, seems to find support in certain statistical correlations between geographic (especially climatic) conditions and social behavior. Crime, increased or decreased efficiency in economic production, and increase or decrease of marriage-rates, seem to be correlated with definite conditions of temperature, atmospheric pressure, air currents, moisture, and so on. I say *seem to be* because I am not sure how many of these correlations will hold after careful analysis of the factors involved. Thus, greater crime during the summer months may not mean any direct effect of temperature on anti-social disposition, but merely greater social opportunity for the commission (and detection) of certain social acts called criminal.

But does not the assumption that summer conditions make for more open-air life and greater opportunity for certain crimes itself take for granted the causation of the social by the physical? Any answer here is confusing unless we clearly distinguish between necessary and sufficient conditions. Given social conditions otherwise the same, a longer day and a milder temperature will bring more people out of doors. But it is hard to say what social effects the mere fact of summer is adequate to produce by itself.

We can see all this more clearly in the usual illustrations of the geographic interpretation of history. The proximity of the sea, it is claimed, explains why the Greeks and Phœnicians were seamen; the presence of certain plants and animals, why certain tribes were agriculturists and hunters; the presence of certain minerals, why certain nations developed certain industries, and so on. Now we may well grant that people cannot fish or sail boats if large bodies of water are inaccessible to them, and that they cannot develop metallurgy if they have no ore. But history amply shows that the mere proximity of the sea will not develop mariners or fishermen (for example, England before the Tudors, or certain parts of Ireland), and that the presence of clay will not make people use pottery. Nor will the presence of certain foods be always followed by their utilization. Thus, many peoples suffering from shortage of food do not utilize the milk of their domestic cattle, the eggs of their fowl, the fish in their rivers, the flesh of certain animals, and so on. The reason for such failure is often attributed to irrational taboos; but often it is due to the more simple consideration that people have not learned to utilize resources which to us are obvious. Is it not true that if we take mankind as a whole throughout its history, the utilization of natural resources is very limited and generally the result of a very slow *process of learning?* The mere presence of the resources is certainly not an adequate cause of men's learning to use them.

In general, those who wish to reduce social phenomena to nothing but physical elements are under the illusion that particular social facts can be derived from physical universals alone. They fail to note the distinction between the necessary and the sufficient conditions of social acts — a distinction which is emphatically explicit in the exact sciences.

2. ARE SOCIAL FACTS BIOLOGIC?

No one, I take it, seriously questions that social phenomena are conditioned by the biologic processes of the human organism. Yet social phenomena are not merely biologic. The cry which is evoked by pain, the turning away of the head from the sight of something frightful, or the turning toward certain other objects, are all biologic facts. But they acquire social significance only when definitely related to the rules or ends of a community. The ceremonials of courtship, marriage, and divorce involve opposite sexes. But the specific character of these ceremonies as courtship, or marriage, or divorce is social and not merely biologic.

All this is very elementary. Yet an astounding number of widespread and influential errors result from overlooking it. Consider, for instance, the Spencer-Fiske theory that prolonged infancy is the cause of the family and of the growth of civilization. Obviously the helplessness of the infant will strengthen the family bond only when *both* parents already have a disposition to care for the infant. It will not affect parents whose relations are not already more or less permanent. The biologic fact of prolonged infancy cannot, therefore, by itself explain the permanent family.

The distinction between social facts and their biologic elements will likewise show the untenability of attempts to find the adequate cause of the family form in the biologic fact of sex. Sex impulse is fitful and variable, and social factors are necessary to explain the diverse rôles that sex plays in family life, in sacred prostitution, celibacy, and so forth.

The confusion between the biologic and the social point of view is increased by the fact that popular biologic thought has a large infusion of anthropomorphism in the form of Lamarckianism, in the Darwinian theory of sexual selection, and the like. Even natural selection is popularly conceived as if it were similar to conscious breeding, as if nature literally selected certain forms because they are the fittest for her pre-conceived purposes. This has led to a most deplorable confusion between biologic and moral considerations. In vain has Huxley clearly and eloquently pointed out (in his lecture on *Evolution and Ethics*) that the phrase " survival of the fittest" has no ethical connotation at all. It is only an analytic proposition to assert that those species survive who in a given environment and under particular conditions are able to breed at a rate sufficiently large to offset the death-rate, and that hence if an unusual cold wave held sway over us those most likely to survive would be the Eskimos, whereas a prolonged heat wave might leave none of us except some miserable Indians on the Amazon. Intellectual discrimination is not an easy virtue where strong moral prejudices can be defended as the Decalogue of (biologic) Science. But from the point of view of logic and scientific method we need have no hesitation in characterizing as downright fallacies most of the explanations of social institutions by the principle of natural selection. Will natural selection explain why the Macedonians and not the Egyptians had certain laws against incest? Is it true that those who have anti-social feelings leave fewer progeny than those who are devoted to the common good? Will those who are devoted and courageous be more likely to leave offspring than those who are selfishly and shrewdly accommodating? To ask these questions is to throw sufficient doubt on purely biologic selection as an explanation of social traits. For it simply is not true that every existing social trait has survived because it has helped the race to survive. Many social maladaptations, for example, prostitution, or war, have persisted through the ages though they in no way make for an increased birth-rate or a decreased death-rate.

Similar to the confusion between biologic and social fitness or adaptation is the confusion between biologic and social heredity. It seemed beyond a shadow of doubt that sentiments, ideas, linguistic and artistic forms, manners, and the like, spread and survive irrespective of whether the great originators of them — saints, prophets, philosophers, orators, artists, gallant ladies, and so on — left any offspring of their bodies. Yet most of the contemporary discussion of social traits seems to assume that social traits are carried along in the germ plasm.[1] This confusion is due to ignoring the difference between biologic heredity through the germ plasm and social heredity as tradition through indoctrination and imitation.

As the rudiments of those questions are precisely the ones that are most generally overlooked, it is well to insist upon them here.

There are two distinct facts of biologic heredity: (1) that offspring resemble their parents more than they resemble other indi-

[1] Cf. McDougall, *The Group Mind.*

viduals of the same species, and (2) that they continue to resemble other individuals of the same species much more than they ever resemble individuals of other species. As individuals of the same species are generally subject to the same environment, it is always difficult to determine to what extent their resemblance is due to the same environment and to what extent it is due to the continuity of germ plasm. Considering the almost infinitesimal amount of direct study of human heredity for an adequately large number of people and generations, and considering how few pure races we can find throughout history, it seems foolish to make any confident assertions about social traits belonging to any human group through biologic heredity. Foolish, in fact, have been nearly all the generalizations about the various races, for example, Gobineau's generalization that the black excel in art and that the Greeks therefore must have had a black strain in their blood, or Lord Acton's generalization that the Semites are monotheists and the Aryans pantheists or polytheists, or the popular generalizations about the social traits of the French, English, and German. The racial composition of the latter peoples has changed relatively little in the last one hundred and fifty years, yet the popular view as to their distinctive cultural characteristics has undergone marked changes. Before the French Revolution great historians like Gibbon could look upon the English as turbulent in contrast with the orderly French. In the nineteenth century it was the French who were looked upon as fickle. The dreamy Germans, having the empire of the clouds at the beginning of the nineteenth century, appeared in a different guise at the beginning of the twentieth century. Yet the great fundamental changes of social life were in the main along the same direction in all three of these countries. Obviously, these social changes since the Industrial Revolution are not to be explained by fixed racial traits; and in general the spread of any social arrangements by imitation or learning — for example, the use of rolling friction, metals, sewing machines, moving pictures, music or even the same language — is independent of race.

3. ARE SOCIAL FACTS EXCLUSIVELY PSYCHOLOGIC?

In recent years there has been a marked effort among economists and political scientists to give their work a psychologic basis. The psychologists, on the other hand, have been abandoning interest in the conscious aspect of phenomena and have gone in for description of the physical and the physiologic aspects of human conduct or behavior. This has led to a blurring of the distinction between the social and the psychologic. The confusion is increased by the fact that psychology as a science denotes three distinct enterprises: (1) the experimental science of psycho-physics, or correlation between mental phenomena and their physical basis; (2) analytic psychology, or description of mental phenomena in terms of their hypothetical elements, by introspective or speculative analytical methods; and (3) social psychology, which is often nothing but the description of diverse social phenomena in somewhat metaphorical and cloudy psychologic language. The first two of these studies clearly belong to the field of natural science, while only the third can appropriately be called a social science.

Social sciences such as economics, politics, and jurisprudence are not primarily concerned (as is psychology) with the individual's psycho-physical responses nor with what will be revealed, by introspection or analysis, as going on in the mind of an individual manufacturer, a political boss, or a judge listening to counsel. Their primary aim, rather, is to establish certain objective relations called economic, political, jural, or the like. A description of the various systems of kinship, of the different ways of distributing land, paying rent, taxes, and so on, clearly belongs to social science and not to psychology. In trying to understand the basis of these relations the contribution of psychology is doubtless of very great importance. But the establishment of economic facts is not the affair of the psychologist but of the economist. The psychologist can give us the psychologic explanation only if he first learns what the economic facts are. No one dreams of maintaining that human traits, habits, motives, hunger, fear, hope, and the like, can be eliminated from social science; but it is the economist not the psychologist who explains why cotton has to be shipped from the South to New England to be sent back as cloth, or why it is cheaper for a merchant in Cincinnati to have his cloth made into garments in New York rather than in his own city.

It is, of course, easy enough to define psychology as the science of all human and, therefore, of all social phenomena. But a unified science will not be produced by such arbitrary definition. The methods used to solve problems of cost-accounting or of legal procedure are not genuinely homogeneous with strictly psychologic methods used in determining the variations of hunger or why people generally start to run when others do.   In the former problems we deal predominantly with abstract measurable relations, in the latter with physiologic processes or analysis of immediate personal feelings.   Hence, if we wish to know the reason for the changes in women's clothes or why Tammany Hall wins so many elections, we are safer in consulting an expert "designer" or a politician than a trained psychologist.

In general, the data from which psychology as a natural science proceeds are relatively simple present facts of direct observation and immediately personal reference.   The data of the social sciences are more complex and refer to objective relations between different people.

4. THE DISTINCTIVE SUBJECT-MATTER OF THE SOCIAL SCIENCES

The social sciences may be said to deal with the life of human beings in their group or associated life.   But is there something that distinguishes this life from that of plant colonies or of social insects studied in biology or natural history?

Three answers have been offered, to wit, (a) that the social sciences deal with volitional conduct and judgments of value while the rational sciences deal with causal relations; (b) that the social sciences deal with concrete historical happenings while the natural sciences deal with abstract or repeatable aspects of natural events; and (c) that the social sciences deal with a peculiar subject-matter which I shall refer to as "tradition" or "culture."

A. THE VOLITIONAL OR TELEOLOGIC CHARACTER OF SOCIAL FACTS
(1) THE RÔLE OF VOLITION

There can be no question that descriptions of social facts are largely in terms of purpose or final cause.   It ought to be equally obvious that the causal relation cannot be eliminated from social considerations.   There is obviously no antithesis between the two points of view if one remembers that when A is the cause of B, A is also a means of bringing about B as an end.   The real issue is whether actual conscious purpose is always a direct and an adequate explanation of social phenomena.

Reflection shows that the actual rôle of conscious purpose in human life has been greatly exaggerated.   The newer psychologic movements protest against the older utilitarian rationalism which supposed that men never acted except out of a desire to bring about a definite end. But the newer theories are themselves only crypto-rationalistic. The subconscious or the unconscious of Freud never acts except in order to bring about desired ends. But human beings are creatures of impulse and may act first and think, if at all, afterward. Lamb's *Origin of Roast Pig* is a true symbol of many social inventions. As human prevision is limited, the achievement of what we set out to accomplish must be largely accidental. But our aims, in fact, are constantly being modified by the course of our achievement. It is pride which makes us read back into our original intention the final (favorable) results attained. Thus, the complacent "self-made" man blindly ignores the unforeseen circumstances that contributed to his achievements; and we all are ready enough to throw the blame for our failures on unforeseeable hindering circumstances.

We must also draw a distinction between the microscopic and the macroscopic view of human purpose, between the little drops of human volition and the general social streams which result from them. Little does the respectable paterfamilias intend, when he begets and rears lusty children, to lay the basis of imperialistic wars or monastic institutions. The voyage of Columbus was undoubtedly one of the causes of the spread of English civilization to America. Yet Columbus no more intended to bring it about than the microscopic globigerina could have planned the chalk cliffs of England which are the result of their life work.

That human volition by itself is, apart from favorable circumstances and mechanisms, inadequate to produce social results, is ancient wisdom. Yet after an event has happened we are prone to look upon the volition as the producing cause. A striking illustration of this fact is the way we explain inventions as due to the need of them. We are inclined to forget the great multitude of human needs that have gone unsatisfied through the ages. A visit to the cemetery of human hopes is needed for sobriety of judgment. Need or necessity may determine what invention will be generally developed; but inventiveness itself is the daughter of exuberant energy and favorable means. The history of science amply illustrates this.

In general, then, we must note that actual volition is not an adequate cause of large social changes.

(2) SOCIAL TELEOLOGY

The exclusively teleological character of social science has been maintained not only from the psychological but also from the moral or jural point of view. Social phenomena are phenomena of conformity to regulation. All human conduct, our goings and comings, what we eat and what we wear, what we say and what we habitually do, are all subject to social control. These actions are, therefore, judged not merely as illustrations of natural sequence in conformity with causal laws, but as conforming or failing to conform to social mores or norms. In general, we may say that the distinctively social point of view regards acts not as events in nature but as problems for us — how to choose the proper means, or to eliminate conflict in our aims. From this point of view the supreme unity of social science is to be sought not in the widest law of causal sequence, but in such a conception of the ultimate social ends as will make possible a coherent science or system of judgments of human conduct.

The foregoing must be defended against the superficial positivism which, on the basis of a misconception of the traditional logic, restricts science to the study of existence and denies the possibility of normative science. We are thus faced with the insistence that economics must be restricted to the study of the causes of actual phenomena (Weber), that ethics as a science can deal only with the causes of certain actual practices (Lévy-Bruhl), and that jurisprudence can deal only with laws or customs which actually prevail (Rolin).

Such a program is neither possible nor desirable. We cannot leave out all questions of what is socially desirable without missing the significance of many social facts; for since the relation of means to ends is a special form of that between parts and wholes, the contemplation of social ends enables us to see the relations of whole groups of facts to each other and to larger systems of which they are parts.

Those who boast that they are not, as social scientists, interested in what ought to be, generally assume (tacitly) that the hitherto prevailing order is the proper ideal of what ought to be. This is seen in the writings of positivists like Comte, Gumplowicz, and Duguit, who heap scorn on the Utopists that are concerned with what ought to be. A theory of social values like a theory of metaphysics is none the better because it is held tacitly and uncritically.

Lévy-Bruhl, who sees that normative considerations cannot be eliminated from ethics, preserves the latter as a rational art. But is not all scientific reasoning a rational art?

If the prejudice against normative science were justified, it would render not only mathematics but all theoretic science impossible. For in developed sciences like physics, we are concerned with a theoretic development of the wider realm of possibility, and thus we must deal with ideal entities such as perfectly free, rigid, continuous, geometric bodies, and with frictionless motion. Only by such theoretic development can we fruitfully apply principles to actual sensible bodies, and see phenomena together in a new light. This is exactly what the study of social ideals does for the purely scientific understanding of social phenomena.[1]

We cannot, however, accept the teleologic character of social phenomena as a complete determinant of what is specifically social. We cannot ignore the fact that some branches of social science, for example, the theory of business cycles, are theoretic in the same manner as the theory of hydrostatic pressure. For an adequate account of the distinctive subject-matter of the social sciences we must take note of the element of tradition, of the ways whereby social conformity is brought about. To understand this we must take into account:

B. THE HISTORICAL CHARACTER OF THE SOCIAL SCIENCES

It has been urged, notably by the followers of Windelband and Rickert, that while natural science deals with abstract aspects of phenomena that can be indefinitely repeated, social science deals with events which are unique. It is rather easy to refute this assertion by pointing to geology as both a historic and a natural science. Yet it would be vain to deny that the understanding of social phenomena requires a more extensive knowledge of the past than is generally the case in physical science. Questions of politics or economics, law or religion, generally refer to some particular historic state of human society.

Since social phenomena thus depend upon historic continuity, there can be no adequate knowledge of them without some reference to the past. It is, however, hasty and false to conclude that the

---

[1] If it be urged that the engineer or the applied physicist also views his field as a series of problems, the answer is that engineering involves problems precisely to the extent that it is concerned with human ends and therefore with social phenomena.

full nature of social phenomena is to be found entirely in their history.

The theory of evolution and the method of explaining all strange customs as "survivals," has strengthened this fallacy of historicism or geneticism. It is to-day, indeed, the favored resort of the intellectually complacent who cannot see that a history of religion, art, labor, war, of the social evil, or the like, is not the same as a solution of the problems which these subjects raise. If history undoubtedly helps us to understand the present, it is just as true that a knowledge of the present and of the permanent nature of things is necessary to understand the past. Can it possibly be more easy to understand why men did things in the little-known past, than why they do them to-day? The dogma that all human history is a continuous evolution from the simple to the complex, is a myth that finds little support in history itself — certainly not in the history of law or language. One suspects that it is precisely because of the absence of adequate knowledge of the past that it is possible for us to project simple stages into it. As we come down to the present and our historical knowledge increases, the certainties of a priori evolutionary history diminish.

The extensive explanation of all sorts of queer social practices as survivals of customs that originally had some use, is a form of inverted- or crypto-rationalism. There is nothing in history to indicate that our ancestors were more rational and more intent on doing things for definite purposes than we are. In any case the weakness of this type of historicism is that it tries to explain the present by the less-known past. It is largely motivated by dissatisfaction with the older rationalistic explanations of existing institutions, illustrated in Blackstone's fanciful "reasons" for the various laws of England. The study of actual history does undoubtedly show that the alleged reasons could not have been operative in originating these laws. Yet it is clearly fallacious to suppose that if we once learn from history how a given law or custom originated, we thereby explain its present existence. For obviously there are many old customs which no longer persist. If any law or custom, then, has survived, it must have something about it that has made it persist longer than other customs. The unusual liability of common carriers to-day may have originated in the fact that in Roman times the actual carrier was a slave, but the rule seems to have survived because of its social utility. Good reasons for social utility are, therefore, not eliminated by real or historical reasons as to origins.

There are, of course, social phenomena of long-time rhythm like the growth (or the decline) of the fundamental institutions of religion, language, social movements, and so forth, that are significantly contemporaneous only if the present includes a large chunk of what for other purposes is the past. But though history is thus a necessary condition for the extension of our knowledge, it will not enable us to dispense with the rational analysis of the present. Social science is this analysis or account of the abstract or logically repeatable aspects of social life.

C. CONCLUSION AS TO SOCIAL TRADITION OR CULTURE

If we keep in mind both the historic and the teleologic aspect of social life, we see an interaction and a mutual dependence between what is and what should be, between the actual historic cause and the ideal of what is desired. The subject-matter of social science thus differs from the subject-matter of natural science not only in introducing the prospective or teleologic point of view, which describes movements in terms of their goals, but in the more specific element of tradition which sometimes takes the form of conscious teaching and learning. We may say that the distinctive subject-matter of the social sciences is culture in the sense defined by Tylor, to wit, "the complex whole which includes knowledge, belief, art, morals, law, custom, and any other capabilities and habits *acquired by man as a member of society.*" I have stressed the last clause because that seems to be the significant clue to the distinction that we are seeking. The substance of culture, such as language, roads, tools, moral habits, and dispositions, are all modifications of the physical and the organic world. What makes them objects of the social sciences is that these modifications take place through social life and are handed on from one generation to another. It may be urged that there must have been a time when there was no human society and that therefore society cannot be an original factor and everything must ultimately be due to nature. But that is really not relevant for our present purpose. The absolute first moment of human society is not a phenomenon within the scope of social science. In the actual scope of the latter all the modifications of nature that we call culture take place under the influence of previous social life or culture. We thus have a distinct field or subject-matter for social science. The form of such science will depend upon the character of the connections between the various elements of the phenomena of culture.

II
The Ideal Goal (Telos) of the Social and the Natural Sciences

So far as science means the rigorous weighing of all the evidence, including a full consideration of all possible theories (which is the true antidote for bias or prejudice), all sciences obviously have the same ideal. But in this sense the efforts of a critical historian like Thucydides are also scientific. A good deal of social and political science is thus scientific only to the extent that history is. When, however, we examine the nature of the general rules employed in evidence or explanation of particular facts, we notice that in the natural sciences these rules are the objects of explicit logical or mathematical development which makes it easier to verify them, while in the social sciences they are apt to be only implicit, and consequently unexamined and of uncertain truth-value. Consider, for example, the explanation of certain social phenomena as due to the gregarious or social instinct, or the explanation of other phenomena as anti-social manifestations of disruptive individualism. If these explanations have any point it is because we assume it to be a law, in the first case, that human beings fall in line and yield to the suggestion of others, and in the second case, that human beings are to some extent intractable, resent dictation, and so on. Obviously, both of these general propositions are to some extent true. But the question of how we shall measure the precise extent of these seemingly opposite laws of human nature has not yet received any treatment comparable in definiteness with that accorded to the laws of physics, chemistry, or physiology.

It is the aim of all natural science to rise above the historical stage and to become theoretic, that is, to attain the form of a theory or system in which all propositions are logically or mathematically connected by laws or principles. Loose words about science being practical, experimental, and inductive cannot permanently obscure this truth, made evident in the history of every branch of physics and biology. No science, for instance, can seem so hopelessly empirical and so immediately practical as chemistry, yet its whole growth through the Periodic and Mozley's Laws has been in the direction of a deductive system.   Modern theories of heredity and variation are doing the same thing for biology.   Clearly, some of the social sciences, for example, economics, aim at the same goal. Yet we can surely survey the history of political science, as the scholarly and genial Professor Dunning did, and come to the melancholy conclusion that two thousand years of effort has brought us no farther than were the Greeks in the day of Aristotle.   Indeed, it seems that professional pride rather than desire for scientific accuracy makes us deny the inferiority of the social to the natural sciences with regard to established and universally verifiable general laws.   This is made manifest in the inferiority of our control over human nature when compared with our progress in the manipulation of physical nature.

The difference between the natural and the social sciences in this respect is not accidental and not readily removed by pious resolution.   In the first place, the subject-matter of the social sciences is inherently more complicated in the sense that we have more variables to deal with than in physics or biology.   In the latter sciences, specimens are more easily obtained; we can experiment more at will, varying the conditions one at a time, and thus we can more readily arrive at definite answers.   In the second place, there is the subjective difficulty of maintaining scientific detachment in the study of human affairs.   Few human beings can calmly and with equal fairness consider both sides of a question such as socialism, free-love, and birth-control.   Opinions on these matters are not viewed with the ethical neutrality with which we view opinions as to the structure of the ether, the atom, and so forth.   Emotional attachment to views which we have always honored, and repugnance toward those views that good people are taught to despise, hinder free scientific inquiry.   For the progress of science always depends upon our questioning the plausible, the respectably accepted, and the seemingly self-evident.   This is in a measure also true when social honor attaches to the holding of certain opinions on physical issues, for example, the Ptolemaic astronomy, or the theory of special creation.   With regard to physical questions, however, the fact that it requires elaborate training to follow them has taught the more intelligent part of the public some humility and the wisdom of suspending judgment.   But how can one admit ignorance on a social question on which every one else has a confident opinion?   One is tempted to say — to parody a remark of Bertrand

Russell — that the reason social scientists do not more often arrive at the truth is that they so frequently do not wish to. The desire to attain the truth is, after all, a late and relatively undeveloped human motive compared with the more vital and voluminous motives of social approval.

Because it is thus impossible to eliminate human bias in matters in which we are vitally interested, some sociologists (for example, the Deutsche Gesellschaft für Soziologie) have banished from their program all questions of value and have sought to restrict themselves to the theory of social happenings. This effort to look upon human actions with the same ethical neutrality with which we view geometric figures, is admirable. But the questions of human value are inescapable, and those who banish them at the front door admit them unavowedly and therefore uncritically at the back door. It is, then, better to aim directly at carrying the critical scientific spirit into the very study of moral values. Only critical reflection and a wider knowledge of the variety of human ideals can shake the naïve confidence in the absoluteness of our contemporary and local ideals. This does not mean that the variability of moral judgment disproves the possibility of a science of ethics any more than variability of vision disproves the possibility of a science of optics. If that which is deemed right at one time and place is deemed wrong at another time and place, it is because the judgment of right and wrong must include regard for the different circumstances. But the persistent confronting of the diversity of historic fact with critical judgments as to values enables us to overcome not only traditional absolutism, but also that narrow empiricism which vainly supposes that we can intelligently determine what is good in specific situations without regard for the ultimate issues involved. This is entirely parallel to the situation in the natural sciences where we must critically confront our experimental findings with general ideas in order to interpret the former and test the latter.

Social science can thus in the long run best attain its goal only when those who cultivate it care more for the scientific game itself and for the meticulous adherence to its rules of evidence than for any of the uses to which their discoveries can be put. This is not to deny that compassion for human suffering and the desire to mitigate some of its horrors may actuate the social scientist. But the social reformer, like the physician, the engineer, and the scientific agriculturist, can improve the human lot only to the extent that he utilizes the labor of those who pursue science for its own sake regardless of its practical applications.

How, indeed, can we improve human affairs unless we know what actually *is*, and what is *better?* How can we attain certain knowledge except by a whole-hearted respect for the rigorous rules of pure science? "He serves all who dares be true." But in the end we must remember that the knowledge of the truth, like the vision of beauty, is a good in itself.

To subordinate the pursuit of truth to practical considerations is to leave us helpless against bigoted partisans and fanatical propagandists who are more eager to make their policies prevail than to inquire whether or not they are right. The pursuit of pure science may not completely prevent our initial assumptions from being biased by practical vital preferences. But this is not to deny that the aloofness involved in the pursuit of pure science is the condition of that liberality which makes men civilized. If it be maintained, as it justly can be, that this ideal is an unattainable one, the only answer is that this is true also of the ideal of beauty, of holiness, and of everything else that is ultimately worth while and humanly ennobling.[1]

III

THE FORM OR METHOD OF RESEARCH IN THE SOCIAL AND THE NATURAL SCIENCES

The great Poincaré once remarked that while physicists had a subject-matter, sociologists were engaged almost entirely in considering their methods. Allowing for the inevitable divergence between the sober facts and heightened Gallic wit, there is still in this remark a just rebuke (from one who had a right to deliver it) to those romantic souls who cherish the persistent illusion that by some new trick of method the social sciences can readily be put on a par with the physical sciences in regard to definiteness and universal demonstrability. The maximum logical accuracy can be attained only by recognizing the exact degree of probability that our subject-matter will allow.

[1] Actuated by the shallow activism of the "business man's" philosophy which conceives perpetual motion to be the blessed life, and by an illiberal or "Puritanic" contempt of pure play or enjoyment, American writers frequently try to ridicule pure science as an "indoor sport." But there is nothing ridiculous about a noble and liberal sport — certainly not so much as in the appeal to the queer jumble of temporarily prevailing prejudices covered by the terms "red-blooded," "mechanistic," "democratic," and "Christian." (Cf. Wolfe's essay in Tugwell's *Trend of Economics*.)

From the fact that social questions are inherently more complicated than those of physics or biology — since the social involves
the latter but not vice versa — certain observations as to metho-
dologic possibilities follow at once.

1. THE COMPLEXITY OF SOCIAL PHENOMENA

In the first place, agreement based on demonstration is less easy
and actually less prevalent in the social than in the natural sciences,
because the greater complexity of social facts makes it less easy to
sharpen an issue to an isolable point and to settle it by direct observation of an indefinitely repeatable fact. We can, for instance, reduce the issue between the Copernican and the Ptolemaic astronomy to the question whether Venus does or does not show phases
like the moon's, and we can settle it by looking through a telescope.
If Venus did not forever repeat her cycle, and if the difference between a full circle of light and one partly covered by a crescent
shadow were not so readily perceived, the matter could not be so
readily settled.

With the greater complexity of social facts are connected (1) their
less repeatable character, (2) their less direct observability, (3) their
greater variability and lesser uniformity, and (4) the greater difficulty of isolating one factor at a time. These phases are so dependent on one another that we shall not treat them separately.

The practical difficulties of repeating social facts for purposes of
direct observation are too obvious to need detailed mention. What
needs to be more often recognized is that social facts are essentially
unrepeatable just to the extent that they are merely historical.
The past fact cannot be directly observed. Its existence is established by reasoning upon assumed probabilities. In the case of
physical history or geology our proof rests on definitely established
and verified laws of natural science. In the case of human history
the principles assumed are neither so definite nor so readily verifiable.

The greater variability of social facts may, if we wish, be viewed
as another phase of their complexity. Any cubic centimeter of
hydrogen will for most purposes of physics or biology be as good as
another. But observation on one community will not generally be
so applicable to another. Even purely biologic facts, for example,
the effects of diet, seem to be more variable in the human than in
other species. In the social realm reasoning from examples is in-

tellectually a most hazardous venture. We seldom escape the fallacy of selection, of attributing to the whole class what is true only of our selected instances. To urge, as some philosophers do, that this is true only because physical knowledge is thinner and depends more upon the principle of indifference, is to urge an interpretation, not a denial, of the fact.

It is, of course, true that for certain social questions we can treat all individuals as alike. Thus, for vital statistics, every birth or death counts the same, no matter who is involved. Likewise, in certain economic or juristic questions we ignore all individual differences. Yet there can be no doubt that the applicability of such rules in the social sciences is more limited and surrounded with greater difficulty than the application of the laws of the natural sciences to their wider material.

J. S. Mill in his *Logic* has raised the interesting question as to why it is that in certain inquiries one observation or experiment may be decisive while in other cases large numbers of observations bring no such certain results. In the main this difference holds between physical and social observation.

I venture to suggest a rather simple explanation of this fact — a fact that puzzled Mill because he did not fully grasp the logic of hypothesis. In any fairly uniform realm like that of physics, where we can vary one factor at a time, it is possible to have a crucial experiment, that is, it is possible to reduce an issue to a question of yes or no, so that the result refutes and eliminates one hypothesis and leaves the other in possession of the field. But where the number of possible causes is indefinitely large, and where we cannot always isolate a given factor, it is obviously difficult to eliminate an hypothesis; and the elimination of one hypothesis from a very large number does not produce the impression of progress in the establishment of a definite cause.

2. THE INFLUENCE OF VARIABILITY OF SOCIAL FACTS

The last observation suggests that the greater complexity and variability of social fact also make its purely theoretical development more difficult. In general, social situations are networks in which one cannot change one factor without affecting a great many others. It is, therefore, difficult to determine the specific effects of any one factor. Moreover, social elements seldom admit of simple addition. The behavior of the same individuals in a large group will not in general be the same as their behavior in a smaller group. This makes it difficult to apply the mathematical methods which have proved so fruitful in the natural sciences. For these mathematical methods depend upon our ability to pass from a small number of instances to an indefinitely large number by the process of summation or integration.

Where the number of units is indefinitely large we can assume continuity in variation. But the application of continuous curves to very limited groups of figures to which our social observation is usually restricted produces pseudo-science, for example, the assertion that if our distribution is skewed we have a proof of teleology.

The relatively small number of observations that we generally have to deal with in the social sciences makes the application of the probability curve a source of grave errors. For all the mathematical theorems of probability refer only to infinite series (for which we substitute as a practical equivalent "the long run"). Where the number is small there is no assurance that we have eliminated the fallacy of selection. The mathematical errors of applying a continuous curve to a discrete number of observations, produces ludicrous results. We can see this clearly when we try to determine the fundamental unit of our investigation, to wit, when are two social events equally probable? It is vain to expect that the crudeness of our observation and the vagueness of our fundamental categories will be cured by manipulation of the paraphernalia of statistical methods.

Physical categories have themselves been clarified by analysis. The dimensions of the different entities that we talk about — energy, action, momentum, and so on — are numerically determined. In the social sciences the very categories that we use are hazy, subject to variable usage and to confusing suggestion. Does law determine the state, or the state make the law? How many thousands of learned men have discussed this and similar questions without fixing the precise meaning of the terms "state" and "law."[1]

It is a familiar observation that the difficulty of framing exact concepts in the social realm causes much confusion through ambiguity. To this it should be added that vague concepts make

---

[1] Before Fourier definitely established the exact "dimensions" of the various physical categories, physicists could dispute (as the Cortesians and the Leibnizians did) as to the proper measure of "living" forces. Social science likewise needs a system of categories the exact dimensions of which are so clear as to make impossible the many confusions of which the example in the text is only one illustration.

possible the constant appeal to vague propositions as self-evidently true. Open any book on social science at random and you will find the author trying to settle issues by appealing to what seems self-evident. Yet most of such self-evident propositions are vague, and when we ask for their precise meaning and for the evidence in their favor, our progress stops. In the natural sciences the questioning of what seems self-evident is relatively simple because when we have a simple proposition we can more readily formulate a true or an exclusive alternative. In social matters where difference of opinion is greater and demonstration more difficult, we cling all the more tenaciously to our primary assumption, so that our assumptions largely mold what we shall accept as facts.

Any one who naïvely believes that social facts come to us all finished and that our theories or assumptions must simply fit them, is bound to be shocked in a court of law or elsewhere to find how many facts persons honestly see because they expected them rather than because they objectively happened. That psychoanalysts, economists, sociologists, and moralists labor more or less in the same situation, the tremendous diversity of opinion among them amply indicates. Will a classical anthropologist admit that some Indians had a patriarchal form of kinship before adopting the matriarchal type? Is it a *fact* that the suppression of certain desires, deliberately or as a result of imitation, necessarily produces pathologic states of mind? One has but to scrutinize such questions to see how much must be assumed before it can be shown that any fact is involved.

Is corporal punishment in schools, or free divorce, an evil or not? Under the influence of general opinions one can readily maintain it as a fact that all the consequences of such practices are evil. But one who refuses to admit that these practices are evils can be equally consistent.

Is the same true in the natural sciences? Certainly not to the same extent. Because theories do not to the same extent influence what we shall regard as physical or biologic fact, false theorems have never been such serious obstacles to the progress of natural science. The statements in popular histories that the Ptolemaic, the phlogiston, or the caloric hypothesis stopped the progress of science have no foundation. On the contrary these and other false theories in physics were useful in suggesting new lines of research. It is this fact that led Darwin to remark that false observations (on which others rely) are much more dangerous than false theories to the progress of science. Now in the social sciences we certainly do not have the elaborate safeguards against false observation that the natural sciences with their simpler material and many instruments of precision find it necessary to cultivate. The very circumstance that social facts are apt to be more familiar makes it easier to be misled as to the amount of accurate knowledge that we have about them.

From another point of view we may express this by saying that in the social sciences we are more at the mercy of our authorities with regard to what are the facts. The social worker or field anthropologist has less opportunity to preserve his specimens than the naturalist or the laboratory worker. If a later social worker or field anthropologist finds the fact to be different from what was reported by his predecessor, there is the possibility not only that they have observed different things but also that the social facts have changed.

In this connection it is well to note that the invention of a technical term often creates facts for social science. Certain individuals become *introverts* when the term is invented, just as many persons begin to suffer from a disease the moment they read about it. Psychiatry is full of such technical terms; and if a criminal is rich enough he generally finds experts to qualify his state of mind with a sufficient number of technical terms to overawe those not used to scrutinizing authorities. The technical terms of natural science are useful precisely because they carry no aroma of approval or disapproval with them. This brings us to:

3. THE RÔLE OF BIAS IN THE SOCIAL SCIENCES

We have referred before to the recognition of this rôle as a commonplace. It is not, however, so often recognized that the greater human interest in social questions itself acts as a powerful deterrent from persistent scientific inquiry. In purely natural questions the trained scientist is apt to be more interested in the soundness of his procedure than in his results. Hence seemingly satisfactory results are frequently most carefully scrutinized by those who obtain them. Interest in human welfare, however, is apt to make the social scientist care more for seemingly helpful results than for the soundness of the methods whereby the results are obtained. Hence much bad science.

Moreover, the practical interest in social problems generally involves so many diverse factors that a thorough study of any one phase will be of little immediately practical avail. Hence there is the temptation to desert the thorough study of abstract phases and to try to arrive at plausible guesses as to the whole outcome. In the applied natural sciences the danger is not so great because our material is more simple and fungible.

4. ARE THERE ANY SOCIAL LAWS?

In view of the paucity of generally recognized laws in social science it is well to ask categorically if the search for them is fully justified. The existence of similarities in different societies at different times and places has been used as a proof of the existence of "a uniform law in the psychic and social development of mankind at all times and under all circumstances."[1] But *similarities* of customs and beliefs, even if they are not superficial or due to the prepossession of the observer, are not laws. As human beings resemble one another in their physical, biologic, and psychologic traits, we naturally expect that their social expressions will have points of resemblance, especially when the outer material is similar. If the number of human traits were known and within manageable compass, the principle of limited possibilities (enunciated by Dr. Goldenweiser) might be a clue to the laws of social life. But even a finite or limited number of facts may be too large for our manipulation.

In the end those who believe in the existence of social laws similar to those of natural science, fall back on the a priori argument of determinism. It is inconceivable, they say, to suppose that anything can be without a cause. This argument involves confusion between determinism in general and the existence of scientific laws. As this confusion is wide-spread, it is well to clear it up here.

The laws of physical science are uniform or invariant relations between successive events. Strictly speaking, no event can repeat itself. What is repeated is a certain pattern of recognizable relations which we identify with the event by the well-known figure of speech which takes the part for the whole. Thus, one instance of the freezing of water is by the principle of indifference, the same as any other instance. Now if we keep this in mind, we can readily see that the existence of physical laws is not the same as universal

[1] Ward, *Pure Sociology*, pp. 53, 54.

determinism. A picture puzzle so constituted that each fragment can fit into only one position illustrates a deterministic system, even if it has no laws or repetition of patterns. What may be termed the organic philosophy of the Hegelians treats the whole world and the phenomena in it from this point of view. The view underlying the mechanical laws of natural science is different. These laws assert not only that certain phenomena always depend upon a very small number of factors but that they depend on nothing else. If the freezing of water depended on everything else there would be no significant point in saying it depended upon temperature and pressure. Physical laws are in fact all expressed in relatively simple analytic functions containing a small number of variables. If the number of these variables should become very large, or the functions too complicated, physical laws would cease to be readily manipulated or applicable. The science of physics would then be practically impossible. If, then, social phenomena depend upon more factors than we can readily manipulate, the doctrine of universal determinism will not guarantee an attainable expression of laws governing the specific phenomena of social life. Social phenomena, though determined, might not to a finite mind in limited time display any laws at all.

Let us take a concrete example. A man says to a woman, "My dear!" The physical stimulus is here a very definite set of sound waves, and we have reason to believe that the physical effect of these waves is always determinate. But what the lady will in all cases say or do in response depends upon so many factors that only an astonishing complacency about our limited knowledge of human affairs would prompt a confident answer. The a priori argument that there must be laws is based on the assumption that there are a finite number of elements or forms which must thus repeat themselves in an endless temporal series. But why may not the repeatable forms and elements be only those which enter our physical laws? What guarantee is there that in the limited time open to us there must be a complete repetition of social patterns as well?

In any case, those who think that social science has been as successful as physical science in discovering and establishing laws, may be invited to compile a list of such laws and to compare the list in respect to number, definiteness, and universal demonstrability, with a collection such as Northrup's Laws of Nature.

5. SOCIAL AND NATURAL CAUSATION

The notion of cause originates in the field of legal procedure. A cause (Greek *Aitia*) is a case or ground for an action. The Stoics, basing themselves on certain notions of Heraclitus, brought the notion of law into the conception of natural happenings. Law to them meant not mere uniformity that just happens to exist, but something decreed by the World-Reason, or Logos. Violations of it are possible but reprehensible. This is still the popular view, which speaks of certain acts as unnatural and of nature punishing all violations of her laws. The notion of a law of nature as a non-purposeful but absolute uniformity, so that a single exception would deny its validity, arises from the modern application of mathematics to physics. The proposition that all x's are y's is simply false if one x is not a y.

Modern physics seeks to attain the latter kind of laws by the process of abstraction. Thus, the proposition that all bodies fall to the earth suggests itself as such a law. But if we remember the behavior of smoke, of birds, or balloons, some modification of this statement is necessary if universality is to be attained. This is achieved in the statement that all bodies attract one another. For in the case of bodies which do not fall we can show the presence of some force which counteracts the attraction of the earth so that the attraction is thus always in being. If the counteracting forces did not themselves operate according to a known law, the law of gravitation would be useless. We can predict phenomena only because the gravitational and the counteracting forces are independently measurable. Unless social forces are similarly measurable and there is some common unit or correlation of social forces, the whole notion of law as employed in the physical sciences may be unapplicable. When religious and economic interests pull individuals in different directions, which force will prevail? Such a question can certainly not be answered on any scientific basis. We do not know how many units of one social force will counteract another. All we can say is that in some cases religious motives prevail over economic ones, in some cases the reverse is true, and in most cases we cannot separate the motives at all.

The difference between social and natural causation is confused by the doctrine that social "forces" are psychic, and that at least one of them, desire, acts like a physical force — indeed, that it obeys the Newtonian laws of motion.[1] Obviously if social phenom-

[1] Ward, *Psychic Factors in Civilization*, pp. 123 and 94.

ena are not merely physical, the term "social force" can at best be only a metaphor and we should be careful to note its real difference from physical force.

This difference is ignored when a popular sociologist speaks of social motion as following the line of least resistance even more closely than does nature herself.[1]   In natural science we know what a straight line is before considering any given physical process.   But what is denoted by the metaphor, the "straight line" or the "line of least resistance" in any given social process, is something that we arbitrarily tell only after the event.   Psychic forces are not physical forces.

If psychic forces operate at all, it is in the way of desire.   Now desire is an actually felt state of mind existing at a definite time but not — except in a metaphorical sense — continuously.   Physical force, on the other hand, is not a temporal event but an abstract aspect of certain physical phenomena, to wit, the product of mass and acceleration.   Moreover, desire can be said to bring about results only if there happens to be some adequate mechanism at hand.   Hence the relation between the desire and what follows does not replace natural causation but is an entirely different non-uniform relation superadded.

Similarly, social forces are not merely psychological.   What is called social causation may be regarded as a teleologic relation. But the fact that in social relations we deal with large groups enables us to depart from individual psychology.   We can thus say with greater certainty that an economic opportunity will be utilized, or that the religion of their fathers will be followed by a large group of persons, than that they will be utilized or followed by a single individual whose specific disposition we do not know.   We cannot tell what a given individual will think of the next war, but we can be fairly certain that every nation will, like the Romans, manage to be convinced that its side is the just one.

Social causation, then, need not be like that of individual purposes.   The overcrowding in cities does not intentionally bring about certain social diseases, any more than the invention of the cotton-gin was intended to bring about the economic changes which led to the fall of the older southern aristocracy or to the political changes which led to the Civil War.   It is of greater importance to recognize that social science is for the most part concerned not like

[1] Ross, E. A., *Foundations of Sociology*, p. 43.

physics with laws expressing the invariant repetition of elements, nor with laws of individual psychic events, but with laws about the relation of very complex patterns of events to one another.

Consider a number of examples of social causations: It is surely significant to inquire as to the effects of density of population. Is feminism a cause or an effect of the greater economic opportunity open to women? Is poverty the cause or the effect of a higher birth-rate? In all such cases a causal relation means some connection not between individual events, or mere sums of such events, but between diverse patterns of distribution, sometimes of the same group of events. If social institutions as specific groups of events are themselves called events, we must distinguish the different levels of the term *events*. It will, however, prevent confusion if we remember that a social institution is a mode of viewing or grouping a number of events and is, therefore, strictly speaking, not a datable event, although the constituent events may occur between two dates.

Thus it is that in social causation the cause does not disappear when it produces an effect, but can be said to continue and to be modified by its effects. A system of education may affect the commerce of a people and the latter in turn may modify the system of education. That is possible because "system of education" is not a single temporal event but a pattern of events actually coeval with the pattern of events called "the commerce of a people." The causal relation or the interaction between them is predominantly a matter of logical analysis of groups of phenomena.

The purely scientific interest is thus best served by isolating some one aspect of social phenomena — for example, the economic, the political, the religious — and tracing the effect of changes in that aspect. Even the historian must select and restrict himself to certain phases of social events. But the practical interest in social outcome is not immediately satisfied by the knowledge of uniform sequences or of the merely necessary conditions of social happenings, which are too numerous to be very interesting. It needs, rather, a knowledge of the quantitative adjustments of *all* the factors necessary to produce a desired effect. This is seldom attainable. We can under certain conditions tell, for example, that a reduction of price or an increase in advertising will (in a high proportion of cases) increase sales. But the variations due to local conditions are very large, and our concrete practical knowledge always involves guess work. Hence, it can never guarantee us against fatal errors.

IV
THE FACULTY OR TYPE OF MENTALITY INVOLVED

The foregoing considerations suggest the element of truth in the Aristotelian view that while physical science depends on theoretical reason (nous), practical social science involves more sound judgment (phroneisis). Sound judgment means ability to guess (or intuit) what is relevant and decisive, and to make a rapid estimate of the sum of a large number of factors that have not been accurately determined. In practice the statesman, the business man, and even the physician may often find the suggestive remark of a novelist like Balzac of greater help than long chapters from the most scientific psychology, since the latter deals with elements, whereas in conduct we deal with whole situations. This frequently gives rise to a philistine anti-rationalism. What is the use of speculating about the ultimate good? Why not, rather, use our intelligence to increase the sum of justice and happiness in actual cases? But *can* decision be intelligent if inquiries as to the ultimate meaning of justice and happiness are prohibited? How will the restricted use of intelligence in that case be different from the uncritical acceptance of traditional judgments as to what is good and what is bad in specific cases?

The efforts of the human intellect may be viewed as a tension between two poles — one to do justice to the fullness of the concrete case before us, the other to grasp an underlying abstract universal principle that controls much more than the one case before us.

No human field shows these forces in perfectly stable equilibrium. The problems of engineering, medication, administration, and statesmanship generally depend more upon not overlooking any of the relevant factors. But in pure science as in personal religion and poetry intense concentration on one phase rather than justice to many is the dominant trait. To the extent that the social sciences aim at the adjustment of human difficulties, they involve more judgment and circumspection. To the extent that they aim at insight or *theoria*, they are at one with pure science and with religion and poetry.

SELECTED REFERENCES

On scientific method generally:

Campbell, N. R.   *The Elements of Physics.*   1920.

Jevons, F. B.   *Principles of Science.*   1877.

Mill, J. S.   *Logic.*   5th ed.   1862.

Morgan, T. H.   *Critique of the Theory of Evolution.*   1916.

Poincaré, H.   *Foundations of Science.*   1913.

Ritchie, D.   *Scientific Method.*   1923.

Thomas, P. F., ed.   *De la Méthode dans les Sciences.*   1910.

On social science:

Wundt, W.   *Logic,* book II.   2d ed.   1895.

Aristotle.   *Works.*   Oxford translations.

Barnes, H. E., ed.   *History and Prospects of the Social Sciences.*   1925.

Barth, P.   *Philosophie der Geschichte als Sociologie.*   1897.

Bernheim, E.   *Lehrbuch der historischen Methode.*   1889.

Boas, Franz.   *Mind of Primitive Man.*   1911.

Cohen, M. R.   "History vs. Value."   *Journal of Philosophy.*   1914.

Comte, Auguste.   *Positive Philosophy.*   3d ed.   1893.

Dennes, W.   *Methods and Presuppositions of Group Psychology.*   1924.

Durkheim, Emile.   *Les Règles de la Méthode Sociologique.*   7th ed.   1919.

Febvre, Lucian.   *A Geographical Introduction to History.*   1925.

Goldenweiser, A.   "Principle of Limited Possibilities in the Development of Culture."   *Journal of American Folk-Lore,* XXVI.   1913.

Hegel.   *Philosophy of Mind,* trans. by Wallace.   1894.

Herder.   *Ideen zur Geschichte der Menscheit.*

Kant.   *Ideen zu einer allgemeinen Geschichte,* trans. by Hastie as *Kant's Principles* (Politics).

Lamprecht, K.   *What is History.*   1905.

Lowie, R. H.   *Ethnology and Culture.*   1917.

Menger, K.   *Untersuchungen.*   1881.

Montesquieu.   *Spirit of Laws.*   1748.   Nugent's translation, 1914.

Pittard.   *Race and History.*   1926.

Small, A. W.   *Origins of Sociology.*   1924.

Schäffle.   *Bau und Leben des Socialen Körpers.*   1881.

Spencer, H.   *Principles of Sociology.*   3d ed.   1885.   Several Editions.

Spranger.   *Lebensformen.*   3d ed.   1922.

Stammler, R.   *Wirtschaft und Recht.*   2d ed.   1906.

Tarde, Gabriel.   *Social Laws,* trans. by Warren.   1907.

Vico, G.   *Scienza Nuovo,* trans. to the French by Mechelet.   1853.

Ward, L. F.   *Psychic Factors in Civilization.*   2d ed.   1906.

Weber, M.   *Aufsätze zur Wissenschaftslehre.*   1922.

CHAPTER XXXIV
THE SOCIAL SCIENCES AND PHILOSOPHY

BY WM. PEPPERELL MONTAGUE

COLUMBIA UNIVERSITY

PHILOSOPHY is the attempt to give preliminary and tentative answers to the kind of questions that have not yet been answered with definiteness and certainty by science. Philosophic questions are vaguer, deeper, and broader than scientific questions and that is why the concepts and theories of philosophy are more speculative and uncertain than those of science. But our powers of discovery and our technique of experimental proof are undergoing continuous improvement with the result that the boundary between philosophy and science is constantly shifting, and that much of the philosophy of yesterday is being incorporated into the science of to-day. The theories of the atomic structure of matter and of the evolution of higher species from lower are notable examples of the transformation of philosophical speculations into scientifically established facts. To reproach philosophy for consisting of unverified speculations is as absurd as to reproach a child for not being a man. As William James pointed out, philosophy must always consist of unsolved problems just because when a problem gets a definite solution it becomes a part of science. And to the query as to why philosophy should persist, two answers may be given: First, the deep importance and the broad insistent interest of a problem are very often inversely proportional to our capacity for solving it scientifically. And whether we like it or not, questions as to the deeper meanings of life and existence will obtrude themselves upon all but the meanest and most prosaic of minds. Philosophy is thus for better or for worse an inescapable incident of human experience. Secondly, philosophy is not only inevitable but also desirable because theories must be formulated by speculative imagination and clarified by analytic discussion before they are ripe for experimental verification. Philosophers are the advance guard of the army of scientists. They spy out the new land as a necessary preliminary to its successful occupation.

Our discussion of philosophy and the social sciences will consist of three sections. In Section I we shall consider the general postulates of social philosophy; in Section II we shall consider one of the major problems of social philosophy: to wit, the problem of property; in Section III we shall speak of the needs for a constructive social philosophy to-day.

I

₍ THE GENERAL POSTULATES OF SOCIAL PHILOSOPHY

First, what is society? And second, what is the end or goal with reference to which social practices are to be evaluated? In answer to these questions we shall set forth two propositions with only so much of justification as may serve to make clear their meaning and to give them a sufficient plausibility to warrant the reader's provisional acceptance of them as postulates.

1. *Society is not an organism in itself but an organization of individuals; and its institutions have value only in so far as they serve the needs of its members.* Chemical atoms are combinations of electrons, physical molecules are combinations of atoms, the living cell is a combination of molecules, the human individual is a combination of cells, and social groups such as families and nations are combinations of individuals. Each of these combinations has a kind of permanence and unity of its own which gives it a relative independence both of the parts which compose it and of the whole of which it is itself a part. But there is only one stage in the entire hierarchy of combinations which gives evidence of rational and purposive activity, and that is the stage of the human individual. On the one hand, if the sub-individual cells of our body possess conscious reason and purpose, they give no signs of it in their behavior; while on the other hand, the hypothesis that any super-individual society of men and women is as such endowed with a collective mind of its own capable of feeling, remembering, and imagining, is a supposition that is probably false and quite certainly useless and even mischievous for both science and philosophy. It is probably false because the existence of a unified consciousness seems to depend upon a much closer and more integrated system of material elements than is found to obtain among the members of any social group. There is, for example, nothing corresponding to a brain and nervous system which would make consciousness as we know it a possibility; and there is nothing in the behavior of such social groups that cannot be explained in terms of its associated members.

The hypothesis of a social or group mind is useless and mischievous as well as false because, even if we were to assume its existence despite the evidence to the contrary, we could make no fruitful use of the assumption. We could not say in what the well-being of such a group-soul would consist, nor whether its values were higher or lower than our own.

In spite of the looseness of the analogies which have suggested this mystical and harmful conception, the acceptance of it has vitiated a great deal of otherwise valid social theory from Plato to Bluntchli. At the present time it operates not openly but in a covert form as the idea that human organizations and institutions have an intrinsic value that is independent of the extent to which they serve the needs of individuals. As against such a view we insist that even the most essential and permanent institutions such as marriage, property, and government are to be evaluated solely in terms of their contribution to the welfare of human beings. Their value is instrumental and secondary, never intrinsic or primary. The individual and only the individual is the consumer of joys and sorrows. His forms of organization are not ends in themselves but means or instruments to his progress. We must not of course misunderstand this as implying that a man should not often sacrifice himself for his country or church or school. It is only that any such sacrifice in behalf of an institution has its ultimate justification in the service rendered by means of the institution to other individuals, present or future. The institution merely as such has no rights and no claim on our allegiance, nor is it sacrosanct or in any degree immune from the freest criticism.

2. *The goal and purpose of all the institutions of society as of all individual conduct should be the maximum happiness or increase of individual life.* Pleasure is the transitory feeling, and happiness the enduring experience accompanying the fulfilment of vital tendency or the actualization of potentiality; and all that can properly be called good consists primarily in such fulfilment of capacity and secondarily in whatever serves as a means or an instrument to that end. As life consists of activity and striving, every attainment of an aim constitutes an increase of life's substance. And we can thus regard moral value or good as *life in the making*, while correspondingly the life actually existing at a given time can be regarded as *good already attained*. I take this conception of moral value to be essentially in harmony both with Professor Dewey's

conception of value as growth, and also with the older utilitarianism of John Stuart Mill.

I think that the reason why the principle has not always been accepted as a postulate of social science and applied ethics, is because of the tendency to transform instrumental values into primary values. Social customs and individual habits which at a given time and under special conditions have resulted in well-being have come by a natural though unfortunate association to be regarded as good in themselves with the consequence that when conditions changed or when new and better instruments were discovered the old ways were blindly and passionately defended, and social progress was retarded. In fact, our entire system of moral and social traditions is cluttered up with taboos or unreasoned rules of conduct which are treated as sacred and unalterable as a result of their having been at one time expedient.

If we can once get a clear popular recognition that moral codes derive all their value from their efficiency to promote the maximum well-being of the maximum number of people under the particular conditions in which they are used, then ethics will cease to be an antiquated branch of theology, and will become the great business of human engineering. From such a change of attitude, there would result two beneficent consequences. First, the whole vast body of secular science could be mobilized and directed to the discovery of better methods of promoting happiness. And, secondly, man's fund of moral and spiritual energy — pitifully small at best — could all be devoted to fruitful realization of human needs instead of being, as at present, largely wasted in the service of outworn shibboleths.

It would be a great mistake to suppose that in making the maximum well-being of human individuals the supreme end in terms of which all social structures and customs are to be evaluated we are in any way belittling either the absolute and imperative nature of the sense of duty on the one hand or what may be called the higher or spiritual side of human character on the other hand. The key virtues are (1) sympathy or love, and (2) enthusiasm or courage; justice is only sympathy universalized by reason, and temperance is only enthusiasm clarified by intelligence. Promotion of these virtues is rightly regarded as more important than any ordinary happiness; but not as is often believed because they are in any way alien to happiness, but rather because they are permanent and intrinsic sources of happiness.   The tree is justified by its fruits, and is cherished because of them; but though its value is in this sense instrumental, it is none the less more important than any one of its fruits just because it is the permanent and necessary condition for all of them.   The moral virtues derive their value primarily from the fact that those who practice them produce happiness in others. But the production of happiness in others is itself a supreme satisfaction or happiness to the producer, because it fulfils the potentialities of his rational and spiritual nature.

II
A Major Problem of Social Philosophy

The institutions or forms of organization which are found in human society are as various and as changing as the needs which they serve.   Among this great mass of more or less transitory social structures there are six which stand out from the rest as being permanent and necessary expressions of human nature.   These six may be listed as follows: property, governmental and inter-governmental adjustments, marriage, education, and religion.   The analysis of these institutions with the comparative evaluations of the variations of which each is susceptible makes up a large part of social philosophy and social science.   As an illustration of the philosophic method of treating social problems I shall consider that institution which by reason of its far-reaching implications for social life and social problems has been regarded as of supreme importance, namely, the institution of property.

Man is distinguished from other animals by the extent to which he attaches to himself objects in his environment that minister directly or indirectly to his needs.   The bee and the squirrel accumulate stores of food for future consumption, and build homes in which it is preserved and in which their young are reared.   It is, however, only in the case of human beings that these usable objects gain a sufficient detachment from their users to be exchanged for one another; and it is only then that they can rightly be called property.   Property can be defined as anything — object, right, or privilege — which is both usable and exchangeable.   A man's property is a kind of extension of his organism, an additional guarantee of power, freedom, and security.   It follows that next in importance to the control of life itself is the control of the social and material means to the fulfilment of life's needs.   If there were enough property for each to have what he desired there would be no difficulty and no problem; but as throughout all animal life the birth-rate exceeds the food-supply, involving a struggle for existence, so analogously in every human community the demand for property exceeds the supply and involves a struggle for economic power. And while the possession of property gives freedom and security, the lack of it gives insecurity and dependence. The difficulties and disorders incident to the primary economic struggle to wrest property from nature have been intensified by the situation that arises when some individuals possess more and others less property than is needed for immediate use. For it then becomes possible for those enjoying a surplus to lend money and land to those suffering a deficit, who in return for the service pay interest and rent. Property used in this way confers upon its owners not only a primary power over nature but a secondary power over other men. They become able to live without working and without diminishing their property, which as principal is not only preserved but actually increased by the income which it draws. Thus to the natural inequalities to be expected from the unequal abilities of men, there are added artificial inequalities due to the power of creditors and landlords to live upon the labor of their debtors and tenants.

The problems intrinsic to this situation have been enormously aggravated by what is known as the Industrial Revolution or the process by which science during the nineteenth century was applied to industry in such a way as to substitute for the hand-tools owned by the workers machine-tools too complicated and too expensive to be divided among those who used them. To the somewhat scattered classes of debtors and tenants there was thus added a much more definitely integrated class of wage-workers. With the increasing industrialization of society the comparatively new group of machine-workers has increased in numbers, in importance, and in class conscious solidarity. And even without the intellectual stimulus of such philosophers as Marx and La Salle it was inevitable that from this new class and their sympathizers there should arise a demand for a revolutionary change in the ownership and control of capital or productive property. The proposed change is of course to consist in replacing the present individual ownership of capital with a collective ownership by the workers, either directly through labor-organizations or indirectly through the general government.

The intensity of the socialist demand is proportioned (1) to the intensity of the suffering of the wage-workers and (2) to the extent to which they have developed a militant class-consciousness. Whether the change is inevitable, and if inevitable whether it is to come slowly and by the orderly methods of parliamentary government or quickly by a violent revolution, are questions that directly or indirectly dominate the politics of the civilized world to-day. As students of social philosophy our interest must be directed to the question of the desirability or undesirability of the threatened change in the institution of property. And within the scope of this article it will of course be possible only to formulate and appraise in the most general terms the principal arguments on each side. To the philosophic defender of socialism a typical capitalistic society appears as a system in which a large class of productive workers are compelled to yield up a part of what they produce to the small class of idlers who own the machines at which the workers must toil to keep from starving. The part of the product which is taken by the owner is called profit. The remainder which the owner returns to the worker after deducting the cost of upkeep is called wages. The owner merely as owner performs no service whatever, and yet he not only lives comfortably on the profits taken from the workers but controls in his own interest all the mechanisms of social life. The injustice and cruelty of this system is equalled by the inefficiency and waste which it involves. For when goods are made for profit rather than for use the capitalist has every incentive to exploit his customers by adulterating his goods, to enter into wasteful competition with rival capitalists in such matters as salesmanship and advertising, and to grind down his employees to the lowest level attainable.

The socialist would replace this cruel and wasteful system by a collective ownership of the means and instruments of production. In such a coöperative commonwealth there would be no wage-slaves and no parasitic idlers. All healthy individuals would be free and all would work, each receiving the equivalent of what he produced, subject only to such modification as might seem to be for the general good. The waste and the chicanery of capitalism as well as the bitter war of classes involved in it would be done away with, and imperfect human beings would live under a system in which there would be a continuous incentive to develop their higher rather than, as now, their lower qualities.

To the socialistic indictment of capitalism on the grounds (1) of its injustice and (2) of its wastefulness, the opponent of socialism replies somewhat as follows:

The profit which the owner of a machine receives is not an unearned increment extorted from what belongs to the workers. One part of it constitutes wages of organization and management, another part can be regarded as wages of risk, a just return for the hazard involved by the owner in using his property to produce goods rather than in consuming it as would be his right. As for the portion of profit that remains after deducting the cost of management and insurance, it constitutes deferred wages for the invention and production of the machinery. The capitalist has either produced the machinery by his own work or has legally inherited or otherwise received it from those who have done so, and hence is entitled to the additional wealth which it makes possible for the workers to produce through its agency. The wages paid the workers amount to more than they could make if left to their own efforts apart from the new machine-tools. They are in no sense wage-slaves, but are free at any time to leave their employment and to produce what they can for themselves.

As for the waste charged against capitalism, one part of it, such as adulteration of goods and other forms of trickery, is the outcome not of any system but of the evil in human nature. The second part of the waste—that which is charged against such activities as competitive advertising and salesmanship — is to a large extent compensated for by the increased needs which advertising creates; and every new need is a new capacity for happiness. Such wastes as remain are inseparable from wholesome business enterprise and register an amount of inefficiency infinitely less than would be involved in production by the state. Socialism, as seen from the standpoint of the defender of capitalism, instead of increasing productivity and making all men free, would result in subjecting the complicated mechanism of business and industry to the inefficiencies and passions of politics. Instead of a system under which the ablest men automatically rise to leadership through an economic natural selection, we should have a system in which political demagogues controlled production. All men would be slaves of a bureaucratic state. And minorities representing ability and originality would be completely at the mercy of thoughtless and passion-driven majorities.

I have tried to present the essential arguments on each side of the controversy as fairly as is possible in such brief compass, and there are two rather obvious comments which I will make before attempting anything like an appraisal of the opposing doctrines.

First, the communistic system, if it worked as well as its advocates believe it would, or even as well as the best examples of existing government ownership, would be superior both in its justice and in its efficiency to capitalism as we have it to-day.   If on the other hand a socialization of production worked out as badly as its opponents believe it would, or even as badly as the worst examples of existing government ownership, it would just as certainly be inferior both in justice and in efficiency to the present competitive system.

Second, whether a socialist régime would work out as a roseate Utopia or as a hideous nightmare, or in some intermediate manner, is a question that can receive no final answer until each type of society in each stage of civilization has tried it by experiment. From Plato to Lenin the arguments on both sides have been propounded with more or less plausibility, but never with finality. With regard to this problem of property as with regard to so many other social problems, we have not advanced from the philosophic stage of speculative discussion to the scientific stage of decisive experiment.

We may venture to come to closer grips with our question if we note that the socialist usually pictures capitalistic enterprise in its late stage, while his opponent usually pictures it in its early stage.

Take the case of a workman who has saved from his earnings a sum of money which he devotes to a productive purpose such as building a sawmill in a community where there is need for one. The venture thrives and his profits from it measure the value of his service to the community.   He employs men from the countryside who make more from the wages paid them than they were making from their own farms.   Nobody loses and everybody is benefited. The owner's profits are in no sense unearned increment and his workers are in no sense wage-slaves.   This sort of capitalism cannot be indicted on the grounds either of injustice or of waste.   The socialist would seem to have no case at all.   But now look ahead a couple of generations and we get a very different picture.   The original entrepreneur has died and his grandchildren are now receiving profits from the mill over and above any service that they render.   Though legal heirs, they are economic parasites.   And as for the wage-workers of the new generation, they have no such opportunity as their grandparents had to return to independent production. The community has become industrialized and the only work that they are capable of performing is the specialized work in the mill. There are more workers than there are jobs; and the new owners of the mill have complete power over their employees. "Wage-slavery" ceases to be a mere piece of rhetoric and becomes a very grim reality. In this phase of capitalism it is the socialist who has all the best of the argument.

Now it is clear that the industrial system of any modern country is a complicated mixture of these two sorts of capitalism. And the strength of the case for socialism varies proportionately with the predominance of the later or sordid type of capitalistic enterprise over the earlier and beneficent type in which the workers are free and the owner's profits are a well-earned return for his enterprise and social service. Unfortunately the course of economic evolution seems to show an unmistakable though irregular trend from the good to the bad type of capitalism, and unless some policy can be found to mitigate the situation, socialism with all its dangers of bureaucratic tyranny and inefficiency would seem both justifiable and inevitable.

Now the crucial evil of the situation does not seem to me to consist so much in the existence of undeserved riches but rather in the existence of inescapable and slavish poverty. The owner of inherited and undeserved wealth may well prove a more efficient and more benevolent manager of his capital than a group of bureaucrats chosen by the majority of the citizens for political reasons. Unless he is an abnormally greedy and stupid person, the man of large means will derive more satisfaction from earning the gratitude and acclaim of his fellows by devoting his wealth to constructive and generous public service than by wasteful and selfish consumption.

On the other hand, no amount either of productive efficiency or of plutocratic benevolence can compensate a community for the indignities suffered by large groups of workers who are dependent for their very lives upon the will of those who own the tools and land with which they must work. Any sort of communism would be preferable to such a system even if it worked as badly as its opponents predict, so long as it guaranteed to every man a decent living and a measure of freedom.

Now there is no reason, either economic or political, why a state should not undertake to abolish the major evil of capitalism — the virtual enslavement of its unemployed and irregularly employed workers — by adopting a policy which we might name "Minimal Communism." I mean a system of state-controlled industries upon which any unemployed worker could fall back no matter how inefficient or otherwise unfortunate he might be. Such a system would in nowise interfere with the prevailing capitalistic society within which it would function, if it were kept economically autonomous and industrially insulated, first, in the matter of the wages paid to its workers, second, in the matter of the disposal of its products. In lieu of ordinary wages there would be only food, shelter, and clothing, supplemented by a small amount of money furnished by the government, so that there would be a constant incentive, though not a degrading necessity, for the workers to return to private employment. In this respect the institution would function as an industrial hospital where all who needed nursing could be cared for, and where none but the incurables would desire to stay permanently. In the matter of goods produced, they should be consumed by the workers and not dumped upon the outside market where they would be in ruinous competition with the products of private capital. Such a system of minimal communism might turn out to be self-supporting, or on the other hand it might prove a very expensive drain on the taxpayers. It would in any event, as a permanent institution, be less costly in money than such temporary palliatives as doles and the comparatively unnecessary public works which are now adopted by the state during periods of sufficiently acute distress. And no matter how great the purely economic cost of our minimal communism, it would be socially worth while, for without destroying capitalism it would remove its most degrading and intolerable feature — slavish dependence and the terror of unemployment that is now suffered potentially and to some extent by all workers, and continuously and acutely by those on the margin of subsistence.

To conclude: The institution of private property confers two sorts of power upon its possessor: first, the power over nature; second, the power over other men. The one power is beneficent and the other sinister. And the major problem in the philosophy of property is the preservation of its power to protect and the destruction of its power to oppress. Pure communism would put each individual at the mercy of the herd. For in depriving a man of property you deprive him of his protection against nature and make him dependent upon the caprice of political passion and its exploitation by demagogues. Pure capitalism, on the other hand, produces a situation in which the luxurious protection of one part of the community is accompanied by a degrading servitude of the other part. If not the minimal communism which I have suggested, then some other measure of similar purport must be sought by the social philosopher as a means of removing at any cost not the riches of the rich but their power to oppress.

III

The Need of Social Philosophy in America To-day

In every age and in every country the rules by which life is conducted are of two distinct kinds. First, there are the rules sanctioned by custom, and second, there are the rules sanctioned by experience and by reason. These two classes of rules are by no means mutually exclusive, but neither are they always in agreement; and when there is conflict between them, social progress consists in a substitution of the rules of reason for those of custom and authority. This is often a difficult matter, for to the natural inertia of the human mind which makes for the perpetuation of customs there is added a slavish veneration for authority which makes men afraid to abandon ancient folk-ways even when new needs and new circumstances cry out for new rules. The demand for change is often met by the claim that the ancient ways were revealed and commanded by God; and this claim for a divine authority, sacrosanct and not to be questioned, is apt to be more insistent in proportion to the unreasonableness of the rules in the support of which it is invoked. When men have good reasons for a policy they welcome free discussion, for they feel that the justness of their cause will win for it an honorable victory in the court of reason. When, on the other hand, men lose faith in the reasonableness of their policies they oppose free inquiry and invoke authoritarian sanctions for beliefs that would otherwise be rejected. Whenever an ethical or a physical hypothesis is promoted to the status of a theological dogma to be accepted on faith, it is safe to infer that its protagonists have themselves lost faith in the possibility of defending it by appeal to reason and experience. The history of science and philosophy is the history of humanity's unending struggle to attain a life of reason and to free itself from the tyranny of its own past.

At the present time and in our own country, this ancient struggle has entered upon a new and more acute phase. The double standard of knowledge is breaking down. The facts of the astronomical and geological evolution of our planet and of the animal origin of our own species, which for fifty years have been commonplaces in the knowledge of the educated classes, have been brought vividly to the attention of those who apparently had been until recently either completely ignorant of them, or who had regarded them as abstract and artificial hypotheses with no real bearing upon the cosmology taught in the Bible. And with the awakening from their dogmatic slumbers of a class which probably comprises a majority of voters in many of our states, the country is confronted with a very real danger to its hard-won achievements in democratic education. It is even possible that the movement represented by the Fundamentalists and by the Ku Klux Klan will develop into a sort of peasant dictatorship or "green terror" more disastrous to the growth of culture than either the "red" or the "white" terrors from which Europe has suffered since the War. Such a catastrophe may seem highly improbable, and yet the mere possibility of it should be sufficient to arouse those interested in the philosophy and science of society to make every effort to prevent it. The prerequisite of prevention is understanding; and although the causes of the present danger are complex I wish to point out two factors which I believe to be causally important, and which I think it within the power of a sound social philosophy to mitigate.

The first of these factors is the authoritarian spirit in which popular theology is promulgated, and the second is the authoritarian sanctions employed in the teaching of ethics. The ultimate desiderata are of course a true theology and a true ethics; but before we can secure these final blessings, we need the instrumental and more easily attainable blessings of a free theology and a free ethics. By a free theology, I mean a theology whose tenets, whatever they may assert, are based upon some sort of experience and defended by some sort of reasoning. And by a free ethics I mean an ethics in which the ideals of life, however they may be conceived, are based upon the needs of man's nature and defended by appeal to his sympathy and intelligence. No matter how mystical the type of experience appealed to, and no matter how fantastic the reasoning by which conclusions are defended, so long as it is any sort of experience and reasoning rather than even the best sort of force and authority, there is hope for progress.

The real trouble with the Fundamentalist theology is not that its beliefs about the origin of man conflict with the beliefs of science. It is rather that the methods employed to justify those beliefs are so opposed to the methods of science that the possibility not only of refuting them, but of proving them is barred out from the start. Is it too much to ask of a man who holds a theory as to the supernatural origin and guidance of the world that he be willing to have that theory discussed freely and fairly without forcibly censoring the expression of views at variance with his own? If he deprives his opponents of the opportunity to state their objections, he deprives himself of the opportunity to refute them. To forbid the teaching of evolution in the high schools and tax-supported universities of a state not only prevents the majority of its citizens from learning the opinions held by the men of science, it prevents also the exposure of whatever falsity those scientific opinions may possess. The recipients of the one-sided teaching are fore-warned but not fore-armed, and when they learn, as they later will learn, the nature of the forbidden doctrines they are powerless to resist or appraise them. The only chance for such a policy is the chance that its victims, or beneficiaries, can be kept throughout their lives from contact with the culture of the outside world.

The consequences of authoritarianism are even more serious for ethics than for religion. For suppose that a youth has been taught that the primary reason for preferring the good life to the life of evil and ugliness is that the former life is commanded by God. If later on that youth comes to doubt the existence of God or the authenticity of his alleged revelation, he will automatically lose the primary reason for preferring good to evil. To the extent that his morals have been founded on his religion, the loss of the latter will result in the loss of the former. The wave of crime which is now sweeping the country is largely owing to the fact that the youth of to-day are abandoning not only the old religious teaching but also the code of conduct based upon it, which is the only code they know. The natural bitterness felt by religious conservatives toward the teachings of science is strengthened by their righteous indignation at the criminals who have strayed from their own fold. But in their anger they forget that it is they themselves rather than their opponents who are largely responsible for the prevalence of crime and the break-down of morale. For the surest way to produce a loss of moral fiber is to base the teaching of morals on a theological foundation that is certain to be challenged.   The remedy which the conservatives are advocating is the impossible one of isolating the youth from all contact with evolutionary science, to the end that by restoring authoritarian religion the authoritarian morality resting upon it may also be restored.   This is the reason for their un-American demand for a religious censorship of science in American schools.

The alternative to the remedy of the conservatives is to emancipate the teaching of moral values from the teaching of theological dogmas, not on the ground that the latter are necessarily false but on the ground that some who are trained in them may come to think them false.   The secularization of moral instruction would not hurt religion and it would remove a great and growing menace to the peace and order of our social life.   It would not hurt religion because any religion that is worthy of respect must rest upon a love of God's goodness rather than upon a fear of his power.   And unless a child is first taught to admire what is good and beautiful in life he cannot properly reverence a supernatural exemplification of it in a Divinity.   And while religion itself would be strengthened rather than weakened by treating moral values on their own merits, morality also, in its practice no less than in its theory, would be measurably advanced if it could be freed from the danger to which it is subjected by being made to rest upon the precarious foundation of theological dogma.

Philosophy has no axe to grind; it destroys no theories, scientific or religious; neither does it prove them.   It advocates the spirit of freedom and fair play in dealing with the deeper problems of existence, and it defends the life of reason both for the individual and for society.   It is my contention that the philosophic spirit and the philosophic life are badly needed in our country to-day.

SELECTED REFERENCES

I. Individualism and utilitarianism.

Donisthorpe, W.   *Individualism: A System of Politics.*   1889.
Faguet, A. E.   *The Cult of Incompetence,* trans. by Barstoe.   1911.
    Questions Politiques.   1899.
Hobhouse, L. T.   *Democracy and Reaction.*   1904.
    Elements of Social Justice.   1922.
    Liberalism.   Home U. Library.   1911.
    Metaphysical Theory of the State.   1918.
    Morals in Evolution.   1906.   New ed., 1915.
    Questions of War and Peace.   1916.

Hobhouse, L. T.   *The Rational Good.*   1921.
　　　　　　　　Social Evolution and Political Theory.   1911.
Kropotkin, P. A.   *Mutual Aid, a Factor in Evolution.*   1904.
　　　　　　　　Anarchism, its Philosophy and Ideal.   1907.
　　　　　　　　Man and the State.
　　　　　　　　Fields, Factories and Workshops.   1913.
Mallock, W. H.   *Aristocracy and Evolution.*   1898.
　　　　　　　　The Limits of Pure Democracy.   1918.
　　　　　　　　Social Reform as Related to Realities and Delusions.   1914.
　　　　　　　　The Critical Examination of Socialism.   1907.
　　　　　　　　Social Equality, Aristocracy and Evolution.   1882.
Mill, J. S.   *Utilitarianism.*   1910 ed.
　　　　　On Liberty.   1859.
Montague, W. P.   "The Missing Link in the Case for Utilitarianism,"
　　　　　　　　Studies in the History of Ideas, vol. II, Columbia
　　　　　　　　University Press.   1925.
Ritchie, D. G.   *Darwinism and Politics.*   1889.
　　　　　　　Principles of State Interference.   1896.
　　　　　　　Natural Rights.   1895.
Spencer, Herbert.   *Man versus the State.*   1884.
Wilde, Norman.   *The Ethical Basis of the State.*   1924.

II. Socialism and property.

Andler, Chas.   *Les Origines du Socialisme d'Etat en Allemagne.*   1911.
Carpenter, Niles.   *Guild Socialism; Historical and Critical Analysis.*   1922.
Cole, G. D. H.   *Social Theory.*   1920.
　　　　　　Self-Government in Industry.   1919.
　　　　　　The World of Labor.   1913.
　　　　　　Guild Socialism.   1921.
Ensor, R. C. K.   *Modern Socialism.*   1910.
Fabian Essays.   By Shaw and others.   1909.
Hobhouse, L. T., and others.   *Property: Its Rights and Duties.*   1915.
Hobson, J. A.   *Evolution of Modern Capitalism.*   1910.
　　　　　　Imperialism.   1902.
　　　　　　National Guilds and the State.
　　　　　　The Social Problem.   1922.
　　　　　　Taxation in the New State.   1920.
　　　　　　Work and Wealth.   1914.
MacDonald, J. Ramsay.   *Socialism and Government.*   1909.
　　　　　　　　The Case for Federal Devolution.   1920.
　　　　　　　　Syndicalism.   1912.
　　　　　　　　The Socialist Movement.   1911.
　　　　　　　　Socialism: Critical and Constructive.   1921.
Tawney, Richard H.   *The Acquisitive Society.*   1920.
　　　　　　　Agrarian Revolution in the 16th Century.   1912.
Tufts, James H.   *Our Democrary, its Origins and its Tasks.*   1917.
Veblen, Thorstein B.   *Theory of the Leisure Class.*   1918.
Webb, Sidney.   *Socialism in England.*   1893.
Webb, Beatrice and Sidney.   *Constitution for Socialist Commonwealth of
　　　　　　　　Great Britain.*   1920.
　　　　　　　　Industrial Democracy.   2 vols.   1897.   Rev.
　　　　　　　　ed.   1911.
　　　　　　　　History of Trade Unionism.   1920.

III. Social control over the individual.

Acton, Lord. *History of Freedom.* 1907, 1909.

Barnes, H. E. *Sociology and Political Theory.* 1924.

Cooley, Chas. H. *Human Nature and the Social Order.* 1902.
 Social Organization. 1909. 2d ed. 1920.
 Social Progress. 1918.

Dickinson, G. Lowes. *The Causes of International War.* 1920.
 Justice and Liberty. 1908.
 War, its Nature, Cause and Cure. 1923.

Figgis, John Neville. *Churches in the Modern State.* 2d ed. 1914.
 Divine Right of Kings. 2d ed. 1914.
 From Gerson to Grotius. 1916.

Follett, Mary P. *The New State.* 1918.

Green, T. H. *Principles of Political Obligation.* 1879.

Herbert, Auberon. *The Right and Wrong of Compulsion by the State.* 1885.

Jenks, Edward. *The State and the Nation.* 1919.
 Government Action for Social Welfare.

Laski, Harold J. *Studies in the Problems of Sovereignty.* 1917.
 Authority in the Modern State. 1910.
 Foundations of Sovereignty. 1921.

Le Bon, Gustav. *La Psychologie Politique et la Défense Sociale.* 1910.
 The Psychology of Revolution. 1913.
 The Crowd. 1917.
 Le Deséquilibre du Monde. 1924.
 The Psychology of Socialism. 1899.
 The World Unbalanced. 1924.

Lecky, W. E. H. *Democracy and Liberty.* 1896.

Lippmann, Walter. *Drift and Mastery.* 1914.
 Liberty and the News. 1920.
 A Preface to Politics. 1913.
 Public Opinion. 1922.
 The Phantom Public. 1925.

Mecklin, John M. *An Introduction to Social Ethics.* 1920.

Montague, F. C. *The Limits of Individual Liberty.* 1885.

Pound, Roscoe. *An Introduction to the Philosophy of Law.* 1922.
 Law and Morals. 1924.
 The Spirit of the Common Law. 1921.

Ross, E. A. *Changing America.* 1912.
 Social Control. 1904.
 The Russian Bolshevik Revolution. 1921.
 The Social Trend. 1922.

Russell, B. *Political Ideals.* 1917.
 Proposed Roads to Freedom. 1919.
 Why Men Fight. 1917.
 Bolshevism: Practice and Theory. 1920.

Trotter, William. *Instincts of the Herd in Peace and War.* 1915.

Wallas, Graham. *The Great Society.* 1904.
 Human Nature in Politics. 1908.
 Our Social Heritage. 1921.

IV. General references.

Barnes, H. E., Merriam, Chas. E., and others. *A History of Political Theories.* (Recent times.) 1924.

INDEX